DEFENSE AND SECURITY

DEFENSE AND SECURITY

A Compendium of National Armed Forces and Security Policies

Volume 1: Angola–Mexico

Edited by

Karl DeRouen, Jr.
Uk Heo

A B C ⬤ C L I O

Santa Barbara, CA   Denver, CO   Oxford, UK

Copyright © 2005 by Karl DeRouen, Jr., and Uk Heo

All rights reserved. No part of this publication may be reproduced, stored in a re-
trieval system, or transmitted, in any form or by any means, electronic, mechanical,
photocopying, recording, or otherwise, except for the inclusion of brief quotations in
a review, without prior permission in writing from the publishers.

Cataloging-in-Publication Data is available from the Library of Congress.

08   07   06   05   10 9 8 7 6 5 4 3 2 1

This book is also available on the World Wide Web as an eBook. Visit abc-clio.com
for details.

ABC-CLIO, Inc.
130 Cremona Drive, P.O. Box 1911
Santa Barbara, California 93116-1911

Production Team

Acquisitions Editor	Alicia Merritt
Project Assistant	Wendy Roseth
Production Editor	Anna R. Kaltenbach
Editorial Assistant	Alisha Martinez
Production Manager	Don Schmidt
Manufacturing Coordinator	George Smyser

It was set in typeface Trump Medieval.

This book is printed on acid-free paper ∞ .
Manufactured in the United States of America

*Dedicated to the memory of Karl DeRouen's grandparents
and to Uk Heo's parents:
Fernand, Agnes, Rosemary, and Sam
and
Mansik and Sunok*

CONTENTS

Preface

This project is designed to fill a niche in the crowded field of international security research. While it is ostensibly a reference set, it is designed to do much more than simply convey encyclopedic information. We have designed this project with a standard set of subheadings that cover a broad range of security/defense issues. Each essay comprises an introduction that covers history and geography, an introductory table of information, regional geopolitics, conflict history, alliance structure, size and structure of the military (including information on the budget), civil-military relations and the role of the military in domestic politics, terrorism, relationship with the United States, the future, and references, recommended readings, and useful country-related Websites. Paul Bellamy wrote an interesting introduction that weaves all the essays together. We also provide a list of acronyms and a chronology.

The project covers over fifty countries from 1945 to mid-2004. We first decided on a list of the most important countries in terms of international politics, size of military, and/or whether it is experiencing conflict (e.g., Angola). Because it is also important to cover smaller countries, we also commissioned two essays with regional foci (Caribbean and Oceania). Rather than try to cover every country in the world, we decided to have longer, more elaborate essays written on a sample of states and regions.

The contributors were asked to be analytic and deliberative—not to simply provide a basic litany of facts. The essays also spend considerable space on topics not typically covered in such projects. For instance, we devote space to defense economics and the role of the defense sector in domestic politics as well as past and current conflicts. The result is a set of quality essays that we are very proud of.

We are also proud of the broad range of contributors who participated in this project. Several countries are represented (Austria, Canada, New Zealand, South Korea, Sweden, and the United States). We also have a broad range of academic institutions in the United States represented. The project boasts two world experts: Ivelaw Griffith from Florida International University and John Henderson from the University of Canterbury in New Zealand are each leading figures in their respective areas. Ivelaw is an expert in Caribbean security, and John's area of interest is Pacific security.

It has been our pleasure to work with a production team at ABC-CLIO: Alicia Merritt, Anna Kaltenbach, and Wendy Roseth.

Karl DeRouen, Jr.
Tuscaloosa, AL
karl.fpdm@lycos.com

Uk Heo
Milwaukee, WI
heouk@uwm.edu

Introduction[1]

Paul Bellamy

Paul Bellamy is a research analyst at the New Zealand Parliamentary Library. Please note that the views expressed in this chapter are those of the author and not necessarily those of his employer.

This introduction leads the reader into the country/region essays contained in the main body of this compendium. The essays are designed to follow a common organizational structure. The introduction of each essay briefly summarizes and discusses the characteristics of various countries according to this systematic framework. The framework examines geography and history, regional geopolitics, conflict history and current conflict, the alliance structure, the size and structure of the military, the military's role in politics, the threat from terrorism, the relationship with the United States, and the future. A thorough understanding of each of these factors is needed if one is to gain a comprehensive understanding of the various defense policies around the world.

Geography and History

Each essay begins with an introduction describing the geography and history. With regard to land size, the Russian Federation (or Russia) is the world's largest country. It spreads over two continents, and the climate varies from subtropical areas to frozen territories. Canada is the second-largest country and shares the world's longest international boundary with the United States, the world's third-largest country. The United States is followed in size by the People's Republic of China (or China). Because of the size of these countries, their geography varies. In contrast are the world's smaller countries. For instance, New Zealand is about the size of the state of Colorado, and Paraguay is about the same size as California. Even smaller are the South Pacific island countries of Fiji, Tonga, and Vanuatu.

The composition and resources of the countries vary. Whereas the United States is comprised of fifty states that include Alaska and Hawaii, the Republic of the Philippines is an archipelago composed of over 7,000 islands, of which 880 are inhabited. The Indonesian archipelago comprises thousands of islands, of which 6,000 are inhabited and another 11,000 are uninhabited. Resources vary too. Saudi Arabia has major oil reserves (although its other resources are limited), and South Africa has major gold resources. Contrasting this, Israel has limited natural resources, and most of China's land is not arable. Countries with limited landmass may have other resources available. Whereas the total land area of New Zealand is only 268,021 sq. km, its maritime Exclusive Economic Zone is 1.3 million square nautical miles (fifteen times its landmass), one of the largest in the world.

As with geography, the history of countries differs and their composition has changed over time. Since around the seventh century Korea existed as a united country under the rule of numerous monarchs. However, the Korean peninsula was divided at the 38th parallel after World War II and remains divided. The roots of the German nation date back to around the eighth century. After World War II Germany was similarly divided but then unified in 1990. Indeed, major changes occurred after World War II as new countries emerged and others gained independence. Independent countries that emerged during this period include Pakistan (1947), India (1947), Israel (1948), Nigeria (1960), and Fiji (1970). More recently, in the 1990s the Soviet Union, Czechoslovakia, and Yugoslavia fragmented into various independent states. East Timor (now the Democratic Republic of Timor-Leste) voted for independence from Indonesia in 1999 and became independent in 2002.

Political systems have also changed since World War II. Communist political systems were established in many countries after the war, such as throughout eastern Europe (in the late 1940s), China (1949), Cuba (1961), and Vietnam (1975). However, many countries have moved away from communism. During upheaval in the 1980s and 1990s the Soviet Union ceased to exist, and democracy was established in the Russian Federation and in other formally communist states such as Poland. There have also been major political changes in noncommunist countries. South Africa has moved from apartheid and held its first multiracial elections in 1994. Countries such as Chile (1990) have moved from military rule to democracy, whereas others such as Pakistan (1999)

have experienced coups. Political reform has been resisted in some countries as well. This is shown by the continuing dictatorship in North Korea.

Regional Geopolitics
Each essay summarizes the diverse range of geopolitical issues countries face. One important issue is geographic location. Pakistan interfaces with three regional systems (south Asia, central Asia, and the Middle East), all of which have an impact on the country. Pakistan also is affected by the geopolitical considerations of China, Russia, and the United States. China has land borders with fourteen countries and border disputes are a major source of tension, although signed border treaties have resolved some issues. For instance, tensions exist over China's ocean border with Vietnam as well as its border with India. Chile has a border dispute with Argentina, while Paraguay's lack of sea access has caused disagreements with its neighbors. Italy faces pressure from other European Union (EU) member states to tighten its border controls as the country is a major destination of immigrants who then migrate to other EU countries. Moreover, border changes have had a major impact on some geopolitical regions. For example, the fall of communism in the Soviet Union and eastern Europe increased the number of Poland's neighbors from three to seven. Indeed, Poland's eastern border now constitutes the front line of the North Atlantic Treaty Organization (NATO).

Regional instability is a source of concern for many countries. The fragmentation of Yugoslavia and resultant conflict had a major impact on regional geopolitics and the security concerns of neighboring countries. The fighting in Iraq since the fall of Saddam Hussein in 2003 and its impact on regional stability is a major concern for Middle Eastern countries. Lebanon's strategic position makes it particularly vulnerable to events in the Middle East. Likewise, Indonesia's neighbors are anxious over the impact of violence within the archipelago on regional stability, and in Brazil there are concerns over violence in Colombia. The potential impact of the fall of the communist regime in North Korea is a major geopolitical issue facing East Asia, and indeed the world, given North Korea's nuclear ambitions. However, violence does not necessarily accompany major state changes. This is shown by the peaceful emergence of the Czech Republic and Slovakia.

Even in regions where conflict is comparatively limited, many issues affect geopolitics. Although the islands of the South Pacific have generally been peaceful following World War II, they face wide-ranging social and environmental issues that are potential sources of instability. Major health concerns have arisen over the spread of HIV/AIDS and the prevalence of Type 2 diabetes. Additional concern has been voiced over rapid population growth, income inequalities, the pressure of customs and traditions, crime, drug and alcohol abuse, and migration. Associated with these issues are the inter-ethnic conflicts and tensions evident in countries such as Fiji.

Conflict History
One method to assess a country's security future is to look at its past involvement in conflict. Some countries experience recurring wars with the same adversary, such as India and Pakistan. Many states that have often been involved in internal (e.g., Indonesia) and external (e.g., Israel) conflict can be expected to experience conflict in the future.

Both world wars caused global suffering. Regions and countries became battlegrounds with a high loss of life and widespread destruction. For instance, Poland suffered heavily during its occupation by Germany in World War II, and two atomic bombs were dropped on Japan. After World War II interstate and intrastate conflict continued. Many countries continue to be involved in interstate conflicts. This involvement has been particularly high among countries such as Syria, Pakistan, Israel, India, and Egypt. This is in contrast to countries such as Switzerland. The Cold War, which dominated much of the twentieth century after World War II, led to various conflicts that involved many countries. The Korean War and Vietnam War are two particularly costly examples of this conflict. Moreover, the Cuban missile crisis of 1962 brought the world close to a nuclear war. Intrastate conflict has been another cause of suffering in countries such as Nigeria, Lebanon, Papua New Guinea, and Argentina. More recently, the fragmentation of Yugoslavia caused much conflict in the 1990s.

Current Conflict
This section summarizes current conflict involvement for each country/region. Conflict continues to threaten many countries and the lives of their people, and thus has a major impact on the international community. According to the Stockholm International Peace Research Institute (SIPRI), there were nineteen major armed conflicts in eighteen locations worldwide in 2003. This was the lowest number for the post–Cold War period with the exception of 1997, when eighteen such conflicts were registered. Four of the nineteen conflicts were in Africa and eight in Asia. SIPRI identified

only two of the nineteen conflicts as being fought between states (SIPRI 2004). These were the conflict between Iraq and the multinational coalition led by the United States and the continuing conflict between India and Pakistan over Kashmir. International concern has been expressed over the continuing conflict in Iraq following the fall of Saddam Hussein. As of August 28, 2004, it was reported that there had been 1,105 coalition deaths in Iraq (Cable News Network [CNN] 2004).[2] The U.S.-led invasion itself has caused much debate, as is later noted. According to SIPRI, fourteen multilateral peace missions were launched in 2003. This was the highest number of new missions initiated in a single year since the end of the Cold War (SIPRI 2004).

Interstate tensions and the threat of conflict are particularly high between some countries. This is shown by the tension between India and Pakistan, which have fought a series of wars since 1948. In 1998 tensions were particularly high as both countries staged nuclear tests. Similarly, tensions remain on the Korean peninsula between the North and South. Both countries have been to war against each other in the past, and the threat of nuclear weapons has emerged with North Korea's nuclear program. The nuclear threat evident in both of these cases is a source of international concern. Another particularly tense relationship remains that between Taiwan and China, which have also experienced conflict. However, it should be noted that some countries, such as New Zealand, do not face a direct military threat.

Intrastate conflict is another major issue. Intrastate conflict continues in Russia and in Colombia. Russian forces in Chechnya continue to face strong opposition despite their efforts since 1999

to subdue resistance. This conflict has not been restricted to Chechnya. In October 2002, Chechen terrorists kidnapped hostages in Moscow, and in June 2004, government buildings were attacked in three towns in Ingushetia, which borders Chechnya. In Colombia a forty-year insurgent campaign to overthrow the Colombian government escalated during the 1990s. An anti-insurgent army of paramilitaries has developed and challenges the insurgents for control of territory and illicit industries such as the drug trade, as well as the government's ability to exert its dominion over rural areas (Central Intelligence Agency [CIA] 2004). According to SIPRI, the volatility of individual intrastate conflicts was shown in 2003 with the sudden and rapid increase of conflict intensity in Burundi, Côte d'Ivoire, Indonesia, and the Philippines (SIPRI 2004).

Alliance Structure

It is important to examine alliance structures to understand international relations and security. According to realist theories of conflict, a key way for a state to augment power externally is through alliance formation. Therefore, to accurately assess a state's strength, these alliances must be taken into account. Alliances also should be analyzed as they can influence the foreign and security policies of countries and, more specifically, their involvement in conflicts.

There are numerous security alliances that vary in terms of both their membership and framework. One of the most important alliances is NATO, which was formed by the 1949 North Atlantic Treaty. The fundamental role of NATO is to safeguard the freedom and security of its member countries by political and military means. In 1999, massive expulsions of ethnic Albanians living in Kosovo provoked an international response, including the NATO bombing of Serbia. NATO currently has twenty-six members from North America and Europe. Bulgaria, Estonia, Latvia, Lithuania, Romania, Slovakia, and Slovenia formally became members in March 2004. NATO is an important alliance for countries such as the United Kingdom and Spain. Indeed, NATO is the only military alliance to which Italy belongs. From 1955 to 1991 the Soviet Union sought to counter NATO with the Warsaw Treaty Organization (WTO) of communist countries.

Other alliances are important to countries. The Organization for Security and Cooperation in Europe has fifty-five participating states from Europe, central Asia, and North America. It is active in early warning, conflict prevention, crisis management, and postconflict rehabilitation. The Association of Southeast Asian Nations (ASEAN) has ten member countries. The Treaty of Amity and Cooperation in Southeast Asia, signed at the first ASEAN summit in 1976, stated that ASEAN political and security dialogue and cooperation should aim to promote regional peace and stability. This was to be done by enhancing regional resilience. Individual security relationships between countries are also important. Following the Soviet Union's collapse, Russia has signed various bilateral and multilateral alliance treaties. Among those are entente agreements with France, Mongolia, and North Korea and neutrality and nonaggression pacts with Moldova and the Ukraine. Other countries that generally cooperate closely on security and defense include New Zealand and Australia and the United States and Canada.

The role of alliances differs within the international community. The neutrality of some countries influences the role of alliances in their foreign policies. Switzerland will not enter into any obligation or military arrangement that could be interpreted as an alliance. However, the Swiss commitment to forego forming alliances pertains only to preventive alliances and not to reactive alliances. Neutral Austria has not joined any military alliance, although it is a member of NATO's Partnership for Peace Programme. Ireland is another neutral country and its foreign policy is likewise affected by this stance. Other countries have not joined military alliances. Venezuela is not a member of any military alliances, though it might have a working relationship with the Cuban military. Other countries have foreign policies that include the principle of nonalignment, as is the case with China.

Security relations are dynamic. Changes in security relations are shown by the impact of the collapse of the Soviet Union, and the subsequent dissolving of the WTO. For example, the Soviet Union was an important ally of Syria. However, with the rapprochement of the Soviet Union with the United States, and the eventual Soviet collapse, there were major changes in Syrian foreign policy as it sought to readjust to the new geopolitical environment. The collapse of the Soviet Union also meant further isolation for Cuba. Moreover, changes have occurred in alliances between the United States and other countries. For instance, after the New Zealand government prohibited visitation by an American naval vessel in 1985, the United States suspended its security obligations under the 1951 Australia-New Zealand-United States (ANZUS) Treaty. Relations have gradually improved between the two countries, but security contact remains restricted.

Size and Structure of the Military

The size and structure of a country's military is another important area to study in order to understand international relations. Military size can be a key indicator of a country's strength, its ability to fulfill its foreign and security policy objectives, and its involvement in conflict. Similarly, the military's structure is important. The military's structure influences its ability to be deployed in conflicts and is indicative of the country's threat perceptions and the priority attached to defense relative to other budgetary demands (such as health and education).

The size of militaries around the world varies extensively. The size of various forces declined with the end of the Cold War, as evidenced by the reduction in the number of military personnel in former adversaries Russia and the United States. More recently, Defense Secretary Geoff Hoon in July 2004 announced large cuts in the UK armed forces as part of modernization plans (British Broadcasting Corporation [BBC], July 21, 2004). However, many countries continue to have large military forces. With over 2 million people in uniform, China has the largest military in the world. India, Pakistan, the United States, Russia, and North Korea all have militaries with more than 1 million personnel. Other military forces are much smaller. Fiji, Papua New Guinea, Tonga, and Vanuatu have military forces with less than 5,000 personnel. Recruitment methods differ between states. Conscription continues in countries such as Egypt, whereas others such as the United States have moved to a professional volunteer force.

As with the number of personnel, the equipment possessed by militaries varies. Both the personnel and equipment of military forces impact their allocated roles and their ability to successfully fulfill these roles. International differences are shown by the unconventional weapons held by some countries. The United States tested the world's first atomic bomb in 1945 and then dropped two such bombs on Japan during World War II. Both the United States and Russia have large nuclear arsenals; other nuclear-armed countries include the United Kingdom, China, France, Pakistan, and India. Other countries, such as North Korea, have undertaken work to develop nuclear weapons. Various treaties have attempted to address the development and the stockpiling of nuclear weapons. For example, the Nuclear Non-proliferation Treaty (NPT) was opened for signature in 1968, entered into force in 1970, and had 187 members in early 2000. Chemical and biological weapons are held by some countries. For instance, it has been reported that Syria has made progress acquiring weapons of mass destruction (WMD). The 2003 invasion of Iraq was in part publicly justified by the perceived threat posed by Iraqi WMD. This justification has been controversial as no such weapons have been found to date (August 2004). In July 2004 the U.S. Senate Intelligence Committee released a report critical of the CIA's prewar estimates of WMD in Iraq. That same month an inquiry report criticized prewar British intelligence on Iraq.

Conventional armaments differ in quantity and sophistication. The divergence in quantity is shown by the major arsenals of large militaries such as those of the United States, China, and Russia, compared with the very limited armaments held by islands in the South Pacific such as Papua New Guinea, Tonga, and Vanuatu. Likewise, the level of weapons technology differs among countries. The United States is a leader in weapons technology. Illustrative of this is the technology being developed to build a national missile defense system, a course of action that has been controversial as the United States has withdrawn from the 1972 Anti-Ballistic Missile (ABM) Treaty. Countries such as Germany, France, Australia, Taiwan, and the United Kingdom also have modern military equipment. However, many defense forces have equipment that is dated and even obsolete. Such forces include those of Paraguay and Vanuatu.

Budget
Levels of defense expenditure can directly influence the size and structure of military forces and, ultimately the combat capabilities of countries. As with the size of the military, expenditure is an indicator of the importance attached to military strength and whether or not the country believes that its security is threatened. More specifically, whether or not the country is involved in a conflict can influence the level of expenditure.

World military spending has increased in recent years. According to SIPRI, world military spending in 2003 increased by about 11 percent in real terms (this was preceded by a 6.5 percent increase in 2002). The institute has calculated that world military spending in 2003 reached $956 billion (in current U.S. dollars). The increase has been primarily attributed to the massive increase in U.S. expenditure since the terrorist attacks of September 11, 2001, namely to cover operations in Afghanistan, Iraq, and antiterrorist activities (SIPRI 2004).

Military spending varies widely among countries. Defense expenditure as a percentage of gross domestic product (GDP) in recent years is estimated to have exceeded 10 percent in North Korea and Saudi Arabia. Contrasting this, expenditure has been estimated at less than 1 percent in Switzerland, Austria, the Philippines, Ireland, Venezuela, and Mexico. As with the percentage of GDP, the actual amount spent on the military can vary. According to SIPRI, in 2003 the world's top five military spenders were: the United States ($417.4 billion or $1,419 per capita), Japan ($46.9 billion or $367 per capita), the United Kingdom ($37.1 billion or $627 per capita), France ($35.0 billion or $583 per capita), and China (an estimated $32.8 billion or $25 per capita) (SIPRI 2004).[3] In comparative terms, expenditure in countries like Tonga (estimated to be less than $5 million in 2001) is very low. However, accurately calculating military expenditure can be difficult. For example, the Chinese People's Liberation Army has extensive off-budget funding as well as revenue from other sources.

Many countries have arms industries. In terms of value, the production of military goods and services predominantly occurs in the United States, Russia, China, and Europe. In both 2001 and 2003 the volumes of major weapons delivered increased. Russia and the United States are the major suppliers. The primary recipients were China and India (in the case of Russia) and Taiwan, Egypt, the United Kingdom, Greece, Turkey, and Japan (in the case of the United States) (SIPRI 2004). The United States is the world's leading supplier of arms and arms transfer agreements, both in terms of total value and as a percentage. The total value of arms transfers in 2002 was $10.2 billion, and the total value of arms transfer agreements in 2002 was $13.3 billion. In 2002, the U.S. share of global arms deliveries was 40.3 percent, and its share of global arms transfer agreements was 45.5 percent. In contrast, countries like Fiji and Tonga have no capability to manufacture weapons.

Military's Role in Politics

The military's role in politics varies among countries. Civilian supremacy is strong in some countries. This is especially the case in established democracies such as the United States and the United Kingdom. However, in some parts of the world the military has often taken the reins of power. This is clearly shown by the experiences of many Latin American countries. In most democracies the head of the military is a civilian, as is the case in the United States. Contrasting this, there are countries with military leaders in power. For instance, the military governs Pakistan and has control over the country's nuclear weapons. Across the border in democratic India, civilians control the strategic weapons. It seems likely that the degree of the military's role in politics helps to shape a nation's defense and security posture.

In the United States, the president is the commander-in-chief. Next in line is the secretary of defense, whose sources of advice include the joint chiefs of staff. This is comprised of one representative from each branch of the military and is headed by the chair of the joint chiefs of staff. Although civil-military relations have not always been smooth, civilian supremacy is strong. Other countries with strong civilian control include Australia, New Zealand, and the United Kingdom. However, there are differences within the frameworks governing civil-military relationships. For instance, in New Zealand the governor-general is the commander-in-chief of the New Zealand Defense Force. The minister of defense is responsible for the armed forces and operates under the prime minister.

Some militaries have major political roles. Under communist rule the militaries of the Soviet Union and WTO were politicized, and the institutions could have a major influence on politics. After the fall of communism major changes occurred that enhanced civilian supremacy. In other countries the military still plays an important role in politics. This is shown by North Korea. Under Kim Jong Il the status of the North Korean military has increased, and the institution has been further politicized to encourage its loyalty. In China there is much integration among the top levels of political and military power. The support of the military is important for the Chinese Communist Party leader, and in 1989 the military played a major role in suppressing protesters perceived to be a threat. Other countries where militaries currently have major political roles include Indonesia, Egypt, the Philippines, and Cuba. Historically, the military has played a major political role in countries such as South Korea and Chile.

A coup is a direct challenge the military can pose to civilian supremacy. Coups have been staged throughout the world and have been frequently experienced by some countries. There have been at least ten military coups in Nigeria since it achieved independence in 1966, seven of which resulted in leadership changes. Indeed, the first civilian transfer of power in Nigerian history occurred in 2003. Likewise, until 1970 a series of coups took place in Syria. Since then, the head of Syria's government has been a military officer except for the first three years of independence. After a 1973 coup, the military dominated politics in Chile until the transition from military rule began in 1988. The legacy of military rule remains, and the former Chilean dictator Augusto Pinochet was arrested in

London for crimes against humanity and human rights violations. (Pinochet was released in 2000.) Countries that have experienced recent coups include Pakistan (1999) and Fiji (2000).

Terrorism

Terrorism has allowed weak or small insurgent groups to become actors in international security. Terrorism has occurred globally following World War II and with increasing frequency since the 1970s. The threat of terrorism has been internationally acknowledged, especially after the attacks of September 11, 2001, and many countries have sought to counter the threat. This in turn has led to changes to the national security structures in various countries. Despite this, terrorist groups remain active, and terrorism continues to occur throughout the world.

Numerous terrorist attacks have occurred in recent years. According to revised U.S. Department of State (DoS) figures there were 208 acts of international terrorism in 2003, an increase from the most recently published figure of 198[4] attacks in 2002 and a 42 percent drop from 355 attacks in 2001. A total of 625 persons were killed in attacks in 2003, less than the 725 killed during 2002. A total of 3,646 persons were wounded in attacks that occurred in 2003, an increase from 2,013 persons wounded during the previous year. The most common types of attack were bombings (119), followed by armed attack (49), kidnapping (14), suicide bomb (14), firebombing (4), assault (3), and arson (3). A total of 201 facilities were attacked (U.S. DoS 2004). The U.S. DoS figures for 2003 indicate that the Middle East was the most targeted region with 321 attacks, followed by Asia (222), western Europe (61), Africa (8), and Latin America (3). No attacks were identified in Eurasia (U.S. DoS 2004). According to the DoS, countries that sponsor terrorism are Libya, Sudan, Cuba, Iran, North Korea, and Syria. Iraq under Saddam Hussein was also identified as a sponsor of terrorism (U.S. DoS 2004).

Many countries have experienced terrorism. Countries that have experienced terrorism historically include the United Kingdom, South Korea, Israel, and Spain. The United States was attacked on September 11, 2001, in the worst international terrorist attack to date (August 2004). Those responsible belonged to the terrorist organization al-Qaeda, and more than 3,000 were killed (U.S. DoS 2002). Major attacks have occurred since 2001, as shown by the experiences of Indonesia and Spain. Various groups in Indonesia have used violence, and Jemaah Islamiyah, an Islamic extremist group, has been identified as a serious threat. In October 2002, two bombs exploded on the island of Bali killing at least 187 international tourists and injuring about 300 others (U.S. DoS 2003). In March 2004, ten bombs exploded in Madrid. These killed 191 people and left at least 1,800 injured. Spain named an Islamic extremist group, the Moroccan Islamic Combatant Group, as the main focus of their investigations (BBC, April 28, 2004).

Countries have taken a wide range of actions to combat terrorism. At the multinational level many states have ratified UN conventions against terrorism. Indeed, the 1999 Convention on the Suppression of the Financing of Terrorism entered into force in record time. Various resolutions have also been passed. For instance, Resolution 1373 obliges states to criminalize the provision of funds to terrorists, freeze the financial assets of people who commit terrorist acts, and prohibit the provision of services to those who participate in terrorism. Individual states have taken additional action. In March 2003, approximately 180,000 personnel from twenty-two different organizations around the U.S. government became part of the Department of Homeland Security. This has been called the largest government reorganization since the beginning of the Cold War (White House, March 2004). Major resources have been committed to law and order organizations as well as the military (as already noted), while legislation including the U.S. Patriot Act of 2001 has been passed. Many other countries, ranging from Russia to Mexico, have taken action against terrorism.

Relationship with the United States
The United States plays a very important role in the international system. Some nations are friendly to the United States while others are largely antagonistic. Where nations stand on this issue is an important defining element of its overall defense posture.

According to former Secretary of State Colin L. Powell, "There is no country on earth that is not touched by America, for we have become the motive force for freedom and democracy in the world. And there is no country in the world that does not touch us" (U.S. DoS 2001). The size of the United States, along with its diplomatic, economic, and military power, contribute to its global influence. The United States maintains diplomatic relations with some 180 countries, and the DoS maintains nearly 260 diplomatic and consular posts around the world. These include embassies, consulates, and missions to international organizations (U.S. DoS 2001).

Security relations between the United States and other countries are illustrated by the U.S.-led security coalition against terrorism. Countries that have contributed to operations in Afghanistan following the downfall of the Taliban regime include Russia, Spain, South Korea, Egypt, Poland, France, and the United Kingdom. Multinational forces are active in Iraq, and their duties include rebuilding the country's infrastructure. Countries that have deployed forces include the United Kingdom, Poland, Japan, New Zealand, Australia, the Czech Republic, and Italy. It was reported in mid-2004 that there were over thirty-five countries working alongside U.S. forces undertaking military and humanitarian operations in Afghanistan and Iraq (the coalition supporting Desert Shield and Desert Storm, 1990–1991 consisted of thirty-six countries) (*Coalition Bulletin* 2004). However, it should be noted that criticism has been leveled at U.S. foreign policy. For instance, France and Germany have openly questioned U.S. actions over Iraq.

Relations between the United States and some countries are especially strong. An important relationship is that between the United States and the United Kingdom. This relationship was strengthened during World War II and remained throughout the Cold War. More recently, the United Kingdom under Prime Minister Tony Blair has been a major supporter of U.S. foreign policy in Iraq and has committed forces to the country. This support has been controversial in the United Kingdom. Likewise, Australian and U.S. relations have historically been close. Australia under Prime Minister John Howard has been supportive of the United States and has deployed forces in Iraq, again a source of domestic controversy. Both the United Kingdom and Australia have emphasized the importance of the United States to international and national security, though relations have not been without problems. In his speech declaring the end of major combat operations in Iraq in May 2003, U.S. President George W. Bush specifically thanked the United Kingdom, Australia, and Poland (White House, May 2003). The security provided by the United States is also important to countries such as South Korea, the Philippines, and Taiwan.

In contrast, relations between the United States and some countries have been especially problematic. This is shown by the poor U.S. relations with North Korea and Iran. President Bush in January 2002 referred to both of these countries (along with Iraq under Saddam Hussein) as constituting an "axis of evil" (White House, January 2002). Historically, U.S.–North Korean relations have been tense. The United States continues to maintain major forces in South Korea and believes that a nuclear-armed North Korea is a threat. Hence, the United States has actively sought to prevent the development of nuclear weapons. North Korea in turn views the U.S. forces in South Korea as a threat and is suspicious of its actions. With regard to Iran, relations have been tense since the 1979 overthrow of Shah Mohammed Reza Pahlevi. Relations have been shaped by U.S. concerns over Iranian development of WMD and support of terrorism. Iranian perceptions have been influenced by U.S. sanctions and concern that, with the occupation of Iraq, the United States has encircled Iran.

Future

Conflict will continue to threaten countries in the foreseeable future. Although President Bush declared that the major combat phase in Iraq was over in May 2003, violence continues. The violence has not ceased since the U.S. transfer of Iraq's sovereignty to an interim government and appears likely to continue in the foreseeable future. In one day of violence alone in late July 2004, at least 110 lives were lost in a Baquda suicide bombing and fighting in south-central Iraq (CNN, July 29, 2004). The possibility that this conflict might spread in the Middle East is a particularly worrying scenario for neighboring countries. Similarly, fighting continues in Afghanistan. Other conflicts that appear unlikely to end in the near future include the second Chechen War and the fighting between Israelis and Palestinians. Historical tensions also exist between countries and appear likely to remain, at least to some degree. These tensions are evident between India and Pakistan and between North Korea and South Korea. However, some countries such as New Zealand are unlikely to face a direct military threat in the near future.

Alliances are likely to continue to play an important international role. This continuing importance is shown by the longevity and growth of NATO. For instance, in June 2004, NATO heads of state and government decided to provide training to Iraq's security forces. The following month, NATO took a first step to further expanding its presence in northern Afghanistan by taking command of provincial reconstruction teams in Mazar-e-Sharif and Maimana.

Changes remain likely in terms of military forces and their budgets. The security policies of various countries continue to change. For instance, major changes have been proposed to the UK military, as has been noted. Internationally, there has been debate regarding the structure of military forces and their suitability for the twenty-first century. This debate is evident in the United States regarding whether the military has adequate resources and suitable equipment to continue its current operations, particularly in Iraq. With regard to budgets, recent trends suggest that global defense expenditures will continue to be high given the demands placed on various military forces by the conflicts in Iraq, Afghanistan, and the war against terrorism.

It is likely that the state of civil-military relations will remain divergent within the international community. Although relations have not been without some tensions, civilian supremacy remains assured in countries such as the United States, the United Kingdom, Australia, and New Zealand. But in other countries there are questions regarding the political role of the military. For instance, the North Korean military's loyalty to Kim Jong Il has been questioned. In various countries where the military has been involved in politics, this role appears likely to continue. These countries include Egypt, Paraguay, the Philippines, and Indonesia.

The war on terrorism is likely to continue in the foreseeable future. DoS figures indicate that the number of terrorist attacks increased in 2003 over 2002 (as has been noted), and various terrorist organizations are likely to remain capable of launching attacks in the future. This is shown by the continued activities of al-Qaeda and the acknowledgment that terrorism remains a serious threat. The independent National Commission on Terrorist Attacks Upon the United States report released in July 2004 shows that, despite American efforts to increase security since September 11, 2001, terrorism remains a threat (National Commission 2004). Moreover, there has been recognition that terrorism is a threat without geographic boundaries, as shown by the 2002 terrorist attack in Bali. It is within this context that countries will continue to seek to address the threat of terrorism.

Finally, the United States will remain a key player within the international community, and hence its international relations will remain important. Given the controversial nature of the decision by the United States to invade Iraq, and the ongoing violence there, it is likely that this conflict will influence the relations other countries have with the United States. Strong relations appear likely to remain between the United States and its key allies, such as the United Kingdom, although some tension is probable. Contrasting this, major change would be required in other countries to establish better relations with the United States. This is shown by the tense relationship between the United States and North Korea.

Notes

1. The information used in this introduction is derived from the following chapters unless referenced.

2. The makeup of this tally was reported as: 974 Americans, 65 Britons, 6 Bulgarians, 1 Dane, 1 Dutch, 1 Estonian, 1 Hungarian, 19 Italians, 1 Latvian, 10 Poles, 1 Salvadoran, 3 Slovaks, 11 Spaniards, 2 Thai, and 8 Ukrainians.

3. Military expenditure is in market exchange rate terms and the figures are at constant (2000) prices and exchange rates.

4. As new information becomes available, revisions are made by the United States to previously published statistics. The U.S. DoS on June 22, 2004, referred to a total of 205 international terrorist incidents in 2002 (U.S. DoS, 2004).

LIST OF ACRONYMS

AA	Anti-aircraft
ABH	Army of the Republic of Bosnia and Herzegovina (Former Yugoslavia)
ABM	Anti-Ballistic Missile
ACCP	Association of Caribbean Commissioners of Police
ACCS	Air Command and Control System
ACDA	Arms Control and Disarmament Agency (USA)
ACLANT	Allied Command Atlantic
ACO	Allied Command Operations
ACS	Association of Caribbean States
ADF	Arab Deterrent Force (Lebanon)
ADM	Assistant Deputy Minister
ADRI	Army of the Republic of Indonesia
AEW	Airborne Early Warning
AF	Agreed Framework (North/South Korea)
AFC	Alliance for Chile
AFP	Armed Forces of the Philippines (Philippines)
AGM	Air-to-Ground Missile
AH	Attack Helicopter
AIFV	Armored Infantry Fighting Vehicle
AIM	Air-Intercept Missile
AIT	American Institute in Taiwan (Taiwan)
ALCM	Air-Launched Cruise Missile
ALINDIEN	*Commandant la zone maritime de de l'Océan Indien* (France)
ALPACI	*Commandant la zone maritime du Pacifique* (France)
ALRI	Navy of the Republic of Indonesia
AMRAAM	Advanced Medium Range Air-to-Air Missile
ANC	African National Congress (South Africa)
ANZAC	Australian and New Zealand Army Corps
ANZAM	Australia and New Zealand in the Malayan Area
ANZUS	Australia-New Zealand-United States
APC	Armored Personnel Carriers
APEC	Asia Pacific Economic Cooperation
ARAMCO	Arabian American Oil Company

ARF	ASEAN Regional Forum
ASA	Association for South East Asia
ASEAN	Association of South East Asian Nations
ASG	Abu Sayyaf Group (Malaysia, Philippines)
ASG	Abu Sayyaf Group (Philippines)
ASMP-A	*Air-Sol-Moyenne Porte* (Ameliore) (France)
ASW	Anti-Submarine Warfare
ATV	Advanced Technology Vehicle (India)
AU	African Union
AURI	Air Force of the Republic of Indonesia
BBC	British Broadcasting Corporation
B.C.	Before Christ
BDF	Barbados Defense Force
BeDF	Belize Defense Force
BERSATU	United Front for the Independence of Pattani (Malaysia, Thailand)
BFA	*Brigade Franco-Allemande* (France)
BICC	Bonn International Center for Conversion
BJP	Bharatiya Janata Party (India)
BLACKSEAFOR	Black Sea Naval Cooperation Task Force (Turkey, et al.)
BNPP	Barisan National Pember-Basan Pattani (Malaysia, Thailand)
BOSS	Bureau of State Security (South Africa)
BR	*Brigate Rosse* (Italy)
BRA	Bougainville Revolutionary Army
BRN	Barasi Revolusi Nasional (Malaysia, Thailand)
BWC	Biological Weapons Convention
CARAT	Cooperation Afloat Readiness and Training
CARICOM	Caribbean Community
CASSIC	*Le Commandement air des Systèmes de Surveillance d'Iinformation et de Communications* (France)
CBMs	Confidence-building measures
CBP	Customs and Border Protection (USA)
CBR	Chemical, Biological, and Radiological
CCC	Civil Contingencies Committee (United Kingdom)
CCP	Chinese Communist Party (People's Republic of China)
CDAOA	*Commandement de la Défense Aérienne et des Opérations Aériennes* (France)
CDI	Defense Intelligence Agency (United States)
CDLR	Committee for Defense of Legitimate Rights (Saudi Arabia)
CDP	Common Defense Policy (Germany)
CDR	Closer Defence Relations (New Zealand)
CDS	Chief of Defense Staff
CDU	Christian Democratic Union (Germany)
CEAA	*Le Commandement des Écoles de l'Air* (France)
CECLANT	*Commandant en chef pour l'Atlantique* (France)
CECMED	*Commandant en chef pour la Méditerranée* (France)

CEMAA	*Le Chef d'État-major de l'Armée de l'Air* (France)
CEMM	*Chef d'État-major de la Marine* (France)
CENTCOM	Central Command (USA)
CENTO	Central Treaty Organization (Pakistan)
CEPD	Council for Economic Planning and Development (Taiwan)
CF	Canadian Forces
CFAC	*Le Commandement de la Force Aérienne de Combat* (France)
CFAP	*Commandement de la Force Aérienne Projection* (France)
CFAS	*Commandement de la Forces Aériennes Stratégiques* (France)
CFAT	*Commandement de la Force d'Action Terrestre* (France)
CFATF	Caribbean Financial Action Task Force
CFC	Combined Forces Command (South Korea)
CFCA	*Le Commandement des Fusiliers Commandos de l'Air* (France)
CFE Treaty	Conventional Armed Forces in Europe Treaty
CFLT	*Commandement de la Force Logistique Terrestre* (France)
CFSP	Common Foreign and Security Policy (European Union)
CHP	*Cumhuriyet Halk Partisi* (Turkey)
CIA	Central Intelligence Agency (USA)
CINC	Commander-in-Chief (United Kingdom)
CINSEC	Caribbean Island Nations Security Conference
CIRA	Continuity Irish Republican Army (Ireland)
CIS	Commonwealth of Independent States
CIWS	Close-in Weapon System
CMAC	Cambodian Mine Action Centre
CMC	Central Military Commissions (China)
CoE	Church of England
COMECON	Council for Mutual Economic Cooperation
CONUS	Continental United States
COW	Correlates of War
CPC	Central People's Commission (North Korea)
CPD	Coalition of Parties for Democracy (Chile)
CPLP	Community of Portuguese-Speaking Countries
CPP-NPA	Communist Party of the Philippines–New People's Army
CSCAP	Council for Security Cooperation in the Asia-Pacific
CSCE	Conference on Security and Cooperation in Europe
CSI	Container Security Initiative (USA)
CSU	Christian Social Union (Germany)
CTBT	Comprehensive Test Ban Treaty (USA)
CTC	Counter Terrorism Committee
CWC	Chemical Weapons Convention
DC	Christian Democrats (Italy)
DCS	Direct Commercial Sales
DDP	Democratic Development Party of Taiwan (Taiwan)
DEA	Drug Enforcement Administration (USA)
DGGN	*Direction Générale de la Gendarmerie Nationale* (France)

DHKP/C	Revolutionary People's Liberation Party/Front (Turkey)
DM	Deutsch Mark
DMoND	Deputy Minister of National Defence (Canada)
DMZ	Demilitarized Zone
DND	Department of National Defense (Philippines)
DND	Department of National Defence (Canada)
DP	Democratic Party (Turkey)
DPP	Democratic Progressive Party (Taiwan)
DPRK	Democratic People's Republic of Korea (USA)
DPRK	Democratic People's Republic of Korea (North Korea)
DRC	Democratic Republic of the Congo
DTA	Democratic Turnhalle Alliance (Namibia)
EADS	European Aeronautic Defense and Space Company
EC	European Community
ECOMOG	Economic Community of West African States Military Observer Group
ECOWAS	Economic Community of West African States
ECSC	European Coal and Steel Community
EEA	European Economic Area
EEC	European Economic Community
EEZ	Exclusive Economic Zone
EFTA	European Free Trade Association
EMF	*États-majors de forces* (France)
EPC	European Political Cooperation
EPR	Popular Revolutionary Army (Mexico)
ERIP	People's Revolutionary Insurgent Army (Mexico)
ESDP	European Security and Defense Policy
ESF	Economic Support Fund (Lebanon)
ETIM	East Turkistan Islamic Movement
EU	European Union
EUFOR	European Force Operation
EUSA	Eighth U.S. Army
EZLN	Zapatista National Liberation Army (Mexico)
FAA	Angola Armed Forces
FALCON	Force Application and Launch from CONUS (USA)
FALPMG	Armed Front for the Liberation of the Marginalized People of Guerrero (Mexico)
FAN	*La Force d'Action Navale* (France)
FAPLA	People's Armed Forces for the Liberation of Angola
FARC	Revolutionary Armed Forces of Colombia
FAWEU	Forces Answerable to Western European Union
FCS	Future Combat Systems (USA)
FDOs	Flexible Deterrence Options
FFA	Forum Fisheries Agency (Solomon Islands)

FLEC	*Frente para a Libertacao do Enclave de Cabinda* (Angola)
FMLN	Farabundo Martí Liberation Front (El Salvador)
FMPs	Force Module Packages
FMS	Foreign Military Sales
FNLA	*Frente Nacional de Libertacao de Angola* (Angola)
FOB	Free on Board
FORFUSCO	*Fusiliers Marins et Commandos* (France)
FPÖ	Freedom Party (Austria)
FRG	Federal Republic of Germany
FTAA	Free Trade Area of the Americas
FTO	Foreign Terrorist Organization
FY	Fiscal Year
FYROM	Former Yugoslav Republic of Macedonia
GASM	Anti-Submarine Action Group (France)
GCC	Gulf Cooperation Council
GDF	Guyana Defense Force
GDP	Gross Domestic Product
GDR	German Democratic Republic (Germany)
GEAR	Growth, Employment and Redistribution Strategy (South Africa)
GHQ	General Headquarters
GIO	Government Information Office (Taiwan)
GMIP	Pattani Islamic Mujahideen Movement or Mujahideen Islamic Pattani Group (Malaysia)
GNP	Gross National Product
GNS	Guyana National Service
GOC	General Officers Commanding (Ireland)
GOLKAR	"Functional Groups" (Indonesia)
GPF	Guyana Police Force
GPM	Guyana People's Militia
GUNT	Transitional Government of National Unity (Chad)
HAL	Hindustan Aeronautics Limited (India)
HARM	High-Speed Anti-Radiation Missile (Taiwan)
HDZ	Croatian Democratic Union (Former Yugoslavia)
HEU	Highly Enriched Uranium
HMS	Her Majesties Ship (United Kingdom)
HQ	Headquarters
HUJI-B	Harakut ul-Jihad-I-Islami/Bangladesh
HUKBALAHAP	*Hukbong Mapagpalaya ng Bayan* (Philippines)
HVO	Croatian Defense Council (Former Yugoslavia)
IAEA	International Atomic Energy Agency
IAF	Indian Air Force
IBERLANT	Iberian Atlantic Command
ICC	International Criminal Court
ICJ	International Court of Justice

ICO	Islamic Conference Organization
ICTY	International Criminal Tribunal for the Former Yugoslavia (Former Yugoslavia)
IDF	Internal Defense Force (Taiwan)
IDF	Israeli Defense Force
IFOR	Implementation Force
IFP	Inkatha Freedom Party (South Africa)
IGO	Intergovernmental Organization
IIPB	Islamic International Peace Keeping Brigade (Turkey)
IISS	International Institute for Strategic Studies
ILMG	Israel-Lebanon Monitoring Group
ILSA	Iran-Libya Sanctions Act
IMET	International Military and Educational Training (USA)
IMF	International Monetary Fund
IMU	Islamic Movement of Uzbekistan
IN	Indian Navy
INC	Indian National Congress
INF	Intermediate-Range Nuclear Forces
INF Treaty	Intermediate-Range Nuclear Forces Treaty
INGU	Interim Government of National Unity (Liberia)
INPFL	Independent National Patriotic Front of Liberia
INTA	National Institute for Aerospace Technology (Spain)
INTERFET	International Force East Timor
INTERPOL	International Criminal Police Organization
IPMT	International Peace Monitoring Team
IRA	Irish Republican Army
ISAF	International Security Assistance Force
ISI	Directorate for Inter-Services Intelligence (Pakistan)
IUCN	World Conservation Union (Pakistan)
JCF	Jamaica Constabulary Force
JDA	Japan Defense Agency
JDAM	Joint Direct Attack Munitions (Taiwan)
JI	Jemaah Islamiyah
JICC	Joint Information Communications Centers
JNA	Yugoslav People's Army (Former Yugoslavia)
JPEO-CBE	Joint Program Executive Office for Chemical and Biological Defense (USA)
JSC	Joint Staff Council (Japan)
KADEK	Kurdistan Freedom and Democracy Congress (Turkey)
KCIA	Korea Central Information Agency (South Korea)
KEDO	Korean Peninsula Energy Development Organization
KFOR	Kosovo Force
KIG	Kalayaan Island Group (Philippines)
KMT	Nationalist Party (Taiwan)
LAF	Lebanese Armed Forces

LC	League of Communists (Former Yugoslavia)
LCM	Landing Craft, Mechanical
LCT	Landing Craft, Tank
LCT/LST	Landing Craft Tank/Landing Ship Tank
LF	Lebanese Front (Lebanon)
LNG	Liquefied Natural Gas
LNM	Lebanese National Movement (Lebanon)
LoC	Line of Control (Kashmir)
LST	Landing Ship, Tank
LTTE	Liberation Tigers of Tamil Eelam (Sri Lanka)
LVF	Loyalist Volunteer Force (Ireland)
MAP	Mutual Assistance Program
MAPHILINDO	Malaysia, Indonesia, Philippines Trilateral Treaty
MARLANT	Maritime Atlantic Formation (Canada)
MARPAC	Maritime Pacific Formation (Canada)
MBA	Military Bases Agreement (Philippines)
MDT	Mutual Defense Treaty (Philippines)
MEF	Malaitan Eagle Force
MERCOSUR	Southern Cone Common Market
MFAT	Ministry of Foreign Affairs and Trade (New Zealand)
MFN	Most-Favored Nation
MI5	UK Security Service (United Kingdom)
MI6	Secret Intelligence Service (United Kingdom)
MID	Militarized Interstate Dispute
MILF	Moro Islamic Liberation Front (Malaysia, Philippines)
MINUGUA	UN Verification Mission in Guatemala
MINURSO	United Nations Mission for the Referendum in Western Sahara
MIRA	Movement for Islamic Reform in Arabia
MITI	Ministry of International Trade and Industry (Japan)
MKEK	*Makina ve Kimya Endüstrisi Kurumu* (Turkey)
MLRS	Multiple Launch Rocket System
MLSA	Mutual Logistic and Support Agreement (Philippines)
MMP	Mixed Member Proportional
MND	Ministry of National Defense (various)
MNLF-BMA	Moro National Liberation Front–Bangsa Moro Army (Philippines, Malaysia)
MOD	Ministry of Defense/Defence (various)
MOF	Ministry of Finance
MOFA	Ministry of Foreign Affairs (Japan)
MONUC	United Nations Observer Mission in the Democratic Republic of Congo
MPFSEE	Multinational Peace Force of South East Europe (Turkey)
MPLA	*Movimento Pouplar de Libertacao de Angola* (Angola)
MRL	Multiple Rocket Launchers (Syria)
MSI	*Movimento Sociale Italiano* (Italy)

MST	Landless Rural Workers Movement (Brazil)
MTAP	Military Training Assistance Program
NAEW	North Atlantic Early Warning
NAFTA	North America Free Trade Area
NAM	Non-Aligned Movement
NAS	Naval Aviation Stations (France)
NASA	National Aeronautics and Space Administration (USA)
NATINADS	European Integrated Air Defense System
NATO	North Atlantic Treaty Organization
NCO	Noncommissioned Officer
NDC	National Defense Commission (North Korea)
NDF	Nationalist Democratic Front (Philippines)
NDFB	National Democratic Front for Bodoland (India)
NDHQ	National Defence Headquarters (Canada)
NDPO	National Defense Program Outline (Japan)
NEACD	Northeast Asia Cooperation Dialogue
NEASeD	Northeast Asian Security Dialogue
NEI	Netherlands East Indies
NEPAD	New Partnership for Africa's Development
NFTC	NATO Flying Training in Canada
NMD	National Missile Defense (USA)
NORAD	North American Aerospace Defense
NORTHCOM	Northern Command (USA)
NPA	East German People's Army (Germany)
NPC	National People's Congress (China)
NPFL	National Patriotic Front of Liberia
NPN	National Party of Nigeria
NPT	Treaty of Non-Proliferation of Nuclear Weapons
NSC	National Security Council (USA, Philippines)
NWFZ	Nuclear Weapons Free Zone
NZDF	New Zealand Defence Force
OAPEC	Organization of Arab Petroleum Exporting Countries
OAS	Organization of American States
OAS	*Organisation de l'Armée Secrète* (France)
OAU	Organization of African Unity
OCU	Operational Conversion Unit (Pakistan)
ODA	Official Development Assistance
ODCCP	UN Office of Drug Control and Crime Prevention
OECD	Organization for Economic Cooperation and Development
OECS	Organization of Eastern Caribbean States
OEEC	Organization for European Economic Cooperation
OEF	Operation Enduring Freedom
OFCs	Offshore Financial Centers
OIC	Organization of the Islamic Conference
ONUMOZ	UN Operations in Mozambique

OPBAT	Operation Bahamas and Turks and Caicos
OPDS	Organ on Politics, Defence, and Security (South Africa)
OPM	Free Papua Movement (Indonesia)
OPT	Occupied Palestinian Territory
OSCE	Organization for Security and Cooperation in Europe
ÖVP	People's Party (Austria)
P2	Propaganda 2 (Italy)
PA	Palestinian Authority
PA	Philippine Army
PAC	Patriot Advanced Capability (USA)
PAF	Philippine Air Force (Philippines)
PAN	National Action Party (Mexico)
PAP	People's Armed Police (China)
PARC	Policy Affairs Research Council (Japan)
PAS	Islamic Party of Malaysia
PC	Communist Party (Chile)
PCI	*Partito Comunista Italiano* (Italy)
PDC	Christian Democratic Party
PDF	Permanent Defense Force (Ireland)
PDI	Indonesian Democratic Party
PDI-P	Indonesian Democratic Party-Struggle
PDN	*Política de Defesa Nacional* (Brazil)
PDPR	Democratic Popular Revolutionary Party (Mexico)
PDRY	People's Democratic Republic of Yemen
PECC	Pacific Economic Cooperation Council
PFLP	Palestinian Front for Liberating Palestine
PfP	Partnership for Peace
PIRA	Provisional Irish Republican Army
PKI	Indonesian Communist Party
PKK	Kurdish Worker's Party
PKK	Kurdistan Labor Party (Syria)
PKK	*Partiye Karkeran Kurdistan* (Turkey)
PKO	Peace Keeping Operations
PLA	People's Liberation Army (China)
PLAAF	People's Liberation Army Air Force (China)
PLAN	People's Liberation Army Navy (China)
PLAN	People's Liberation Army of Namibia
PLF	Palestine Liberation Front
PLO	Palestinian Liberation Organization
PMG	Peace Monitoring Group (New Zealand)
PN	Philippine Navy
PNG	Papua New Guinea
PNGDF	Papua New Guinea Defense Forces
PNP	Philippine National Police
PNR	National Revolutionary Party (Mexico)

POW	Prisoner of War
PPD	Party for Democracy (Chile)
PPP	Purchasing Power Parity
PPP	United Development Party (Indonesia)
PRC	People's Republic of China
PRD	Party of the Democratic Revolution (Mexico)
PRI	Party of the Institutional Revolution (Mexico)
PRM	Party of the Mexican Revolution (Mexico)
PRSD	Radical Social Democratic Party (Chile)
PS	Socialist Party (Chile)
PSI	*Partito Socialista Italiano* (Italy)
PT	Workers' Party (Brazil)
PTBT	Partial Test Ban Treaty (USA)
PULO	Pattani United Liberation Organization (Malaysia, Thailand)
PVA	People's Volunteer Army (China)
RAF	Red Army Faction
RAM	Reform Armed Forces Movement (Philippines)
RAMSI	Regional Assistance Mission to Solomon Islands
RDF	Reserve Defense Force (Ireland)
RDLETC	Regional Drug-Law Enforcement Training Center
RFA	Royal Fleet Auxiliary (United Kingdom)
RFMF	Republic of Fiji Military Forces
RIRA	Real Irish Republican Army (Ireland)
RMA	Revolution in Military Affairs (USA)
RN	National Renewal (Chile)
RNC	Republic of Northern Cyprus
ROC	Republic of China
ROCCISS	Regional Organized Counter Crime Information Sharing System
ROK	Republic of Korea
RSA	Republic of South Africa
RSI	*Repubblica Sociale Italiana* (Italy)
RSIP	Royal Solomon Islands Police
RSS	Rashtriya Swayamsewak Sangh (India)
RSS	Regional Security System
RUC	Royal Ulster Constabulary (United Kingdom)
RUF	Revolutionary United Front (Sierra Leone)
RZ	Revolutionary Cells
SAARC	South Asian Association for Regional Cooperation
SADC	Southern African Development Community
SADCC	Southern African Development Coordinating Conference
SADF	South African Defense Force
SALT	Strategic Arms Limitation Talks
SAM	Surface-to-Air Missile
SANDF	South African National Defense Force
SANG	Saudi Arabia's National Guard

SDA	Party of Democratic Action (Former Yugoslavia)
SDF	Self Defense Forces (Japan)
SDS	Serbian Democratic Party (Former Yugoslavia)
SEATO	South East Asian Treaty Organization
SFOR	Stabilization Force in Bosnia and Herzegovina
SIGINT	Signal Intelligence
SIPAM	System for the Protection of the Amazon (Brazil)
SIPRI	Stockholm International Peace Research Institute
SIVAM	System for the Vigilance of the Amazon (Brazil)
SLBM	Submarine Launched Ballistic Missiles
SLOC	Sea Lines of Communication (Taiwan)
SME	Small and Medium Size Enterprise
SORT	Strategic Offensive Reduction Treaty
SOUTHCOM	United States Southern Command
SPD	Social Democratic Party (Germany)
SPÖ	Socialist Party (Austria)
SSBN	Fleet Ballistic Missile Submarine
SSU	Special Service Unit
START	Strategic Arms Reduction Treaty
START II	Strategic Arms Reduction Treaty II
SWAPO	South West Africa People's Organization
TACC	Theater Air Control Center
TAF	Turkish Armed Forces
TDS	Tonga Defense Service
TEU	Treaty of European Union
TGF	Turkish General Staff
TKNU	North Kalimantan National Army (Indonesia, Malaysia)
TLF	Turkish Land Forces
TNI	National Army of Indonesia
TNI-AL	National Navy of Indonesia
TNI-AU	National Air Force of Indonesia
TPFDD	Time-Phased Forces Deployment Data
TPVM	Third Party Verification Mechanism (Democratic Republic of the Congo)
TRA	Taiwan Relations Act (USA)
TTDF	Trinidad and Tobago Defense Force
TTIC	Terrorist Threat Integration Center (USA)
UAE	United Arab Emirates
UAR	United Arab Republic
UAV	Unmanned Aerial Vehicle
UCK	Kosovo Liberation Army (Kosovo) or National Liberation Army (Macedonia) (Former Yugoslavia)
UDA	Ulster Defense Association (Ireland)
UDI	Independent Democratic Union (Chile)
UK	United Kingdom

ULFA	United Liberation Front for Assam (India)
ULIMO	United Liberation Movement for Democracy (Liberia)
UMNO	United Malays National Organization
UN	United Nations
UNAMET	UN Mission to East Timor
UNAMIR	UN Assistance Mission for Rwanda
UNASOG	UN Anzou Strip Observer Group
UNAVEM	UN Angola Verification Mission
UNC	UN Command
UNDOF	UN Disengagement Observation Force (Syria)
UNEF	UN Emergency Force
UNFICYP	UN Peacekeeping Force in Cyprus
UNIFIL	UN Interim Force in Lebanon
UNIIMOPG	UN Iran-Iraq Military Observer Group
UNIMSET	UN Mission of Support in East Timor
UN-ISAF	UN International Security Force
UNITA	*União Nacional para a Independência Total de Angola* (Angola)
UNMEE	UN Mission in Ethiopia and Eritrea
UNMISET	UN Mission in Support of East Timor
UNMOP	UN Mission of Observers in Prevlaka
UNO	UN Organization
UNOMIG	UN Observer Mission in Georgia
UNOMIG	UN Mission in Georgia
UNOMIL	UN Observer Mission in Liberia
UNOMSIL	UN Observer Mission in Sierra Leone
UNOSOM	UN Operations in Somalia
UNOSOM II	UN Operations in Somalia II
UNPROFOR	UN Protection Force
UNRWA	UN Relief and Works Agency
UNSC	UN Security Council
UNSCOM	UN Special Commission
UNTAET	UN Transitional Administration in East Timor
URNG	Guatemalan National Revolutionary Unity
USA	United States of America
USAF	U.S. Air Force
USAID	U.S. Agency for International Development
USFK	U.S. Forces in Korea
USN	U.S. Navy
USSR	Union of Soviet Socialist Republics
UTA	*Union des Transports Aériens de Guinée* (France)
UTO	United Tajik Opposition (Tajikistan)
UVF	Ulster Volunteer Force (Ireland)
VFA	Visiting Forces Agreement (Philippines)
VMF	Vanuatu Mobile Force
VPF	Vanuatu Police Force

WEAG	Western European Armaments Group
WEAO	Western European Armaments Organisation
WEU	Western European Union
WMD	Weapons of Mass Destruction
WSK	*Wytwornia Spzetu Komunikacyjnego* (Poland)
WTO	Warsaw Treaty Organization
WTO	World Trade Organization
WWI	World War I
WWII	World War II
WZO	World Zionist Organization

CHRONOLOGY: IMPORTANT INTERNATIONAL AND SECURITY EVENTS 1945–2004

Min Ye and Paul Bellamy

1945

February   Soviet leader Joseph Stalin, British Prime Minister Winston Churchill, and U.S. President Franklin Roosevelt met in Yalta to discuss postwar arrangements.

May   VE Day—Victory in Europe Day.

July   The United States conducted the world's first nuclear test.

           U.S. President Harry Truman, British Prime Minister Clement Atlee, and Stalin met at Potsdam to further discuss postwar arrangements. The conference ended the following month.

August   The United States dropped the first atomic bomb on Hiroshima, Japan.

           The Soviet Union declared war on Japan.

           The United States dropped the second atomic bomb on Nagasaki.

           Japan surrendered unconditionally to the Allies.

           Indonesia declared independence.

October   The United Nations was founded.

1946

April   Syria declared independence.

July   The Philippines became independent.

December   The French Fourth Republic was established.

1947

August   Pakistan obtained independence.

India obtained independence.

October   The First Kashmir War between India and Pakistan started. The war ended in January 1949.

1948

January   Indian leader Mahatma Gandhi was assassinated.

March   Belgium, Britain, France, Luxembourg, and The Netherlands signed the Treaty of Brussels.

April   The Charter of the Organization of American States was signed and the Organization of American States (OAS) was established.

May   Israel was declared an independent state. Arab states invaded Israel. Israel signed separate armistices in 1949.

June   The Berlin blockade started. The blockade ended in May 1949.

August   The Republic of Korea (South Korea) was established.

September   The Democratic People's Republic of Korea (North Korea) was established.

1949

April   The Republic of Ireland was established.

The North Atlantic Treaty was signed. NATO was formed.

May   The Federal Republic of Germany (West Germany) was established.

August   The Soviet Union detonated its first atomic bomb.

October   The People's Republic of China (China) was established.

The German Democratic Republic (East Germany) was established.

December   Following defeat in the Chinese civil war, the Nationalist Party of China fled to Taiwan and established Taipei as the new capital of the Republic of China.

1950
February   China and the Soviet Union signed the Treaty of Friendship, Alliance, and Mutual Assistance.

June   The Korean War began.

1951
August   The U.S.-Philippines Mutual Defense Treaty was signed.

September   The ANZUS Treaty was signed.

              The Treaty of Mutual Cooperation and Security between Japan and the United States was signed.

1952
February   Turkey joined NATO.

April   Under the Treaty of San Francisco, the United States ended its occupation of Japan, and Japan gained its full independence.

1953
March   Stalin died.

July   The Korean War ended.

October   The U.S.-South Korea Mutual Defense Treaty was signed.

1954
May   French forces at Dien Bien Phu surrendered to the Viet Minh.

August   The first Taiwan Straits crisis started. China stopped shelling Quemoy and Matsu islands in May 1955. A second (1958–1959) and third crisis (1995–1996) ultimately followed.

July   The Japanese Self-Defense Forces were founded.

              At the Geneva Conference, Vietnam was divided into North Vietnam and South Vietnam.

September   Australia, France, Great Britain, New Zealand, Pakistan, the Philippines, Thailand, and the United States signed the Southeast Asia Treaty Organization (SEATO). SEATO was disbanded in 1977.

December   The Mutual Defense Treaty between the United States and Taiwan was signed.

1955

February   The Baghdad Pact was signed. Iraq, Turkey, Iran, Pakistan, and Britain were members of the pact.

May   West Germany joined NATO.

                The Warsaw Treaty Organization was established.

1956

March   Pakistan became an Islamic republic.

July   Egypt announced the nationalization of the Suez Canal Company.

October   Israel invaded the Sinai Peninsula.

                Britain and France bombed Egypt to force it to reopen the Suez Canal.

November   The Soviet Union sent troops into Hungary, crushing the Hungarian reform movement.

                The UN General Assembly adopted a resolution calling for Britain, France, and Israel to withdraw from Egypt.

December   Japan became a member of the United Nations.

1957

January   Israel withdrew from the Sinai Peninsula.

March   Egypt reopened the Suez Canal.

                The Treaty of Rome was signed. The European Economic Community (EEC) was established.

August   The Federation of Malaya obtained independence.

1958

May   The North American Aerospace Defense Command was created.

October   The Fifth Republic constitution of France was introduced.

1959

January   Cuban president Fulgencio Batista was overthrown by forces led by Fidel Castro.

                The United States recognized the new Cuban government of Castro.

1960

February   France detonated its first atomic bomb.

May   A U.S. U2 spy plane was shot down by the Soviet Union.

August   Cyprus obtained independence.

October   Nigeria obtained independence.

1961

January   The United States ended diplomatic relations with Cuba.

April   Cuban exiles failed to overthrow Castro at the Bay of Pigs.

May   The Republic of South Africa came into existence.

July   The Soviet Union and North Korea signed the Treaty of Friendship, Cooperation and Mutual Assistance.

China and North Korea signed the Treaty of Friendship, Cooperation and Mutual Assistance.

August   The Berlin Wall was built.

September   A coup was staged in Syria and the country's withdrawal from the United Arab Republic was announced.

December   Castro declared that Cuba was a communist country.

India invaded Goa.

1962

January   Cuba's membership in the OAS was suspended.

March   The war between Algeria and France ended.

July   Algeria was pronounced independent.

August   Jamaica gained independence.

Trinidad and Tobago gained independence.

October   The Cuban missile crisis occurred.

The China-India War over territorial disputes started. China declared a unilateral cease-fire in November 1962.

1963

January   France and Germany signed the treaty on Franco-German cooperation (also known as the Elysee Treaty).

June   The United States and the Soviet Union signed a Memorandum of Understanding to establish a direct "hotline" communications link between the two nations for use in a crisis.

August   The United States, Britain, and the Soviet Union signed the Partial Test Ban Treaty.

November   President John F. Kennedy was assassinated.

1964

January   China and France established diplomatic relations.

August   U.S. destroyers reported attacks by North Vietnam in the Gulf of Tonkin.

October   China successfully detonated its first atomic bomb.

1965

March   The first U.S. combat troops arrived in South Vietnam.

June   Japan and South Korea signed the Treaty on Basic Relations.

August   The second Indo-Pakistani War began. A cease-fire was accepted by both countries the following month.

1966

March   French president Charles de Gaulle announced France's complete withdraw from NATO's military command.

May   Chinese leader Mao Zedong launched the Cultural Revolution.

            China exploded its first hydrogen bomb.

            Guyana gained independence.

October   A military encounter occurred between Guyana and Venezuela over the occupation by Venezuela of Guyana's portion of Ankoko Island.

1967
June   The Six Days' War between Israel and Arab states occurred.

                     The Soviet Union dropped diplomatic relations with Israel after the Six Days' War.

August   ASEAN was established by Indonesia, Malaysia, the Philippines, Singapore, and Thailand.

1968
January   Political liberalization (the "Prague Spring") started in Czechoslovakia.

                     Communist forces launched the Tet Offensive in South Vietnam.

July   The NPT was signed.

August   The troops of Warsaw Pact countries (except Romania) led by the Soviet Union invaded Czechoslovakia in order to end the political liberalization.

1969
March   A military clash occurred between Chinese and Soviet troops over the disputed Damansky/Zhenbao Island.

August   British troops were deployed in Northern Ireland.

1970
April   The United States invaded Cambodia.

October   The October Crisis of Quebec, Canada, occurred.

                     Fiji obtained independence.

1971
February   South Vietnamese troops invaded Laos with the help of the United States.

March   Pakistan sent troops to East Pakistan to suppress an uprising.

August   India and the Soviet Union signed the Treaty of Peace, Friendship and Cooperation.

October   China joined the United Nations and Taiwan was expelled.

December   Bangladesh was established after Pakistani forces surrendered in East Pakistan.

1972

January   Pakistan withdrew from the Commonwealth (the intergovernmental organization headed by the British sovereign).

February   President Richard Nixon visited China.

March   Bangladesh and India signed the Treaty of Friendship.

May   The Strategic Arms Limitation Talks were held.

            The ABM Treaty between the United States and Soviet Union was signed.

July   The Simla Agreement on Bilateral Relations between India and Pakistan was signed.

September   Arab terrorists killed Israeli athletes at the Olympic Games in Munich.

            Martial law was announced by Philippine president Ferdinand Marcos.

1973

January   Denmark, Ireland, and the United Kingdom entered the EEC.

            Ferdinand Marcos became President for Life of the Philippines.

            The United States signed a peace treaty ending its involvment in Vietnam.

March   The last U.S. soldiers left Vietnam.

June   The Conference on Security and Cooperation in Europe was formally opened in Helsinki.

September   A military coup led by Augusto Pinochet overthrew the democratically elected government of Chile.

October   The Yom Kippur War occurred between Israel and Arab states.

1974

July   Turkey landed forces in Cyprus.

            The treaty between the United States and the Soviet Union on the limitation of underground nuclear weapons tests was signed.

November   The Irish Republican Army bombed a pub in Birmingham, England.

1975

April   The Lebanese civil war started. The war ended in October 1990.

Pol Pot took power in Cambodia and established the Democratic Republic of Kampuchea. Subsequently, the "killing fields" were experienced by Cambodians.

Communist forces captured Saigon and South Vietnam surrendered.

November   Angola obtained independence.

The Spanish dictator Francisco Franco died and Prince Juan Carlos assumed the position of king and head of state.

East Timor declared independence.

December   Indonesia invaded East Timor.

1976

January   Spain and the United States signed the Treaty of Friendship and Cooperation.

June   The Soweto riots occurred in South Africa.

September   Mao Zedong died.

1977

July   Deng Xiaoping was restored to his offices in China.

September   Panama and the United States signed a treaty on the status of the Panama Canal.

Fifteen countries signed the NPT.

November   Egyptian President Anwar Sadat visited Israel.

1978

March   Israeli forces invaded Lebanon.

September   Egypt and Israel signed the Camp David peace accords.

December   A crisis occurred between Argentina and Chile over the Beagle Channel. The Act of Montevideo was signed the following month to ease tensions.

Vietnam invaded Cambodia and overthrew the Pol Pot regime.

1979

January	China and the United States established diplomatic relations.
	The shah of Iran left the country for exile.
February	Ayatollah Khomeini became the religious leader of Iran.
	The China-Vietnam War started. The war ended the following month.
March	The Egyptian-Israeli peace treaty was signed in Washington.
June	The treaty between the United States and Soviet Union on the Limitation of Strategic Offensive Arms was signed.
October	South Korean president Park Chung Hee was assassinated.
November	In Iran, radical students invaded the U.S. Embassy in Tehran and took Americans hostage.
December	The Soviet Union invaded Afghanistan.

1980

January	Egypt and Israel established diplomatic relations.
April	The United States dropped diplomatic relations with Iran.
May	The Kwangju Uprising in South Korea was suppressed.
September	Iraq invaded Iran. The eight-year Iran-Iraq War began.
October	Syria signed the Treaty of Friendship and Cooperation with the Soviet Union.

1981

January	The American hostages in Tehran were released after 444 days in captivity.
	Greece entered the EEC.
June	Israel attacked and destroyed an Iraqi nuclear reactor near Baghdad.
September	Belize gained independence.
October	Egyptian President Anwar Sadat was assassinated.
	Hosni Mubarak became president of Egypt.

December   Wojciech Jaruzelski declared martial law in Poland.

1982
April   Argentina invaded the Falkland Islands.

May   Spain joined NATO.

June   Israel invaded south Lebanon.

                The Argentine troops in the Falkland Islands surrendered to British forces.

1983
January   Colombia, Mexico, Panama, and Venezuela initiated the Contadora Group.

March   President Ronald Reagan proposed the Strategic Defense Initiative.

May   An accord on Israel's withdrawal from Lebanon was signed.

September   Korean Air Lines Flight 007 was shot down by a Soviet fighter.

October   A suicide bombing of the U.S. and French barracks in Beirut took place.

                The United States invaded Grenada.

                The first democratic election was held in Argentina after seven years of military rule.

1984
January   Brunei obtained independence.

October   Indian prime minister Indira Gandhi was assassinated.

December   Britain and China signed the Sino-British Joint Declaration regarding the future of Hong Kong.

1985
February   New Zealand declined to allow a U.S. guided missile destroyer to visit under its antinuclear policy.

March   Mikhail Gorbachev became the general secretary of the Soviet Communist Party.

May   Argentina and Chile signed a treaty at the Vatican over island disputes in the Beagle Channel.

July   In New Zealand, agents of the French secret service sank the *Rainbow Warrior*, flagship of the environmental group Greenpeace.

November   Argentina and Brazil signed the Foz de Iguazú Declaration.

1986

January   Portugal and Spain entered the EEC.

February   The Single European Act was signed.

              Philippines dictator Ferdinand Marcos was ousted.

April   The United States launched an air attack on Libya.

December   Foreign ministers of Argentina, Brazil, Colombia, Mexico, Panama, Peru, Uruguay, and Venezuela held a meeting to establish a body for political consultation and coordination. This was later called the Rio Group.

1987

November   A bomb exploded aboard Korean Air Lines Flight 858.

December   The treaty between the United States and the Soviet Union on the elimination of their intermediate-range and shorter-range missiles was signed.

1988

July   The USS *Vincennes* shot down Iran Air Flight 655.

August   Pakistan President Mohammad Zia ul-Haq died in a plane crash. The U.S. ambassador was also killed in the crash.

December   Pan Am Flight 103 crashed after a bomb exploded on board.

1989

January   The Free Trade Agreement between Canada and the United States came into effect.

              Cuban troops began to withdraw from Angola.

February   The last Soviet troops left Kabul, Afghanistan.

June   Iranian religious leader Ayatollah Khomeini died.

              The Chinese government used the military to suppress the democratic movement in Beijing.

The political movement Solidarity won the first free election in Poland.

November   The Berlin Wall was opened.

The Velvet Revolution began in Czechoslovakia, leading to the peaceful overthrow of the communist government.

December   President Nicolae Ceausescu was overthrown and executed in Romania.

The United States invaded Panama.

1990
January   Panama leader General Manuel Noriega was captured by U.S. forces.

February   South African president Frederik Willem de Klerk declared that apartheid had failed.

Nelson Mandela was released from Victor Verster prison.

West and East Germany reached an agreement for a two-stage plan of re-unification.

Argentina and Britain resumed diplomatic relations.

March   Patricio Aylwin became the first democratically elected Chilean president since 1973.

April   Trinidad, Tobago, and Venezuela signed the Delimitation Treaty to settle the territorial dispute over the Gulf of Paria.

May   North and South Yemen were united into a single state, the Republic of Yemen.

August   Iraq invaded Kuwait.

October   East Germany was absorbed into the Federal Republic of Germany.

November   The Treaty on Conventional Armed Forces in Europe was signed by NATO and Warsaw Pact states.

The UN Security Council passed Resolution 678. This required Iraqi leader Saddam Hussein to withdraw his forces from Kuwait by January 15, 1991.

1991
February   Czechoslovakia, Hungary, and Poland formed the Visegrad Group.

	Kuwait was liberated by a U.S.-led coalition.
May	Lebanon and Syria signed the Treaty of Brotherhood, Cooperation, and Coordination.
June	Slovenia and Croatia declared independence from Yugoslavia.
	Boris Yeltsin won the first popular presidential election in the Russian Federation.
July	The WTO was officially dissolved.
	The Strategic Arms Reduction Treaty between the United States and the Soviet Union was signed.
August	The State Emergency Committee staged an unsuccessful coup in the Soviet Union.
September	The Soviet Union recognized the independence of Estonia, Latvia, and Lithuania.
October	An agreement was reached at the Paris conference regarding peace and democracy in Cambodia.
December	The Commonwealth of Independent States was founded.
	Gorbachev resigned as president of the Soviet Union. The Supreme Soviet officially dissolved the Soviet Union.

1992

February	The Treaty on European Union (also known as the Maastricht Treaty) was signed.
	U.S. President George H. W. Bush and Russian President Yeltsin held their first meeting since the dissolution of the Soviet Union.
March	Bosnia declared its independence from Yugoslavia.
June	The UN conference on the environment and development (the "Earth Summit") was held.
September	The first democratic election in Angola was held.
October	The peace agreement of Mozambique was signed, ending a long civil war.

December   Kim Young-Sam won the presidential election in South Korea.

U.S. troops were sent to Somalia.

1993
January   Czechoslovakia was divided into two independent sovereign states, Slova-kia and the Czech Republic.

The United States and Russia signed the Treaty on Further Reduction and Limitation of Strategic Offensive Arms.

February   A terrorist bomb exploded beneath the World Trade Center in New York City.

May   Elections were held in Cambodia under the supervision of the UN Transitional Authority in Cambodia.

July   In the Japanese general election, politicians formed the first non-Liberal Democratic Party (LDP) government. This ended the thirty-eight-year dominance of the LDP in Japanese politics.

September   Israel and Palestine signed the Oslo Accords.

October   In Somalia, eighteen U.S. soldiers and hundreds of Somalis were killed in a gun battle.

Conflict occurs between forces under Yeltsin and opponents in the Russian Parliament.

November   The official ceremony for the creation of the Eurocorps was held in Strasbourg.

1994
January   The North American Free Trade Agreement, including the United States, Canada, and Mexico, went into effect.

April   Rwanda President Juvenal Habyarimana and Burundi President Cyprian Ntayamira were killed in a plane crash. Genocide followed in Rwanda.

The first multiracial election was held in South Africa.

May   Nelson Mandela became the first black president of South Africa.

July   North Korean leader Kim Il Sung died. His son, Kim Jong Il, succeeded him.

Israel and Jordan signed the Washington Declaration.

The first meeting of the ASEAN Regional Forum took place.

October   The United States and North Korea signed the Agreed Framework. This ended the first Korean peninsula nuclear crisis.

Israel and Jordan signed a peace treaty.

December   The first Chechen War began. The war ended in 1996.

1995
January   The Mercado Commun del Sur, a customs union between Argentina, Brazil, Paraguay, and Uruguay, came into effect.

Austria, Finland, and Sweden joined the EU.

Chinese President Jiang Zemin spelled out the mainland's stance in his "Eight-Point Offer" to Taiwan.

July   President Bill Clinton announced the normalization of U.S. relations with Vietnam.

October   The second referendum on Quebec's independence was held (the first was held in 1980). The proposal of seccession was defeated.

November   Israeli prime minister Yitzhak Rabin was assassinated.

December   The General Framework Agreement for Peace in Bosnia and Herzegovina (also known as the Dayton Peace Accords) was signed.

1996
March   The first direct presidential election was held in Taiwan.

September   The Comprehensive Test Ban Treaty was opened for signature.

The Taliban stormed the presidential palace in Kabul, the capital of Afghanistan.

October   The first New Zealand general election under the Mixed Member Proportional voting system took place.

November   Switzerland joined NATO's Partnership for Peace.

1997

May   NATO and Russia signed the NATO-Russia Founding Act.

July   Britain handed over sovereignty of Hong Kong to China.

October   The Burnham Truce marked the end of an armed struggle by Bougainville separatists in Papua New Guinea. A permanent cease-fire was signed in April 1998.

1998

April   The British and Irish governments, and various Northern Ireland political parties, signed the Belfast Agreement (also known as the Good Friday Agreement).

May   India announced that it had conducted a series of nuclear tests.

               Indonesian president Thojib Suharto resigned.

               Pakistan announced that it had conducted nuclear tests.

August   The U.S. embassies in Kenya and Tanzania were bombed by terrorists.

               The Real Irish Republican Army carried out the Omagh bombing in Northern Ireland.

October   Israel and Palestine signed the Wye River Accords.

               The former Chilean dictator Augusto Pinochet was arrested in London for crimes against humanity and human rights violations. Pinochet was released in 2000.

1999

February   The Rambouillet talks were held to address conflict in Kosovo. The talks ended the following month.

               India and Pakistan signed the Lahore Agreement.

March   The Czech Republic, Hungary, and Poland joined NATO.

               NATO started bombing Serbia to force it to withdraw from Kosovo.

June   Slobodan Milosevic accepted the autonomy plan of Kosovo and Serbian forces withdrew.

September	Peacekeeping troops led by Australia were sent to East Timor to restore order and stop violence.
October	General Pervaiz Musharraf led a military coup and took control of Pakistan.
	Russian ground forces advanced into Chechnya.
December	China and Vietnam signed the Vietnam-China Treaty on Land Border.
	Russian president Yeltsin resigned and named Vladimir Putin as acting president. Putin was elected president in March 2000.

2000

February	North Korea and Russia signed a new Treaty of Friendship.
March	Chen Shui-bian won the presidential election of Taiwan.
May	A coup was staged in Fiji. Two previous coups had occurred in 1987.
	Israeli troops withdrew from Lebanon.
October	Milosevic was overthrown in Serbia.

2001

January	Joseph Estrada resigned as president of the Philippines.
February	The Treaty of Nice was signed.
April	The Black Sea Naval Cooperation Task Group Agreement was signed in Istanbul.
	Tensions arose between the United States and China after a Chinese fighter and a U.S. surveillance plane collided.
June	Milosevic was extradited to the International Criminal Tribunal for the Former Yugoslavia at The Hague.
September	Terrorists attacked targets in the United States including the World Trade Center in New York City and the Pentagon in Washington, D.C.
November	The Northern Alliance seized Kabul in Afghanistan. The alliance had received support from the United States.
December	Terrorists attacked the Indian Parliament in New Delhi.

The United States granted China permanent normal trade relations status.

2002

January   The united European currency (the Euro) replaced the national currency of twelve EU states.

          In his State of the Union address, President George W. Bush called Iran, Iraq, and North Korea an "axis of evil."

April   Cease-fire negotiations were concluded in Angola. The Angola civil war ended.

May   The NATO-Russia Council was established.

          East Timor gained independence.

          President Bush and President Putin signed the Strategic Offensive Reductions Treaty.

June   The United States formally withdrew from the ABM Treaty.

September The Bush administration released the National Security Strategy for the United States of America.

          Switzerland joined the United Nations.

October   Two bombs exploded in the town of Kuta on the island of Bali, Indonesia.

          Chechen terrorists kidnapped hostages in Moscow. The crisis was ended three days later through use of force by the Russians.

November China and ASEAN signed a code of conduct in the South China Sea to maintain peace and stability.

          The UN Security Council passed Resolution 1441, forcing Iraq to disarm.

December The Bush administration released the National Strategy to Combat Weapons of Mass Destruction.

          Chile and the United States signed the U.S.-Chile Free Trade Agreement.

2003

January   North Korea withdrew from the NPT.

March   Forces led by the United States invaded Iraq.

April	Coalition forces seized control of Baghdad.
	North Korea admitted that it had nuclear weapons.
May	President Bush declared that the major combat phase in Iraq had ended.
July	The Inter-American Convention against Terrorism entered into force.
October	Malaysian prime minister Mahathir Mohamad resigned after twenty-two years in power.
December	Saddam Hussein was captured in Iraq.

2004

March	Terrorist bombings took place in Madrid.
	Bulgaria, Estonia, Latvia, Lithuania, Romania, Slovakia, and Slovenia formally became members of NATO.
May	Cyprus, the Czech Republic, Estonia, Hungary, Latvia, Lithuania, Malta, Poland, Slovakia, and Slovenia joined the EU.
June	The United States transferred sovereignty of Iraq to an interim government.
July	The International Court of Justice ruled that the barrier Israel was building to seal off the West Bank violated international law.
	The U.S. Senate Intelligence Committee released a report critical of the CIA's prewar estimates of WMD in Iraq.
	An inquiry report was critical of prewar British intelligence on Iraq.
	The independent National Commission on Terrorist Attacks Upon the United States released its findings. The report found that the United States had failed to understand the gravity of the threat posed by radical Islamists.
August	There was extensive fighting between the Shiite cleric Muqtada al-Sadr's Mehdi army militia and U.S. and Iraqi forces in the Najaf region, Iraq.
	Traces of explosives were found in the wreckage of two aircraft that crashed almost simultaneously after departing from Moscow.

References

British Broadcasting Corporation (BBC). 2004. *Timeline: Madrid Investigation.* April 28. http://news.bbc.co.uk/2/hi/europe/3597885.stm (accessed July 20, 2004).

———. 2004. *20,000 Posts Go in Defence Cuts.* July 21. http://news.bbc.co.uk/2/hi/uk_news/3912283.stm (accessed June 16, 2005).

Cable News Network (CNN). 2004a. *Iraq Suicide Blast Kills 68.* July 29. http://www.cnn.com/2004/WORLD/meast/07/28/iraq.main/index.html (accessed July 30, 2004).

———. 2004b. *War in Iraq—Forces: U.S./Coalition Casualties.* http://www.cnn.com/SPECIALS/2003/iraq/forces/casualties/index.html (accessed August 29, 2004).

Central Intelligence Agency (CIA). 2004. *Colombia.* http://www.cia.gov/cia/publications/factbook/geos/co.html (accessed July 30, 2004).

Coalition Bulletin—A Publication of the Coalition Fighting on Global War on Terrorism. 2004. http://www.centcom.mil/Operations/Coalition/Bulletin/bulletin13.pdf (accessed June 2004).

National Commission on Terrorist Attacks Upon the United States. 2004. *The 9/11 Commission Report.* http://i.a.cnn.net/cnn/US/resources/9.11.report/911ReportExec.pdf (accessed June 16, 2005).

Stockholm International Peace Research Institute (SIPRI). 2004. "SIPRI *Yearbook 2004.*" http://editors.sipri.se/pubs/yb04/aboutyb.html (accessed June 16, 2005).

United Nations. *Selected United Nations Activities to Address Terrorism—September 2001–2002.* http://www.un.org/News/dh/infocus/overview.htm (accessed July 27, 2004).

United States Department of State (U.S. DoS). July 2001. *Diplomacy—The State Department at Work.* http://www.state.gov/r/pa/ei/rls/dos/4078.htm (accessed July 29, 2004).

———. 2002a. *Diplomatic Support for Operation Enduring Freedom.* 2002. http://www.state.gov/coalition/cr/fs/12805.htm (accessed July 29, 2004).

———. 2002b. *Patterns of Global Terrorism 2001—The Year in Review.* http://www.state.gov/s/ct/rls/pgtrpt/2001/pdf/ (accessed July 29, 2004).

———. 2003. *Patterns of Global Terrorism 2002—The Year in Review.* http://www.state.gov/s/ct/rls/pgtrpt/2002/pdf/ (accessed July 29, 2004).

———. 2004. *Patterns of Global Terrorism 2003—The Year in Review* (rev.), June 22. http://www.state.gov/s/ct/rls/pgtrpt/2003/33771.htm (accessed July 29, 2004).

White House. January 2002. *President Delivers State of Union Address.* http://www.whitehouse.gov/news/releases/2002/01/20020129-11.html (accessed June 16, 2005).

———. May 2003. *President Bush Announces Major Combat Operations in Iraq Have Ended.* http://www.whitehouse.gov/news/releases/2003/05/iraq/20030501–15.html (accessed July 29, 2004).

———. March 2, 2004. *President Highlights a More Secure America on First Anniversary of Department of Homeland Security.* http://www.roadway.com/homeland/pdfs/highlights.pdf (accessed June 17, 2005).

———. July 2004. *Homeland Security.* http://www.whitehouse.gov/homeland/ (accessed July 29, 2004).

Contributors

Michael Barutciski
Assistant Professor
York University
Toronto, Ontario
Canada

Paul Bellamy
Research Analyst
Parliamentary Library, New Zealand
Parliament
Wellington, NZ

Sheryl Boxall
Research Assistant–Post Graduate
    Student
University of Canterbury
Christchurch, NZ

Alex Braithwaite
Ph.D. Candidate
Pennsylvania State University
University Park, PA

Woondo Choi
Research Professor
Institute of East and West Studies
Yonsei University
Seoul, South Korea

Eben J. Christensen
Ph.D. Candidate
University of Wisconsin, Milwaukee
Milwaukee, WI

Elizabeth P. Coughlan
Assistant Professor
Salem State College
Salem, MA

Karl DeRouen, Jr.
Associate Professor
University of Alabama
Tuscaloosa, AL

Balkan Devlen
Ph.D. Candidate
University of Missouri, Columbia
Columbia, MO

Kihong Eom
Lecturer
Iowa State University
Ames, IA

P. D. Finn
Graduate Student
University of Wisconsin, Milwaukee
Milwaukee, WI

Faten Ghosn
Pennsylvania State University
University Park, PA

Kenneth Ray Glaudell
Assistant Professor
Cardinal Stritch University
Milwaukee, WI

Ivelaw L. Griffith
Professor and Dean
Florida International University
Miami, FL

John Henderson
Associate Professor
University of Canterbury
Nw South Wales, Australia

Shale Horowitz
Associate Professor
University of Wisconsin,
   Milwaukee
Milwaukee, WI

Christopher E. Housenick
American University
Washington, DC

Timothy D. Hoyt
Associate Professor of Strategy
   and Policy
U.S. Naval War College
Newport, RI

Neal G. Jesse
Associate Professor
Bowling Green State
   University
Bowling Green, OH

Kyle A. Joyce
Ph.D. Candidate
Pennsylvania State University
University Park, PA

Tatyana A. Karaman
Assistant Professor
Samford University
Birmingham, AL

Franz Kernic
Associate Professor

University of Innsbruck
Vienna, Austria

Dong-hun Kim
Ph.D. Candidate
University of Iowa
Iowa City, IA

Joakim Kreutz
Research Assistant
Uppsala University
Uppsala, Sweden

Dong-Yoon Lee
Research Professor
Sogang University
Seoul, South Korea

Ronald R. Macintyre
Senior Lecturer
University of Canterbury
New South Wales, Australia

Rodelio Cruz Manacsa
Ph.D. Candidate
Vanderbilt University
Nashville, TN

Justin L. Miller, Ph.D.
El Paso, TX

Daniel S. Morey
Ph.D. Candidate
University of Iowa
Iowa City, IA

Özgür Özdamar
Ph.D. Candidate
University of Missouri,
   Columbia
Columbia, MO

Brandon C. Prins
Assistant Professor

Texas Tech University
Lubbock, TX

Steven B. Redd
Assistant Professor
University of Wisconsin, Milwaukee
Milwaukee, WI

Terence Roehrig
Associate Professor and Chair,
    Department of Political Science
Cardinal Stritch University
Milwaukee, WI

Marc R. Rosenblum
Assistant Professor
University of New Orleans
New Orleans, LA

Trevor Rubenzer
Ph.D. Candidate
University of Wisconsin,
    Milwaukee
Milwaukee, WI

Kanishkan Sathasivam
Assistant Professor
Salem State College
Salem, MA

Christopher Sprecher
Assistant Professor

Texas A&M University
College Station, TX

Hans Stockton
Assistant Professor
University of St. Thomas
Houston, TX

Jonah Victor
Ph.D. Candidate
Pennsylvania State University
State College, PA

Darius Watson
Ph.D. Candidate
SUNY Albany
Albany, NY

Kyle V. Wilson, Jr.
Graduate Student
University of Wisconsin, Milwaukee
Milwaukee, WI

Jung-Yeop Woo
Ph.D. Candidate
University of Wisconsin, Milwaukee
Milwaukee, WI

Min Ye
Ph.D. Candidate
University of Wisconsin, Milwaukee
Milwaukee, WI

DEFENSE AND SECURITY

Angola

Jonah Victor

Geography and History

With its vast natural resource holdings, Angola is one of the most richly endowed countries in Africa; yet a history of almost constant civil war and poor governance has left Angola underdeveloped and impoverished. With 481,000 square miles of land, Angola is the seventh largest country in Africa.

Formerly a colony of Portugal, Angola won independence in 1975. Its long coastline straddles the west coast of the continent between relatively prosperous southern Africa and perennially volatile central Africa. To the north, Angola's small coastal province of Cabinda is separated from the mainland by a narrow stretch of the Democratic Republic of the Congo. Angola borders the Republic of Congo (Congo-Brazzaville), the Democratic Republic of the Congo (Congo-Kinshasa), Namibia, and Zambia. Each of these four countries was colonized by a different European power (France, Belgium, Germany, and Great Britain, respectively) and together the Europeans were responsible for drawing the boundaries between their territories. The population of Angola is concentrated largely in the western half of the country, principally in Cabinda Province and the cities of Luanda (the capital) and Huambo.

The Portuguese arrived in Angola in 1483, but did not fully consolidate control over the entire country until the early twentieth century. Since independence, Angola has been governed by dictatorship. The Popular Movement for the Liberation of Angola (MPLA), first a rebel movement and later a political party, has controlled the government since independence. The MPLA was Marxist in origin and allied Angola with the communist bloc during the Cold War. From 1975 to 2002, the MPLA waged a bloody, protracted struggle against the insurgent National Union for the Total Independence of Angola (UNITA), led by Joseph Savimbi.

The current president and leader of the MPLA, Eduardo Dos Santos, has held power since 1979. In July 2003, Dos Santos declared that nationwide elections would be held in 2004 or 2005, and that he would not run as a candidate. As of 2005 these elections had been postponed until 2006 amid wrangling between the MPLA and UNITA over election rules. The county has held elections only once, during a cease-fire in 1992. A 220-member parliament dominated by the MPLA was elected with UNITA winning 70 seats. In a presidential election the same year, Dos Santos defeated Savimbi, but UNITA rejected the results and resumed fighting. The legislature has little real power, but occasionally it passes legislation proposed by opposition parties, including UNITA.

The press in Angola is severely restricted, yet religious freedom is widely respected (Freedom House 2004). In 2003 the International Institute for Strategic Studies declared that "Angola had not proven itself as a fully functioning state" (IISS 2003b, 302). The Angolan government is considered among the most corrupt in the world and quite deficient in governance in comparison with other African countries. In 2004 the World Bank ranked Angola below the global fifteenth percentile in government effectiveness and below the tenth percentile in regulatory quality, rule of law, and control of corruption. Human Rights Watch (2004) claims that from 1997 to 2002, $4.22 billion in government oil revenues that could have been used for social expenditure remained unaccounted for by the Dos Santos administration.

Angola has been relatively stable since the death of Joseph Savimbi in 2002, but consequences of the conflict between the MPLA and UNITA linger as obstacles to development. While around half of the 4.1 million Angolans that had been internally displaced have returned to their places of origin, about 375,000 Angolans remain refugees in other countries (Freedom House 2004). As many as 7 million landmines deployed during the conflict may still cover Angola, creating the largest landmine problem in the world. The education system is severely deficient, and the weak healthcare system was overwhelmed by an epidemic of the fatal Marburg virus in 2005. The transportation infrastructure of paved roads and railroads has not improved since the eve of independence.

Possibly the largest obstacle to sustaining the relative peace is the need to continue the demobilization of tens of thousands of UNITA soldiers—in addition to

---

Sidebar 1   Critical Source of Oil

In recent years, Africa has become an important source of oil for the United States. Angola, with an estimated 30 billion barrels, has by far the greatest oil reserves in Africa. In 2002, 15 percent of U.S. oil imports came from sub-Saharan Africa, and this proportion is expected to rise to 25 percent by the year 2015. Approximately two-thirds of these African oil imports to the United States come from Angola. Across all goods, the United States is sub-Saharan Africa's largest single-country market, purchasing more than 21 percent of the region's exports in 2002.

Sources
U.S. Dept. of Commerce-International Trade Administration. 2004. "US-African Trade Profile."
U.S. Dept. of State. 2003. *Congressional Budget Justification for Foreign Operations.*

---

child soldiers used by both UNITA and the Angolan government—who must be reintegrated with their families and brought back into Angolan society. Former rebels have been provided agricultural toolkits with which to start their own farms or been given the chance to join the armed forces of Angola.

Despite the challenges, hope for Angola rests on its great economic potential. It currently stands as the sixth largest economy in Africa. In 2002, when the civil war ended, Angola experienced a 17 percent growth in gross domestic product, the highest on the continent (World Bank 2003). Oil reserves were first developed in Cabinda in 1957, and offshore oil is known to exist as far south as Luanda. Angola is currently the second largest oil producer in Africa after Nigeria. It is the

Sidebar 2   Demobilizing Child Soldiers

Since 2002, Angola has been demobilizing soldiers from decades of civil war by utilizing a strategy of reintegrating former rebels and government troops into civilian society by providing them with crop seeds, agricultural tools, and instruction in farming. In 2004, however, Human Rights Watch criticized the demobilization program employed for child soldiers as being ineffective. As many as 11,000 children fought in final years of the civil war, and Human Rights Watch reports that some child soldiers recruited during the war still remain in the Angolan armed forces. The organization also reported that child soldiers generally have not received the same level of resettlement assistance as that given adult soldiers.

Source
Human Rights Watch. 2004. "Child Soldier Use 2003." http://www.hrw.org.

fourth largest producer of diamonds in the world. Yet it remains the thirteenth least developed country worldwide. Only 3 percent of arable land is currently being farmed (ibid.). In 2004 the gross domestic product per capita at purchasing power parity was estimated at $2,100 (CIA 2003).

Regional Geopolitics

The end of civil wars in Angola and Mozambique has solidified southern Africa's status as the most stable and prosperous region of sub-Saharan Africa led by the economic powers of Botswana and South Africa. Still, instability, poverty, refugee flows, illegal small arms trade, poor governance, and the pandemic of HIV/AIDS offer daunting challenges to the political and economic development of the region. In 2003 a famine threatened 13 million people in the region. The average HIV infection rate is 20.6 percent of adults. A poor household with an infected member is estimated to see income decline by as much as 40 to 60 percent (IISS 2003b).

Despite clashes between several countries during interventions in Congo-Kinshasa, the states of southern Africa look to strengthen cooperation in development and regional security. Since the end of the Cold War, the ideological divide between Marxist and free market governments has largely disappeared. Today, southern Africa is free of states holding or developing nuclear weapons. South Africa once had a nuclear weapons program, but it ceased development and completely disarmed in the early 1990s. Most southern African countries downsized their militaries in the 1990s. South Africa and Zimbabwe made the most drastic cuts in the size of their armed forces, although Botswana and Namibia continued to develop and expand their military capabilities. In many instances, cuts in the military coincided with expansions of national police forces.

The older generation of southern African leadership was bonded by close personal ties. During the rebellions against the rule of Europeans and white settlers in the 1960s and 1970s, many of the political and military leaders of the 1970s through 1990s in Angola, Mozambique, Namibia, South Africa, and Zimbabwe lived and trained together in the refugee and military camps of Botswana, Tanzania, and Zambia, building lifelong relationships and friendships (Honwana 1997). Much of the current leadership of

Table 1   Basic Statistics

Type of government	Presidential-parliamentary republic
Population (millions)	10.8 (2003)
Religion	Indigenous beliefs 47%, Roman Catholic 38%, Protestant 15%
Main industries	Oil, diamonds, refined petroleum products, gas, coffee
Main security threat(s)	Cabinda Insurgency, state failure, regional instability
Defense spending (% GDP)	9.8% (FY 2002)
Size of military (thousands)	129–131
Number of civil wars since 1945	4
Number of interstate wars since 1945	1

Sources

Central Intelligence Agency Website. 2003. CIA *World Factbook*. http://www.cia.gov/cia/ publications/factbook/ (accessed May 15, 2005).

International Institute for Strategic Studies (IISS). 2003a. *The Military Balance 2003–2004*. London: IISS and Oxford University Press.

southern Africa does not have these connections (Robert Mugabe of Zimbabwe is one of the last of that generation). However, cooperation in the region has expanded through the rise of formal intergovernmental organizations.

The expansion of the Southern African Development Community (SADC) has fostered cooperation between states on matters of security, economics, and environmental protection. SADC includes Angola, Botswana, Congo-Kinshasa, Lesotho, Malawi, Mauritius, Mozambique, Namibia, Seychelles, South Africa, Swaziland, Tanzania, Zambia, and Zimbabwe. The Organ on Politics, Defence and Security (OPDS) is the sub-organization of SADC responsible for coordinating the prevention, management, and resolution of conflict in the region. Buzan (1997) predicts that SADC may become influential enough to expand into a security regime for all of sub-Saharan Africa.

South Africa was labeled a pariah state by most African countries and politically isolated during the apartheid era. Today it is clearly the major power of the re-

gion, having a gross domestic product three times greater than the rest of SADC combined (Angola is the second largest economy in SADC) and it plays a key leadership role. In fact, the military of South Africa is so much larger than that of any other SADC member that members are concerned that it might dominate a future regional security regime. The fact that the leadership of South African armed forces remains inundated by an apartheid era elite might be troublesome to other SADC members if they were to assume a regional leadership role. SADC members are also concerned that Western powers have encouraged South Africa to use its hegemonic status to maintain stability in the region.

Democratization continues to spread in southern Africa. South Africa has been a democracy only since 1994, but with two successful elections, prospects for continued stability are bright. Botswana is Africa's most enduring democracy, and over the past decade it has had one of the world's fastest growing economies. However, Botswana is now challenged with the world's highest HIV/AIDS infection rate, estimated to have spread to over one-third of the adult population (CIA 2003). The microstates of Lesotho and Mauritius also stand as examples of successful democracies. Mozambique's long civil war ended in 1992. After a successful UN peacekeeping mission, and despite massive poverty, it has continued down the road to stability and democracy.

Among southern African countries, Zimbabwe could potentially be the most destabilizing to the region. With a devastated economy—75 percent unemployment and 200 percent inflation in 2003—the potential for state failure is high. That would likely become a regional crisis (IISS 2003b, 299).

State collapse and conflict in Congo-Kinshasa has loomed to the north as a major security threat to the region since 1997. In 2003 the conflict subsided, but no clear path to stability is in sight. For several years the civil war created a rift between Angola, Namibia, and Zimbabwe, which defended the Congolese government; and Uganda and Rwanda, which fought on the side of rebel forces. Neighboring states had withdrawn their troops from Congo-Kinshasa by the end of 2003.

Conflict Past and Present

Conflict History

Angola has been involved in only one full-scale interstate war. However, since its independence in 1975 it has been plagued almost constantly with internal conflict. During the Angolan civil wars, China, Cuba, South Africa, the Soviet Union, the United States, and Zaire each intervened at various times with military support or assistance to either the side of the government or the side of the rebels. Recently Angola has launched several of its own military interventions in neighboring countries.

Angola was a colony of Portugal, winning independence relatively late. The Portuguese arrived in 1483, but did not consolidate control over the entire country until the early twentieth century. Starting in the 1960s a series of rebellions led by a variety of factions sought to drive out the Portuguese. Because so many factions were fighting independently, Portugal found the rebellion in Angola more costly than colonial wars in any other colony. Each of the four major rebel groups was sponsored either by major powers or by neighboring African countries. By 1974 the Portuguese military had become frustrated with its collective colonial wars and overthrew the government in Lisbon. The new government made a hasty retreat from many of its colonial possessions. Unlike the decolonization procedures of the British and French, the Portuguese did not negotiate a handover agreement with any one faction in Angola, or attempt to establish a transitional government.

When the Portuguese left Angola on November 11, 1975, the Popular Movement for the Liberation of Angola (MPLA), the National Front for the Liberation of Angola (FNLA), and the National Union for the Total Independence of Angola (UNITA) each struggled for control of the new state. In the beginning, the Marxist MPLA controlled the capital of Luanda. The FNLA and UNITA allied to oust the MPLA, with the help of South African forces and the support of China, the United States, and Zaire (now Congo-Kinshasa). However, China and the Soviet Union intervened to solidify the MPLA's foothold, and by 1976 the MPLA had become recognized by most of Africa as the legitimate government of Angola.

From that point, the war with UNITA continued without pause until the early 1990s. In the early 1980s, UNITA was able to capture considerable territory. By 1984 they controlled 35 percent of the country.

Cuba and the Soviet Union continued their support for the MPLA, while UNITA continued its guerilla activity in southern Angola. Over time, a total of 300,000 Cubans served in Angola. The size of the Cuban force peaked in 1988, when a force of 61,000 were deployed in the country.

The MPLA government supported the South West Africa People's Organization (SWAPO), an insurgent group in Namibia fighting for independence from South Africa. From 1977 to 1984, South Africa retaliated by launching several interventions into southern Angola, in which several SWAPO bases were located. Initially South Africa agreed to withdraw troops from Angola in 1984, but the plan failed; South Africa continued to support UNITA efforts. In 1987 and 1988 the MPLA launched a series of offenses against UNITA in southern Angola, and South Africa sent 3,000 troops into Angola to help UNITA repel the MPLA from their territory. In 1988 and 1989, the MPLA government, Cuba, and South Africa worked to reach a cease-fire and nonaggression pact. The three parties negotiated the withdrawal of South African and Cuban troops from Angola. The South African withdrawal was completed in 1988, but the Cuban withdrawal continued until 1991.

In 1991, Portugal, the Soviet Union, and the United States joined efforts to bring the MPLA and UNITA to the negotiating table. The two sides agreed to a cease-fire, a nationwide election, and the creation of a unified army that would integrate both MPLA and UNITA troops, but with an air force and navy remaining under MPLA control. The new Angola Armed Forces (FAA) was to be jointly commanded by MPLA and UNITA generals.

An election was held in 1992, but when it was announced that the MPLA had a strong lead in the early returns, UNITA leader Joseph Savimbi declared the election fraudulent and withdrew his troops from the FAA. UNITA remobilized and launched an offensive that quickly captured 60 percent of the country. The war raged on and off for the next decade, despite a series of further peace attempts and threats of military intervention by South Africa and Zimbabwe. In late 1994 the MPLA and UNITA signed the Lusaka Protocol, and in 1997 they joined together in a short-lived government of national unity. By 1998, however, the UNITA insurgency resumed.

UNITA had been utilizing neighboring Zaire as a conduit to smuggle out diamonds, bring in arms, and establish rear bases. In 1997 the Angolan government decided to send troops to the aid of Laurent Kabila and his insurgency in Zaire (now Congo-Kinshasa). UNITA also deployed troops into Zaire, but to defend the ruling regime of Mobutu Sese Seko. Anticipating defeat, UNITA forces retreated into neighboring Congo-Brazzaville. Mobutu was ultimately overthrown by Kabila, and the new Democratic Republic of the Congo was established. Following that, Congo-Brazzaville, which was governed by an administration that had been friendly to both UNITA and the Cabindan Liberation Front (FLEC) rebels in Angola, flamed into civil war. The Angolan government deployed 3,000 troops to aid the insurgents in Congo-Brazzaville and helped overthrow the democratically elected government.

In February 2002, UNITA leader Joseph Savimbi was killed in battle. Two months later, a cease-fire was negotiated, and the civil war between the MPLA and UNITA effectively ended. The government of Angola then granted amnesty to all UNITA troops.

In Congo-Kinshasa, rebel forces marched against the new Kabila government in 1998. Angola sent as many as 2,500 soldiers with tanks, armed trucks, transport and attack helicopters, and possibly MiG fighter aircraft to defend the Congolese government, along with forces from Namibia and Zimbabwe. Rwanda and Uganda intervened and fought on the side of the rebels.

A much smaller internal conflict remains ongoing in Cabinda province—an enclave on the coast separated from the mainland of Angola by a strip of territory belonging to Congo-Kinshasa. The FLEC has been fighting a separatist movement for the independence of Cabinda since colonial times.

*Current and Potential
Military Confrontation*

Internally, the FLEC separatist movement in Cabinda continues to be a security threat to the Angolan government. Although the FLEC claims membership in the thousands, it is estimated to include about 600 insurgents with small arms (ibid., 205). To some extent, the government of Angola has co-opted the secessionists in the province with patronage payouts. The FLEC is further disadvantaged from the loss of a friendly government in neighboring Congo-Brazzaville. However, Cabinda produces more than 50 percent of Angola's oil, and the province's full economic potential cannot be realized until the threat is eliminated. The end of the conflict with

UNITA has allowed the military to concentrate significant forces in Cabinda.

A longer-term threat is a future "resource war" such as the one fought between the MPLA and UNITA. A resource war is a distinctive threat because it typically becomes highly protracted. Essentially, a resource war is a conflict in which one or both sides are able to finance their armaments and armies through the sale of natural resources. In the case of UNITA, after South Africa and the United States had ceased support, they funded their insurgency by capturing diamond mines and smuggling gems out through Zaire. Between 1992 and 1998, UNITA derived $3.7 billion from diamond sales and at one point controlled 90 percent of Angola's diamond exports (Renner 2002, 33). The MPLA used oil revenue to fund much of their military.

Diamond mining does not require great infrastructure or a skilled labor force. It is not like a factory that needs to be constructed and then supplied with steady shipments of raw materials. Some diamonds can be mined without sophisticated technology. Angola's offshore oil wells are also a strategic resource during times of civil war, as they can easily be protected from rebel forces. It is reasonable to assume that a future insurgency might capture and exploit mineral resources to support a rebellion. Although the weakness of the state makes Angola highly susceptible to a future civil war, there is no apparent movement at this time to launch a nationwide rebellion.

The government of Angola is, at present, at peace with neighboring governments. The MPLA helped fight to install the current regime of Congo-Brazzaville and defend the regime of Congo-Kinshasa. Angola has a formal defense pact with Namibia, and good relations with Zambia.

However, considering the instability in the two Congos, conditions are not unlikely to change. An interstate conflict is unlikely to stem from an attack by a neighboring country, but rather from an intervention launched by Angola that could once again place it at odds with other countries in southern Africa.

Alliance Structure

Angola's alliance priorities have shifted dramatically since the end of the Cold War and may do so again with the conclusion of the UNITA insurgency in 2002. In recent years Angola has sought military cooperation primarily with governments of Marxist or communist heritage, Lusophone (Portuguese-speaking) countries, and countries of southern Africa.

From 1976 to 2002, the top security priority of the Angolan government was to defeat the UNITA insurgency. The government was allied with the communist bloc, receiving assistance from the Soviet Union and Cuba in the form of weapons and military training. In addition, Cuba sent forces to Angola to help combat UNITA and defend the MPLA government. On the side of UNITA, South Africa sent troops to fight the MPLA government, and from 1985 to 1991 the United States gave UNITA $60 million worth of military assistance.

Angola had a formal treaty of entente with the Soviet Union from 1976 to 1991. Formal treaties of nonaggression were signed with Hungary (from 1981 to 1989) and East Germany (from 1979 to 1989), likely coinciding with Hungary and East Germany sending military advisors to train MPLA forces. A third treaty of nonaggression was signed with Zaire (1979 to 1982). A defense pact existed with Mozambique, Tanzania, and Zambia from 1976 to 1999. In 1999, when Congo-Kinshasa was under assault from Uganda and Rwanda, a defense pact was signed between Angola, Congo-Kinshasa, Namibia, and Zimbabwe.

The members of the Southern African Development Community (SADC) continue to increase their defense ties. Angola has been a leading proponent of increasing security cooperation among the members of SADC. In August 2003, the fourteen countries signed a mutual defense pact that permits SADC members to intervene in conflicts in neighboring countries.

Even though the Angolan government no longer espouses Marxist-Leninism, it still seeks to maintain close relations with communist and former communist countries. In 1999, Angola signed an accord for military cooperation with Russia that provides for the training of the Angolan army, air force, and navy, as well as for improving Angola's military technology. In 2002, Angola signed a five-year military cooperation protocol with Cuba for training and technical assistance that includes sending Angolan officers to Cuban military academies. Angola is also seeking to improve relations with China, North Korea, and Vietnam, but at the current time cooperation mostly concerns economic issues.

Angola was formerly a Portuguese colony, and since independence it has maintained close relations with Portugal and other Lusophone countries, both through the Community of Portuguese-speaking Countries (CPLP) and on a bilateral basis. In October 2003, Angola and Portugal concluded several accords to extend military cooperation. Portugal plans to train Angolan soldiers for peacekeeping operations, offer medical assistance to the military, help in efforts to remove landmines, and expand Angola's transportation infrastructure. In turn, Angola has assisted smaller Lusophone countries. In 2003, talks took place between Angola and East Timor to arrange for the training of Timorese military and police in maintaining internal security. In recent years, Angola has trained military officers from the island state of Sao Tome and Principe.

In the 1990s, Angola became increasingly concerned about the instability of its neighbors and the ability of UNITA to operate from within the border regions of Congo-Brazzaville and Congo-Kinshasa. In 1997, Angola, Namibia, and Zimbabwe joined to support the Kabila government in Congo-Kinshasa against several insurgencies and the interventions of Burundi, Rwanda, and Uganda. In return for Zimbabwe's support, the Angolan government has publicly praised President Robert Mugabe's controversial land reform policies. Angola was believed to have initially deployed as many as 7,100 troops at the beginning of the intervention (Berman and Sams 2000, 180). Zambia and Angola share a common border, and the migration of Angolan refugees has been a security issue. Despite recent animosity stemming from the Angolan interventions into Congo-Brazzaville and Congo-Kinshasa, relations with the governments of Congo-Brazzaville and Uganda have improved.

Size and Structure of the Military

Since the end of the UNITA insurgency, Angola's military has been undergoing a radical transformation. The 1994 Lusaka protocol calls for a new FAA that integrates the army of the MPLA regime (the People's Armed Forces for the Liberation of Angola [FAPLA]) with demobilized UNITA forces. UNITA forces have been granted amnesty and largely demobilized. The FAA was to be led by one UNITA general and one MPLA general. The officer corps of UNITA was to be integrated in accordance with existing vacancies into the organization of the FAA. The original integration plan was for former UNITA troops to join only the army, but not the navy or air force.

Military service is by conscription. The total active armed forces of Angola are estimated to fall between 129,000 and 131,000 members. That includes an army of 120,000, a navy of 3,000, and an air force of 6,000 to 8,000. The navy is based at Luanda. The fleet is in disrepair, and, apart from an amphibious support ship, there are unlikely to be any operational vessels. The air force is estimated to have 105 combat aircraft, mostly of Sukhoi and MiG varieties, but the actual number of operational planes is unknown. The air force also has sixteen armed helicopters and as many as fifty other helicopters, mostly of Russian and French origin. A rapid reaction paramilitary police force numbers about 10,000 (IISS 2003a).

The president is the commander-in-chief of the FAA. Following the heritage of the FAPLA, the FAA follows Soviet military doctrine. However, that could change as Western countries become increasingly involved in developing Angola's armed forces. The country is divided into six military districts: North, South, East, Central and West, Luanda, and Cabinda (ISS 2002).

From 2001 to 2002, the defense budget decreased from $410 to $386 million. However, the actual defense expenditure in 2002, outside the official budget, was estimated at $1 billion. When considering military expenditure as a proportion of GDP, it decreased from 17 percent in 2001 to 10 percent in 2002 (IISS 2003a).

Most arms transfers to Angola have come from former communist countries. From 1999 to 2003, Belarus, Bulgaria, Kazakhstan, Peru, Russia, and Slovakia all made major arms deliveries to Angola. As late as 1998, Ukraine sold to the UNITA rebels several helicopters and fighter jets (ibid.).

Currently, Angolan officers are trained at the Institute for Military Defense. Portugal is expected to help Angola establish a new military administration school for the armed forces, as well as to expand training assistance to prepare Angolan forces for peacekeeping operations. South Africa cooperates with the FAA on technical training and telecommunication programs. Cuba and Russia have also assisted in technical training. For the last several years, the United States has trained many Angolan officers through its International Military Education and Training program.

Civil-Military Relations/The Role of the Military in Domestic Politics

Despite a turbulent history, Angola is rare among African countries for never having experienced a military coup d'état. In its entire history Angola has been ruled by only two different leaders, and both came to power from within the MPLA. The reason for this might be attributed to the country's being in a state of almost constant civil war since independence. This state of war has served to distract the military's attention from the governance of the regime to focusing on successfully thwarting the many insurgencies. It has also served to give the military a high budget priority, so that it was not lacking in financial support from the governing regime. The height of militarization in Angola, before the end of the war with UNITA, came in the late 1980s and early 1990s, peaking in 1991, when almost 16 percent of the total population was serving in the armed forces (COW).

Now, with the majority of the country at peace and only a small conflict in Cabinda, the probability of a military coup has significantly increased. Angola's conditions of high poverty, poor economy, underdeveloped civil society, and high ethnic diversity make it highly prone to a coup in the future if a new enemy is not found to occupy the military's focus. To that end the government may be tempted to continue interventions in neighboring countries. Although the strategic reason that Angola intervened in Congo-Kinshasa was to eliminate UNITA support networks, Angolan soldiers fought in exchange for the right to pillage the locals of money and food (Howe 2001, 99). With President Dos Santos expected to step down in the near future, there is no certainty that the leaders of the military will show his successor the same level of loyalty they showed him.

In the 1990s, Angola was notable for its use of mercenary soldiers to combat the UNITA insurgency. From 1993 through 1996, the Executive Outcomes Corporation was commissioned by the MPLA government to field 550 soldiers as well as to train 5,000 Angolan troops and 30 pilots in motorized infantry, artillery, engineering, signals, medical support, sabotage, and reconnaissance. Executive Outcomes was initially hired in early 1993 by Heritage Oil and Gas, a British company, to capture the towns of Kefekwena and Soyo from UNITA. After a successful mission, the MPLA government was encouraged to contract Executive Outcomes directly in late 1993. The Executive Outcomes force disbanded in 1996, and many of the mercenaries not only remained in Angola but also entered into the service of UNITA against their former employers (ibid., 199).

The funding of both government and rebel forces in Angola has been closely linked to the oil and mineral mining industries. Even though the government paid Executive Outcomes $40 million for their services, that fee was supplemented by granting the company valuable mining rights. That included the rights to the Yetwene diamond mine in northeast Angola, which is estimated to earn $24 million per year (ibid., 205).

Private security continues to be an important industry in Angola. Angolan law requires that foreign diamond companies hire their own security to protect their property and operations. The government pressures companies to contract with either Teleservices or Alpha–5, two Angolan firms. The principal shareholders of both are Angolan government officials (ibid., 220).

Terrorism

Angola has not been publicly known to harbor or support global terrorist groups. It lies far from North Africa, east Africa, and the Sahel—the regions of Africa most often suspected of offering refuge to al-Qaeda, Hamas, and other Middle Eastern terrorists. That said, the government of Angola has been particularly outspoken in its support of global efforts to combat terrorism. After the September 11, 2001, attacks on the United States, Angola expressed strong support for the U.S. action in Afghanistan. Angola has recently urged the SADC to combat terrorist activities in southern Africa by improving legal and internal security cooperation between member states.

The Angolan leadership's antiterrorism rhetoric may stem from its own domestic concerns. During the civil war, the MPLA government often characterized the UNITA insurgency as a terrorist group. UNITA was known to attack civilian targets. In the largest incident, UNITA ambushed a passenger train near Luanda in August 2001, claiming more than 250 lives. In 2002, the MPLA government successfully lobbied SADC to declare UNITA a terrorist organization.

Although the war with UNITA has ended, it might be expected that Angola will continue its support for regional and global efforts to combat terrorist groups. As the long-standing regime has combated insurgencies for most of the history of independent Angola, the government may hope for international support in combating future insurgencies under the guise of fighting terrorism.

Relationship with the United States

After a history of enmity with the United States, both the United States and Angola are taking a pragmatic path toward reconciliation and cooperation. In 2002, Angola supplied 10 percent of all oil imports to the United States (IISS 2003b, 302). Overall, the United States is by far Angola's leading export destination. The largest American direct investment in Angola is made by Chevron-Texaco. The view of the United States as an enemy by the government of Angola stems from U.S. support of UNITA from 1985 to 1991. The United States sought to help overthrow the MPLA government—a Soviet and Cuban ally during the Cold War. In 1986 the Reagan administration delivered

$10–15 million in military aid to UNITA, funneled through Zaire.

The Clinton administration awarded the Angolan government full diplomatic recognition in 1993. In 1997 the United States strongly condemned Angola's intervention in the Congo-Brazzaville civil war. Although its government no longer follows a doctrine of Marxist-Leninism, Angola remains friendly to countries with Marxist heritage, including Cuba and North Korea, neither of which enjoys normal diplomatic relations with the United States.

It might be suspected that while Angola is publicly slow to warm relations with the United States, it is privately interested in increasing economic and defense cooperation. As new ties are forged, however, an air of mutual suspicion lingers over the relationship. Angola vocally supported the U.S. invasion of Afghanistan in October 2001 and condemned the World Trade Center attacks. In the spring of 2003, when the United States was building support for a war on Iraq, the Bush administration fought hard to earn Angola's vote on the UN Security Council.

The United States publicly named Angola on its "coalition of the willing" list—countries from around the world supporting the U.S. position. However, Angola was dropped from the list one day later. It was widely suspected that Angola wished to be a silent supporter and that the public announcement was a mistake on the part of the Bush administration. The support of President Dos Santo for the U.S. position was unpopular among Angolans. According to the U.S. Department of State's 2003 Congressional Budget Justification for Foreign Operations, the official interests of the United States in Angola are "regional sta-

bility, democracy, human rights, humanitarian assistance, and open markets" (U.S. Department of State 2003, 191).

U.S. security assistance to Angola has gradually been increasing. For the past several years, the U.S. military has been training Angolans in the removal of the millions of landmines that cover Angola. As of 2003, the United States began funding an International Military Education and Training (IMET) program for Angola. The goal of the IMET program is to develop professionalized militaries by training foreign officers. Among other things, the IMET program teaches students human rights ethics, the English language, U.S. culture, and respect for civil-military relations. Prior to the recent cooperation, the United States had trained only five officers (all in 1997) under IMET. The U.S. Department of Defense also hopes to supply the Angolan military with equipment with which to enhance de-mining operations and conduct civic action programs.

Each year the United States spends millions of dollars on healthcare programs in Angola, including HIV/AIDS education and testing programs and programs to improve children's health. The United States has supported developmental assistance programs in Angola, especially in the training and development of the agricultural sector.

Although the road to cooperation between the United States and Angola has been long, more progress might be expected in coming years. If President Dos Santos steps down in the near future, as he suggested he will, and free and fair elections are held, the willingness of the U.S. government to support Angola will likely increase. The Bush administration has expressed interest in becoming more involved in the development of Africa and the fight against HIV/AIDS. This move is strongly motivated by its "War on Terrorism." Failing and collapsing states in Africa are seen as potential refuges for terrorist groups. Alleged unfettered operations by al-Qaeda and other groups in Somalia are a prime example of what the United States hopes to prevent in other parts of Africa. The enormous oil and mineral resources of Angola provide an economic incentive for the United States to become engaged, but U.S. companies may be wary of investing in Angola until the pervasive culture of political corruption has been curtailed.

The Future

The death of UNITA rebel leader Joseph Savimbi in 2002 seems to have signaled an end to the three decades of conflict that have torn apart Angola. However, unless the government can prove its legitimacy by rebuilding the country and transitioning to democratic rule, prospects for Angola are not bright. The spread of AIDS, poor governance, economic underdevelopment, the threat of future insurgencies, and regional instability all loom on the horizon as obstacles to establishing Angola as a major power of Africa. Yet with its vast mineral wealth and fertile land, Angola has the natural resources necessary for prosperity. The Angolan government has demonstrated a desire to be more engaged in regional and continent-wide economic and security cooperation. The end of both the Cold War and the UNITA insurgency is likely to invite unprecedented engagement by industrialized countries around the world in the development of the country.

The HIV/AIDS epidemic is a top economic and security threat to most countries in Africa. The spread of the disease burdens an already weak healthcare system and reduces the workforce. When HIV/AIDS spreads in the military it cripples the readiness of the armed forces to respond to security threats. There are indications that the issue is being addressed by the government with the support of the international community, however, as the rate of condom use in Angola to prevent the spread of the disease is reported to have increased from 83 percent to 93 percent from 2002 to 2003 (ibid., 192). Even if Angola is able to respond effectively, the spread of HIV/AIDS through the militaries of other southern African countries may hinder the ability of SADC to coordinate effective conflict management and resolution.

The pervasive government corruption and the underdevelopment of Angola need to be remedied before significant economic progress can take place. The largely unskilled workforce and undeveloped infrastructure will limit the sort of progress that can occur. The transportation infrastructure across the country has not significantly improved beyond what the Portuguese built before independence. As of 1998 there had been no growth in the road density of Angola since 1974, and only 25 percent of roads were paved (World Bank 2003). The railway system is limited to the western coast of the country, around Luanda, and few roads travel into what was UNITA territory. This deficiency both limits economic activity and hampers the government's ability to govern and control the western half of the country.

Although there is no present indication that UNITA will remobilize and return to war, in the near future Angola will remain highly prone to future insurgencies and civil war. The sprawling territory and uneven population distribution of

Table 2   Key Events

1975	Independence from Portugal; civil war begins
1976	MPLA establishes control of the capital, Luanda
1979	Eduardo Dos Santos becomes president
1988	Number of Cuban troops in Angola peaks; South Africa withdraws troops
1991	Cease-fire negotiated between MPLA and UNITA; Cuba withdraws troops
1992	Parliamentary and presidential elections held; results of presidential election disputed; conflict resumes
1993	Executive Outcomes Corporation hired by MPLA to fight UNITA
1994	MPLA and UNITA sign Lusaka Peace Accord
1997	Angola aids the overthrow of Mobutu Sese Seko in Zaire
1998	Angola intervenes in Congo-Kinshasa civil war; UNITA insurgency resumes
2002	Death of Joseph Savimbi; end of UNITA insurgency

Angola prompt Africa scholar Jeffrey Herbst to characterize the political geography as one of the most difficult in Africa to govern (Herbst 2000, 150–151). It is simply very difficult for the government of Luanda to project its power across the country. That, combined with an undeveloped infrastructure, will make it difficult for the government to prevent state failure. African countries that are less economically developed and have high military spending are found to be more likely to experience civil war than other countries (Henderson 2000). Although in Angola the economy has been poor and military spending high in the recent past, both have shown trends of changing for the better in recent years (World Bank 2003).

The internal conflict in Cabinda against FLEC rebels remains ongoing, despite assertions from the Angolan government that the insurgency has all but ended. In reality, the insurgency remains small and isolated from most of the country. This war will remain costly in terms of military resources and the potential oil wealth of Cabinda, which could otherwise be extracted, but it will not consume the majority of the country in a state of war as did the UNITA insurgency. More than a thousand former FLEC soldiers have been granted amnesty and reintegrated into Angola society. In late 2003, Angolan military officials met with officials from Congo-Brazzaville and Congo-Kinshasa to discuss strengthening borders in the Cabinda region and enhancing security cooperation to contain the FLEC.

Recent interventions of the Angolan military into Congo-Brazzaville and Congo-Kinshasa have established a precedent of preemptive defense policy. These precedents suggest that the government will not hesitate to deploy further military interventions into neighboring countries. Such action will be taken to defend Angola from regional instability and prevent Angolan rebels from organizing in neighboring countries. The stability of Congo-Kinshasa seems unlikely to improve significantly in the near future, and it should be expected that Angola will remained involved there. Military interventions increase the opportunity for Angola to come into conflict with other countries in southern and central Africa. However, with increasing conflict management coordination among SADC members, Angola may be less likely to operate unilaterally.

At this time, Angola's relations with other countries in the region are improving as the Angolan government seeks greater economic and security cooperation. Angolan policy is expected to remain favorable toward expanding the roles of intergovernmental organizations such as the African Union and SADC.

One positive development is the 2003 launch of the African Peer Review Mechanism by the New Partnership for Africa's Development (NEPAD), a coalition of states from across sub-Saharan Africa. Angola has joined sixteen other states in volunteering to be subject to a peer review of the quality of political, economic, and corporate governance in the country. This will be published in an official report that will assess whether each country is making progress in political and economic development.

Angola is not prepared at the present time to participate significantly in regional peacekeeping operations. However, current training and professionalization of the military by both Portugal and the United States are expected to prepare Angola to participate in the future. Participation in UN peacekeeping missions is particularly attractive to poor countries, as the government will receive about $1,000 per month per soldier. The money does not go directly to the individual soldier but often helps governments to finance the military.

For the first time since independence, a new regime may come to power when President Dos Santos's long rule ends in coming years. Increasing engagement with Western countries is likely to pressure the Angolan government to hold free and fair elections. Although the economic potential for Angola is unlimited, a new leader will need to overcome the pervasive culture of corruption and con-tinue postwar healing and reconstruction in order to be successful. The success of future regimes will determine whether Angola is to become a leader in African security and development or a dysfunctional burden to the region in the new century.

References, Recommended Readings, and Websites

Books

Berman, Eric, and Katie Sams. 2000. *Peacekeeping in Africa: Capabilities and Culpabilities.* Geneva: United Nations.

Buzan, Barry. 1997. "Regions and Regionalism in Global Perspective." In *Defensive Restructuring of the Armed Forces in Southern Africa*, G. Cawthra and B. Moller, eds. Aldershot, UK: Ashgate.

Ciment, James. 1997. *Angola and Mozambique: Postcolonial Wars in Southern Africa.* New York: Facts on File.

Copson, Raymond. 1994. *Africa's Wars and Prospects for Peace.* London: M. E. Sharpe.

Duke, Lynne. 2003. *Mandela, Mobutu, and Me.* New York: Doubleday.

Furley, Oliver, and Roy May, eds. 2001. *African Interventionist States.* Aldershot, UK: Ashgate.

Henderson, Errol. 2000. "When States Implode: The Correlates of Africa's Civil Wars, 1950–1992." *Studies in International Comparative Development* 35:28–47.

Herbst, Jeffrey. 2000. *States and Power in Africa.* Princeton: Princeton University Press.

Heywood, Linda. 2000. *Contested Power in Angola.* Rochester: University of Rochester Press.

Honwana, Joao. 1997. "Between Hope and Despair: Southern Africa's Security." In *Defensive Restructuring of the Armed Forces in Southern Africa*, G. Cawthra and B. Moller, eds. Aldershot, UK: Ashgate.

Hooper, Jim. 2002. *Bloodsong!: An Account of Executive Outcomes in Angola.* London: Collins.

Howe, Herbert. 2001. *Ambiguous Order: Military Forces in African States.* Boulder, CO: Lynne Rienner.

Human Rights Watch. 1999. *Angola Unravels: The Rise and Fall of the Lusaka Peace Accords.* New York: Human Rights Watch.

International Institute for Strategic Studies (IISS). 2003a. *The Military Balance.* London: Oxford University Press.

International Institute for Strategic Studies (IISS). 2003b. *Strategic Survey.* London: Oxford University Press.

Laremont, Ricardo. 2002. *The Causes of War and the Consequences of Peacekeeping in Africa.* Portsmouth, NH: Heinemann.

Mendes, Pedro. 2003. *Bay of Tigers: A Journey through War-Torn Angola.* London: Granta Books.

Mullins, A. F. 1987. *Born Arming: Development and Military Power in New States.* Stanford, CA: Stanford University Press.

Renner, Michael. 2002. *The Anatomy of Resource Wars.* Washington, DC: Worldwatch.

Reno, William. 1998. *Warlord Politics and African States.* Boulder, CO: Lynne Rienner.

Articles

Agence France Presse. "Uganda Hails Angola as 'Important Factor' in Central Africa." October 16, 2003.

"Angola Hints Could Abstain on UN Iraq Resolution, Calls War 'Inevitable.'" March 10, 2003.

"Luanda Calls for Terrorist 'Observers' in Southern Africa." December 17, 2001.

"Death Toll Rises to 259 after UNITA Attack on Angolan Train." August 18, 2001.

Angola Press Agency. "Defense Minister Concerned about Higher Military Training." December 24, 2003.

"Ministers Council Approves Military Protocol Signed with Cuba in 2002." December 16, 2003.

"Cabinda: Programme of Support to FLEC ex-Soldiers Started." November 29, 2003.

"Angola, DR Congo, Congo Forces' Chiefs Meet over Sub-regional Security." November 25, 2003.

"Interior Minister Calls on Major Attention to Border Patrolling." November 21, 2003.

"Military Authorities Sign Accords." October 22, 2003.

"Military Administration School for Army." October 21, 2003.

"Angola to Help Train East Timorese Police Officers." September 9, 2003.

"Initiative for Military Cooperation Launched." July 31, 2003.

"Angolan, Cuban Defence Officials in Talks over Training of Military Personnel." March 12, 2003.

Pan African News Agency. "SADC Leaders Sign Protocol on Regional Security." August 27, 2003.

Websites

Angola Ministry of Defense: http://www2.ebonet.net/minden/.

Angola Ministry of Foreign Affairs: http://www.mirex.ebonet.net/.

Angola Mission to the United Nations: http://www.un.int/angola/.

Angolan Press Agency: http://www.angolapress-angop.ao/.

Central Intelligence Agency (CIA). 2004. *The World Factbook:* http://www.cia.gov.

Correlates of War Project (COW): http://cow2.la.psu.edu.

Embassy of Angola in the United Kingdom: http://www.angola.org.uk.

Embassy of Angola in the United States: http://www.angola.org.

Freedom House: http://www.freedomhouse.org.

Institute for Security Studies (ISS). 2002. "Arms Analysis: Angola." http://www.iss.co.za/af/arms/103ang.html. Accessed February 7, 2004.

United Nations. 2003. "Progress Report on the Global Response to the HIV/AIDS Epidemic." http://www.unaids.org.

U.S.-Angola Chamber of Commerce: http://www.us-angola.org.

U.S. Department of State. 2003. *Congressional Budget Justification for Foreign Operations:* http://www.state.gov.

World Bank. 2003. *World Development Indicators:* http://www.worldbank.org.

Argentina

Joakim Kreutz

Geography and History

The territory of present-day Argentina was originally controlled by two indigenous communities, the Diaguita and the Guarani, as well as by nomadic tribes, when the first Spaniard, Juan de Solis, landed in 1516. Despite resistance from the indigenous groups and scarcity of building materials, further Spanish expeditions returned to the mouth of the Rio de la Plata in search of gold and silver. Buenos Aires was founded in 1536 but did not become a permanent settlement until 1580.

After nearly 200 years, Buenos Aires became an integral part of the Spanish colonial system as the capital of the newly created viceroyalty of the Rio de la Plata. After a brief spell under British rule in 1806, the city of Buenos Aires declared independence in 1810. Between 1816, the official founding year of the republic of Argentina, and 1824, there was a war of independence between Spanish forces, centralists, and local administrations advocating a federal state. Competition between centralists and federalists continued until President Bartolamé Mitre made Buenos Aires the capital of Argentina in 1862.

President Nestor Kirchner has led the Republica Argentina since May 25, 2003, with Daniel Scioli serving as vice president. The president is both chief of state and head of government, and is elected for a period of four years. In addition, Argentina has a bicameral legislature (Congreso Nacional). The two houses consist of a 72-seat Senate and 257-seat Chamber of Deputies. The highest court is the Supreme Court, consisting of nine judges appointed by the president with Senate approval. The country is divided into a federal capital (Buenos Aires) and twenty-three provinces-each with its own governor, legislature, and judiciary.

Argentina is the second largest country in South America, located at the eastern side of the southern tip of the continent, bordering Chile, Bolivia, Brazil, Paraguay, and Uruguay. The total area is 2,766,890 square kilometers, consisting of rich plains (Pampas) in the northern half, flat to rolling plateau (Patagonia) in the south, and rugged mountains (the Andes) along the western border with Chile.

Argentina is rich in natural resources, as the Pampas are very fertile, and lead, zinc, tin, copper, iron ore, manganese, petroleum, and uranium are present. In the last few years Argentina has experienced a severe economic crisis, leaving the GDP at U.S.$404 billion, or U.S.$10,500 per capita, and an unemployment rate above 20 percent in 2002 (CIA *World Factbook* 2004; Latin America Bureau 2004).

Table 1   Basic Statistics

Type of government	Presidential republic
Population (millions)	38.7 (2003)
Religion	Roman Catholic (92%)
Main industries	Food processing, motor vehicles, consumer durables, textiles, chemicals and petrochemicals, printing, metallurgy, steel
Main security threats	Deteriorating economy, corruption, criminality
Defense spending (% GDP)	1.4 (2001)
Size of military (thousands)	69.9 (2002)
Number of civil wars since 1945	3
Number of interstate wars since 1945	1

Sources

Central Intelligence Agency Website. 2005. CIA *World Factbook.* http://www.cia.gov/cia/publications/factbook/ (accessed May 15, 2005).

Eriksson, Mikael, ed. 2004. *States in Armed Conflict 2002.* Uppsala: Uppsala Publishing House.

Stockholm International Peace Research Institute (SIPRI). 2003. *SIPRI Yearbook 2003: Armaments, Disarmament and International Security.* London: Oxford University Press.

Regional Geopolitics

Argentina is one of the founding members of the United Nations, and it accepts all of the purposes and principles espoused in the UN charter. Argentina has also been active in the last decade in participating in international and regional peacekeeping missions. It is a member of several other international organizations and has been a major force in the creation of MERCOSUR (Mercado Común del Sur), a regional customs union incorporating Argentina, Brazil, Uruguay, and Paraguay, with Chile and Bolivia as associated members.

Increased economic and political cooperation in the region has led to a situation in which geopolitical tensions are lower than ever before. In the past, however, Argentina had a history of treating neighboring countries as potential enemies rather than potential allies, leading to rivalries.

In the Argentine Constitution of 1853, the British sovereignty of the Falkland Islands (Islas Malvinas) and dependent territories was contested. Following the civil wars, Argentine forces briefly occupied the islands, but since 1833 they have been under British rule. Since the nationalist rule of Juan Perón in the 1940s, the inclusion of the islands into Argentina has been a foreign policy priority. The Falklands were invaded by Argentina in 1982, but less than three months later the invading forces were defeated.

After the return of democratic government in Argentina in 1983, high-level activity for improving relations with Great Britain was initiated. Several joint declarations were signed regarding confidence-building measures in 1989–1990, and in 1995 Argentina ceded the right to settle the dispute by force. There is still a strong wish in parts of the society to annex the islands, and offers have been made to the islanders about financial incentives for accepting Argentine sovereignty (Millett and Gold-Biss 1996, 26, 243–246; Hunter 1996, 16).

The main enduring military rivalry has been between Argentina and Chile. The two countries share a long, mountainous, and basically unguarded border that at some places has been disputed. Traditionally, and especially during military rule, Argentina has worried that the access to natural resources could tempt Chile into an invasion. The Chilean army has also usually been considered the strongest in the region, a fact that has fueled Argentine suspicions. An attack would be easy to plan, as an invading force could easily cross the vast spaces of Patagonian plains and attack Buenos Aires from the south; the territory is too large for the Argentine military to cover adequately.

The rivalry between the two countries has focused mainly on competition over the Beagle Channel near the Kap Horn, as the channel is a key passage between the Pacific and the Atlantic (Mares 1998, 81). The contest led to a crisis in 1978, when both the Argentine and Chilean armies were ready to go to war over the issue; intervention and mediation from the Vatican defused the situation. After continuous involvement by the pope, the two countries settled the dispute in the mid-1980s through the Treaty of Peace and Friendship, and a series of meetings among high-level military commanders were initiated.

Another border dispute between the two countries, over the Laguna del Desierto in the same area, led to a breakdown of relations in 1965. In the late 1980s, the dispute was handed over to international mediators who, in 1994, declared that the territory should belong to Argentina (Millett and Gold-Biss 1996, 246–252).

Another relationship that at times has been strained is that with Brazil. The border territory between the two countries has been poorly defined, but most of the contested area has been in relation to the use of natural resources. Since Brazil and Argentina are the two largest states with traditionally the strongest economies in South America, this competition has been linked mainly to economic development and growth. During the economic success of the "Brazilian miracle" in the 1960s and 1970s, the Argentine leadership became very suspicious of their neighbor and its suspected expansionist policy (ibid., 245). When Brazil and Paraguay in 1966 signed an agreement to build a hydroelectric plant in Itaipú, the Argentineans reacted angrily. The proposed facility would be located only twenty-three kilometers from the Argentine border and would severely limit the downstream water supply. The tense situation between the countries persisted even though the three military governments signed an agreement on the issue in 1979 (Mares 1998, 82).

Relations in the region have improved significantly since the change to democratic government in the countries, starting with the signing by Brazil and Argentina of the Foz de Iguazú Declaration in 1985, when both committed to developing nuclear power for civilian purposes only. The year following, the presidents met and agreed on a plan for an Argentine-Brazilian Economic Integration Program (ABEIP) that later was joined by Paraguay and Uruguay and developed into MERCOSUR.

Since the mid-1980s there have also been periodic bilateral meetings between senior representatives of the Argentine and Brazilian general staffs, discussing matters of common interest and planning specific measures, such as military-to-military cooperation to exchange information and plan joint arms manufacturing. Those meetings later included representatives of Paraguay, Uruguay, and Chile as observers. In recent years there has also been increased police cooperation in the border area of Brazil, Argentina, and Paraguay, because there have been claims of terrorist hideouts and widespread smuggling and criminality in the region (Hirst 2002, 1; Hunter 1996, 2; Mares 1998, 91; Millett and Gold-Biss 1996, 25, 252–255).

Conflict Past and Present

Conflict History

After Argentina declared independence on July 9, 1816, there followed eight years of independence wars, as there was disagreement over whether the new state should be federalist or centralist under the leadership of Buenos Aires. Spanish troops were also involved in these wars, with the intention of remaining in control of some Argentinean provinces. Following defeats by the armies of Simon Bolívar in Gran Colombia, and San Martin in Argentina, the Spaniards were forced to leave South America in 1824.

Disagreement over the domestic political organization in Argentina continued and led to several conflicts as Buenos Aires temporarily seceded from the country between 1853 and 1862. Conflicts also arose with the indigenous people until the brutal "Conquest of the Desert" in 1879–1880, which virtually removed the "Indian Problem" and opened Patagonia for settlement. The borders of the newly created states in South America were not yet fixed, however, and skirmishes followed, especially with neighboring Uruguay. More territory was incorporated after Argentina had allied with Brazil and Uruguay in fighting Paraguay during the War of the Triple Alliance, 1865–1870 (Huser 1998, 1; Armed Conflicts Event Data; Hunter 1996, 11).

In 1880 the Argentine borders were basically in place, but domestically there was a lack of cohesion. Most of the population consisted of recently arrived immigrants, and there was a strong political and social division between the growing urbanity of Buenos Aires and the rural provinces. Following the example of the strongest military power in the region at the time, Chile, Argentina approached Prussian military experts for advice on building a military organization. That led to the establishment of mandatory military service in 1901 and a professional military role in the development of the Argentine nation (der Ghougassian and Carneiro 1998, 6; Hunter 1996, 15). As a consequence, the military organizations were highly active in the large-scale programs instigated for increasing literacy among the lower classes and building infrastructure. The military "class" was held in high esteem by society at large, as the perception (not least among themselves) was of their being the protectors of the state (Barber and Ronning 1966, 124–125).

Experiences during the early period of democracy in Argentina, from 1916 to 1930, led to an activist approach to domestic politics among the military, based upon that self-perceived role of protecting the state. During that period, radical movements, populism, and electoral fraud marred democratic leadership. Socialist and anarchist organizations clashed with paramilitary groups formed by large landowners with the help of parts of the military elite (der Ghougassian and Carneiro 1998, 5). At the same time, the military leadership was being distanced physically from society as special residential areas and social clubs were created for staff and their families; as the military branches became increasingly involved in business projects, the occasional civilians invited were large landowners or the industrial elite. When the economy worsened, and President Yrigoyen wanted to cut increases in military salaries and pensions, the military removed him from power in 1930 and announced new elections without Yrigoyen's Radical Party. This began a period of some fifty-five years in which the military leadership on several occasions intervened into the political life of the country. Until 1983, only eight of twenty-three de facto presidents were civilian, and only six of those had been elected (see Table 2).

During World War II, the United States and Great Britain put diplomatic pressure on Argentina to join in the fight against the Axis Powers. Although the conservative government at the time seemed to be taking an increasingly pro-British stance in its foreign policy, a military coup in 1943 made sure that the country remained neutral in the conflict. In the military coalition government that followed, the career of the young colonel Juan Perón quickly accelerated as his popularity was fostered through connections with the labor movements (Millett and Gold-Biss 1996, 248). Argentina finally declared war on the Axis, but it has been suggested that it was more due to a wish to be a charter member of the United Nations, and an attempt to avoid losing prestige in the postwar order (Huser 1998, 1).

Perón went on to win the presidential elections in 1946 and established a personalized authoritarian leadership. That was accompanied by random acts of charity often involving Perón's popular wife, Eva (or Evita), establishing a connection between the government and the lower classes. By assuming control over appointments in the military, Perón tried to assure himself of loyalty from the armed

forces. This increased civilian input into what was considered internal organizational matters eventually led to discontent among high-ranking officers, and Perón was overthrown in September 1955 by General Pedro Aramburu in the third coup attempt since 1951.

After an unsuccessful countercoup the following year the popular Peronist party was banned, leading to the formation of smaller guerrilla groups such as FAP (Fuerzas Armadas Peronistas) and FAR (Fuerzas Armadas Revolucionarias) (der Ghougassian and Carneiro 1998, 5). New elections were held, but the military stepped in again to remove the president in 1962. In the ensuing elections the winner, Arturo Illia, only narrowly managed more votes than the blanks. Continuing bad economic performances led to a new military takeover in 1966. At the same time the military became increasingly worried after the successful example of the Cuban revolution, not least by the part played by Argentine Ernesto "Che" Guevara and his subsequent announcement of spreading the revolution throughout Latin America (Koonings and Kruijt 1999, 128).

The technocratic solutions to the economic crisis was to stabilize society through banning all political parties, suppressing unions and labor's demands, and strengthening the "anticommunist" ideology of the state with the support of the Catholic Church. The communist security threat was played up by the United States as young officers were sent to the U.S. Southern Command in Panama and Fort Bragg, North Carolina, to undergo antisubversive training.

Political repression led to the radicalization of the opposition, as the Peronist supporters started to form more active guerrilla groups such as the Monteneros, who

Table 2   Seventy-Five Years in the Hot Seat—the Presidents of Argentina Since 1928

Year	Name	Mil./Civ.	Basis for power**
1928	H. Irigoyen	Civilian	Elected
1930	J. E. Uriburu	Military	Coup
1932	A. P. Justo	Civilian	Elected
1938	R. M. Ortiz	Civilian	Elected
1942	R. S. Castillo	Civilian	Appointed
1943	P. P. Ramírez	Military	Coup
1944	E. Farrel	Military	Coup
1946, 1951	J. D. Perón	Military/Civilian*	Elected
June 1955	E. Lonardi	Military	Coup
September 1955	P. E. Aramburu	Military	Coup
1958	A. Frondizi	Civilian	Elected
1962	J. M. Guido	Military	Coup
1963	A. H. Illia	Civilian	Elected
1966	J. C. Onganía	Military	Coup
1970	R. Levingston	Military	Coup
1971	A. Lanusse	Military	Coup
March 1973	H. J. Cámpora	Civilian	Elected
July 1973	R. A. Lastri	Military	Coup
September 1973	J. D. Perón	Civilian	Elected
1974	I. Perón	Civilian	Appointed
1976	J. R. Videla	Military (Proceso)	Coup
March 1981	R. E. Viola	Military (Proceso)	Appointed
December 1981	L. F. Galtieri	Military (Proceso)	Coup
1982	R. B. Bignone	Military	Appointed
1983	R. R. Alfonsín	Civilian	Elected
1989, 1995	C. S. Menem	Civilian	Elected
1999	F. De la Rúa	Civilian	Elected
December 2001	R. Puerta	Civilian	Appointed
December 2001	A. R. Saá	Civilian	Appointed
December 2001	E. Camano	Civilian	Appointed
2002	E. Duhalde	Civilian	Appointed
2003	N. Kirschner	Civilian	Elected

* Perón had participated in the military government in the years before his election, but was running as a civilian.

** Not all elections were free and fair and included all parties. When the previous leader (civilian or military) was forced to resign due to military involvement, it is recorded as a coup.

Sources

Alston, Lee J., and Andrés A. Gallo. 2003. "The Erosion of Rule of Law in Argentina, 1930–1947: An Explanation of Argentina's Economic Slide from the Top 10." http://www.ssrn.com/abstract=463300.

Roehrig, Terence. 2002. *The Prosecution of Former Military Leaders in Newly Democratic Countries: The Cases of Argentina, Greece, and South Korea.* Jefferson, NC: McFarland and Company.

Solimano, Andrés. 2003. "Development Cycles, Political Regimes and International Migration: Argentina in the Twentieth Century." Santiago: UN Economic Development Division.

started to attack foreign-owned corporations and organize large-scale strikes, together with labor unions (der Ghougassian and Carneiro 1998, 6). Even more radical organizations, such as the ERP (Ejército Revolucionario del Pueblo, the People's Revolutionary Army), emerged and started attacking police and military installations toward the end of the decade (Koonings and Kruijt, 1999, 127).

Continuing civil unrest led to new coups in 1970 and 1971, until the military decided to withdraw from the government and invite Perón to return and compete in elections. Two elections were held in 1973, with Juan Perón competing in and winning the second to reassume the presidency. The Peronist movement had no ideological unity, however, and thus his authoritarian moves when in power against the leftist labor movements came as a surprise to many of his supporters. At the same time, ERP stepped up their attacks on the military and announced the formation of a liberated zone in the northern province of Tucumán (ibid., 128).

In July 1974, the aging Perón died of a heart condition and was succeeded by his new wife, Isabel. She had little political experience and gave the military a free hand in dealing with political discontent. The army started attacking the ERP, while the police joined forces with right-wing paramilitary groups such as AAA (Argentine Anticommunist Alliance) to focus on the Monteneros and other left-wing Peronist groups. Between July 1974 and March 1976, more than a thousand people were killed in political violence. As the military stepped up its attempts to capture, torture, and execute the *guerrilleros*, the ERP announced the indiscriminate killing of military officers as a reprisal.

Certain spectacular incidents—such as the attack on an army captain and his three-year-old daughter in December 1974, and the placing of a bomb under the bed of General Cardozo by his daughter's classmate in 1976—shocked the military establishment and pushed them toward even harsher counterinsurgency measures (ibid.). As the violence escalated, opposition alliances were made. After limiting their attacks toward Peronist right-wing groups and the police in the early 1970s, the Monteneros joined forces with ERP in 1975 with the aim of overthrowing the government.

By then, the military had already made plans for a large-scale project to assault the revolutionary left. In February 1975, a secret decree ordered the army to annihilate the Marxist insurgency in Tucumán through Operation Independence. The tactics used were inspired by the French fight against insurgencies in Indochina and Algeria decades earlier. Commander General Vilas reversed Mao Zedong's statement that the guerrilla must operate like a fish in the water. The repressive tactics he used were a way of killing the fish by draining the water through special civilian-clad task forces (*grupos de tarea*) that raided houses and abducted suspects, while regular armed forces combed the populated rural areas.

Anyone might have been accused of collaborating with the enemy, and torture was used extensively. The tactic proved successful in Tucamán, and from October 1975 onward it was employed in the rest of the country. In 1975 the various militaries of the region—many also being in charge of government—signed the so-called Plan Condor Agreement, which created cross-border cooperation against left-wing insurgents. Argentina,

Brazil, Chile, Uruguay, Bolivia, and Paraguay all signed the agreement, but joint operations against the opposition were not limited to the territories of those countries (McDermott 2003, 39). The increasing violence, combined with an ever-worsening economy with an annual inflation rate of some 300 percent, made many Argentineans relieved when Isabel was removed in a military coup on March 24, 1976 (Koonings and Kruijt 1999, 130–131).

A military coalition government consisting of one general, one admiral, and one air force brigadier under the official name Proceso (Proceso de Reorganización Nacional) was installed. The first and foremost goal for the Proceso was to crush the "terrorist subversives" of the left, with particular attention given to the Montoneros and ERP guerrillas. What followed has been known as the Dirty War, as institutionalized state terror followed.

From 1976 to 1983 at least 8,960 people disappeared, although some human rights groups claimed that the number was closer to 30,000 (Vanished Gallery). There was also widespread use of torture and other human rights abuses (CONADEP 1986). Even though the Dirty War defeated the left-wing guerrillas, it instigated popular discontent in the form of human rights activists. Most notable were the Madres de Plaza de Mayo (the Mothers at the Plaza de Mayo), who from September 1977 on staged weekly protests calling for knowledge about their "disappeared" relatives.

Desperate to obtain public support, the Proceso government launched several large-scale projects, among them hosting the Soccer World Cup in 1978 (Glanville 1993, 211), as the economy deteriorated. The foreign debt more than doubled between 1980 and the end of 1982 (Statistical Yearbook 1992). In desperation to remedy the situation, there were intramilitary coups twice in 1981. Given that backdrop, the decision was made to invade the Falkland Islands.

Sidebar 1   Violence, Soccer, and Politics

By far, the most popular spectator sport in Argentina is soccer. In Buenos Aires, some rival teams even have stadiums that are located within sight of each other. Passion for the sport has led to violent incidents between rival gangs of soccer fans, or *barra bravas*, which resulted in the deaths of twenty-nine people during the 1990s. These fan groups have links to part of the clubs' management, and have been used to "influence" elections of club presidents. Following clashes in August 2003 between fans of the Boca Juniors and the Chacarita Juniors, which injured seventy-one fans, the soccer league was suspended for two weeks. It was later reported that some of the Chacarita *barra bravas* had been paid to start the fight in the Boca "Bombonera" stadium. This was an attempt to hurt the reputation of Boca's club president, Mauricio Macri, who at the time was campaigning to be elected mayor of Buenos Aires Capital Federal on a strong law-and-order platform.

Sources

González, Gustavo. 2003. "Special Report: Football Violence, but No Red Card." www.insidecostarica.com, June 16, 2003.

Peronius, Olof. 2004. "Mot alla odds." *Offside* 2:74–96.

———. "Fan Violence Halts Argentine Season." Sports Network, September 10, 2003.

Several other factors played into the decision to attack the Falkland Islands in 1982. The Argentine government calculated that the British were not truly interested in the islands at the time, as they had removed full British citizenship for islanders in 1981 and had withdrawn the ice-patrol ship HMS *Endurance* in early 1982. The situation seemed analogous to the way in which India acquired Goa in 1961 without much international opposition, and Argentina sensed possible political support from the United States. Following the election of President Reagan, with his foreign policy based on anticommunism rather than the human rights issues of the Carter administration, U.S.-Argentine relations had improved. The basic tactics for the invasion were based on the assumption that the islands could be invaded quickly; then Argentina would be in a position to negotiate a settlement with Great Britain.

On April 2, 1982, Argentine forces seized the islands almost without resistance, claiming that the invasion was a response to British demands for documentation from Argentine workers at the nearby South Georgia Islands (Millett and Gold-Biss 1996, 246). At the same time, the Argentine mission to the United Nations was lobbying hard to get the USSR and China to veto any attempt to bring up the issue in the Security Council, something that proved unsuccessful; the United Nations called for a withdrawal of Argentine forces.

On April 31, the United States declared its support of Great Britain in the conflict, an announcement that was taken by the Argentine government as a surprise and a betrayal. On May 21 the United Kingdom counterattacked, and between that date and June 14, when the Argentine forces surrendered, 1,500 Argentineans were killed; Argentina's military forces proved themselves poorly equipped and unprepared for war (Mares 1998, 87). Domestically, this defeat eroded the last bastion of belief in the military government. In public opinion, it had now become clear that the military had failed both in running the economy and in running a war. The junta resigned in June, leaving the task of administrating the transformation to civilian rule to a member of the engineering corps, General Reynaldo Bignone.

In the 1983 elections, the Radical Party candidate, Raúl Alfonsín, won 52 percent of the vote after promising that he would hold the military leadership accountable for the Dirty War (Hunter 1996, 11). In December 1983, Alfonsín installed the CONADEP (Comisión Nacional Sobre la Desaparición de Persona), with a mandate to inquire into the fate of the disappeared. The Presidential Commission heard more than 5,700 witnesses in nine months and in 1984 published its findings in a report entitled *Nunca Más* (*Never Again*) (CONADEP 1986).

Even though Alfonsín's original intention was to restrict the people on trial to the top leadership, thousands of cases of atrocities committed during the Dirty War were filed in Argentine courts between 1984 and 1987 (Hunter 1996, 13). The civilian government cut military spending to the point where officers usually had to get a second job and there was increased discontent among younger officers. In April 1987, a group calling themselves the Carapintadas (the "painted faces") rebelled under the leadership of Lt.-Col. Aldo Rico. The group pointed out that the rebellion was not a coup attempt but a demonstration of grievances among the armed forces. The Argentine public responded with mass demonstrations in support of the civilian government, but the Carapintadas managed to make a deal with the government: no one with a rank lower than that of colonel during the Dirty War would be prosecuted under the Obendencia Debida (Due Obedience) Law.

The Carapintadas rebelled twice again in 1988 and once more in December 1990, when they were defeated by other troops loyal to the government. In 1989, Carlos Menem became president, and his policy for reconciliation between the civilian leadership and the military establishment involved amnesty for jailed officers as well as a major restructuring of the armed forces (ibid., 13–14; der Ghougassian and Carneiro 1998, 6). During the 1990s, several NGOs campaigned against the two amnesty laws adopted in the late 1980s. In 2001, federal judges declared the laws unconstitutional, but the cases were appealed to the Supreme Court. Following his inauguration in 2003, President Kirchner vocally supported a reopening of investigations into the Dirty War. In August 2003, both chambers of the Congress voted to annul the two amnesty laws adopted in 1986–1987 (Human Rights Watch 2003).

*Current and Potential
Military Confrontation*
Argentina has had an enduring rivalry with Chile over several contested border areas in Patagonia. Relations between the countries have improved steadily in the last decades, as there has been a growing trend of cooperation within the Southern Cone, both in relation to military and economic problems as well as in reference to criminality and terrorism. Several agreements have been signed, including the Memorandum of Understanding of 1994, which established an Argentine-Chilean Permanent Security Committee (Ministerio de Defensa 1998).

Argentina is still contesting the British sovereignty of the Falkland Islands, but the country has officially renounced the right to settle the dispute by force. The government claims that the islands are under British occupation, and it has repeatedly called for meetings about settling the conflict by incorporating the islands into Argentina ("Argentina Calls for Resumption," 2004). The majority of the inhabitants on the Falkland Islands consider themselves part of Britain and are against any such settlement. It is unlikely that Argentina would be willing to jeopardize trade relations between MERCOSUR and the European Union, as the country's priority in the near future must be to increase economic growth.

Because the civilian administration has managed to create a new identity for the armed forces, and because the military has not intervened in domestic politics during the instability of the last five years, it may be inferred that the risk of another coup attempt is marginal. During the administration of President Menem, concessions to the military such as the general amnesty made the armed forces loyal to the government. The current president, Nestor Kirchner, and several of his main advisors were part of the persecuted leftist movements during military rule, and the new administration has quickly moved to appoint new officers rather than place "Menem's men" in key positions (McDermott 2003, 38).

Alliance Structure
As part of finding a new identity for the Argentine armed forces, the National Defense Law in 1989 established that par-

ticipation in peacekeeping missions become part of the formal military statement. In February 1990 the United Nations sent a request to Argentina to supply fast patrol boats to the ONUCA (UN Observer Mission in Central America), which became the start of large-scale involvement in peacekeeping and observer missions.

Argentina became the only Latin American country to provide troops for operations Desert Shield and Desert Storm in the Iraq-Kuwait conflict, and throughout the decade Argentina was involved in operations in Angola, El Salvador, Western Sahara, Cambodia, Croatia, Somalia, Cyprus, Bosnia-Herzegovina, Haiti, Eastern Slavonia, and Guatemala (Huser 1998, 2–4; Millett and Gold-Biss 1996, 28–29).

After the brief outbreak of hostilities in 1995 on the border between Ecuador and Peru, the Argentine military participated in a non-UN observatory mission (MOMEP—The Military Observer Mission Ecuador-Peru). Later the same year, the CAECOPAZ (Centre Argentino de Entrenamiento Conjunto para Operaciones de Paz: Argentine Joint Peacekeeping Operations Training Centre) opened for joint peacekeeping simulation programs (Huser 1998, 4–7).

The focus of international participation has served several purposes for the Argentine military: it has restored some self-esteem and re-created an identity for the country; it has given individual officers a chance for extra financial rewards; and it has supplied necessary training in the field. An important and proud day for the armed forces was February 17, 1997, when Brigadier General Evergisto de Vergara was announced as the commander of the UN peace contingent in Cyprus with—among others—British troops under his command (ibid., 4–5).

In 2002, Argentina participated in the UN missions in Bosnia-Herzegovina, Yugoslavia/Kosovo, the Middle East (UNTSO), Cyprus, the Western Sahara, Iraq/Kuwait, East Timor, Guatemala, Ethiopia/Eritrea, the Democratic Republic of the Congo, and Croatia (*SIPRI* 2003). Because of improving relations with the United States in the 1990s and involvement in many U.S.-led operations, Argentina has been pursuing a path toward NATO membership. At a state visit in 1997, U.S. president Bill Clinton announced that Argentina was a "major non-NATO ally" (a title officially granted in February 1998), the first country to receive that status since the end of the Cold War. The plans for even closer ties to NATO were abolished, however, when the Peronist Party lost the presidential elections in 1999, and relations with the United States have cooled during the recent economic crisis (Huser 1998, 8).

Argentina has also been an active member within the Organization of American States (OAS) since its establishment in 1948. In the 1990s the organization established several means of institutionalized cooperation, such as the OAS Commission on Hemispheric Security and the Defense Ministerial of the Americas. At the Defense Ministerial Summit of the Americas in Santiago de Chile in 1998, the Commission on Hemispheric Security was asked to identify ways and means of revitalizing and strengthening inter-American security-related institutions. This led to a Declaration in 2002 by the OAS general assembly, which declared that hemispheric security encompasses political, economic, social, health, and environmental factors (OAS 2002). The OAS has recently adopted treaties relating to arms control, and it established

CICTE (Comité Interamericano contra el Terrorismo: Inter-American Committee against Terrorism) in 2002. In July 2003, the Inter-American Convention against Terrorism came into effect.

After the attacks on the United States on September 11, 2001, Argentina and Brazil lobbied successfully to invoke the Rio Pact, or TIAR (Tratado Interamericano de Asistencia Recíproca: Inter-American Treaty of Reciprocal Assistance), of 1947 and participated in the ensuing U.S. mission in Afghanistan (Hirst 2002, 2; Arnson 2003, 120; OAS 2004).

Economic cooperation within the MERCOSUR framework was supplemented by a political declaration of MERCOSUR as a Peace Zone, signed by the presidents of Argentina, Brazil, Uruguay, Paraguay, Bolivia, and Chile in 1998 (Argentina White Paper 2000). This has so far led to the establishment of a zone free of weapons of mass destruction, but the economic development in the region is at present more prioritized. MERCOSUR is involved in trade negotiations with the European Union and is working toward the possible future establishment of an FTAA (Free Trade Area of the Americas).

Size and Structure of the Military

The Argentine Armed Forces consisted in August 2002 of 69,900 troops. Of that number, the army registered 41,400, the navy 16,000, and the air force 12,500. There were no reserves formally established or trained, as the country abolished mandatory military service in 1995. Argentina also had 31,240 paramilitary forces under the administration of the Ministry of Interior, consisting of 18,000 gendarmes and 13,240 Prefectura Naval (coast guard).

The Argentine military is organized under the civilian leadership of the president and the Ministry of Defense. During the last decades there has been an unofficial policy of noninvolvement in the Defense Ministry and the Chief of Staffs, for each branch has in effect a large degree of independence in organizational matters. During the short tenure of the present Kirchner administration, there has been a major initiative to remove people appointed during the Menem years, known for "soft" treatment of the military. During the first months of his presidency, Kirchner appointed new heads of the army, the navy, and the air force, as well as several federal police chiefs and new heads for the intelligence agency (McDermott 2003, 38–39).

The largest branch of the military is the army, which consists of three corps and a strategic reserve that includes the Army HQ Escort and the Presidential Escort. The second largest is the navy, which is divided into four different commands: the surface fleet, submarines, marines, and naval aviation; the administrative branch is divided into an Atlantic, a Center, and a Southern region. In addition to a base in Buenos Aires, the navy has headquarters in Puerto Belgrano (Center), Mar del Plata (Atlantic), and Ushaio (South), as well as a shipbuilding base in Rio Santiago. The surface fleet command consists of five destroyers, eight frigates, two mine countermeasure vessels, one amphibious vessel, and fourteen patrol and coastal combat ships, as well as eleven smaller support and miscellaneous vessels. The submarine command is also based in Mar del Plata. It consists of three units: two *Santa Cruz* (TR-1700) and one *Salta* (T-209/1200).

Of the 16,000 troops in the navy, some

2,500 belong to the marines, which are divided into two fleet forces and one supporting amphibious battalion. Trelew and Punta Indio (training) are the main bases for naval aviation, consisting of 2,000 troops. The naval aviation arm has at its disposal twenty-five combat aircraft and twenty-three armed helicopters.

Argentina's air force is also divided into four commands: the Air Operations, Air Regions, Logistics, and the Personnel Command for training. The air force has a total of 130 combat aircraft of different sizes and 29 armed helicopters. The aircraft are divided as follows: five strategic squadrons, one defense squadron, two tactical squadrons, one survey and reconnaissance squadron, and six transport and tanker squadrons. All helicopters are designated for search-and-rescue operations (*The Military Balance* 2002).

Budget

As mentioned earlier, partly to restrict the military influence into the civilian sector, and partly as a result of a neoliberal economic policy, most of the assets of the armed forces were privatized during the presidencies of Alfonsín and Menem. During the same period military spending was also greatly reduced, to less than 2 percent of the increasing GDP. That was accompanied by a new security perception in which scenarios regarding the border with Chile, the dispute over the Falklands, and domestic opposition all became less likely to lead to armed conflict. Despite the abolition of a conscript force, the main part of the budget has gone to cover personnel costs, inasmuch as the military traditionally has been responsible for funding retired staff as part of the defense budget. In 1996 it was reported that there were 100,000 active soldiers, but that approximately 80 percent of the annual military budget went to cover salaries and pensions for a total of 500,000 men (Goni 1996, 2).

In the last part of the twentieth century, military spending was at a consistent level of around U.S.$4.3 billion (as of 1999), or 1.3 percent of GDP (as of 2000), changing only with the economic crisis of 2001–2002. The defense budget was fixed at 3.3 billion pesos for 2002, but, inasmuch as the currency peg to the dollar was lifted, that effectively led to a decrease from U.S.$3.3 billion to U.S.$940 million.

One of the consequences of the economic crisis was that a number of planned air force modernization projects were shelved in 2003. Even though the economy recovered better than expected in 2003, the high rate of unemployment has made it unlikely that Argentina will increase military expenditures. Inasmuch as most of the budget still goes to personnel costs, it is difficult to reduce spending substantially. The International Monetary Fund is pressuring Argentina to cut public spending in order to be able to reduce the foreign debt; cuts in military spending are likely to follow (CIA *World Factbook*; Perlo-Freeman 2003; *The Military Balance* 2003).

Civil-Military Relations/The Role of the Military in Domestic Politics

After the return of democratic rule in 1983, Presidents Raúl Alfonsín and Carlos Menem launched a number of large-scale initiatives to increase civilian control over the armed forces. The powers of the Ministry of Defense were strengthened, especially in relation to personnel matters, control of military expenditures,

Sidebar 2   Life in an
Economic Crisis

A consequence of previous economic troubles was that Argentineans had to work multiple jobs, while the last decade instead has seen a wave of unemployment. The failed efforts to manage the economy have led to an increased lack of trust in political institutions and a feeling that the Argentinean quality of life has declined. This is largely attributed to unemployment, increased criminality, and drug and alcohol use.

Despite the transition to democracy, the percentage of Argentineans expressing great confidence in at least one political institution has fallen from 76 percent in 1981 to 20 percent in 2001. During the same time, the number of poor people in the country has more than quadrupled. It appears that poverty is beginning to become institutionalized, as most advertised jobs require high school education while only one quarter of the poorest 20 percent of the population completes secondary school.

Sources
Narayan, Deepa, and Patti Petesch, eds. 2002. *Voices from the Poor from Many Lands*. Washington, DC: World Bank.
Berensztein, Sergio. 2003. "When All Politics Becomes Local: Argentina after the Crisis." Paper presented at the Conference on Rethinking Dual Transitions: Argentine Politics in the 1990s in Comparative Perspective. Weatherhead Center for International Affairs, Harvard University, March 20–22, 2003.

the personnel in the armed forces dropped in number from 175,000 in 1983 to 65,000 ten years later. The senior leadership was especially targeted, most of the generals being forced into retirement in the 1980s. Organizational changes also meant that the numbers were cut at the top, from seventy generals in 1983 to only thirty-two in 1995 (Hunter 1996, 12–16).

As suggested by the nature of the liberalized economic policies, almost all of the military industrial and arms-producing sectors were privatized between 1990 and 1997 (Brömmelhörster and Paes 2003, 21–22). In the adoption of the new National Defense Law of April 1988, the military was removed from any involvement in domestic security. At the same time, police and border patrols were removed from military authority (Millett and Gold-Biss 1996, 120–151).

The new mission statement for the Argentine military was focused primarily on defense of the national territory, but complemented with a series of secondary missions. These were participation in international peacekeeping, as well as participation in a supporting role in internal operations (logistical support in counternarcotics operations and relief in case of natural disasters) (Ministerio de Defensa 1998). Following the new mission statement, the armed forces began restructuring its organizations during the 1990s, as the government under Menem applied an unofficial "hands-off" policy in relations to decision making on the use of military budget or staff appointments (Hunter 1996, 19).

In 1995 the policy of conscription was abolished and a system of voluntary service (Servicio Voluntario Militar), open for men and women, instituted (Huser 1998, 6; Balza 1996, 65). Involvement in

and the development of a national defense policy. The military budget was cut from 32 percent of public sector expenditures in 1982 to 18 percent in 1990, and peacekeeping has led to a new approach and status for the Argentine armed forces, and they are aware of the reputation of their history of involvement in domestic policy. This stance has been most vocal in relation to U.S. suggestions that the military be more involved in fighting narcotics trafficking, international crime, and terrorism; the armed forces have been clear in rejecting such proposals. At the most, the military has been willing to provide logistical support to the Gendarmerá Nacional (border guard), the Prefectura Naval (coast guard), and the federal and provincial police forces (Huser 1998, 6; Hunter 1996, 5).

Terrorism

The first cases of terrorism in Argentina can be said to have been the activities of the Monteneros and ERP and the right-wing paramilitary groups in the early 1970s (Saavedra 2003, 196). A group that declared themselves the remains of the leftist guerrillas attacked a military base in 1989.

In 1995–1996 another group, calling itself OPR (Organización Revolucionaria del Pueblo), took responsibility for some bombings of public places and a failed assassination attempt on former president Alfonsín in March 1996. According to intelligence analysts, they were a group of anarchists wanting to destabilize society in general, without having any political goals (der Ghougassian and Carneiro 1998, 6).

Other incidents of political violence were brought to worldwide attention with the 1992 and 1994 bombings of a Jewish Community Center and the Israeli Embassy in Buenos Aires. Some suggested that the groups behind these incidents were formed within—and took cover among—the large Muslim population in the Triple Border area between the cities of Puerto Iguazu (Argentina), Ciudad del Este (Paraguay), and Foz du Iguacu (Brazil). The majority of these Muslims had migrated into Argentina during the large immigration waves of the early twentieth century. Other sources, however, claimed that the bombings had links to parts of the former Carapintada military movement (Hirst 2002, 4; der Ghougassian and Carneiro 1998, 6).

It is claimed that between 12,000 and 70,000 "Arab Muslims," mostly of Lebanese ancestry, live in the Triple Border area. The region has been described by official sources as a "free zone and safe haven for drug dealers, arms smugglers, international organized crime figures, money launderers, and representatives of terrorist groups" (Saavedra 2003, 208).

It has also been suggested that part of the revenue from these operations has been used to support Hezbollah, Hamas, and al-Qaeda groups mainly active in the Middle East. The terrorist threat in the region seems more to stem from the economic backing that the area delivers to groups abroad, and U.S. sources from the State Department, CIA, and DIA have encouraged activities to stop the smuggling and money laundering. Following the establishment of the CICTE, there has been an increase in cross-border police cooperation regarding terrorism, especially focusing on the Triple Border, which, according to some sources, is at present the most heavily policed area in South America (ibid., 208–209; Hirst 2002, 4).

Relationship with the United States

The Argentine relationship with the United States has for the most part been uneasy. Unlike European influence on the military development of the region, which was requested, the growing importance of good relations with the United States has been viewed with suspicion. Even though Argentina has happily participated in U.S.-initiated regional organizations such as the OAS and the CAA (Conference of American Armies), the general opinion has been that the United States is a possible competitor as a regional power (Millett and Gold-Biss 1996, 245; Kjonnerod 1995, 205).

During World War II the United States put pressure on Argentina to join the Allied side, something that there was strong opposition against within the Argentine armed forces because of longstanding ties with Germany and the perceived economic benefits of neutrality. It took almost until the war had ended before Argentina declared war on the Axis, and even that was supposedly a controversial decision intended mainly to make Argentina one of the founding members of the United Nations. The military government at the time also sought the international prestige of belonging to the victorious side.

The United States saw the growing popularity of Juan Perón as a threat because of his anti-U.S. stance and linkages to the labor organizations. The postwar U.S. ambassador to Buenos Aires, Spruille Braden, instigated a campaign against Perón, trying to link him to fascism. Needless to say, because of the huge popularity of Perón, that approach led to bad relations between the two countries in the ensuing years (Millett and Gold-Biss 1996, 247–248).

Another area in which Argentina became annoyed with the United States was in relation to the latter's arms export policy of the 1950s and 1960s. The re-fusal of the United States to supply anything but light weapons to Latin America led to the development of increasing domestic arms production in Argentina from 1967 and onward. As the violence in the early 1970s partly targeted foreign companies as well as the U.S. embassy in Buenos Aires , the United States was initially positively inclined toward the military coup in 1976.

When increasing numbers of reports on the atrocities of the Dirty War came out, the relationship became tense, especially when the Carter administration declared that promotion of human rights was the main foreign policy goal of the United States. In 1977, U.S. transfers of arms and aid to Argentina were stopped, and relations continued to suffer (Arnson 2003, 13–14). When the United States imposed economic sanctions against the Soviet Union following the invasion of Afghanistan, Argentina not only refused to participate but even tried to increase their exports to the Soviet market (Hudson 1999, 176; Ginsberg 1989, 76).

The declaration of the Reagan administration that anticommunism was the main U.S. foreign policy incentive led to improved relations, but when the United States chose to back Britain in the Falklands conflict in 1982, the Argentine leadership felt betrayed. Following the demise of the communist threat and the election of Carlos Menem as president in 1989, Argentina pursued a dedicated policy of improving relations with the United States and established the country as a reliable U.S. partner in a new order. Partly this was the activist approach to international forces under U.S. command, but it was also visible through Argentina's increased attention to the U.S. foreign policy goal of counternarcotics efforts and increases in arms exports from the United States to Argentina.

Beginning in 1995 there has been a series of joint military exercises under the name Fuerzas Unidas, incorporating staff and forces from the United States, Argentina, Brazil, Paraguay, and Uruguay (Millett and Gold-Biss 1996, 255–256; Mares 1998, 94–95). Relations reached their high point in 1997–1998, when Argentina was proclaimed a "major non-NATO U.S. ally" (Huser 1998, 7–8); Argentina's intention was then to apply for membership in NATO.

After Menem's successor as the Peronist party candidate lost the election in 1999, the idea of NATO membership was forgotten as economic developments overtook any other foreign policy goals. The economic recession in Argentina became severe after a sudden halt of capital influx in 1998, and in 1999, Brazil devalued the real. The peso at the time was pegged to the U.S. dollar, and the devaluation effectively meant that Argentina lost the only market in which they had a trade surplus (Focal 1999, 6).

As the crisis spread throughout Argentine society, the United States refused to grant any financial aid. Arguably, the U.S. stance worsened the situation through the adoption of measures to protect U.S. domestic steel production, hurting Argentina's export industry. In 2001 the United States and the World Bank held back on previously agreed upon help packages, leading to mass withdrawals from banks in Argentina and social unrest in Buenos Aires. The peso's peg to the dollar was abandoned in January 2002, and the peso was floated in February. As a consequence the exchange rate plunged (the peso's dollar value increased some 200 percent), inflation picked up,

and there were devastating effects on Argentine retirement funds (Hirst 2002, 3; Arnson 2003, 115–116; CIA *World Factbook* 2004). Economic relations between the United States and Argentina have started to recover but the political closeness that persisted before the economic crisis has disappeared.

However, the strong support from Argentina in relation to the U.S. "War on Terror" and the persistent close military cooperation show that in relation to security policy, the two countries have very good relations. There has been a shift from the Menem years, as the present administration has made a point of pursuing an independent Argentinean foreign policy, with its main focus on South America. The United States has been annoyed with the good relations established between Argentina and Cuba, as well as with the socialist Brazilian president, Lula, and the anti-American Venezuelan president, Chavéz (Briggs 2004).

The Future

Recovery from the economic crisis is the first and foremost necessity for creating stability within Argentine society. In 2003 the economy began to recover as a result of a strong demand for exports; unemployment decreased, and inflation stabilized at around 4 percent by the end of the year. However, there still exist fundamental economic problems in Argentina that have to be dealt with and that are likely to influence society in the future. The foreign debt is still a problem, as are a high rate of poverty and the effects of the breakdown of retirement funds, a crisis not yet fully experienced. There is also a growing problem with corruption, which has been in the public spotlight thanks to the evolving independent news media. That has led, among other things, to investigations into illegal arms shipments to Croatia and Ecuador, with allegations against ministers, former ministers, and high-ranking army officials (Falcoff 2002, 7; Focal 1999, 5; Hudson 1999, 179–180).

Another security threat connected to the economic situation is increasing criminality. During the 1990s there was increasingly severe fighting among gangs, drug dealers, and soccer fans in Buenos Aires, exacerbated by access to more modern weapons. There is a growing black market industry of hostage-taking, carjackings, and more advanced operations. At the same time, more and more minors are involved in criminal activity (der Ghougassian and Carneiro 1998, 8).

Argentina has not had a history of much organized crime, but there are some suggestions that structures created by soccer supporters are increasingly taking control over the illegal businesses of hostage-taking and drug trafficking. During the 1960s some fans of soccer teams in Argentina started organizing themselves into groups referred to as *barra bravas* (the Brave Fans), with the intention of fighting other fans. Over time those groups became increasingly powerful in "soccer-political" areas such as the elections of club presidents, in which they often were active to put pressure on members to vote for a specific candidate. There have been suggestions that similar tactics have been used in local elections, as Argentine politicians like to present themselves as supporters of a particular club. The level of organization of some *barra bravas* can be compared to that of paramilitary units, and it is not unlikely that there is a connection between those groups and more organized crime (Giulianotti et al. 1994, 37–72; der Ghougassian and Carneiro 1998, 7–8).

References, Recommended Readings and Websites

Books

Arnson, Cynthia J., ed. 2003. "Argentina-United States Bilateral Relations." Woodrow Wilson Center Report on the Americas No. 8.

Atkins, G. Pope. 1999. *Latin America in the International Political System*. 3d ed. Boulder, CO: Perseus Books.

Barber, William F., and C. Neale Ronning. 1966. *Internal Security and Military Power*. Columbus: Ohio State University Press.

Bodemer, Klaus, Sabine Kurtenbach, and Klaus Meschkat, eds. 2001. *Violencia y regulación de conflictos en América Latina*. Caracas: Nueva Sociedad.

Brömmelhörster, Jörn, and Wolf-Christian Paes, eds. 2003. *The Military as an Economic Actor: Soldiers in Business*. Basingstoke: Palgrave Macmillan.

CONADEP (The National Commission of the Disappeared). 1986. *Nunca Mas (Never Again)*. London: Faber and Faber.

Eriksson, Mikael, ed. 2004. *States in Armed Conflict 2002*. Uppsala: Uppsala Publishing House.

Ginsberg, Roy. 1989. *Foreign Policy Action of the European Community: The Politics of Scale*. Boulder, CO: Lynne Rienner.

Giulianotti, Richard, Norman Bonney, and Mike Hepworth, eds. 1994. *Football, Violence and Social Identity*. London: Routledge.

Glanville, Brian. 1993. *The Story of the World Cup*. London: Faber.

Kjonnerod, L. Erik, ed. 1995. *Hemispheric Security in Transition: Adjusting to the Post 1995 Environment*. Washington, DC: National Defense University Press.

Koonings, Kees, and Dirk Kruijt, eds. 1999. *Societies of Fear: The Legacy of Civil War, Violence and Terror in Latin America*. London: Zed Books.

Kurtenbach, Sabine, Klaus Bodemer, and Detlef Nolte, eds. 2000. *Sicherheitspolitik in Lateinamerika: Vom Konflikt zur Kooperation?* Opladen: Leske and Budrich.

Mares, David R., ed. 1998. *Civil-Military Relations: Building Democracy and Regional Security in Latin America, Southern Asia, and Central Europe*. Boulder, CO: Westview Press.

Millett, Richard L., and Michael Gold-Biss, eds. 1996. *Beyond Praetorianism: The Latin American Military in Transition.* Coral Gables, FL: North-South Center Press.

Narayan, Deepa, and Patti Petesch, eds. 2002. *Voices from the Poor from Many Lands.* Washington, DC: World Bank.

Norden, Deborah L. 1996. *Military Rebellion in Argentina: Between Coups and Consolidation.* Lincoln: University of Nebraska Press.

Pion-Berlin, David. 1997. *Through Corridors of Power: Institutions and Civil-Military Relations in Argentina.* University Park: Penn State University Press.

Roehrig, Terence. 2002. *The Prosecution of Former Military Leaders in Newly Democratic Countries: The Cases of Argentina, Greece, and South Korea.* Jefferson, NC: McFarland and Company.

Silva, Patricio, ed. 2001. *The Soldier and the State in South America.* New York: Latin American Studies Series.

SIPRI Yearbook 2003. 2003. Stockholm/London: Stockholm International Peace Research Institute, Oxford University Press.

Statistical Yearbook 1990–1991. 1992. New York: UN Department of Economic and Social Information and Policy Analysis.

The Military Balance 2002–2003. 2003. London: International Institute for Strategic Studies, Oxford University Press.

Articles/Papers

Alston, Lee J., and Andrés A. Gallo. 2003. "The Erosion of Rule of Law in Argentina, 1930–1947: An Explanation of Argentina's Economic Slide from the Top 10." *http://www.ssrn.com/abstract=463300.*

Balza, Martin Antonio. 1996. "Argentine Military Culture." *Joint Force Quarterly* 11:64–66.

Berensztein, Sergio. 2003. "When All Politics Becomes Local: Argentina after the Crisis." Paper presented at the Conference on Rethinking Dual Transitions: Argentine Politics in the 1990s in Comparative Perspective. Weatherhead Center for International Affairs, Harvard University, March 20–22, 2003.

Briggs, Jebediah. 2004. "Argentina's Kirchner: Latin America's Most Dynamic Leader in 2003." Council on Hemispheric Affairs—Memorandum to the Press 04-04. *http://www.coha.org/NEW_PRESS_RELEASES/New_Press_Releases_2004/04.04_Kirchner_2003_Leader.htm.*

Der Ghougassian, Khatchik, and Leandro Piquet Carneiro. 1998. "Connecting Weapons with Violence." *ISS Monograph 25.* Pretoria: Institute for Security Studies.

Domínguez, Jorge. 1999. "Argentina, NATO's South Atlantic Partner." *NATO Review* 1:7–10.

Falcoff, Mark. 2002. "The Future for Democratic Institutions in Latin America." Paper presented at the Bretton Woods Committee Conference in Washington, D.C., 12.12.2002. *http://www.brettonwoods.org/Falcoff.pdf.*

Focal: Canadian Foundation for the Americas. 1999. *Argentina after the Menem Decade.* Policy Paper 99-15. *http://www.focal.ca/english/publicat_1999.htm.*

Goni, Uki. 1996. Argentina's Military Up for Sale. *http://www.ukinet.com/media/text/index.htm.*

Hirst, Monica. 2002. An Overview of the Impact of September 11 on Latin America. *Social Science Research Council—After September 11 Archive. http://www.srrc.org/sept11/essays/hirst.htm.*

Hudson, Peter. 1999. "Menem's Argentina: Economic Miracle or Quick Fix?" *The Washington Quarterly* 4:175–180.

Human Rights Watch. 2003. "Argentina: Senate Votes to Annul Amnesty Laws." *http://www.hrw.org/press/2003/08/argentina082103.htm.*

Hunter, Wendy. 1996. "State and Soldier in Latin America: Redefining the Military's Role in Argentina, Brazil, and Chile." *United States Institute of Peace Report.* 10/96. *http://www.usip.org/pubs/peaceworks/pwks10.html.*

Huser, Herbert C. 1998. "Democratic Argentina's 'Global Reach': The Argentine Military in Peacekeeping Operations." *Naval War College Review.* 3. *http://www.nwc.navy.mil/press/Review/1998/summer/rtoc-su8.htm.*

McDermott, Jeremy. 2003. "Shaking up Argentina's Military." *Jane's Intelligence Review* 8:38–39.

Ministerio de Defensa. 1998. "Libro Blanco de la República Argentina." http://www.ser2000.org/protect/libro-argentina/defa-indice.htm.

Ministerio de Defensa. 2001. "Revisión de la Defensa 2001." http://www.pdgs.org.ar/featured/fea-revi-indice.htm.

OAS (Organization of American States). 2002. "Declaration of Santiago, Chile, November 18–22 2002." http://www.oas.org.

Perlo-Freeman, Sam. 2003. "Survey of Military Expenditure in South America: Background Paper for the SIPRI Yearbook 2003." http://projects.sipri.se/milex/mex_s_america_bg_03.pdf.

Peronius, Olof. 2004. "Mot alla odds." *Offside* 2:74–96.

Saavedra, Boris. 2003. "Confronting Terrorism in Latin America: Latin America and United States Policy Implications." *Security and Defense Studies Review* 2:192–220.

Solimano, Andrés. 2003. "Development Cycles, Political Regimes and International Migration: Argentina in the Twentieth Century." @Ref:Santiago: UN Economic Development Division.

Articles/Newspapers

González, Gustavo. "Special Report: Football Violence, but No Red Card." www.insidecostarica.com, June 16, 2003.

———. "Fan Violence Halts Argentine Season." Sports Network, September 10, 2003.

———. "Argentina Calls for Resumption of 'Sovereignty Talks.'" Mercopress, January 1, 2004. http://www.mercopress.com/Detalle.asp?NUM=3070. http://www.sportsnetwork.com.

Websites

Argentina Ministerio de Defensa: http://www.mindef.gov.ar/.

Armed Conflicts Event Data: http://www.onwar.com/aced/index.htm.

Central Intelligence Agency (CIA). *The World Factbook* (visited 2004-04-07): http://www.cia.gov.

CONADEP (Comisión Nacional Sobre la Desaparición de Persona: National Commission on the Disappearance of Persons): http://www.nuncamas.org/.

Constitución de la Nación Argentina (1994): http://www.georgetown.edu/pdba/Constitutions/Argentina/argen94.html.

Constitution of the Argentine Nation (1853): http://www.oefre.unibe.ch/law/icl/ar00000_.html.

Human Rights Watch: http://www.hrw.org.

Latin American Bureau: Argentina (visited 2004-04-07): http://www-lab.org.uk/?lid=83.

MERCOSUR: http://www.mercosur.org.uy/.

Organization of American States: http://www.oas.org/.

The Vanished Gallery: http://www.yendor.com/vanished/.

Australia

Alex Braithwaite

Geography and History

Covering a territory of some 2,966,200 square miles, Australia ranks as the sixth largest country in the world; yet, with a projected population of just 20.05 million, it has a population density of a mere 6.65 persons per square mile—as compared with 74 in the United States and 629 in the United Kingdom. Australia consists of a wide variety of landscapes, including deserts in its interior, hills and mountains, and tropical rain forests. Much of its land is almost uninhabited, with the bulk of the population concentrated along the eastern coast (including the cities of Brisbane and Sydney, the largest city, and Canberra, the capital), the southeastern coast (including Melbourne), and the southwestern coast (including Perth).

The ethnic makeup of this population is 95 percent Caucasian, 4 percent Asian, and 1 percent Aborigine. In respect to religion, 26.1 percent of Australia's population are Anglican, 26 percent Roman Catholic, 24.3 percent other Christian, 11 percent non-Christian, and the remaining 12.6 percent are of other religious affiliations (CIA 2005). These statistics are demonstrative of a nation founded upon large-scale migration from the United Kingdom, Western Europe, and North America that has experienced increasing incoming Asian populations since the establishment of communist regimes in China and elsewhere on the Asian continent.

Australia's history stretches back long before the arrival of settlers from Europe. It is believed that the first humans may have arrived before 40,000 B.C.E. Prior to the arrival of early European explorers in the fifteenth and sixteenth centuries, aboriginal Australians had developed significant trade and cultural links with various East Asian populations and had populated many regions within the Australian territory, bringing with them a variety of languages and traditions. Modern Australia gained independence on January 1, 1901, having been a member of the British Empire since the first British settlements were established in 1788 with the arrival of Captain Arthur Phillip and the "First Fleet"; their agenda was to establish a penal colony (Clarke 2002). The years under colonial rule can be crudely summarized as being defined by a struggle to establish a national identity (with the white Europeans—mainly the British—endeavoring to re-create European life at the expense of indigenous populations and in denial of the new regional setting); after 1850 it can be summarized by the rush for gold.

Since gaining independence, Australia has continued to recognize the British monarch as sovereign and has maintained an active role in the British Commonwealth. Following the Westminster

Table 1   Basic Statistics

Type of government	Federal parliamentary democracy recognizing the British monarch as sovereign
Population (millions)	20.05 (2004)
Religion	Anglican 26.1%, Roman Catholic 26%, other Christian 24.3%, non-Christian 11%, other 12.6% (2003)
Main industries	Mining, industrial and transportation equipment, food processing, chemicals, steel
Main security threat(s)	Regional instability from civil conflict in Philippines; water rights issues with East Timor; drug production in Tasmania; and involvement in war against terrorism via campaigns in Afghanistan and Iraq
Defense spending (% GDP)	2.9% (2002)
Size of military (thousands)	51 (2001)
Number of civil wars since 1945	0
Number of interstate wars since 1945	5

Sources

Australian Bureau of Statistics. 2005. http://www.abs.gov.au/ (accessed May 17, 2005).

Central Intelligence Agency Website. 2005. CIA *World Factbook*. http://www.cia.gov/cia/publications/factbook/ (accessed May 17, 2005).

Correlates of War Project. 2005. http://cow2.la.psu.edu/ (accessed May 17, 2005).

World Bank. 2005. http://www.worldbank.org/data/countrydata/aag/aus_aag.pdf (accessed May 17, 2005).

model, with minor modifications in the U.S. mold, Australia's political system has matured into a federal parliamentary democracy with universal and compulsory voting from the age of eighteen, often referred to as the "Washminster" hybrid (see Sidebar 1).

The present structure comprises three sections of government. The federal government—headed by the prime minister, presently John Howard, and governor-general, Michael Jefferey, and consisting of publicly elected upper (senate) and lower (government) chambers—has jurisdiction over national issues such as foreign affairs, immigration, defense, telecommunications, social security, and finance. The six state governments in turn determine policy in regard to schooling, policing, hospitals, and general community services. Finally, there are some 900 local government councils.

Throughout the twentieth century, Australia's democratically elected officials have deployed a variety of military and peacekeeping forces overseas to aid with ongoing and recently concluded conflicts—including World War I, World War II, Korea, and Vietnam. Since World War II, greater importance has been placed upon formal and informal ties with the United States and East Asia than with the former colonizer, Great Britain. In that time Australia prospered economically, and it has been able to maintain and step up its proactive role in global affairs—perhaps most notably via its assorted actions on behalf of the United Nations. More important, Australia has advanced domestically.

Since the conclusion of World War II, Australia has opened its doors more readily to immigration from non-European regions—especially Asia. Moreover, in

1967, fully sixty-six years after federation and independence, Aborigines gained the right to vote (ibid.). Thus while the contentious issues of immigration and race are by no means settled, they do now occupy a far more important (read democratic and visible) position in Australian politics.

In the post–Cold War era, Australia faces the proliferation of a variety of security threats that represent the manifestation of global issues at the regional level. There is additionally, however, an expectation that as they integrate more economically and politically with the nations of the East Asia–Pacific region, they will be able to shed some of the sense of vulnerability that has long dictated foreign policy-making in Australia.

Although distant from the West in terms of geography, Australia enjoys levels of development and prosperity much closer to those of the West than of the majority of its immediate regional neighbors. The life expectancy of 80.4 years, a gross national income (GNI) of U.S.$386.5 billion, and GNI per capita of U.S.$19,740 (World Bank 2003 est.) are comparable to those of much of Western Europe and North America. Underpinning this advanced level of development is an industrial base consisting of mining, the production of industrial and transportation equipment, food processing, textiles, chemicals, and iron and steel. Additionally, Australia maintains one of the more advanced agricultural production economies, thanks largely to its sheer size and low population density (CIA 2003). As was also true of military relations, Australia's heavy dependence upon Great Britain for overseas investment and trading relations during the first half of the twentieth century was replaced by a rapid diversification of relationships in the wake of World War II. By the first quarter of 2003, Australia had an increasing trade deficit of a little more than AUS$4 billion, which consisted of surpluses with Japan, the United Kingdom, South Korea, New Zealand, Taiwan, and Singapore (with Japan, New Zealand, and South Korea as the three biggest export markets) and deficits with China and the United States.

Australia's distance from the West also offers an interesting quandary in terms of foreign policy-making. The majority of nonaboriginal Australians have tended—since the times of the original British settlements in 1788—to view Australia as a distant extension of European affairs (Edwards 1997). Over the past half-century, however, the focus of Australian attention has often been reoriented toward parts of East Asia and the Pacific region—

such as during the Pacific phase of World War II, the Korean and Vietnamese campaigns, Malaysian and Indonesian efforts toward decolonization, and the more recent rumbling of domestic strife in East Timor.

Thus, to a large extent, Australia's foreign and security policies are increasingly characterized by an inherent contradiction. On the one hand, Australia has consistently maintained close ties with the United Kingdom and the United States, in order to guarantee security against the invasion of their seemingly isolated territory. On the other, the country has attempted to forge closer ties and greater influence within the affairs of a multitude of states within the Asia-Pacific region—from where (at least during the Cold War) the threat of communist invasion was the greatest.

Regional Geopolitics

The history of Australia's regional geopolitics is a story fraught with self-perceived vulnerability. In the latter half of the nineteenth century, Anglo-Saxon Australians feared the dilution of their cultural heritage at the hands of non-British immigration. During World War II the fear was that the rapidly approaching Japanese would invade—an outcome that was only narrowly avoided in 1942, when the Japanese bombed Australia but did not reach land.

It follows, therefore, that an important consideration when assessing the nature of Australia's present-day regional geopolitics is to address this issue of vulnerability—or at least the perception of vulnerability. Dalrymple (2003) concludes that while Australians appear to have a stronger self-image and are more confident that the twenty-first century offers an opportunity for a more independent approach to foreign policy-making, there remains a sense that Australia is vulnerable because of its isolation from those states with which it shares a common history and heritage.

Australia's present-day geopolitics is defined largely by the proliferation of "global" issues at the regional level (White 2003). As Australia continues to play a central role in global affairs, the regional security burden appears greater than ever. State failure, international terrorism, conflict over water rights, the proliferation of weapons of mass destruction (WMD), and the migration of displaced peoples are all prominent affairs throughout the international system that are particularly noteworthy within Australia's regional geopolitics.

In the years since the end of the Cold War, Australia has increasingly put regional matters ahead of those of a more global nature. This stems largely from recognition of the fact that their traditionally strong ties with the United States have been relaxed somewhat, replaced by a newfound ability to assimilate themselves more closely with regional powers such as China and Japan. Initially it appeared as though economic affairs would overtake the importance of military affairs (Mediansky 1997)—a dynamic that was of concern for those who recognized Australia's declining economic power through the 1980s. In the short time since the attacks upon New York, Washington, D.C., and Pennsylvania on September 11, 2001, however, it has become clear that military affairs have once again gained a position of priority in foreign affairs in Australia—and elsewhere around the globe.

In an age of unrelenting globalization a variety of states within Australia's regional neighborhood face the unenviable task of adapting (developing) or drowning (falling foul to a variety of crime-based alternatives to statehood). The viability of a number of neighbors—notably Papua New Guinea and the Pacific Islands (including the Solomon Islands)—is so questionable that Australia provided more than $1 billion in official development assistance in the 2003–2004 financial year. This aid program—concentrated to a large extent in Southeast Asia (Papua New Guinea is the largest single recipient) and the Pacific Islands—followed fast upon the heels of a regional mission to restore law and order in the Solomon Islands (State Department 2004).

The threat caused by international terrorism will be discussed in greater detail below. In a broad sense, however, it is possible to note that Australia has played and will continue to play an important role as an ally of the United States and its ongoing "War on Terrorism." At the same time, however, Australia has a more specific terrorist threat at the regional level. White (2003) argues that the threat against Australian citizens and property at home and abroad is now greater than ever before, due, in no small part, to the presence of a number of extremist Islamic terrorist organizations in nearby Indonesia. White additionally notes that Australia's action in attempting to nurture some form of participatory democracy in Jakarta will be key to its ability to counter that threat.

In September 1999, acting under a UN Security Council mandate, Australia led an international coalition to restore order in East Timor following Indonesia's withdrawal. The threat of instability caused by the vacuous remnants of state structure in East Timor certainly acted to motivate Australian intervention. Addition-

ally important, however, were concerns regarding the distribution of rights to the oil and gas resources of the Timor Sea—as dictated by the Timor Gap Treaty (Dalrymple 2003). This case is important not only in terms of the distribution of tangible goods (oil, gas, and water) but also in terms of the perceived morality of Australian foreign policy. For many years, opponents (mainly domestically) have been critical of the tendency for governments to ignore the poor record of human rights in Indonesia in return for stability in the relationship that safeguards the above-mentioned water rights. Dalrymple (ibid.) notes that a reversal of that ignorance may improve domestic sentiment but could come at the cost of reaffirming some key differences between Australian and East Asian foreign policy goals and management techniques.

A little further afield, yet nonetheless key to regional geopolitics is the issue of the vertical proliferation of WMD in North Korea (especially in terms of nuclear capabilities) and the threat of their horizontal proliferation into the hands of terrorists in the broader region (White 2003). Although it is the case that Australia may not be individually targeted and threatened by the vertical proliferation of nuclear weapons within North Korea, that does threaten to upset the regional balance of power. Already it appears as though Chinese activism on this issue is more considerable than the Japanese response—which has necessarily been masked by their consideration of U.S. preferences. Thus it appears that if they are successful in mitigating North Korean aggression, China may be successful in placing itself atop both economic and diplomatic regional hierarchies (ibid.). In respect to horizontal proliferation of WMD, no specific threats exist. Yet it is clear that given Australia's primary terrorist concerns—as participant in the ongoing war on terrorism and as neighbor to Indonesia—such proliferation could be of no discernible benefit.

A final emerging concern that is shaping Australia's regional geopolitics addresses the migration of displaced peoples. Recent government efforts—particularly under Prime Minister Keating—have begun to establish legislation, akin to that in the United States, to protect Australia's borders. This legislation is directed specifically toward peoples of Iran, Iraq, Afghanistan, and East Timor, smuggled across the seas from neighboring Indonesia (Dalrymple 2003).

On a less threatening note, the global trend toward integration is also matched regionally for Australia. A priority for all recent governments in Canberra has been achieving a balance between traditional ties to the United Kingdom and United States and those emerging within the East Asia–Pacific region. Australia's fifteen-year membership in APEC lies at the heart of this new integration movement and is considered, by many, to represent the lifeblood for the future Australian economy; already, New Zealand, Japan, and South Korea are the three largest markets for Australian exports (Australian Bureau of Statistics 2005).

Conflict Past and Present
Conflict History
Prior to Australian independence in 1901, Australian troops—under British command—were deployed to aid imperial campaigns in the Sudan, the Boer War, and against the Boxers. After gaining independence, Australia maintained close ties with the British armed forces and had its troops, in the hundreds of thousands, deployed to fight in both the World Wars at the behest of the Commonwealth. These troops were fundamental to Allied campaigns at Gallipoli during World War I and at Timor and Crete during World War II.

The year 1942 represents the only time that Australian home soil has been threatened by invasion: Japanese bombing missions led to the deaths of a few hundred Australians and fell just narrowly short of opening the door to the insertion of troops (Dalrymple 2003). In the wake of the achievement of peace in the Pacific, Australia additionally contributed up to 45,000 troops toward the British Commonwealth Occupation Force (BCOF); they were stationed in defeated Japan from 1946 to 1951.

Australia was then second, after the United States, to proffer troops toward the UN-led actions on the Korean Peninsula between 1950 and 1953. These troops were taken from those previously stationed in Japan as part of the BCOF. In a subsequent assignment, Australian forces contributed toward the British effort at putting down the attempted communist revolt in Malaya from 1948 to 1960—deploying troops toward cargo runs, leaflet drops, and mopping-up duties from 1950 to 1960 (Dennis and Grey 1996). Moreover, having earlier supported the revolt that led to Indonesian independence from the Dutch in 1949, Australia, under Commonwealth command, combated the Indonesian-supported invasions of Sarawak and Borneo between 1963 and 1965 (ibid.). They later sent troops to assist South Vietnamese and U.S. forces in Vietnam. In the years since the end of the Cold War, Australia has contributed most notably toward coalition forces in the Persian Gulf conflict of 1991, in Yugoslavia in the mid-1990s, in Afghanistan in 2001, and in Iraq in 2003.

At a lower level, Australia has been party to a half-dozen militarized interstate disputes (MID) involving a variety of force levels. They used force unilaterally against Portugal briefly in 1941 and multilaterally alongside the United Kingdom against Thailand between 1942 and 1945. In the post–Cold War years, Australia joined a coalition of states showing military force in order to persuade North Korea to back away from its ambitious nuclear program between 1993 and 1995, showed force to deter the ousted Indonesian government from using its military in East Timor in 1999, and used force in a brief dispute with Norway in 2001—in what was most likely a dispute over fishing rights (Ghosn and Palmer 2003).

Although Australia has a long history of involvement and participation in international conflicts, the country has not suffered domestic violence that would register on most social science data-collection radars. That is not to say, however, that Australia has seen no civil strife. Indeed, ever since the first European settlements there has been civil strife between white settlers and aboriginal populations. That strife, in fact, is central to Australia's modern history and has, at its most serious, resulted in near-genocidal campaigns that at one time saw the aboriginal population fall from the 1788 figure of a few hundred thousand to a nadir of only 60,000 at the middle of the last century. Even though the aboriginal response has never been sufficiently strong to threaten the Canberra government, various guerrilla efforts prior to independence kept the six colonial settlements on their toes.

Current and Potential Military Confrontation

As has been stated, Australia's geographical isolation minimizes the number of threats directed against its immediate security. At the same time, however, a range of overseas military and peacekeeping deployments mean that Australia is participating in ongoing conflicts and will possibly become embroiled in future engagements. For example, Australian forces are currently involved in U.S.-led coalition forces in Afghanistan (since 2001) and Iraq (since 2003). They are also participating in a broad range of UN missions in, among other places, the Middle East, Kashmir, the former Yugoslavia, East Timor, and the Solomon Islands. Of those, the greatest threat to Australian national security is posed by the potential for Indonesian aggression toward East Timor.

Alliance Structure

Across security, economic, and diplomatic realms, Australia is currently party to a great number and wide variety of international agreements and obligations. Smith (1997) has put the number at 920 treaties, 400 of which were multilateral; more than 300, mainly bilateral, were signed between 1985 and the end of the century alone. It is possible, nonetheless, to boil this list down to a handful of economic, military, and diplomatic ties that have been, in the years since Australia gained its independence, most influential in the determination of Australia's foreign and security policies.

For at least four decades after independence, many elements of Australian political society—especially within conservative ranks—favored a union with the

United Kingdom for the sake of foreign policy matters. Indeed, it would appear as though Prime Minister Menzies (1939–1941 and 1949–1966) favored such a relationship as late as 1950 (Edwards 1997). Clearly, the security that Australians felt they gained from this relationship was sufficiently significant as to pave the way for Australia's entry into a variety of military campaigns under British command far from their own soil in the name of defending their own interests.

Australia has long held a number of long-standing arrangements with the United Kingdom and neighboring New Zealand—both within and outside of the Commonwealth of Nations. For example, 1944 saw Australia conclude an agreement with New Zealand dealing with the security, welfare, and advancement of the independent territories of the Pacific (the ANZAC pact). They have also held a variety of agreements with the United Kingdom and New Zealand to ensure the security of former British dependencies in Singapore and Malaysia.

Since the decline of British influence, Australia also has had a variety of arrangements within the broad spectrum of military/security alliances with the current hegemon, the United States. The Australia, New Zealand, United States (ANZUS) security treaty, for example, was formed initially as a defense pact with New Zealand between 1944 and 1951 that was joined by the United States after 1951. According to the treaty, each party agreed to defend against armed attack in the Pacific area against any of them. The three nations also pledged to maintain and develop individual and collective capabilities to resist attack. When, in 1985, New Zealand refused rights to the United States to port nuclear-capable vessels, the three-way

ANZUS meetings were replaced by bilateral meetings between the United States and Australia; those have continued, to this day, maintaining the agreements of the ANZUS alliance.

Although Australia and New Zealand continue to maintain significant bilateral ties in respect to the security provisions of the ANZUS treaty, New Zealand's defiance in the face of U.S. demands has been met by considerable criticism from the Australian government. Australia's official line continues to prioritize the relationship with the United States, while New Zealand has maintained a staunchly critical stance, opposed to many U.S. actions. This divergence between Australian and New Zealand policy was first witnessed by their differing responses to requests to port U.S. naval vessels; it has more recently become apparent in regard to the provision of forces toward the ongoing campaigns in Afghanistan and Iraq by the United States.

The period since the outset of World War II has witnessed Australian involvement in ententes with the United States, the United Kingdom, New Zealand, France, Pakistan, Thailand, and the Philippines between 1954 and 1977 (Pakistan exited in 1973), and with Indonesia since 1995 (Gibler and Sarkees 2004). It also appears that they earlier had formalized defensive and offensive treaty obligations during the final three years of World War II (1942–1945) with the United States, the United Kingdom, Canada, Cuba, Haiti, the Dominican Republic, Honduras, El Salvador, Nicaragua, Panama, Guatemala, the Soviet Union, South Africa, Iran, China, and New Zealand (Leeds et al. 2002).

In regard to international economics, Australia has been party to APEC since 1989. APEC promotes trade and investment liberalization, business facilitation, and economic and technological cooperation among its twenty-one members, and it is Australia's foremost regional economic alliance structure. Although Prime Ministers Hawke, Keating, and Howard have shared that opinion, there has been a general reluctance among the wider population to pursue closer regional ties (Mediansky 1997). Representatives are also frequent participants in meetings of the Commonwealth Regional Heads of Government and the Pacific Islands Forum, and have led the way in promoting the interests of the Cairns Group, consisting of a number of countries pressing for agricultural trade reform in World Trade Organization (WTO) negotiations (State Department 2003).

Australia is also an active participant in the Association of South East Asian Nations (ASEAN) and its Regional Forum (ARF), alongside Malaysia, Indonesia, the Philippines, Singapore, and Thailand. Under the auspices of that organization, each of these nations commits to promoting regional cooperation on security issues. ASEAN has played a significant part in the task of nation-building in the region and was central in reacting to recent concerns in Papua New Guinea and East Timor. Australian forces have participated in a variety of UN operations, including peacekeeping, disarmament negotiations, and narcotics control.

Size and Structure of the Military
Size and Structure
Australia has rarely faced a direct threat to its national security. It has long been, however, concerned about that potential. Moreover, Australia has frequently contributed troops to Allied- and UN-led combat and peacekeeping operations, and it has, accordingly, maintained a significant force level in order to do so. The Correlates of War (COW) project lists Australia's total military armed forces at a consistent level of 6,000 to 8,000 during the interwar period, reaching a peak in World War II of some 680,000 and then declining in the postwar period to the 1950 level of 38,000. Accommodating a number of overseas deployments, their Cold War force increased by 1953 to 57,000, and by 1970 to 86,000. Following the Vietnam War, numbers again fell. Between 1973 and 1998, the figure remained fairly consistently between 65,000 and 73,000. Since the turn of the century it appears that the figure has continued to drop; in 2001 it was down to 51,000 (COW 2005), and in 2003 it was estimated at 53,650 (IISS 2003).

The figures detailed above encompass the three main branches of the Australian Armed Forces: (1) The Royal Australian Navy (RAN) and Women's Royal Australian Naval Service (WRANS) consist of a fleet comprising squadrons, flotillas, and task forces that collectively total 12,850 personnel; (2) The Australian Army and Australian Women's Army Service (AWAS) consist of subunits (battalions, companies, platoons, and sections) that collectively make up formations (army, corps, divisions, and brigades) that number 26,600 troops; and (3) The Royal Australian Air Force (RAAF) and Women's Royal Australian Air Force (WRAAF) consist of a number of sections that combine to form flights, squadrons, wings, and groups. The air force consists of some 14,200 personnel, according to recent records (ibid.).

The navy is composed of Maritime and Naval Systems commands and is headquartered out of Sydney, with additional bases in Darwin, Cairns, Stirling, Flinders, Jervis Bay, and Noura. In addition to a variety of patrol and counter-forces, Australia currently possesses six tactical Collins submarines and eleven frigates. Australia's Land, Special Operations, and Training commands of the army are equipped with 71 Leopard 1A3 battle tanks, 255 ASLAV-25 light armored vehicles, and 364 M-113 armored personnel carriers. The air force consists of main Air and Training commands that lead a force including 53 F-111 strike and reconnaissance wings, 71 F/ A-18 tactical/fighter wings, and 33 Hawk 127 training wings (ibid.).

Despite its distance from many war zones, Australia has a rich history of contributing armed forces to UK-, U.S.-, and UN-led campaigns across all regions of the world. Combat deployments and casualties incurred during those deployments are summarized in Table 2.

Prior to independence, Australia's citizenry contributed troops for British campaigns in the Sudan (770 troops), the Boer War (16,463), and the Boxer Rebellion (560). Since gaining independence, Aus-tralia has deployed hundreds of thousands of troops to serve overseas in World War I (331,781), World War II (575,799), the Korean War (17,164), the Malayan Emergency (7,000), the Indonesian Confrontation (3,500), and the Vietnam War (50,001) (Australian War Memorial 200).

As of 2000, Australia had also led the way in contributing troops to UN-led peacekeeping and observation forces (see Sidebar 2) in Indonesia (1947–1951), Korea (1948–1956), Israel and neighboring territories (since 1948), Kashmir (since 1949), Congo (1960–1964), Irian (1962–1963), Yemen (1963–1964), Cyprus (since 1964), the Sinai Peninsula (since 1973), Syria (since 1974), Lebanon (since 1978), Zimbabwe (1979–1980), the Persian Gulf (1988–1999), Namibia (1989–1990), Cambodia (1989–1993), Western Sahara (since 1991), Somalia (1992–1995), the former Yugoslavia (1992–1995; since 1997), Mozambique (1992–1995), Rwanda (1993–1996), Bougainville (1994; 1997–1999), Haiti (1994–1995), Guatemala (1997), East Timor (since 1999), and the Solomon Islands (2000) (Department of Veteran's Affairs 2005).

Table 2   Australia: Key Overseas Combat Deployments and Casualties

Years	Conflict	No. Troops	Battle-Deaths
1896–1898	British Campaigns in the Sudan	770	9
1899–1902	Boer War	16,463	606
1900	Boxer Rebellion	560	6
1914–1919	World War I	331,781	61,720
1939–1945	World War II	575,799	39,366
1950–1953	Korean War	17,164	339
1951–1960	Malayan Emergency	7,000	36
1963–1966	Indonesian Confrontation	3,500	15
1964–1973	Vietnam War	50,001	520

Sources
Australian War Memorial. 2005. http://www.awm.gov.au/atwar/statistics.
Dennis, P., J. Grey, E. Morris, R. Prior, and J. Connor, eds. 1995. *The Oxford Companion to Australian Military History*. Melbourne: Oxford University Press.

By 2003, Australia's overseas deployments were the most wide ranging since the end of the Vietnam War. Under Operation Falconer, Australia has contributed some 2,000 personnel, 14 F/A-18 combat aircraft, 1 C-130 transporter P-3 patrol aircraft, 2 frigates, and a 500-man Special Forces task group. In the summer of 2003, Australia additionally committed more than 2,000 military and police personnel to the regional operation to bring stability to the Solomon Islands.

The value of each of these overseas deployments is most clearly demonstrated when one examines the costs that have been incurred as a result. Australia suffered battle deaths in all of the major conflict campaigns to which the country deployed troops: 9 in the Sudan, 606 in the Boer War, 6 during the Boxer Rebellion, 61,720 in World War I, 39,366 in World War II, 339 in Korea, 36 in Malaya, 15 in Indonesia, and 520 in Vietnam. In more than fifty years of peacekeeping missions, they have additionally lost 7 deployed troops.

Budget

Recent assessments list Australia's military budget (across the three component parts: the Australian Army, the Royal Australian Navy, and the Royal Australian Air Force) at U.S.$9.9 billion (IISS 2003)—the twelfth largest globally (CIA 2003). The 2003 budget, buoyed by general economic growth, included provisions for increases in defense and national security spending. Recent growth in the military budget is part of a broader package of provisions set to see growth at 3 percent per annum over the next five years (IISS 2003).

The COW project additionally offers a longer range assessment of the evolution of Australia's military budget. The data demonstrates that the budget increased at a fairly constant rate after settling by 1950 at $250 million, increased up to and during the Vietnam War, and then accelerated from $1 billion (1967) to a little over $9 billion at the turn of the century. After a review in 2000 of Australia's future defense needs, the government made a commitment to increase defense spending by 3 percent a year for the next ten years—largely in reaction to the recent evolution of policy regarding international terrorism (State Department 2003). The government's white paper detailed specifically that the budget would receive an increase of AUS$500 million in 2002 and 2003, keeping it in line with a 1.9 percent proportion of Australia's total government budget (Reith 2001).

The growth of the military budget—placing Australia's defense budget at 2 percent of its GDP—made possible the development of plans to procure wide-bodied air tankers, upgraded defenses for Chinook and Black Hawk helicopters, and Wedgetail early warning and control aircraft (IISS 2003). Overall, Australia is a net importer of military technology; there have been, however, a number of key domestic procurements: four of the navy's front-line frigates are of the new Australian-built ANZAC class, with four more under construction. Moreover, each of their six submarines is of the new, indigenous Collins class. The Royal Australian Air Force's F/A-18 fighter—built in Australia under license from the U.S. manufacturer—is their principal combat aircraft. In June 2002, Australia additionally announced that it intended to become a research and development (R&D) partner in the U.S.-led Joint Strike Fighter Program (State Department 2003). The bulk of Australia's remaining military hardware is supplied through contracts in the United States, the United Kingdom, and Canada (IISS 2003).

Civil-Military Relations/The Role of the Military in Domestic Politics

Australia has enjoyed a great deal of domestic stability since gaining independence at the beginning of the twentieth century. Consequently, the threat of military coup has never emerged. That is in large part the result of the fact that governance of the military falls into the hands of the public via the democratic election of representatives.

Although there are no direct threats to domestic stability, there remains a significant history of public disapproval toward decisions to deploy military force overseas. World War I conscription, for example, was met by two bitter referendums that highlighted great internal division within Australian society (Smith 1997; Robson 1969). Moreover, the loss of 2,800 personnel in Vietnam is commonly viewed as having provoked widespread public disapproval (Mackie 1976; Millar 1991). Indeed, public disapproval grew to the point where in 1969 a majority were against continued participation. In both instances, however, as well as during the current campaigns in Afghanistan and Iraq, public support for the troops themselves has remained very high.

Terrorism

The impact of terrorism upon Australian national security is a rather ambiguous affair. As with other forms of conflict, there has been no substantial history of terrorist campaigns on the territory of Australia, nor is there an immediate danger that it will occur. At the regional level, however, Australian concerns were heightened by the November 2002 bombings on Bali that cost the lives of 202 people, a number of whom were Australians. There is, additionally, a slim chance that the continued failure of state structures in Timor, Bougainville, and the Solomon Islands might aid the maturation of extremist terrorist organizations, and that Australia may be targeted by such groups.

Additionally, there remains the potential for danger by association. Australia's continued support of the war on terrorism—in the time since the Bali bombings—poses the possibility for reactive attacks against Australian troops stationed across the globe. Specifically, given the apparent increase in al-Qaeda attacks against Western military and diplomatic deployments across the Middle East, there is some level of expectation that Australian forces serving in Afghanistan and Iraq, as well as peacekeeping troops in various parts of the region, might be subject to terrorist attack.

Beyond these rather ambiguous threats to Australian national security, the issue of terrorism, at home and abroad, will remain as a central component of any future foreign or security policy. The Australian government will continue to draw links between terrorist threats and the regional proliferation of WMDs—as Defense Minister Reith did in March 2001 while visiting China (Reith 2001). Moreover, the global threat of terrorism will be cited as motivation and justification for the continued escalation of Australia's military budget (ibid.).

Relationship with the United States

Australia, to a greater extent than any of the other former British colonies, maintained close ties with the United Kingdom after independence, largely to the detriment of their relations with other nations—especially those in their own region. Indeed, it wasn't until 1940 that diplomatic missions were set up in Washington, D.C., Tokyo, and Ottawa; they had been established thirty years earlier in London (Edwards 1997). It was shortly afterward—not coincidentally at a time when many would claim that Britain's influence in global affairs was beginning to dwindle—that the orientation of Australian foreign policy swung toward that of the United States (Bell 1988).

For quite some time it appeared that the conservative political machine in

Australia—especially under Prime Minister Menzies in the 1940s and 1950s—was able to convince the country at large of the need for Australia to participate wholeheartedly in campaigns alongside the United Kingdom and the United States. Indeed, Australia's current participation in Afghanistan and Iraq might suggest that this willingness persists.

The sentiment has not gone unchallenged, however. Over the past century or so since independence, a variety of movements among liberals, nationalists, socialists, and religious radicals have been critical of the tendency for the government to place Australian troops in the line of fire in what they describe as "other people's wars." Resistance to such actions was first noteworthy when ANZAC troops were deployed to the Mediterranean during World War I and was perhaps at its greatest during the Vietnam campaign (Edwards 1997). This resistance has resulted in an increasing tendency for governments to show a tougher stance against what could be claimed to be "bullying" by the United Kingdom and the United States. Accordingly, there has been a move toward developing regional ties in the place of maintaining dependence upon the West—although Dalrymple (2003) places a question mark next to the effectiveness and popularity of that endeavor.

The ANZUS arrangement, to which both Australia and the United States prescribe, has no integrated defense structure or dedicated forces. However, in fulfillment of ANZUS obligations, Australia and the United States conduct a variety of joint activities. These include military exercises ranging from naval and landing exercises at the task-group level to battalion-level special forces training, the assignment of officers to each other's armed services, and standardizing, where possible, equipment and operational doctrine. The two countries also operate several joint defense facilities in Australia (Albinski 1997).

Following the terrorist attacks on the United States on September 11, 2001, Australian prime minister Howard invoked the ANZUS Treaty for the first time on September 14, 2001. Subsequently, Australian defense forces were among the earliest participants in Operation Enduring Freedom in Afghanistan, and they later contributed toward coalition military action against Iraq in Operation Iraqi Freedom. Moreover, Australian military and civilian specialists are actively participating in the reconstruction of Iraq. New Zealand's continued refusal to act in a similar fashion in behalf of the U.S. "War on Terrorism" again demonstrates the overtly bilateral nature of the modern iteration of the ANZUS treaty.

Relations between the two states are multifaceted. From a financial point of view, the value of bilateral trade between the two states reached $20 billion in 2002. Given the size of this relationship, it is unsurprising that the two sides occasionally endure friction. For example, the United States has communicated concerns about Australian quarantine barriers to imports of cooked chicken, fresh salmon, and some fruits, about changes in Australian law governing intellectual property protection, and about Australian government procurement practices (State Department 2003). Both countries continue, however, to share a commitment to liberalizing global trade and have, accordingly, worked together very closely in the World Trade Organization (WTO) and the Asia-Pacific Economic Cooperation (APEC) forum.

Diplomatically, recent presidential visits to Australia (in 1991 and 1996) and Australian prime ministerial visits to the United States (in 1995, 1997, 1999, 2001, 2002, and 2003) have underscored the strength and closeness of the alliance. This was additionally confirmed in 2001, when the two parties concluded negotiations over, and signed, a new tax treaty and a bilateral social security agreement.

The Future

From an immediate national security perspective, many of the factors that define Australia's current geopolitics require ongoing consideration and management. Unresolved disputes from the fallout of East Timor, for example, will remain upon Australia's policymaking plate. The division of rights over the Timor Sea and the sharing of its oil and gas resources with Indonesia will require particularly close attention, as will the government's general stance on the management of relations with Indonesia (Dalrymple 2003). Additionally, despite strict controls over areas within Tasmania known to be home to the production of a variety of banned opiate products, it is likely that Tasmania will remain one of the world's major suppliers of such products; thus Australia will increasingly be subject to expectations from the United States to heighten its war on the international drug trade.

From a more general point of view, Edwards (1997) predicts a future in which growing confidence sees Australia increasingly acting independently of the United Kingdom and the United States in respect to foreign policy. In the economic sphere this will likely emerge in the form of a renewed attempt to become more tightly integrated within the APEC environment. In respect to military and security obligations, this pursuit of self-reliance (a popularly supported sentiment) will likely be faced with recognition of the need for preservation of traditional alliance relationships (Dalrymple 2003). Thus it is likely to be key that the government is quickly and persuasively able to demonstrate the inherent value of Australia's regional partnerships.

In the years ahead, it will also become increasingly important for all states to recognize that a variety of "new issues" (including environmental degradation, health epidemics, and refugee migration) require actual rather than just hypothetical action. Moreover, these actions require a global perspective rather than simply a local one—as would appear to determine Australia's pursuit of natural resources in the East Timor Sea and enhanced legislation to secure the country's borders against illegal immigration. Fundamental to the achievement of these global collective goals—and perhaps Australia's most valuable role in forthcoming relations—may be their ability to forge an improvement in relations between China and the West. In an address to the National Defense University of China in Beijing in March 2001, Australian minister of defense Alan Reith, MP, alluded to that fact:

Australia places a high priority on our relationship with China—as the country with the fastest growing influence on the region. . . . [We] recognize that we have some different perceptions—for example on the role of the United States in the region—but we also have common interests in a stable and cooperative international environment. (Reith 2001, 5)

References, Recommended Readings, and Websites

Books
Albinski, H. S. 1970. *Politics and Foreign Policy in Australia: The Impact of Vietnam and Conscription.* Durham, NC: Duke University Press.
———. 1997. "Australia and the United States." In *Australian Foreign Policy: Into the New Millennium,* F. A. Mediansky, ed. South Melbourne: Macmillan Education Australia, pp. 183–196.
Beaumont, J., C. Waters, D. Lowe, with G. Woodward. 2003. *Ministers, Mandarins, and Diplomats: Australian Foreign Policy Making, 1941–1969.* Melbourne: Melbourne University Press.
Bell, C. 1980. *Agenda for the Eighties: Contexts of Australian Choices in Foreign and Defense Policy.* Canberra: Australian National University Press.
———. 1988. *Dependent Ally: A Study in Australian Foreign Policy.* Melbourne: Oxford University Press.
Bridge, C., ed. 1991. *Munich to Vietnam: Australia's Relations with Britain and the United States since the 1930s.* Melbourne: Melbourne University Press.
Camilleri, J. A. 1976. *An Introduction to Australian Foreign Policy.* 3d ed. Milton, Queensland: Jacaranda.
Chalk, P. 2001. *Australian Foreign and Defense Policy in the Wake of the 1999/2000 East Timor Intervention.* Santa Monica, CA: Rand.
Chiddick, J. P. 1977. *Australia and the World: A Political Handbook.* South Melbourne: Macmillan.
Clarke, F. G. 2002. *The History of Australia.* Westport, CT: Greenwood.
Coonan, H. 2001. "The Role of Upper Houses: Is Washminster Washed Up?" In *Beyond the Republic: Meeting the Global Challenges to Constitutionalism,* C. Sampford and T. Round, eds. Sydney: Federation Press.
Cotton, J., and J. Ravenhill. 2001. *The National Interest in a Global Era: Australia in World Affairs 1996–2000.* Oxford: Oxford University Press.

Dalrymple, R. 2003. *Continental Drift: Australia's Search for a Regional Identity.* Aldershot, England: Ashgate.

Dennis, P., and J. Grey. 1996. *Emergency and Confrontation: Australian Military Operations in Malaya and Borneo 1950–1966.* Sydney: Allen and Unwin.

Dennis, P., J. Grey, E. Morris, R. Prior, and J. Connor, eds. 1995. *The Oxford Companion to Australian Military History.* Melbourne: Oxford University Press.

Edwards, P. G. 1992. *Crises and Commitments: The Politics and Diplomacy of Australia's Involvement in South East Asian Conflicts, 1948–1965.* North Sydney: Allen and Unwin.

———. 1997. "History and Foreign Policy." In *Australian Foreign Policy: Into the New Millennium,* F. A. Mediansky, ed. South Melbourne: Macmillan Education Australia, pp. 3–12.

Evans, G. J. 1992. *Australia's Foreign Relations in the World of the 1990s.* Carlton, Victoria: Melbourne University Press.

Grant, D., and G. Seal. 1994. *Australia in the World: Perceptions and Possibilities.* Perth: Black Swan.

Grey, J. 1990. *A Military History of Australia.* Cambridge: Cambridge University Press.

International Institute for Strategic Studies (IISS). 2003. *The Military Balance: 2003–2004.* Oxford: Oxford University Press.

Mackie, J. A. C. 1976. *Australia in the New World Order: Foreign Policy in the 1970s.* Melbourne: Nelson, in association with the Australian Institute of International Affairs.

McKernan, M., and M. Browne, eds. 1988. *Australia: Two Centuries of War and Peace.* Sydney: Allen and Unwin.

Mediansky, F. A. 1992. *Australia in a Changing World: New Foreign Policy Directions.* Botany, Australia: Maxwell Macmillan Publishing Australia.

———, ed. 1997. *Australian Foreign Policy: Into the New Millennium.* South Melbourne: Macmillan Education Australia.

Millar, T. B. 1991. *Australia in Peace and War: External Relations since 1788.* 2d ed. Botany, Australia: Australian National University Press.

Pettit, D., and A. Hall. 1978. *Selected Readings in Australian Foreign Policy.* Malvern, Victoria: Sorrett.

Robson, L. L. 1969. *Australia and the Great War, 1914–1918.* Melbourne: Macmillan.

Rumley, D. 1999. *The Geopolitics of Australia's Regional Relations.* Boston: Kluwer Academic Publishers.

Smith, G., D. Cox, and S. Burchill. 1996. *Australia in the World: An Introduction to Australian Foreign Policy.* New York: Oxford University Press.

Smith, H. 1997. "Politics of Foreign Policy." In *Australian Foreign Policy: Into the New Millennium,* F. A. Mediansky, ed. South Melbourne: Macmillan Education Australia, pp. 13–32.

Articles

Gibler, Douglas M., and Meredith Sarkees. 2004. "Measuring Alliances: The Correlates of War Formal Interstate Alliance Data Set, 1816–2000." *Journal of Peace Research* 41:211–222.

Leeds, B. A., J. M. Ritter, S. McLaughlin, and A. G. Long. 2002. "Alliance Treaty Obligations and Provisions, 1815–1944." *International Interactions* 28:237–260.

White, H. 2003. *Beyond the War on Terror: Australian Defence Policy in an Age of Uncertainty.* Unpublished Manuscript: Australian Strategic Policy Institute.

Websites

Australian Bureau of Statistics (ABS): http://www.abs.gov.au/.

Australian Department of Foreign Affairs and Trade: http://www.dfat.gov.au/.

Australian Foreign Ministry: http://www.foreignminister.gov.au/.

The Australian War Memorial: http://www.awm.gov.au/atwar/statistics.

Bristow, D. 2001. "Australia's Defence Renewal": http://www.global-defence.com/2001/RSpart1.html.

The British Broadcasting Corporation: http://news.bbc.co.uk/1/hi/world/asia-pacific/country_profiles/1250188.stm.

Central Intelligence Agency (CIA), *World Factbook:* http://www.cia.gov/cia/publications/factbook/geos/as.html.

The Correlates of War Project: http://cow2.la.psu.edu/.

The Department of Veteran's Affairs (DVA): http://www.dva.gov.au/commem/commac/studies/anzacsk/res1.htm.

Economist, The: http://www.economist.com/countries/Australia/.

Ghosn, Faten, and Glenn Palmer. 2003. "Codebook for the Militarized Interstate Dispute Data, Version 3.0." Online: http://cow2.la.psu.edu.

Reith, P. 2001. *Australian Defence Policy: Address to the National Defence University, China.* Beijing, March 1. Downloaded from: http://www.minister.defence.gov.au/ReithSpeechtpl.cfm?CurrentId=546.

The State Department: http://www.state.gov/g/drl/rls/shrd/2004/43109.htm.

The Worldbank: http://www.worldbank.org/data/countrydata/aag/aus_aag.pdf.

Austria

Franz Kernic

Geography and History

Austria is situated in the heart of Europe. For centuries it has held an important strategic position at the crossroads of Central Europe, with many easily traversable Alpine passes and valleys, among them the Danube River. Important transportation and traffic lines from Eastern Europe to southern Germany and Western Europe crisscross the country.

Austria is a fairly small country. Its territory encompasses 83,858 square kilometers (32,368 square miles), approximately one-eighth the size of Texas. The country is located north of Italy and Slovenia and south of Germany, the Czech Republic, and Slovakia. Austria also has common borders with Hungary in the east and with Liechtenstein and Switzerland in the west. As much as two-thirds of its terrain is made up of mountains (Alps), with the Grossglockner its highest point (3,798 meters). Along the eastern and northern margins, it is mostly flat or gently sloping. Of the total area, 20 percent consists of arable land, 29 percent pasture, 44 percent forest, and 7 percent is barren. Most of Austria's population is concentrated in the eastern lowlands and in or around its capital, Vienna. Natural resources are iron ore, oil, timber, magnesite ($MgCO_3$), lead, coal, lignite, copper, and hydropower.

Austria is a German-speaking country (about 98 percent), with most people of German origin and a few of smaller ethnic groups, particularly Croatians, Slovenes, Hungarians, Czechs, Slovaks, and Roma. Because of the multinational and multi-ethnic character of the Austro-Hungarian Empire and the role played by migration in Central Europe, both past and present, the roots of most Austrians living in the eastern part are in fact multinational and multicultural. Once at the center of power in Europe, Austria was reduced to a small, independent state and republic after the defeat of the large Austro-Hungarian Empire in World War I.

In other words, Austria in its modern form was created as the German-speaking rump of the empire after all the other nationalities established their own countries in 1918. Today Austria has a federal form of government. It is divided into nine provinces or federal states (*Bundesländer*). Austria is governed under the revised 1929 constitution (original constitution of 1920). It has a mixed presidential-parliamentary form of government. Austrian politics since World War II has been dominated by two major parties, a left-of-center Socialist Party (SPÖ) and a right-of-center People's Party (ÖVP), as well as three smaller parties: a Communist Party, the Freedom Party (FPÖ), which in the year 2000 joined a coalition with the People's Party, and the Greens. Since the year 2000, the People's

Party and the FPÖ have been ruling the country.

Austria is a prosperous country. It joined the European Union in 1995 and the Euro monetary system in 1999. The country, with its well-developed free-market economy, enjoys a high standard of living. It is one of the most tourist-dependent countries in Europe. Economically it is closely tied to the other EU member states, especially to Germany. In terms of GDP per capita, Austria is one of the richest countries, not only of the European Union but also in the world. The GDP real growth rate is approximately 1.1 percent (2002 est.) and the GDP per capita (purchasing power parity) approximately U.S.$27,900 (2002 est.). The GDP composition by sector reads as follows: agriculture, 2 percent; industry, 33 percent; and services, 65 percent (2002 est.) (CIA *World Factbook* 2003).

Recently Austria has been facing an economic slowdown caused by a general regression of the economy in the Western world and increased competition from other EU countries, as well as Central and Eastern European states. In the last year the Austrian government has undertaken a number of privatization efforts and has been working hard on a budget consolidation program in order to meet the Maastricht criteria of the EU monetary union, as well as to bring down its total public sector deficit.

The country's unemployment rate has been relatively stable during recent years. In comparison with other EU member states, Austria has recorded a remarkably low unemployment rate. Undoubtedly tourism plays a major role in its economy. Austria's main export partners are EU countries: Germany, with approximately 36 percent, Italy, France, Hungary, and Switzerland, and the United States.

Regional Geopolitics

Both World War I and II dramatically changed the political landscape of Europe and reshaped regional geopolitics in Central Europe as well. The Republic of Austria was proclaimed shortly after the end of World War I. The state itself was in

Table 1   Key Statistics

Type of government	Federal republic
Population (millions)	8.1 (2003)
Religions	Catholics (78%), Protestants (5%), Muslims and others (including no denomination, 17%)
Main industries	Construction, machinery, food, chemicals, communications equipment, tourism
Main security threat(s)	Organized crime, ethnic conflicts in the region (Balkans)
Defense spending (% GDP)	0.8 (2002)
Size of military (thousands)	106 (2003)
Number of civil wars since 1945	none
Number of interstate wars since 1945	none

Sources

Austrian MoD, 2005, Webpage: http://www.bmlv.gv.at (accessed May 17, 2005).

Central Intelligence Agency Website. 2005. CIA *World Factbook*. http://www.cia.gov/cia/publications/factbook/ (accessed May 15, 2005).

Federal Press Service (Austria), 2000, Austria, edited by the Federal Chancellary, Vienna.

fact nothing more than the German-speaking part of what remained of the large Austro-Hungarian Empire of the past. In the 1920s, Austria—and particularly its capital, Vienna—had to become accustomed to the tremendous changes of the postwar order. The country's inhabitants had to reconcile themselves to the fact that Austria's identity was in transition, moving from its previous position at the center of a large and multinational empire to a new status, whereby it became just a little backwater republic of Central Europe. Of course, Austria tried to overcome its isolated position after World War I by attempting to merge with its much bigger neighbor, Germany, but that political aim was quickly ruled out by the Allied powers. Remaining under Italian protection and relying on foreign loans to secure stability, the young Austrian republic experienced an economic crisis, the Crash of 1929, that brought about an authoritarian regime a few years later.

Despite its very limited political power in Central Europe, Austria continued playing a decisive role in Europe's political landscape of the 1920s and 1930s. Geopolitically it remained situated between two major powers, both of which were undergoing tremendous changes in their own political systems: Germany, in the north, and Italy, in the south. Of course, the general power struggle in Europe in the 1930s imposed significant changes on the small country between the greater powers and evolving new political movements. Austria was occupied by German troops in March 1938 and became part of the German Reich, though the *Anschluss* was welcomed by a majority of the Austrian population shortly thereafter, partly on account of economic reasons. A few months later World War II started, and Austria became heavily involved in fighting the war.

World War II ended with the defeat of the German Reich and an occupation of the territory of former Austria by Allied troops. Because of its strategic position in Central Europe, the Austrian territory was divided into four occupation zones. In order to avoid separation, the Austrian government, which had already been established shortly after the war, sought to regain political independence and sovereignty by all means at its deposal. Austria's 1955 State Treaty brought the long-desired independence and the withdrawal of Allied troops. Shortly after the State Treaty, Austria declared itself "permanently neutral," a status that had been a condition of Soviet military withdrawal. Because of its neutrality Austria did not join any military alliance, although it did become a member of the United Nations shortly after regaining its national sovereignty, accepting the goals and principles of the UN charter.

Since the early 1960s, Austria has maintained its nonaligned and neutral position with respect to military activities, although it has also strongly supported UN activities dedicated to the maintenance of peace and stability around the globe. Its foreign and security policies followed the general principles of what has become known as an "active policy of neutrality," aiming at serving as an impartial mediator in major political conflicts and building bridges between East and West. One may see the Kennedy-Khrushchev summit conference, which was held in Vienna on June 4, 1961, as one positive achievement of this specifically Austrian diplomatic mediating policy during the Cold War.

Undoubtedly, the withdrawal of Allied forces, as a result of the State Treaty of

1955, dramatically affected the general strategic situation in Central Europe. The two neutral countries in the heart of Europe—Switzerland and Austria—in effect split the defense system of NATO into northern and southern tiers. It was exactly this strategic advantage that caused the political leaders of the Soviet Union to accept Austria's proposal to establish some kind of "buffer zone," built up by the two neutral countries, between NATO and the Warsaw Pact, which cut off links between NATO forces in southern Germany and northern Italy. The strategic planning of the Cold War period even showed that "if Warsaw Pact forces had chosen to violate Austrian neutrality by driving westward through the Danube Basin, they would have been able to outflank strong NATO defenses on the central front and avoid a contested Danube River crossing in Bavaria. A second line of potential Warsaw Pact attack ran along the southern flanks of the main Alpine range from the Hungarian Plain leading into northern Italy" (http://reference.allrefer.com/country-guide-study/austria/austria155.html).

The geopolitical situation has changed dramatically since the end of the Cold War. Old enmities have been resurrected, and new tensions have come into existence all across Europe. Among Austria's neighbors, the Republic of Yugoslavia fell apart, leading to a civil war and a serious crisis in the Balkans; Czechoslovakia peacefully split up into two new states a few years later. With the rise of the post–Cold War order in Europe, new security threats emerged and new geopolitical patterns developed. When Austria joined the European Union in 1995, it once again took over an important strategic position with respect to both bridging Western Europe and the other Central and Eastern European states and securing the outer EU border toward the east and southeast.

After successfully growing from six to fifteen members, the European Union accomplished its largest enlargement ever in terms of scope and diversity. Ten new member states—Cyprus, the Czech Republic, Estonia, Hungary, Latvia, Lithuania, Malta, Poland, the Slovak Republic, and Slovenia—joined the EU on May 1, 2004. This enlargement again has changed the strategic position of Austria, moving it from a more marginal member situated somewhere in the eastern part of the union to a state right in the center of an enlarged EU.

Conflict Past and Present
Conflict History
Austria has had a long war-fighting tradition, and many military conflicts have had an impact on the country's historical and political development. Because of its geographic and strategic location, the region that today forms the state territory of Austria has witnessed many wars and battles since the Celtic people from Western Europe settled in the eastern Alps around 400 B.C.E. The Celtic state, Noricum, which developed around the region's ironworks in the second century B.C.E., was occupied by the Romans a few years B.C.E. and made into the northern frontier of the Roman Empire. For more than four centuries the Roman power, backed by well-organized military forces, guaranteed political and social stability in the region. During the general decline of the Roman Empire and the establishment of new settlements of Germanic tribes, including the Ostrogoths, Visigoths, and Vandals, south of the Danube, Noricum gradually became indefensible; much of

its Roman or Romanized population left the region. Around the year 500, the Roman era in the eastern Alps ended.

The name Austria (*Österreich*) dates back to the Middle Ages and derives from the word *Ostarrichi* (literally, Eastern Realm), which was the name for a small margravate roughly corresponding to the present-day province of Lower Austria. The territories that constitute modern Austria were a complex feudal patchwork during the time of the establishment of the Holy Roman Empire, which brought Christianity back to Central Europe. In the final years of the reign of Emperor Otto the Great (tenth century), the small margravate named Ostarrichi was formed within Bavaria. It was detached from Bavaria and became a separate duchy in 1156. Until 1246 the Duchy of Austria was one of the extensive feudal possessions of the Babenberg family.

When the Habsburgs acquired this territory, as well as other territories in the eastern Alpine-Danubian region, "Austria" subsequently became an informal way to refer to all the land possessed by the so-called House of Austria. From the late Middle Ages until the end of World War I in 1918, the political and social development of the region was closely linked with the reign of the Habsburgs. As a consequence, Austrian history—with its huge number of internal as well as external wars—can, for that very long period of time, also be seen as the concrete outcome of the tremendous struggle of the Habsburgs for power.

As a result Austria has a very long tradition of war-fighting, even though the Habsburgs themselves realized early that a policy of territorial expansion frequently can be much better performed by marriage than through the use of military force (*tu, felix Austria, nube*; see Sidebar).

In short, the reign of the Habsburgs in the territory that is occupied by Austria today started with a battle between Otakar, the king of Bohemia, and Rudolf von Habsburg, and ended with the defeat of the Austrian-Hungarian Empire after World War I.

Sidebar 1   Austrian Catch Phrase

Bella gerant alii, tu, felix Austria, nube!—*Let others wage war, you, happy Austria, marry!* This popular phrase is a historical reference to Austria enlarging its empire through marriage instead of waging war. The Austro-Hungarian Empire lasted until the end of World War I in 1918.

Source
http://www.aboutaustria.org/history/habsburg.htm

Undoubtedly, the Habsburgs increased their influence and power through both strategic alliances ratified by marriages and war. Because of the large territorial extension of the Habsburg Empire and its tremendous amount of power in Europe, nearly all major conflicts and wars in Europe were either directly related to the Habsburgs or had an effect on that family's policies and political ambitions in Europe. It is important to note that the Habsburgs inherited not only the Hereditary Lands but also the Franche-Comté, The Netherlands, Spain, and the Spanish Empire in the Americas. But one of the greatest threats to the Habsburgs came from the East.

Challenged on both sides—in the west by France and on his eastern borders by the Turkish Ottoman Empire—Emperor Charles V divided his realm geographically in 1522 to achieve more effective rule. The western half remained under Charles V's direct control, and the eastern half, the Hereditary Lands, were to be administered by his brother, Ferdinand (r. 1522–1564). This territorial division effectively created two branches of the Habsburg Dynasty: the Spanish Habsburgs, descended through Charles V, and the Austrian Habsburgs, descended through Ferdinand.

In the sixteenth century, defense against military threats from the expanding Ottoman Empire was one of the most vital political and military tasks for the Habsburgs, who wished to maintain stability in Europe and to remain in power. In the early sixteenth century, Turkish troops reached and attacked Vienna. It was quite obvious that Turkey's ultimate objective was the conquest of Europe. After the Turkish siege of Vienna in 1529, the Habsburgs began to reorganize the empire's defense system in the east and to establish a solid bulwark against future threats from Turkey in Hungary. The peace agreement signed with the Turks in 1562 brought the military conflict to an end, although the treaty itself was not long lasting; conflict broke out again in 1663. The Turkish siege of Vienna in 1683 did not bring the Turks a breakthrough or success. On the contrary, Habsburg forces were able to move into central Hungary. By the end of the seventeenth century, the Ottoman Empire had been eliminated as a power in Central Europe.

However, the Habsburg Empire was involved in many more military conflicts than these rivalries with the Ottoman Empire. Among the huge number of wars that the Habsburgs fought, the following played an important role in Austrian history: the Thirty Years' War (1616–1648), the War of the Spanish Succession (1701–1714), the War of the Austrian Succession (1740–1748), the Napoleonic Wars, and, finally, World War I, which brought the Habsburg Empire to an end. In addition, the Habsburgs also fought a number of internal or civil wars. They had to deal with a number of revolutionary movements, as well, particularly in the years after the French Revolution, as well as struggles between the various national and ethnic groups inside the political framework.

World War I led to the end of the Austro-Hungarian Empire and the birth of the first Austrian republic. On November 11, 1918, Karl, the last Habsburg emperor, renounced any role in the new Austrian state. A few days later, the new state of Austria was proclaimed, and a democratic political system was implemented, Austria thus becoming a republic. The political situation of the new state was characterized by a combination of external and internal conflicts and threats. Externally, the republic was included in the general power game of the post–World War I European landscape. Whereas the Austrians wanted to establish close links with Germany or even become part of a larger Germany, the Allied states did not like that option and instead imposed a number of political restrictions in the treaties signed after the end of the war.

Internally, the young Austrian republic had to cope with a number of economic and social problems. With only limited experience in democratic procedures and policymaking, internal conflict soon arose and even led to severe fights between the different political powers and parties. In 1934, Austria witnessed a civil war that came right after the implementation of an authoritarian political system that replaced democracy (see Table 2). The growing political strength of the

Table 2   Interstate and Civil Wars Since 1918 (Austria)

1934	Civil War
March 1938	"Anschluß"—occupation of Austria by German troops
1939–1945	World War II

Nazis in Germany as well as in Austria and worsening economic conditions heavily influenced the political situation in Austria in the 1930s.

Growing German pressure on Austria after Hitler came to power and became the German *Reichskanzler* led to a final attempt by the Austrian government to save the country's independence and sovereignty. The Austrian government was not strong enough, however, to succeed. In March 1938, German troops invaded Austria, and the country became part of the German Reich. A few months later, World War II began.

Current and Potential Military Confrontation

Since the reestablishment of Austria as a fully independent and sovereign state in 1955, the country has experienced a rather peaceful and stable period of development with no internal or external military conflicts. However, the larger strategic issues of the Cold War overshadowed both the external and internal political development of the country. The prevailing threat perceptions of the 1950s through the 1980s all depended on the general pattern of the East-West conflict. Austria was in a way squeezed into its little space between the two heavily armed military forces of NATO and the Warsaw Pact. Consequently, the most evident military threat was tied to scenarios of attack or invasion through one of the opposing parties and their armed forces.

Regardless of its neutral status, Austria clearly showed sympathies for the Western democracies—for example, opposing the Soviet invasion of Hungary in 1956 and of Czechoslovakia in 1968. During the Cold War, major conflict scenarios resulted from such political events, or the likelihood of the outbreak of similar conflicts (such as Yugoslavia) in the countries neighboring Austria. Austria's efforts to make itself a bridge between East and West helped—at least economically and diplomatically—to achieve a relatively high and secure position in the Cold War political order.

Internally, since the end of World War II, Austria has successfully implemented a democratic order as well as a special system of political cooperation and crisis management that has made possible peaceful and stable political development. This system of political cooperation, established during the occupation years and economic reconstruction, was aimed at close cooperation and interaction between the representatives of the major economic interest groups—the so-called commission of the social partners. It required unanimous decisions and was established on a permanent basis, thus becoming a powerful stabilizing force in Austrian society. Up to the present day, Austrian society has not witnessed any serious social or political threat, or momentum toward destabilization.

In sum, one can hardly imagine any potential military confrontation or conflict in Central Europe today. In addition, the ongoing process of political integration and enlargement of the European Union brings Austria closer to its neighbors in the East and Northeast. New threats and risks are to a very large extent related only to terrorism, migration, minor ethnic conflicts (particularly in the East or Southeast of Europe), illegal drug trafficking, and organized crime. Such threats will in the near future require additional efforts in policing but will probably not stop the ongoing process of downsizing the armed forces and reducing the size of the military establishment in Austria. This situation has recently led to an evaluation of the current and potential military threats to the Austrian state that was performed by the Austrian government. The evaluation concluded that Austria had to prepare for future external military operations—perhaps even outside the territory of an enlarged European Union—in order to secure stability and peace in the world, but that it will remain "surrounded by friends" in the near future.

Alliance Structure

As mentioned above, Austria has been a neutral country since 1955 and thus has never joined any kind of military alliance. That is the case with the North Atlantic Treaty Organization (NATO), although Austria became a member of NATO's Partnership for Peace Program (PfP) in 1995. Austria entered the European Union on January 1, 1995.

Austria's status of neutrality is closely linked with its post–World War II history and its people's desire to regain independence and sovereignty after ten years of occupation by Allied forces, from 1945 until 1955. In the spring of 1955, the political landscape of Europe began to change: at that point Austria immediately realized it might have a chance to avoid separation, which more and more seemed to be an unavoidable outcome of the emerging Cold War structure in Central Europe. It also stood to put an end to its status of occupation by the four foreign nations—that is, the United States, the United Kingdom, France, and the Soviet Union. In particular, the concept of permanent neutrality, following the example of Swiss neutrality, seemed to be a perfect way to open the door for future independence and also to convince the political leaders of the Soviet Union that a future sovereign, independent, and nonaligned Austria would not pose any threat to the Eastern European communist political systems and the newly founded Warsaw Pact.

Political negotiations were conducted successfully, and exactly one day after the Warsaw Pact Treaty was signed, Austria regained independence. Under the State Treaty, signed in Vienna on May 15, 1955, a number of restrictions were imposed that affected the buildup of the Austrian armed forces (Austria was, for example, prohibited from possessing any self-propelled or guided missiles or guns with a range of more than thirty kilometers). In the so-called Moscow Memorandum of 1955, Austria had also stated its intention to declare its neutrality as soon as the last soldier of an occupation power left the country.

On October 26, 1955, the government in fact passed a law in which Austria declared of its own free will its permanent neutrality. Article 1 of the Federal Constitution Law on the neutrality of Austria states that "for the purpose of the permanent maintenance of its external independence and for the purpose of the inviolability of its territory, Austria, of its own will, declares its permanent neutrality, which it is resolved to maintain and defend with all the means at its disposal. In order to secure these purposes, Austria will never in the future accede to any military alliances nor permit the establishment of military basis of foreign states on its territory" (Federal Constitutional Law of October 26, 1955, Article 1).

Since 1955, the Austrian government has frequently asserted that it alone is competent to define Austrian neutrality. In the mid-1950s, the government referred primarily to the example of Switzerland's status of neutrality, which should be followed in general terms—that is, particularly as far as it defined a neutrality that had to be militarily defended, thus requiring the buildup of military forces to defend the borders as well as the territory of the country in case of foreign attack. In this respect, one can argue that Austria has interpreted its posture as a neutral state in Europe with terms similar to those used by Switzerland.

At the same time, however, Austria has never followed the rather narrow and strict interpretation of Switzerland when it comes to questions of "ideological neutrality" or the formation of the UN system. In the year following the formation of the Cold War bipolarity, with two major military alliances facing each other in Europe, Austria deliberately adopted a more liberal interpretation of its neutrality, thus allowing a more active policy of political and military involvement in world politics. The term "active neutrality policy" (*aktive Neutralitätspolitik*) became commonplace in Austria, characterizing the country's will to take over new roles in global politics—such as, for example, participating in international peacekeeping and humanitarian aid mis-

sions led by the United Nations, or promoting Vienna as the third UN HQ city in the world after New York and Geneva.

After the end of the Cold War, Austria had to rethink its traditional concept of neutrality and to adapt it to the new security environment of the post–Cold War era. Although Austria did not participate directly in more robust peace-enforcement missions or other UN-backed action—such as, for example, the Gulf War in 1991—it at least indirectly supported the Western alliance by providing financial assistance or by granting expanded overflight authority for troops involved in the war.

A few years later, public discussion on Austria's future membership in the European Union also caused a heated debate on the continued appropriateness of Austrian neutrality. In that context, the question was raised whether Austria should still adhere to its status as a neutral country or, rather, abolish that status and join NATO. Furthermore, after Austria's entry into the European Union, a slowly developing common European security and defense policy led to a completely new interpretation of Austrian neutrality. The new expression of European solidarity—instead of neutrality within the framework of pan-European security—was introduced in public language, although the term has never made its way into the Austrian legal system as an amendment to or change of the Federal Constitutional Law of 1955 on Austria's neutrality.

To sum up, neutrality, once ingrained as part of the Austrian cultural identity, has been called into question since the end of the Cold War. Concurrently, Austria has played an increasingly prominent role in European affairs, particularly with the development of a common security and defense policy for the European Union. This clearly indicates a general dilemma in Austria's security and defense policy, which has not yet been overcome. On the one hand, the country still adheres to its traditional concept of neutrality and remains to a very large extent isolated and militarily nonaligned; on the other, it agrees to a number of mutual agreements in the security and defense agenda that in fact imply the end of its neutrality. The most important agreement in this context is undoubtedly Austria's readiness to participate in the EU Rapid Deployment Force and its future missions.

Sidebar 2   Austria: The "Peacekeeping Country"

Since the early 1960s, peacekeeping has become an important role for the Austrian armed forces. During the Cold War, Austria was one of the countries that made available the largest number of troops for UN peacekeeping operations. Since the Congo UN peacekeeping mission in 1960, Austria has deployed military peacekeeping units to Cyprus, Cambodia, former Yugoslavia, Albania, the Golan Heights, and other areas in the Middle East. All in all, more than 40,000 Austrians to date have served in the UN peacekeeping troops all over the world as soldiers, military observers, civilian police officers, and civilian experts.

Source
Erwin Schmidl. 2001. "Die österreichische Teilnahme an der UN-Friedensoperation in Zypern seit 1964." *Österreichisches Jahrbuch für internationale Politik* 18:63–73.

During the Cold War, Austria's military commitment to UN-led peacekeeping operations was of high national priority. The country's involvement in international peacekeeping started in 1960, when the army sent a medical team to the Congo. Since the mid-1960s, Austria has provided military forces, medical units, and observers to UN peacekeeping operations in Cyprus and other areas in the Middle East. To date more than 40,000 Austrians have served under the UN flag (see Sidebar). Austria will continue to play an active part in UN peace support operations in the future as well as in the tasks incorporated into the Amsterdam Treaty of the European Union (particularly the so-called Petersberg tasks)—that is, to participation in humanitarian actions, rescue operations, and peacekeeping missions, as well as in crisis management operations and peace-making measures. Austria has an equal share in the planning and decision-making process of such activities within the European Union's frameworks of Common Foreign and Security Policy (CFSP) and European Security and Defense Policy (ESDP).

Size and Structure of the Military

As of 2003, the Austrian armed forces had a total strength of approximately 106,600 people. Of that number, 34,600 soldiers serve on active duty (including approximately 17,400 active and short-term soldiers; there are approximately 17,200 conscripts, excluding approximately 9,500 civilians) (*Military Balance*, 2003–2004). Approximately 1 million Austrians have had reserve training but no further military commitment. Austria still adheres to compulsory military service, which was introduced in 1955 when Austria regained its sovereign status and independence after having been occupied by the Allied forces for the decade following the end of World War II. Conscription is for a seven-month period, with liability for at least another thirty days and reservist refresher training spread over eight to ten years (with sixty to ninety days' additional training for officers, NCOs, and specialists). Annually some 30,000 conscripts undergo military training (Austrian Ministry of Defense Homepage, 2004).

Austria started the process of downsizing its total mobilization strength in 1992. During the last decade, the total number of soldiers included in the total mobilization plan of the armed forces has been reduced from approximately 200,000 to roughly 110,000. Without prior mobilization, there are up to 35,000 troops available. In addition, Austria has set up rapid deployment units of some 1,500 to 2,000 personnel for international commitments and peace support operations, including PfP, UN, Organization for Security and Cooperation in Europe (OSCE), and EU military operations. Approximately 1,000 of them are presently deployed to a number of areas, such as Bosnia, the Golan Heights, and Afghanistan.

The commander-in-chief of the Austrian armed forces is the federal president of the Republic of Austria; the minister of defense exercises command and control and is advised by the chief of the defense staff (*Generalstabschef*). Subordinate to the minister and the MoD military staff are Land Force Command, the Air Force Command, the Special Operations Command, and the Austrian International Operations Command, as well as the Service Support Command and the C^{3}I Command. The National Defense Academy, located in Vienna, the Maria Theresia Military Academy in Wiener Neustadt, other weapon schools, and a number of agencies complete the Austrian military establishment (ibid.).

Presently, the Austrian Army is structured in five brigades (two mechanized brigades and three infantry brigades) and nine provincial military commands. The mechanized brigades are equipped with Leopard 2/A4 main battle tanks. One of three infantry brigades is earmarked for airborne operations. The second is equipped with Pandur wheeled armored personnel carriers, and the third infantry brigade specializes in mountain operations. The artillery units are brigade-directed. M-109 armored self-propelled guns equip the artillery battalions (ibid.).

The air force forms part of the army (army aviation), and an Austrian navy does not exist. The army aviation's main tasks are to maintain sovereignty over the country's airspace; provide reconnaissance, transport, liaison, and combat support for the ground troops; and act in an emergency relief capacity both at home and abroad (ibid.). Austria's army aviation comprises three aviation and three air defense regiments with about 6,850 personnel (including approximately 2,240 conscripts), more than 150 aircraft, including 23 Draken interceptors and Saab 105s, and a number of fixed and mobile radar stations. The air defense system, called Goldhaube (Golden Hat), was installed at the end of the 1980s when Austria bought 24 Saab J-35OE Draken interceptors from Sweden and introduced them into service. The air defense system has been operational ever since, with two Saab 105s or Draken permanently ready for takeoff in order to intercept unidentified aircraft entering Austrian airspace.

The three aviation regiments consist of a number of squadrons equipped with Augusta-Bell 212 helicopters, Augusta-Bell 206A Jet Rangers, Augusta-Bell 204Bs, and Bell OH 58B Kiowas. Further aircraft and helicopters include the Shorts SC-7 Skyvan Series 3Ms, Pilatus PC-6/B2H2 Turbo Porters, S-70 Black Hawks, as well as a number of Alouettes IIIs (mainly used for rescue and emergency tasks). In 2003 Austria ordered 18 Eurofighters, which will be delivered in the course of the next years: 4 airplanes in 2007, 12 airplanes in 2008, and the remaining 2 in 2009. The costs for these 18 planes are approximately 1.959 billion Euro (ibid.). In addition, in February 2004 the Austrian minister of defense started negotiations with Switzerland in regard to buying additional F-5 Tiger aircraft in order to secure the Austrian airspace until the year 2008.

Recently, the Austrian government has set up a commission for a comprehensive reform of the Austrian defense system and armed forces. The meetings of the reform commission started in spring of 2004 and a final report was issued later that year. It is very likely that the Austrian military will undergo tremendous structural changes in the near future. In addition, it is also noteworthy that a broad public discussion on conscription and the future role of the Austrian armed forces and European defense system (European Security and Defense Policy) has been started, as well as public consideration of the question of whether Austria should join NATO or adhere to its traditional status of neutrality.

Today, Austrian soldiers and troops are participating in a number of international missions and peace support operations, including, for example, European Force Operation Concordia (EUFOR-CONCORDIA) in Skopje, Kosovo; International Security Force (KFOR) in Pristina, with some 525 troops; UN Disengagement Observer Forces in Syria (UNDOF), with approximately 367 soldiers; UN Peacekeeping Force in Cyprus (UNFICYP); and the UN Mission in Ethiopia and Eritrea (UNMEE).

Budget
Austrians have been traditionally reluctant to allocate significant sums for improving the nation's defense system. That attitude still prevails today in public life, causing the military establishment serious trouble when the acquisition of expensive military equipment seems unavoidable. In particular, the question of whether Austria really needs to buy new interceptors for the armed forces has always caused endless public debate and demonstrations. In past decades, the military establishment was frequently forced to postpone large-scale equipment acquisitions and to accept compromises in quantity and quality of new material and maintenance standards.

Within the last decade, the government has tried to maintain a relatively constant defense budget. In the future, anticipated lower expenditures for personnel will permit some expansion in equipment, military technology, and new aircraft. In the 1980s and 1990s, personnel costs absorbed almost half of the budget; operations consumed approximately 32 percent of funding, and investment only 17 percent. The current downsizing process is aiming at a tremendous reapportionment of these numbers.

Austria's defense spending as a proportion of the gross national product is still among the lowest in Europe. During the decade from 1981 to 1991, annual defense outlays were in the range of 1.0 to 1.5 percent of GNP. The Austrian defense budget in 2002 was 1.7 billion Euro (approximately 1.7 billion Euro for 2003).

Civil-Military Relations/The Role of the Military in Domestic Politics

Civil-military relations in Austria are characterized by a clear predominance of civilian power over the military. The Austrian military establishment forms part of the administration system of the Austrian state; all military-related law forms part of the general Austrian legal system. In 1955, the Austrian armed forces were established on the basis of a compulsory military system. Conscription still plays an important role in Austrian society because it is generally viewed as the best way of guaranteeing the integration of the armed forces and the officers' corps into the democratic system of Austrian society and the avoidance of the formation of a small state within the state. Recently, however, conscription has been called into question because Austria needs more troops for military operations abroad and fewer soldiers for national defense. For this purpose, an all-volunteer force seems inevitable.

In addition, the traditional Austrian defense system was established upon a militia system, in which soldiers were permanently trained for national defense tasks over a period of from 10 to 20 years. Austria's defense system of the 1970s and 1980s was linked with the idea of area defense, with so-called key zones for territorial defense. Since the end of the Cold War, the militia system has gradually lost its importance and is about to be abolished.

Under Article 79 of the constitution, the Austrian army is entrusted with the military defense of the country. Insofar as the legally constituted civil authority requests its cooperation, the army is further charged with protecting constitutional institutions and their capacity to act, as well as with protecting the democratic freedoms of the inhabitants and maintaining order and security. Finally, rendering aid in disasters and mishaps of extraordinary scope, and participating in international peace support operations, are also listed as tasks for the armed forces.

Terrorism

Terrorism, in its modern form as a militant strategy to achieve certain political aims by threatening and using violence, has never played an essential role in Austrian society. Nevertheless, Austria has had to deal with a small number of terrorist actions on its territory. Probably the most shocking terrorist attack that ever occurred in Austria was the OPEC takeover on December 21, 1975, when a group of terrorists attacked the assembled ministers and delegates at the Vienna OPEC meeting. The attack was led by Carlos the Jackal, a Venezuelan terrorist whose real name was Ilich Ramirez Sanchez. Three people were killed during the attack; the victims were an OPEC employee, an Iraqi bodyguard, and an Austrian policeman.

Other notable terrorist attacks were the kidnapping of a Sabena airplane on its way from Vienna to Tel Aviv via Athens on May 8, 1972; the kidnapping of the "Chopin-Express" train from Moscow to Vienna in Bratislava close to the Austrian border; and the assassination of the Turkish ambassador in Vienna in 1975. The latter event took place on October 22, 1975, when three armed terrorists from a group called the Armenian Victorious Army rushed into the Turkish embassy in Vienna and killed the ambassador of Turkey. The three terrorists managed to disappear after the shooting.

Most terrorist attacks in the 1970s and 1980s were related to political issues, mainly to the Middle East crisis, the Turkish-Kurdish problem, or the question of the status of South Tyrol (former part of Austria) in Italy. In the 1990s, Austria was hit by a wave of letter bombs with a racist background. Most letter bomb attacks targeted immigrants or immigrant-related groups across the country, leading to a number of deaths and injuries. Police suspected that neo-Nazis were behind those attacks. Most of the attacks came to an end when police arrested one suspect in 1997.

Today, Austria appears to be a relatively safe place, and cannot be seen as one of the likely major targets for terrorist attack. However, because of its geopolitical situation and the many international organizations, including many UN agencies, headquartered in Vienna, there may remain at least a minimum chance of the country's becoming a target for terrorists.

Relationship with the United States

Austria has enjoyed a very good relationship with the United States since the end of World War II. Between 1945 and 1955, U.S. troops were stationed in parts of Austria, because the United States was one of the four occupation powers responsible for the rebuilding of Austria's democratic state. During the period of occupation, the United States was generally perceived as a nation that was truly willing to help Austria and economically support the Austrian population. In fact, foreign U.S. aid under the auspices of the Marshall Plan helped in effectively rebuilding the state and Austrian society.

Since regaining independence in 1955, Austria has never understood its neutrality in an ideological sense. The country clearly showed that it wanted to be viewed as part of the Western world with a democratic system and free market–oriented economy. Together with the Western European countries, it has belonged to a single economic, political, and cultural system; it has also shared most of the common Western values. However, continued close cooperation with the United States did not destroy differences of opinion—such as, for example, with respect to capital punishment, the use of military force, or issues of environmental policy. In recent years Austria has even intensified its military cooperation with the United States, although the country still hesitates to give full support to many U.S.-led military operations, particularly when such missions are not backed by UN resolutions. In this context it must be mentioned that—especially with respect to the currently ongoing "War on Terrorism" and the U.S. intervention in Iraq—public attitudes in Austria toward U.S. foreign policy and military actions have become more and more critical.

The Future

The post–Cold War political order has revealed new threats and risks with respect to Austrian and European security. The Balkan region, in particular, became very unstable, with a high potential for deadly ethnic conflicts and struggles. Moreover, dramatic changes and tensions in the nation-state system of the former Yugoslavia contributed strongly to new risks in the form of local and ethnic conflicts close to the Austrian border. Defense of the country's border and prevention of spillover from the Yugoslav civil war into Austrian territory became primary tasks of the Austrian armed forces in the early 1990s.

Border observation is still the preliminary task of the Austrian armed forces at home; this is performed daily and will remain an important task in the near future. Disaster relief operations have also played an important role and that, too, will continue. Austria is even willing to pay much more attention to disaster relief units in order to prepare for more international missions in cases of emergency or crises abroad. A third task for the armed forces, which have gained influence and importance in recent years, is participation in international military operations. This will become the main task of the future and will be the biggest challenge for the current restructuring process of the Austrian armed forces. In this respect, it can be foreseen that Austria will gradually move away from its traditional system of universal conscription and introduce at least a mixed-manning system or eventually even abolish conscription and establish an all-volunteer-force.

In general, Austria will continue to play an important role in the European Union, particularly with respect to the EU enlargement process. But it will not play a decisive role in the emerging European security and defense system. As a non-NATO member and with its unclear but still remaining status as a neutral country with limited military resources and capabilities, Austria, instead of participating in large-scale military operations, will probably seek other niches for its defense and foreign policy.

References, Recommended Readings, and Websites

Books
Arndt, Sven W. 1982. *Political Economy of Austria.* Washington, DC: American Enterprise Institute.
Bartlett, Christopher J. 1996. *Peace, War, and the European Powers, 1814–1914.* New York: St. Martin's Press.
Bischof, Günter, and Anton Pelinka, eds. 1993. *Austria in the New Europe.* Contemporary Austrian Studies, No. 1. New Brunswick, NJ: Transaction Books.
Bridge, F. R. 1990. *The Habsburg Monarchy among the Great Powers, 1815–1918.* New York: Berg.
Dachs, Herbert, et al., eds. 1991. *Handbuch des politischen Systems Österreichs.* Vienna: Manz.
Evans, Robert, and John Weston. 1984. *The Making of the Habsburg Monarchy, 1550–1700: An Interpretation.* Oxford: Clarendon Press.
Fitzmaurice, John. 1990. *Austrian Politics and Society Today: In Defence of Austria.* New York: St. Martin's Press.
Jelavich, Barbara. 1969. *The Habsburg Empire in European Affairs, 1814–1918.* Chicago: Rand McNally.
———. 1987. *Modern Austria: Empire and Republic, 1815–1986.* Cambridge: Cambridge University Press.
Johnson, Lonnie. 1989. *Introducing Austria: A Short History.* Riverside, CA: Ariadne Press.
Kann, Robert A. 1977. *A History of the Habsburg Empire, 1526–1918.* Berkeley: University of California Press.
Kernic, Franz, and Jean M. Callaghan. 2002. "Politische Identität und allgemeine Wehrpflicht in Österreich." In *Europas Armeen im Umbruch,* Karl W. Haltiner and Paul Klein, eds. Baden-Baden: Nomos, pp. 179–203.
Klose, Alfred. 1987. *Machtstrukturen in Österreich.* Vienna: Signum.
Leeper, Alexander Wigram Allen. 1941. *A History of Medieval Austria.* London: Oxford University Press.
Macartney, Carlile Aylmer. 1968. *The Habsburg Empire, 1790–1918.* London: Weidenfeld and Nicolson.
Neuhold, Hanspeter, and Heinz Vetschera. 1984. *Austria's Security Policy,* Geneva: UNIDIR.
Nick, Rainer, and Anton Pelinka. 1984. *Parlamentarismus in Österreich.* Vienna: Jugend und Volk.
———. 1993. *Österreichs politische Landschaft.* Innsbruck: Haymon Verlag.
Pelinka, Anton. 1998. *Austria: Out of the Shadow of the Past.* Boulder, CO: Westview Press.

Nick, Rainer, and Sieglinde Rosenberger. 2003. *Österreichische Politik: Grundlagen—Strukturen—Trends*. 2d ed. Vienna: WUV.

Rauchensteiner, Manfried, ed. 1980. *Das Bundesheer der Zweiten Republik: Eine Dokumentation*. Vienna: Bundesverlag.

Steiner, Kurt, ed. 1981. *Modern Austria*. Palo Alto, CA: Society for the Promotion of Science and Scholarship.

Stourzh, Gerald. 1980. *Geschichte des Staatsvertrages 1945–1955*. Graz: Styria.

Stuhlpfarrer, Karl. 1987. *Austria: Permanently Neutral—Austrian Foreign Policy since 1945*. Vienna: Federal Press Service.

Sully, Melanie A. 1990. *A Contemporary History of Austria*. London: Routlege.

Sweeney, Jim, and Josef Weidenholzer, eds. 1988. *Austria: A Study in Modern Achievement*. Aldershot, UK: Avebury.

Tapié, Victor Lucien. 1971. *The Rise and Fall of the Habsburg Monarchy*. New York: Praeger.

Zöllner, Erich. 1970. *Geschichte Österreichs: Von den Anfängen bis zur Gegenwart*. Vienna: Verlag für Geschichte und Politik.

Articles and Journals

Federal Press Service. 2000. *Austria: Facts and Figures*. Vienna: Bundespressedienst. (for document see: http://www.austria. gv.at/e/)

Federal Press Service. 1990. *Religions in Austria*. Vienna: Bundespressedienst.

Federal Press Service. 1988. *The First Republic,1918–1938*. Vienna: Bundespressedienst.

Binter, Josef. 1989. "Neutrality, European Community and World Peace: The Case of Austria." *Journal of Peace Research* 26, no. 4 (November 1989): 413–418.

Callaghan, Jean M., and Franz Kernic. 2001. "Conscription and Citizenship Identity in Austria and Switzerland." *Österreichische Militärische Zeitschrift* (ÖMZ), no. 2:189–198.

Der Soldat. Vienna: Austrian Ministry of Defense. *Österreichische Militarische Zeitschrift*. Vienna: Austrian Ministry of Defense. *Schriftenreihe der Landesverteidigungsakademie*. Vienna: Austrian Ministry of Defense, National Defense Academy.

Fender, Peter. 1986. "Die österreichische Wehrstruktur." *Vierteljahresschrift fuer Sicherheit und Frieden* (S+F) 4, no. 3:133–137.

Kernic, Franz. "The Participation of Soldiers in Austrian Politics: Possibilities and Conditions." *Politics and Society in Germany, Austria and Switzerland* 2, no. 1–2:59–69.

Military Balance, 2003–2004. London: International Institute for Strategic Studies.

Statistisches Jahrbuch für die Republik Österreich. Vienna: Österreichisches Statistisches Zentralamt.

Truppendienst. Vienna: Austrian Ministry of Defense.

Websites

Austria—A Country Study: http://lcweb2. loc.gov/frd/cs/attoc.html.

Background Note: Austria (U.S. Department of State): http://www.state. gov/r/pa/bgn/index.cfm%3Fdocid=3165.

Bundesheer (Austrian Armed Forces): http://www.bundesheer.com/.

CIA *World Factbook* 2003: Austria: http:// www.cia.gov/cia/publications/factbook/ geos/au.html.

Country Studies: Austria: http:// countrystudies.us/austria/.

History of Austria: http://www. countryreports.org/history/austhist.htm.

Ministry of Defense: Austria: http://www. bmlv.gv.at.

Terror & Attentate in Austria: (Österreich) http://www.emergency-management.net/terror_austria.htm.

Study and Country Guide: Austria: http:// reference.allrefer.com/country-guide-study/austria/.

Brazil

Justin L. Miller

Geography and History

Occupying almost half of the South American continent, Brazil is slightly smaller than the United States, with a total area of 8,511,965 square kilometers and a land area of 8,456,510 square kilometers. It shares a common boundary with every South American country except for Chile and Ecuador, neighboring French Guiana, Suriname, Guyana, Venezuela, and Colombia to the north; Peru and Bolivia to the west; and Paraguay, Argentina, and Uruguay to the southwest. The terrain of Brazil includes dense forests in its northern regions. In fact, forests cover approximately half of the country, with the largest rain forest in the world located in the Amazon Basin. Brazil also has a semiarid region along the northeast coast; mountains, hills, and rolling plains in the southwest; and coastal lowland.

Brazil is the most populous country in South America and the fifth largest in the world, with an estimated 182 million inhabitants. The country's capital, Brasilia, with its population of 2.1 million, is dwarfed by the major industrial giants in the south-central region. In fact, the overwhelming majority of Brazil's population is concentrated in the area stretching from the state of Minas Gerais to Rio Grande do Sul, which includes the major cities of São Paulo (17.9 million) and Rio de Janeiro (10.7 million). Brazil is predominantly (80 percent) Roman Catholic, the remainder of the country being Protestant or following practices derived from African religions. The Brazilian population is made up of Portuguese, Africans, and various other European, Middle Eastern, and Asian immigrant groups, as well as indigenous peoples of Tupi and Guarani language stock. The official language is Portuguese, while English, French, German, and other European languages also are spoken.

Brazil gained its independence in 1822 following three centuries under Portuguese rule; it became a constitutional democracy in 1889. The democratic period ended with a military coup in 1930 that brought to power Getulio Vargas (1930–1945, 1951–1954), a civilian, who would lead a fifteen-year dictatorship. The military successfully replaced Vargas in 1954 with another civilian president. In 1964 the military removed President João Goulart and began a twenty-one-year period of military governance.

Brazil returned to democracy in 1985 with indirect presidential elections. The president-elect, Tancredo Neves, died before he could assume office, and therefore the presidency went to his vice presidential running mate, José Sarney. The 1988 constitution officially reestablished competitive presidential and legislative elections, and Brazil completed its transition to a popularly elected government in 1989, when Fernando Collor de Mello won in the first direct presidential election in almost three decades. President Collor was impeached after a major corruption scandal and replaced by his vice president, Itamar Franco. Fernando Henrique Cardoso, a leftist academic and opposition politician under the military dictatorship, won the presidential election in 1994 and again in 1998. After campaigning for the presidency four times, Luiz Inácio Lula da Silva, commonly known as Lula, was elected president in 2002.

Today Brazil is a federal republic; it contains twenty-six states and a federal district. The federal government, which consists of executive, legislative, and judicial branches, is granted broad powers by the 1988 constitution. The executive branch has a president, elected for four years, with the right to reelection for an additional four-year-term. Brazil has a bicameral legislature, with 81 senators, three for each state and the Federal District, and 513 deputies. A number of political parties are represented in the federal government; as of 2003, fifteen parties had seats in the legislature (U.S. Department of State 2003).

Brazil has capitalized on its large labor pool to exploit its vast natural resources, making it the largest economic power in South America. Its mineral resources are extensive and include large iron and manganese reserves, which are important sources of industrial raw materials. Other exploited minerals include deposits of nickel, tin, chromite, bauxite, beryllium, copper, lead, tungsten, zinc, and gold (ibid.). In addition, Brazil has one of the most advanced industrial sectors in South America. The major industries are textiles, shoes, chemicals, cement, lumber, iron ore, tin, steel, aircraft, motor vehicles and parts, and other machinery and equipment. Brazil is also one of the world's leading producers of hydroelectric power (CIA *World Factbook* 2004).

Table 1   Brazil: Key Statistics

Type of government	Federative republic
Population (millions)	182 (2003)
Religion	Roman Catholic (80%, 2002)
Main industries	Textiles, shoes, chemicals, cement, lumber, iron ore, tin, steel, aircraft, motor vehicles and parts, other machinery and equipment
Main security threats	Illicit drugs; unruly region at convergence of Argentina-Brazil-Paraguay borders; uncontested dispute with Uruguay over islands
Defense spending (% GDP)	2.3% (2002)
Size of military (thousands)	287
Number of civil wars since 1945	0
Number of interstate wars since 1945	0

Sources

Central Intelligence Agency Website. 2005. CIA *World Factbook.* http://www.cia.gov/cia/ publications/factbook/ (accessed May 15, 2005).

International Institute for Strategic Studies (IISS). 2003. *The Military Balance 2003–2004.* London: IISS and Oxford University Press.

Throughout the 1980s and 1990s, Brazil struggled with high inflation, foreign debt, and currency instability. In fact, inflation devalued the Brazilian currency to the point that it was virtually worthless, forcing reform in 1994 in which the cruzeiro was replaced by the real. Brazil's economy recovered, although not without difficulties. The Brazilian economy was under critical stress in 2002 on account of economic uncertainties leading up to the election of Lula and his left-wing Worker's Party (PT), as well as the 35 percent depreciation of the real and reduced foreign investment (dropping to $1.6 billion, $6 billion below the previous year's total). The IMF rescued Brazil, stepping in with a record $30 billion program. Brazil's 2002 GDP was estimated at $499.4 billion (1.5 percent growth), and although the economic crisis has subsided, high poverty rates and massive income inequality still plague the country (U.S. Department of State 2003).

Regional Geopolitics

Brazil has not been involved in a conflict with any of its neighbors for more than a century. Prior to the 1980s, Argentina, Brazil's historical rival, was considered the most likely external threat. However, the two countries consolidated their ties in the 1980s and are now fully integrated economic partners. Brazil continues to have an uncontested dispute with Uruguay over certain islands in the Quarai/Cuareim and Invernada boundary streams, and the resulting tri-point with Argentina.

As a result of Brazil's proximity to Colombia, a greater security concern is a potential spillover of Colombia's civil war, whether from rebels seeking sanctuary or from the Colombian military in pursuit; any cross-border incursions violate Brazil's sovereignty. Consequently, Brasilia has been a vocal critic of the U.S.-supported Plan Colombia, which is aimed at cracking down on Colombian drug traffickers and producers. Although some in the Brazilian government see further Colombian turmoil as undermining regional stability, many others fear that it eventually could force the drug trade—as well as refugees and guerrillas—across the border into the Brazilian Amazon (Rabasa and Chalk 2001, 90–91).

Indeed, as a result of the escalation of the war on drugs in the Andean region, drug traffickers have redirected their shipment routes through Brazil and are increasingly using the country as a conduit for narcotics destined for Africa and the lucrative European market. Brazil's long and porous borders, as well as its developed infrastructure and banking system, make it a highly attractive transit country for Andean cocaine. Moreover, many narco-traffickers and producers have sought haven in Brazil, leading to the development of closer ties between drug lords in both Brazil and Colombia (*Military Balance, 2003–2004*, 177). In 2000, Brazil responded to these problems by launching a three-year plan named Operation Cobra, a unified effort between the military and federal police to patrol the border with Colombia.

The steady rise in drug trafficking has been disastrous for Brazil, which is rapidly becoming one of the world's largest markets for Colombian, Bolivian, and Peruvian cocaine. Indeed, an increasing amount of cocaine HCI is flooding the streets of São Paulo and major Brazilian cities where *basuco* and crack cocaine are used among the youth (U.S. Department of State 2002). Brazil has also witnessed an upsurge in drug-related violence, particularly in Rio de Janeiro, by drug gangs such as the Red Commandos, which control many of the cities' principal favelas, or shantytowns. As Larry Rohter noted in a *New York Times* article on April 27, 2003, these drug gangs "boast that they have become a 'parallel power,' and to demonstrate their strength and the government's weakness, they periodically force stores, banks, schools, offices and markets not to open for business."

Sidebar 1   Brazilian Airspace Policy

A major surge in violence committed by drug gangs in the Brazilian major cities of São Paulo and Rio de Janeiro, and the steady rise in trafficking through the Amazon region, together prompted the Brazilian government to adopt a policy in 2004 allowing the military to shoot down aircraft transporting illegal drugs in its airspace. The United States has expressed concern over such policies in Latin America since a Peruvian jet accidentally shot down an aircraft carrying an American missionary and her child in 2001.

Source
Larry Rohter. 2004. "Brazil Carries the War on Drugs to the Air," *New York Times*, July 25: 6. http://www.nytimes.com (accessed July 25, 2004).

There is also concern about the tri-border area, where Brazil, Paraguay, and Argentina converge. The tri-border area is considered a principal region for money-laundering, arms and drug trafficking, software piracy, and other criminal activity, and it is allegedly a haven for militant Islamist organizations.

Conflict Past and Present
Conflict History
Historically, Brazil has been reluctant to involve itself in international conflicts. In World War I, Brazil first announced neutrality; it was drawn into the war only after German U-boats began sinking Brazilian freighters. Their military role remained limited primarily to naval patrols in the South Atlantic. Likewise, in World War II, Brazil again opted for neutrality until its freighters began to be torpedoed. Brazil's contribution in that war, however, was much more substantial, and included dispatching combat troops to Europe.

Since 1945 the armed forces of Brazil have not been engaged in international combat, even refusing, at times, calls for military assistance. For instance, in the 1950s, Brazil declined to participate in the Korean War, and in September and October 1990, it refused to assist in the military blockade of Iraq following the Iraqi invasion of Kuwait, although Brazil's position was influenced by the fact that a number of Brazilians were being held hostage there. In compliance with UN Security Council Resolution 661, however, Brazil effectively cut off exports to Iraq and Kuwait.

Despite this reluctance, however, Brazil has sent troops on UN and OAS peacekeeping operations. In 1956 troops were dispatched to the Suez Canal at the request of the United Nations, and then to the Belgian Congo in 1960. In 1965, Brazil accepted an invitation from the OAS to send troops to intervene in the Dominican Republic's civil war as part of the Inter-

American Peace Force. In the 1990s, Brazil became even more active in UN multinational peacekeeping efforts, participating in Angola, Cyprus, El Salvador, Mozambique, the former Yugoslavia, and Rwanda. Most recently, Brazil deployed military forces to East Timor (ibid. 2003).

Current and Potential Military Confrontation

Brazil's principal strategic vulnerability is on the Brazil-Colombia border, from leftist narco-insurgents such as the Revolutionary Armed Forces of Colombia (FARC) seeking sanctuary in the vast, largely uncontrolled Amazon region, as well as from cross-border drug trafficking.

Historically, the Brazilian government has been reluctant to incorporate the armed forces into the war against drugs, despite pressure from the United States for the past two decades to militarize its counterdrug efforts. The military has maintained that it is primarily a law enforcement matter, and therefore the responsibility of the federal police. It also fears the massive corruption that typically accompanies counterdrug operations, and an increased U.S. military presence in Brazil.

The role of the military is slowly changing, however, as Brazil is increasingly becoming involved in the Colombia conflict by strengthening its military activities on the Brazil-Colombia border in order to prevent spillover and to curb drug trafficking. Much of Brazil's military effort in the Amazon region involves the newly constructed radar system, built by the U.S-based Raytheon Corporation, called the System for the Vigilance of the Amazon (SIVAM), which monitors communication, air traffic, maritime movement, and border activity of all types. One observer has noted that, while SIVAM was "originally designed to control deforestation," it "has become the focal point of Brazil's military operations, involving more than 20,000 troops that occasionally expel paramilitary guerrillas from inside Brazil's porous borders" (Johnson 2003, 84–85). Furthermore, as the Brazilian government slowly incorporates the armed forces into the drug war for the first time, it is also more willing to share intelligence with other countries.

In addition to the problems on the Brazil-Colombia border, there is also a possibility of internal confrontation with domestic terrorist groups. Although not typically considered "terrorists," the drug gangs of Rio de Janeiro and São Paulo have increasingly turned to violence to protect their interests in the lucrative drug trade, particularly in the favelas. The growing influence of these groups and their ever-expanding ties to international criminal organizations have led to a growing fear of a possible "Colombianization" of Brazil, in which terror, crime, and corruption incapacitate the government and law enforcement.

There is also civil unrest with the increasingly militant Landless Rural Workers Movement (MST), who are calling for land redistribution. Following the election of Luiz Inácio Lula da Silva to the presidency, a victory for the left-wing Worker's Party, there was an escalation of violence by the MST in the Brazilian countryside; thus far, the Brazilian government's efforts to crack down on the movement have been unsuccessful.

Alliance Structure

Brazil is a charter member of the United Nations, and it has been a member of the

UN Security Council four times. Brazil has played a significant role in the consolidation of the Zone of Peace and Cooperation of the South Atlantic, which has been recognized by the international community as a valuable mechanism for the promotion of dialogue and cooperation among the Atlantic coastal countries of West Africa and South America in the pursuit of the common goals of peace, social and economic development, and protection of the environment. Furthermore, Brazil is a member of the Conference on Disarmament (CD), the International Atomic Energy Agency (IAEA), the Missile Technology Control Regime (MTCR), the Nuclear Suppliers Group (NSG), and the Organization for the Prohibition of Chemical Weapons (OPCW).

Traditionally a leader in the inter-American community, Brazil plays an important role in collective security efforts and economic cooperation in the Western Hemisphere. Brazil is a member of the Organization of American States, a group of states that adopted a charter in 1948 with the objective of strengthening peace and security in the region. Brazil is also a party to the Inter-American Treaty of Reciprocal Assistance (the Rio Treaty). In 1995, Brazil—with Argentina, Chile, and the United States—became a guarantor of the Peru-Ecuador peace process, verifying compliance with cease-fire agreements (SIPRI).

Brazil continues to expand economic relations with its neighbors. It is a founding member of the Amazon Pact, the Latin American Integration Association (ALADI), and the economic bloc MERCOSUR, the Common Market of the South. Set up as a customs union in 1995 among Brazil, Argentina, Uruguay, and Paraguay, MERCOSUR is currently one of the most important industrial sectors among the developing countries; it attracts significant investment from around the world. Chile and Bolivia are associate members.

Size and Structure of the Military

The armed forces of Brazil have a total of 287,600 active servicemen and women, including 48,200 conscripts. In addition, Brazil has 1,115,000 trained first-line reserves, and 225,000 second-line. The army (Exército Brasileiro) is by far the largest of Brazil's three branches of armed forces, with 189,000 full-time duty personnel (40,000 conscripts), followed by the air force (Força Aérea Brasileira) with 50,000 (5,000 conscripts). The total number of servicemen and women in the navy (Marinha do Brasil) is 48,600, which includes 1,150 naval aviation, 14,600 marines, and 3,200 conscripts (*Military Balance, 2003–2004*, 181–182). In the event of an emergency, the military can call on the "military police," who are uniformed police officers responsible for maintaining public order and controlled by the individual state governments. The armed forces are unified under the civilian-led Ministry of Defense, which was created in 1999 with the purpose of directing national defense policy and integrating the three military branches.

Brazil remains the only country in Latin America to have an aircraft carrier. Recently Brazil replaced the retiring carrier, the *Minais Gerais*, with the forty-year-old former French carrier *São Paulo*. At 32,000 tons, the *São Paulo* is almost double the size of its predecessor; it carries fifteen Skyhawk fighter aircraft (ibid., 2002–2003, 169). The Brazilian Navy also operates four SSK *Tupi*-class submarines and has plans for a *Tikuna*-class submarine in the near future. In 2002 the Brazilian Army enhanced its capability by creating the 1st Special Forces Brigade, with specialized units including Psychological Operations and Nuclear, Biological, and Chemical detachments, which are in addition to the existing Special Forces battalion and Special Operations Center (ibid., 2003–2004, 178–182). Brazil abandoned its nuclear weapons program in the early 1990s and has bolstered its commitment to nonproliferation.

Brazil has contributed troops to a number of UN peacekeeping missions in the Middle East, the former Belgian Congo, Cyprus, Macedonia, Mozambique, Angola, and East Timor (U.S. Department of State 2003). In 2003, Brazil maintained its military presence in East Timor as part of the UN Mission of Support in East Timor (UNMISET), whose mission is to provide assistance to the administrative structures of the Timorese government, interim law enforcement, and overall security. Furthermore, Brazil continued sending military observers to UN missions in Europe and Latin America. In Europe, military observers were dispatched to Croatia to monitor the demilitarization of the Prevlaka peninsula as a part of the UN Mission of Observers in Prevlaka (UNMOP), and to Cyprus to participate in the UN Force in Chipre (UNFICYP), whose mission is to supervise cease-fire lines, maintain a buffer zone between the Greek Cypriot and Turkish Cypriot communities, and undertake humanitarian activities. In the Americas, military observers support the UN Verification Mission in Guatemala (MINUGUA), to verify compliance with human rights agreements (SIPRI).

The military's role is not limited to defense and peacekeeping efforts, however. The armed forces participate in a number of development and civic-action activities.

The army in particular assists in the construction of roads, bridges, and railroads, and engages in education and health care programs.

Budget

Brazil's defense expenditures have remained at low levels since the 1950s, which can be attributed to the perception that the country has few external threats. In 2002, Brazil spent U.S.$9.7 billion on defense, which is approximately 2.3 percent of its GDP, slightly above the average for Latin America (1.69 percent) (*Military Balance, 2003–2004*, 338). This low level of spending is partly the result of Brazil's heavy debt burden. Following market uncertainty leading up to the election of Lula as president, the fiscal situation stabilized, but the new administration continued to struggle with the debt crisis. Consequently, Lula has tightened the defense budget. For instance, he deferred the much-anticipated F-X BR fighter procurement program until 2004.

Other air force projects have not been affected, such as the U.S.$270 million purchase of twelve EADS CASA C-295 transport aircraft, or the upgrade of seven P-3 maritime patrol aircraft to seven P-3BR standard. However, the navy was forced to halt construction of its *Barroso*-class corvette and *Tikuna*-class diesel-electric submarines, which were seen as a springboard toward development of a nuclear-powered submarine. The army has also been affected by the budget cutbacks, impeding its modernization efforts and forcing it to release 44,000 conscripts (ibid., 310–311).

In 2002, Brazil finally implemented the U.S.$1.4 billion project known as SIVAM. Begun in 1995, the system was designed to monitor a variety of interests in the Amazon region, including illegal incursions into Brazilian territory. In 2002, Brasilia created a separated government agency, the System for the Protection of the Amazon, or SIPAM, to maintain SIVAM and to coordinate information sharing between federal and local governments and other interested parties.

Brazil is a major exporter of military weapons. In the 1980s, Brazil became one of the leading arms exporters among developing countries, supplying to all regions of the world. Brazil's three largest firms, Avibrás Aerospace Industry (Avibrás Indústria Aeroespacial S/A), Engesa (Engenheiros Especializados S/A), and Embraer (Empresa Brasileira da Aeronáutica) were established in the 1960s. However, these companies did not begin to export on a large scale until the late 1970s and early 1980s, as the demand for armaments in the developing world increased. Hundreds of other firms in Brazil began to contribute either directly or indirectly to arms production.

Between 1985 and 1989, Brazil became the world's eleventh largest exporter of arms, selling the majority of its weapons to the Middle East. In the latter half of that decade, Iraq became the overwhelming recipient of Brazilian arms transfers. Consequently, the termination of the Iran-Iraq War in 1988 dealt a harsh blow to the Brazilian arms industry. Coinciding with the end of that war, the global demand for armaments declined, and the Brazilian government under President Collor began to withdraw much state support for the arms industry, leading to the privatization of Embraer, the Brazilian Aeronautics Company. In 1990, two leading major Brazilian manufacturers, Engesa and Avibrás, filed for bankruptcy as a result of those international and domestic developments (Library of Congress 1997).

The Brazilian arms industry has not climbed back to its previous robust form of the 1980s, and much of its arms producing capabilities have dissipated. In fact, no Brazilian companies in 2000 were listed among the hundred largest arms producing companies. Nevertheless, Brazil continues to export a significant amount of military weaponry, ranking thirty-sixth in the period between 1998 and 2002 among all countries and non-state actors in the world with regard to exports of major conventional weapons (SIPRI).

The Brazilian aeronautics industry has been quite successful. Embraer is one of the largest aircraft manufacturers in the world, supplying military aircraft to more than twenty air forces for surveillance, combat, and training. The aeronautics company was Brazil's largest exporter between 1999 and 2001, and the second largest in 2002. In 2002 it employed more than 12,161 people and contributed to the creation of over 3,000 indirect jobs (Embraer).

In addition, Avibrás paid off much of its debt, and it continues to work with the manufacturing of rockets and multiple-launch rocket systems (MLRS), such as the Artillery Saturation Rocket System (Astros II). The company manufactures the SKYFIRE-70, a new generation of high-performance 70-mm (2.75-inch) rocket, and it recently revealed that it is developing a new model of its Astros, called Astros III (Air Force Technology 2004). When Engesa was dismembered following its economic crisis in the early 1990s, its ordinance-related firms were taken over by the state and integrated with Imbel (Indústria de Material Bélico do Brasil), which is a public company tied to the Defense Ministry and the Brazilian Army. Imbel is the oldest war matériel industry of Latin America; it manufactures and supplies military matériel worldwide (Imbel 2004).

Civil-Military Relations/The Role of the Military in Domestic Politics

For much of the twentieth century, the military was very influential in Brazil's political and economic development. From 1945 to 1964, the military intervened in the political process on a number of occasions, and in fact, civilians often called on military support during crises. Moreover, there were military coups in 1945, 1954, and 1964, and coup attempts in 1955 and 1961. Prior to 1964 the military always stepped down after it had replaced the executive leadership with a more suitable civilian leadership—such as in 1954, when the military removed President Getúlio Vargas from office. Although the military was unable to block João Goulart from winning the presidency in 1961, the economic turmoil of his administration, accompanied by the rising influence of radical political elements, paved the way for the coup of March 31, 1964, which drastically changed the role of the military in domestic politics.

For the first time, the military actually assumed political power. Goulart was replaced with General Humberto Castelo Branco, initiating a period of military government that would last until 1985. During that period the military imposed its candidates for president and governors, and an accommodating congress or an electoral college approved them. The Branco presidency lasted until 1967, followed by that of Artur da Costa Silva (1967–1969), Emílio Garrastazú Médici (1969–1974), Ernesto Geisel (1974–1979), and João Baptista de Oliveira Figueiredo (1979–1985).

Figueiredo's inauguration in 1979 marked the beginning of *abertura* (political opening), the process of restoring the political rights that had been revoked. Many of the country's exiles were allowed to return, and the public's demand for redemocratization accelerated. Figueiredo steadily guided the opening process, while balancing the hard-liner and moderate factions within the high ranks of the military. In 1982 the country held direct elections for state governors, the first such elections since 1965, initiating the transition to civilian rule (Arceneaux 2001, 143–182).

After a twenty-one-year period of military rule, in 1985 the armed forces ceded power to a civilian government under the direction of José Sarney. However, the civilian leadership's authority over the armed forces did not significantly expand until after the Sarney period. Sarney's weak political base, the result in part of his nonelectoral route to the presidency, encouraged his dependency on the armed forces and impeded his ability to challenge influential military officers.

Following the first direct presidential election held in twenty-nine years, Fernando Collor de Mello took office in 1990; he began to redefine the role of the military while taking bold steps to expand civilian authority. One of his more significant institutional changes was to replace the military-controlled National Intelligence Service (SNI) with a civilian-led Secretariat of Strategic Affairs (SAE). Collor also cut defense spending, trivialized the military ministers, and reduced the military's influence over various nuclear programs (Hunter 2000, 111–112). However, as Collor's impeachment approached, Itamar Franco began to work more closely with the military officers. Consequently, once he had taken office,

President Franco did little to expand civilian authority over the military. While Collor distanced himself from influential military officers, Franco appointed various retired military officers to positions within his cabinet. Franco's reliance on the military was in part due to the economic and political chaos that marked his administration, and the fact that his presidency did not rest on a popular mandate: he was not directly elected to office.

Fernando Henrique Cardoso (1994–2002) continued this rapprochement, restoring military salaries and facilitating modernization of the armed forces. However, military influence continued to erode. In November 1996, President Cardoso announced the promulgation of the National Defense Policy (Política de Defesa Nacional—PDN). The PDN stressed that civilian leaders are in charge of determining military policy, and that the military should reorient toward external, rather than internal, defense (Hunter 2000, 114–115). The PDN was a key step in the creation of a civilian-led Ministry of Defense, a project that was completed in 1999. These and other institutional changes dramatically reduced the influence of the military on government decision-making during the Cardoso presidency.

The military remains under civilian control, both in law and practice. It is important to note, however, that while the Brazilian military is far less influential now than in the initial transition to civilian rule, it continues to exercise influence over issues beyond simply defense and security—issues such as land policy and indigenous rights (ibid., 38–39). However, the military is not attempting to regain political power, but rather is focusing more on budget issues and adapting to the new security environment. Common markets, nuclear weapons agreements, and the end of the Cold War drastically affected the military's perception of its role. Moreover, given the lack of a potential conflict with countries such as Argentina, or with domestic subversive groups, many outsiders see the Brazilian military as increasingly irrelevant. The military has responded by successfully redefining its mission, and it has turned its attention to the Amazon region to prevent spillover of the Colombian conflict and to combat international crime; it also continues to participate in various peacekeeping roles in the Western Hemisphere and overseas.

Terrorism

Narco-terrorism has become an increasing concern for Brasilia because of Brazil's close proximity with Colombia and the rising violence by domestic drug trafficking organizations. However, in light of the U.S.-led "War on Terrorism," the international community has given greater attention to the unruly tri-border area and the activities of Islamic extremist organizations.

The tri-border area emerged as an important commercial region in the early 1970s, when Brazil and Paraguay were seeking to exploit the energy-generating potential of Igauçu Falls and to attract tourism. The countries established a free-trade zone in Paraguay's Ciudad del Este, which is separated from Brazil's Foz do Igauçu by the Paraná River. Since then the area has become a center for lawlessness and organized crime. The principal criminal activities in the region are money-laundering, arms and drug trafficking, and software piracy. Moreover, the tri-border area is home to one of the largest Arab communities in Latin America, with the overwhelming majority being of Lebanese descent. These communities remain tightly knit, providing an ideal environment for terrorist organizations in which to raise funds, recruit, and plan attacks within a web of ethnic and religious sympathizers.

A number of terrorist organizations allegedly operate in the tri-border area, including Egypt's al-Gama'a al-Islamiyya (Islamic group) and al-Jihad (Islamic Jihad), al-Qaeda, Hamas, Hezbollah, and al-Muqawamah (the Resistance), a pro-Iran wing of Hezbollah. Hezbollah is alleged to have the most significant presence, deriving a substantial amount of income from illicit activities (such as drug trafficking) in the tri-border area and using local businesses and financial institutions for the purpose of money-laundering.

Furthermore, there have been reports of direct Iranian government support of Hezbollah activities in the region, such as the bombings of the Israeli embassy in Buenos Aires on March 17, 1992, and a Jewish Community Center, the Argentine-Israeli Mutual Association (AMIA), in Buenos Aires on July 18, 1994. News media reports of the arrests of a few individuals with connections to al-Qaeda, and reported identification of al-Qaeda members by Argentine intelligence, suggest an al-Qaeda presence in the region. Al-Qaeda's alleged activities include the trafficking of arms, drugs, and uranium, as well as money-laundering (Library of Congress 2003, 1–2).

In late 2001 various intelligence and law enforcement agencies began to monitor the tri-border area closely, leading to an exodus of Arabs. Reportedly, thousands of Arab members of the Islamic community have fled to other Arab population centers in Latin America.

Relationship with the United States

The United States was the first country to recognize Brazil's independence, in 1822, and the two countries have traditionally enjoyed friendly, active relations encompassing a broad political and economic agenda. Brazil supported the Allies in World War II, fighting alongside the United States in Western Europe, and U.S.-Brazil relations remained close in the postwar period. In 1952 the United States became the provider of most of Brazil's major weapons and military training, as a result of the signing of the Military Assistance Agreement.

However, the tenor of U.S.-Brazilian security relations has not always been steady. Relations deteriorated in the late 1960s and 1970s as Brazil became increasingly assertive and nationalistic in its foreign policy. In 1975, Brazil became the first Latin American country (with the exception of Cuba) to recognize the

---

Sidebar 2   Tri-Border Money-Laundering

The notorious tri-border area (where Brazil, Paraguay, and Argentina meet) is a center for the money-laundering activities of organized crime groups—particularly in the Brazilian city of Foz do Iguaçu and the Paraguayan city of Ciudad del Este. Although the amount of money laundered each year is impossible to determine, it is estimated to be in the billions.

Source
The Library of Congress. 2003. *Terrorist and Organized Crime Groups in the Tri-Border Area (TBA) of South America.* Washington, DC: Federal Research Division, Library of Congress.

communist-backed insurgents in the Angolan civil war, and Brazil voted in the United Nations to equate Zionism with racism, reflecting its increasing reliance on Arab oil imports. The United States also feared Brazil's rising nuclear program, increasing Brazilian-German nuclear cooperation, as well as Brazil's potential to facilitate an arms race in the Third World. In addition, there was mounting concern in Washington over human rights issues and Brazil's increasing trade deficit with the United States. These concerns prompted the Carter administration to restrict U.S. arms trade to Brazil and to pressure the Brazilian government to end its nuclear weapons program and defend human rights. In 1977, Brazil responded by renouncing the U.S.-Brazilian bilateral military accord of 1952 (Buckman 2001, 58).

Relations began to normalize in the 1980s as the United States and Brazil sought to improve security ties, reflecting changes in both countries and in the international system. In Brazil, President João Figueiredo (1979–1985) continued the process of political liberalization, eventually leading to the transfer of power to a civilian-led government in 1985. During the Reagan administration the United States became more pragmatic in the security relationship, moving away from President Carter's human rights policies. As military relations between the two countries strengthened, the United States and Brazil signed a memorandum of understanding on industrial-military cooperation, on August 31, 1983. Nevertheless, a number of tensions remained in the 1980s, including disagreement over Brazil's nuclear weapons program and the steadily increasing drug trade.

U.S.-Brazilian relations strengthened again in the 1990s as the countries developed a mutual trust, particularly in the area of nonproliferation. This trust grew out of Brazilian accession to the various multilateral control regimes, such as the Missile Technology Control Regime, the Nuclear Suppliers Group, the Conventions on Chemical and Biological Weapons, the Nuclear Nonproliferation Treaty, the Comprehensive Test Ban Treaty, and the Safeguards Agreement between Brazil, Argentina, the International Atomic Energy Agency, and the Brazilian-Argentine Agency for the Control and Accounting of Fissile Materials. Furthermore, President Cardoso had several meetings with President Clinton, and he met with President George W. Bush soon after his inauguration. In 2002, Brazil benefited from Washington's appropriation of $782 million to combat emerging terrorist and related threats in the Andean region and also to improve economic conditions (*Military Balance, 2003–2004,* 176).

Deepening U.S.-Brazil cooperation was carried over into Lula's administration as well. In December 2002, President Bush invited then president-elect Lula to Washington for a meeting. Lula again visited Washington for a summit on June 20, 2003, and there were numerous other high-level contacts between the two countries during that period. The major topics of discussion and cooperation included trade and finance, hemispheric economic integration, and the Free Trade Area of the Americas (FTAA). In fact, at one time opposed to the FTAA, Lula and the PT have moderated their stance as market liberalization and economic stabilization significantly enhanced Brazil's growth prospects. Other issues have in-

Table 2   The Drug Trade in Brazil

Main threat	Conduit for South American (Colombian, Bolivian, and Peruvian) cocaine and heroin
Cocaine seizures	9415.200 kg (2002)
Illicit cultivation	Cannabis grown primarily for domestic consumption; minor coca cultivation in the Amazon region
Financial activity	Significant money-laundering through the financial system and in the tri-border area
Government programs	Large-scale eradication program to control cannabis; inter-agency Colombia border-security program (COBRA); several anti-corruption operations; monitoring system of the Amazon (SIVAM)

Sources

Central Intelligence Agency Website. 2005. CIA *World Factbook.* http://www.cia.gov/cia/publications/factbook/ (accessed May 15, 2005).

United Nations Office on Drugs and Crime. 2004. "World Drug Report 2004."

U.S. Department of State. 2003. *International Narcotics Control Strategy Report.* http://www.state.gov/g/inl/rls/nrcrpt/.

cluded nonproliferation and arms control, human rights, and environmental issues (U.S. Department of State 2003).

Counterterrorism and counternarcotics also remain at the top of the agenda. The United States and Brazil have increased cooperation in developing antiterrorist initiatives, such as with the signing of the Inter-American Convention against Terrorism in July 2003. Signed by thirty-three OAS member states, the convention is aimed at sharing information and carrying out joint training (*Military Balance, 2003–2004*, 176). Brazil continues to express interest in active cooperation, particularly intelligence sharing and coordination with the United States in counternarcotics activities. Bilateral agreements form the basis for drug control cooperation between the United States and Brazil. Bilateral programs that took place in 2002 included cooperation with the Regional Intelligence Center of Operation Cobra, the International Drug Enforcement Conference (IDEC), Operation Alianza 8 and 9, and Operation Seis Fron-

teiras IV. In addition, Brazil and the United States are parties to a bilateral extradition treaty, signed in 1961 (U.S. Department of State 2002).

The Future

South America's largest, most populous country and leading economic power consolidated its democracy over the last two decades. Calming many skeptics who doubted his ability to move Brazil forward, Lula, the leader of the leftist Worker's Party, has taken a pragmatic and moderate approach to his presidency. The civilian leadership has effectively eroded the authority of the once-influential military, which now seems content with its role of defending Brazil from external threats. However, Brasilia will continue to struggle with pressing societal issues, including high poverty rates, massive income equality, rising illicit drug consumption, and land redistribution, which have the potential to generate internal conflict that might lead some to call for an increased military presence in domestic affairs.

Brazil's major security issues are in the Amazon region, and the country continues to focus on preventing spillover from Colombia's civil war and curbing narcotics trafficking. In doing so, Brazil continues to expand Operation Cobra toward other border areas as well, including Suriname and Guyana in the north, and Argentina and Paraguay in the south. This expansion will significantly improve Brazil's ability to combat drug trafficking and production, and it will facilitate cooperation and unified counterdrug strategies with its neighbors and the United States. The multifaceted SIVAM project is also being heralded as an opportunity for cooperation and trust, with the potential to reduce criminal trafficking and prevent illegal cross-border migration of insurgents. Brazil is also demonstrating a strong willingness to share intelligence and fund counternarcotics programs, thereby playing an increasing role in unified hemispheric security efforts.

The United States now has less influence in its relationship with Brazil than it did in the post–World War II period. Given Brazil's large economy and industrial base, as well as its population of 182 million people, Brasilia can exert leverage in South America, although the United States continues to dominate U.S.-Brazil relations. There has, however, been increased cooperation between the two countries in a number of security-related areas. Indeed, Brazil is slowly coming to grips with its problem of narco-terrorism and understands that further cooperation with the United States is necessary to suppress the growing power of criminal organizations operating within its borders.

References, Recommended Readings, and Websites

Books

Arceneaux, Craig L. 2001. *Bounded Missions: Military Regimes and Democratization in the Southern Cone and Brazil.* University Park: Pennsylvania State University Press.

Bacchus, Wilfred A. 1990. *Mission in Mufti: Brazil's Military Regimes, 1964–1985.* New York: Greenwood Press.

Buckman, Robert T. 2001. *Latin America.* 35th ed. Harpers Ferry, WV: Stryker-Post Publications.

Conca, Ken. 1997. *Manufacturing Insecurity: The Rise and Fall of Brazil's Military-Industrial Complex.* Boulder, CO: Lynne Rienner.

Davis, Sonny B. 1996. *Brotherhood of Arms: Brazil–United States Military Relations, 1945–1977.* Boulder, CO: University Press of Colorado.

Hunter, Wendy. 1997. *Eroding Military Influence in Brazil: Politicians against Soldiers.* Chapel Hill, NC: University of North Carolina Press.

———. 2000. "Assessing Civil-Military Relations in Post-Authoritarian Brazil." In *Democratic Brazil: Actors, Institutions, and Processes*, Peter R. Kingstone and Timothy J. Power, eds. Pittsburgh: University of Pittsburgh Press.

Library of Congress. 2003. *Terrorist and Organized Crime Groups in the Tri-Border Area (TBA) of South America.* Washington, DC: Federal Research Division, Library of Congress.

The Military Balance, 2002–2003. London: International Institute for Strategic Studies.

The Military Balance, 2003–2004. London: International Institute for Strategic Studies.

Rabasa, Angel, and Peter Chalk. *Colombian Labyrinth: The Synergy of Drugs and Insurgency and Its Implications for Regional Stability.* Santa Monica, CA: RAND, 2001.

SIPRI Yearbook 2003. New York: Humanities Press.

Skidmore, Thomas E. 1988. *The Politics of Military Rule in Brazil, 1964–85.* New York: Oxford University Press.

Smallman, Shawn C. 2002. *Fear & Memory in the Brazilian Army &*

Society, 1889–1954. Chapel Hill: University of North Carolina Press.

Stepan, Alfred C. 1990. *Military in Politics: Changing Patterns in Brazil.* Princeton: Princeton University Press.

Articles/Newspapers

Filho, João R., and Daniel Zirker. 2000. "Nationalism, National Security, and Amazônia: Military Perceptions and Attitudes in Contemporary Brazil." *Armed Forces & Society* 27, no. 1:105–129.

Johnson, Elizabeth. May 2003. "The Taming of the Amazon." *Foreign Policy* 136:84–85.

Rohter, Larry. 2003. "Rio's Drug Wars Begin to Take Toll on Tourism." *New York Times*, April 27, Section 5:3.

Websites

Air Force Technology: http://www.airforce-technology.com.

Brazilian Air Force: http://www.aer.mil.br.

Brazilian Army: http://www.exercito.gov.br.

Brazilian Department of the Federal Police (Departamento de Polícia Federal): http://www.dpf.gov.br/.

Brazilian Embassy in Washington, D.C.: http://www.brasilemb.org/.

Brazilian Ministry of Defense: http://www.defesa.gov.br.

Brazilian National Antidrug Secretariat (Secretaria Nacional Anti-Drogas): http://www.senad.gov.br/.

Brazilian Navy: http://www.mar.mil.br/.

Central Intelligence Agency. *The World Factbook:* http://www.cia.gov.

Defesanet (Defense Electronic Publication in Brazil): http://www.defesanet.com.br.

Embraer: http://www.embraer.com.

Imbel (Indústria de Material Bélico do Brasil): http://www.imbel.gov.br.

Library of Congress. 1997. *Brazil—A Country Study.* Washington, DC: Federal Research Division, Library of Congress: http://www.loc.gov.

Segurança e Defesa (Security and Defense Magazine): http://www.segurancaedefesa.com/.

Stockholm International Peace Research Institute (SIPRI): http://www.sipri.se.

UN Office on Drugs and Crime. *World Drug Report 2004:* http://www.unodc.org/unodc/world_drug_report.html.

U.S. Department of State. 2003. *Country Background Notes: Brazil:* http://www.state.gov/r/pa/ei/bgn/1972.htm.

U.S. Department of State. 2002. *International Narcotics Control Strategy Report:* http://www.state.gov/g/inl/rls/nrcrpt/.

Canada

Balkan Devlen

History and Geography

Canada is the second largest country in the world after Russia; it is almost as big as the continent of Europe. Canada covers more than 3.8 million square miles (approximately 9.2 million square kilometers), almost 7 percent of the world's land mass. Bordered by three oceans—the Pacific, Arctic, and Atlantic—it has a total coastline of 146,000 miles (243,791 kilometers). It shares the world's longest international boundary (5,335 miles or 8,893 kilometers) with the United States to its south and northwest.

Canada has a population of roughly 32 million, and about 90 percent of it is concentrated within 100 miles of the U.S. border. Canada is an ethnically diverse country. Roughly a quarter of the population has French origins, mostly concentrated in the province of Quebec, and another quarter has British origins. The rest of the population has either mixed or other origins, mainly European, Asian, and African. Indigenous peoples (Amerindians) constitute roughly 2 percent of the total population. Canada has two official languages: English, which about 60 percent of the population speaks, and French, which 23 percent of the population speaks.

The first people entered what is now Canada around 10,000 B.C.E., having traveled over the Bering Strait. Around the year 1000, Leif Ericsson briefly established a colony in Vinland, the Viking colony of L'Anse aux Meadows in Newfoundland, Canada. Later, in 1534, the French led by Jacques Cartier began to explore inland and set up colonies. Under Samuel de Champlain the first settlement was made in 1608, which would later grow to be Quebec City.

During the Seven Years War, the British gained control of Quebec City after the Battle of the Plains of Abraham in 1759; they took Montreal in 1760. With the Treaty of Paris in 1763, France ceded almost all of its Canadian territory to the British. After the American War of Independence, several thousand Loyalists—people who remained loyal to Britain—escaped to Canada. During the War of 1812, the United States made unsuccessful attempts to invade Ontario. That war, which lasted until 1814, was essentially a stalemate. Two rebellions, in 1837 and 1838, followed the War of 1812 but were easily suppressed by the British.

Canada became independent from the United Kingdom with the British North America Act of 1867. The Constitution Act of 1982 is the current legal framework for Canada. Canada is a confederation with parliamentary (bicameral) democracy, and the chief of state is Queen Elizabeth II, represented by the governor-general. The House of Commons has 301 members, Ontario and Quebec having the largest num-

Table 1   Canada: Key Statistics

Type of government	Confederation with parliamentary democracy
Population	32,805,041 (July 2005 estimate)
Religion	Roman Catholic (46%), Protestant (36%), Other (18%)
Languages	English 59.3% (official), French 23.2% (official), and other 17.5%
Main industries	Transportation equipment, chemicals, processed and unprocessed minerals, food products, wood and paper products, fish products, petroleum, and natural gas
Gross domestic product (GDP)	CAD$1.228 trillion (2003)
Main security threats	Proliferation of WMD; international terrorism; environmental and humanitarian crises around the globe
Defense spending (% GDP)	1.2 (2003)
Size of military (thousands)	52 (2003)
Number of civil wars since 1945	none
Number of interstate wars since 1945	2

Wars are based on the number of wars where Canadian Forces have served in combat abroad. The two are the Korean War and the first Gulf War in 1991. Peacekeeping operations are not included.

Sources
Central Intelligence Agency Website. 2005. "CIA World Factbook."
    http://www.cia.gov/cia/publications/factbook/geos/ca.html (accessed May 15, 2005).
International Institute for Strategic Studies (IISS). 2003. *The Military Balance 2003–2004.*
    London: IISS and Oxford University Press.

ber of representatives—103 and 75, respectively. Canada is divided into ten provinces and three territories. The provinces are Alberta, British Columbia, Manitoba, New Brunswick, Newfoundland and Labrador, Nova Scotia, Ontario, Prince Edward Island, Quebec, and Saskatchewan. The territories are the Northwest Territories, Nunavut, and the Yukon. The provinces have a reasonably large amount of autonomy from the federal government, while the territories have somewhat less. Each of the provinces and territories have their own unicameral legislatures.

Canada is one of the wealthiest countries in the world, with GDP of almost $1 trillion (PPP) (purchasing power parity) and $29,300 GDP per capita (PPP) (CIA *World Factbook* 2004). Vast amounts of natural resources, a highly educated skilled labor force, and a high-tech industrial complex ensure Canada's economic prospects for the future. Manufacturing, mining, and service sectors drive economic growth, and Canada enjoys a substantial trade surplus. Canada is also a member of the 1994 North American Free Trade Agreement (NAFTA) and has various bilateral free trade agreements with other countries around the globe.

Finally, Canada is a founding member of the North Atlantic Treaty Organization (NATO) and has extensive and deep bilateral defense and security relations with the United States, mainly through NORAD. Canadian Forces have some 52,300 active personnel, and defense spending is around 1.2 percent of the

GDP, one of the lowest among NATO members.

Regional Geopolitics

Canada shares the longest demilitarized border in the world, with the United States. Bordering three oceans—the Atlantic, Pacific, and Arctic—Canada has a coastline of more than 240,000 kilometers that keeps it away from the major flashpoints in the world. During the Cold War era, however, the potential of a thermonuclear war between the United States and the USSR made Canada a target. However, since the end of the Cold War, the possibility of such a nuclear attack seems distant. In short, it is plausible to argue that Canada is located in one of the safest regions of the world.

Despite that fact, there are geopolitical issues that can threaten Canada's national interests. Such threats can be divided into three broad categories: Arctic security and environmental concerns, fishing rights, and border security.

Arctic security, especially surveillance of the Northwest Passage, is important for Canadian sovereignty claims on the Arctic regions. The heart of the issue is who controls international shipping through the Northwest Passage (Huebert 2003). Increasing concerns over global warming and its effects on the Arctic, together with environmental concerns, constitute a long-term, serious problem for Canadian national interests. The Department of National Defence 1994 Defence Policy White Paper (available at the Department of National Defence Website, hereafter DND), which is currently the basic reference document for Canadian defense and security policy, places environmental surveillance within national security priorities.

According to the 1994 Defence Policy White Paper, the protection of fisheries is important in securing Canadian economic interests in the oceans. Both the air force and navy patrol the Canadian continental shelf in order to prevent predatory foreign fishing activities, and they are ready to engage in protective actions to prevent abuses within the 200-mile exclusive fishing zone.

After the events of September 11, 2001, the status of the demilitarized border between the United States and Canada, which runs for more than 6,500 kilometers, became an issue of concern. Apart from cross-border illegal activities such as drug trafficking, the possibility of terrorist infiltration into the United States from Canada raises doubts on the security of the border. Although as of yet there has been no such infiltration, U.S. officials express concerns over Canadian immigration procedures and argue that liberal policies could provide a backdoor for terrorists to the United States through Canada (DND 2004).

Conflict Past and Present

Conflict History

Beginning with the establishment of the first colony by Samuel de Champlain in New France in 1608 and continuing until the eighteenth century, wars in Canada were mainly between indigenous tribes and French settlers, with the exception of minor skirmishes with the British. Nevertheless, three times during the eighteenth century, the French and English North American colonies found themselves at war with one another in local offshoots of larger European conflicts—the War of the Spanish Succession (1702–1713), the War of the Austrian Succession (1744–1748), and the Seven Years War (1756–1763).

When the British defeated the French in the Battle of the Plains of Abraham in 1759, French control in North America ended. At the end of the Seven Years War, the entire area of New France was given to the British.

During the American War of Independence (1776–1783), the United States attempted to take Quebec and some posts in the Maritimes but was repelled by superior British power. In 1812 the United States declared war on Britain and attacked Upper Canada. The war raged on for two years along the border of Upper Canada and in the Great Lakes. In December of 1814, the opponents signed a peace treaty. The borders that had existed before the war remained as they were. Tensions escalated once more during the U.S. Civil War (1861–1865); the Trent crisis of 1861–1862, in which war was averted, was the last Anglo-American military confrontation in North America.

Since the British North America Act of 1867 no war has been fought on Canadian soil, despite the fact that Canada did participate in world wars, the Korean War, and various military operations under the banner of NATO and the United Nations. The only exception was the Northwest Rebellion of 1885, which was suppressed by the militia (Wise 2001, 23). Canadians also took part in the Boer War of 1899–1902 between the British Empire and the Boers in South Africa, as a part of the British Empire.

Soon after World War I broke out, Canada sent the first contingent to England, and Canadian troops had their first battle in the Second Battle of Ypres in 1915. Canada had four divisions in Europe during World War I and lost more than 60,000 soldiers on the battlefields. Canadian troops contributed significantly in the battles of Mount Sorrel, Somme, Vimy Ridge, Passchendaele Ridge, Cambrai, Amiens, and Mons (Veteran Affairs Canada 2004). In 1918 more than 630,000 men were enlisted to fight in World War I, and almost 100,000 troops were fighting in Europe (Morton 2001). Apart from human costs, the participation in World War I resulted in an increase in gross national debt from $544 million in 1914 to almost $2.5 billion in 1919 (ibid.).

World War I had two major effects on Canadian society. It was the first time that Canadians paid such a great cost in both material and human terms. This strengthened the international prestige of Canada and contributed to the growth of independent nationhood within the British Commonwealth. Second, the conscription crisis of 1917—in which Quebec, almost unanimously, was opposed to the idea—left deep traces in the psyche of Canadian society (Wise 2001).

When World War II broke out in September 1939, Canada once again stood by the United Kingdom, declaring war on Germany on September 15, 1939. More than a million Canadians served during World War II on a variety of fronts, including the Battle of Britain, the Battle of the Atlantic, the defense of Hong Kong, the raid on Dieppe, the conquest of Sicily, in Normandy, and in the Pacific (Veteran Affairs Canada 2004). Over 45,000 Canadians lost their lives during those battles. Canada again faced a conscription crisis during World War II, and in a national plebiscite, all provinces except Quebec voted in favor of conscription. The conscripts were sent overseas with the 1944 Normandy landings. After the end of the war, Canada emerged as one of the strongest military and economic powers in the world, at least for some time (Morton 2001).

Canadian troops went overseas to fight once again with the Korean War in 1950. Some 26,791 troops served in that war, the largest contribution as a percentage of the population after the United States; Canada lost 1,558 soldiers. Canada also took part in the 1991 Gulf War. The country sent two destroyers, a supply ship, and a CF-18 squadron to the region. When the air war began, Canada's planes were integrated into the coalition force, providing air cover and attacking ground targets. It was the first time since the Korean War that Canadian forces had participated in combat operations. Canada did not suffer any casualties in the Gulf War (DND 2004).

Canada took part in almost every UN peacekeeping operation after 1947; of NATO operations, the total is currently seventy-two, excluding currently active operations around the world (ibid.). The details of Canadian involvement in peacekeeping operations and NATO will be discussed below.

Current and Potential Military Confrontation

With the end of the Cold War, there seemed to be no imminent threat to Canadian security. However, the absence of a major nuclear war between the United States and the Soviets did not make the twenty-first century any more benign than the previous one (Delvoie 2002). There are several conventional and unconventional external security threats for Canada, as well as an important internal problem that could pose a threat in the future—namely, the Quebec issue.

According to Strategic Assessment 2003 (DND 2004), the external threats to Canadian security can be divided into three broad categories: international terrorism, proliferation of nuclear weapons, and the post-Saddam Middle East. The terrorism issue will be discussed separately below.

The proliferation of weapons of mass destruction (WMD) represents two major challenges for Canada (Delvoie 2002; Ross 1996). First is the possibility of a WMD attack against North America by terrorist groups or rogue states. Given the unstable political situation in most of the former Soviet republics and in southern Asia, it is possible that some terrorist groups could acquire nuclear materials or various biological and chemical agents in order to build a WMD. In addition, several states around the world are known to pursue nuclear weapons programs, such as North Korea, Iran, and Libya. As Delvoie (2002) and Harvey (2000) argue, there is no reason to think that Toronto or Montreal will be spared in a nuclear attack by one of those so-called rogue states against North America.

Second, such weapons development represents a challenge to the principles of the nonproliferation agreements, of which Canada perceives itself the most prominent advocate (DND 2004; Harvey 2000; Axworthy 1997). Thus the proliferation of WMDs is also seen as a serious blow to Canadian-led nonproliferation initiatives and Canadian prestige in the international arena (DND 2004).

The future of post-Saddam Iraq and the Middle East is not clear yet. This unpredictability has serious consequences for Canadian security. The most important ones are the possibility of disruption of oil supplies from the Middle East in the case of a regional war, widening of the gap between the United States and its

European allies over U.S. policies in the Middle East, and early withdrawal of the United States from Iraq because of increasing casualties, leaving Iraq and the Middle East in turmoil (ibid.).

Although not spelled out in Department of National Defence documents, the issue of Quebec represents a potential internal security challenge to Canada. The Quebec province, a majority of whose residents speak French, was one of the four founding provinces of Canada. In 1774, the British Parliament passed the Quebec Act, which allowed Quebec to maintain the French Civil Code as its judicial system and sanctioned the freedom of religious choice, allowing the Roman Catholic Church to remain. However, the tensions remained, and the 1960s witnessed the Quiet Revolution in Quebec. The Quiet Revolution was a period of social and political change that saw the decline of the Roman Catholic Church's influence and the emergence of a separatist movement (See 2001).

During the 1960s a terrorist group known as the Front de libération du Québec (FLQ) launched a series of bombings, robberies, and attacks on government offices. Their activities reached a peak during the October Crisis of 1970, when James Cross, the British trade commissioner to Canada, was kidnapped along with Pierre Laporte, a provincial minister and vice premier who was murdered a few days later. The FLQ was crushed after that incident. However, the separatist movement continued to increase its influence, but using nonviolent methods.

Two referendums for Quebec independence, in 1980 and 1995, took place. In the 1995 referendum vote, Quebec independence was defeated by a very slim margin (less than 1 percent). Quebec still did not ratify the Constitution Act of 1982. The specter of an independent Quebec represents a serious problem for the future of Canada, as that could lead to disintegration of the federation. Such a movement, in the event of an independent Quebec, could come from western provinces such as Alberta; the Quebec issue is the single most important domestic security challenge to Canada (See 2001).

Alliance Structure

Canada has always relied on alliances to protect itself and defend its national interests (Keating 2002; Murray 1994). Canadian defense policy rests on two major pillars: a close bilateral relation with the United States, and active involvement in multilateral security institutions, primarily in NATO. This section will focus on Canadian involvement in NATO.

Canada is one of the founding members of NATO, and for most of the Cold War saw NATO as the primary mechanism for collective security of the West (Keating 2002; Murray 1994). However, according to Keating (2002), there is more in NATO for Canada. He argued that a multilateral alliance among Western powers not only reduces the cost of Canadian defense but also prevents isolation of Canada within a bilateral defense pact.

However, soon after NATO was established, the United States virtually dominated the alliance, and thus Canadian aspirations about keeping the United States in check by using a multilateral setting failed (ibid.). Nevertheless, NATO continued to play a central role in Canadian defense policy. As Haglund (1997, 466) points out, in the early years of NATO

Canada was one of the most important contributors to Western European defense, which included a well-equipped brigade and an air division with a total of 240 aircraft. In short, during the 1950s and early 1960s, Canada was a producer of security in Europe.

However, as Western Europe recovered and reached a state in which it could protect itself, the Canadian contribution began to diminish. Haglund (1997, 468–471) offers three reasons for the apparent disengagement of Canada from the "central front." First, it became too expensive for Canada to sustain high levels of military readiness for European defense, especially when it has responsibilities in the air defense of North America. Second, for Canada, NATO should be something more than just another military alliance. However, that vision of Canada was not shared by the rest of the members, which created disillusionment on the part of Canadian policymakers about NATO. Nevertheless, Canada continued to view NATO as a forum for political influence within the West. Third, Canadians believe that as Western Europeans recover from war they could and should be more responsible for their own defense.

This disengagement reached its peak when Canada decided, unilaterally, to withdraw its troops from Europe in 1992 (ibid., 471). Despite a decreasing commitment to European defense, Canada stayed in NATO and contributed substantially to its peacekeeping and peacemaking operations after the Cold War. Why? Keating (2002, 161) argues that the main reason for continued, albeit diminished, Canadian involvement since the late 1960s was the desire to "keep a seat at the table." It was the desire to contribute to East-West dialogue during Détente, establishing a footing in the transformative structures of the post-Détente era, and finally, having a voice in post–Cold War security architecture in Europe.

Canada can influence the events in the international arena through its political capabilities, which are based on its involvement in multilateral security institutions, primarily NATO, rather than through the display of military prowess (ibid.). Furthermore, by contributing substantially to peacekeeping and peacemaking operations after the Cold War, Canada has ensured its image as a Middle Power and furthered its advocacy of cooperative security in the international arena.

Canada has contributed to almost every peacekeeping and peacemaking operation under the auspices of the United Nations or NATO since the end of the Cold War

Table 2   Canada and Peace Operations

Number of troops deployed overseas	3,800 (July 2004)
As a percentage of total strength	6.5% (July 2004), the second highest within NATO
Ranking in contribution to UN operations	19th out of 83 countries (June 2004)
Number of past peace operations	72 (since 1947)
Current operations	17
Number of deaths on peace operations	122 (August 2003), the highest rate in the world

Sources
Ross, Cameron. 2004. "Future Defence and Security Challenges: A Canadian Perspective." *Journal of Military and Strategic Studies* (spring).
http://www.forces.gc.ca/site/operations/current_ops_e.asp.

(DND 2004). Canada contributed to the Implementation Force (IFOR) and later to the Stabilization Force (SFOR) in Bosnia after 1995, to monitor the implementation of the 1995 Dayton Agreement. In addition, Canada took part in the 1999 Kosovo War as a member of NATO and contributed to the Kosovo Force (KFOR), which was established afterward.

According to the Department of National Defence, Canadian Forces were, as of February 18, 2004, involved in thirteen international operations; the total number of troops in those operations was 3,931 (ibid.). The most significant of those operations were the NATO-led ISAF in Afghanistan, which has 2,243 Canadian troops, and SFOR in Bosnia, with 1,192 troops (that latter contingent is made up of a mechanized infantry battalion group, a National Support Element, a National Command Element, a detachment of Griffon helicopters, an engineer design and works team, and military police) (ibid.).

Apart from peacekeeping and peacemaking operations, Canada also has an initiative called NATO Flying Training in Canada (NFTC), aimed at providing NATO nations with military pilot training, and a Military Training Assistance Program (MTAP), which is the main Canadian contribution to the Partnership for Peace (PfP) (ibid.).

According to the Department of National Defence, Canada's current commitments to collective defense under NATO are as follows: in peacetime, the Canadian Forces (CF) assign a ship to NATO's Standing Naval Force Atlantic, contribute personnel to the NATO Airborne Early Warning System and various NATO headquarters, and participate in NATO tactical, operational, and strategic-level military exercises on an ongoing basis (ibid.).

In the event of a crisis that threatens the security of a NATO nation, Canada provides an infantry battalion group for NATO's Immediate Reaction Force, a naval task group consisting of up to four combatants (that is, warships and submarines), and a support ship, a brigade group, and a wing of fighter aircraft and a squadron of tactical transport aircraft (ibid.). Furthermore, Canada would mobilize additional national resources in order to fulfill Canada's commitment to NATO under Article 5, if and when necessary.

In short, it can be argued that despite the end of the Cold War and decreasing Canadian involvement in collective defense, NATO remains the main venue for Canadian participation and contribution to international peace and stability, especially through peace support missions.

Size and Structure of the Military
Size and Structure
Canada has had a unified armed force since 1968, the only example of one within NATO (Murray 1994, 84). Canadian Forces have a total strength of 52,300 active personnel, of which the army (land forces) has 19,300, the navy (maritime command) 9,000, and the air force (air command) 13,500; some 10,500 are not identified by service. The number of paramilitary troops is 9,350, which includes the Canadian Coast Guard and the Department of Fisheries and Oceans. The total number of reserves is 36,900 (Military Balance 2004, 36–37).

Formally speaking, the governor-general—as the representative of the queen—is the commander-in-chief of the Canadian Forces. However, in practice, the Canadian defense establishment is headed by the minister of National Defence (MoND), who is accountable and responsible to the Parliament (DND 2004). Unlike the United States, Canada has a single defense staff, including both civilian and military personnel; the organization of the defense establishment is simple when compared with that of the United States (Murray 1994, 79).

The daily management of the National Defence Department (DND) is jointly handled by the deputy minister of National Defence (DMoND), who is a civilian, and the chief of the Defence Staff (CDS), who is the highest-ranking military man—a four-star general—in the defense organization (DND 2004). DMoND is generally responsible for the bureaucratic sphere within the department, while CDS is responsible for the operational command and control of the Canadian Forces (Murray 1994, 78). DMoND and CDS are assisted by the vice chief of the Defence Staff and the deputy chief of the Defence Staff in the management of National Defence Headquarters (NDHQ) (ibid.).

The number of assistant deputy ministers (ADM) is eight, and they are on an equal organizational level with the deputy chief of the Defence Staff. Their responsibility areas are finance and corporate services, infrastructure and environment, information management, matériel, policy, human resources, science and technology, and the Office of Critical Infrastructure Protection and Emergency Preparedness (DND 2004). The commanders of major operational commands—that is, army, navy, air force, and reserves—report to the deputy chief of the Defence Staff. There are several committees and councils within the NDHQ that develop and coordinate defense policy and programs, including the Defence Council, the Defence

Management Committee, the Armed Forces Council, and the Program Control Board (Murray 1994, 78).

Apart from annual defense planning reports, strategy assessments, and military assessments, two basic documents form the basis of current defense policy, the 1994 Defence Policy White Paper, which is the guiding document to date, and Strategy 2020, which sets forth long- and short-term objectives for the next two decades (DND 2004).

According to the DND, the fundamental goals of the Canadian Forces (CF) are defending Canada by protecting Canadian territory, airspace, and maritime areas of jurisdiction, and helping civil authorities during national emergencies (ibid.). The CF contribute to the defense of North America by protecting the Canadian approaches to the continent together with the United States, and by promoting Arctic security (ibid.). The CF also contribute to international security by participating in multilateral operations through international organizations such as the United Nations and NATO, supporting humanitarian relief efforts and helping to restore conflict-devastated areas, and participating in confidence-building measures such as arms-control programs (ibid.).

Maritime Command, based in National Defence Headquarters, Ottawa, operates fleets on both the Atlantic and Pacific coasts. The Maritime Atlantic formation (MARLANT) is based in Halifax, Nova Scotia, and the Maritime Pacific formation (MARPAC) is based in Esquimalt, British Columbia, on Vancouver Island. Naval Reserve Headquarters is located in Quebec City, Quebec (ibid.).

The Land Force Command is based at National Defence Headquarters in Ottawa, Ontario. Reporting to the command are four geographically dispersed areas: Land Force Western Area, encompassing British Columbia and the Prairie Provinces, with its headquarters in Edmonton, Alberta; Land Force Central Area, encompassing the province of Ontario, with its headquarters in Toronto; Land Force Quebec Area, encompassing the province of Quebec, with its headquarters in Montreal; and Land Force Atlantic Area, encompassing the Atlantic Provinces, and whose headquarters is located in Halifax, Nova Scotia (ibid.).

The field forces of the command are concentrated predominantly in three multipurpose brigade groups. The First Canadian Mechanized Brigade Group is based in Edmonton, Alberta. The Second Canadian Mechanized Brigade Group is based in Petawawa, Ontario. The Fifth Groupe-brigade mécanisé du Canada is based in Valcartier, Quebec. These formations have common territorial defense and domestic operations responsibilities, but each could be tasked to undertake or provide forces for peacekeeping or contingency operations abroad. Units of the Land Force, which are not normally resident within the brigade groups, include an Air Defense Regiment and an Engineer Support Regiment, both based in Gagetown, New Brunswick. The Joint Task Force Headquarters and a National Command Element (for international operations) are based at the Joint Operations Group garrisoned in Kingston, Ontario, and are the responsibility of the deputy chief of the Defense Staff (ibid.).

The reserve force elements of the Land Force are currently organized into ten brigade groups: three are located in Land Force Western Area; three in Land Force Central Area; two in Land Force Quebec Area; and two in Land Force Atlantic Area (ibid.). The chief of the Air Staff is located at National Defence Headquarters in Ottawa. The operational air wings and squadrons are commanded by an operational level headquarters, First Canadian Air Division, located in Winnipeg, Manitoba (ibid.).

The Canadian Air Force has 104 CF-18 fighters for operational missions. These are divided among four fighter squadrons, two each at Cold Lake, Alberta, and Bagotville, Quebec. The squadrons perform primarily an air defense role. With the provision of precision guided munitions, the squadrons maintain a fighter bomber attack capability in support of maritime and land operations. Two of these CF-18 squadrons are available for contingency operations anywhere in the world (ibid.). The Canadian Air Force commitment to NATO includes a wing composed of two fighter squadrons, a squadron of tactical transport aircraft (all based in Canada), and personnel support of the NATO Airborne Early Warning System (ibid.).

Canada's air force provides general-purpose support to the land forces, with three tactical helicopter squadrons located in Edmonton, Alberta; Petawawa, Ontario; and Valcartier, Quebec. It also maintains a training squadron in Gagetown, New Brunswick, and reserve squadrons at St. Hubert, Quebec, and Borden, Ontario (ibid.). The air force provides support to the navy for undersea warfare, surveillance, search and rescue, and other tasks. Three maritime patrol squadrons and a training unit are equipped with Aurora long-range patrol aircraft. Two maritime helicopter squadrons and a training squadron are equipped with Sea King shipborne helicopters (ibid.).

There is additional general-purpose air support to maritime, land, and national tasks. One strategic transport and VIP squadron is located in Trenton. Three tactical transport squadrons operate with Hercules aircraft, while one additional squadron operates five air-to-air refueling-capable Hercules aircraft. Finally, four search-and-rescue squadrons and a rescue unit fly from Comox, Edmonton, Trenton, Greenwood, and Gander, Newfoundland, with search-and-rescue helicopters and Hercules and Buffalo aircraft. There are two composite squadrons at Comox, British Columbia, and Greenwood, Nova Scotia, for combat support, electronic warfare training, and coastal patrol (ibid.).

Budget
The defense budget for fiscal year 2004 was approximately $9.8 billion, which was 1.2 percent of the GDP (ibid.). The baseline budget can be broken down as follows: $4 billion (39 percent) for personnel costs; $3.2 billion (31 percent) for operations and maintenance; $1.5 billion (19 percent) for procurement and construction; $1.1 billion (11 percent) for statutories, grants, and contributions; and $153 million for R&D (all values are in U.S. dollars) (ibid.). However, in the fiscal year 2005 an additional $10.2 billion was allocated over the next five years, the largest increase in a five-year period in the previous 20 years (ibid.). $2.4 billion of this new funding was to expand the Canadian Forces by 5,000 troops and 3,000 reserves within the next five years. $2 billion was for capital investment, particularly for specialized facilities for the JFT2, Canada's elite anti-terror unit (ibid.).

In terms of Canadian dollars, defense spending has fluctuated between $11 billion and $13 billion since 1993 (SIPRI Yearbook 2003). However, when it is compared as a percentage of GDP, Cana-

dian defense spending was 1.8 percent of total GDP in 1993; as of 2003, it was 1.2 percent (ibid., 353). Again, in constant U.S. dollars (2000), Canadian defense spending went down from $9.9 billion in 1993 to $8.1 billion in 2002 (ibid., 347). These low levels of defense spending have been a matter of debate within the defense community since the end of the Cold War (Bland 1999; Harvey 2000; Macleod et al. 2000).

It is important to note that, since 2001, Canada's contribution to the so-called "War on Terrorism" through Operation Apollo and Operation Athena in Afghanistan has cost more than $722.5 million. When that is taken into account—together with an additional increase of $10.2 billion over the baseline budget in 2005 over a five-year period—it is plausible to argue that we could witness an increase in Canadian defense spending in the coming decade, mainly because of the "War on Terrorism."

Canada does not have nuclear weapons and is an important advocate of nuclear nonproliferation treaties. Key pieces of army equipment include 114 Leopard Tanks, 193 Armored Combat Vehicles (Cougar), 266 Armored Vehicles General Purpose (Grizzly), 199 Armored Personnel Carriers (wheeled, Bison), 1,171 M133 Armored Personnel Carriers, 651 Light Armored Vehicle III, 203 Reconnaissance Vehicles (Coyote), 76 Self-Propelled Artillery (M109), and 28 Towed Artillery (LG1). Key pieces of navy equipment include 4 Destroyer 280 (Iroquois class), 12 frigates (Halifax class), 4 Upholder submarines (Victoria class), 12 Maritime Coastal Defense Vessels (Kingston class), and 2 Auxiliary Oiler Replenishments. Key pieces of air force equipment are 120 CF-18 (104 of them are operational), 32 CC-130 (Hercules), 6 CC-144, 5 CC150,

18 Aurora, 28 Sea King, 98 Griffon, and 12 Labrador (DND 2004).

Several new procurement and modernization projects hope to get a share from the defense budget each year. Those projects include, but are not limited to, modernization of CF-18 and CP-140 Aurora aircraft, strategic air-to-air refueling capability projects, afloat logistics and sealift capability projects, frigate equipment life extension (FELEX) projects, Canadian search-and-rescue helicopter projects, tactical command control and communications system projects, and light utility vehicle wheeled projects (ibid.). In line with that, Budget 2004 specifically included the following equipment acquisitions: 66 Mobile Gun Systems to replace the aging Leopard tank fleet, 28 new Maritime helicopters, Unmanned Aerial Vehicles and Counter Bombardment Radars, and 800 Mercedes G-Wagons (ibid.). Furthermore, Budget 2005 envisioned the acquisition of new medium-capacity helicopters, logistic trucks, and utility aircraft to be used in the Arctic (ibid.)

As has been argued in various DND reports, several of those projects should be accomplished if Canada would like to continue to make a meaningful contribution to international security and assert and defend its sovereignty, land, and maritime borders. The modernization of the Canadian Navy, Air Force, and Army should be accelerated (ibid.).

Civil-Military Relations/The Role of the Military in Domestic Politics

The Canadian military is effectively under civilian control, and that is evident from the fact that it has unified defense staff, unlike that of most NATO nations. Murray (1994) argues that Canada is an unmilitary society in which the key word is compromise. Canada has never in its history experienced a military coup, and as Keating (2002) has argued, Canadian Forces are generally seen as supporting elements of political and economic goals rather than being a tool for military power projection. Furthermore, CF also have the duty to assist civilian authorities during natural disasters, conduct search-and-rescue missions, and

Sidebar 1   The Somalia Incident

Since 1960, the Airborne Regiment of the Canadian armed forces has contributed to almost all of the peacekeeping operations. So when Somalia plunged into chaos in 1992, Canada provided three Commando units from the Airborne Regiment (approximately 900 soldiers) to the UN peacekeeping force. This, however, would be the last mission of the Airborne Regiment.

In the spring of 1993, a young Somalian prisoner named Arone died in the custody of Canadian military. The soldier charged with the Somali's killing. The Canadian Department of National Defence started an inquiry but ended it before it was completed as rumors about a cover-up emerged in the media. Allegations of racist activities within the regiment also surfaced. This "Somalia incident" caused a public uproar and, finally, the Canadian Airborne Regiment was disbanded on 15 March 1995.

Sources
http://en.wikipedia.org/wiki/Somalia_Incident.
http://archives.cbc.ca/IDD-1-71-723/conflict_war/somalia/.

protect Canadian ocean fisheries (DND 2004).

In 1993, however, the image of the CF was seriously shattered with the torturing and killing of a Somalian teenager by members of the Canadian Airborne Regiment. A huge inquiry was launched by the Parliament, and the final report of the Somalia Commission of Inquiry was submitted to the government in June 1997 (ibid.). The report suggested that there was a cover-up in the killing of the boy in March 1993 that went up to the headquarters in Ottawa. This issue created uproar among the public and led to the restructuring and reconsideration of military training, procurement, and organization.

Terrorism

Domestic terrorism is not an issue for Canadian security; however, the Canadian Department of National Defence perceives the threat of international terrorism as one of the top priorities after September 11. The Department of National Defence argues that U.S. national security strategy and U.S. Homeland Security should be taken into account while devising policies to counter international terrorism. As Delvoie (2002) argues, the problem with international terrorism for Canada is less about a possible direct attack on Canadian soil or against Canadians abroad than about the new strategic realities of the post-9-11 world. U.S. preoccupation with the "War on Terrorism" for the near future in its international security policy puts a strain on the structure of the international system and casts doubts on the viability and usefulness of the Euro-Atlantic alliance (DND 2004). This volatility in the international system could hurt Canadian interests in general, ranging from Canadian initiatives on arms control agreements to international trade.

CF have their Joint Task Force–2, a federal counterterror unit, and it contributed to the "War on Terrorism" through Operation Apollo, bilateral arrangements with the United States on the issues of immigration, border security, intelligence sharing, surveillance, and so forth (ibid.).

Relations with the United States

Canada has a long and complex history with the United States. The relations had a poor start with the American War of Independence and the U.S. invasion of Canada in the War of 1812. However, starting from the mid-nineteenth century, the previous animosity disappeared; as the United Kingdom declined as a global superpower, Canada and the United States became close partners. As will be discussed, Canada played an important role for the defense of North America during the Cold War.

In economic terms, U.S.-Canadian relations are extremely close and extensive. The United States is the biggest trading partner of Canada, with $1.4 billion in trade each day (CIA World Fact Book 2004). Since 1988, Canada has had a free trade agreement with the United States, which is the largest foreign direct investor in Canada, amounting to almost 75 percent of total foreign direct investment (ibid.). With such a massive trading relationship, trade disputes between the two countries are inevitable. U.S. firms have complained about subsidies to softwood lumber and Canadian cultural restrictions on magazines and television. Canadians have complained about such things as the ban on beef since a single case of mad cow disease was discovered in 2003, and high U.S. agricultural subsidies (Wikipedia 2004).

The United States and Canada also have resolved several issues involving fisheries. The two countries submitted a Gulf of Maine boundary dispute to the International Court of Justice in 1981 and accepted the court's October 12, 1984, ruling that demarcated the territorial sea boundary. In 1990 the United States and Canada signed a bilateral Fisheries Enforcement Agreement, aimed at deterring illegal fishing activity. The United States and Canada signed a Pacific Salmon Agreement in June 1999 that settled differences over implementation of the 1985 Pacific Salmon Treaty for the next decade (ibid.).

There is very close cooperation on security and defense issues between Canada and the United States, not seriously affected by differences in foreign policy. Canada has always been an advocate of multilateralism; it was opposed to the war in Vietnam in the 1960s and 1970s, maintained relations with Cuba despite U.S. protests, and in 2003 opposed the war in Iraq.

Nevertheless, according to the DND, the United States is Canada's most important ally and defense partner. Defense and security relations between the two countries have been characterized as long-standing and highly successful. This relationship is unique and underpinned by close economic interdependence and common values. It also acknowledges the security provided through Canada's close proximity to the world's only superpower (DND 2004). It has been argued that this special relationship is a real bargain for Canada, as it could not enjoy such a level of security with its own resources (Macleod et al. 2000). The responsibility

of Canada in this relationship is to make certain that its territory will not be used to launch an attack on the United States (ibid.). The following figures from DND represent the level of cooperation and interdependence between the United States and Canada: there are more than 80 treaty-level defense agreements, more than 250 memoranda of understanding between the two defense departments, and approximately 145 bilateral forums in which defense matters are discussed (DND 2004).

But are relations always smooth? Not necessarily, because Canadians do not always share either U.S. threat perceptions or U.S. views on how to counter threats (Macleod et al. 2000). Therefore, generally speaking, Canada tries to limit U.S. ambitions, while preserving the friendly nature of the relationship (ibid.). What then is the historical trajectory of the relationship? Murray (1994, 63–66) identifies two broad periods since World War II: the era of convergence and cooperation between the United States and Canada (1940–1964), and the era of independence and divergence in defense policies (1965–present). According to Murray (ibid.), the era of convergence started with the Ogdensburg declaration, which created the Permanent Joint Board on Defense, the senior advisory body on continental security, and reached its peak with the creation of the North American Aerospace Defense Agreement (NORAD) in 1958. Murray (ibid., 64) argued that after 1964 the nature of the Soviet threat to North America changed from bombers to missiles, thus changing the orientation of the continental defense system. The new U.S. strategy of flexible response also contributed to the increasing divergence between Canada and the United States. After that period, Canada tried to demonstrate its difference from the United States in terms of international security policy, without upsetting its privileged relationship with its neighbor to the south.

The reason for the divergence is twofold. First, Canada wants to pursue an independent foreign and security policy not only because of concerns over sovereignty but also because the domestic image of Canada is based on "being different from the Americans." That plays an important role in the formation of Canadian identity, and Canada persists in the desire to differentiate itself from the United States in several policy areas. Second, the threat perceptions and proper policy options for the United States and Canada have diverged at an increasing speed since the end of the Cold War. During the Cold War, the enemy was common and the threat seemed imminent. However, with the end of the Cold War, the strategic priorities of the United States evolved, and the attacks of 9–11 placed the "War on Terrorism" at the top of U.S. security and foreign policy.

For Canada, on the other hand, although international terrorism is a security threat, it is not a direct threat against the Canadian homeland but a threat to Canadian values. For Canadians, the issues of nonproliferation, arms control, environmental problems, and the concept of human security occupy a more central role than those of rogue states or international terrorism (Macleod et al. 2000). Increasing U.S. unilateralism is in sharp contrast with Canadian commitment to multilateral institutions and security regimes, and over-reliance by the United States on military power contradicts the Canadian culture of compromise, negotiation, and consultation.

For example, the United States did not sign the Land Mine Ban Treaty (spon-sored and promoted by Canada), has withdrawn from the ABM treaty, refuses the jurisdiction of the International Criminal Court, and refuses to sign the Kyoto Protocol. In short, the U.S. way of doing things, especially since 2001, is in contradiction with the way Canadians like to handle things, and with the perceptions of the majority of the Canadian public about themselves and the world.

Despite those differences, however, Canada still preserves its special relationship with the United States. Macleod et al. (ibid.) argue that the main reason is not the huge gains from that close relationship but the enormous costs that Canada would incur if it decided to reduce the level of cooperation and pursue a more independent security and defense policy. Such a move would probably have a devastating impact on the Canadian defense budget, reputation, and capabilities.

Currently there are two major issues in U.S.-Canada defense relations: the future of NORAD, and the Canadian contribution and involvement in the National Missile Defense (NMD). NORAD was established on May 12, 1958, to monitor and defend North American airspace. The agreement must be renewed every five years. The commander-in-chief is a U.S. general appointed by and responsible to both the president of the United States and the prime minister of Canada. The deputy commander is always a Canadian general. Since its establishment, NORAD has been the center of U.S.-Canada defense relations, and Canada has benefited greatly from this relationship (Murray 1994; Macleod et al. 2000).

However, with the creation of the Northern Command (NORTHCOM) in April 2002, the United States unified the continental U.S. defense commands. Subsequently, the commander of NORAD also became the commander of NORTH-COM. Soon it became evident that the United States was planning to integrate NORAD into this structure (Byers 2003). That also raised the issue of placing a sizable portion of the CF—not only the air force but also the army and navy—under the operational control of a permanent, integrated U.S. command structure; NORTHCOM provides the institutional and legal basis for such an action (ibid.).

This resulted in a controversy within the Canadian defense establishment, and Byers argued that such an action would have serious consequences for Canada, ranging from sovereignty concerns over the Arctic to legal problems in the international arena (ibid.). The future of this issue, and thus NORAD, is, however, unclear; it is highly likely that the United States will not be willing to tolerate two parallel structures for the defense of North America and will push Canada to expand its current defense cooperation with the United States by integrating NORAD into NORTHCOM and placing Canadian Forces under operational control of the United States.

Related to the issue of the future of NORAD is the Canadian role in NMD. According to the DND's Strategic Assessment 2003, missile defense has been a priority of the Bush administration since early 2001. The 9–11 terrorist attacks, together with the proliferation of WMD and missile technology, have intensified research into an operational missile defense system. To that end, the United States withdrew from the 1972 Anti-Ballistic Missile Treaty. Currently, U.S. plans are to make the system partially operational by 2007 (DND 2004).

Given Canada's long-standing relations with the United States, especially within

---

Sidebar 2   Canadian Armed Forces

Do you know that you can seat the entire Canadian Army in a hockey rink and you will still have empty seats? It is true; the combat forces of Canada consist of about 25,000 people. The army has 14,000, the air force 6600, and the navy 4000. The Saddledome has about 17,000 seats, so the entire combat forces of the Canadian Army could be seated there with room left for most of the navy!

Source
Ross, D. A. 1998. "Canada's Functional Isolationism." *International Journal* 54, no. 1 (Winter): 120–142.

---

the framework of NORAD, it seems plausible that Canada will take part in NMD without much trouble. However, the reality is not like that. The issue became a hot topic among academics and policy-makers alike (Harvey 2000; Gizewski 2001; Haglund 2001). Proponents argue, with considerable force, that Canada's role in missile warning and aerospace defense would become meaningless if the country did not participate in missile defense. Furthermore, they argue that it will cost very little for Canada, and that even if Canada refuses to participate, the United States will go ahead anyway, because NMD does not need Canadian soil or aerospace to function properly. Thus it is a matter of political endorsement rather than technical or financial contribution, in the eyes of the United States (Harvey 2000). Advocates of NMD suggest that Canadian refusal might result in exclusion of Canada from NORAD, and the country could lose its privileged relationship with the United States (ibid.; Macleod et al. 2000).

On the other hand, opponents argue that taking part in such a project would undermine the ABM treaty and other arms-control treaties, and could hurt Canada's image in the international arena (Gizewski 2001). They also point out possible legal and domestic problems related to Canadian participation in NMD. However, it seems as though the advocates have the upper hand, since in May 2003, Canada agreed to enter into discussions with the United States on the possibility of participation in its missile defense program (DND 2004). Despite all the foot-dragging Canada probably will participate in NMD, because what Brooke Claxton, Canadian minister of defense in 1953, said is still valid today: it was "very difficult indeed for the Canadian government to reject any major defense proposals which the United States government presents with conviction as essential for the security of North America" (cited in Macleod et al. 2000, 354).

The Future

Canada is one of the wealthiest countries in the world, strategically located near the world's only superpower; the future of Canadian security, economy, and society seems crystal clear. A highly educated citizenry, rich natural resources, and a strong, industrially based economy are the major forces that will ensure the future of Canada. However, the same cannot be said for the future of the Canadian Forces.

A mismatch between the aspirations of multipurpose, combat-capable CF and low levels of defense spending has haunted CF for more than a decade. Despite the rhetoric of modernizing the

Canadian Forces, the government almost always underfunds the defense budget, and that leads to the erosion of military capabilities. For example, currently Canada does not have strategic airlift capability that could be used in overseas operations, nor does it have a powerful navy that could project power in three oceans (Boutilier 2003; Bland 1999). Canadian troops in overseas missions are ill equipped, with insufficient intelligence capabilities, medical resources, and logistics support (Bland 1999, 160–165). Various projects have been canceled or delayed significantly as a result of insufficient funds, thus increasing the speed of erosion of Canadian military capabilities (Bland 1999). If this trend continues for the next decade, it is very optimistic to argue that the targets in Strategy 2020 (DND 2004) will be met.

The next five to ten years look volatile and unpredictable internationally. That could lead to an isolationist policy on the part of Canada, more cutting of the defense budget, and continued heavy reliance on the United States for the country's defense. Eventually the CF could be reduced to a peacekeeping force that has no independent force projection capabilities, unable to defend and protect Canada's borders or maritime or aerospace interests. Erosion of Canadian military capability could also cost it its "place on the table," as we have already started to see with the exclusion of Canada from the Contact Group during the Yugoslav crisis of 1992–1995. That could in turn effectively threaten the sovereignty of Canada. As has been said in the 1994 Defence Policy White Paper: "[In] the final analysis it may be said that a nation not worth defending is a nation not worth preserving" (ibid.).

References, Recommended Readings, and Websites

Books

Bryden, Penny, Raymond Blake, and Michael Tuckers, eds. 2000. *Canada and the New World Order: Facing the New Millennium*. Toronto: Irwin.

Government of Canada. 1995. *Canada in the World*. Ottawa: Government of Canada.

Hampson, Fen Osler, Michael Hart, and Martin Rudner, eds. 1999. *Canada among Nations 1999: A Big League Player?* Toronto: Oxford University Press.

Keating, Tom. 2002. *Canada and World Order: The Multilateralist Tradition in Canadian Foreign Policy*. Canada: Oxford University Press.

Military Balance. 2004. *Military Balance 2003–2004*. London: IISS.

Morton, D. 2001. "Canada's Military Experience in the Twentieth Century." In *Canadian Military History since the 17th Century*, Yves Tremblay, ed. Ottawa, Canada: National Defense.

Murray, Douglas J. 1994. "Canada." In *The Defense Policies of Nations: A Comparative Study*, 3d ed., Douglas J. Murray and Paul R. Viotti, eds. Baltimore: Johns Hopkins University Press.

See, Scott W. 2001. *The History of Canada*. Westport, CT: Greenwood Press.

SIPRI. 2003. *SIPRI Yearbook 2003*. New York: Oxford University Press.

Wise, S. F. 2001. "Canada and War, 1600–2000." In *Canadian Military History since the 17th Century*, Yves Tremblay, ed. Ottawa, Canada: National Defense.

Articles

Axworthy, Lloyd. 1997. "Canada and Human Security: The Need for Leadership." *International Journal* 52, no. 2 (spring): 183–196.

Bland, Douglas L. 1999. "A Sow's Ear from a Silk Purse: Abandoning Canada's Military Capabilities." *International Journal* 54, no. 1 (winter): 143–174.

Boutilier, James A. 2003. "The Canadian Navy and the New Naval Environment in Asia." *International Journal* 58, no. 1 (winter): 181–199.

Byers, Michael. 2003. "Canadian Armed Forces under United States Command." *International Journal* 58, no. 1 (winter): 89–114.

Chapnick, Adam. 2000. "The Canadian Middle Power Myth." *International Journal* 55, no. 2 (spring): 188–206.

David, Charles-Philippe, and Stephane Roussel. 1998. "Middle Power Blues: Canadian Policy and International Security after the Cold War." *ARCS* 28, nos. 1–2 (spring–summer): 131–156.

Delvoie, Louis A. 2002. "A Not So Benign New Century: Conventional Security Challenges to Canadian Interests." *International Journal* 57, no. 1: 19–35.

Dewitt, D. B. 2000. "Directions in Canada's International Security Policy." *International Journal* 55, no. 2 (spring): 167–187.

Gizewski, Peter. 2001. "The International Politics of Missile Defense: A Response to Harvey." *International Journal* 56, no. 3 (summer): 527–532.

Haglund, D. G. 1997. "The NATO of Its Dreams?" *International Journal* 52, no. 3 (summer): 464–482.

———. 2001. "Yesterday's Issue? National Missile Defense, Canada, and the Allies." *International Journal* 56, no. 4 (autumn): 688–698.

Harvey, Frank P. 2000. "The International Politics of National Missile Defense: A Response to Critics." *International Journal* 55, no. 4: 545–566.

Huebert, Rob. 2003. "The Shipping News Part II: How Canada's Arctic Sovereignty Is on Thinning Ice." *International Journal* 58, no. 3 (summer): 295–308.

Jockel, Joe, and Joel Sokolsky. 2000. "Lloyd Axworthy's Legacy." *International Journal* 56, no. 1 (winter): 1–18.

Macleod, Alex, Stephane Roussel, and Andri Van Mens. 2000. "Hobson's Choice: Does Canada Have any Options in Its Defense and Security Relations with the United States?" *International Journal* 55, no. 3 (summer): 341–354.

Maloney, S. M., and Scot Robertson. 1999. "The Revolution in Military Affairs." *International Journal* 54, no. 3 (summer): 443–462.

Ross, Cameron. 2004. "Future Defence and Security Challenges: A Canadian Perspective." *Journal of Military and Strategic Studies* (spring).

Ross, Douglas A. 1996. "Canada and the World at Risk: Depression, War, and

Isolationism for the 21st Century?"
International Journal 52, no. 1 (winter):
1–24.

———. 1999. "Canada's Functional
Isolationism." *International Journal* 54,
no. 1 (winter): 120–142.

Sens, Allen. 1995. "Saying Yes to
Expansion: The Future of NATO and
Canadian Interests in a Changing
Alliance." *International Journal* 50, no.
4: 675–700.

Stairs, Denis. 1999. "Canada and the
Security Problem." *International
Journal* 54, no. 3 (summer): 386–403.

Websites

Central Intelligence Agency. *The World
Fact Book:* http://www.cia.gov.
Accessed March 1, 2004.

Department of National Defence (DND),
Canada. "1994 Defence Policy White
Paper": http://www.forces.gc.ca/
admpol/eng/doc/white_e.htm. Accessed
March 1, 2004.

Department of National Defence (DND),
Canada. "Strategic Assessment 2003":
http://www.forces.gc.ca/admpol/eng/
doc/strat_2003/sa03_index_e.htm.
Accessed March 1, 2004.

Department of National Defence (DND),
Canada: http://www.forces.ca. Accessed
March 1, 2004.

NATO: http://www.nato.int.

NORAD: http://www.norad.mil.

Veteran Affairs Canada: http://www.
vac-acc.gc.ca. Accessed March 1, 2004.

Wikipedia: http://www.wikipedia.com.
Accessed March 15, 2004.

The Caribbean

Ivelaw L. Griffith

History and Geography

The histories of the four countries discussed here—Belize, Guyana, Jamaica, and Trinidad and Tobago—are, like the history of the Caribbean as a whole, admixtures of the drama of power and power pursuits of European nations and later the United States. They are also the story of the powerlessness of people indigenous to the region and transplanted as slaves and indentured servants from Africa and Asia. Discussions of the chronology of the histories often begin with 1492 and the voyage of Christopher Columbus. Yet, as Franklin Knight (1978) rightly underscores in his seminal *The Caribbean: The Genesis of a Fragmented Nationalism*, peoples, nations, and cultures existed in Belize, Guyana, Jamaica, Trinidad and Tobago, and elsewhere in the region prior to the arrival of Columbus and his fellow adventurers.

The sad fate of those peoples, nations, and cultures is a direct outcome of the policies and actions of the colonizers and sundry political pirates and economic privateers. Colonial pursuits for property, power, and prestige witnessed countless wars, territorial conquests and exchanges, and degrees of direct and indirect rule and misrule between the late fifteenth century and the mid-to-late twentieth century, when the countries secured political independence from their colonial over-lords. Belize secured its independence in 1981, and Guyana's was granted earlier, in 1966. The year 1962 witnessed the two other territories gaining their right to independent nationhood. In all cases, political independence marked new—and often sad—chapters in their national histories, as political elites faced the realities of governing nations in an environment in which the dominant powers rejected their radical political and economic philosophies—especially in Guyana and Jamaica. Moreover, in some cases—notably Guyana and Jamaica—domestic political rule witnessed political violence, political misrule, and increased economic deprivation. Trinidad and Tobago had the first attempted army coup before even a full decade of independent rule, in 1970.

In geographical terms, Belize and Guyana are mainland territories; the former is in Central America and the latter northern South America. Jamaica and Trinidad and Tobago are island states; the former is in the Greater Antilles, and the latter is a twin-island republic in the Lesser Antilles. The four nations differ dramatically in size and topography. For instance, Belize covers 22,970 square kilometers, while its mainland counterpart, Guyana, covers 214,970. As to Jamaica, it is 11,424 square kilometers, while Trinidad and Tobago is 5,182. Although Belize and Guyana are not island states, they

Table 1   Belize: Key Statistics

Type of government	Parliamentary democracy
Population	266,440 (July 2003 estimate)
Religion	Roman Catholic 50%, Protestant 27%, other 14%, none 9%
Main industries	Garment production, food processing, tourism, construction
Main security threats	Territorial claim by Guatemala; drug trafficking
Defense spending (%GDP)	1.87%
Size of military	1,050 active and 700 reserves
Numbre of civil wars since 1945	0
Number of interstate wars since 1945	0

Sources

Central Intelligence Agency Website. 2003. "CIA World Factbook." http://www.cia.gov/cia/publications/factbook/ (accessed May 15, 2005).

International Institute for Strategic Studies (IISS). 2003. *The Military Balance 2003–2004.* London: IISS and Oxford University Press.

have historically been defined—and have defined themselves—as Caribbean largely because of the common British rule and political culture—although all four of the countries have experienced political rule in at least part of their present territory by at least one other European power. The region's most powerful defining geographical and identity feature is the Caribbean Sea, which has an area of 1,049,500 square miles and north-south width ranging from 380 to almost 700 miles. One of its channels, that across the submarine ridge south of the Virgin Islands, is more than 6,000 feet deep.

Regional Geopolitics

The geopolitical context and significance of the Caribbean lies, generally, in its possession of strategic materials, in the loca-

Table 2   Guyana: Key Statistics

Type of government	Constitutional republic
Population	702,100 (July 2003 estimate)
Religion	Christian 50%, Hindu 35%, Muslim 10%, other 5%
Main industries	Bauxite, sugar, rice milling, timber, textiles, gold mining
Main security threats	Territorial claims by Venezuela and Suriname; drugs
Defense spending (%GDP)	1.7%
Size of military	2,000
Number of civil wars since 1945	0
Number of interstate wars since 1945	0

Sources

Central Intelligence Agency Website. 2003. "CIA World Factbook." http://www.cia.gov/cia/publications/factbook/ (accessed May 15, 2005).

International Institute for Strategic Studies (IISS). 2003. *The Military Balance 2003–2004.* London: IISS and Oxford University Press.

Table 3   Jamaica: Key Statistics

Type of government	Parliamentary democracy
Population	2,695,867 (July 2003 estimate)
Religion	Protestant 61%, Roman Catholic 4%, others, including Rastafarians 35%
Main industries	Tourism, bauxite, textiles, light manufactures, agriculture
Main security threats	Drug trafficking and production; crime and violence
Defense spending (%GDP)	NA%
Size of military	2,830 active and 953 reserves
Number of civil wars since 1945	0
Number of interstate wars since 1945	0

Sources

Central Intelligence Agency Website. 2003. "CIA World Factbook." http://www.cia.gov/cia/
publications/factbook/ (accessed May 15, 2005).

International Institute for Strategic Studies (IISS). 2003. *The Military Balance 2003–2004.*
London: IISS and Oxford University Press.

tion of vital sea lanes of communication, and in the security networks of powerful states in the area. As regards strategic materials, Caribbean states own and produce natural resources that are important for military and civilian purposes, such as petroleum and natural gas, bauxite, gold, nickel, silver, and diamonds. For instance, Trinidad and Tobago and Venezuela produce large quantities of petroleum, and Barbados, Cuba, and Suriname have small oil industries. The Dominican Republic, Guyana, Jamaica, and Suriname produce bauxite, and there is gold mining in Cuba, Guyana, the Dominican Republic, and Suriname. Moreover, Trinidad and Tobago produces some 16 billion cubic meters of liquefied natural gas (LNG) annually.

Table 4   Trinidad and Tobago: Key Statistics

Type of government	Parliamentary democracy
Population	1,104,209 (July 2003 estimate)
Religion	Roman Catholic 29%, Hindu 24%, Anglican 16%, Muslim 6%, other 25%
Main industries	Petroleum, chemicals, tourism, manufacturing, cement
Main security threats	Maritime dispute with Barbados; drug trafficking; crime
Defense spending (%GDP)	1.4%
Size of military	3,000
Number of civil wars since 1945	0
Number of interstate wars since 1945	0

Sources

Central Intelligence Agency Website. 2003. "CIA World Factbook." http://www.cia.gov/cia/
publications/factbook/ (accessed May 15, 2005).

International Institute for Strategic Studies (IISS). 2003. *The Military Balance 2003–2004.*
London: IISS and Oxford University Press.

Sidebar 1   Caribbean Resources

Caribbean countries possess some key strategic resources. For instance, tiny Trinidad and Tobago is among the world's top-five producers of liquefied natural gas, and Venezuela is among the world's top-ten oil producers. Four of the world's top-ten producers of bauxite, which is key to the manufacture of alumina and aluminium (aluminum), are in the Caribbean: Guyana, Jamaica, Suriname, and Venezuela. Indeed, it was in the Caribbean—in Jamaica—that commercial mining of bauxite began, in 1854.

In relation to sea lanes, two of the world's major "choke points" are in the Caribbean area: one is the Panama Canal, and the other is the Caribbean Sea. The canal, which started operations in August 1914, links the Atlantic and Pacific oceans. The canal has both military and civilian value. From a U.S. military perspective, it remains useful for the rapid transit of military supplies from one theater to another, particularly in a "two major regional contingency scenario." In addition, the efficiency and routine operations of the canal continue to be of critical commercial importance to the United States, as more than 10 percent all U.S. trade passes through the canal (Binnendijk and Kjonnerod 1997). It also is widely accepted that while the canal is now less important to the United States than two decades ago, other countries are still very dependent on it, among them Chile, Ecuador, and Japan. For instance, according to the commander of the U.S. Southern Command (SOUTHCOM), in his March 2004 congressional testimony, Chile is the fourth heaviest user of the canal.

Once ships leave the canal from the Pacific Ocean, they must use one or more of the several Caribbean Sea passages en route to destinations in the United States, Europe, Africa, and elsewhere. The Florida Strait (between Key West, Florida, and Cuba), Mona Passage (between the Dominican Republic and Puerto Rico), Windward Passage (between Cuba and Haiti), St. Vincent Passage (between St. Lucia and St. Vincent and the Grenadines), Anegada Passage (between the British territories Anegada and Sombrero), and the Yucatan Channel (between Cuba and the Mexican Yucatan) are the principal passages for ships entering or leaving the Caribbean. Needless to say, the strategic significance of the Caribbean Sea predates the creation of the Panama Canal.

In terms of security networks, up until the early 1990s the United States considered the Caribbean its "southern flank," its "strategic rear." (Now the region is considered the "Third Border" of the United States.) A considerable force presence was maintained there, mainly in Puerto Rico, at the Atlantic threshold of the Caribbean; in Panama, at the southern rim of the Caribbean Basin; and in Cuba—at Guantánamo Bay—on the northern perimeter. In 1990, for instance, the United States maintained 4,743 military and civilian personnel in Puerto Rico, 20,709 army, navy, and air force personnel in Panama, and 3,401 naval personnel in Cuba. Other bases and installations were also maintained throughout the region. Much has changed since 1990, however, including strategic redesign and force redeployment. Puerto Rico is now home to fewer forces, and SOUTHCOM relocated from Panama to Miami in 1997. Guantánamo, long viewed as having little strategic value, began to serve essentially as a political beachhead in the hemisphere's last remaining communist outpost. However, 9–11 changed things somewhat; Guantánamo became an important detention center as the United States prosecuted its 9–11 and counterterrorism battles (Lakshmanan 2003, 3A).

Of course, the United States has not been the only "big power" with security networks in the area. Notable in this respect were the bases and networks maintained by the USSR, especially in Cuba. During the heyday of the Cold War the Soviet military presence in Cuba included modern docks and repair facilities, airport facilities for reconnaissance aircraft, and satellite and other surveillance operations. The twenty-eight-square-mile intelligence facility at Lourdes had three functions: monitoring U.S. missile tests; intercepting satellite communications; and relaying microwave communications between the USSR and its diplomatic posts in the Western Hemisphere. At the time, the Lourdes facility was reputedly the largest such operation the Soviets maintained outside the USSR. As the USSR collapsed, in September 1991 President Mikhail Gorbachev announced discussions with Cuban officials about the withdrawal of 11,000 troops from the island; the Soviet military presence was progressively reduced from November 1991 onward. However, the Lourdes facility was maintained until October 2001, when President Vladimir Putin ordered it closed (Gonzalez 1982; Glasser 2001).

Border and territorial disputes dot the region's geopolitical landscape. Both land and maritime controversies are involved. It is important to note that while the term "border disputes" generally is used to refer to the controversies over land and sea, the disputes in which Caribbean states are involved are not all border disputes, which are controversies between states over the alignment of land or maritime boundaries. Some controversies, such as those between Venezuela and Guyana, and between Suriname and Guyana, are really territorial disputes—that is, controversies arising from claims to land or maritime territory. The most serious disputes involve Venezuela and Guyana, Suriname and Guyana, and Guatemala and Belize. Some casual observers of the Caribbean might be startled to learn the number of nations with unresolved maritime or land disputes. The list includes Antigua and Barbuda and France relating to Guadeloupe, Jamaica and Colombia, Cuba and Haiti, Suriname and France relating to French Guiana, Dominica and Venezuela, Cuba and the United States, Haiti and Jamaica, Haiti and the United States, Jamaica and Honduras, Jamaica and the United States, Jamaica and Nicaragua, St. Kitts and Nevis and Venezuela, St. Lucia and Venezuela, and St. Vincent and the Grenadines and Venezuela. Some countries are involved in multiple disputes. For example, Guyana is facing a claim by Venezuela for the western five-eighths of its territory of 214,970 square kilometers and another by Suriname for 15,000 square kilometers to the east.

Sidebar 2   Guyana

Venezuela has a territorial claim against Guyana for five-eighths of the country's 214,970 square kilometers of land, and Suriname's claim is for 15,000 square kilometers.

The long-standing Guatemalan claim against Belize is also a massive one. A milestone in efforts to settle that dispute was reached in 2002 with an agreement that grew out of negotiations facilitated by Paul S. Reichtler for Guatemala and Shridath Ramphal for Belize, under the auspices of the Organization of American States (OAS). The Ramphal-Reichtler proposals pertain to five main items: land issues; maritime issues; a development trust fund; trade, investment, and functional cooperation; and transitional arrangements. As to the fifth, the two nations took the settlement process one step further in signing an agreement about the transition process and confidence-building measures on February 7, 2003. Later that same month, OAS officials went to the two countries to establish an OAS office in the Adjacency Zone that will verify any transgressions of confidence-building measures as the agreement is implemented.

However, in August 2003, Guatemala told the OAS that it was abandoning aspects of the 2002 agreement. Nevertheless, delegations headed by the vice ministers of foreign affairs of the two countries met in October 2003 in Washington, D.C., along with OAS assistant secretary general Luigi Einaudi to review the implementation of the confidence-building measures specified in the February 2003 agreement. They reported that the majority of the measures are being successfully applied, and they agreed to develop and execute those few measures that had not yet been activated. That same day OAS secretary general César Gaviria presided over the first meeting of the Group of Friends of Belize-Guatemala, an advisory body to the secretary general on the various initiatives for achieving a peaceful resolution of the territorial dispute. It comprises Argentina, Brazil, Canada, Ecuador, El Salvador, Jamaica, Mexico, Nicaragua, Spain, Sweden, the United Kingdom, and the United States. Japan also participated in the first meeting as an observer.

The Guyana-Suriname dispute developed medium to high intensity in 2003. After a lull of nearly three years, the dispute took a fairly dramatic turn in March 2003, when the Guyana Defense Force (GDF) deployed the GDF Coast Guard flagship, *M.V. Essequibo* from the eastern town of New Amsterdam, to patrol the waters off the Guyana-Suriname border following publication by Suriname of a map showing the disputed area as part of its territory. In response, Suriname's defense minister, Ronald Assen, placed the Suriname Defense Force navy on "alert" status. Moreover, in February 2004, Guyana announced its decision to pursue a settlement of the maritime component of the dispute with Suriname in the UN Law of the Sea arena, citing frustration with hostile and delaying tactics by Suriname in its efforts to settle the matter diplomatically (Canadian Broadcasting Corporation 2003; Denny 2004).

Another important part of the region's geopolitics involves the business of drugs. The Caribbean is a bridge or front between North and South America. The drug trade is massive. In relation to only cocaine, the United Nations Office on Drugs and Crime in the Caribbean reported that the "total trade balance (exports-imports) in the Caribbean for illegal drugs as calculated using 2001 figures gives a total of U.S.$3,447 billion. By adding the estimated total internal for drugs in the region we obtain a total drugs GDP for the Caribbean of U.S.$3,684 billion. The weight of the total drugs industry GDP in the region when compared to the overall Caribbean region GDP (U.S.$108.681 billion) is 3.4%."

In addition, "the total illicit drugs GDP figure mentioned above, when compared with the national GDP figures from Caribbean Community (CARICOM) countries, is surpassed only by Jamaica and Trinidad and Tobago. With the total illicit drug exports transiting the region estimated at approximately U.S.$4,800 million in 2001, this figure almost triples total CARICOM petroleum export earnings (also the number one export income earning sector) for 2000 and in fact surpasses the total of the top five CARICOM domestic exports in 2000" (UN Office on Drugs and Crime Caribbean Regional Office 2003, 6–7).

The geonarcotics dynamics partly explain why the region is such a key corridor for drug trafficking between South and North America. In terms of North America, the United States is the principal destination, both for drugs coming from the Caribbean and drugs coming through it. For instance, in February 2003 the UN Office on Drugs and Crime reported that close to 90 percent of drugs seized within the Caribbean during 2001 were destined for the United States. Moreover, in September of the same year the U.S. Drug Enforcement Administration reported that in 2002 an estimated 27 percent of the 544 metric tons of export-quality cocaine available to the United States flowed through the Caribbean corridor (UN Office on Drugs and Crime Caribbean Regional Office 2003; U.S. Drug Enforcement Administration 2003).

It is important to observe that drugs in the Caribbean have a security connection not simply because of the size of the problem. The connection exists essentially for four reasons. First, drug operations have multiple consequences and implications, such as marked increases in crime, systemic and institutionalized corruption, and arms trafficking, among other things. Second, the operations and their consequences have increased in scope and gravity over the last two decades. Third, they have dramatic effects on agents and agencies of national security and good governance, in military, political, and economic ways. And fourth, drugs precipitate sovereignty infringement of many countries, by both state and nonstate actors (Griffith 1997; Bernal et al. 2000).

Conflict Past and Present
Conflict History
Thankfully, the conflict history of Belize, Guyana, Jamaica, and Trinidad and Tobago since independence is minuscule. Although there has been jingoism in Guatemala over the claim against Belize, especially at times of presidential elections, and occasional minor skirmishes between military and law enforcement units of the two countries, there has been no war or major military hostility. The fact that the United Kingdom maintained a deterrent naval and army presence in Belize for close to a decade certainly has contributed to this desirable outcome. Similarly, except for the minor military encounter between the defense forces of Guyana and Venezuela over occupation by Venezuela of the Guyana portion of Ankoko Island in October 1966, five months after independence, there has been no significant interstate military engagement between the two nations. Illegal overflights by the Venezuelan Air Force allegedly occurred regularly during the 1970s and 1980s, and over the years there have been illegal cross-border entries by Venezuelan forces and seizures of

Venezuelan commercial vessels by Guyana's military.

Guyana successfully used military force against Suriname in 1967, ejecting a detachment of the Suriname Defense Force from the New River Triangle after their illegal occupation of that territory. Over the years diplomatic and low-level military and police hostility periodically has marred relations between Guyana and Suriname, but the two nations have avoided major military conflict over the disputed territory. Although there are maritime disputes between Jamaica and several nations, including Haiti, Honduras, Nicaragua, and the United States, Jamaica has never been engaged in interstate conflict. Trinidad's often high-decibel dispute with Venezuela over the Gulf of Paria was settled by treaty in April 1990. That dispute had been the reason for low-level hostile action between the Venezuelan navy and the Trinidadian coast guard on several occasions. Despite the treaty, however, illegal fishing by fishermen of both nations continues to result in expulsions and arrests by the naval forces of the two nations.

Current and Potential Military Confrontation

Although all of the four countries under examination here—Belize, Guyana, Jamaica, and Trinidad and Tobago—have been involved in territorial or political disputes, they have not been in, nor are they now engaged in, rivalries in the sense used by Paul Diehl and Gary Goertz: "a relationship in between two states in which both use, with some regularity, military threats and force as well as one in which both sides formulate foreign policy in military terms" (Diehl and Goertz 2000, 4). Thus, although the maritime disputes between Guyana and Suriname and between Trinidad and Tobago and Barbados were taken before the United Nations during the spring of 2004, neither past behavior nor current developments suggest any reason to anticipate that the disputes will develop to the point of military conflict.

Alliance Structure

The countries discussed here do not have military alliances, although they do have varying kinds and degrees of military relationships with a variety of nations, including the United States, the United Kingdom, China, Canada, India, France, and Brazil. The agreements and memorandums of understanding pertain significantly to counternarcotics operations, military education and training, intelligence sharing, and military grants and sales.

Size and Structure of the Military

Belize

Belize is atypical of countries in the Caribbean and the Third World in that the formal establishment of its defense force predated it independence as a nation state, which occurred in 1981. Because of the territorial dispute with Guatemala, which was examined earlier, the Belize Defense Force (BeDF) was formed on January 1, 1978. Its nucleus came from the British Honduras Volunteer Guard and the elite Belize Police Special Service Unit, both of which were disbanded at the time of the army's creation. Overall policy direction of the force is the responsibility of the Belize Defense Board, comprising the deputy prime minister, who serves as chairman, the permanent secretary, Ministry of Defense, the BeDF commandant, the BeDF deputy commandant, and the head of the Defense Secretariat at the Ministry of Defense. There is also an eight-member Commissions Board that advises the head of state on appointments to commissions and appointments up to the rank of major on the army side and lieutenant commander on the maritime side. The defense minister, in consultation with the prime minister, makes appointments beyond the rank of major.

Organizationally, the BeDF is composed of the following core elements: Headquarters Company, Support Group, two regular battalions, one reserve battalion, air wing, maritime wing, cadet corps, and military band. Headquarters Company, located at Price Barracks near the Belize International Airport, is responsible for overall force command and operation. The Support Company, the BeDF's specialist elements, comprises the Mortar, Signal, Reece, and the Combat Engineer units, while the Combat Engineer Platoon undertakes construction and renovation but also has a unit called the Explosive Ordnance Device Team, tasked with bomb disposal and demolition. The two battalions are styled First Battalion and Second Battalion, respectively. The first has a headquarters company and three rifle companies, and the second also has three rifle companies. They are involved in territorial defense along the southern and western borders with Guatemala, training, and routine guard duties. The reserve component, called the Third Battalion or the Volunteer Battalion, has its headquarters at Price Barracks and comprises three rifle companies and two detachment platoons.

A commander heads the small BeDF Maritime Wing. It is very poorly equipped, yet it has a mandate to patrol and pursue territorial defense, search and rescue, counternarcotics, and other missions in some 40,000 square miles of sea. *The Military Balance* for 2003–2004 describes its total assets as "14 armed boats." What that publication fails to indicate is that most of those boats are out of commission at any one time, and that most of the arms are ancient, nonfunctional, or both. The Maritime Wing operates ostensibly from bases in Belize City and three other locations. The Air Wing, which is also undermanned and underequipped, had a 2004 inventory of five aircraft: two propeller-driven Britten-Norman Defenders; one Cessna, a 1995 gift from the governor of Quintana Roo, Mexico; one Slingsby T3A Firefly, which was donated by the United Kingdom in 1995; and one T67–200 Firefly.

As *The Military Balance* for 2003–2004 rightly points out, the BeDF has no armed combat aircraft or military helicopters. Over the years, foreign forces, notably the Flight Army Air Corps of the British Army Training Support Unit Team, have provided logistics support. The Cadet Corps was created in July 1981 out of the Belize Cadet Corps, itself formed in 1977. With headquarters at Price Barracks, it has detachments in Belize City, San Ignacio, Orange Walk Town, Corozal Town, Dangriga, and Punto Gorda. As to the military band, it was formed in January 1978 from the former Belize Volunteer Guard Band, which itself dated to 1947 as part of the North Caribbean Force (Battalion of Belize).

As is the case with other defense forces in the Caribbean, the defense force in Belize also supports the civilian police force in coping with crime. Moreover, the BeDF participates in ceremonial functions related to independence day celebrations, the opening of parliament, and visits of heads of states, among other things. It also is engaged in civic and national development activities, such as road repair and environmental clean-up. The BeDF is not a significant player on the international scene. However, it did participate in peacekeeping in Haiti during late 1994–early 1995 (Griffith 1993; *Military Balance 2003–2004*; Phillips 2004).

Guyana

Like Belize, Guyana faced territorial claims, by Venezuela and Suriname, long before independence in May 1966. Thus Guyana found it necessary to establish a standing army when the military defense mandate of the British ended at independence. That army is the Guyana Defense Force (GDF). It was created by passage of the 1966 Defense Act, just four days before independence. Simultaneously, its precursors, the British Guiana Special Service Unit (BGSSU) and the British Guiana Volunteer Force (BGVF), were abolished. The military in colonial Guyana had a history traceable to 1778, when the first militia was created. Also, as was the case with other West Indians, Guyanese were drafted into the British imperial army. For example, the British Guiana Militia, later called the British Guiana Regiment, was part of Britain's South Caribbean Force during World War II.

As independence drew close and plans for the standing army developed, the BGVF and the BGSSU were natural and appropriate sources from which to draw officers and regular ranks for the new security outfit. Personnel were selected from those forces for training at the Mons Officer Cadet School and elsewhere in England. Local training was provided at Atkinson Field Base (now Camp Stephenson) near the country's main international airport, and at the Tacama Training Camp in the Berbice region. The GDF headquarters were established in Thomas Lands, in the northern part of the capital, Georgetown. It is now called Camp Ayanganna.

Although the legal birth date of the GDF is May 22, 1966, its operational birthday on November 1, 1965, is the one traditionally observed. The Defense Act of 1966—the army's enabling legislation—gives the GDF a rather broad mandate: "The Force shall be charged with the defense of and maintenance of order in Guyana *and with such duties as may from time to time be defined by the Defense Board*." Using that broad legal authority, the political elites identified several specific roles for the GDF, the most important of which were to maintain the integrity of the country's borders and defend against aggression; to assist in the maintenance of law and order when required; and to contribute to the life of the country by engaging in engineering and other projects and providing a labor/rescue organization in an emergency.

Forbes Burnham, Guyana's dominant leader from 1964 until 1985, is credited with articulating a security strategy called "Defense in Depth." His conception of security was multidimensional, with military, political, economic, and psychological facets. In the military area, it was envisaged that military defense would be provided by the defense establishment plus ordinary citizens, organized, armed, and trained for territorial defense. There was also a civil defense component, focusing on the protection of citizens and their property. Economic defense pertained to safeguarding supplies of goods, fuel, and other commodities needed for survival, while psychological defense entailed maintaining the morale of the population and neutralizing the efforts of enemy propaganda and misinformation. It should also be observed that

Forbes Burnham progressively turned the security services into instruments of political rule, serving partly as guarantors of regime security and not just national security.

In political terms, the GDF falls under the portfolio of the minister of defense, a position traditionally held by the president. Nevertheless, the Defense Act vests policy responsibility for the army's command, administration, and discipline in a Defense Board. The president, who is also commander-in-chief, heads the six-member board, which includes the minister of home affairs, who is responsible for the police and the prisons, among other things, and the GDF chief of staff. Over the decades since independence, Guyana has developed a multidimensional national security establishment. Between 1990 and 1992, the policy-making framework was expanded with the creation of the position of national security adviser to the president. Brigadier David Granger, a one-time GDF force commander, was named the first national security adviser. However, following his election in October 1992, President Cheddie Jagan abolished the position.

Operationally, the chief of staff heads the GDF, with overall command responsibility for the army. But for fifteen years, day-to-day administrative and logistical matters were under the charge of the force commander, the number-two official in the GDF hierarchy. The roles of chief of staff and force commander had been merged until 1972, when they were separated as the GDF expanded. However, there was a reorganization of the military services in 1987 in which the two roles were again combined.

As part of that reorganization, the former Defense Secretariat, the chief of staff's office, was merged with the Force Headquarters, the force commander's office. Moreover, regarding the multidimensionality of the security establishment, for close to two decades Guyana's military and law enforcement agencies—principally the GDF, the Guyana Police Force (GPF), the Guyana National Service (GNS), and the Guyana People's Militia (GPM), but also the Guyana Prison Services and the National Guard Service—formed part of an umbrella agency called the Disciplined Services of Guyana. The National Guard Service, which had been created in 1980 to protect state property against theft, vandalism, and sabotage, was absorbed into the Guyana Police Force in August 1991. The Disciplines Services approach, which also had served partisan political purposes by President Forbes Burnham and (less so) by President Desmond Hoyte, was abandoned once political rule changed in 1992.

The GDF has always been involved in civil engagement and national development, especially in areas of road construction and maintenance, and training and logistics support to the agriculture, mining, and fishing sections, thus engaging in what some consider scab labor in times of industrial disputes involving governmental agencies. These were notable aspects of the "army of the people" approach of the Forbes Burnham and Desmond Hoyte governments, and have been less prominent since 1992.

Especially during the presidency of Hugh Desmond Hoyte (1985–1992), there was notable involvement in regional security assistance. For instance, a contingent of military engineers was sent to Jamaica in September 1988 in the wake of Hurricane Gilbert; a joint-services detachment, with GDF, GPM, and GNS personnel, was sent to the Eastern Caribbean in 1989, following the destructive trail of Hurricane Hugo; and a GDF detachment was dispatched to Namibia from June 1989 to April 1990, as part of the UN Special Monitoring Force. In addition, a Joint Services Relief Task Force went to Montserrat from February to April 1990 to build thirty-two houses and repair schools. Moreover, in August 1990, a forty-member contingent from the GDF's First Infantry Battalion spent two weeks in Trinidad aiding internal security in the aftermath of the attempted coup there. Also of note is that a Guyana Police Force contingent spent a year in El Salvador between March 1992 and March 1993 as part of a UN Observer Mission. The GDF also contributed forces to the CARICOM Battalion, which performed postintervention duties in Haiti during late 1994 and early 1995.

According to the defense headquarters in Georgetown, the GDF maintains a wide range of bilateral and some multilateral relationships. For instance, the relationship with the People's Republic of China entails training in China for senior and midrank officers in several areas, high-level military exchange visits, and grants of military supplies. Guyana-U.S. military contacts involve specialist training at U.S. military academies through its International Military Education and Training (IMET) program, and military assistance with transportation, communications, and maritime equipment. The GDF also participates in the annual exercise called TRADEWINDS, which is sponsored by the United States.

Moreover, Guyana makes available its Jungle and Amphibious Training facilities to U.S. forces and hosts port call visits by U.S. Coast Guard vessels. It does the same for British forces, and also benefits from training in British military schools. Al-

though the relationship with the French does not involve training in French military academies, Guyana provides Jungle and Amphibious Training facilities and host naval vessels, and it conducts exchanges with the French military. GDF officers also benefit from training offered by Brazil, Canada, India, and Venezuela. The relationship with Brazil is more diversified than with Venezuela, for understandable reasons, and involves training in Brazil, support for the GDF Coast Guard, intelligence exchange cross-border activities, and high-level military exchange visits (Guyana Defense Force 2004).

Jamaica

The Jamaica Defense Force (JDF) became operational in July 1962, just weeks before Jamaica's independence from Britain on August 6, 1962. Its core element was the Jamaica Regiment, a key component of the West Indies Regiment (WIR), the defense outfit of the ill-fated West Indies Federation (1958–1962). The First Battalion of the WIR was based in Jamaica. The JDF was conceived as an integrated army, with a coast guard and an air wing, although the latter was not created until 1963. Headquarters were established at Up Park Camp, Kingston, with companies in Kingston, Montego Bay, Mandeville, and May Pen. The JDF falls under the portfolio of the Ministry of National Security, with its operational head as the chief of staff.

The JDF initially comprised the Force Headquarters, two regular units, and the Jamaica National Reserve. In order to improve command and control, in 1973 the Support and Services Battalion was formed to incorporate all the support units of the former Headquarters and Support units. In 1977 the renamed JDF Air Wing and JDF Coast Guard, previously subunits of Support and Services Battalion, were made autonomous. In the same year the JDF Construction Squadron, which initially consisted of noncombatant soldiers and which was raised to support a government minidam program, was established as a subunit of the Support and Services Battalion. Seventeen years after the formation of the Jamaica Regiment, another regular infantry battalion increased its size, when the Second Battalion of the Jamaica Regiment was formed in 1979. In similar responses to both internal and official civil needs, the engineering elements of the JDF were both upgraded and consolidated in 1991 with the formation of the First Engineer Regiment, incorporating the JDF Engineer Unit and the JDF Construction Squadron.

The JDF now comprises the following eight major units, in order of precedence:

- The First Battalion—the Jamaica Regiment, an infantry unit.
- The Second Battalion—the Jamaica Regiment, an infantry unit.
- The Support and Services Battalion, comprising the Medical Reception Station, Pay Office, Jamaica Military Band, Information Systems Center, Military Records Section, Training Depot, Workshop, and the Transport Unit.
- The JDF Air Wing.
- The JDF Coast Guard.
- The First Engineer Regiment, comprising the Field, Construction, Support, and Maintenance squadrons and a Power Plant Troop. Interestingly, the Power Plant Troop is tasked with operating the Jamaica Public Service Company's supplementary power-generating barge in Kingston, the Jamaican capital.
- The JDF Intelligence Unit.
- The Third Battalion of the Jamaica Regiment (National Reserve).

In keeping with one of its designated roles, the JDF has supported the Jamaica Constabulary Force (JCF), the national civil police organization, in the maintenance of law and order. The JDF and the JCF have a long history of joint operations, dating to July 1962. However, passage of the Suppression of Crime (Special Provisions) Act in 1974 gave the JDF-JCF collaboration a new dimension. The JDF was permitted to cordon off any area of the island while the JCF conducted house-to-house searches. In addition, the JDF assisted Jamaican water-supply development from 1983 to 1985 with the construction of a major water pipeline from Yallahs, St. Thomas, to the Mona Reservoir in St. Andrew. Between March 1993 and July 1995 the Engineer Regiment repaired more than 55 kilometers of farm roads in several parishes of Jamaica. Ever since its formation the force has helped essential services during industrial disputes. The JDF is also very active in environmental protection.

The JDF Coast Guard is trained and equipped to deal with marine oil spills, and, interestingly, it sent one officer and a senior rate to Alaska in 1990 to assist with the clean-up of the *Exxon Valdez* oil spill. Also on the international front, the JDF was part of the coalition of regional forces that restored democracy to Grenada between 1983 and 1985. It was also a part of the multinational force that intervened in Haiti in 1994 to assist in the restoration of democracy and subsequently provided a contingent for peacekeeping duties there, serving for the first time under the flag of the United Nations. Beyond that, troops were deployed to Antigua, Dominica, and St. Lucia after the devastation of Hurricane Hugo in 1989, to the Bahamas following Hurricane Andrew in 1992, and to Antigua, Barbuda, and Anguilla in 1995 following Hurricane Luis.

An important recent development is the adoption of the NATO Continental Staff System, from July 2003. The essence of the Continental Staff System is a combination of letters and numbers, which indicate the level and purpose of a given appointment. For example, at command headquarters there will be a number of principal staff branches—Personnel, Intelligence, Operations, Training, Finance, and Logistics—numbered 1 through 6. The adoption of the Continental Staff System, which entailed significant change to the JDF's operating structure, required the standardization of the JDF's operating structure in line with the system used by NATO and the armed forces, with which the JDF maintains close ties through training, exercises, and diplomatic arrangements, including the forces in Canada, the United Kingdom, the United States, and some CARICOM countries. With the full implementation of the Continental Staff System, the JDF will move away from the old system of using two branches, the General Staff (G) Branch and the Adjutant Quartermaster (A) Branch, and will reconfigure the headquarters into four branches (Griffith 1993; Jamaica Defense Force 2004).

Trinidad and Tobago

The British overlords in Trinidad and Tobago disbanded the regiment after World War II, in 1947. But as the August 31, 1962, independence date approached, it became clear to Trinidadian leaders that they would need to create a standing army. Thus the Trinidad and Tobago Defense Force (TTDF) was created, primarily from the Second Battalion of the West Indies Regiment. The legal birth date is June 1, 1962, when the Trinidad and Tobago Defense Act took effect. The army was formed with a set of modest objectives: to perform ceremonial functions; to aid in providing internal security; and to provide for a token show of force in the event of an external attack.

Trinidad did have a legitimate reason to fear an external security threat, no matter how attenuated. The basis of that fear lay in the dispute with Venezuela over the Gulf of Paria. Nevertheless, it was readily appreciated that the army could not provide any credible defense against a serious external attack. Hemispheric and international networks were considered vital to the country's defense. Official thinking was that defense against foreign aggression was to be met by (1) membership in the Organization of American States; (2) geographic placement under the military umbrella of the states composing the North Atlantic Treaty Organization; and (3) membership in the United Nations.

The security services were reorganized after an army mutiny in 1970, following passage of several laws modifying the 1962 Defense Act. In that respect a major piece of legislation was the Defense (Amendment) Act of 1979, which created the position of chief of defense staff, with responsibility for both the ground force and the coast guard. It also established a five-member Defense Council headed by the national security minister and including the chief of staff, the attorney general, and the permanent secretary of the Ministry of National Security. According to Section 5 of the 1979 legislation, the Defense Council "[s]hall be responsible under the general authority of the Minister [of National Security] for the command, administration, and discipline of and all matters relating to the Force," except that "the responsibility of the Council shall not extend to the operational use of the Force for which responsibility shall vest in the Chief of Defense Staff subject to the general or special direction of the Minister."

The 1979 amendment also created a Commissions Board to advise the president, through the national security minister, on appointments to commissions and promotions up to the rank of major/lieutenant commander. The 1962 Defense Act had made no provision for community service activities. Consequently, the army had a limited role in national life and in fact had very few contacts with the populace prior to the 1970 mutiny. The postmutiny changes introduced community service projects. The army has even been used to deliver fuel oil, sugar, and other supplies during major strikes in the oil and sugar industries. Thus the original mission statement was a far cry from the current one: "To contribute to the maintenance of a safe and secure environment for the well being of the people of Trinidad and Tobago, and to assist in the promotion of hemispheric and international security and development, with a well equipped force, trained in a broad range of disciplines and actively involved in community development."

The TTDF, still popularly called the Trinidad Regiment, is a defense force with ground, air, and maritime units. Policy is the responsibility of the Defense Council, with political direction flowing from the minister of National Security. The president of the republic is commander-in-chief, but operational command of the force lies with the chief of

Defense Staff, who holds the rank of brigadier general and operates from force headquarters at Chaguaramas, where the principal units are Personnel (J1), Intelligence (J2), Operations and Training (J3), Logistics (J4), Civil/Military Relations (J5), and Information Systems (J6). The main components of the TTDF are the regiment, the coast guard, and the Volunteer Defense Force. The TTDF presently is reviewing its strategic plan seeking to align its plan with the government's 2020 vision. To that end the TTDF has proposed a five-year strategic plan to develop its land force to brigade strength, its maritime force from coast guard status to that of a navy, and an independent air force.

With regard to community involvement, the TTDF continues to manage the Civilian Conservation Corp, which attracts young people with only a primary school education. In addition, the TTDF has been tasked to manage three other community programs: Military Led Academic Program, Military Led Youth Partnership and Reorientation Training, and National Service. These three programs were due to begin during 2004, and the TTDF had already submitted the concept papers to establish them. The Defense Force Steel Band and Military Band continue to be popular and in demand for many community activities, strengthening the interface between the defense force and the general population (Trinidad and Tobago Defense Force 2004). The air wing operates out of bases at the Piarco International Airport in Trinidad and the Crown Point Airport in Tobago, while the coast guard has its headquarters at Staubles Bay, Trinidad. The TTDF has extended training assistance to other Caribbean countries, especially in coast guard operations. The Trinidad and Tobago Coast Guard has helped train officers for similar units in Jamaica, Barbados, and Antigua, among other places, both in Trinidad and in the nations concerned. As might be expected, Trinidad and its army have received foreign military assistance, primarily from Britain, but also from the United States, Canada, and even from a country about which Trinidad has been deeply suspicious, Venezuela.

Trinidad has the dubious distinction of being the first English-speaking Caribbean country in which military officers challenged the legitimate political rulers, almost succeeding in overthrowing them. The April 1970 mutiny occurred in the context of social unrest beginning the previous February 26. The unrest involved student protests and black power activism precipitated by a sense of frustration caused by increased economic deprivation, among other things. On April 21, 1970, two Sandhurst graduates, lieutenants Raffique Shah and Rex Lasalle, turned their weapons against Lt. Colonel Henry Christopher and Captain Julian Spencer, the ranking TTDF officers at the army base at Chaguanas. Other officers helped subdue the mutineers, but in the process Shah's rifle fired a shot.

That shot was interpreted by others in the plan as a signal to act. Subsequently, the ammunition bunker was occupied, and Shah and Lasalle were freed. Negotiations between the rebels and the government led to their surrender on May 1. There was a lengthy trial by a tribunal composed of military officials from Ghana, Nigeria, Singapore, Uganda, and Guyana. Shah was sentenced to twenty years in prison on mutiny and treason convictions. Lasalle was given fifteen years, and thirty of the eighty-five other soldiers involved were given lesser terms. Shah and Lasalle were freed later,

as their convictions were overturned by the Trinidad and Tobago Court of Appeals on legal technicalities. The other mutineers were also released (Griffith 1993; Trinidad and Tobago Defense Force 2004).

Civil-Military Relations/The Role of the Military in Domestic Politics

Neither Belize nor Guyana—nor Jamaica nor Trinidad and Tobago—has witnessed any political rule by the military, although, as explained earlier, a section of the military in Trinidad and Tobago did try to seize power in 1970, and, also as explained above, the Forbes Burnham government in Guyana co-opted the military forces in exercising political rule. That very fortunate situation, especially when compared with those in neighboring Latin America, derives from several factors. One is the small size of the military establishments. A second is the nonpraetorian and noncaudillo political culture developed under British colonial rule. There is no reason to believe that this situation will change anytime soon. The democratic culture is strongly entrenched in each of the countries, and there is both respect for and acceptance of civilian control of security and law enforcement agencies.

Terrorism

None of the countries under discussion—Belize, Guyana, Jamaica, and Trinidad and Tobago—are on either the UN or the U.S. list of terrorist nations. (Cuba is the only Caribbean country listed on the U.S. list of terrorist-sponsoring states. Although Cuba undoubtedly has engaged in such actions in previous decades, there has been no independent corroboration of the U.S. claim over the last few years.) Nor do any of the four countries harbor any terrorist organization. Occasionally, there have been accusations in relation to Jamaat-al-Muslimeen, the Black Muslim organization in Trinidad that tried to overthrow the government in Trinidad and Tobago in July 1990. There also have been charges of linkages between that group and cells and organizations in the Middle East. But no credible evidence has been provided to support those charges. The fact that Guyana and Trinidad and Tobago have fairly sizable populations of nationals who follow Islam, and of people of Middle Eastern descent, is reason for the United States to monitor developments there.

Within the wider Caribbean politics and law enforcement, officials have raised the prospects of several likely threat possibilities: that the region's maritime and air networks could be used for conveyance of terrorist operatives and operational assets; that terrorists could use the region's banking and other financial systems to finance their pursuits; and that regional port or air facilities could be used to stage terrorist operations, either targeted to places in the region or elsewhere. Thus, because of their very limited military and law enforcement capabilities, the geopolitical connections to the United States, and the tourism and offshore banking industries there, these countries are vulnerable to use by terrorists as staging grounds for campaigns directed against the United States or other countries. Needless to say the region has not been immunized against terrorism, even before September 11, 2001. For instance, in the postindependence period in Trinidad and Tobago there were "ideologically Zionist" bombings, and in Guyana

scholar-politician Walter Rodney was assassinated in June 1980.

The most devastating terrorist incident within the Caribbean occurred in October 1976, when a bomb aboard a *Cubana Air* flight from Guyana to Cuba was detonated shortly after the flight departed Barbados, where it had made a transit stop. All seventy-three people onboard—fifty-seven Cubans, eleven Guyanese, and five North Koreans—were killed. Anti-Castro exiles based in Venezuela later claimed responsibility for the action. In August 1998, while on a visit to Barbados, President Fidel Castro of Cuba dedicated a monument to the victims of the incident. Moreover, Cuba suffered a dozen bombings of tourist locations during 1997, allegedly orchestrated by anti-Castro Cuban exiles in Miami and Central America. Elsewhere in the region, there have been "*independentisa* bombings" by the *Macheteros* in Puerto Rico, and "nationalist bombings" in Guadeloupe (Griffith 2004).

Relationship with the United States

Overall, the relations between the countries discussed here and the United States are positive, with economic and trade interests, counternarcotics, and counterterrorism making for wide-ranging bilateral and multilateral dealings. For instance, the United States gets sixty-five percent of its liquefied natural gas (LNG) from Trinidad and Tobago, and plans are underway both to expand LNG production and the LNG trade with the United States. Moreover, all four countries have counternarcotics agreements with the United States, covering things such as overflight by its military aircraft, the boarding of suspect ships by its coast guard in these countries' territorial waters, and entry into their territory by its military and law enforcement forces to investigate drug operations.

However, some of the countries, and the regional organization called CARICOM of which they are members, have serious disagreements with the United States on several issues. The list includes relations with Cuba, political developments in Haiti, the creation of the International Criminal Court (ICC), which was the brain-child of A. N. R. Robinson, a former president of Trinidad, and intervention in Iraq. Free trade matters, notably the FTAA, and the issue of criminal deportations to the Caribbean also have been areas of contention that will continue to have traction. In the case of deportations, the numbers involved are relatively high for the small jurisdictions, as Table 5 shows. None of the countries under review is under U.S. sanction, except that in relation to Jamaica and Trinidad and Tobago, their signature of the ICC treaty has led to U.S. suspension of military sales and grants.

The Future

The key security developments to be watched pertain to recent developments

Table 5   Criminal Deportees from the United States, January 1997 to October 2003

Country	Number of criminal deportees	Average age when entered U.S.*	% of deportees 13 years or older at entry into U.S.	% of deportees 18 years or older at entry into U.S.	Average age when deportee returned to country of origin	% of deportees that entered U.S. without immigrant visa
Antigua and Barbuda	170	19.6	76	54	34	60
Bahamas	546	22	79	67	32	86
Barbados	286	16.7	65	38	34	46
Dominica	106	19.2	76	54	33	43
Dominican Republic	12,366	22.9	86	67	34	56
Grenada	100	19.5	70	50	34	61
Guyana	813	19	71	47	33	40
Haiti	2,138	20.1	77	54	33	65
Jamaica	8,001	22.47	83	65	34	60
St. Kitts and Nevis	107	18.3	73	51	35	44
St. Lucia	112	22.3	78	63	32	65
St. Vincent and the Grenadines	104	22.77	85	62	33	64
Suriname	21	24.65	95	70	33	81
Trinidad and Tobago	1,164	19.26	72	48	36	49
Summary	26,034	21	82	63	34	58

Note: *This is the average age for deportees with known dates of entry.

Source
U.S. Bureau of Citizenship and Immigration Services, December 2003.

on the Guyana-Suriname dispute, the Belize-Guatemala dispute, counternarcotics, organized crime, geopolitical vulnerability in relation to terrorism, and the prospect that poverty can precipitate political instability. The dispute between Guyana and Venezuela seems headed for an appreciable lull if not a resolution following the visit to Guyana by President Hugo Chavez in February 2004, during which he publicly denounced "the military solution" and offered to aid Guyana's pursuit of economic development in the disputed territory. Relations with the United States will continue to experience highs and lows, but they are critical for the economic and political stability of the countries reviewed here and the region as a whole.

References, Recommended Readings, and Websites

Books and Articles

Bernal, Richard L., J. Leslie Winsome, and Stephen E. Lamar. 2000. "Debt, Drugs, and Structural Adjustment in the Caribbean." In *The Political Economy of Drugs in the Caribbean*, Ivelaw L. Griffith, ed. London: Macmillan.

Binnendijk, Hans, and L. Erik Kjonnerod. 1997. "Panama 2000." *Strategic Forum* 17 (June). http://www.ndu.edu/inss/strforum/SF117/forum117.html.

Canadian Broadcasting Corporation. 2003. "Guyana Sends Gunboat into Waters Disputed with Suriname," March 23. Available at http://www.cbc.ca/cp/world/030314/w031464.html.

Central Intelligence Agency. 2004. *The World Factbook 2003*. Washington, DC.

Denny, Patrick. 2004. "Guyana Goes to UN to Settle Maritime Row with Suriname." *Stabroek News*, February 26:1.

Diehl, Paul F., and Gary Goertz. 2000. *War and Peace in International Rivalry*. Ann Arbor: University of Michigan Press.

Glasser, Susan B. 2001. "Russia to Dismantle Spy Facility in Cuba," *Washington Post*, October 18:A34.

Gonzalez, Edward. 1982. *A Strategy for Dealing with Cuba*, Rand Corporation, R-2954-DOS/AF, September.

Griffith, Ivelaw L. 1993. *The Quest for Security in the Caribbean: Problems and Promises in Subordinate States*. Armonk, NY: M. E. Sharpe.

———. 1997. *Drugs and Security in the Caribbean: Sovereignty under Siege*. University Park: Pennsylvania State University Press.

———, ed. 2004. *Caribbean Security in the Age of Terror: Challenge and Change*. Kingston, Jamaica: Ian Randle.

Guyana Defense Force. 2004. Communication from Col. Kemraj Persaud to Ivelaw Griffith. March.

International Institute for Strategic Studies. 2003. *The Military Balance 2003/04*. London.

Jamaica Defense Force. 2004. The Jamaica Defense Force, available at http://www.jdfmil.org.

Lakshmanan, Indira. 2003. "Ex-detainees: Guantánamo not Bad," *Miami Herald*, March 27:3A.

Phillips, Dion E. 2004. "Defense, Internal Security and the Other Roles of Belize's Military." *Defense and Security Studies Review* 4, no. 1 (spring). http://www.ndu.edu/chds/journal/.

Trinidad and Tobago Defense Force. 2004. Communication from Col. Edmund Dillon to Ivelaw Griffith. March.

UN Office on Drugs and Crime Caribbean Regional Office. 2003. *Caribbean Drug Trends 2001–2002*. Bridgetown, Barbados, February.

U.S. Drug Enforcement Administration. 2003. *The Drug Trade in the Caribbean: A Threat Assessment*. DEA-03014, September. http://www.usdoj.gov/dea/pubs/intel.htm.

Recommended Readings

Arthur, Prime Minister Owen. 2002. "Address" at the Inaugural Session of the 32nd General Assembly of the Organization of American States. Bridgetown, Barbados, June 2.

Black Britain. 2004. "Barbados and Trinidad Go to UN Arbitration," February 18. Accessed February 28, 2004 from http://www.blackbritain.co.uk/News?News.asp?i.

Bryan, Anthony T., J. Edward Greene, and Timothy M. Shaw, eds. 1990. *Peace, Development, and Security in the*

Caribbean. New York: St. Martin's Press.

Byron, Jessica. 2003. "Rethinking International Relations: Changing Paradigms or More of the Same? A Caribbean Small State Perspective." In *Governance in the Age of Globalization: Caribbean Perspectives*, Kenneth O. Hall and Denis Benn, eds. Kingston: Ian Randle.

Duncan, Neville. 2003. "Governance in Small Societies: The Importance of Strong Democracy." In *Governance in the Age of Globalization: Caribbean Perspectives*, K. O. Hall and Denis Benn, eds. Kingston: Ian Randle.

Heine, Jorge, and Leslie Manigat, eds. 1990. *The Caribbean and World Politics*. York: Holmes and Meier.

Knight, Franklin W. 1978.*The Caribbean: The Genesis of a Fragmented Nationalism*. New York: Oxford University Press.

Knight, W. Andy, and Kenneth B. Persaud. 2001. "Subsidiarity, Regional Governance, and Caribbean Security." *Latin American Politics and Society* 43, no. 1 (spring):29–56.

Manigat, Leslie. 1988. "The Setting: Crisis, Ideology, and Geopolitics." In *The Caribbean and World Politics*, Jorge Heine and Leslie Manigat, eds. New York: Holmes and Meier.

Ramphal, Shridath. 2003. "Governance and the New Imperium." In *Governance in the Age of Globalization: Caribbean Perspectives*, Kenneth O. Hall and Denis Benn, eds. Kingston: Ian Randle.

Richards, Peter. 2004. "CARICOM Delayed by Boundary Dispute." *OCNUS.NET*, Feb. 24. Accessed Feb. 27, 2004, http://www.ocnus.net/artman/publish/article.

Rosenau, James N. 1998. "Hurricanes Are Not the Only Intruders: The Caribbean in an Era of Global Turbulence." In *From Pirates to Drug Lords: The Post–Cold War Caribbean Security Environment*, Michael C. Desch, Jorge I. Domínguez, and Andrés Serbin, eds. Albany: State University of New York Press.

Serbin, Andrés. 1990. *Caribbean Geopolitics: Towards Security through Peace?* Boulder, CO: Lynne Rienner.

Young, Alma H., and Dion E. Phillips, eds. 1986. *Militarization in the Non-Hispanic Caribbean*. Boulder, CO: Lynne Rienner.

Websites
CARIBBEAN REGIONAL
Association of Caribbean Commissioners of Police: http://www.accpolice.org/.
Association of Caribbean States: http://www.acs-aec.org/.
Caribbean Community (CARICOM): http://www.caricom.org/.
Caribbean Customs Law Enforcement Council: http://www.cclec.org.lc/.
Caribbean Maritime Institute: http://www.cmi.edu.jm/.
Caribbean Media Network: http://www.caribbean-media.net/.
Caribbean Shipping Association: http://www.caribbeanshipping.org/archway/front.htm.
Institute of International Relations: http://sta.uwi.edu/socasci/iirt/index.htm.
Regional Security System: http://www.rss.org.bb/index.htm.

BELIZE
Belize Central: http://www.belizecentral.com/.
Belize-Guatemala Relations: http://www.belize-guatemala.gov.bz/.
BelizeNet: http://www.belize.net/search/npl.cgi.
Government of Belize: http://www.belize.gov.bz/.
The Belize Times: http://www.belizetimes.bz/.
University of Belize: http://www.ub.edu.bz/.

GUYANA
Guyana and Caribbean Political and Cultural Center for Popular Education: http://www.guyanacaribbeanpolitics.com/.
Guyana News and Information: http://www.guyana.org/.
Guyana Outpost: http://guyana.gwebworks.com/guyana.shtml.
Land of Six Peoples: http://www.lasalle.edu/~daniels/guyexp/gy1001.htm.
Ministry of Foreign Affairs: http://www.sdnp.org.gy/minfor/.
University of Guyana: http://www.sdnp.org.gy/uog/.

JAMAICA
International Centre for Environmental and Nuclear Sciences: http://www.icens.org/.
Jamaica Defense Force: http://www.jdfmil.org/.

Jamaica Information Service: http://www.
   jis.gov.jm/.
Jamaicans for Justice: http://www.
   jamaicansforjustice.org/.
Ministry of Foreign Affairs and Foreign
   Trade: http://www.skillsreturn.gov.jm/.
Ministry of National Security and Justice:
   http://www.mnsj.gov.jm/.
University of the West Indies, Mona:
   http://www.uwimona.edu.jm/.

TRINIDAD AND TOBAGO
Government of Trinidad and Tobago:
   http://www.gov.tt/.
National Emergency Management
   Agency: http://www.nema.gov.tt/.
Trinicenter: http://www.trinicenter.com/.
Trinidad and Tobago Defense Force:
   http://www.ttdf.mil.tt/.
University of the West Indies, St.
   Augustine: http://www.uwi.tt/.

Chile

Franz Kernic

Geography and History

Chile, situated in southwestern Latin America, has existed as a national entity since 1810, when it declared its independence from the Spanish empire. In terms of geographical coordinates, this rather narrow country stretches from the northernmost city of Arica, situated close to the Peruvian border, to the Strait of Magellan and the world's southernmost town, Puerto Williams. In the west, Chile borders the South Pacific Ocean with a coastline of 6,435 kilometers, while in the east the Andes Mountains form a kind of natural border (with Bolivia and Argentina as neighbors). Because of its location, Chile has long held a strategic position, particularly in terms of sea lanes between the Atlantic and Pacific oceans (Strait of Magellan, Beagle Channel, and Drake Passage).

With an area of 756,945 square kilometers (approximately 292,200 square miles), the country is larger than Texas and nearly twice the size of California; its territory stretches a distance similar to that between San Francisco and New York. Geographically, the terrain is characterized by a desert in the north, a fertile central valley, numerous volcanoes and lakes toward the south, and a rough coastline. In the northern and central part of Chile, the Andes Mountains occupy from a third to a half of the width of the territory, thus representing a significant barrier to transportation and communications, both within the country and with respect to its neighboring country, Argentina.

The vast majority of Chileans are descended from the European invaders of the sixteenth and seventeenth centuries and the Indian tribes and peoples resident in this area at the time of the Spanish conquest. Undoubtedly, the politics of the Spanish conquest and the colonial period have shaped the social, political, and economic structure, as well as the religious life of the country, and they have had a long-lasting influence on its political system. Despite the very strong impact of the European people and culture on Chile's history, economy, social life, and political system, the country's distinctive culture has survived a number of wars, as well as the violence and repression of its recent history.

Most Chileans are of Spanish ancestry, although there have also been small but influential communities of Irish, English, and German immigrants, as well as groups from Italy, Croatia, France, and the Middle East. Indigenous traditions persist in certain regions and parts of Chile, particularly in the southern-central area and the Andean foothills (where there are approximately 400,000 indigenous inhabitants, mostly of the Mapuche tribe). About 85 percent of Chile's population lives in urban centers, with 40 percent living in the metropolitan area of greater Santiago (pop. 5.2 million). The annual population growth rate is approximately 1.0 to 1.5 percent (CIA Factbook 2005; UN *World Statistics Pocketbook* and *Statistical Yearbook*, Human Development Report 2003).

From the sixteenth until the early nineteenth century, Chile's economy was shaped by the global economic policy of the Spanish Empire and its politics of conquest and colonialism. In the process of establishing the postcolonial order, Chile became a role model for many other Latin American states, especially in the area of economic and industrialization policy and practices. Nitrate mines in areas conquered during the War of the Pacific at the end of the nineteenth century became an important source of huge revenues for Chilean society. The so-called nitrate economy ushered Chile into the industrial age and modernization. However, what Loveman (2001) has dubbed "the legacy of Hispanic capitalism"—particularly the fact that in Chile, as in many other Latin American countries, the benefits of capitalism were not widely distributed across the population—has also shaped the country's social stratification and forced Chilean society not only to cope with certain economic difficulties and internal political dissensions but also to deal with tensions between a small minority of wealthy Chileans and the vast majority of the territory's population.

In the early 1970s the socialist government of Salvador Allende attempted to renew Chile's political and social systems as well as its economic policies, but its ambitions quickly came to an end when a military coup succeeded and Allende himself was assassinated (or committed suicide) in the fall of 1973. During the following years of Pinochet's dictatorship (1973–1990), Chile pursued decidedly laissez-faire economic policies and moved toward a largely free-market economy. Thenceforth, the country vigorously pursued expanded trade opportunities and soon became one of Latin America's most competitive and rapidly growing economies. The military regime clearly shifted toward liberalization of domestic economy, privatization of public enterprises and services, increases in domestic and foreign private investment, and export promotion (with a strong emphasis on the Asian market).

With its return to democracy in 1990, Chile became a relatively politically stable and rather economically prosperous South American state. During the early 1990s, Chile even enjoyed the reputation of being a general role model for economic reform, with growth in real GDP at around 8 percent. Economic growth continued at an accelerated rate until the so-called Asian crisis in 1997–1999 (approximately one-third of Chilean exports went to Asia in the mid- and late 1990s). In addition, the country's economy also suffered under the effects of a recession caused by the general financial crisis of the global market and a global economic slowdown leading to lower export earnings. For the first time in more than fifteen years, Chile experienced negative economic growth, but it soon recovered from those negative effects on its economy. During the last few years, economic growth rebounded to 3.1 percent in 2001 and 2.1 percent in 2002, but began a slow recovery in 2003, growing 3.2 percent and accelerating to 5.8 percent in 2004 (CIA World Factbook 2005).

At the end of 2002, Chile signed a free trade agreement with the United States. Nevertheless, the government has never given up its commitment to export-led, free-market policies.

Economically, Chile has a GDP (that is, gross domestic product, or the value of all final goods and services produced within a nation in a given year, derived from purchasing power parity—PPP—calculations) of $169.1 billion (2004 est.) with a per capita income of $10,700 (2004 est.) (ibid.). The annual real growth rate is around 2 to 3 percent (2002–2003 est.). As already pointed out, Chile's economy is characterized by a high level of foreign trade, with copper as its principal export. Natural resources are copper, timber, iron ore, nitrates, precious metals, molybdenum, and hydropower. The country's agricultural products include wheat, potatoes, corn, sugar beets, onions, beans, fruits, livestock, and fish. Its economy is divided among the following major sectors: agriculture, 13.6 percent; industry, 23.4 percent; and services, 63 percent (2003, ibid.). Unemployment remains high in Chile. The traditional range is 4 to 6 percent, although it reached a high of 11 percent nationwide in the late 1980s, thus putting pressure on the overall standard of living. On the other hand, one may also note that the share of Chileans with incomes below the poverty line fell from 46 percent of the population in 1987 to 23 percent in 1998.

Since the early twentieth century, Chile's economy has been highly dependent on its exports. Copper has been among the most important goods, with a production of approximately 3,707,000 metric tons in the year 1998 (http://www.sunsonline.org/trade/process/followup/1998/12180398.htm). In the last decades, nontraditional exports have grown faster than those of copper and other minerals. In 1975 nonmineral exports made up just over 30 percent of total exports, whereas they now account for about 50 percent.

The most important nonmineral exports are forestry and wood products, fresh fruit and processed food, fish meal and seafood, and other manufactured products. Chile's export markets are fairly balanced among Europe, Asia, Latin America, and North America.

The politics of Spanish conquest and colonialism have also shaped Chile's political system and left the country with a strong "authoritarian legacy." Since the conquest, social and political struggles, internal and external wars, and a general polarization of political views and attitudes, as well as tensions between the different classes, have been at the core of Chilean history. In the nineteenth century, Chile developed a truly national political system that paved the way for modernization and impressive economic growth. Chile established a parliamentary-style democracy at the same time. However, the political and constitutional conflicts within Chilean society that had developed in the process of establishing the postcolonial order largely remained unsolved. Political influence in Chile has continuously tended to protect the interests of the ruling oligarchy and has helped to maintain the established class system; it has even at times helped to widen the gap between the wealthy upper class and the vast majority of the Chilean population. In the twentieth century, times of dictatorship were followed by civilian juntas installed by the military, or attempts at establishing a more democratic system.

Following the military coup in 1973 that overturned the socialist Salvador Allende government, which had been in power since 1970, Chile was ruled by a military regime headed by General Augusto Pinochet (see Sidebar). His regime remained in power until 1990. The first years of the Pinochet regime were marked by serious human rights violations. In its later years, however, the regime gradually permitted greater freedom of assembly, speech, and association, and it moved slowly toward the restoration of civilian government and democracy. General Pinochet was denied a second eight-year term as president in a national plebiscite in 1988. In 1990 the democratic government of President Patricio Alywin took over power from the military, although the military-imposed 1980 constitution still remained in place.

That constitution was promulgated on September 11, 1980, after being approved in a national plebiscite. It became effective on March 11, 1981 (amended in 1989, 1993, and 1997). It states that the president of the republic is both the chief of state and head of government. The bicameral national congress (*congreso nacional*) consists of the senate (*senado*) with 49 seats (38 elected by popular vote, 9 designated members, and 2 former presidents who serve six-year terms and are senators for life) and the chamber of deputies (*cámara de diputados*) with 120 elected members (http://www.senado.cl/).

In the 1993 election, Eduardo Frei Ruiz-Tagle of the Christian Democratic Party was elected president for a six-year term; he took office in March 1994. Recardo Largos followed him as president after winning the December 1999 elections. Largos, a socialist who had vigorously opposed the Pinochet dictatorship from exile, took office in March 2000. After 1990, Pinochet himself stayed on as commander of the army, and then, in March 1998, he became a "senator for life" (Chile's constitution provides that former presidents who have served at least six years shall be entitled to a lifetime senate seat). Surprisingly, in October 1998,

---

Sidebar 1   Chilean Coup—11 September 1973

Chile's armed forces, headed by General Augusto Pinochet Ugarte, seized power on 11 September 1973. This military coup, with covert U.S. support, resulted in President Allende's death and the establishment of military dictatorship in Chile. General Pinochet and the armed forces took control of the country. The mostly military cabinet quickly put an end to Chile's "road to Marxism," which had started a few years earlier with the Marxist Salvador Allende being elected president.

In 1974, Pinochet assumed the position of head of state and became the undisputed leader of the country. Civil liberties were restricted at the same time. During the first two years of military rule in Chile, about 80 percent of the cabinet posts were held by military officers. Chilean democracy was destroyed. The events of 11 September 1973, mark a tremendous change in Chilean history, as the new political rule soon resulted in a general militarization of political life in Chilean society.

Source
Pino, Miguel González, and Arturo Fontaine Talavera, eds. 1997. *Los mil días de Allende*, Santiago de Chile: Centro de Estudios Públicos.

Pinochet was arrested in London at the request of a Spanish judge for crimes against humanity and human rights violations. That event resulted in a new and broad public debate on the issue of "truth and justice" with regard to human rights violations in Chile's recent past.

Today, Chile's political landscape is characterized by a wide array of competing political parties that tend to form coalitions when congressional elections are held, because the election system rewards coalition slates. Major political parties are the Alliance for Chile (Alianza) or APC, including RN and UDI; the Christian Democratic Party (PDC); the Coalition of Parties for Democracy (*Concertacion* or CPD); the Communist Party (PC), which did not win a congressional seat in the last election; the Independent Democratic Union (UDI); the National Renewal Party (RN); the Party for Democracy (PPD); the Radical Social Democratic Party (PRSD); and the Socialist Party (PS). The political parties with the largest representation in the current Chilean Congress are the centrist Christian Democratic Party and the center-right National Renewal Party (http://www.electionworld.org/election/chile.htm).

Regional Geopolitics

The Spanish invaders of the sixteenth century were driven into the territory that modern Chile now occupies by the hope of finding extensive gold and silver resources. Although they were not particularly lucky in that regard, they soon recognized the agricultural potential of Chile's central valley. In fact, agriculture and hunting had already played a crucial role in all the Indian cultures that had inhabited the area before the Spanish conquest. When, centuries later, the country's potential for wealth through the exploitation of valuable natural resources (such as nitrate and copper) was discovered, the enormous geopolitical consequences for the country became obvious, causing a number of internal and external conflicts and wars. Chile's strong economy and its rapid economic growth in the past, as well as its enormous recent boost

in international business and trade, can be at least partially explained by its natural resources and its strategic position, particularly with respect to major sea lanes.

The northern Chilean desert contains great mineral wealth, primarily copper and nitrates. Chile's leading export of the nineteenth century was nitrate. Above all else, the Chilean economy of the middle and late nineteenth century depended upon mineral exports. When synthetic nitrates began to be produced, the Atacama Desert became responsible for Chile's leading export, copper. Most of the country's nitrate and copper exports came from mines in this area. This economic development clearly shows the geopolitical importance of that region, which consequently has been disputed by Chile and Bolivia since the mid-nineteenth century. The conflict was partially resolved by a treaty in 1866, but a few decades later Bolivia lost "all the territory and riches under dispute, along with its access to the Pacific, when it was defeated by Chile in the War of the Pacific" (Loveman 2001, 124). As a result of the war, the Atacama corridor came to Chile in 1884, but it has been disputed among Chile, Peru, and Bolivia ever since. Being aware of the enormous natural resources of the Atacama, Bolivia still continues to press Chile and Peru to restore the corridor. On the other hand, Chile demands water rights to Bolivia's Rio Lauca and Silala Spring.

The relatively small central area of Chile dominates the country in terms of population and agricultural resources. Fruits, agriculture, and wine have always played a major economic role there. The area is also the historical center, from which Chile expanded until the late nineteenth century, when it incorporated its northern and southern regions. Fishing, sheep, livestock, oil, and natural gas have been of importance in southern Chile. "This part is rich in forests and grazing lands and features a string of volcanoes and lakes. The southern coast is a labyrinth of fjords, inlets, canals, twisting peninsulas, and islands. It also has small, rapidly declining petroleum reserves, which supplied about 8% of Chile's domestic requirements during 1996" (http://en.wikipedia.org/wiki/Demographics_of_Chile).

Because of the country's unique geopolitical and strategic situation in Latin America, boundary problems dominate a considerable portion of Chile's history. The most important international boundary disputes, which have continued over the last centuries, have concerned the Beagle Channel islands in the south, the territory of the Atacama Desert, the Tacna-Arica question in the north, the country's territorial claims in Antarctica (Chilean Antarctic Territory), and, finally, the Easter Island question in the Pacific. These boundary problems must still be seen as major sources of potential conflict. They have been the main concern of Chile's foreign policy and diplomacy for the last one hundred years, particularly with respect to its foreign relations with Chile's neighboring countries of Peru, Bolivia, and Argentina (but also partially overlapping U.S. and British claims—for example, Antarctica).

There can be no doubt that the expansion of mainland Chile in the nineteenth century resulted in tremendous economic advantages for the country and its population. Chilean governments realized early on the enormous importance of possessing those territories, not only for strengthening the country's economic and geostrategic position as a basis for communication and defense but also for future economic prosperity and general social and political development within Latin America. Geopolitical thinking had always played a major role in Chilean society and politics; that became more important than ever when the Pinochet military junta took over power in 1973.

A general revival of geopolitical concepts in the early Pinochet years also reaffirmed the position of Easter Island in Chile's strategic thinking. "Growing acceptability of a 320-kilometer (200-mile) economic limit for territorial waters . . . provoked Chilean interest in the Pacific Ocean as a future resource base. The enactment of Supreme Decree No. 346 on 5 June 1974 officially named the waters off Chile as the 'Sea of Chile,' and confirmed the nation's maritime avocation" (Porteous 1981, 234). To date, Chile has not given up its strategic thinking about the Pacific, nor its intention of maintaining its sphere of influence in Oceania. Chile's geographical position has made it a natural maritime power since the late nineteenth century. Therefore, for more than a century the country has tried to reach out far into the west of the Pacific Ocean and to maintain control of its strategic position in the south, where the Atlantic and Pacific meet.

Conflict Past and Present

Since the early sixteenth century, military conflicts and political struggles have been at the heart of Chilean history. It is true that "the territory occupied by the Chilean nation is the prize of military conquest" (Loveman 2001, 8). It is, of course, also the case that Spanish conquistadors took the land from a variety of indigenous peoples in the sixteenth century, and that ever since Chile's history has shown a long string of wars and military conflicts. Recurrent warfare characterized the colonial period. "Spanish religious and government authorities periodically negotiated peace treaties with Indian leaders in what became a ritualized system of conferences (*parlamentos*) and peace accords (*paces*), followed by breaches of the agreement and renewed conflict" (ibid., 58). Continuing conflicts and occasional major insurrections (1655, 1723) resulted in important peace negotiations and treaties in 1647, 1651, 1738, 1756, 1760, 1764, 1767, and 1794 (ibid.).

In September 1810 the creation of a national junta was proclaimed, and the door to freedom and independence was opened. Nevertheless, Chile had to fight for its independence for almost a decade. Four years of civil war (1810–1814) and uncertain advances toward independence were followed by the so-called *Reconquista*—that is, the Spanish attempt to reimpose arbitrary rule through force of arms (1814–1817)—and, finally, a prolonged struggle during the time of the Bernardo O'Higgins dictatorship (1817–1823); Chilean independence was formally proclaimed on February 12, 1818. Even O'Higgins's dictatorship did not really contribute to introducing a long-lasting period of stability and peace.

The 1820s were instead characterized by the continuation of political uncertainty and instability, the chaotic succession of governments, political crises, and, finally, even a civil war (1829–1830). Those internal conflicts and crises were soon accompanied by external military conflicts, and they led to the extension of Chile's national territory—achieved mostly by the use of force. In sum, nineteenth-century Chilean conflicts can be characterized as a combination of internal and external conflicts and wars, starting with the struggle for independence and the *Reconquista*, followed by numerous political crises and civil wars during the two decades following the year 1810. The war with the Peru-Bolivia confederation occurred in 1836–1839, followed by electoral violence and coup threats in the mid-1840s, civil wars in 1850–1851 and 1858–1859, the War with Spain (1865–1866), the War of the Pacific (1879–1884), the civil war of 1891, and numerous failed rebellions and a state of siege in the years 1893–1894 (see Table 1).

In the War of the Pacific (1879–1883), Chilean armed forces defeated Bolivian and Peruvian forces. When the country incorporated much of the Atacama Desert into its national domain as a result of that war, it gained access to and control of an important territory with great national resources.

Despite their large number and high intensity, the conflicts, civil wars, and political revolts of the nineteenth century brought little social change to Chilean society; its social structure remained almost unchanged, thus preserving the essence of the stratified colonial social, political, and administrative system. The general dispute about the basic character of the constitution and the balance of power in the postcolonial order

Table 1   Major Wars and Militarized Interstate Disputes (Chile)

1836–1839	War against Bolivia and Peru (Peruvian Confederation)
1865–1866	Spanish-Chilean War
1879–1884	War of the Pacific (Chile against Peru and Bolivia)
1977–1984	Beagle Dispute between Chile and Argentina

remained widely unsolved, as did the tensions between the small minority of wealthy Chileans and the vast majority of the population. The system of presidential power eventually predominated (important steps forward in establishing a new constitutional order were made in 1822 and 1828), but wealthy landowners continued to control the political, social, and economic life in Chile. Even in that respect, however, a certain pattern of political and constitutional conflicts and polarizing political views within the Chilean society developed, which would recur often during the nineteenth and twentieth centuries.

The War of the Pacific did not only enlarge Chilean territory by more than a third; it also accelerated the process of establishing a modern nation-state with its own political identity. Chilean soldiers occupied Lima in 1881. In the same year, Chile signed a treaty with Argentina confirming Chilean sovereignty over the Strait of Magellan. With the end of the War of the Pacific, the victorious Chileans dictated a harsh settlement to Peru and Bolivia in 1883 (the Treaty of Ancón). A few years later, they began to establish a standing army. After a comprehensive reform of its armed forces, the military became an important and powerful element of national life and Chilean society. Toward the end of the nineteenth century, the Chilean government consolidated its position in the south by persistently suppressing the Mapuche Indians.

The years 1924–1932 brought a break in constitutional and political stability. By the 1920s, growing tensions between the social classes had become a new threat to the political order and stability of the country. The emerging middle and working classes had become powerful enough to elect a reformist president and to launch new social programs that favored their own interests. The military coups of 1924 and 1925, however, put a quick end to all plans of social reform. Instead, continuing political and economic instability led to a new dictatorship under the rule of General Carlos Ibañez (1924–1932). It was not until the restoration of constitutional rule in 1932 that a strong middle-class party could emerge and gain power in Chile. That new party, the so-called Radical Party, soon turned into a key force in coalition governments for the next twenty years (1932–1952). The end to the Radical Party presidencies came in 1952, when Carlos Ibañez came to power; he ruled until 1958.

Chile's politics between 1952 and 1973 may again be characterized by a certain pattern of cyclical political and social violence and political ruptures, as well as military coups. The most important event in recent Chilean history occurred in 1973, when, on September 11, the armed forces overthrew President Allende in a military coup and seized power. The military coup cut short the Chilean "road to socialism" under the socialist Allende. For the next seventeen years, Chileans lived under military dictatorship (1973–1990). General Pinochet's regime even continued to influence everyday life in the 1990s, when two elected presidents governed the country and the transition period toward civilian rule had already come into place.

The internal political and social conflicts that became so obvious in Chile in the mid and late twentieth century were accompanied by a number of serious border conflicts during the time of Pinochet's military rule. Over the course of the last two centuries, the extension of the Chilean national domain by different means—both militarily as well as peacefully—has led to numerous conflicts with its neighboring countries, as well as with the international community. To date, the territories that Chile acquired in the nineteenth century, particularly during the War of the Pacific (1879–1884), have remained a source of friction and potential conflict among Chile, Peru, and Bolivia. Another important source of conflict resulted from the fact that Chile also claims substantial portions of Antarctica (lat. 53°W—90°W) and Easter Island, located in the middle of the Pacific Ocean and formally taken over by the Chileans in 1888.

In addition, a long-lasting border dispute with Argentina, dating back to the late nineteenth century, was renewed during Pinochet's regime, thus increasing the probability of war between the two nations. In the 1980s, the previously agreed upon principle regarding the separation of Chile's sphere of influence (the Pacific) from Argentina's (the Atlantic) was once again called into question. The conflict about the Beagle Channel islands nearly led to a war between the two nations that could finally be resolved only through papal mediation, in 1984. However, a few years later, armed incidents occurred again when oil was discovered in the disputed territory.

Alliance Structure

With the transition to civilian democratic rule in the early 1990s, Chile again became an important and active participant in the international political arena. Economically, it has already played a crucial international role during the time of military dictatorship because of Pinochet's vigorously pursued expanded trade policies. Consequently, Chile joined a number of cooperative international trade organizations and became a full member of the Asia-Pacific Economic Cooperation Forum (APEC) and the Pacific Economic Cooperation Council (PECC). For many years, Chile has been an active member of the Rio Group. It became an associate member of MERCOSUR in 1996 and signed free trade agreements with many other Latin American countries, Mexico, the United States, and Canada. Finally, the country signed the Framework Cooperation Agreement with the European Union.

On many occasions, Chile has proven to be a strong proponent of pressing ahead with negotiations for a Free Trade Agreement of the Americas (FTAA). It not only supported the implementation of the 1994 Summit of the Americas but also hosted the second Summit in Santiago four years later. In sum, the Chilean government is actively seeking to promote the country's exports on the global market.

Politically, Chile has been an active member of the United Nations and the UN family of agencies for many years. It has also participated in various UN peacekeeping activities and international UN programs (e.g., UNSCOM in Iraq, and presently in Haiti). The country served on the UN Security Council from 1995 until 1997. In 1993, a Russian Foreign Intelligence Service report listed Chile as possibly having a chemical weapons program. However, this claim has not been confirmed. In that context, it must be mentioned that Chile ratified the Chemical Weapons Convention (CWC) in 1996. In recent years, Chile has established quite good relations with other Latin American countries. The Chilean government has diplomatic relations with most countries, including Cuba, but maintains only consular relations with Bolivia. Chile's border disputes still influence its relations with Peru and Bolivia.

Size and Structure of the Military

The Chilean armed forces were quite small throughout the middle decades of the nineteenth century. Before the war with Bolivia and Peru, the army counted fewer than 2,500 men under arms. But then the War of the Pacific changed that situation dramatically. Rapid military victories against Bolivia and Peru as well as the acquisition of the northern territories "and the persistent Argentine border dispute now gave a new mission to the Chilean military. The threat of conflict with Peru and Bolivia or with Argentina made military preparedness a national concern" (ibid., 151). The professionalization and modernization of the Chilean military, following the Prussian model of how to establish modern armed forces, started immediately after the War of the Pacific in the mid-1880s and led to the establishment of a strong military organization in Chile.

Rapidly, a new professional military elite emerged, gradually taking over a crucial role in Chilean politics and society. That development, of course, also entailed serious consequences for Chile's already existing tendency toward authoritarian rule. The professionalization of the Chilean armed forces must be seen as an important prerequisite for the country's future development toward authoritarianism and military rule, which became a familiar pattern in Chilean political life throughout the twentieth century. Undoubtedly, the armed forces—with their growing numbers of personnel, better equipment, and well-organized professional military training—became an increasingly dominant political force.

The growth in personnel indicated not only the growing strength and power of the military organization but also a certain degree of permanent militarization in Chilean politics and society. Gradually, the Chilean army became "the army of the state. Out of the political situation from the time of its progressively oriented intervention in the years 1925–32 emerged an army that included all social classes, just as the state appeared to be one that represented the whole people" (Rouquié 1987, 229).

Nevertheless, the Chilean armed forces rapidly developed their own special values, traditions, and views toward politics. There can be no doubt that this professionalized, well-organized military, based on extensive military training and specific socialization systems for the officers, engendered strong links between the officer corps and the state. Consequently, the officers displayed strong loyalty to the state as well as to their military institution or units; that strong loyalty evolved into a belief system, in which officers frequently viewed the military as much better prepared and organized for fulfilling the necessary political tasks of the country than most civilian institutions. As a result, the issue of the balance or imbalance between civilian and military institutions in Chilean politics and society became one of the most crucial concerns of twentieth-century Chilean history.

Today, the Chilean Ministry of Defense is composed of the following military branches: first, the three military forces (*fuerzas armadas*)—the army, the navy (including naval air, coast guard, and marines), and the air force—and second, the internal security forces (*fuerzas orden y seguridad*) of the Chilean National Police (*Carabineros de Chile*) and the Investigative Service or Investigations Police. The aim of the latter is to protect domestic order and security. After the 1973 military coup, the Chilean national police were incorporated into the Ministry of Defense. Under the 1980 constitution, all military forces enjoy a large degree of legal autonomy. Upon return to civilian rule after 1990, the police were placed under the operational control of the Interior Ministry, but remained under the nominal control of the Ministry of Defense.

The armed forces are subject to civilian and democratic control exercised by the president through the minister of Defense. "The Ministry of National Defense directs and coordinates its subordinate organizations for the accomplishment of their assigned missions at the domestic security and environmental level, particularly safeguarding public order during elections and plebiscites, in compliance with Article 18 of the Constitution, and fulfilling the specific tasks assigned to each of them, in any of the scenarios that correspond to a state of exception, as foreseen by the Constitution and Constitutional Organic Law 18,145 for States of Exception" (Ministry of Defense, 7).

According to Chile's national defense plan, the most important defense objectives are the preservation of the independence and sovereignty of the country; the maintenance of Chile's territorial integrity; contributing to the preservation of the rule of law; the safeguarding, strengthening, and renewal of the country's cultural and historical identity; contributing, in a well-balanced way, to the development of national power; strengthening the citizen's commitment to defense, and contributing to the preservation and promotion of international peace and security in accordance with national interests (ibid.).

Another important institution in the defense sector and the security- and military-related decision-making process is the National Security Council (*Consejo de seguridad nacional*—Cosena). In addition to Cosena, two other bodies, whose functions are specifically limited to the advisory level, deal with matters of national defense and security: the Politico-Strategic Advisory Council (*Consejo asesor político-estratégico*—CAPE) and the Internal Security Advisory Council (*Consejo asesor de seguridad interior*—CASI). CAPE is entrusted with long-range planning for the defense and external security of the state, while CASI deals with internal security planning (http://www.globalsecurity.org/military/world/chile/mod.htm).

Chile's estimated total military manpower available (men from 18 to 49 years) is 3,815,761 (2005 est.); the military manpower fit for military service (men from 18 to 49 years) is 3,123,281 (2005 est.); the military manpower of male citizens reaching military age annually is 140,084 (2005 est.) (CIA Factbook, 2005 est.). The armed forces have a total strength of 77,300 personnel on active duty, including 22,400 conscripts and about 50,000 reservists (Military Balance 2003–2004). Terms of service are one year in the army and twenty-two months in the navy and air force. The 47,700-person army is organized into six divisions, one separate brigade, and an air wing. The 19,000-person navy, including 3,500 marines and 1,000 conscripts, also operates its own naval aircraft with approximately 600 personnel. The fleet is allocated to four naval zones and is composed of a number of surface vessels and submarines. The manpower of the air force, which consists of five air brigades, is about 10,600 personnel, including 700 conscripts. The

Carabineros or national police, have a total manpower of about 36,800 and are responsible for public order and safety as well as border security, while the much smaller civilian Investigations Police are responsible for criminal investigations and immigration control (ibid.).

Budget

For many decades, Chile's armed forces have benefited substantially from financial aid programs and other kinds of military support from the U.S. government. Military cooperation with the United States had already played a crucial role in the pre-Pinochet era and became even more important in the 1970s and 1980s. In the late 1980s, Chile also collaborated with the United Kingdom firm Royal Ordnance to develop the Rayo (Lightning) multiple launch artillery rocket (Foss 1990, 695). Defense expenditures increased dramatically with the 1973 coup and the following military rule.

In recent years, Chile's defense budget increased slightly and came to approximately U.S.$1.1 billion in 2002 and $1.2 billion in 2003. "However, total defense spending in 2002 was closer to $2.8 billion when extra budgetary items are considered, including approximately $233 million devoted to defense from the proceeds of Chile's 2002 copper exports. Chile's Army Commander Lieutenant-General Juan Cheyre outlined, under '*Plan Bicentenario*,' proposals to modernize the army through the procurement of main battle tanks, armored personnel carriers, antitank helicopters and new command-and-control systems. Around $1 billion would need to be earmarked for this modernization program, which is scheduled for completion by 2010. The Chilean government, though, has indicated a preference to prioritize

the navy and the air force" (Military Balance 2003–2004, 311).

Civil-Military Relations

When the Chilean government contracted the German lieutenant-colonel Emil Körner to become subdirector at the Military Academy (*Escuela Militar*) and to direct the modernization of Chilean military education in 1885, the country launched the general process of the professionalization and modernization of its armed forces following the Prussian model; it also formed a new military elite and officer corps, entailing serious consequences for the future development of civil-military relations. But Chile went even a step further and tried to "export" the new model of a professional military to other Latin American countries. Therefore we witness the curious "phenomenon of 'second-hand' Prussianization carried out by the Chilean army in several countries of the continent. In Ecuador, Colombia, El Salvador, and Venezuela, Chilean military missions were called upon to reorganize and to 'Europeanize' the national army" (Rouquié 1987, 83).

In the twentieth century, the Chilean military not only grew in personnel and equipment but also became a dominant political force. Frequently, the officer corps became disillusioned with civilian rule and intervened in politics. The 1920s, in particular, brought a number of military coups, followed by military dictatorship, various military and civil-military juntas in the early 1930s, and a failed coup by General Ariosto Herrera on August 25, 1939. In general, one can observe all across the twentieth century a pattern of cyclical military interference in the spheres of politics and social life in Chile, and a strong tendency among the officer corps to do so in order to maintain order and security.

The most important military coup in recent Chilean history was the putsch against President Allende in September 1973. There can be no doubt that the capture of the army was already at the center of all domestic political and social confrontations in the early 1970s, when the socialist government came into power. Its rule was based on public support of a small majority. At the beginning, the army "loyally supported Allende and guaranteed the continuation of the socialist experience in the name of the defense of the Constitution. This was also to be the death knell of Popular Unity and the democratic regime. No one was unaware that most of the generals were not sympathetic to socialism" (ibid., 241). Not surprisingly, it was the military that overthrew Salvador Allende and the Popular Unity regime in the coup of September 11, 1973.

In his book *Legacy of Hispanic Capitalism*, Brian Loveman pointed out that "unlike the military-dominated governments in Argentina, Uruguay, Brazil, and Peru during the 1970s and early 1980s, the Chilean government came to be identified even more closely with the personalist control of one officer rather than the institutional control of the country by the armed forces" (Loveman 2001, xv). In fact, the Chilean military dictatorship (1973–1990) was bound primarily to one person in power, General Augusto Pinochet, who transformed the armed forces into what was in practice a personal dictatorship by the commander-in-chief of the Chilean Army.

The military government maintained the country under a state of siege for the next five years, and then under various military-dominated "regimes of excep-

tions" until the plebiscite of 1988. "According to Karen L. Remmer, it was a combination of political shrewdness and favorable circumstances that "allowed Pinochet to take full advantage of Chilean military traditions and outmaneuver his rivals" (Remmer 1989, 131). "The expression of career opportunities and related politicization of the military institution unquestionably helped Pinochet maintain the support of the officer corps after 1973. At the same time, however, the incorporation of military officers into government inevitably entailed professional costs—costs that became particularly obvious in the wake of the 1988 plebiscite" (ibid., 133).

The transition away from military rule started in 1988, when Pinochet was defeated in a plebiscite and restoration of civilian government started. But even then the legacy of the military regime continued to significantly influence the political, economic, and social life in Chile; the 1980 constitution remained in place, though changed to ease provisions for future amendments and to diminish the role of the National Security Council by equalizing the number of civilian and military members (four members each). Although two elected presidents governed Chile during the decade from 1990 to 2000, they achieved virtually no change in the military-imposed political system with respect to the question of how to serve the cause of justice on behalf of the victims of the huge number of human rights violations committed in Chile's recent past.

After Pinochet was arrested in London in October 1998, things began to change. Since 2000, President Ricardo Lagos's government has been continuously confronted with demands for "truth and justice" regarding the human rights violations of the past—particularly with respect to those violations committed by the armed forces. There can be no doubt that military and police personnel were involved in countless human rights violations during the Pinochet era. Moreover, it was the military that directly negotiated the terms of the transition back to civilian government. Even today the military still maintains strong influence over civilian and public life.

The new government is still confronted with the dilemma of how to deal with the political legacy of large-scale human rights violations and how to balance civil-military relations in a way that gives both power and legitimacy to civilian rule. New strategies and methods for democratic and civilian control of the armed forces must be developed and put into place to restrict military participation in policy matters outside the security and defense sector.

Terrorism

To date, the "War on Terrorism" has not played any significant role in Chilean politics. Because of Chile's geopolitical situation, the country has not yet become a major target for Islamic terrorist attack. However, on many occasions Chile has stressed the importance that the country attaches to the global debate on terrorism and the significance of the role of the United Nations in the adoption of the measures needed to combat it. Recently, a number of official documents and conferences have addressed the issues of global and regional terrorism and called for immediate action to protect the country from terrorist threats. In this context, the aim of protecting shipping and aviation, in particular, from terrorist attack has become a key issue for both governmental and business representatives.

It is important to mention that September 11 has a distinctive but quite different meaning for Chileans, because that date also reminds them of the anniversary of the military coup of 1973, when the Chilean military seized power. In recent years, the days around September 11 have been a very active period for public demonstrations in Chile that sometimes resulted in violent protest. Regarding the country's recent history, terrorism may rather be seen in the light of state-terrorism or state-sponsored terrorism. From that perspective, terrorism is simply one of the effects of an authoritarian rule or dictatorship based primarily on the exercise of force and violence.

On the other hand, in nondemocratic societies it is often the case that governmental organizations, including police and military forces, argue that the real terrorist threat comes from left-wing and other extremist networks or organizations that have the political aim of destabilizing the country and destroying law and order. In fact, organized left-wing "subversion" and right-wing "counterterror" played a role in Chile from the 1970s until the late 1980s, but they almost completely vanished with the return of civilian government in 1990.

Relationship with the United States

The relationship between the United States and Chile has been very close for most of the twentieth century. Today relations seem even better than in the past, particularly since the signing of a free trade agreement in December 2002. Economic prosperity and increasing trade have made Chile a very attractive trade partner for the United States. Chile and the United States have developed strong economic ties, and the United States has become one of Chile's largest foreign investors. In addition, the two countries have established close links in the security and defense sector.

During the Cold War, Chile benefited greatly from various U.S. military assistance programs. The purpose of those military aid programs during the Cold War was "to convert the armies of the hemispheric defense into forces of internal order mobilized against Communist subversion, thus contributing to the security of 'the free world'" (Rouquié 1987, 137). Under the auspices of these programs, a considerable number of Chilean officers were trained at U.S. military schools, such as, for example, the U.S. Army School of the Americas. Thus the officers were at least indirectly also educated toward a certain understanding of what *political democracy* and *free world* mean and, as Rouquié pointed out, subjected at the same time to a specific brand of anticommunism and pro-American indoctrination (ibid., 136; see Sidebar). "Beginning in 1965, particularly all Chilean officers took training programs in American schools. From 1950 to 1970, 4,374 Chilean military men were trained in Panama or the U.S." (Rouquié, 242). In total, the Chilean military received in military aid programs from the United States about $169 million between 1946 and 1972 (ibid.).

Chile's political journey throughout the twentieth century from oligarchy to democracy and military dictatorship following the 1973 overthrew of Allende's socialist government has always been influenced in one way or another by the United States. With the beginning of the twentieth century, U.S. power and influence in Latin America was clearly on the rise. After World War II, the United States became even more powerful. Start-

---

Sidebar 2   Fighting Communism

During the 1960s, counterinsurgency training and anti-communist indoctrination were extended to the Chilean armed forces. In this context, U.S. military aid began to play a crucial role.

"Beginning in 1965, practically all Chilean officers attended training programs in American schools. From 1950 to 1970, 4,374 Chilean military men were trained in Panama or in the U.S."

Source
Rouquié, Alain. 1987. *The Military and the State in Latin America.* Berkeley: University of California Press. p. 242.

---

ing with the Rio Pact in 1947 (with Chile as an important member state) and the development of the Organization of American States (OAS) a year later, the U.S. "battle against communism" included the Latin American continent in the evolving pattern of Cold War international politics.

Chile soon became an important partner for the United States in its new alliance system, and a bilateral defense pact was signed in the early 1950s. The exchange of military equipment and services with Chile continued until the 1975 report on Chile of the U.S. Senate's Select Committee on Intelligence, which documented that the United States had "covertly engaged for a decade in [a] massive and sustained campaign against [Salvador Allende] and the Left in Chile" (Lowenthal 1990, 34). The report also revealed that "Washington first promoted an abortive military coup and then considered and apparently attempted bribery to prevent Allende's formal selection by the Chilean congress" (ibid.). There can be no doubt that U.S. political and military efforts were significant in preparing the way for the 1973 coup and the following military rule under General Pinochet.

Since 1990, Chile has been enjoying the fruits of restored democratic policies, which were then highly welcomed by the United States. The United States was not only among the first countries that applauded the rebirth of the Chilean democracy; it was also on the forefront when it came to the issue of trade partnership, foreign investment, and new international solidarity and cooperation in the security and defense area—as well as Chile's future participation in a number of new international security and military programs initiated by the U.S. government. In this respect, continuous dialogue takes place between both countries in bilateral commissions (covering defense, global security, agriculture, trade and investment, and bilateral issues).

Finally, as pointed out by the U.S. State Department, "[T]he warm relationship enjoyed by the United States and Chile today contrasts with the difficult period of relations during Augusto Pinochet's military regime from 1973 to 1990. A 1976 car bomb attack in Washington, DC, which killed Orlando Likelier, former Chilean ambassador to the United States and a member of President Salvador Allende's cabinet, and U.S. citizen Ronny Moffitt, caused a sharp deterioration in relations, including a ban on security assistance and arms sales to Chile. In response to a commitment by President Alvin's government to pursue the Likelier-Moffitt case within the Chilean judicial system, President Bush lifted the sanctions. A Chilean court subsequently convicted two Chilean military officers of having ordered the assassination. The goal of U.S. foreign policy in Chile is to pursue expanded economic relations and to cooperate on a range of bilateral and multilateral issues of interest. Above all, the United States believes that an economically strong and democratically healthy Chile will benefit the entire hemisphere" (U.S. Department of State, Background Notes: Chile, August 1999, released by the Bureau of Western Hemisphere Affairs). Today, one may conclude that U.S. hegemony in the Western Hemisphere, particularly with respect to Chile, is far from eroding.

The Future

The road ahead still looks difficult with respect to preventing future conflicts, both within Chilean society and internationally. Regarding the agenda of promoting political tolerance and democracy, as well as the issue of reconciliation of conflicts from the past, one may even argue that Chile is still facing new challenges and threats. In order to resolve the lingering damage of the country's authoritarian legacy, Chile must continue to seek social justice, reconciliation, and stable democratic conditions. Additionally, the territorial disputes of the past remain at least partially unresolved and a potential source of friction and conflict for the future.

A few years ago, Chile adopted and published a White Book on its security and defense policy for the twenty-first century (*Libro de la Defensa Nacional de Chile*), in which the government clearly outlines new security threats, recent changes in the whole security environment, the country's primary security goals and national interests, and new tasks for the armed forces. The armed forces themselves presented a new program for modernizing their equipment in order to meet the new challenges of the twenty-first century. International cooperation in the security and defense area still remains at the core of all new concepts and the country's policies.

References and Recommended Readings

Books

Alexander, Robert J. 1978. *The Tragedy of Chile.* Westport, CT: Greenwood Press.

Arriagada, Genaro. 1991. *Pinochet. The Politics of Power.* Boulder, CO: Westview Press.

———. 1998. *Por la razón or por la fuerza. Chile bajo Pinochet.* Santiago: Editorial Sudamericana Chilena.

Barros Arana, Diego. 2000. *Historia General de Chile.* 10 vols. Santiago: Editorial Universitaria.

Collier, Simon, and William F. Sater. 1996. *A History of Chile, 1808–1994.* Cambridge: Cambridge University Press.

Díaz Albónico, Rodrigo, ed. 1987. *El tratado de paz y amistad entre Chile y Argentina.* Santiago: Editorial Universitaria.

Drake, Paul, and Iván Jaskic, eds. 1991. *The Struggle for Democracy in Chile.* Lincoln: University of Nebraska Press.

Fitch, J. Samuel. 1998. *The Armed Forces and Democracy in Latin America.* Baltimore, MD: Johns Hopkins University Press.

Fuentes, Claudio, and Carlos Martin. 1998. *La nueva agenda argentino-chilena.* Santiago: FLASCO.

García, Pio, ed. 1974. *Las fuerzas armadas y el golpe de estado en Chile.* México: Siglo veintiuno editores.

Hickman, John. 1998. *News from the End of the Earth: A Portrait of Chile.* New York: St. Martin's Press.

Kornbluh. Peter. 2003. *The Pinochet File: A Declassified Dossier on Atrocity and Accountability.* New York: New Press.

Loveman, Brian. 1999. *For la Patria: Politics and the Armed Forces in Latin America.* Wilmington, DE: Scholarly Resources.

———. 2001. *The Legacy of Hispanic Capitalism.* 3d ed. New York: Oxford University Press.

Lowenthal, Abraham F. 1990. *Partners in Conflict: The United States and Latin America in the 1990s.* Rev. ed.

Baltimore, MD: Johns Hopkins University Press.

Mares, David R. 2001. *Violent Peace: Militarized Interstate Bargaining in Latin America.* New York: Columbia University Press.

Military Balance 2003–2004. Edited by the International Institute for Strategic Studies (IISS). London.

Muñoz, Heraldo. 1986. *Las relaciones exteriores del gobierno militar Chileno.* Santiago: PROSPEL-CERC.

Nunn, Frederick M. 1976. *The Military in Chilean History: Essays on Civil-Military Relations, 1810–1973.* Albuquerque: University of New Mexico Press.

Pion-Berlin, David. 2001. *Civil-military Relations in Latin America: New Analytical Perspectives.* Chapel Hill: University of North Carolina Press.

Porteous, J. Douglas. 1981. *The Modernization of East Island.* Victoria, BC: University of Victoria.

Quiroga, Patricio, and Carlos Maldonado. 1988. *El prusianismo en las fuerzas armadas chilenas. Un estudio histórico 1885–1945.* Santiago: Ediciones Documentas.

Rauch, George von. 1999. *Conflict in the Southern Cone: The Argentine Military in the Boundary Dispute with Chile, 1870–1902.* Westport, CT: Praeger.

Remmer, Karen L. 1989. *Military Rule in Latin America.* Boston: Unwin Hyman.

Rouquié, Alain. 1987. *The Military and the State in Latin America.* Berkeley: University of California Press.

Talbott, Robert D. 1974. *A History of the Chilean Boundaries.* Ames: Iowa State University Press.

UN *World Statistics Pocketbook* and *Statistical Yearbook.* 2003. Human Development Report, ed. United Nations Statistics Division. New York: United Nations Press.

Valenzuela, J. Samuel. 1997. *La Constitución de 1980 y el inicio de la redemocratización en Chile.* Kellogg Institute, Working papers 242. South Bend, IN: University of Notre Dame.

Varas, Augusto, and Claudio Fuentes. 1994. *Defensa nacional, Chile 1990–94. Modernización y desarrollo,* Santiago: FLACSO.

Vergara Quiroz, Sergio. 1993. *Historia social del ejército de Chile.* 2 vols. Santiago: Universidad de Chile.

Witker, Alejandro. 1978. *Chile: Sociedad y política. Del Acta de la Independencia a nuestros días.* México: Universidad Nacional Autónoma de México.

Zeitlin, Maurice. 1984. *The Civil Wars in Chile.* Princeton: Princeton University Press.

Articles

Foss, Christopher S. 1990. "UK-Chile rocket test launched." *Jane's Defense Weekly* (13 October):695.

Fuentes, Claudio, and Carlos Martin. 1992. "Chile-Argentina después de Marzo de 1990: Hacia la cooperación o el conflicto." *Fuerzas Armadas y Sociedad* 7 (July–September):3–17.

Hunter, Wendy. 1998. "Negotiating Civil-Military Relations in Post-Authoritarian Argentina and Chile." *International Studies Quarterly* 42:295–318.

Websites

Background Note: Chile (U.S. Department of State, August 1999, released by the Bureau of Western Hemisphere Affairs): http://www.state.gov/r/pa/ei/bgn/1981.htm.

Chile—A Country Profile (Library of Congress): http://lcweb2.loc.gov/frd/cs/cltoc.html.

Chile—CIA Factbook 2005: http://www.cia.gov/cia/publications/factbook/index.html.

Chile—The State of Chile: http://www.estado.cl/.

Chilean Air Force (Background Information): http://orbat.com/site/air_orbats/orbats/Chilean%20Air%20Force%20FACh.pdf http://www.fach-extraoficial.com/.

Chilean Air Force: http://www.fach.cl/.

Chilean Army: http://www.ejercito.cl/.

Chilean Carabineros: http://www.carabinerosdechile.cl/main.htm.

Chilean Military (Background Information): http://www.nationmaster.com/country/ci/Military.

Chilean Navy: http://www.armada.cl.

Government of Chile: http://www.presidencia.cl/. http://www.segegob.cl/.

Ministry of Defense: http://www.defensa.cl/.

National Congress of the Republic of Chile: http://www.congreso.cl/.

Revista Fuerzas Armadas y Sociedad (Journal): http://www.eurosur.org/FLACSO/fasoc.html.

Senate of the Republic of Chile: http://www.senado.cl/.

White Book on National Defense (Libro de la Defensa Nacional de Chile): http://www.defensa.cl/paginas/public/libro_2002/index.htm.

China

Min Ye

Geography and History

China is approximately 3.7 million square miles (960 million square kilometers) in size, making it the fourth largest country in the world. The topography of China descends like a staircase from west to east. Plateaus and high mountains characterize China's western and central topography. The eastern coast is composed primarily of plains, deltas, and hills. Regional geographic variation in China leads to uneven population distribution: more than 90 percent of the population lives on less than 40 percent of the land. Nearly one-third of China's territory is desert, and only 13 percent of the land is arable. As a result, China could not produce sufficient food for its people until the early 1980s.

China, with more than 1.29 billion people, is the world's most populous country. The population is composed of more than fifty ethnic groups, although the Han constitute approximately 92 percent of the population. Officially China is an atheistic country, yet there are large numbers of followers of Buddhism and Daoism, an indigenous religion that was born and developed in China. In recent years China has experienced a relaxation of restrictions on religious practices, resulting in gains for Christianity and Islam. So far, Muslims account for 1 to 2 percent of the population, whereas Christians constitute 3 to 4 percent (CIA World Factbook 2004).

As the oldest extant civilization in the world, China has a history that can be traced back about 3,500 years. Beginning in 221 B.C.E., the Shi Huang-ti united the country under a highly centralized dynastic system. During the two thousand years that followed, China experienced nine feudal dynasties. Chinese civilization flourished for many centuries, leading the Chinese people to believe that China was the center of the world (in Chinese, *China* means the "Central Kingdom").

When the Manchu people established the last dynasty, the Qing Dynasty, in 1644, China was still one of the most powerful states in the world. However, China began to lag behind when the industrial revolution spread across the West. In 1840, Great Britain defeated the Central Kingdom in a war over the opium trade and imposed the Nanjing Treaty. Under the terms of that treaty, China agreed to cede Hong Kong, pay large reparations, and open its ports for trade. In the following years, other powers pressed China to grant similar privileges, either through wars or treaties. As a result, China became the de facto colony of those powers at the beginning of the twentieth century.

In 1911, the Qing Dynasty was overthrown in a revolution led by the Nationalist Party (KMT), and the Republic of China (ROC) was established. Historians often contend that the KMT never effectively governed China because of the civil wars among warlords, the communist intransigence, and the Japanese invasion of World War II. KMT rule on the mainland ended when the party was defeated by the Soviet-supported Chinese Communist Party (CCP) in the Chinese Civil War (1946–1949). On October 1, 1949, Mao Zedong, leader of the CCP, proclaimed the People's Republic of China (PRC) in Beijing. The KMT, along with 2 million of its followers, fled to Taiwan and has continued its rule there under U.S. protection.

Mao subsequently established a communist regime in China and adopted a foreign policy of "leaning to one side" of the Soviet-led communist camp. His regime embraced a set of political and economic systems that originated from the Soviet Union. In 1958, Mao announced a new economic movement, "the Great Leap Forward," the idea of which was to increase the speed of economic growth by diverting excess labor from agriculture to industry. Farmers were mobilized to produce steel, the symbol of industrialization, with backyard furnaces. The Great Leap Forward turned into an economic disaster, however. Production of nonsteel goods fell dramatically. In addition, lack of labor and farm implements resulted in sharp declines in agricultural output, which led to the nationwide famine in 1958, 1959, and 1960. An estimated 4 to 40 million people lost their lives (the Wikipedia Encyclopedia, http://en.wikipedia.org/).

The failure of the Great Leap Forward severely damaged Mao's prestige within the party. Some Chinese leaders, such as Liu Shaoqi and Deng Xiaoping, even considered removing Mao from any real power. To restore his power base and oust his rivals, Mao launched the Cultural Revolution in 1966. His aim was to use the masses—mainly the young students known as the Red Guards—to purge his rivals in the party. Although Mao successfully eradicated most of his political rivals, China remained on the verge of anarchy for the next decade. All economic activities were halted to make way for "revolution" and "class struggle." Schools shut down, transportation was disrupted, and central and local governments were taken over by the Red Guards. Millions of public officials and intellectuals labeled as "counter-revolutionaries" were sent to rural labor camps, where they were tortured or killed. Clashes between different factions within the Red Guards were common.

The scope of the political catastrophe was far reaching. The economy collapsed. A generation of Chinese people did not receive any formal education. Although there is no official causality figure, it is estimated that about 33 million people were either directly or indirectly killed during the Cultural Revolution (ibid.).

The disaster ended with the death of Mao in 1976. Deng Xiaoping reassumed power in 1978 and shifted the country's emphasis from massive political focus to economic development. China launched a market-oriented economic reform program, which in turn propelled the country into a new era marked by rapid economic growth. After more than two decades of sustained development, China's GDP quadrupled to more than $6 trillion in 2003, making China the second largest economy in the world. In spite of those advances, however, China is still a poor country in per capita terms, per capita income being $5,000 (measured on a purchasing power parity—PPP—basis) (CIA World Factbook 2004).

Economic liberalization was accompanied to a lesser extent by political liberalization, resulting in some democratic reform. However, political reform increased expectations, especially among students. In the spring of 1989, university students in Beijing gathered to mourn the death of the former general secretary, who had been forced to resign in 1987. The students' activity later developed into a demonstration against corruption and a rally for democratic reform. Intellectuals and urbanites joined the demonstrations, which spread throughout most major cities.

In Beijing thousands of university students gathered in Tiananmen Square, the symbol of the CCP's rule. Failing to convince the students to leave the square, the government declared martial law and brought the armed forces into Beijing. In the early morning of June 4, the demonstrations in Tiananmen Square were ended by force. More than a hundred people, most of them civilians, died during the conflict. At the same time, sympathizers within the government, including the general secretary of the CCP, were purged.

After the Tiananmen Square Incident, Jiang Zemin was selected as the new general secretary. Although Deng was officially retired from all official positions, he still held substantial influence behind the scenes until his death in 1997. Jiang continued most of Deng's "reform and open-up" policies in the following years. In 2003, Jiang passed the position of general secretary to Hu Jintao. Following Deng's example, Jiang retained the title of president of the Central Military Commissions, the highest commander of the military.

In the wake of the Cold War, China is one of the few remaining communist countries, with a hybrid of liberal economics and authoritarian politics. According to the country's constitution, the National People's Congress (NPC) is the

Table 1   China: Key Statistics

Type of government	Authoritarian, communist
Population (millions)	1,287 (July 2003 est.)
Religion	Daoist (Taoist), Buddhist, Muslim 1% to 2%, Christian 3% to 4% (2003)
Main industries	Iron and steel, coal, machine building, armaments, textiles and apparel, petroleum, cement, chemical fertilizers, footwear, toys, food processing, automobiles, consumer electronics, telecommunications
Main security threats	Territory disputes with the Philippines, Vietnam, Malaysia, India, and Japan; the separatist movements of several minority ethnic groups; the Taiwan Question
Defense spending (% GDP)	4.3% (FY 2002)
Size of military	2,310,000
Number of civil wars since 1945	1
Number of interstate wars since 1945	5

Source
Central Intelligence Agency Website. 2004. "CIA World Factbook 2004." http://www.cia.gov/cia/publications/factbook/geos/ch.html (accessed May 15, 2005).

supreme organ of state power, and the State Council is the executive body of government. In reality, however, the government is subordinate to the Communist Party; its role is to implement CCP policy. The CCP still dictates most aspects of political and social life through its large networks. The core decision-making agency of the CCP is the standing committee of the Politburo.

Regional Geopolitics

China spans from the Asia-Pacific region to Central Asia. It also shares borders with South Asian states such as India and Pakistan. After the Cold War, regional security improved substantially. Tight economic ties have offered the policy-makers a new perspective on disputes, increasing interdependence among countries in those regions. Despite the improvements, however, several regional security issues remain.

The first regional security issue concerns the territorial disputes between China and its numerous neighbors. China has land borders with fourteen countries (Afghanistan, Bhutan, Burma, India, Kazakhstan, Kyrgyzstan, Laos, Mongolia, Nepal, North Korea, Pakistan, Russia, Tajikistan, and Vietnam), and ocean borders with seven countries (Brunei, Indonesia, Japan, Malaysia, the Philippines, Singapore, and South Korea). Some of the borders are maintained by tradition, without reference to formal treaties. However, other borders were drawn according to treaties signed by previous Chinese governments. Beijing has never recognized those agreements, calling them the unequal treaties signed under imperial threat.

Before the 1990s, China's only formally demarcated borders were with Burma and Mongolia. During the Cold War, border disputes accounted for roughly half of China's interstate conflicts. In the 1990s, China altered its policy and took a more diplomatic approach to border issues. So far, China has signed border treaties and solved territorial disagreements with Russia, Vietnam, Kazakhstan, Kyrgyzstan, and Tajikistan. But several issues, including disputes over the Spratly (Nansha) Islands with several Southeast Asian states, the Diaoyu/Uotsuri Islands with Japan, the ocean border with Vietnam, and the border with India, are still unresolved. Because of the history and complexity of these issues, they are likely to remain unresolved for the foreseeable future.

The situation in the Korean Peninsula is China's second concern. The current tension is related to North Korea's nuclear program. In 1993, North Korea refused to allow the International Atomic Energy Agency (IAEA) to conduct special inspections of two facilities suspected of being used for its nuclear program. As the tension deepened, the United States considered the possibility of an air strike against those facilities. The crisis ended when the United States and North Korea signed the Agreed Framework in 1994. North Korea agreed to halt its nuclear program on the condition that the United States provided energy assistance, as well as economic and diplomatic compensation (Niksch 2002). However, delays and disputes threatened the Agreed Framework almost from its inception. The situation deteriorated further in January 2002, when President Bush referred to North Korea as part of the "axis of evil." In response, North Korea declared that it would restart its nuclear reactors. In January 2003, North Korea formally withdrew from the Nuclear Non-proliferation Treaty (NPT).

In South Asia, the India-Pakistan conflict, their nuclear arms race, and the hostility between China and India are the key geopolitical issues. The India-Pakistan conflict has endured over the five decades since their establishment in 1948. The territorial dispute over Kashmir lies at the heart of the India-Pakistan rivalry. It has led to three major wars and numerous minor conflicts. Even today India and Pakistan frequently exchange fire across the cease-fire line of Kashmir. Their military confrontation stimulated the nuclear arms race. In May 1998, India conducted five nuclear tests and declared itself a nuclear state. In response, Pakistan conducted six nuclear explosions.

The hostility between India and China has it origin in the brief border war of 1962; half a million troops continue to be stationed along the China-Indian border. Several days before India's nuclear test in 1998, India's defense minister, Fernandes, declared that China was India's number one threat. India has also accused China of helping Pakistan develop its missiles, a claim that both China and Pakistan have denied. Tensions have eased in recent years, however, and high-level visits have promoted bilateral relations. But because of problems rooted deep beneath the surface, it is hard to be overly optimistic about the future relationship between China and India.

Long before the military campaign in Afghanistan caught the world's attention surrounding the various issues in Central Asia, the rise of Islamic extremism became a serious threat there. Shortly after the division of the Soviet Union, Tajikistan descended into a bloody civil war between the government and the radical Islamic movement, the United Tajik Opposition (UTO). In 1997, a peace deal that arose under UN mediation set in motion the process of national reconciliation. However, military clashes still take place from time to time.

The Taliban's victory in the Afghan civil war further complicated matters. As a result of ideological and material support from the Taliban, Islamic extremist movements rapidly swept through the region. The best-known radical Islamic group is the Islamic Movement of Uzbekistan (IMU). Founded in 1999, the IMU originally aimed to establish an Islamic state in Uzbekistan. Later the IMU moved its base to Afghanistan and expanded its goal to toppling all the secular governments in Central Asia and creating a Central Asian Islamic state. The influence of Islamic extremism has even spilled over the border into China and Russia. The military force of the IMU was seriously degraded during the antiterrorist war in Afghanistan. However, as a political power, the IMU still has a wide base and remains a potential threat in this region.

The last major problem is the division between Taiwan and Mainland China. Hostility between Taiwan and the Mainland dates back to the Chinese Civil War (1946–1949), when the defeated KMT fled to Taiwan and retained its rule there. Shortly after the outbreak of the Korean War, the United States intervened in order to contain communist expansion. Thus Beijing, Taipei, and Washington formulated a subtle balance across the straits. Before the 1990s, both Beijing and Taipei adhered to the "One China" principle, maintaining that there was only one legitimate authority over both the Mainland and Taiwan. However, in the mid-1990s the Taiwanese government began to deviate from the "one China" stance and has gradually accelerated its pace toward independence. In 1999, Taiwanese president

Lee Teng-hui for the first time publicly stated that the relationship across the Taiwan Straits should be discussed on a "special state-to-state" basis. In 2000, the pro-independence Democratic Progressive Party (DPP) defeated the KMT in the presidential election. Despite Beijing's basic policy toward Taiwan of "one country, two systems, and peaceful unification," China has not abandoned its option of using force as a means to secure unification. China's policy, along with Taiwan's increasingly aggressive stance, makes the issue a potential source of conflict in the region.

Conflict Past and Present

Conflict History

China's Civil War (1946–1949) resulted in a split between the mainland, governed by the CCP, and the island of Taiwan, ruled by the KMT. Unification was at the top of Beijing's agenda after the establishment of the PRC. However, that process was disrupted by the outbreak of the Korean War. Under the order of U.S. president Truman, the Seventh Fleet was sent into the straits. The United States intended to neutralize the Taiwan Straits and prevent attack on its forces from either side. The comparative strength of the U.S. fleet served to isolate conflict to the KMT-occupied offshore islands of Jinmen (Quemoy) and Mazu, eight miles from the mainland. Before the 1990s, there were two crises in the Taiwan Straits.

The first Taiwan Straits Crisis occurred between August 11, 1954, and May 1, 1955. In February 1953, the Eisenhower administration changed Truman's neutralization policy and lifted the blockade of the Taiwanese side, making it possible for Taiwan to attack the mainland. By Au-

gust 1954, 73,000 troops had been sent to Jinmen and Mazu. In response, the People's Liberation Army (PLA) began shelling the two islands in September. The conflict also extended to some major coastal mainland cities. On January 18, 1955, the PLA captured the KMT-held Yijiangshan Island, 210 miles north of Taiwan. In response, President Eisenhower and Secretary of State Dulles publicly threatened to use nuclear weapons to retaliate against further aggression by Beijing. On April 23, 1955, Beijing expressed its will to negotiate on this issue. Eight days later China stopped the bombardment, and the first Taiwan Straits Crisis ended.

The second Taiwan Straits Crisis occurred three years later. The background of this crisis is complicated. First, the U.S. military assistance broke the military balance across the straits, rendering the military situation of Jinmen and Mazu favorable to the KMT side. Secondly, the political struggle within the CCP resulted in a hard-line stance on the Jinmen and Mazu issue. On August 23, the PLA resumed bombardment of these islands and prepared to invade them. Fierce fighting occurred in the sea and air around Jinmen and Mazu. The United States took a strong stance in its defense of Taiwan, sending more naval vessels to the straits and publicly threatening to begin a nuclear strike against major mainland cities if the PLA invaded Jinmen and Mazu. Beijing tried to avoid direct military confrontation with U.S. forces. Chinese Premier Zhou Enlai suggested an ambassadorial-level meeting to negotiate an end to the crisis on September 6, 1958. In October, the Chinese defense minister also offered to stop bombarding for a week while negotiations took place. In January 1959, the PLA stopped the bombardment. After that crisis, the straits entered a relatively calm era.

In addition to the two Taiwan Straits Crises, China also engaged in five other interstate wars: the Korean War (1950–1953), the China-India border war (1962), the Vietnam War (1965–1969), the China-Soviet border war (1969), and the China-Vietnam border war (1979) (see Table 2 for a brief summary).

Soon after the establishment of the PRC, the Korean War broke out on June 25, 1950. After several initial victories, North Korea's attempt to unify the country was set back by international intervention. After the Inchon landing on September 15, 1950, the situation in the Korean Peninsula was completely reversed: U.S.-led UN troops not only recovered all the territory of South Korea but also approached the North Korea–China border, the Yalu River. Worrying about a U.S.-dominated Korea along its industrial center in Manchuria, China entered the war after consulting with the Soviet Union.

Some 380,000 Chinese soldiers, in the name of the People's Volunteer Army (PVA), crossed the Yalu River on October 19, 1950. This unexpected assault by the PVA quickly pushed back the badly divided UN troops (Weintraub 2000). On January 4, 1951, the PVA recaptured Seoul, the capital of South Korea, and in May some Chinese troops even reached the 37th parallel. However, inferior equipment and a backward supply system prevented the PVA from advancing any farther. The war ultimately stalemated along the 38th parallel, where it had started. On July 27, 1953, the Korean War Armistice Agreement was signed, and the Korean War ended without a peace treaty. The Korean War was the most brutal war in the history of the PRC: approximately half a million Chinese soldiers died. As a result, the relationship between China and the United States was frozen in the following two decades.

The Sino-Soviet border disagreement can be traced back to the seventeenth century. Since the Treaty of Nerchinsk of 1689, China has signed a total of twenty-four treaties with Russia, demarcating their 6,875-mile (11,000-kilometer) border. In Beijing's view, all the treaties, except the initial agreement, were unequal: the weak Qing Dynasty was forced to accept the czar's incursion into China's 600,000-square-mile (1.5-million-square-

Table 2   Major Conflicts

Name	Rival	Date	PRC Casualties
The Korean War	U.S., UN, ROK	Oct. 1950 to July 1953	500,000
The China-India Border War	India	Oct. 1962 to Nov. 1962	500
The Vietnam War	U.S.	June 1965 to July 1970	6,000
The China-Soviet Border War	Soviet Union	March 1969	150
The China-Vietnam Border War	Vietnam	Feb. 1979 to Mar. 1979	21,000

Sources
Correlates of War Project, University of Michigan. http://www.umich.edu/~cowproj/ (accessed May 14, 2005).
Chen, Jian. 1995. "China's Involvement in the Vietnam War, 1964–1969." *China Quarterly* 142: 356–387.

kilometer) territory. The Sino-Soviet honeymoon between 1949 and 1958 temporarily ended that dispute. As Sino-Soviet relations cooled, however, because of ideological controversies, the territorial dispute emerged as an outlet of mutual hostility.

A military clash occurred in March 1969, when the two sides used thousands of troops to compete for control of the Damaksky/Zhenbao Island in the Ussri River. The conflict swiftly spread along the longest border in the world—from northeastern to Central Asia. Sino-Soviet tension was so high, in fact, that at one point in the conflict the Soviet Union considered a "surgical strike" on China's nuclear facilities in Xinjiang. Because both China and the Soviet Union were nuclear powers, there was a tacit limitation on both sides regarding the use of force, and full-scale war was averted. In September 1969, premiers of both countries met in Beijing and agreed to resume the border demarcation negotiations. However, several rounds of negotiations made no progress, and sporadic clashes extended into the 1980s. The border clashes reordered China's view of national security, causing it to regard the Soviet Union, rather than the United States, as the major threat. That eventually led to the normalization of the China-U.S. relation in the 1970s. Until the demise of the Soviet Union, there were still 700,000 Soviet troops deployed in the Far East, confronting a million Chinese counterparts across the border.

China was also involved in the Vietnam War, although to a lesser degree than the Korean conflict. After the escalation of the Vietnam War following the Tonkin Gulf Incident in August 1964, China decided to aid North Vietnam at the request of the Vietnam Communist Party. Because of the lessons learned from the Korean War, China chose a different way to engage in Vietnam. In particular, China selected three avenues of participation: dispatching engineering troops to construct and maintain the defense and transportation networks; sending in antiaircraft artillery forces to defend strategic targets; and providing military materiel (Chen 1995). In 1965, the first group of Chinese engineering and antiaircraft artillery troops entered North Vietnam. Before withdrawing all of its forces in 1969, China had dispatched 320,000 troops to Vietnam. According to Chinese statistics, Chinese antiaircraft artillery troops fought 2,154 battles with U.S. air forces. Moreover, the Chinese Air Force attacked U.S. aircraft that invaded Chinese airspace, shooting down twelve U.S. planes. China suffered nearly six thousand casualties in the war (Whiting 2001).

After the Vietnam War, the relationship between Vietnam and the Soviet Union tightened. In 1978, Vietnam joined the Council for Mutual Economic Cooperation (COMECON) and signed the Treaty of Friendship and Cooperation with the Soviet Union. That concerned China, because the Chinese government viewed the Soviet Union as the most dangerous threat to its security. In December 1978, Vietnam invaded Cambodia and overthrew the Chinese-backed Pol Pot regime. That action also provoked Beijing. Frequent border clashes and the Vietnamese government's expulsion of 250,000 ethnic Chinese completely destroyed the "brotherly comrades" relationship between the two countries (Tretiak 1979). After a massive propaganda assault, Beijing decided to teach the Vietnamese a lesson. Approximately 120,000 Chinese troops entered Vietnam from several places along

Sidebar 1   China's Defense Industry

Until the early 1980s, Chinese leaders believed that a third world war was inevitable. The construction of China's defense industry was guided by a need to prepare for an "early, major, and nuclear war." In the 1960s and 1970s the Chinese government undertook a costly relocation of approximately 55 percent of defense industries to the interior mountainous area. Nearly half of China's national investment was allocated to the "Third Front" project. The remote location and poor infrastructure, however, later prohibited the development of these industries during the reform era. At present, most of these defense industries are staggering under heavy debt, antiquated equipment, funding decreases, and brain-drain, particularly of technicians and skilled workers.

Sources

Frankenstein, John, and Bates Gill. 1996. "Current and Future Challenges Facing Chinese Defense Industries." *China Quarterly* 146: 394–427.

Gurtov, Mel. 1993. "Swords into Market Shares: China's Conversion of Military Industry to Civilian Production." *China Quarterly* 134: 213–241.

the border on February 17, 1979. After several fierce battles, the PLA penetrated twenty-five miles into Vietnam and seized Long Son, a major city in northern Vietnam. Chinese troops advanced to within approximately a hundred miles of Hanoi. On March 6, China declared the war a success and withdrew its forces. Some 21,000 casualties were reported in the war.

China's war with Vietnam served to push the Vietnamese into an even closer alliance with the Soviets. The aftermath of the war extended into the early 1980s, with both sides continuing to exchange fire and launch military raids onto the other's territory. In addition to the low-intensity conflicts along the land border, the Chinese and Vietnamese navies fought over islands in the South China Sea.

At the end of the Cold War, relations between the two communist countries were swiftly restored. Both sides committed to negotiation instead of military means to settle territorial disputes. In December 1999 they signed the Vietnam-China Treaty on Land Borders, finally solving the demarcation problem. Both nations also promised to iron out their disagreements over the islands through cooperation and negotiation.

China has also experienced an ongoing rivalry with India. The conflicting border claims date back to the nineteenth century. Although the establishment of new governments in both countries led to a friendly relationship in the early 1950s, discord over the border issue triggered a series of military clashes in the disputed regions in the late 1950s. Unable to solve the problem through political negotiations, China resorted to arms. On October 20, 1962, nine divisions of Chinese troops launched an attack against the Indian forces defending the 1,062-mile (1,700-kilometer) border. The well-equipped and better-trained Chinese soldiers quickly wiped out the Indian posts and rooted out organized resistance. By November 21, the PLA had seized most of the disputed regions and repelled several Indian counterattacks. After achieving its goal and wishing to avoid heavy resistance in the Indian plains, China declared a unilateral ceasefire on November 22, 1962, and withdrew its troops back to the line of control established on November 19, 1959. Each side suffered approximately 500 casualties during the brief war.

The following years witnessed recurring conflicts of varying intensity along the Sino-Indian border. As a result, China occupied the western sector of the disputed regions, Aksai Chin, whereas India took the eastern sector, Arunachal Pradesh. In 1986, after a border clash, India promoted Arunachal Pradesh from union territory to state. That led to another round of tensions. In 1987, 400,000 Chinese and Indian troops were deployed along the border. In the meantime, negotiations on the border issue were also under way. Some progress was made in 1994, during the Chinese premier's visit to New Delhi, when an accommodation was reached to improve "confidence-building measures" (CBMs) at the border.

Current and Potential
Military Confrontation

As China shifted its emphasis to economic development in the late 1970s, a major goal of Chinese foreign policy was to build a peaceful external environment. China has taken a more practical approach toward solving disputes with other countries. As a result, the country has settled many of its disputes through negotiation. In addition, Beijing also renounced the use of force in its remaining disputes. Taiwan remains an exception to that rule, however. Beijing still maintains its right to use force under certain circumstances. Since the situation in Taiwan has become highly uncertain in recent years, the Taiwan Straits are the potential flashpoint that could involve the PRC in conflict and alter its future development.

During the 1990s relations across the Taiwan Straits changed extensively. The rapid growth of trade and investment engendered closer economic ties between China and Taiwan. However, the political environment in Taiwan brought more uncertainties. One salient change in the policies of the Taiwanese government in the 1990s was that it gradually deviated from adherence to the "one China" principle. On several occasions Taiwanese leaders expressed the view that Beijing should treat Taiwan as a state, rather than as a province. Some high-ranking Taiwanese officials also conducted personal visits to other countries. Beijing regarded them as a challenge to the "one China" principle and decried the visits as a step toward independence.

The situation became explosive in 1995 and 1996, resulting in the third Taiwan Straits Crisis. In June 1995, Taiwan's president, Lee Teng-hui, made a private visit to the United States. In an address at Cornell University, his alma mater, Lee advocated the "One China, One Taiwan" policy to replace the "one China" policy. Moreover, Taiwan's first free multiparty presidential election would be held in March of the following year, and Lee would run for president as the KMT candidate. The pro-independence Democratic Progressive Party (DPP) candidate was also allowed to participate.

To express irritation at Lee's visit to the United States and to dissuade pro-independence voters, Beijing conducted a series of missile tests and military exercises in the period from July 21, 1995, to March 23, 1996, and deployed more troops in the coastal region of the straits. The PLA conducted missile tests using mobile, nuclear-capable short- and intermediate-range missiles. The target regions covered the airline and shipping routes of Taiwan's major ports, which demonstrated the PLA's capacity to blockade the island in time of war. One of the missiles landed just thirty miles from Taipei. The landing exercises also targeted Taiwan. In the largest military exercise, 160,000 soldiers, 200 landing craft, and 100 other ships were mobilized. In reaction, the United States sent two aircraft carrier battle groups to the straits to monitor these tests and exercises. The exercises did not achieve their goal. Lee was re-elected as president with 54 percent of vote.

After the DPP candidate, Chen Shuibian, won the presidential election in 2000, the situation in the Taiwan Straits became more complex. Although Chen promised not to declare independence as long as Beijing did not use military force against Taiwan, he adopted many policies that, in Beijing's eyes, pushed Taiwan closer to actual independence. In 2002, Beijing revised its Taiwan policy, emphasizing that unification cannot be delayed *sine die*. This was a strong signal of Beijing's hard-line stance in the face of an increasingly uncertain political situation in Taiwan. According to the Taiwan Relations Act of 1979, the United States committed to the peaceful solution of the Taiwan problem. In this sense, Taiwan's movement toward independence may give rise to a military reaction from Beijing. That, in turn, may lead to military intervention from the United States. This dynamic game constitutes the most dangerous threat to the peace and stability of the Asia-Pacific region.

Alliance Structure

In February 1950, China signed the Treaty of Friendship, Alliance, and Mutual Assistance with the Soviet Union. The aim of the China-Soviet alliance is to "prevent a repetition of aggression and breach of the peace by Japan or any other

state which might directly or indirectly join with Japan in acts of aggression" (PRC, Ministry of Foreign Affairs, www. fmprc.gov.cn). A similar treaty was signed with North Korea in July 1961. According to the treaty, when one party to the treaty is in a state of war, the other will provide military and economic assistance. These treaties reflected China's growing concern at that time about military encirclement and possible military intervention by the United States and its allies (Chen 1992).

The Sino-Soviet alliance did not last long. After the death of Stalin, China rejected Khrushchev's destalinization policy. The ideological dispute ultimately gave rise to the overt breakup of the two parties in March 1965, when the CCP refused to attend the convocation of a World Congress of Communist Parties. Soon the ideological rift escalated into military conflict along the frontier, and the Soviet Union gradually replaced the United States as the top threat to China in the later years of the Cold War. Thus, after 1958 the Sino-Soviet alliance existed only on paper. On April 3, 1979, the NPC stated that the treaty would not be extended after it expired in 1980.

China also has an alliance with North Korea that remains in effect today. However, it is different from the "teeth-and-lip" relationship following the Korean War. In Pyongyang's view, China's economic reform is a deviation from communist doctrine. On China's side, economic interests have replaced ideology as the principal consideration guiding its foreign policy. That shift led to China's establishment of formal diplomatic relations with South Korea in 1992. Pyongyang was angered by Beijing's action, feeling betrayed by its socialist comrade for the sake of economic interests. The relationship between Beijing and Pyongyang quickly cooled. In the years following China's recognition of South Korea, there were almost no high-level visits between Beijing and Pyongyang. That contrasted sharply with the flourishing China–South Korea relationship.

However, peace and stability on the Korean Peninsula is of vital interest to China. The Korean Nuclear Crisis refreshed the status of North Korea in China's foreign policy agenda. North Korea's collapse would not be in China's interest, as it would bring floods of refugees, border conflicts, and a pro-U.S. Korea at China's border. On the other hand, an isolated Pyongyang has realized that China is its only friend in the world. Chinese economic and military aid is indispensable for its survival. The bilateral relationship has started to recover since Kim Jong Il's secret visit to China in 2000. North Korea even planned to make some modest economic reform following China's example. However, China has made it clear that it will not be bound by its alliance if North Korea invades the South.

Size and Structure of the Military

Since the establishment of the PRC, China has maintained the largest standing army in the world. Until the early 1980s, China still had more than 4 million people in uniform. There are two factors that account for the scale of the Chinese army. The first is the military strategy of the PLA. Before the mid-1980s, Mao's theory of people's war formed the basis for PLA doctrine. According to that theory, men, rather than weaponry, will determine the outcome of war. The second reason was China's evaluation of the Cold War environment. Chinese leaders believed that a third world war was inevitable; thus the PLA should always be ready for an "early, major, and nuclear war" (Deng 1993). In 1985, China changed its military doctrine from preparing for a world war to handling limited local conflicts along its borders. Following that transition, China began to streamline its army. Since the 1980s, China has reduced the size of its army by 1.5 million. Presently, the PLA has approximately 2.31 million soldiers.

Although China had the largest military force in the world, its military technology remained far behind that of the advanced industrial nations. After the Gulf War in 1991, China became more aware of the technology gap and systematically began to modernize its military forces by such means as cutting the military's size, increasing R&D inputs, and procuring modern weapons and technologies from abroad (mainly Russia and Israel). Those efforts have narrowed and even eliminated the gap in some areas. On the whole, however, China is still estimated to be ten to twenty years behind the other major military powers (Shambaugh 1996).

China's military forces are composed of ground forces, the navy (including naval infantry and naval aviation), the air force, and the Second Artillery Corps (the strategic nuclear force). China also has a 1.1-million member paramilitary, the People's Armed Police (PAP). It undertakes police duties but keeps the same regulations and benefits from the same treatment as the PLA. In time of war, the PAP can also conduct some military operations.

With more than 1.8 million soilders, China has the world's largest ground force. The army is composed of twenty-one army groups. About 20 percent of China's ground forces have the capacity for "rapid reaction" and can be quickly deployed in the country without significant training. The army has a formidable weaponry inventory that includes approximately 10,000 tanks, 4,000 armored vehicles, and 25,000 artillery guns and multiple rocket launchers (MRLs). But most of the equipment is obsolescent and badly maintained. For example, more than 8,000 Chinese tanks are the outdated Russian T54/55s and their Chinese version, Type 59/69/79. Some of this armor has been in service for more than thirty years. Since the 1980s, China has developed some new models, including the Type 80, Type 85, and Type 90-II. The performance of the newest Type 90-II is similar to that of the Russian T-72. However, because of the limited budget, it is unlikely that the Chinese will update the bulk of their weaponry inventory. The country may keep a smaller but a more modern weaponry inventory.

The People's Liberation Army Air Force (PLAAF) is the third largest air force in the world, with approximately 4,350 aircraft and 470,000 airmen. It is estimated that the PLAAF has 3,000 fighters (1,900 J-6/MiG-19, 720 J-7/MiG-21, 222 J-8I/II/III, and 55 J-11/Su–27SK), 440 gound-attack aircraft Q-5 (modified MiG-19), and 449 bombers (307 H-5/Il–28 and 142 H-6/Tu–16) (Moore 2000). Qualitatively, the PLAAF is the weakest branch of the PLA. A large portion of China's jets was produced before 1973 and is not well maintained. To accelerate the modernization of the air force, China recently purchased a small number of high-quality Su–27 and Su–30 aircraft from Russia and obtained the production license for the Su–27. China has also developed a new type of fighter, the J-10, on its own. The J-10 is said to be "a hybrid of the U.S. F-16 A/B with some Chinese and Israeli *Lavi* elements" (Shambaugh

1996, 294). But these efforts will not change the general weakness of the PLAAF in the near future.

Presently, the People's Liberation Army Navy (PLAN), with its 250,000 sailors, 63 submarines, 18 destroyers, and 35 frigates, is capable of coastal defense but is still far away from a "bule water" project. As do the other branches of the PLA, the PLAN suffers from obsolete equipment and poor maintenance. Although the PLAN has benefited most from the recent increase in China's defense spending, it still lags behind the other major navies in the region, such as the Japanese naval Self-Defence Force, the Indian Navy, the Navy of the ASEAN, as well as the Taiwanese Navy.

Nuclear weapons remain an important part of the Chinese arsenal. On October 16, 1964, China successfully tested its first atomic bomb. Two years later, it launched its first nuclear missile. In June 1967, China detonated a hydrogen bomb. At present, China's nuclear inventory includes 120 land-based, 130 air-based, 20 submarine-launched, and 120 nonstrategic nuclear weapons (NRDC Nuclear Notebook, 2003). However, its nuclear weapons stockpile is composed primarily of short- and intermediate-range missiles. Only the land-based weapons have intercontinental capacities (Manning et al. 2000). China continues its efforts to modernize its nuclear system in order to guarantee the necessary level of deterrence. For instance, the successful test of the DF-31 missile in 1999 equipped China with the capacity to reach targets in the western United States. In general, however, China's nuclear weapons are intended to manage primarily peripheral security concerns, such as the border dispute with India and the tension in the Taiwan Straits.

The PLA's status in China's political system is rather ambiguous. The PLA is not responsible to the Department of Defense, which is in charge only of the defense industry, military facilities construction, and foreign military affairs. The PLA is under the command of the Central Military Commissions (CMC). Technically there are two CMC, but the two have nearly identical membership: one belongs to the CCP and the other to the state. Specifically, the CMC includes four general departments: the General Staff Department, the General Logistics Department, the General Political Department, and the General Armament Department. Chinese territory is demarcated into seven military regions: Beijing, Jinan, Guangzhou, Lanzhou, Nanjing, Shenyang, and Chengdu. The commander of each military region is under the direct command of the CMC and the four general departments.

Budget
China's official defense budget has grown at a more than 10 percent annual rate in the past decade. By official accounts, defense spending increased from $6.8 billion in 1992 to $20.5 billion in 2002. The defense budget in 2002 represented 1.5 percent of GDP. It is important to recognize, however, that the PLA has a great deal of off-budget funding as well as revenue from other sources that covers much of the military procurement and R&D budget. PLA-owned enterprises also contribute a large amount of profit each year. Taking those extra budgetary sources into account, China's actual defense budget might be four to ten times the official figure (Federation of American Scientists, www.fas.org). According to CIA estimates, China's defense budget in 2002 was $56 billion, 4.3 percent of

China's GDP. The PLAN constitutes approximately 35 percent of the budget. The ground forces and the PLAAF each receive approximately 29 percent of the budget, while the Second Artillery Corps receives 7 percent.

China is an important military exporter on the world market. Before China instituted significant economic reforms, its military exports were more ideological than financial, aiming to sustain China's influence in the Third World (Byman and Cliff 1999). Since the 1980s, however, China has behaved more like an entrepreneur in the global arms trade. During the 1980s the Iran-Iraq War provided a huge market for cheap, low-tech Chinese weapons. As a result, in 1987 China became the fourth largest supplier of conventional arms in the world. However, China's arms sales diminished sharply as the Iran-Iraq War ended. In addition, the Gulf War fully exposed the disadvantages of low-tech weaponry in modern conflicts. More countries began turning to high-tech weapons or to the less expensive Russian advanced arms. China's ranking in the world military market dropped to twelfth place in 1999, with $300 million of arms exports (WMEAT).

China has also been charged with transferring nuclear, biological, and chemical weapons and technologies. Under rising international pressure (mainly from the United States), China restricted its arms sales in recent years and acceded to the Nuclear Non-proliferation Treaty (NPT) in March 1992. China was the last of the declared nuclear powers to accede.

As one of the five permanent members of the UN Security Council, China held a negative attitude toward UN peacekeeping operations prior to the end of the Cold War (Fravel 1996). That situation has gradually changed in the post–Cold War

Sidebar 2   China's Military Budget

Few analysts accept China's official military budget, given the need to sustain its 2.3 million–member standing army, 1.1 million–person paramilitary forces, 1.5 million–member militia, and an ambitious plan to modernize its conventional and nuclear weaponry. It is an open secret that the PLA (People's Liberation Army) raises funding through many other channels. Much of the military research and development and procurement budget is funded under other budgetary headings within the central and local governments.

The PLA is also one of the few armies in the world that is allowed to run a business. The PLA owns more than 10,000 companies, whose roles range from self-sufficient farming and food production to health services, property management, transport services, hotel management, and tourism. These off-budget revenues constitute a substantial portion of China's actual military expenditure, and are estimated to be several times more than the officially announced budget allocation.

Sources
Waller, Digby. 1996. "Estimating Non-Transparent Military Expenditures: The Case of China." *Defense and Peace Economics* 8:225–241.
Wang, Shaoguang. 1999. "The Military Expenditure of China, 1989–98." *SIPRI Yearbook 1999*. 334–352.

Civil-Military Relations/The Role of the Military in Domestic Politics

In China, the military not only functions as the national defender but also plays an indispensable role in politics. One distinction of China's civil-military relations is the high degree of integration among the top levels of political and military power (Paltiel 1995). This special relationship has been in place since the birth of the PLA in 1928 as the military branch of the CCP. Mao often repeated: "The political power (of the CCP) grows out of the barrel of a gun" in one of his well-known dicta, and "the party commands the gun, and the gun must never be allowed to command the party" in another. Similarly, Deng required that "the army will in the final analysis be loyal to the party." The fact that the party and the military have intertwined opens the door for the military to intervene in intraparty political struggles (Mora 2002).

Support from the military is indispensable for a CCP leader wishing to consolidate his power within the party. The military is also reserved as the last resort in the political field whenever it is necessary. In this context, the PLA, as Joffe describes it, is a "Party-army with professional characteristics"—that is, "the political and military leaderships have been locked in a symbiotic relationship at the top of the power structure, but the modernization of the armed forces and their professionalism have produced a functional separation at the lower level" (1996, 300).

In the history of the PRC, military involvement in politics is by no means rare. One representative case is the military's embroilment in the political struggles of the Cultural Revolution. At the end of the Cultural Revolution, the PLA functioned as the ruling agency of civil affairs at the local provincial level (ibid.). Since

era. China joined the Special Committee on Peacekeeping Operations in September 1988 and sent its first "Blue-helmet" troops to Cambodia in 1992. In the succeeding years, China participated in twelve other peacekeeping operations, dispatching more than 2,000 personnel.

Deng assumed power in 1978 the military has gradually withdrawn from civil affairs, and its political importance has decreased. However, as a result of the nature of the party-military relationship, it is impossible to rule out the military's influence on future political discourse. The most recent example of a strong military role in Chinese politics is the Tiananmen Square Incident of 1989. The military cracked down on the mass demonstration in Beijing, while supporting the conservative faction within the party.

Terrorism

The East Turkistan Islamic Movement (ETIM), which argued for the establishment of an independent Islamic Uighur state (East Turkestan) in Xinjiang Province, is treated as the most dangerous terrorist organization by the Chinese government. It is reported that during the 1990s the ETIM committed a series of terrorist acts, resulting in more than six hundred causalities (China Daily 2002). China declared that there is a connection between the ETIM and Bin Laden's al-Qaeda organization. Al-Qaeda is charged with training the ETIM fighters in its Afghan bases. On September 11, 2002, the UN Security Council, under the joint request of China, the United States, Afghanistan, and Kyrgyzstan, listed the ETIM as a terrorist group. So far, China has acceded to eleven international antiterrorism conventions. China also has bilateral antiterrorism consultations with the United States, Russia, Britain, France, India, and Pakistan.

Relationship with the United States

The China-U.S. relationship can be evaluated in three different stages: confrontation (1949–1972), cooperation (1972–1989), and "partial cooperation and partial friction" (1990–present) (Chang 2000, 62).

The CCP's attempts to form a relationship with the United States date back to the early 1940s. That relationship did not initially develop, because the CCP felt humiliated "when the Americans did not even bother to give Mao a reply" (Hao and Zhai 1990, 95). After some hesitation, Mao decided to align with the Soviet Union. That was due not only to ideological orientation in the context of the Cold War but also to the firm commitment by the United States to the KMT in the Chinese Civil War. Prior to the 1970s, China and the United States viewed each other as enemies. China built military alliances with the Soviet Union and North Korea and took part in military operations against the "American imperialists" in the Korean Peninsula, North Vietnam, and the Taiwan Straits. In turn, the United States adopted a containment policy toward "Red China," including diplomatic isolation, military encirclement, and trade embargo.

The deterioration of Sino-Soviet relations, culminating in the border conflicts in 1969, altered Chinese leaders' worldview. The Soviet Union replaced the United States as the greatest threat to Chinese security. Obviously, containing Soviet influence was in line with the interests of the United States. This constituted the common ground that formed the basis of China-U.S. rapprochement. President Nixon's visit in 1972 opened a new era of Sino-U.S. relations, leading the two countries to treat each other as strategic partners. China-U.S. relations entered a "golden age" in the following two decades. Cooperation quickly expanded from security issues to cultural, economic, and even military issues. Despite the fact that China was a communist state, it enjoyed a rather high level of military cooperation with the United States, including technology and weapons transfers, personnel exchange at different levels, and intelligence sharing (Ross 1999).

The Tiananmen Square Incident and the end of the Cold War marked another turning point in the U.S.-China relationship. Shortly after soldiers shot demonstrators in Beijing, the Bush administration suspended all high-level contacts with China and imposed economic sanctions. In response, China accused the United States of attempting to overthrow the Chinese government by means of "peaceful transition" and mobilized the sentiment of anti-Americanism among the public by appealing to Chinese nationalism (Li 1997, Xu 2001, Zhao 2002a, and 2002b).

In subsequent years, Sino-U.S. relations were characterized by partial cooperation and partial confrontation. There are two factors that account for that transition. First, the absence of a Soviet threat highlighted the existing and potential controversies between China and the United States. Moreover, for the United States, victory in the Cold War "could not be deemed complete for as long as China . . . remained led by a communist party" (Pablo-Baviera 2003, 341). Preoccupied with the idea of constructing a multipolar international system, China refuses to accept U.S. global hegemony. It fears that what occurred in Yugoslavia, Afghanistan, and Iraq could happen in China should the United States remain dominant. The mix of cooperation and confrontation was reflected in both the economic and political fields. As economic ties between the two countries quickly improved (for example, in 2002, the

United States was China's largest investor and second largest trading partner), disputes over the U.S. trade deficit, China's poor protection of intellectual property rights, China's most-favored-nation (MFN) status, and China's entry into the World Trade Organization (WTO) formed another theme of bilateral economic relations throughout the 1990s.

The situation is most complex and sensitive in the political area. During President Clinton's visit to Beijing in 1997, a "constructive strategic partnership toward the 21st century" was forged. China and the United States also cooperated on many international issues, including the Korean Peninsula Nuclear Crisis and peace-building efforts in Cambodia. On the other hand, the United States has consistently criticized China's poor human rights record, the repression of dissidents, and the transfer of military technologies. China, in turn, protested against U.S. intervention in its internal affairs.

On two occasions, tensions between China and the United States threatened to become more than rhetorical. The first incident occurred during the third Taiwan Straits Crisis, when the United States dispatched two air carrier battle groups to the Taiwan Straits to demonstrate its commitment to defending Taiwan. That constituted the most dangerous military confrontation between the two countries since the Vietnam War. The bombing of a Chinese embassy during NATO air strikes of Belgrade in 1999 triggered the second incident. The embassy building was destroyed, and three Chinese citizens were killed. Mass demonstrations against the United States spread to all the major Chinese cities, with the government's acquiescence.

The September 11 terrorist attacks against the United States partially altered the course of Sino-U.S. relations. The antiterrorist war deflected, at least temporarily, the attention of the United States away from bilateral controversies. China became an important partner in the global antiterrorism coalition. In the meantime, China is watching with some anxiety as the United States increases its military presence in Central Asia and asserts its leadership in the international war on terrorism. Based on the existing constellation of shared and divergent interests, the future of U.S.-China relations is likely to be characterized by a mixture of confrontation and cooperation.

The Future

To the Chinese public, the history of modern China (prior to the establishment of the PRC) is one of being looted, invaded, and oppressed. Chinese history continues to be a catalyst for current efforts to restore the power of the Central Kingdom. China's economic prosperity provides the means to assert power in the international arena. From that point of view, it is not hard to understand the concerns of many countries, including the United States, about China's potential to challenge the current international order. How to evaluate China's future role has become the core argument among Washington's China policy-makers. The question of whether China should be considered a challenger or an ally when it accumulates enough power is beyond the scope of this chapter. However, there is no doubt that a politically stable and economically prosperous China not only benefits the 1.2 billion Chinese but also contributes greatly to the peace and development of the Asia-Pacific region and, possibly, the world.

China's military buildup continues to center on concerns of the "China threat." China, in the near future, is unlikely to alter its emphasis on economic development. Although China never slows its efforts to modernize its military forces, military modernization is secondary to economic development. According to Chinese official figures, China's military expenditures in 1978 were 9 percent of those of the United States. In 2002, after several years of record-level growth, that figure declined to 6 percent. If we examine per capita military expenditures, the gap is dramatically larger. The per capita military expenditure of the United States in 2002 was $1,500, and that of China only $28. Another trend that may well continue is China's change in its foreign policy toward its neighbors. Once the "second most dispute-prone state of the major powers in the post–Second World War period" (Johnson 1998, 9), China now prefers negotiation and discussion as the means to resolve its disputes with other countries.

The only exception is in the Taiwan Straits. The third Taiwan Straits Crisis (1995–1996) was a good example of how dramatically the situation in the straits could change Beijing's course of development. As the DPP government pushes Taiwan toward independence, there is less room left for peaceful negotiation and discussion. A military showdown between the Mainland and Taiwan would have severe repercussions for the entire Asia-Pacific region.

References, Recommended Readings, and Websites

Books
Arase, David, ed. 2003. *The Challenge of Change: East Asia in the New Millennium*. Berkeley: Institute of East Asian Studies, University of California.

Byman, Daniel L., and Roger Cliff. 1999. *China's Arms Sales: Motivations and Implications.* Santa Monica, CA: Rand.

Deng, Xiaoping. 1993. *The Selected Works of Deng Xiaoping (Deng Xiao Ping Wen Xuan).* Vol. 2. Beijing: The People's Press.

Fairbank, John King. 1992. *China: A New History.* Cambridge: Belknap Press of Harvard University Press.

Joffe, Ellis. 1987. *The Chinese Army after Mao.* Cambridge: Harvard University Press.

Kan, Shirley. 2003. *China: Possible Missile Technology Transfers.* New York: Novinka Books.

Lampton, David M. 2001. *The Making of Chinese Foreign and Security Policy: In the Era of Reform, 1978–2000.* Stanford, CA: Stanford University Press.

Manning, Robert A., Ronald Montaperto, and Brad Roberts. 2000. *China, Nuclear Weapons, and Arms Control: A Preliminary Assessment.* New York: Council on Foreign Relations.

Moore, Frank W. 2000. *China's Military Capabilities.* Cambridge, MA: Institute for Defense and Disarmament Studies.

Niksch, Larry A. 2002. "North Korea's Nuclear Weapons Program." In *Korea: Current Issues and Historical Background,* Edgar V. Connor, ed. New York: Nova Science Publishers.

Ross, Robert S. 1999. "Engagement in US China Policy." In *Engaging China: The Management of an Emerging Power,* Alastair Iain Johnson and Robert S. Ross, eds. New York: Routledge.

Weintraub, Stanley. 2000. *MacArthur's War: Korea and the Undoing of an American Hero.* New York: Free Press.

Zagoria, Donald S., ed. 2003. *Breaking the China-Taiwan Impasse.* Westport, CT: Praeger.

Zheng, Yongnian. 2004. *Globalization and State Transformation in China.* Cambridge, MA: Cambridge University Press.

Articles
Chang, Johannes Han-Yin. 2000. "China-US Relations: The Past as Looking Glass." *American Studies International* 38:62–79.

Chen, Jian. 1995. "China's Involvement in the Vietnam War, 1964–69." *China Quarterly* 142:356–387.

Cossa, Ralpha, and Jane Khanna. 1997. "East Asia: Economic Interdependence and Regional Security." *International Affairs* 73:219–234.

Ding, Arthur S. 1996. "China's Defense Finance: Content, Process and Administration." *China Quarterly* 146:428–442.

Frankenstein, John, and Bates Gill. 1996. "Current and Future Challenges Facing Chinese Defence Industries." *China Quarterly* 146:394–427.

Fravel, M. Taylor. 1996. "China's Attitude toward U.N. Peacekeeping Operations since 1989." *Asian Survey* 36:1102–1121.

Gurtov, Mel. 1993. "Swords into Market Shares: China's Conversion of Military Industry to Civilian Production." *China Quarterly* 134:213–241.

Hao, Yufan, and Zhihai Zhai. 1990. "China's Decision to Enter the Korean War: History Revisited." *China Quarterly* 121:94–115.

Joffe, Ellis. 1996. "Party-Army Relations in China: Retrospect and Prospect." *China Quarterly* 146:299–314.

Johnson, Alastair Iain. 1996. "Prospects for Chinese Nuclear Force Modernization: Limited Deterrence versus Multilateral Arms Control." *China Quarterly* 146:548–576.

———. 1998. "China's Militarized Interstate Dispute Behavior 1949–1992: A First Cut at the Data." *China Quarterly* 153:1–30.

Li, Hongshan. 1997. "China Talks Back: Anti-Americanism or Nationalism? A Review of Recent 'Anti-American.'" *Journal of Contemporary China* 6:153–160.

Mora, Frank O. 2002. "A Comparative Study of Civil-Military Relations in Cuba and China: The Effects of Bingshang." *Armed Forces & Society* 28:185–209.

NRDC Nuclear Notebook. 2003. "Chinese Nuclear Forces, 2003." *Bulletin of the Atomic Scientists* 59:77–80.

Pablo-Baviera, Aileen San. 2003. "The China Factor in US Alliances in East Asia and the Asia Pacific." *Australian Journal of International Affairs* 57:339–352.

Paltiel, Jeremy T. 1995. "PLA Allegiance on Parade: Civil-Military Relations in

Transition." *China Quarterly* 143:784–800.

Shambaugh, David. 1996. "China's Military in Transition: Politics, Professionalism, Procurement, and Power Projection." *China Quarterly* 146:265–298.

Tretiak, Daniel. 1979. "China's Vietnam War and Its Consequences." *China Quarterly* 80:740–767.

Waller, Digby. 1996. "Estimating Non-transparent Military Expenditures: The Case of China." *Defense and Peace Economics* 8:225–241.

Wang, Shaoguang. 1996. "Estimating China's Defense Expenditure: Some Evidence from Chinese Sources." *China Quarterly* 147:889–911.

Whiting, Allen S. 2001. "China's Use of Force 1950–96, and Taiwan." *International Security* 26:103–131.

Xu, Guangqiu. 2001. "Anti-Western Nationalism in China, 1989–99." *World Affairs* 163:151–162.

Zhao, Dingxin. 2002a. "An Angle on Nationalism in China Today: Attitudes among Beijing Students after Belgrade 1999." *China Quarterly* 172:885–905.

_____. 2002b. "Student Nationalism in China." *Problems of Post-Communism* 49:16–28.

Websites

Armed Conflict Event Data. Sino-India War 1962–1963: http://www.onwar.com/aced/data/india/indiachina1962.htm.

Center of Defense Information. Nuclear Weapons Database: Chinese Nuclear Delivery Systems. http://www.cdi.org/issues/nukef&f/database/chnukes.html.

Chen, Jian. 1992. "The Sino-Soviet Alliance and China's Entry into the Korean War (A working paper of Cold War International History Project). http://wwics.si.edu/topics/pubs/ACFAE7.pdf.

China Daily. "China Discloses the Truth of the 'East Turkestan,'" September 12, 2002. http://www1.chinadaily.com.cn/gb/doc/2002–09/12/content_27551.htm.

Chinese National Defense White Paper. http://www.globalsecurity.org/military/library/report/2003/wmeat9900/18724.pdf.

CIA. World Factbook. http://www.cia.gov/cia/publications/factbook/.

Correlates of War Project, University of Michigan. http://www.umich.edu/~cowproj/.

Federation of American Scientists (FAS). Military Analysis Network: First Taiwan Straits Crisis Quemoy and Matsu Islands. http://www.fas.org/man/dod–101/ops/quemoy_matsu.htm.

Federation of American Scientists (FAS). Military Analysis Network: Sino-Soviet Border Clashes. http://www.fas.org/man/dod–101/ops/war/prc-soviet.htm.

Federation of American Scientists (FAS). Weapons of Mass Destruction: China's Nuclear Weapons. http://www.fas.org/nuke/guide/china/nuke/.

Ministry of Foreign Affairs of the People's Republic of China. Conclusion of the 'Sino-Soviet Treaty of Friendship, Alliance and Mutual Assistance.' http://www.fmprc.gov.cn/eng/ziliao/3602/3604/t18011.htm.

People's Daily. Jiang Zemin's speech in the 15th National Conference of the CCP, 1997. http://www.people.com.cn/GB/shizheng/252/5089/5093/20010430/456848.html.

Piero, Scaruffi. Wars and Casualties of the 20th Century. http://www.scaruffi.com/politics/massacre.html.

Virtual Information Center. China's Weapons Sales—Special Report. http://www.vic-info.org/RegionsTop.nsf/0/3c3cc99bcf75f4c58a256a8f00744233?OpenDocument.

World Military Expenditures and Arms Transfers (WMEAT). Arms Transfer. http://www.globalsecurity.org/military/library/report/2003/wmeat9900/18724.pdf.

Colombia

Joakim Kreutz

Geography and History

In 1499, one of Christopher Columbus's companions, Alonso de Ojeda, arrived at the Guajira peninsula. The local tribes produced some accomplished gold work and pottery, giving rise to the legend of El Dorado, and several expeditions followed from bases in northern present-day Colombia. The indigenous tribes were at first tolerant of the Spaniards, but they became hostile when the colonists wanted to enslave them and confiscate their land. In 1544 almost all of the territory was under Spanish control, incorporated into the viceroyalty of Peru. The administrative province was changed in 1739, when present-day Colombia, Venezuela, Ecuador, and Panama formed the New Granada. Increasing resistance toward slavery and the Spanish monopoly led to several uprisings, until independence was achieved in 1819 after an armed struggle led by a Venezuelan, Simón Bolívar. The newly created Union of Gran Colombia collapsed in 1830, establishing the states of Colombia (including the territory of present-day Panama), Venezuela, and Ecuador.

President Alvaro Uribe Velez has led the Republica de Colombia since August 7, 2002, with Fransisco Santos serving as vice president. The president is both chief of state and head of government and is elected for a period of four years. The cabinet consists of a coalition of the two dominant parties, the PL (Partido Liberal, the Liberal Party) and the PSC (Partida Social Conservador, the Conservative Party), and some independents.

In addition to the head of government and cabinet, Colombia has a bicameral congress. The two houses consist of a 102-seat senate and a 166-seat house of representatives, whose members are elected for four-year terms. The judicial branch is divided into four coequal judicial organs: the Supreme Court of Justice in relation to criminal law, the Council of State for administrative law, and the Constitutional Court. The fourth organ is the Higher Council of Justice, which administers and disciplines the civilian judiciary and nominates judges for the other three organs. The three sister courts and congress elect members for the Higher Council of Justice. The country is divided into a capital district (Distrito Capital de Bogota) and thirty-two *Departamentos*.

Colombia is located in northern South America, being the link to Panama and Central America. It is the only South American country bordering both the Caribbean Sea and the Pacific Ocean. Apart from the northern connection to Panama, the country is bordered by Venezuela and Brazil in the east and by Peru and Ecuador in the south. The country's total area is 1,138,910 square kilometers, including the territories of Isla de

Table 1   Colombia: Key Statistics

Type of government	Republic
Population (millions)	42 (2003)
Religion	Roman Catholic
Main industries	Textiles, food processing, oil, clothing and footwear, beverages, chemicals, cement, gold, coal, emeralds.
Main security threats	Current civil war against the left-wing guerillas FARC-EP and ELN. In July 2003, the right wing group AUC begun demobilization as part of a recently agreed peace process
Defense spending (% GDP)	3.8 (2001)
Size of military (thousands)	158 (2002)
Number of civil wars since 1945	1 (ongoing as of 2003)
Number of interstate wars since 1945	0

Sources

Central Intelligence Agency Website. 2003. "CIA World Factbook." http://www.cia.gov/cia/publications/factbook/ (accessed May 15, 2005).

Eriksson, Mikael, ed. 2004. *States in Armed Conflict 2002*. Uppsala: Uppsala Publishing House.

International Institute for Strategic Studies (IISS). 2002. *The Military Balance 2002–2003*. London: IISS and Oxford University Press.

Perlo-Freeman, Sam. 2003. "Survey of Military Expenditures in South America: Background Paper for the SIPRI Yearbook 2003." http://projects.sipri.se/milex/mex_s_america_bg_03.pdf.

Malpelo, Roncador Cay, Serrana Bank, and Serranilla Bank. Colombia (in its west and north) consists of flat coastal lowlands, central highlands that rise into the high Andes mountains, and lowland plains toward the eastern border. The climate is tropical in the coastal and eastern lowlands and cooler in the highlands. The highlands are subject to volcanic eruptions and occasional earthquakes, as well as occasional droughts.

Colombia has some natural resources such as petroleum, natural gas, coal, iron ore, nickel, gold, copper, emeralds, and hydropower. Oil production is currently suffering some decline, as there is a need for new exploration. Colombia's other main export, coffee, has also suffered recently because of increased international competition and bad harvests (CIA World Factbook 2004).

Regional Geopolitics

Historically Colombia has focused its attention toward the north and east, and relations with countries other than the United States, Panama, and Venezuela largely have been neglected. Because for most of the last century the United States controlled the Panama channel, not many initiatives or troubles were experienced with the countries in Central America.

It was not until Colombia decided to pursue a policy of subregional economic integration in the 1960s that relations with neighboring countries became a prime interest. In 1969, Colombia signed the Cartagena Agreement, establishing the Andean group, which eventually led to the establishment of the LAFTA (Latin American Free Trade Association) and ALADI (Asociación Latinoamericana de

Integración, Latin American Integration Association) in 1980. During the administration of President Betancur (1982–1986), Colombia initiated the Contadora Group in 1983 with Mexico, Venezuela, and Panama, with the longstanding goal of establishing peace in Central America.

During the last decades, there has been increased publicity around a dispute between Nicaragua and Colombia concerning the maritime boundary involving 50,000 square kilometers in the Caribbean Sea, including the Archipelago de San Andres y Providencia and Quita Sueno Bank. The basis of that disagreement is that Nicaragua does not acknowledge a treaty signed in 1928, the Barcenas-Esguerra Treaty, which established Colombian sovereignty over the area, as Nicaragua at the time was under U.S. occupation. In December 2001, Nicaragua filed a complaint over the issue in the International Court of Justice, and it is an ongoing case at present (International Court of Justice 2004).

Ever since the breakup of Gran Colombia in 1830, there has been a special relationship between Colombia and Venezuela. That has manifested itself both in the form of cross-border trade and economic cooperation and in rivalry over resources. The longest running and most serious rivalries concern border disputes in the oil-rich Golfo de Venezuela. The situation almost led to open conflict when Colombia in the late 1960s attempted to negotiate contracts with foreign oil companies to do offshore exploratory drilling in a contested area. The Venezuelan government pointed out that the Golfo was a Venezuelan inland waterway, and in 1971 the two countries agreed to suspend further operations in the area until they had reached a final agreement. The dispute

was not settled, and in 1979 talks to establish stricter boundary limits began.

During the first half of the 1980s, there were several shooting incidents in the area, and both countries mobilized troops along the border and engaged in a minor arms race. After unsuccessful talks in 1986 the conflict almost led to armed clashes in 1987, after claims were made that a Colombian warship had crossed the border and both countries mobilized (U.S. Library of Congress 1988). The Venezuelan military was superior at the time, but after the U.S.-sponsored military buildup in the late 1990s, Colombia now has military superiority over its neighbors.

Because of the tense relations between the two countries, the Venezuelan government has been suspicious of the renewed intensity of U.S. involvement in the region resulting from the Plan Colombia, launched in 2000. The Colombian government has suggested during the last decade that Venezuela is supporting the Colombian insurgent movement FARC-EP by allowing them to have bases across the border. Even though those claims usually have been denied, there has been some evidence of Venezuelan troops supporting FARC-EP and even participating in FARC-EP operations on Colombian territory. There have also been links between the Colombian paramilitary units AUC and armed Venezuelan right-wing groups, and in June 2002, AUC leader Carlos Castano confirmed that clashes between AUC and FARC-EP took place on the other side of the border (Valenzuela 2002, 6).

Another area that has seen much cross-border activity has been in Ecuador, inasmuch as the U.S.-sponsored Plan Colombia, aimed at drug trafficking and the left-wing guerrillas FARC-EP and ELN, has one of its headquarters at the Ecuadorian military base in Manta. FARC-EP has stated that the United States is pursuing a strategy aimed against the guerrillas, and that Ecuador is central to that aim because there are U.S. troops stationed not only in Manta but also in Lago Agrio, Tulcan, and Esmeraldas. Other reports claim that paramilitary opponents of FARC-EP have bought land in Ecuador and initiated training of the local population (Valenzuela 2002, 5–6).

The intense civil conflict in Colombia and the drug trafficking in the area have spilled across the borders to all neighboring states, and during the last five years there has been a military buildup along the Colombian border. Venezuela has increased its military spending, Ecuador has reinforced its border patrols, and Brazil launched operation Co-Bra in 2000 to strengthen its military presence in the Amazonian region (ibid., 6)

Conflict Past and Present

Conflict History

After the breakup of Gran Colombia in 1830, an uneasy state-building process started in Colombia. Following a short civil war in 1840, the Creole elites started to organize in the 1840s into two main parties: the conservatives, who wanted a centralist state, and the liberals, who proposed a federal solution. The struggle between the two turned violent, and the country suffered eight civil wars and more than fifty armed insurrections in the second half of the nineteenth century. The situation culminated in the "Thousand Days War" (La Guerra de los Mil Días), which led to more than 50,000 deaths, property damage, and the ruin of the national economy in 1899–1902. In November 1902 a peace treaty was signed, but the Colombian government was still not able to prevent Panama, with U.S. back-

ing, from leaving the republic and gaining independence the following year (Scott 1913).

At the time, Chile's Prussian-trained army was the strongest in South America. Colombia contacted Chile for help with organizing its army along similar lines, creating a conscription army with an unspoken mission to protect and correct society. The Prussian-Chilean influence was soon overtaken by the influence of the United States as U.S. companies became involved in the growing oil industry. Good relations between the countries led to an outspoken policy by the Colombian government to follow the U.S. lead in foreign policy and security matters. During the first decades of the twentieth century, the Colombian elite was intent on avoiding a resumption of civil conflict, but there were border incidents with Peru on several occasions leading to shorter military campaigns in 1911, 1922, and 1932–1933 (ibid.).

During the 1940s, the close working relationship between the ruling conservatives and the liberals suffered, as there was a growing public discontent over social inequalities. That fostered the career of the left-wing liberal Jorge Eliécer Gaitán, who declared himself an independent candidate in the presidential election of 1946 on a platform of social reform; he later became leader of the Liberal Party. Gaitán became a symbol for a growing left wing within the Liberal Party, which refused to distance itself from communist and social democratic movements in Latin America (Rudqvist 2002, 9).

During the Ninth Pan American Conference, held in Bogota in 1948, Gaitán was assassinated. The event led to mass rioting, and Gaitán supporters lynched the assassin. The masses then continued by destroying most of downtown Bogota and attacking government and U.S.-owned belongings. The conservative leadership answered with severe repression, including banning public meetings and replacing all Liberal Party governors. In 1949 the congress was forcibly shut down and the Liberal Party boycotted the ensuing elections. Liberals and peasants organized themselves into self-defense groups against the conservative paramilitary forces, and throughout the country violent clashes erupted.

The Conservative Party lost power in a military coup in 1953, leading to the dictatorship of General Rojas Pinilla, who tried to end the violence and implement social reforms inspired by the populist activities of Perón in Argentina. Those measures led to a temporary decrease in the fighting, but after the military government responded in authoritarian style to new outbreaks of rural violence, the repression worsened.

As opposition against the military government spread, negotiations were initiated between exiled conservative and liberal party leaders, and in 1957 the two groups signed the San Carlos Agreement, creating a coalition Frente Nacional (national front) with a rotating presidency, the first president being a conservative. A plebiscite was held on the agreement, and in August 1958 the newly elected congress appointed the first Frente Nacional president.

The period from 1948 to 1958 is usually referred to as La Violencia (the Violence), and it has been claimed that there were 300,000 political killings over the period (Restrepo et al. 2003, 4–5). Toward the end of La Violencia, the peasant and left-wing armies had managed to create autonomous areas in several parts of the country. In those areas, land abandoned by its former owners had been redistributed to the poorer rural population. During the Frente Nacional of 1958–1974 there was more political stability, but low-intensity violence continued—especially in the rural areas in the 1960s, as the new government tried to reinstate land to its former owners. That led to a refusal of the peasant armies in some areas to recognize the new government and the continuation of the armed organizations.

Even though the political confusion of La Violencia was over, many of the conditions that had provided the setting for the violence were still in place. There was a growing discontent with the social inequalities of Colombian society and the concentration of land ownership. The success of the Cuban revolution provided inspiration for several left-wing movements, as well as a reason for a government offensive against "communist enclaves" (UCDP database 2004). In 1964 an estimated 100 armed insurgent groups existed in Colombia, all with different backgrounds. Below are the main actors in the conflict.

The ELN (Ejército de Liberación Nacional, National Liberation Army) was formed in 1964 by a group of students who had returned from Cuba, and it soon became the most popular guerrilla movement, with an outspoken goal of overthrowing the government. Part of its popularity stemmed from the leadership of Camilo Torres, a Catholic priest of the National University in Bogotá and one of the founders of its Sociology Department. After issuing an anticapitalist "Platform for a Movement of Popular Unity," Torres was fired from his position at the university and joined the ELN; he was killed in combat in February 1966.

After a government offensive in 1964—sponsored by the U.S. Plan LASO (Latin

American Security Operation) and aimed at the leftist self-defense groups in the regions of Marquetalia, Pato, Riochiquito, and Guyabero—the remaining members decided to join forces under the name Bloque Sur (the Southern Block). At the second conference of the Bloque Sur in 1966, the group established an armed wing under the name FARC (Fuerzas Armadas Revolucionarias de Colombia, Revolutionary Armed Forces of Colombia), with a proclaimed revolutionary agenda (García-Durán 2004; Restrepo et al. 2003, 5; UCDP database 2004; Molano 1994, 67–68).

At the same time, there was an internal ideological struggle within the PCC (Partido Comunista Colombiano, Communist Party of Colombia) that in the mid-1960s led to the creation of the splinter group PCML (Communist Party of Colombia Marxist-Leninist). Influenced by the Chinese Cultural Revolution, a group of students decided to form an armed wing, the EPL (Ejército Popular de Liberacion, Army of Popular Liberation) for the movement in 1965. EPL announced their intention to carry out a prolonged popular war, modeled on the Maoist revolutionary experience. It took until 1967 before the EPL performed any armed activities (UCDP database 2004).

As the civil conflict worsened, former dictator Rojas Pinilla returned from exile in Spain and announced his candidacy in the presidential elections of 1970 for the newly formed party ANAPO (Alianza Nacional Popular, National Popular Alliance). After four re-counts, the Frente Nacional conservative-liberal candidate Misael Pastrana Borrero narrowly defeated Pinilla. Strong claims were made about election fraud (Bushnell 1993, 230, 291), and political tensions within the country worsened as the economy stalled

in the early 1970s. Disgruntled ANAPO members created the M-19 (Movimento 19 de Abril, The 19th of April Movement) in 1972, taking the name from the election day of 1970. The M-19 became famous when in 1974 they stole the sword of the national liberator Simón Bolívar from his exhibit.

The M-19 continued to pursue tactics based around social disturbance through spectacular attacks, or *golpe revolucionario publicitario*, while the other groups focused on rural guerrilla war, with the EPL suffering most during the government offensives of the 1970s. As the conflict continued, and with large parts of the country under rebel control, there was an increase in narcotics production and export from Colombia: first marijuana; from 1975 on, cocaine; and eventually heroin. Large drug-producing facilities were established in territory under FARC control against a tax to the guerrillas to continue their struggle. In government-controlled areas, a similar fee for protection was paid to the civilian paramilitary forces and so-called Intelligence Hunter/Killer teams, which had been established in the 1960s (Koonings and Kruijt 1999, 143–144; HRW 1996; Colombiawar 2003).

In this environment, it was considered necessary for large landowners and the drug lords to create their own paramilitary protection forces. On December 3, 1981, a helicopter over the city of Cali dropped leaflets announcing the formation of the group MAS (Muerte a Secuestradores, Death to Kidnappers). Some members of the drug-trafficking Medellín cartel had organized the group after the M-19 had kidnapped one of their relatives. Other parts of society tired of war took notice. Following the initiative of the local mayor, a meeting of local businessmen, politicians, cattle ranchers, and oil company representatives decided to form another group, also named MAS, in Puerto Boyacá in 1982. The Colombian Army was happy to supply training and tactical support, and the paramilitary groups began their campaign to "cleanse" the area of subversives.

One of the most influential groups was the ACCU (Autodefensas Campesinas de Córdoba y Urabá, Peasant Self-defense Groups of Córdoba and Urabá), led by Fidel "Rambo" Castano, who managed to force FARC out of the Magdalena Medio region in 1985 only to take over their functions and collect protection fees. Soon Castano and his brothers also became directly involved in controlling the drug business (HRW 1996; Koonings and Kruijt 1999, 150; Van do Stadi 1990, 39).

The administration of President Belisario Betancur (1982–1986) began investigations into the paramilitary activity but also initiated a peace process with the guerrillas. In 1984, a truce was proposed and a general amnesty offered. FARC and parts of the ELN signed the truce, and FARC established a political party, the Union Patriótica (Patriotic Union, UP) that competed in the 1986 elections (Rabasa and Chalk 2001, 71). The M-19 also signed a truce but spectacularly resumed their struggle as a group of commandos seized control of the Palace of Justice in Bogota in November 1985. In the ensuing twenty-eight-hour battle with police and army troops, 128 people were killed, including 12 politicians and 41 M-19 members (Carrigan 1993, 14).

Because of the high income to be made by involvement in illegal businesses such as drug trafficking, extortion, and kidnappings, the various rebel groups barely suffered any loss of capabilities from the diminishing external support when the

---

Sidebar 1   Criminals or Rebels?

In the Colombian civil war, all nongovernmental parties, including the paramilitaries, have track records of being involved in kidnappings-for-ransom and in the drug-trafficking industry. According to local NGO Fundación Pais Libre, during 2002 there were 936 kidnappings by FARC-EP, 776 by ELN, and 180 by AUC. Some of these were politically motivated, but the majority were a means of funding the struggle.

Another important source of revenue is the narcotics industry. Since the end of the large "cartels" of Medellín and Cali, the main drug traffickers are now some 200 smaller groups. Many operate on territory controlled by rebels or paramilitaries that sometimes participate in the business. These choices, however, seem to be made locally, as in some areas that the coca business simply is "taxed" like other businesses, while local rebel commanders in other regions have told farmers not to grow coca.

Sources
Crocker, Chester A., Fen Osler Hampson, and Pamela Aall, eds. 2001. *Turbulent Peace*. Washington, DC: U.S. Institute of Peace.
HRW (Human Rights Watch). 2003. *You'll Learn Not to Cry*. New York: Human Rights Watch.

Cold War ended, and there was a cut of support from the Soviet Union, Cuba, and China. The dependence on drugs for income, however, had had an effect on the tactics used, as both paramilitaries and guerrillas were dependent on controlling certain territories to provide an income to continue fighting. Already during the truce in the mid-1980s, there had been an increase of political violence, aimed mainly at members of the Union Patriótica but also against trade unionists and other political activists. The paramilitary groups committed most of those murders, which, for example, practically exterminated the UP, with links to the military, local political leaders, and drug traffickers. After FARC ambushed the military at Puerto Rico in June 1987, the cease-fire was effectively over and the conflict escalated (Bergquist et al. 2001, 6; Koonings and Kruijt 1999, 152–153; Restrepo et al. 2003, 7; García-Durán 2004).

Toward the end of the 1980s, M-19 decided to lay down its arms and participate in the 1990 elections, and several other smaller groups—such as the EPL, the Quintín Lame group, and the PRT (Revolutionary Workers' Party)—followed as Colombia adopted a new constitution in 1991. After the M-19 peace agreement, FARC quickly expanded into urban areas and created a subgroup called RUAN (Red Urbano Antonio Narino, Antonio Narino Urban Network) to foster relations between the rural guerrillas and the groups operating in Bogotá. Being the only remaining rebel organizations, FARC and ELN started to coordinate their activities under the acronym CGSB (Coordinadora Guarillera Simón Bolívar). The joint guerrilla group participated in some negotiations with the government, but those peace talks were suspended after a series of attacks by FARC on politicians in 1991–1992 and subsequent military offensives by the government (Rabasa and Chalk 2001, 72; Rudqvist 2002, 25).

With the help of the paramilitary groups, the drug barons and other large landowners expanded their territory—estimated at being from a third to a half of the arable land in 1984 and 1997—at the expense of the rural peasant population. The paramilitary groups—while still at times working closely with the armed forces—became increasingly independent, and in 1989 participation in "self-defense groups" was declared illegal and the president referred to the paramilitaries as "terrorist organizations" (Rudqvist 2002, 16; HRW 1996; Kurtenbach et al. 2000, 201; Leech 1999, 8).

After the "war on drugs" became a primary foreign policy goal for the United States, and the National Drug Control Strategy of 1989 singled out Colombia, Peru, and Bolivia as the prime focus, there was increasing pressure on the Colombian government to focus on counternarcotics operations (Bouley 1999, 1–2). Annoyed by the increasing pressure, the drug-trafficking cartels launched a bombing campaign against government officials. Violence between cartels also increased in the late 1980s, as they tried to expand their share of the market.

As conflict between the guerrillas and counternarcotics operations escalated in the late 1980s and early 1990s, so did other forms of criminality. The abundance of small arms and the long-standing violence and uncertainty over authority in some areas led to a culture in which an increasing part of the population took justice into their own hands. According to the Comisión Columbiana de Juristas and the Colombian National Police, there were almost 300,000 homicides in Colombia in 1998–2000, as compared with fewer than 25,000 political homicides and approximately 15,000 battle-related deaths within the same period. Kidnappings also became a lucrative business for rebel and criminal groups during that period (Rudqvist 2002, 78).

*Current and Potential
Military Confrontation*

The conflict continued during most of the 1990s. FARC-EP was the largest of the guerrilla groups, controlling large areas as well as being active in urban operations. There has been occasional coordination between FARC-EP and the ELN, which is the other active rebel group. Partly because of the intense campaign against the drug lords and partly because of fighting between the different cartels, the guerrillas and the paramilitary groups acquired direct control over most of the business. In 1994 the leader of the paramilitary group ACCU, Fidel Castano, disappeared during an arms-gathering expedition in Panama and was replaced by his younger brother Carlos. Under the leadership of Carlos Castano, extensive connections were made with other paramilitary organizations, which led to the establishment of the alliance AUC (Autodefensas Unidas de Colombia, the United Self-Defense Forces) (Montalvo 2000).

Since 1997, the AUC has been a fully organized national actor with strong interests in the drug business, as well as pursuing a partly independent agenda based on an anti-leftist ideology and the rejection of structural reforms regarding land ownership. It should also be noted that the AUC has been the fastest growing actor in the conflict during the last decade, and that the groups in the alliance had substantial support from the general public (Kreutz 2005).

The relationship between the Colombian armed forces and the AUC has been complicated. It was soon recognized that the paramilitary groups consisted to a large extent of people with a background in the armed forces. In the early to mid-1980s, the establishment of self-defense groups was a legal and useful method of gaining the upper hand against the guerrillas. As the paramilitaries grew stronger and started to expand their activities to attacks on alleged supporters of the guerrillas, it became clear that the government had to act against them. Several reports, however, have shown that—even if the AUC during the late 1990s to a lesser extent was acting in tandem with the Colombian armed forces—they shared some common goals and strategies. It was an unspoken rule that AUC members were allowed, for example, to travel without problem through military checkpoints.

In a way, the appearance of the AUC helped the Colombian armed forces clean up their previously questionable human rights record. On several occasions, it was claimed that the military used the threat of AUC action in their inquiries into FARC-EP hideouts. That implicit threat grew as the AUC became increasingly notorious for its methods of torture and mass execution. After public outrage resulted following several large massacres of civilians in guerrilla-dominated areas by paramilitaries in 1997–1999, the AUC publicly committed itself not to massacre or kill large numbers of individuals and to increase their "selectiveness." That did not stop the AUC, however, from attacking civilians, but made them change tactics slightly, so as not to leave several bodies at the same location. In 2001–2002, most of the bodies discovered executed in the jungle were found alone or in pairs (Restrepo et al. 2003, 24; Bodemer et al. 2001, 179–186).

In the mid-1990s the Colombian public became increasingly vocal in their demand to end the conflict, and a citizen's group managed to attract 10 million supporters for the Mandate for Peace in 1997. The peace movement received a great deal of attention in the 1998 presidential elections, prompting the newly elected Andrés Pastrada to initiate peace talks (García-Durán 2004; Ceballos 2001). To foster the process, a 42,000-square-kilometer *zona de despeje* (demilitarized zone) was established for the purpose of peace talks. As negotiations slowly progressed the AUC became visibly stronger, and the Colombian armed forces were modernized as a result of the implementation of the U.S.-sponsored Plan Colombia. Following the events in the United States on September 11, 2001, and the ensuing proclamation of the "War on Terrorism," sectors within the government and the armed forces opposed to a negotiated settlement became more influential (García-Durán 2004).

At the same time, ELN and FARC-EP continued to disrupt the process through sabotage and attacks on political leaders to gain an advantage in the negotiations, culminating when FARC-EP hijacked a commercial airliner with a senator aboard in April 2002. President Pastrana reacted by withdrawing from the peace talks and ordering a military offensive into the demilitarized zone. The guerrillas withdrew to bases in the border area with Venezuela, where they had strong public support following a wave of cross-border attacks on civilians by the AUC in the late 1990s to control drug routes.

In the 2002 elections, Pastrana's failure with the peace process led to him losing office to Alvaro Uribe, who campaigned under the slogan "Firm Hand, Big Heart." The presidential campaign was marred by violence, assassination attempts, and kidnappings from all sides, aimed at politicians, media sources, and election workers. Symptomatically, as Uribe was being inaugurated, FARC-EP launched an

---

Sidebar 2   The Failed Negotiations

Following the strong peace movement in the mid-1990s, the administration of President Pastrana initiated peace talks. A demilitarized meeting zone comprising five municipalities (42,000 square kilometers, or roughly the size of Switzerland) was set up as the fighting was "allowed" to continue in the rest of the country. An ambitious agenda was drafted concerning twelve issues and forty-eight sub-issues that were considered important to the actors.

On 5 October 2001, the parties signed a pre-agreement for the conclusion of negotiations, but other dynamics meant that the political backing of the process was rapidly decreasing. Factors contributing to these dynamics were an increasing number of paramilitary groups, provocative rebel acts, substantial U.S. military aid, and the "War on Terror" that singled out FARC-EP as the most dangerous terrorist group in the hemisphere. In early 2002, the peace process disintegrated.

Source
García-Durán, Mauricio, ed. 2004. "Alternatives to War—Colombia's Peace Processes." *Accord* 14. Conciliation Resources, http://www.c-r.org/.

---

attack aimed at the presidential palace but instead hitting a nearby slum. Uribe declared his willingness to negotiate with both paramilitaries and guerrillas if they first declared a cease-fire; he increased military spending and launched a large-scale military offensive. In December 2002 the AUC declared a cease-fire and started negotiations with the government. In an attempt to provoke the AUC into resuming the armed struggle, FARC-EP soon launched an offensive aimed at the paramilitaries (Restrepo et al. 2003, 5; UCDP database 2004).

After seven months of secret negotiations between government representatives and AUC leaders, the AUC, the government, and church representatives signed the "Accord of Santa Fe De Ralito to Contribute to Peace in Colombia" in July 2003. That agreement stipulated the demobilization of the AUC by December 31, 2005. Some parts of the AUC rejected the accord, but in late 2003 two of the other major paramilitary groups, Bloque Aliado Vencedores de Arauca and the Bloque Central Bolívar, signed similar agreements. At present, it is not exactly clear what concessions have been made in relation to the paramilitaries, and several commentators have expressed their concern about the process. At the end of 2003, however, it had been observed that just over 1,000 former paramilitaries had demobilized under the terms of the agreements (UCDP database 2004; García-Durán 2004).

Following the resumption of armed conflict, FARC-EP and ELN agreed in August 2003 to form a military alliance, with FARC-EP being the superior group, with an estimated 17,000 troops. ELN consisted of some 5,000 men. The conflict was still active as of December 2003, and it has escalated in intensity since the mid-1990s, as can be seen in Table 2.

Military offensives during Uribe's presidency have managed to recapture part of the previously guerrilla-held territory, but there have also been signs that the groups, especially FARC-EP, have changed tactics. FARC-EP has become more active in committing terrorist attacks, and in acting within urban areas not necessarily inside Colombia. In February 2003, two bombs (at the Colombian consulate and

Table 2   Intensity and Escalation of the Conflict 1990–2002

Estimated troop sizes (average) for conflict actors

Year	No. of deaths	Gov.	AUC	FARC	ELN
1990	1,820	133,000		5,500	2,200
1991	1,860	134,000		5,500	1,750
1992	2,036	139,000		6,000	2,750
1993	1,560	139,500		3,500	1,000
1994	1,375	146,400		5,700	2,500
1995	1,330	146,400		5,700	2,500
1996	1,582	143,000		5,700	2,500
1997	1,741	143,000	2,000	6,400	2,750
1998	2,417	144,000	4,000	11,000	4,500
1999	2,710	153,000	5,300	13,500	4,500
2000	3,101	158,000	8,000	12,500	4,500
2001	3,245	158,000	11,500	17,500	4,000
2002	4,036	158,000	15,000	17,500	4,250

Sources

Kreutz, Joakim, ed. 2005. "Dictionary of Non-state conflict in the World." www.ucdp.uu.se.
Restrepo, Jorge, Michael Spagat, and Juan F. Vargas. 2004. "The Severity of the Colombian Conflict: Cross-Country Datasets versus New Micro Data." http://personal.rhul.ac.uk/pkte/126/.
Uppsala Conflict Data Program Database. www.ucdp.uu.se.

the Spanish embassy) detonated in the Venezuelan capital of Caracas, and leaflets proclaimed that the small Venezuelan group FBL was responsible. FBL is—according to most analysts—nothing more than a FARC-supported militia based in the border region between the two countries (UCDP database 2004; Webb-Vidal 2003, 14–15; McDermott 2003b, 17).

Alliance Structure

Colombia has been a member of the United Nations since November 5, 1945, and recognizes the UN charter with all its obligations. Partly because of its relationship with the United States, but also as a means of contributing to the United Nations, the Colombian armed forces soon committed themselves to multinational operations. A ground unit participated in the UN force in Korea, and a battalion was part of the UN emergency force sent to the Gaza Strip in 1956–1958. Since then the Colombian military has been more restrictive in its international involvement, but since 1978 there has been an infantry battalion participating at the non-UN observer mission in Egypt/Israel.

For a long time, the Colombian focus on the United States as the prime foreign policy ally led to a rejectionist stance toward growing regional integration. Lately, Colombia has assumed a more active role in the OAS (Organization of American States), of which the former Colombian president, Gaviria, became president in 1994 and was re-elected in 1999.

During the 1960s the country adopted a policy of economic openness to the region, which corresponded to a greater willingness for political involvement. In 1969 Colombia signed the Cartagena Agreement establishing the Andean group, together with Bolivia, Chile, Ecuador, and Peru. In 1973 the membership was expanded to Venezuela, but Chile left the organization in 1976. Cooperation eventually led to the establishment of the LAFTA (Latin American Free Trade Association) and ALADI (Asociación Latinoamericana de Integración, Latin American Integration Association) in 1980.

In 1983, Colombia initiated the Contadora Group with Mexico, Venezuela, and Panama and continued to expand its institutionalized foreign political relations through the Group of Eight (today the Rio Group), and the Non-Aligned Movement. In relation to military cooperation, Colombia is not part of any regional alliance, but it has a close working relationship with the United States.

Size and Structure of the Military

In August 2002, the Colombian military consisted of 158,000 troops. Of that number, the army constituted 136,000, the navy 15,000 (including 100 naval aviation and 10,000 marines), and the air force 7,000. In addition, the country had 60,700 reserves and 104,600 police. Voluntary paramilitary groups such as the AUC that have some connections to the armed forces have been described extensively in the section on the present conflict. Some 74,700 of the military were conscripts, as there are twelve to eighteen months of mandatory service.

Since 2002, military intelligence has been boosted with a network of civilian informants. The initiative consisted of handing out radios and paying minimum wage for civilians working part-time throughout the country (McDermott 2002, 20).

According to the recently announced new Democratic Security and Defense

Policy, there is an ongoing restructuring of the armed forces. Conscription procedures will be reformed, and there will be more "equality" concerning the time served. In the new policy there is also an increased focus on professionalization of the armed forces, more specifically in reference to improving mobility of the forces and increasing the quality of training, equipment, and intelligence (Mindefensa 2003, 37–38).

Most of the conscripts (63,800) were active in the army (Ejercito Nacional). The army also had at its disposal some 100 helicopters. Lately the military has introduced the concept of High Mountain Battalions, consisting of integrated infantry and artillery units. The idea behind these troops is to close down movements of guerrillas and drug traffickers, and they are designed to fight without air support because of the weather conditions in the areas in which they are deployed. In 2001–2003, three of the proposed five battalions became operational (McDermott 2003b, 17).

One infantry battalion from the army participated in the Multinational Force and Observers peacekeeping mission in Egypt/Israel in 2002. The MNO is a non-UN mission established by the 1978 Camp David Accords and the 1979 Peace Agreement between Egypt and Israel. Colombia has participated with one infantry battalion since the beginning of the mission. In 2003 it was reported that the Colombian battalion (COLBATT) consisted of 31 officers, 58 noncommissioned officers, 265 soldiers, and 3 civilians. Together with a battalion from the United States and another from Fiji, COLBATT was responsible for monitoring part of the Egypt/Israeli border area. The force is lightly equipped, as most of the mission consists of monitoring the area (Military Balance 2002–2003; Multinational Force and Observers homepage).

The navy (Armada Nacional) had its main ocean base in Cartagena in the Caribbean Sea, and in Buenaventura and Málaga for the Pacific. It also had established river bases in Puerto Leguízamo, Barranca-bermeja, Leticia, Puerto Oocue, Puerte Inirida, and Puerto Carreno, with the last being the headquarters for the Tri-Service Unified Eastern Command. The navy included 4 submarines, 2 each of the *Pijao* (T-209) and the *Intrepido* (SX-506) types, and 4 corvettes. Most of the naval vessels, however, were patrol and coastal combatants (total 27), divided into 5 offshore, 9 coastal/inshore, and 13 riverine patrol boats. The navy also incorporated some 10,000 marines, and a small unit for naval aviation comprising 8 aircraft, 4 helicopters, and 100 troops.

The air force (Fuerza Aerea Colombiana) comprised some 7,000 troops, including 3,900 conscripts. There were a total of 58 combat aircraft and 23 armed helicopters, with the majority organized in the tactical air support and military air transport commands. There were also two squadrons of a total of 18 aircraft (*Mirage* and *Kfir*) devoted to air combat, and a substantial command for air training. The air force is modern and still improving, as part of the U.S. aid has been in the form of the donation of a helicopter fleet (Military Balance 2002–2003; McDermott 2003b, 21). It should be noted that the National Police are in charge of internal security as well as normal policing duties. That means that police forces perform internal operations, usually armed with automatic weapons and without backing of artillery or in large numbers, mainly in urban areas.

Following the election of President Uribe in 2002, he instigated an offensive against guerrillas that led to an increase in the number of police officers and the creation of "peasant platoons." The latter consist of conscripts performing their military service in their local area as support units for police and regular troops. It was reported in late 2003 that some 8,000 peasant soldiers were deployed, but the intention was to increase that number to 15,000 in 2006 (McDermott 2003b, 16; Restrepo et al. 2003, 6).

Budget
The defense budget stayed at around U.S.$1.7 billion in the years 2000–2002, even though fluctuation of the currency shows less stability when viewing the budget in pesos. When President Uribe won the election in 2002, he did it with promises of acting forcefully against the guerrillas, and one of his first acts as president was to impose a new "war tax," effectively boosting defense spending for 2002 by 20 percent. The 2003 budget included a raise for defense spending of 12 percent, while other departments' allocations were frozen or reduced in an attempt to reduce the budget deficit.

In 2002 there were about fifteen military advisors from the United States present in Colombia implementing the Plan Colombia military aid program, passed into law in 2000. Originally, at least 75 percent of the plan, worth a total of U.S.$1.3 billion—of which U.S.$642 million was designated for assistance to Colombia's security forces—was supposed to target counternarcotics activities. Criticism emerged that the Colombian government used the aid in relation to the civil war rather than the original purpose.

Following the attacks on the United States on September 11, 2001, the activities under Plan Colombia were converted into the "War on Terrorism," and the distinction between end-use of the aid was removed in August 2002. Starting in 2002 the United States also expanded its military operations in Colombia through the Pipeline Protection program. As part of that effort (U.S.$99 million for 2002–2003, and another U.S.$147 million for 2004), more than seventy U.S. Special Forces will train two elite battalions of Colombian soldiers to protect a pipeline, partly owned by the U.S.-based Occidental Petroleum Company. Finally, as part of the March 2003 "emergency supplemental" foreign aid package designated to pay for the Iraq war, an additional U.S.$104 million was included for Colombia (García-Durán 2004; Military Balance 2002–2003; Perlo-Freeman 2003).

Civil-Military Relations/The Role of the Military in Domestic Politics

At present, Colombia has been in conflict for so long that the state of war is "normal" and has been institutionalized into governmental structures. Even though the guerrilla groups, criminal gangs, and paramilitary forces at times have managed to disturb civil society, there is a clear constitutional design in place. Despite their country's tumultuous past, Colombians are proud of the fact that the country is one of the most stable democracies in Latin America and has had very few periods of military involvement into politics.

The armed forces of Colombia have not considered themselves "superior" to civilian politicians, as has been the case in many other South American states. The civil wars in the nineteenth century were fought largely between conservative and liberal paramilitary groups, as the military were more focused on defense against possible attacks by other countries. In the period of peace from 1902 to 1948, the army took pride in being apolitical.

There were brief movements toward a possible military intervention into politics on two occasions toward the end of the period. In 1936 the Liberal president Alfonso Lopez tried to intervene into the promotion procedures of the army in an attempt to change the perceived Conservative bias among the officer corps. Disgruntled officers started planning for a coup, but the conspiracy was discovered before it came into effect. Eight years later a coup attempt was launched during the second presidential term for Lopez, but loyal forces defeated it.

Following the large-scale repression initiated by the Conservative government in the first years of La Violencia, a split occurred within the army leadership. During the proclaimed dictatorship of Laureano Gomez, some military officers took places in the cabinet and participated in the campaign. Others played critical roles in how the armed forces had taken sides in the conflict. Again following the transformation of the police force from the Ministry of Defense to the Ministry of Interior (directly under the control of the Conservative Party), some officers had enough. The 1953 coup by armed forces commander Rojas Pinilla was partly an attempt to depoliticize the armed forces. The police were transformed back from the Ministry of Interior to the Ministry of Defense as a means of imposing some control on the force, under the supervision of the military minister of defense. The police are still considered part of the defense ministry but act completely independently from the army.

After Pinilla tried in 1957 to influence the election process, a short-lived military junta took power and quickly negotiated the transfer of political power to the Frente Nacional. Since 1958 there have been no signs that the armed forces in Colombia have had any intention of intervening in the political process. That can be explained partly by the strong position military issues have had on the agenda during the period, as there has been an ongoing conflict in the country. It was a tradition that the position of minister of defense was given to a military commander until the 1990s, and the civilian government has usually been restrictive in interfering with how the armed forces have allocated their budget and resolved personnel questions (Fishel 2000, 51–52).

Since the administration of President Gaviria (1990–1994), a civilian has held the position of minister of defense. The chain of command runs from the president, who is also commander-in-chief, through the minister of defense, to the commander of the armed forces. Excluded from the chain of command is the civilian vice minister of defense, who still carries the responsibility for day-to-day functions such as the budget. In 2003 it was declared that the Defense Ministry should be restructured according to the new policy goals (Fishel, 2000, 53–54; Mindefensa 2003, 34).

In 2003 the Colombian government published the "Democratic Security and Defense Policy," a framework document for the long-term basic security strategy. It declares that "the general objective of the Democratic Security and Defense Policy is to strengthen and guarantee the rule of law throughout Colombia, through the reinforcement of democratic authority" (Mindefensa 2003, 12).

To implement the policy, a new government structure was announced whereby the president and the cabinet, representatives of the armed forces, and the police would convene in the National Defense and Security Council. Similar structures would be set up on a regional level. The new structure would also incorporate a Joint Intelligence Committee that reports to the president or the minister of defense and that consists of the directors of the intelligence services. This plan would also be copied on a regional level. Finally, the document pointed out the need to restructure the defense ministry to pursue new policy goals, and that process is currently under way (ibid., 33–34).

Terrorism

The Colombian conflict has a long history of terrorist activity, as the long period of La Violencia proved. The actions of groups such as M-19 in the 1970s to 1980s were followed by a bombing campaign by the drug cartels around 1990. That was allegedly the first time that linkages with international terrorist groups were explored, as Spanish bomb experts from ETA (Euskadi Ta Askatasuna) were hired to train the Medellín cartel. Most of the urban movements signed peace agreements with the government in 1990–1991, leaving a vacuum that was explored by the FARC-EP.

During most of the 1990s, the focus was on more "traditional" warfare, with most of the terrorist activity aimed at opposing political figures or suspected informers and supporters. The ELN was the most active group using this tactic, mainly targeting infrastructure such as oil pipelines. During the peace process in 1999–2001, there were nevertheless more terrorist attacks, and in June 2001 a FARC-EP official declared that the group was prepared to take the war to the cities.

Following the breakdown of peace talks, both the Colombian government and the U.S. State Department referred to FARC-EP, ELN, and the AUC as terrorist organizations. The United States also indicted both the AUC leader Carlos Castano and the FARC-EP leadership in their absence for drug trafficking (García-Durán 2004; Mindefensa 2003, 23–24; McDermott 2003a, 22).

The strength of the three groups, and the fact that they all have controlled, and to a certain extent still control, territory in Colombia makes them different from the traditional notion of terrorist organizations. With only one of a few possible exceptions, they have only acted within Colombia within an active conflict that sets the Colombian groups aside from the general perception of "terrorism" that is characterized by uneven distribution of capabilities between the actors. They use the tactics of terrorists, but that has been the case for many actors in the Colombian conflict for a long time.

Some links have been made to other groups and international terrorism. In 2003 two bombs exploded in the Venezuelan capital Caracas, allegedly orchestrated by FARC-EP and a Venezuelan group. After a bombing campaign by FARC-EP leading up to the presidential elections in May 2002, it was reported that European-manufactured explosives had been used, supposedly supplied by the terrorist organizations IRA (Irish Republican Army) and ETA (Euskadi ta Askatasuna).

Relationship with the United States

Colombia is arguably the country in South America that historically has had the best relations with the United States. Even though relations between the two were strained at the beginning of the twentieth century because of the U.S. involvement in the secession of Panama, increasing trade links between the countries led to the Colombian policy of Res Pice Polum (Follow the North Star) in the early 1920s. The United States began to provide military training to the Colombian armed forces even before World War II as part of President Roosevelt's "Good Neighbor" policy.

As the close relationship continued, Colombia supplied troops to the U.S.-led UN force in the Korean War (1950–1953), as well as to the UN Emergency Force in Suez (1956–1958). Following the end of La Violencia in 1958, Colombia became a major recipient of U.S. aid for industrialization and economic development, as well as in fighting left-wing insurgency movements. After a brief period in the late 1970s to early 1980s when Colombia decided to pursue a regionalized foreign policy and therefore angered the United States by establishing ties with Cuba and the Sandinista government in Nicaragua, the second half of the decade once again led to improved U.S.-Colombian relations.

After President Reagan in the late 1980s declared drug trafficking a threat to national security and designated the Pentagon responsible for international counternarcotics policy, increased attention has been given to Colombia. The so-called Andean Strategy announced by President Bush, Sr., in 1989 led to a great involvement of U.S. counternarcotic agencies in Colombia. The most publicized event was when U.S. intelligence in 1993 managed to track the mobile phone call of Pablo Escobar, head of the Medellín cartel, which subsequently led to his being shot by Colombian police. During the presidency of Ernesto Samper (1994–1998), Colombia was removed from the list of prioritized countries after it became clear that Samper had received campaign contributions from the Cali cartel. U.S. aid continued for the antinarcotics police.

In 1998, as President Pastrana took office, U.S. aid increased again, and in 2000 the ambitious Plan Colombia was launched. The plan consisted of a U.S.$1.3 billion package of military aid that was restricted to the war on drugs and with a limited role for U.S. advisors. Colombian armed forces were initially criticized in the United States, and by the Venezuelan president, Hugo Chávez, for using the aid in the civil war rather than against drug traffickers. Since the events of September 11, 2001, in the United States, and the ensuing proclamation of a "War on Terrorism," military aid to Colombia has been included as part of a larger U.S. commitment. In this environment, the hard-line stance of Colombian president Uribe toward insurgent groups has suited the presently good relations between the United States and Colombia (McDermott 2003c, 20–21; García-Durán 2004; U.S. Library of Congress 1988).

The Future

Despite the strong emphasis on battling drug trafficking from Colombia and some setbacks for FARC-EP and ELN in their campaigns, the two insurgent groups still have the potential to continue fighting in the foreseeable future. It has been claimed that income from the kidnappings alone brings in more than U.S.$100 million annually, which is more than enough to maintain the present level of war (McDermott 2003, 18). The recent government offensive has been successful in regaining control of some territory in the countryside, but it has been inefficient in targeting urban groups. Even though the government launched a large-scale campaign to prevent violence in relation to the local elections in 2003, that was largely unsuccessful.

The strength of the opposition organizations is such that it is unlikely the war can be won in a traditional sense—especially since the growing budget deficit eventually will lead to a downsizing of Colombian military spending. To end the conflict there must be a negotiated settlement, but there is a risk that if the government initiates such a process, the AUC may return to arms. Because of the economic advantages for some actors involved in illegal businesses, it can also be questioned whether the conflict at present is based on political ideas or greed.

The current attempt to demobilize the AUC is definitely a good development for increasing security in Colombia. As the current president, Uribe, is generally considered a "hard-liner" with a lot of support among the armed forces and paramilitary groups, the question is how willing the former combatants may be to commit to not taking up arms again under a new government.

The most important objective at present is to re-establish a civil society and the rule of law in the country, as a possible return of large-scale criminality is likely to lead to paramilitary forces reforming. Stopping acts of terrorism and narcotrafficking is also important, but for the Colombian general public to resume faith in society, there must be an end to the criminality and a lowering of the homicide rate. There is such an abundance of arms available in Colombia, and such a long history of conflict, that it is hard to assess from the outside how to end the fighting.

References, Recommended Readings, and Websites

Books

Atkins, G. Pope. 1999. *Latin America in the International Political System.* 3d ed. Boulder: Perseus Books.

Bagley, Bruce M., and William O. Walker, eds. 1995. *Drug Trafficking in the Americas.* Coral Gables: University of Miami Press.

Bergquist, Charles, Ricardo Penaranda, and Gonzalo G. Sanchez, eds. 2001. *Violence in Colombia 1990–2000: Waging War and Negotiating Peace.* Wilmington, DE: Scholarly Resources.

Bodemer, Klaus, Sabine Kurtenbach, and Klaus Meschkat, eds. 2001. *Violencia y regulación de conflictosen América Latina.* Caracas: Nueva Sociedad.

Bushnell, David. 1993. *The Making of Modern Colombia: A Nation in Spite of Itself.* Berkeley: University of California Press.

Carrigan, Ana. 1993. *The Palace of Justice: A Colombian Tragedy.* New York: Four Walls Eight Windows.

Crocker, Chester A., Fen Osler Hampson, and Pamela Aall, eds. 2001. *Turbulent Peace.* Washington, DC: U.S. Institute of Peace.

Eriksson, Mikael, ed. 2004. *States in Armed Conflict 2002.* Uppsala: Uppsala Publishing House.

HRW (Human Rights Watch). 1996. *Columbia's Killer Networks: The Military-Paramilitary Partnership and the United States.* http://www.hrw.org/reports/1996/killertoc.htm.

HRW (Human Rights Watch). 2003. *You'll Learn Not to Cry.* New York: Human Rights Watch.

Koonings, Kees, and Dirk Kruijt, eds. 1999. *Societies of Fear: The Legacy of Civil War, Violence and Terror in Latin America.* London: Zed Books.

Kurtenbach, Sabine, Klaus Bodemer, and Detlef Nolte, eds. 2000. *Sicherheitspolitik in Lateinamerika: Vom Konflikt zur Kooperation?* Opladen: Leske and Budrich.

Mares, David R., ed. 1998. *Civil-Military Relations: Building Democracy and Regional Security in Latin America, Southern Asia, and Central Europe.* Boulder, CO: Westview Press.

Military Balance 2002–2003. 2002. London: International Institute for

Strategic Studies, Oxford University Press.

Molano, Alfredo. 1994. *Trochas y Fusiles,* Bogotá: El Áncora Editores.

Rabasa, Angel, and Peter Chalk. 2001. *Colombian Labyrinth: The Synergy of Drugs and Insurgency and Its Implications for Regional Stability.* Arlington, VA: Rand Corporation.

Rudqvist, Anders, ed. 2002. *Breeding Inequality—Reaping Violence: Exploring Linkages and Causality in Colombia and Beyond.* Uppsala: Collegium for Development Studies.

Scott, William R. 1913. *The Americans in Panama.* New York: Statler Publishing.

Silva, Patricio, ed. 2001. *The Soldier and the State in South America.* New York: Latin American Studies Series.

SIPRI Yearbook 2003. 2003. Stockholm/London: Stockholm International Peace Research Institute, Oxford University Press.

UNHCR Report 2002. *International Protection Considerations regarding Colombian Asylum-seekers and Refugees.* Geneva: UN High Commissioner for Refugees.

Valenzuela, Pedro. 2002. *Conflict Analysis: Colombia, Bolivia, and the Andean Region.* Stockholm: SIDA (Swedish International Development Cooperation Agency).

Zartman, I. William, ed. 1995. *Elusive Peace: Negotiating an End to Civil Wars.* Washington, DC: Brookings Institution.

Articles/Papers

Bouley, Eugene E. 1999. "Human Rights and the War on Drugs in Latin America." Paper presented at the annual meeting of the Academy of Criminal Justice Sciences in Orlando, Florida (March).

Chernick, Mark W. 2001. "The Dynamics of Columbia's Three-Dimensional War." *Conflict, Security and Development* 1:93–100.

Fishel, John T. 2000. "Colombia: Civil-Military Relations in the Midst of War." *Joint Force Quarterly* (summer):51–56.

García-Durán, Mauricio, ed. 2004. "Alternatives to War—Colombia's Peace Processes." *Accord* 14. Conciliation Resources, http://www.c-r.org/.

Kreutz, Joakim, ed. 2005. "Dictionary of Non-State Conflict in the World." http://ucdp.uu.se.

Leech, Garry. 1999. "Fifty Years of Violence." *Colombia Journal Online* (May). http://www.colombiajournal.org.

McDermott, Jeremy. 2002. "Colombia Imposes Democratic Authority." *Jane's Intelligence Review* 10:20–23.

———. 2003a. "Nightclub Attack Demonstrates FARC's New Urban Capability." *Jane's Intelligence Review* 3:22–23

———. 2003b. "Uribe Gains the Upper Hand in Colombia's Guerrilla War." *Jane's Intelligence Review* 12:16–21.

———. 2003c. "USA Faces Colombian Dilemma." *Jane's Intelligence Review* 4:18–21.

Mindefensa (Ministerio de Defensa Nacional). 2003. "Democratic Security and Defense Policy." http://www.mindefensa.gov.co/politica/documentos/seguridad_democratica_eng.pdf.

Montalvo, Samia. 2000. "Paramilitaries, Drug Trafficking and U.S. Policy in Colombia." *Dollars and Sense* (July/August). http://www.thirdworldtraveler.com/South_America/Paramilitaries_Colombia.html.

Perlo-Freeman, Sam. 2003. "Survey of Military Expenditure in South America: Background Paper for the SIPRI Yearbook 2003." http://projects.sipri.se/milex/mex_s_america_bg_03.pdf

Restrepo, Jorge, Michael Spagat, and Juan F. Vargas. 2003. "The Dynamics of the Colombian Civil Conflict: A New Data Set." Paper given at the conference "Revolutions, Old and New," Villa Gualino, Italy (June).

———. 2004. "The Severity of the Colombian Conflict: Cross-Country Datasets versus New Micro Data." http://personal.rhul.ac.uk/pkte/126/.

U.S. Library of Congress. 1988. *Colombia: Country Study.* http://countrystudies.us/colombia/.

Webb-Vidal, Andrew. 2003. "Embassy Bombs Mark New Phase in Venezuelan Crisis." *Jane's Intelligence Review* 4:4–17.

Articles/Newspapers

Ceballos, Miguel. 2001. "It Is Ultimately up to Ordinary Colombians to Bring Change to Colombia." *Cnn.com Special.* http://www.cnn.com.

Van do Stadi, Dominique C. 1990. "Colombian Journalists vs. Drug Terrorists." *World Press Review* (January):39.

Websites
Armada Nacional de Colombia. Colombian Navy: http://www.armada.mil.co/.
Armed Conflicts Event Data: http://www.onwar.com/aced/.
Autodefensas Unidas de Colombia: http://www.colombialibre.org/.
Central Intelligence Agency (CIA). The World Factbook: http://www.cia.gov (accessed March 15, 2004).
Colombiawar.org—Documentation from the Colombian Conflict 1928–1973: http://www.icdc.com/~paulwolf/colombia/colombiawar.htm.
Ejercito Nacional de Colombia. Colombian Army: http://www.ejercito.mil.co/.

Fuerza Aérea Colombiana. Colombian Air Force: http://www.fac.mil.co/.
Fuerzas Armadas Revolucionarias de Colombia: http://www.farcep.org/.
International Court of Justice (ICJ): http://212.153.43.18/icjwww/icj002.htm (accessed March 9, 2004).
Ministerio de Defensa Nacional. Colombian Ministry of Defense: http://www.mindefensa.gov.co/.
Multinational Force and Observers: http://www.mfo.org.
Presidencia de la República de Colombia. Colombian President: http://www.presidencia.gov.co/#.
UCDP (Uppsala Conflict Data Program) Armed Conflict Database: http://www.pcr.uu.se/basicSearch/index.php (accessed May 22, 2004).
U.S. Library of Congress Data: Colombia Country Study: http://countrystudies.us/colombia/ (accessed May 8, 2004).

Cuba

Christopher E. Housenick

Geography and History

Western civilization first charted Cuba when Christopher Columbus landed on that Caribbean island on October 28, 1492. It was more than four hundred years later that Cuba first gained its independence from Western colonial powers, following the Spanish-American War, on May 20, 1902. Since then this small island country has been surrounded by tumultuous security and foreign policy concerns. In Cuba's domestic scene, revolution and violent uprisings have played a significant role in politics and security over the past 150 years. On the international front, conventional war, great power politics, and even the threat of nuclear war have influenced the security concerns and policies of this Caribbean island of just over 11 million people.

Geographically, Cuba is the largest Caribbean island nation, being roughly the size of Pennsylvania. It is a generally flat country with some rolling hills, a few mountains, and a warm, tropical climate (U.S. State Department 2005; CIA *World Factbook* 2005). The most important element of Cuba's geography is its proximity to the U.S. mainland, being only ninety miles off the coast of Florida. That short distance creates many of the difficulties in relations between the two states. Forty years of military conflict, trade embargoes, and illegal immigration have kept ten-

sions high between Cuba and the United States, even after the conclusion of the Cold War.

In present-day Cuba, security concerns are well intertwined with the economic situation. For the better part of the Cold War, Cuba was able to spend approximately 4 percent of its GDP on its military and defense forces, while also receiving military subsidies and equipment free from the Soviet Union, making it one of the most militarized states in the Western Hemisphere. After the disintegration of the Soviet Union, that important source of funds and military matériel evaporated. Cuba is only now beginning to stabilize from the loss of those assets, with a military force approximately one-fifth its Cold War magnitude. It remains to be seen for how long the Cuban military will maintain their current size.

It is also important to note that, while Cuba is a communist country, there are some elements of this state that differ from those of their European and Asian communist counterparts. In particular, religion remains a part of life in Cuba. Official record-keeping on the religious denominations of Cuban citizens ended in 1959 with the revolution, and the communist regime did shut down some four hundred Catholic schools in 1962 (U.S. State Department 2003). Since then, however, there has been a reemergence of religion in

Table 1   Cuba: Key Statistics

Type of government	Communist state
Population (millions)	11.2 (2003)
Religion	Roman Catholic (85% in 1959, prior to Communist regime)
Main industries	Agriculture (sugar, tobacco), raw materials (petroleum, nickel, steel, cement)
Main security threats	Illegal refugees leaving for, and tense relations with, the United States
Defense spending (% GDP)	1.8% (2003)
Military size (thousands)	60
Number of civil wars since 1945	1
Number of interstate wars since 1945	1

Sources
U.S. Central Intelligence Agency. CIA *World Factbook,* 2005. http://www.cia.gov/cia/publications/factbook/geos/cu.html (accessed May 23, 2005).
Sarkees, Meredith Reid (2000). "The Correlates of War Data on War: An Update to 1997." *Conflict Management and Peace Science* 18, no. 1: 123–144.
International Institute for Strategic Studies (IISS). 1990, 2001. *The Military Balance.* London: Oxford University Press.

Cuba. In 1991, Catholics were allowed to apply for membership in the Communist Party, and in 1992 the Cuban constitution was amended to make Cuba a secular, rather than an atheist, state (ibid.). Those reforms were dramatic enough to warrant a papal visit in January 1998. This role of religion is in sharp contrast to the Soviet model, wherein religious practice was a borderline criminal activity.

Regional Geopolitics

The regional politics of Cuba, with its Caribbean, Central, and South American neighbors, has been an area of tension and concern ever since Castro's revolution. Since that time Cuba has played an active military and financial role in revolutionary movements across the Caribbean basin. In 1962, Cuba supplied arms to a group of twenty Venezuelan guerrillas in order to overthrow their government (Falk 1986, 30–31). In 1966, Che Guevara (one of Castro's fellow revolutionaries and for-mer minister of industry) went to Bolivia to begin a revolutionary movement there. Both of those early attempts at revolution were failures, and Cuba took a break from actively supporting those groups until the late 1970s.

Starting in 1977, Cuba supported the Sandinista guerrillas in Nicaragua by sending thousands of civilian and military personnel to assist in that movement (Bethell 1993, 145). When the Sandinista movement ultimately succeeded in 1979, Havana increased support for other insurrectionist movements across Central America and the Caribbean. Several hundred civilian and military personnel were sent to Grenada when a revolutionary government came to power there, and in 1980, Fidel Castro began to commit resources to the support of the Farabundo Marti National Liberation (FMLN) in their struggle for supremacy in El Salvador (ibid.). Those international commitments ultimately led to direct conflict between the United States and Cuba in

Grenada, when the U.S. invaded that island in October 1983. Fortunately the invasion did not spark a larger scale military conflict between the two nations.

Current regional relations between Cuba and its neighbors are best described as trilateral. There are bilateral relations between Cuba and other nations, but those bilateral relationships are observed, shaped, tempered, and commented on by the opinions and reactions of the United States. For instance, the current Venezuelan government under Hugo Chávez possesses a very close relationship with Fidel Castro, permitting hundreds of teachers and doctors into Venezuela to help improve conditions in downtrodden regions in that country (*Economist*, "Another Cuba" 2003). However, the United States expressed its deep concern over that apparent closeness, and worries surfaced in early 2004 when Chávez expressed the idea that his administration might nationalize the state banking system. Bringing the bank under governmental control would serve as a signal to many states that Venezuela would be moving dangerously close to a Cuban model of governance—a situation that the United States and other states will closely monitor.

There are two major regional concerns prevalent today. The first is the trafficking of illegal drugs through Cuban waters. While Cuban law stipulates the death sentence for those convicted of drug trafficking (and that policy is implemented), the location of Cuba between the drug-producing countries of Central and South America and the U.S. mainland makes it a very attractive site for refueling on the way to the United States.

The second regional concern is the flow of refugees across the Caribbean. With the United States only ninety miles from Cuba (and in view of the policy of not returning those who successfully land on U.S. soil), there are a large number of refugees that brave the Florida straits. Such attempts at illegal immigration can often ignite tensions between Cuba and the United States. One very public case, the Elian Gonzalez incident of 1999–2000, exemplifies how this conflict can escalate quickly into an international incident.

Conflict Past and Present
Conflict History
Cuba's history is marked by war and conflict, both external and internal. As early as 1868, Cuba began to press for independence from Spain. In October of that year, Carlos Manuel de Céspedes, a plantation owner from the Eastern Cuban town of Bayamo, formed an army to fight against the Spanish and declared independence for several reasons: "the inability of Cuban Creoles to serve in their own government, excessive taxation, corruption, the lack of religious liberties, suppression of the press and the denial of the rights of petition and assembly" (Staten 2003, 32). The movement went so far as to petition Secretary of State William Seward and President Ulysses S. Grant for annexation and eventual inclusion of Cuba into the United States (Pérez 2003, 51).

Throughout this early rebellion there was little noticeable U.S. attention or involvement, for two important reasons. First, weariness after the U.S. Civil War made armed conflict unthinkable to policymakers at that time. Second, there was little regard for Cuba's separatists because of their stance on slavery; during this early revolution Cuba still practiced and supported slavery, thereby distancing itself from the United States, which had abolished the practice only a few years earlier (ibid., 53). This insurrection lasted almost ten years, until February of 1878, when the rebel forces and the Spanish signed an armistice, the Peace of Zanjon (Smith 1994, 4).

While there was no open warfare in Cuba, difficult living and economic conditions set the stage for another war of independence from Spain. In 1884, the U.S. consul in Havana reported that "out of the twelve or thirteen hundred planters on the island, not a dozen are said to be solvent" (Staten 2003, 34; Pérez 2003, 56). By 1888, Cuba was in even greater economic disarray; its share of the world sugar market had plummeted from approximately 30 percent just two decades prior to just over 10 percent (Smith 1994, 29).

At this low economic point, the United States began to invest heavily in Cuba. Able to purchase businesses inexpensively, U.S. investors in Cuba did just that, following the sugar price collapse. The result was improved economic conditions on the island. Growth was spurred even further in 1890, when the McKinley Act ended taxes on imported sugar and molasses. With those barriers down, economic interdependence between the two countries flourished. "By 1894, the United States had invested more than $50 million in Cuba, purchased 87 percent of Cuba's exports and accounted for almost 40 percent of the island's imports" (Staten 2003, 36). When an economic setback came in the late 1890s, most Cubans (and many U.S. investors) blamed their difficulties on Spain, fomenting another round of revolutionary war in Cuba.

In April 1895, exiled revolutionaries from the first civil war with Spain returned to Cuba to begin another revolution (Smith 1994, 9). Open warfare erupted almost immediately, and both sides began to use draconian practices to win the war. Under General Valeriano Weyler in early 1897, the Spanish began a policy of internment. They relocated much of the rural Cuban population to camps just outside major population centers, often resulting in epidemics of smallpox, yellow fever, typhus, dysentery, cholera, and measles (ibid., 19). They also began to make use of "scorched earth" approaches, burning villages to the ground, in order to cut rebels off from their supplies (Staten 2003, 38).

The insurgent strategy was a guerrilla-style campaign to "create maximum economic and social dislocation and thereby undermine Spain's resolve" (Smith 1994, 17). Following that policy, the insurgents also destroyed many plantations for not providing support to their forces. Despite all the brutality, the United States did not take an active role to resolve the situation for several years. It took a major event for the United States to enter the war: that event was the explosion that destroyed the USS *Maine* in Havana Harbor on February 15, 1898. While details and explanations of what destroyed the ship vary, 260 sailors of her crew of 355 in total died that day (Staten 2003, 38). The event catapulted public sentiment toward war, and after a few final diplomatic avenues failed to avert conflict, Congress declared war against Spain on April 25, 1898.

The war was relatively short, lasting a mere six months and ending in U.S. victory. Spanish troops never fought on continental U.S. soil, and U.S. troops never set foot on the Iberian peninsula—the war was fought almost exclusively in Cuba. For the United States, only 345 soldiers were killed in action or eventually died from combat wounds; Spain lost 775 to direct military combat (Cirillo 2004, 32;

and Sarkees 2000, respectively). One important footnote to this war was that both the United States and Spain lost more troops to disease than to direct combat. For the Spanish, estimates were that for every soldier killed in combat with either the rebels or the United States, ten more died of various diseases (Smith 1994, 14). For the United States, disease claimed 2,565 lives, more than seven times the number killed by hostile fire (Cirillo 2004, 32). On December 10, 1898, Spain and the United States signed the Treaty of Paris, ending the war between those two countries and passing control of Cuba from Spain temporarily to the U.S.

Cuba's economy was devastated by the civil war. Before the war there had been 1,100 sugar mills in Cuba; by 1898 there were only 207 still functioning (Staten 2003, 40). Over the next four years the United States worked to prepare Cuba for independence, which began in 1902 with the election of Tomás Estrada Palma to the presidency. However, the peace was short-lived, as corruption quickly became a difficulty in Cuban politics. "The 1904 elections for the Cuban national legislature were marred by fraud, and in 1905 Estrada intimidated his opponent into withdrawing from the election and was reelected president" (ibid., 47). Such acts undermined the democratic system in Cuba, giving rise to a third insurrection in four decades. In 1906, after determining that the current Cuban government under Estrada would be unable to resolve the situation, the United States deployed military forces to Cuba to restore peace. By 1909, Cuba had reestablished democratic governance, and the United States again withdrew from internal Cuban affairs.

Over the next forty years, Cuba was relatively peaceful. While there were in-

Sidebar 1   Cuban Independence

Cuban efforts to garner American support for their independence from Spain began long before the Spanish-American War. In 1868, Carlos Manuel de Céspedes petitioned Secretary of State William Seward and President Ulysses S. Grant for annexation and eventual inclusion of Cuba into the United States. War weariness and the continuing practice of slavery in Cuba prevented the United States from taking this offer seriously.

The number one killer of Spanish and American soldiers during the Cuban struggle for independence was not enemy gunfire, but disease. Over the 30 years of quelling rebellions on Cuba, the Spanish lost more than ten times the number of soldiers to various tropical illnesses than to enemy combat. Likewise, the United States lost more than seven times the number of soldiers to disease than to enemy combat during the Spanish-American War.

Sources
Cirillo, Vincent J. 2004. *Bullets and Bacilli: The Spanish-American War and Military Medicine.* New Brunswick: Rutgers University Press.
Pérez, Louis A., Jr. 2003. *Cuba and the United States: Ties of Singular Intimacy.* Athens: University of Georgia Press.
Smith, Joseph. 1994. *The Spanish-American War: Conflict in the Caribbean and the Pacific 1895–1902.* New York: Longman Publishing.

stances of strikes, riots, protests, and even some insurrections, none of them rose to the level of conflict seen surrounding the independence of Cuba. In the 1930s, however, one of the more important elements of Cuban politics had risen to the forefront—the role of the Cuban military. Political leaders had made use of the army ever since independence from Spain in order to control rioters and protestors, as well as to supplement the labor force during strikes. With such a prominent role in society, the military became intertwined in all aspects of Cuban economic, social, and political life. In the 1930s, however, a leader would emerge that would maintain the Cuban military's influence in domestic politics for years to come. That leader was Fulgencio Batista.

In 1933 domestic difficulties manifested themselves in Cuba, and the democratically elected government stepped aside. The military stepped in to maintain order, and Batista became the accepted but not the official leader of Cuba in 1933, after the bloodless "Sergeants Revolt." Batista was the true locus of power in Cuban domestic politics. "For the rest of the decade [1933 to 1940] Batista ran Cuban affairs, working through the easy mechanisms of puppet presidents and supine administrations" (Simmons 1996, 255).

In 1940, Batista himself ran for and won the presidency in a fair election. He served one term as president, losing his reelection campaign in 1944 to Grau San Martín (ibid., 256). In 1952, after eight years of corrupt and ineffective leadership by San Martín, Batista again ran for the presidency. When it became apparent that he could not win the election fairly, Batista ordered the *golpe*, a military coup against the sitting president. With the aid of a number of junior military officers, he led a bloodless expulsion of President Carlos Prío Socarrás, thus ending the legacy of democracy in Cuba and laying the foundation for the rise of another political leader's assent—Fidel Castro (ibid.).

In 1952, after being infuriated by the *golpe*, a group of 165 young Cubans devised a plan to overthrow the Batista government. Led by the twenty-seven-year-old Fidel Castro, the operation had the central objective of attacking and holding the Moncada Barracks. Their plan was that once they captured that installation, thereby seizing the weapons stored there, they would distribute them to the local population, sparking a popular uprising (Pérez-Stable 1993, 53). After almost a year of planning, waiting, and immense secrecy, the attack on the barracks was a complete failure. All the members of the uprising were captured; many were tortured and killed, while the others were imprisoned. Even in failure, however, Castro became a national figure. In 1954, Batista gave amnesty to and released many political prisoners, including Castro and his supporters (now called the July 26th Movement).

By 1957, a number of groups actively participated in armed opposition to the Batista government and took action in Cuba. "In March [1957], under the leadership of José Antonio Echevarría, the Revolutionary Student Directorate (DRE) attacked the Presidential Palace with the objective of assassinating Batista. The students came perilously close to success" (ibid., 57). By 1958 open armed hostilities were the norm in Cuba, and on New Year's Eve, Batista fled Cuba, leaving Fidel Castro and his July 26th Movement in power as 1959 began.

Castro's successful revolution set the table for what would become the Bay of Pigs fiasco. Initial U.S. opinions of Castro varied, but by the summer of 1959, the Eisenhower administration decided that Castro's regime was a problem and planned "to take every possible step to try and eliminate that revolution" (Blight and Kornbluh 1998, 37). At that point, the U.S. Central Intelligence Agency (CIA) began to devise a plan for the overthrow of the Castro regime that paralleled the revolutionary movements of Cuba's past. The original plan was simple and consisted of two parts. The first was to create an opposition movement on Cuba; given the history of the state and the confusion surrounding the power vacuum created by Batista's abdication, creating that organization did not appear very difficult. Once the opposition movement was in place and ready, the second part of the operation would commence in the form of a small-scale military action. The original concept for the military action was to parachute-drop a small invasion force of 300 Cuban ex-patriots into Cuba (Blight and Kornbluh 1998). Their attack, combined with the preparations by anti-Castro opposition movements, would trigger a counterrevolution against Castro.

Over the next year and a half, the CIA revised and altered the plan for invading Cuba several times. One of the operational parameters implied during Eisenhower's tenure and enunciated clearly by the Kennedy administration was "that U.S. involvement in the invasion be denied" (Nathan 2001, 48). That consideration of plausible deniability gave rise to many changes to the military side of the plan, making it almost unrecognizable from its original form. Planners abandoned the initial strategy of an airdrop almost immediately. The large number of specialty military aircraft necessary to transport 300 soldiers and their equipment for an airborne assault would have immediately implicated the United States. Instead of the airdrop, planners decided to use a more common approach—a naval assault.

A second important change to the invasion plan was to alter the size of the military force that would land on Cuba.

In 1960, the Cuban military's equipment was improving dramatically. "The Soviet Union was pouring vast quantities of equipment into Cuba, including artillery, tanks, trucks, and anti-aircraft weapons" (Hawkins 1998, 12). The improved capabilities of the Cuban army made it necessary to expand the invasion force from 300 to approximately 1,500.

Also complicating the planning stages of this operation was that it spanned two presidential administrations. It was originally conceived during the Eisenhower administration, and CIA head Allen Dulles had to reassure newly elected President Kennedy: "At least 25 percent of the Cuban population, once learning of the strike, would rise in revolt against Castro" (Thompson 1992, 111). Between the revolt and the military attacks, popular opinion in policy circles held that Castro would fall from power and a pro-U.S. and potentially democratic government would arise in its place.

On April 14, 1961, the Cuban ex-patriots (now called Brigade 2506) boarded their ships bound for Cuba. On April 15, the United States attempted to fulfill another operational necessity—air superiority. For an amphibious operation to be successful, policymakers deemed that the entire Cuban Air Force and the runways they utilized had to be destroyed. A group of B–26 bombers (flown by CIA pilots) attacked key airfields and caused some casualties and damage but failed to destroy the Cuban Air Force; almost all the targeted runways were left still functional. From that point, the plan began to unravel quickly. One of Castro's mantras was that the United States had every intention of ruling the Cuban people. When the air strikes started, the Cuban citizenry took this as evidence of Castro's position, allowing him to act swiftly against his opponents on the island and consolidate his power. On April 16 the communists rounded up most of the 2,000 CIA agents operating in Cuba and 20,000 of their sympathizers, quelling any uprising before it could begin (Blight and Kornbluh 1998).

Instead of landing in a country primed for revolution, the ex-patriots landed at Bahía de Cochinos (Bay of Pigs) against a unified and defiant country in the early hours of April 17. The Cubans scrambled the remnants of their air force, attacking the landing force, sinking two ships, and chasing away the supply ships of the exiles. At this point the United States had to make a decision whether or not to support the invasion directly from the aircraft carrier USS *Essex*. Deciding against the expansion of the conflict, Kennedy did not send air support to help the ex-patriots. With no air support and no supplies, there was no chance that the invasion force of exiles could succeed. By April 19 the fighting was over, with the Cuban army killing 100 soldiers and capturing the remaining 1,300 invading members of Brigade 2506.

Overall, the failed invasion was a political windfall for Castro. In a matter of a few days he was able to solidify his government, purge the country of almost all his opposition, and establish his reputation for powerful leadership. These results, however, led to a fateful decision that would create more international conflict: the Soviet Union decided to place nuclear weapons in Cuba. That decision would lead to one of the most analyzed and discussed crises in international relations—the Cuban Missile Crisis. Superpower politics would surround Cuba, but this Caribbean nation would be the stage, not one of the actors in this drama.

Sidebar 2 Bay of Pigs Invasion

The original concept for the Bay of Pigs Invasion was to parachute drop a small invasion force of 300 ex-patriots into Cuba. This air drop portion of the plan changed almost immediately, because it would have taken so many aircraft to transport the Cuban ex-patriots that it would have been impossible for the United States to maintain its denial of involvement or responsibility.

The final operation plan was to amphibiously land 1,500 soldiers on the Cuban beach. Another reason the size of the invasion force increased dramatically was because the Soviet Union began supplying the Cuban military with larger quantities of and better-quality weapons in late 1960 and early 1961.

Even with the dramatic increase in the number of ex-patriot soldiers landing on the beaches of Cuba for the Bay of Pigs invasion, this operation was a disaster for the Unites States. The CIA failed to destroy the Cuban air force and President Kennedy withheld direct air support from the USS *Essex*. Within two days of their landing, the Castro regime killed 100 invading Cuban exiles and captured 1,300 more.

Sources
Blight, James G., and Peter Kornbluh. 1998. *Politics of Illusion: The Bay of Pigs Invasion Reexamined*. Boulder, CO: Lynne Rienner Publishers.

By May of 1962, the United States had established operational nuclear missile bases in Turkey. With a number of nuclear weapons so close to the Soviet Union, this prompted Khrushchev to consider placing nuclear weapons in Cuba. Having already approved the deployment of surface-to-air missiles there earlier that same year, it seemed only a logical extension and reciprocity for U.S. actions. Therefore, the Soviet Union decided to establish medium-range nuclear weapons bases in Cuba. One important question remained—how many missiles to deploy in Cuba. The Soviet Union decided that forty-two medium-range nuclear missiles would be an adequate show of military force to deter any U.S. aggression against Castro and his regime (Nathan 2001, 77).

By August 1962, construction in Cuba had begun: "The Soviets were developing a huge military base in Cuba protected not only by MiG fighters, light bombers, and cruise missiles for costal defense but also by a ring of surface to air missiles" (ibid., 82). While aware of the construction, the United States did not determine what purpose the base served until mid-October. On October 16 of that year, a U–2 aircraft took another series of pictures examining the construction of bases in Cuba. "U.S. analysts counted eight large MRBM transporters and four erector launchers already in firing positions" (ibid., 93).

Policymakers in the United States quickly decided that they had three primary paths of military response. The first was a massive air strike, attempting to absolutely destroy every nuclear missile site in Cuba. The second was a full-scale invasion of the island. The third and finally agreed-upon method of dealing with the Cuba situation was to create a naval "quarantine," a ring of warships stopping all naval traffic into and out of Cuba (Allison and Zelikow 1999, 115–120). Conceptually, this quarantine was identical to a naval blockade; however the term "naval blockade" is considered an open act of war according to international law, thereby necessitating a

change in terminology. After several tense days of position taking and negotiations, Kennedy and Khrushchev came to an agreement that removed the missiles from Cuba. Neither Castro nor anyone else in his regime was involved in the negotiations over the missiles.

For a few years after the missile crisis, the situation in Cuba was rather tranquil. Domestic strife was low, and international encounters were few and far between. By the late 1960s, however, Cubans would find themselves involved in international conflicts away from their home island. During the 1960s, a phenomenon of warfare by proxy arose between the superpowers. While they avoided direct conflict, they made use of guerrilla organizations and revolutionary movements across the globe to fight one another.

In 1961 a civil war against Portuguese colonialism struck Angola, and by late 1966, Cuban military advisors were in that country (James 1992, 59). By 1974, over 12,000 Portuguese soldiers would be dead and another 40,000 wounded when Portugal declared the end of their colonial rule in Angola (ibid., 41). During the war against Portugal and in the power vacuum immediately afterward, there were three parties that vied to rule Angola: the National Front for the Liberation of Angola (FNLA), the National Union for the Total Independence of Angola (UNITA), and the Popular Movement for the Liberation of Angola (MPLA). Each of these organizations had its own major power backers: the FNLA received support from China, UNITA received support from the United States, and the MPLA received assistance from the Soviet Union and Cuba (ibid., 41–63). In 1975, Cuba decided to send 36,000 troops to Angola to support the MPLA

(Bethell 1993, 143). The Cuban intervention (with Soviet logistical and material support) resulted in a victory by the MPLA in 1976.

In January 1978, Fidel Castro answered a request from the Ethiopian government, which was quickly losing its war against a Somali invasion. Intervention there helped save the Ethiopian government from being overrun. These troops would remain in Africa well into the 1980s, when they finally returned home to Cuba at the end of hostilities. In many cases across Africa, Cuban and Soviet military advisors would find themselves working side by side in their efforts to shape conflict outcomes.

Current and Potential Military Confrontation

The forecast of conflict seems to follow two paths—international conflict and domestic conflict. Looking first at international conflict, the possibility of a full-scale war between Cuba and the United States (or anyone else) does not seem to be a realistic possibility. After the collapse of the Soviet Union, Cuba was forced to reduce the size of its military dramatically. In 1991, the Cuban military had 297,000 members. By 1995, that number had been cut by more than three-quarters to a mere 70,000 troops, and it seemed to have settled at approximately 60,000 soldiers in 2004 (Singer et al., 1972 [2004]; and CIA *World Factbook* 2003, respectively). With this reduction in troop strengths and shrinking military budgets, the practice of sending Cuban soldiers abroad—as was popular in the 1970s— also came to an end. The relatively small military force of 60,000 soldiers is necessary on the home island in order to maintain political control over the citizenry of Cuba; it cannot afford to be fighting in Africa or Central America. From the U.S. perspective, strategies to attack and occupy Cuba have not been made public, if they exist at all. Therefore, it would seem that a full-scale invasion of and subsequent war in Cuba is not a possibility in any foreseeable future.

Certain policies of both Cuba and the United States create tensions, however, as well as incidents that can erupt into interstate conflict on a scale smaller than war. For instance, on February 24, 1996, Cuban planes shot down two small aircraft over international waters. These aircraft were owned and operated by the "Brothers to the Rescue" organization, a private group of U.S. citizens that patrols the Florida straits looking for refugees adrift, in order to assist them in reaching the United States (Brothers to the Rescue 2005). That sort of incident, combined with the always high tensions surrounding the U.S. naval base at Guantánamo Bay, is indicative of the sort of international dispute that might arise between the United States and Cuba in the future.

Looking at domestic conflict, given Cuba's history of civil unrest and revolution, the potential always exists for another bout of domestic political unrest and civil war. However, most policy analysts hold that a direct revolution against Fidel Castro in the near future is rather unlikely. Generally speaking, any and all possibilities for a twenty-first-century domestic insurrection or civil war in Cuba surround the idea that Fidel Castro passes from office because of natural causes. As of 2004, any foreseeable replacement would probably be perceived as weak, illegitimate, or both.

One prominent set of circumstances surrounds Raúl Castro, Fidel's brother. He is next in the line of succession for the Cuban presidency (Staten 2003, 137), as well as being second in the military chain of command, serving as "General of the Army" and "Minister of the Revolutionary Armed Forces [FAR]" (Rabkin 1991, 76). However, the "problem with Raúl is that he is only four years younger than his brother and is neither popular nor respected among most Cubans" (Staten 2003, 138). Without the respect given to—or the charisma of—his brother, Raúl Castro would need to solidify his control quickly in order to establish his legitimacy; most analysts assume that his most likely method of consolidating control would be for Raúl to increase the repression against dissenters. Combining his lack of charisma and respect with increasing political repression would be a potentially combustible mix that could result in another Cuban civil war.

In a second possible succession scenario, the Cuban exile community could step in and administer Cuba after the end of the Castro regime. This group possesses a tremendous amount of economic clout, because the exile communities in the United States pour much-needed doses of hard currency into Cuba's economy. However, because of the lack of diplomatic ties, this community has little political credit with either the government or the military establishment. The exiles "lack legitimacy among Cubans in general and with the FAR" (ibid.). Without such legitimacy, Cuba could fall into a civil war under the watch of the exile community. In either of these scenarios, circumstances exist that could propel Cuba into a civil war after the passing of Fidel Castro.

The current defense posture of Cuba is to maintain the status quo and the Castro regime in Cuba. Their efforts to shape the international environment through revolution and direct military action are things of the past. The doctrine of the Cuban military has changed from a static defense of the island nation to a "retreat into Cuba's mountains and rural areas" (ibid., 132). Instead of facing an invasion at the beaches as they did during the Bay of Pigs operation, the Cuban military would fight an invading force using a guerrilla-style campaign, avoiding large military confrontations.

Alliance Structure

Cuba was a signatory to only one formal military alliance throughout its history. From 1936 until 1962, Cuba was part of the Organization of American States (Gibler and Sarkees 2004). One of the first and foremost purposes of this organization as outlined in Article 1 of Chapter 1 of its charter is that all members are pledged to defend the sovereignty, the territorial integrity, and the independence of all states of the Americas (OAS Website 2004). Cuba aligned itself with much of Central and South America against the growing threat of war across the globe. This formal alliance was strained after the communist revolution in 1959 and lasted only until the Cuban Missile Crisis in 1962, when the United States lobbied the other members and narrowly had Cuba suspended from the alliance organization. "By resolution of the Eighth Meeting of Consultation of Ministers of Foreign Affairs (1962) the current Government of Cuba is excluded from participation in the OAS" (ibid.). Cuba is still technically a member of the organization, however; with a regime change or noticeable regime reform it is conceivable that Cuba could be reinstated into this organization on short notice.

During its history, Cuba has aligned itself with both the United States and the

Soviet Union. From the time of its independence until the 1959 revolution, Cuba was generally aligned with the United States. The two countries were major trading partners, and Cuba was the recipient of large amounts of U.S. investment. During World War II, relations between the two countries were strong: "Cuba and the United States signed no less than nine military agreements during the war" (Staten 2003, 65). While those agreements were not formal military alliances, they do indicate a positive relationship between Cuba and the United States at that time. However, those ties ended after Batista abdicated.

After Castro's revolution, Cuba cooperated heavily with the Soviet Union. The failed Bay of Pigs invasion consolidated Castro's regime, overcoming a major concern for leaders in Moscow. By 1962 the Soviet leadership was confident and supportive enough of Castro and the Cuban government to begin building and deploying nuclear weapons on the island. However, with the agreements between the United States and the Soviet Union regarding that crisis, Cuba was shut out of the negotiation process by both their U.S. adversaries and their supporters in Moscow. That fact would strain the relationship between Cuba and the Soviet Union until the late 1960s.

It is an important distinction that during their time of alignment with the Soviet Union, Cuba was not a formal Warsaw Pact member. Unlike the states of Eastern Europe, Cuba was never a puppet government of Moscow, but an autonomous decision-making entity. This relationship runs counter to the popular perceptions of the Havana-Moscow relations during this time (ibid., 114). Cuban decision-makers, without consulting Moscow, sent troops to Angola and Ethiopia in the 1970s to provide assistance during those civil and interstate wars. Cuba also decided to send a large number of civilian technical specialists to Africa and other Third World countries during the 1970s, without instructions and sometimes in the face of opposition from Moscow.

With the Cold War over, Cuba currently finds itself without a major political alliance. While relations between the United States and Cuba have had minor relaxation periods, several recent legislative acts and charged political rhetoric make it appear that there are no immediate plans for a restructuring of the relationship; it would take rather extraordinary circumstances for that situation to change in the near future.

Size and Structure of the Military

The Cuban military establishment possesses three broad categories. First there is the Revolutionary Armed Forces (FAR), which is the standing military. Currently, the FAR has approximately 47,000 soldiers in the army, 9,500 in the air force, and 3,500 in the navy (Cuban Armed Forces Review 2005). Second, there are the Territorial Troops Militia, and finally the Army of Working Youth. Each of these three groups has undergone severe changes since the end of the Cold War, and will be discussed in turn.

From 1959 until the early 1990s, Cuba possessed a greater percentage of their population serving in the military than most other nations in the world. In 1985, Cuba had 29.5 soldiers per one thousand people. The average for developing nations in that same year was a mere 4.9 per thousand, while in the developed world there were an average of 9.8 soldiers per thousand people (Rabkin 1991, 77). During this time, the army had approximately 135,000 active duty members with a similar number in their ready reserves (ibid., 76). Most of the troops sent abroad to Angola, Ethiopia, and Grenada came from these ready reserves, in order to maintain a strong domestic presence to retain control. Since the end of Soviet funding, the Cuban army has been downsized greatly. Now consisting of approximately 47,000 members, this organization is a shell of its former self. Sending troops abroad is a thing of the past, and one of the only remaining missions for the Cuban army is to maintain the Castro regime.

The Cuban navy was well equipped by the Soviet Union, including *Foxtrot*-class diesel submarines and *Koni*-class frigates (Cuban Armed Forces Review 2005). After the severe cuts of the 1990s, however, the navy suffered severe cutbacks in equipment and personnel. The submarines and frigates have been decommissioned, thereby limiting Cuba's naval activities to coastal defense and little else. The navy has approximately 3,500 members now, including 550 naval infantry (ibid.). That is more than a 50 percent reduction in the number of sailors since the end of the Cold War.

The Cuban air force still flies some of the best fighter planes built by the Soviet Union. They have MiG 29 Fulcrum and MiG 23 Flogger aircraft, which are technically superior to those of most air forces in Central America and the Caribbean (ibid.). The difficulty for the Cuban air force is that fewer than two dozen fixed-wing attack aircraft are in service (ibid.; Defense Intelligence Agency 2005). Much as with the army and navy, the number of Cuban air force personnel has diminished from the Cold War high to approximately 9,500 members, a more than 50 percent decrease.

The second element of the Cuban military establishment is the Territorial Troops Militia. In 1980, Fidel Castro created this national militia with a very wide scope of membership, including both men beyond the military retirement age of fifty and women. At its inception, this force received rudimentary military training and totaled almost 1.5 million members. After the Cold War, however, the force changed fundamentally. While still maintaining a large number of members, they receive very little if any military training or equipment (Staten 2003, 118). Therefore the Territorial Troops Militia does not count toward estimates of Cuban military troop strength, even though approximately 10 percent of the Cuban population are members.

The third and smallest element of military strength in Cuba is the Army of Working Youth. This organization consists primarily of younger conscripts; it is most often employed in the agriculture industry, year-round, in order to provide cheap labor. In 2000 this organization consisted of approximately 65,000 members (Cuban Armed Forces Review 2004). Its members receive even less formal training than the Territorial Troops Militia, and they appear to serve little if any military function. Again, this paramilitary organization does not count toward published estimates of Cuban military strength, because of the emphasis placed on their labor; however, if pressed by an outside attack, the members of this organization could be pressed quickly into military service.

For all these branches of the Cuban military, it is important to note that, while the size of these services has decreased since the end of Soviet support, the country still possesses large amounts of military matériel. Cuban submarines

Table 2   Cuban Military Strength, Cold War and Post–Cold War Eras

	Cold War (1984–1991)	Post–Cold War (2003)
Army	270,000	47,000
Navy and Air Force	27,000	13,000
Total	297,000	60,000

Sources
Cuban Armed Forces Review: http://www.cubapolidata.com/cafr/cafr.html.
Rabkin, Rhoda P. 1991. *Cuban Politics: The Revolutionary Experiment.* New York: Praeger.
Singer, J. David, Stuart Bremer, and John Stuckey. 1972. "Capability Distribution, Uncertainty, and Major Power War, 1820–1965." In *Peace, War, and Numbers*, Bruce Russett, ed. Beverly Hills, CA: Sage, pp. 19–48. (Article of Reference for National Materials Capability Data Set Version 3.0, 2004.)

and frigates were not sent back to Russia when funding dried up, but were mothballed; some estimates hold that 70 percent of Cuba's tanks and artillery are similarly stored (ibid.). Therefore, it is theoretically possible that if Cuba were attacked or defense expenditures increased from an economic windfall, the basic materials for fighting could be given to new soldiers from these current inventories.

Budget
The Cuban military budget, much like the size of the military, has undergone dramatic reductions since the end of the Soviet era. During the Cold War, examining Cuba's military budget was a difficult endeavor. The Soviet Union provided a wealth of military material for free. Rifles, tanks, advanced fighter aircraft, submarines, and frigates were sent to the island nation at no charge. By not having to pay out of the state budget for these items, Cuba was able to acquire expensive military matériel while maintaining a strong social welfare system and managing some form of economy. During this time, Cuba spent approximately $1.69 billion a year on the military (IISS 1990).

After the dissolution of the Soviet Union, that substantial source of free military equipment no longer existed. All Cuban military spending is now on the books, unlike in the Cold War era. The military budget seems to have stabilized at approximately $735 million, which is less than half the Cold War allotment (ibid., 2001).

Civil-Military Relations/The Role of the Military in Domestic Politics
Military personnel and former military members play an important role in Cuban domestic politics. Fidel Castro is the commander and chief of the Cuban military, much like the president in the United States, while Raúl Castro serves as second in command (Rabkin 1991, 76). Historically, the military also has a rather high concentration of representation in both the central committee and on the Politburo; in 1984, every general in the Cuban military was a member of the central committee (ibid., 77).

The military also plays an important economic role in Cuba, thus entrenching it more deeply into society. Often the military would assist in harvesting crops, helping to spur economic development. However, in recent years the military has diversified its economic efforts and become intertwined with many new endeavors. The chairman of the board for the Business Administration Group (Grupo Administración Empresarial, or GAESA) is Division General Julio Casas Regueiro, second in command and confidant to Raúl Castro (Cuban Armed Forces Review 2004). The boardroom for GAESA is located on the fourth floor of the Armed Forces Ministry in Havana; this corporation administers a large number of companies with great diversity in their holdings. For instance, the GAESA company Gaviota operates more than thirty hotels throughout Cuba, with eleven more under construction (ibid.). Other companies under the GAESA umbrella include import-export firms, tourism companies, maritime industries, and gas stations (ibid.). Therefore the military has significant impact on the economic well-being of Cuba.

It is also worth noting that the military could increase its own funding if Cuban development plans succeed. Recent economic plans have been to foster growth in the tourism industry in Cuba. As mentioned before, the military has holdings in many tourist hotels and sites across the island. If that industry increases, it is conceivable that proceeds from these hotels could finance a resurgence in both the size and training of the Cuban military.

Terrorism

The current state of Cuban support for or opposition to terrorism is a matter of controversy. Cuba maintains that the actions of the United States against Cuba constitute terrorist acts. On the Ministry of Foreign Affairs website, the Cuban government claims that there has been a long and extensive list of terrorist incidents carried out by the United States against Cuba: "[O]ur authorities [have] learned of 16 other plots to assassinate the President of Cuba, 8 plots to try to kill other leaders of the Revolution and 140 other terrorist plots hatched between 1990 and 2001" (Cuban Ministry of Foreign Affairs 2005). Internationally, claims by Cuba against the United States for acts of terrorism have gone unanswered.

Looking at the terrorist question from the U.S. perspective, the U.S. Department of State holds that "Cuba continued to provide safe haven to several terrorists and U.S. fugitives and maintained ties to state sponsors and Latin American insurgents" (U.S. State Department 2005). Two Colombian insurgent groups, the Revolutionary Armed Forces of Colombia (FARC) and the National Liberation Army (ELN), once received monetary support and training from Cuba. While this active support has disappeared, they still possess offices in many capitals, only one of which is Havana (Council on Foreign Relations 2005). The United States also asserts that a number of Basque separatists have dealings with Cuba (U.S. State Department, "Overview of State-Sponsored Terrorism" 2005).

One concern for U.S. policymakers regarding Cuba and terrorism is the rapid growth and potential threat of their biotechnology field. In attempting to reinvigorate their economy, Cuba has invested billions of dollars in this field, and it now possesses the third largest biotechnology industry in the world (Council on Foreign Relations 2005). This causes concern for U.S. policymakers because technology used to make prescription medications can also be used in the production of biological weapons. While there have been no formal declarations that Cuba intends to follow that course of action, their modern facilities would be able to produce biological weapons quickly, easily, and in vast quantities if the Havana government chose to do so.

Relationship with the United States

This essay has already examined several areas of current difficulty in U.S.-Cuban relations. Potential dangers and difficulties surround the shipment and transportation of illicit drugs, their past history of international conflict, the ever-present problem involving refugees from Cuba to the Florida coast, and the concerns and debates surrounding international terrorism; all strain relations between these two states.

Since 1962 the United States has maintained a formal trade embargo against Cuba, covering the vast majority of all goods and services. In addition, neither state has direct embassy connections with the other; however, both states have "interests sections" within the Swiss embassies and maintain diplomatic ties through those channels (U.S. State Department Website 2005). Since the early 1990s direct flights from Cuba to the United States have been allowed on a limited basis, allowing family members to visit each other and for a limited number of businesspeople to meet with their counterparts in Cuba.

Even with the trade embargo in place, there are rather large economic connections between the United States and Cuba. The trade embargo does not include foodstuffs or medical supplies; the United States was Cuba's tenth largest trading partner in 2002, based on trade in only those two commodities (*Economist*, "The Americans Have Come" 2003). This relationship is unlikely to change in the foreseeable future, because of the essential nature of the commodities traded. The United States would not want to appear as withholding food and medical supplies from a state in difficult times, and the Cuban government would not want to create the sort of domestic discontent that a severe lack of food or medical supplies could foment.

Domestic U.S. politics are an ever-present concern in U.S.-Cuban relations. The Cuban exile community has become an important player in Florida politics, with Hispanics now making up 16.8 percent of Florida's population (U.S. Census Bureau 2005). With such a large concentration in the state, the Cuban population has become a pivotal, decisive coalition in Florida. Any U.S. presidential candidate running for election or reelection must cater to this group or run the risk of losing Florida, a major battleground state in the Electoral College. In view of the state's twenty-seven electoral votes in the 2004 election, and a margin of victory for George W. Bush of fewer than 1,700 votes (out of 5.96 million votes cast) in the 2000 presidential election (U.S. Federal Election Commission Website 2005), U.S. presidents and candidates alike must listen to and enact the policies of the Cuban community in Florida in order to win the national election. The consensus of the Cuban communities in Florida is to maintain the embargo and economic pressure on Cuba; presidents of the United States have followed that policy for more than forty years, regardless of their political party or other dispositions.

The Future

The future of Cuba hinges on the physical health and regime of Fidel Castro. As long as he remains in power, it appears that there will be little change in Cuba's defense and foreign policies. After Fidel Castro passes from the scene, there is potential for dramatic changes in relations between Cuba, the United States, and the rest of the world. What those changes could look like is rather uncertain; however, it appears clear that until there is some form of regime change, the status quo will be maintained.

Much of Cuban policy will be decided by the actions of the United States. United States domestic interest groups often lobby both the White House and Congress to bring greater pressure to bear on Castro and his regime. Those pressures surface in a variety of forms. In early 2004 the United States announced plans to increase restrictions on maritime traffic between Florida and Cuba, a move that will reduce the hard currency flows into the small nation. That surely will create tension and animosity between the two governments, setting the scene for more diplomatic, political, and perhaps even military conflicts.

References, Recommended Readings, and Websites

Books

Allison, Graham, and Philip Zelikow. 1999. *The Essence of Decision: Explaining the Cuban Missile Crisis.* New York: Longman.

Bethell, Leslie, ed. 1993. *Cuba: A Brief History.* New York: Cambridge University Press.

Blight, James G., and Peter Kornbluh. 1998. *Politics of Illusion: The Bay of Pigs Invasion Reexamined.* Boulder, CO: Lynne Rienner Publishers.

Cirillo, Vincent J. 2004. *Bullets and Bacilli: The Spanish-American War and Military Medicine.* New Brunswick, NJ: Rutgers University Press.

Falk, Pamela S. 1986. *Cuban Foreign Policy.* Lexington: D.C. Heath.

Guimarães, Fernando Andersen. 1998. *The Origins of the Angolan Civil War.* New York: St. Martin's Press.

Horowitz, Irving Louis, and Jamie Suchlicki, eds. 2003. *Cuban Communism, 1959–2003.* New Brunswick, NJ: Transaction Publishers.

International Institute for Strategic Studies (IISS). 1990, 2001. *The Military Balance.* London: Oxford University Press.

James, W. Martin, III. 1992. *A Political History of the Civil War in Angola 1974–1990.* New Brunswick, NJ: Transaction Publishers.

Janis, Irving Lester. 1983. *Groupthink: Psychological Studies of Policy Decisions and Fiascos.* Boston: Houghton Mifflin.

Nathan, James A. 2001. *Anatomy of the Cuban Missile Crisis.* Westport, CT: Greenwood Press.

Pérez, Louis A., Jr. 2003. *Cuba and the United States: Ties of Singular Intimacy.* Athens: University of Georgia Press.

Perez-Stable, Marifeli. 1993. *The Cuban Revolution: Origins, Course, and Legacy.* New York: Oxford University Press.

Rabkin, Rhoda P. 1991. *Cuban Politics: The Revolutionary Experiment.* New York: Praeger.

Simmons, Geoff. 1966. *Cuba: From Conquistador to Castro.* New York: St. Martin's Press.

Smith, Joseph. 1994. *The Spanish-American War: Conflict in the Caribbean and the Pacific 1895–1902.* New York: Longman Publishing.

Staten, Clifford L. 2003. *The History of Cuba.* Westport, CT: Greenwood Press.

Thompson, Robert Smith. 1992. *The Missiles of October: The Declassified Story of John F. Kennedy and the Cuban Missile Crisis.* New York: Simon and Schuster.

Articles

The Economist. 2003. "The Americans Have Come." January 2: 41.

———. 2003. "Another Cuba?" July 10: 47.

Gibler, Douglas M., and Meredith Sarkees. 2004. "Measuring Alliances: The Correlates of War Formal Interstate Alliance Data Set, 1816–2000." *Journal of Peace Research* 41: 211–222.

Hawkins, Jack. 1998. "An Obsession with 'Plausible Deniability' Doomed the 1961 Bay of Pigs Invasion from the Outset." *Military History* 15, no. 3:12–15.

Sarkees, Meredith Reid. 2000. "The Correlates of War Data on War: An Update to 1997." *Conflict Management and Peace Science* 18, no. 1:123–144.

Singer, J. David, Stuart Bremer, and John Stuckey. 1972. "Capability Distribution, Uncertainty, and Major Power War, 1820–1965." In *Peace, War, and Numbers*, Bruce Russett, ed. Beverly Hills, CA: Sage, pp. 19–48. (Article of Reference for National Materials Capability Data Set Version 3.0, 2004.)

Websites

Brigade 2506 Website: http://www. brigada2506.com/index.html.

Brothers to the Rescue: http://www. hermanos.org/.

Center for Defense Information. "Cuba: Bioweapons Threat or Political Punching Bag?": http://www.cdi.org/ terrorism/cuba-pr.cfm.

Council on Foreign Relations. "Terrorism: Questions and Answers": http:// cfrterrorism.org/home/.

Cuban Armed Forces Review: http://www. cubapolidata.com/cafr/cafr.html.

Cuban Government Official Website: http://www.cubagob.cu/ingles/default. htm.

Cuban Ministry of Foreign Affairs: http://www.cubaminrex.cu/English/.

Defense Intelligence Agency. "The Cuban Threat to U.S. National Security": http://www.defenselink.mil/pubs/ cubarpt.htm.

Granma Internacional (Cuban Communists Party's Newspaper): http:// www.granma.cu/ingles/.

Organization of American States (OAS): http://www.oas.org/main/english/.

U.S. Census Bureau Website: http://www. census.gov/.

U.S. Central Intelligence Agency. CIA *World Factbook*, 2005. http://www. cia.gov/cia/publications/factbook/geos/ cu.html.

U.S. Federal Election Commission. "2000 Official Presidential General Election Results." http://www.fec.gov/ pubrec/2000presgeresults.htm.

U.S. State Department: http://www.state. gov.

U.S. State Department. "Overview of State-Sponsored Terrorism": http:// www.state.gov/s/ct/rls/pgtrpt/2000/ 2441.htm.

Egypt

Kyle Wilson

Geography and History

Egypt's defense policy has formed as a function of its geography. Because of enduring rivalry with Israel, Egypt has had to make political decisions that protect its interests. Having fought several wars with Israel, Egypt realized that the battlefield was not the appropriate forum for settling their dispute. Thus its peace treaty with Israel represents Egypt's situation reflecting defense policy. Although Egypt, unlike many Western countries, does not publicize its defense policy, there has been important work completed on the issue since the United States began supporting Egypt with military assistance. Egypt's defense policy depends on the leadership of the president, who retains control over the armed forces. The interaction between geography and type of government makes Egypt's defense policy an interesting combination of personality and location.

Major geographical features in Egypt include the Nile River, the Sahara Desert, the Red Sea, and the Mediterranean Sea. The Nile River is the world's longest, at 3,470 miles from its source, Lake Victoria. It travels through Uganda and Sudan to reach the Mediterranean coast. Throughout Egypt's history, the Nile River has been central to the lives of those who have lived on its banks, from the time of the pharaohs to the present day. The Sahara Desert is the world's largest, extending from the Atlantic Ocean to the Red Sea. It covers nearly 3.5 million square miles and extends about 1,000 miles north to south and about 3,200 miles east to west. Egypt borders Libya (to the west), Sudan (to the south), the Gaza Strip (to the east) and Israel (also to the east). Egypt also borders the Mediterranean Sea to the north and the Red Sea (to the east).

Egypt achieved its first autonomy from the United Kingdom on February 28, 1922, and realized full autonomy after World War II. As the largest Arab state, with a population of 77,505,756 (July 2005 est.), Egypt remains one of the most important Muslim states in the world. At the crossroads between Africa and Asia, Egypt has one foot in each world—which often puts it in difficult situations, as both a mediator and a participant within the Middle East. Egypt's republican, secular government sets it apart from its neighbors, which are guided by authoritarian rulers or promote Islam as the cornerstone of justice. The Arab Republic of Egypt remains a model for other Middle Eastern countries, but unfortunately, Mubarek has weakened Egypt's republican institutions by not allowing true participation in government (U.S. Department of State, 2002). The dominant religion in Egypt is Islam, mainly Sunni, at 94 percent, with the remainder being Coptic

Christians and others (CIA *World Fact-book* 2003; CIA *World Factbook* 2005; Metz 1991, 95–103).

Egypt has a gross domestic product of $268 billion (2002 est.), mainly from its textiles, food processing, tourism, chemicals, hydrocarbons, construction, cement, and metals industries. The country maintains a substantial negative trade imbalance, with exports totaling $7 billion (free on board value, 2002 est.) and imports totaling $15.2 billion (free on board value, 2002 est.). The main export commodities include crude oil and petroleum products, cottons, textiles, metal products, and chemicals; the main import commodities include machinery and equipment, foodstuffs, chemicals, wood products, and fuels. The economy is composed of agriculture (17 percent), industry (34 percent), and services (49 percent). Within the agriculture sector the main crops include cotton, rice, corn, wheat, beans, fruits, vegetables, cattle, water buffalo, sheep, and goats. Along with a negative trade imbalance, Egypt also maintains an international debt of $30.5 billion. Although its trade balance and debt overhang are substantial, Egypt does receive substantial

Official Development Assistance (ODA) of $2.25 billion, mainly from the United States (CIA *World Factbook* 2003).

As the home of one of the world's great civilizations, Egypt is the protector of great monuments including the Great Pyramids and the Sphinx. Egypt's role in history has been extensive, ranging from the dynasties in ancient Egypt, through the Middle Ages and the rise of Islam, and in the present day as a leader in the Middle East. Evidence of life within the fertile region abutting the Nile extends back about 6,000 years. This civilization included prominent names such as Cleopatra, Ramses, and Tutankhamun, and today Egyptologists study the many great mysteries that have yet to be explained. Because of the strategic location of the Nile River, the ancient civilization of Egypt fell to several other great civilizations, including the Ptolemies, Greeks, Romans, Arabs, Fatamids, Mamluks, Ottoman Turks, the French under Napoleon Bonaparte, and the British. The British ceded control over what is today Egypt nominally in 1922 and finally in 1954. Egypt, which had been under foreign domination for years, finally realized self-

Table 1 Egypt: Key Statistics

Type of Government	Arab republic: president dominates government
Population (millions)	74.7 (2003)
Religion	Muslim (mostly Sunni) 94%, Coptic Christian and other 6%
Main Industries	textiles, food processing, tourism, chemicals, hydrocarbons, construction, cement, metals
Main security threat(s)	Israel, Muslim extremists, terrorism
Defense spending (% GDP)	4.1% (FY 1999)
Size of military (thousands)	443 (2001)
Number of civil wars since 1945	0
Number of interstate wars since 1945	6

Sources
CIA *World Factbook* 2003; Bonn International Center for Conversion (BICC); Eriksson, Wallensteen, and Sollenberg 2003.

determination. Under the leadership of Gamel-Abdul Nasser, Egypt rose to a leadership position in the Arab world that it still holds today (Metz 1991, 3–89).

Regional Geopolitics

Egypt resides in a complex region where enduring rivalries complicate efforts to realize a just and lasting peace. Wars have occurred regularly in the region, creating mistrust and outright hatred between neighbors. The central issue within the region is the Arab-Israeli conflict, which has caused several wars between Israel and its neighbors, changing the borders in the region several times. Israel has controlled the Sinai and Southern Lebanon, and it still controls the Golan Heights of Syria, the Gaza Strip, and the West Bank (including East Jerusalem).

As the largest Arab state that shares a border with Israel, Egypt has participated in four wars with Israel, in 1948, 1956, 1967, and 1973. Other Arab states also participated in those wars, including Syria, Saudi Arabia, and Iraq. Egypt has since signed a permanent peace agreement with Israel, leading other countries to resign themselves to a form of détente with Israel. Syria still demands the return of the Golan Heights, however, while Lebanon, which only recently regained sovereignty over its southern region, demands that Israel halt its air attacks on Lebanese soil. Arab unity can also be seen in the United Nations, where there is consistent pressure on Israel to abide by Security Council resolutions 242, 338, and other pertinent requirements under international law.

Making the region more insecure, the Middle East has also witnessed three wars involving Iraq (1980–1988, 1991, and 2003) that have involved not only regional states such as Iran and Kuwait but also international coalitions established to reverse Iraq's annexation of Kuwait in 1991 and to end the rule of Saddam Hussein in 2003. During the First Gulf War, Hussein strategically fired SCUD missiles into the heart of Israel in the hope that Israel would retaliate, thus expanding the conflict. The most volatile situation in the Middle East remains the Israeli-Palestine conflict, which continues to cause bloodshed despite multiple attempts to forge a just and lasting peace between the parties to the dispute. Thus the security situation in the Middle East is fluid and could easily deteriorate into regionwide warfare (Tabbara 2003).

Conflict Past and Present

Conflict History

More than 100,000 Egyptian troops fought in World War II, mainly under British supervision in defensive and administrative tasks. There were also Egyptians integrated into the British air forces, but the British did not trust the Egyptians, because of their early indecision in declaring war on the Axis powers. The Suez Canal was a vital waterway for the Allies during the war, and the British utilized Egyptian forces to defend it as a strategic asset. Italy attacked Egypt early in 1940 but was repelled by the British. Germany's Afrika Korps also moved on British assets in Egypt, but in a turning point in the Africa campaign, British troops defeated the Germans in Al Alamayn in October 1942. Egypt maintained neutrality through much of the war, despite the huge presence of British military personnel. Eventually King Faruk declared war on the Axis powers in February of 1945. During this period the Egyptian military expanded greatly, and after the war the groundwork was laid for its importance in Egyptian society. Although the war ended in 1945, the British remained to protect the Suez Canal (Metz 1991, 295–296).

Since 1945, Egypt has participated in six armed conflicts. Table 2 lists them in the order in which they occurred. Egypt was one of the main combatants in the first Arab-Israeli War, which began in 1948 upon the declaration of the establishment of the state of Israel by David Ben-Gurion. Egypt sent an invasion force of 7,000 men to end the existence of the foreign, Zionist entity that had arisen to their east. After moving to within thirty-five kilometers of Tel Aviv, the fledgling capital of the state of Israel, in the fall of 1948, Egypt's now 18,000 men were pushed back to the Sinai Peninsula by Israeli forces. In late 1948, a UN-sponsored armistice was agreed to between Egypt and Israel. Soon after, a cease-fire line was agreed to that left the West Bank in the hands of Jordan and the Gaza Strip in the hands of Egypt. The poor performance of the Egyptian military in this war led to a revolution against the king and government, which were blamed for the humiliating loss to Israel. That revolution eventually led to the leadership of Gamal Abdul-Nasser (ibid., 296).

The 1956 war placed Egypt against the United Kingdom, France, and Israel, because on July 26, 1956, Nasser made the decision to nationalize the Suez Canal. The United Kingdom and France considered the Suez Canal as the vital link between the Mediterranean and the Red Sea, and as such it was essential to the security of the West. In that vein, it was necessary to ensure that Western vessels would always have free and unfettered access to the Suez Canal. Upon Nasser's announcement of the nationalization of the canal, the United Kingdom, France, and Israel began secret negotiations on how to retake the waterway, despite the fact that Egypt promised to keep the canal open and to compensate the stockholders of the Suez Canal Company, owner of the canal. Behind the scenes, Egypt's disappointment at the West's withdrawal of loans for the construction of the Aswan High Dam may have led to the nationalization. Under the threat of invasion by France and the United Kingdom, Egypt not only gained the support of the USSR, Eastern Europe, and much of the Third World in its battle against imperialism but also gained financial support from the USSR for the construction of the Aswan High Dam.

As the United Kingdom, France, and Israel began an invasion, however, most countries were shocked to see Israel participate in the war. Once the world realized what was occurring, there was near universal condemnation of the war and calls for immediate cessation of hostilities—including calls from the United States and the USSR. It went so far as the United States threatening sanctions and the USSR threatening rocket attacks. Due to Egypt's strategic position between the Mediterranean and the Red Sea, in control of the Suez Canal, the United States and USSR both felt it in their national interest to protect this asset. Therefore, on December 26, 1956, the United Kingdom and France, under extreme economic and political strain, completed their withdrawal.

Table 2   Armed Conflicts since 1945

1948	Arab-Israeli War
1956	Suez Crisis
1962	Yemeni Civil War
1967	Second Arab-Israeli War
1973	Third Arab-Israeli War
1991	Operation Desert Storm

Israel was less willing to withdraw from the territory it controlled in the Sinai Peninsula and decided to do so only after destroying everything along its escape route. Filling the void as Israel withdrew was the UN Emergency Force (UNEF), mandated with monitoring the cease-fire line. Because of Israel's refusal to permit the force onto its territory, UNEF monitored the cease-fire from the Egyptian side of the border (ibid., 296–297).

Another war that is rarely mentioned is Egypt's participation in the Yemeni civil war from September 1962 until the June 1967 war. It was during this war that Egypt used chemical weapons against the troops of the Saudi-backed royalist faction. Relations between Egypt and Saudi Arabia plummeted at the outset of the war and remained fractured for several years afterward. The resources that Egypt invested in the war weakened its ability to defend itself and contributed to the defeat it suffered in 1967 (ibid.).

While Egypt was involved in the Yemeni civil war, tensions continued to rise between Arabs and Israelis, especially between Egypt and Israel. To strengthen themselves against the growing Israeli threat, Egypt and Syria signed a five-year defense pact. With that agreement Egypt and Syria felt more secure. But with Egypt's realization, based on Soviet intelligence, that Israel was mobilizing its forces to the border region, Syria and Egypt reciprocated. It would have been diplomatically difficult for Egypt to launch an attack on Israel with the UNEF monitoring the cease-fire line. Pressure by Egypt's Arab brethren increased, however, as they questioned Egypt's leadership in the movement to free the Palestinian people from Israeli oppression. That pressure materialized in calls for Egypt to expel the UNEF peacekeepers and act on the rheto-

ric of "Arab Nationalism" that Egypt had been preaching since the 1956 Suez Crisis.

On May 16, 1967, Nasser asked the UNEF to leave Egyptian soil and also threatened to close the Strait of Tiran, Israel's only access to the Red Sea. These actions signaled to Israel that Egypt was planning for war by removing the cease-fire monitors (UNEF) and blockading Israel's access to the sea. Also, Jordan and Iraq signed a defense agreement with Egypt, intensifying Israel's beliefs that war was encroaching from all sides. Nasser's generals urged him to strike first and deliver a crippling blow to the Israeli armed forces. Instead he waited, in an attempt to reach a negotiated settlement that would return the Sinai Peninsula to Egypt. While Nasser continued to look for a diplomatic solution, Israel struck deep inside its Arab enemies, crippling their ability to counterattack. Israel eventually found itself in control of all of the Sinai, the West Bank (including all of Jerusalem), the Gaza Strip, and the Golan Heights of Syria (ibid., 297–299).

As a result of its embarrassing defeats in previous wars with Israel, Egypt was not expected to be able to organize an effective attack on Israel in the 1973 War. Initially Anwar Sadat was in favor of peace, but his attempts at negotiating a peace with Israel fell on deaf ears within Israel. Arab Nationalism continued to grow, leading to growing demands for removing Israel from the holy city of Jerusalem. Since Israel would not negotiate on account of its strong position, Sadat believed that the Arab countries would have to attack Israel and reverse the gains that Israel had made in 1967. By going to war, Sadat could mute his domestic critics and give him a stronger position in the Arab World.

Although many did not see Sadat's preparations for war, there were three clear signs that war was the option that Sadat had chosen. First, on July 17, 1972, Sadat expelled 15,000 Soviet advisors to ensure that his preparations for war remained secret, and so that the USSR could not pressure Egypt to stop its war preparations internally. Second, on December 28, 1972, Sadat created permanent war committees to carry on his goal of removing Israel from Egypt's territory. Third, on March 26, 1973, he assumed the position of prime minister and formed a new government, which allowed him to continue preparations for war without oversight from the legitimately elected government. After completing these preparations, on October 6, 1973, Egypt launched a successful surprise attack on Israel. Syria also joined in on the attack. Sadat chose this date because Israel was celebrating Yom Kippur, a religious holiday, and was not prepared for an attack. Egypt planned well for the invasion, not only in timing but also in military innovation. The crossing of the Suez Canal took only four hours, because of the availability of bridges and water cannons on boats, used to break through the large sand dunes that Israel had constructed as defensive barriers (ibid., 299–302).

On October 17 Arab oil producers decided to retaliate against the Western supporters of Israel with an initial 5 percent cut in oil output and additional cuts each month until Israel withdrew from Palestinian territory. The United States, under President Richard Nixon, was the main supporter of Israel. During the 1973 War the United States airlifted $2.2 billion in arms to Israel. In retaliation for that support, Saudi Arabia initially increased its oil production cuts to 10 percent and eventually implemented a total block on oil exports.

Although Israel was shocked by the invasion and suffered losses at first, it was able to counterattack with the support of the U.S. arms transfers. This counterattack led to the near surrounding of the Egyptian Third Army in the Sinai Peninsula. After Sadat learned that the Third Army was surrounded, he pleaded with the Soviet Union for assistance. The Soviets negotiated in behalf of the Egyptians with the United States and believed that they had received promises for a cease-fire at the current military position. In coordination with this agreement the UN Security Council passed Resolution 338, which called for a cease-fire within twelve hours.

Egypt agreed to the resolution, but Israel claimed that Egypt had violated the cease-fire and used that pretense to complete its encirclement of the army of nearly 45,000 men. The action infuriated the Soviet Union, which had believed that the cease-fire would be respected, and it threatened to intervene unilaterally. Upon that threat the United States went to high alert; however, the United Nations was able to deploy a peacekeeping force in time to ease tensions between the superpowers. Although Syria did not agree with Egypt's decision to end the campaign to regain Arab territory, it finally agreed to end the war. Egypt suffered 8,000 killed in action but won a victory for Egyptian and Arab morale in initially shocking the Israelis. After the war negotiations began for a permanent peace with Israel (ibid.).

Iraq's aggression toward a fellow Arab state brought Egypt into Operation Desert Storm as part of a U.S.-led coalition. Egypt took a leadership role in the aftermath of Iraq's invasion of Kuwait by calling together the leaders of the Arab world for an emergency summit of the

League of Arab States in August 1990. The majority of Arab States supported a call for Iraq to withdraw from Kuwait immediately. Also, per Saudi Arabia's request for international assistance, the League of Arab States authorized the creation and deployment of an Arab force to the region. Egypt would send 35,000 men with its own resources and be an important force in driving Saddam Hussein out of Kuwait (*Europa* 2003, 1480; Berman and Sams 2000, 422–423).

Current and Potential Military Confrontations

Egypt and Sudan have competing claims over the Halaib Triangle (southeast Egypt, northeast Sudan). Most recently the dispute has intensified because of Egyptian claims of Sudanese complicity in the assassination attempt on the life of Hosni Mubarak in Addis Ababa, Ethiopia, in 1995. Accordingly, Egypt restricted access to the area by enforcing visa and permit requirements in contravention to a bilateral agreement of 1978. The Organization of African Unity also accused Sudan of complicity in the assassination attempt and demanded that the country turn over the suspects to face legal action in Egypt. Sudan retaliated to Egypt's permit and visa requirements for Sudanese citizens by implementing their own requirements on Egyptian citizens.

From this low point in Sudanese-Egyptian bilateral relations both leaders, Hosni Mubarak and Omar al-Bashir, began to look for ways to improve relations. At the Arab League summit in 1996 the two men discussed bilateral issues and came to an understanding, but, after the summit, Egypt proclaimed that Sudan was not abiding by the agreement, since Sudan was harboring Egyptian terrorists. Eventually, through substantial diplomatic discussions, Egypt and Sudan began gradually to reopen ties between the two countries. By September 2000 the two countries had again exchanged ambassadors and signed several bilateral cooperation accords. Despite the improvement in relations, however, a final status agreement on the Halaib Triangle is not today in place. Because of Sudan's continuing internal civil war, it is likely not in Sudan's interest to create animosity between itself and Egypt. Once peace is realized in Sudan and the country has had an opportunity to rebuild, it may have more resources with which to negotiate a final settlement for the region. Until then the situation remains tenuous, yet stable (*Europa* 2003, 1484; Ronen 2003, 81–98).

Since 1992, Egypt has been battling a determined Islamic fundamentalist movement that supports the overthrow of the secular Egyptian government. These groups include the Vanguard of Conquest, the Muslim Brotherhood, Islamic Jihad, and Jama'ah al-Islamiyah. The Egyptian government claims that these groups have ties to al-Qaeda and present a threat to the peace and stability of Egypt, a linchpin for the peace and security of the Middle East. Many of the attacks by these groups have been on foreign tourists and investors, both important groups to the economic well-being of Egypt. Although Egypt had claimed that these groups were under control, the massacre at Luxor in 1997 clearly showed to the world that Egypt does not have the situation in hand.

In its attempt to control the situation, Egypt has put the country in a state of emergency that has been renewed several times. This allows the government to detain possible fundamentalists without the legal rights usually afforded to prisoners in Egypt. With the rise of the second Intifada in the West Bank and Gaza

Strip, there was a call for these fundamentalists in Egypt to focus their resources on freeing the Palestinian people
from Israeli oppression. That issue will
continue to plague Egypt until the government improves the disparity between
rich and poor, especially between Muslims and Christians, as well as opening
the political process to more people (*Europa* 2003, 1481–1482; U.S. Department
of State 2004).

As a leader in the Arab world, Egypt
could be strongly affected by the Palestinian conflict. Throughout its history
Egypt has championed the cause of the
Palestinian people, both peacefully and
nonpeacefully. The potential for conflict
in the Middle East is high, despite Egypt's
signing of a peace accord with Israel. If
tensions in the Occupied Territories intensify, Egypt may be forced to move beyond diplomatic solutions and resort to
war, as it has done in the past. Although
the likelihood that Egypt would jeopardize its relationship with the United
States remains low, it is a possibility that
cannot be ignored.

Alliance Structure

Egypt's proximity and involvement in
several conflicts in the Middle East has
necessitated membership in several military alliances with its fellow Arab states.
That, coupled with Nasser's Arab Nationalism movement, has led to several close
relationships with its neighbors. As the
key proponent of Arab Nationalism,
Egypt joined forces with countries such as
Syria, Yemen, and Libya. During Nasser's
reign Arabs were united in their dislike
for Israel and were willing to join forces.
Egypt was unable to overcome Israel's
military superiority, however, because
the USSR was unwilling to provide mili-

tary assistance at the level and quality of
what Israel received from the United
States.

Arab unity over Israel has manifested
itself in many ways—economic, social,
and political. Within the political realm
the creation of the Arab League as an alliance against the Israelis was the main
military alliance in the Middle East.
Under that umbrella the Arab states attempted to create a United Arab Command, but the grandiose vision never materialized. Egypt united with Syria in the
United Arab Republic from 1958 to 1961.
In this union Egyptian president Nasser
was elected in a plebiscite to rule over all
Egyptians and Syrians. Over time Nasser
attempted to instill the principles of socialism among the Syrian people. As
Nasser was trying to implement nation-
alizations, redistribution of wealth, and a
common currency, the Syrians decided to
secede from the United Arab Republic
(Metz 1991, 65–66; *Europa* 2003, 1479).

During the same period Egypt was also
in a union with Yemen called the United
Arab States. The results of that union
were the same as with Syria, but more
devastating for Egypt. Egypt became entangled in civil war after the union disintegrated (Metz 1991, 66). Although Egypt
and Syria had signed a five-year defense
pact in November 1966 to ward off the Israeli threat, in the war of 1967 neither
side was able to succeed against the Israelis, leading to the obsolescence of the
defense agreement (ibid., 68). In 1972,
Egypt, Libya, and Syria created the Federation of Arab Republics, to protect themselves from the Israeli threat, but that attempt, like the other attempts at Arab
unity, did not last (*Europa* 2003, 1479).
An important moment in Egypt's history
was its decision to make peace with Israel; however, the repercussions were

costly to its stature in the Arab world. The entire Arab community, represented by the Arab League, expelled Egypt following the peace accords and implemented sanctions. Egypt's exile from the Arab League lasted from 1979 to 1987. At the end of this exile, Egypt worked to gain prominence again in the Arab world by initiating peace proposals that it hoped would bring peace between Palestinians and Israelis.

Size and Structure of the Military

Size and Structure
The armed forces are led by the president, who holds the title of supreme commander of the armed forces. The president relies on the advice of his closest advisors and can call on the expertise of the National Defense Council. Beneath the president lie the minister of defense, who is the commander-in-chief of the armed forces, and the minister of military production, usually the same person. Reporting to him is the chief of staff of the armed forces and commander-in-chief of the army. (The army plays a central role in the Egyptian armed forces.) The other branches (navy, air force, and air defense forces) have a commander-in-chief who reports to the chief of staff of the armed forces. Within each service there is a chief of staff who reports to his respective commander-in-chief. The Egyptian Army is divided into Central (Cairo), Eastern (Ismalyiya), Western (Mersa Matrum), Southern (Alexandria), and Northern (Aswan) zones. The Central Zone controls the reserves and the Republican Guard, while the Eastern Zone controls the 2nd and 3rd Field Armies (Metz 1991, 305–306).

In regard to the Egyptian infantry the overall personnel performance remains high, with various problems that are indicative of the militaries of middle-income countries. Soldiers are well trained and well supplied professionals that can execute corps level operations in a coordinated manner. The Egyptian Army's equipment includes a basic kit that is complete and includes uniform, load-bearing equipment, AK-47, and ammunition. The size of the active Egyptian Army is 310,000, which includes four armored divisions, seven mechanized divisions, and one infantry division. The military is experienced in a wide range of operations, including multinational peace operations that include the following: UNOSOM II, MINURSO, ONUMOZ, UNPROFOR, and UNAMIR. As of March 2005, Egypt was contributing a total of 122 peacekeepers as part of UN missions. That included fifty-one civilian police, fifty-four military observers, and seventeen troops (United Nations 2005). Egypt also contributed two heavy divisions to Operation Desert Storm, deploying its own air transport assets. The military is attempting to increase interoperability with NATO forces; it has obtained night operations capability and equipment, while maintaining a healthy (physically) armed forces.

The military leadership, the officer corps, relies on highly concentrated decision making within the senior officer corps, while the junior officers either do not, or are not permitted to, display much initiative. At least two years of advanced professional training or education are standard for officers, while many have also received additional foreign training through International Military Education and Training (IMET). Noncommissioned officers (NCOs) receive specialized and command school training but do not have a leadership or decision-making role. Most

NCOs are given rigid and specialized tasks (Berman and Sams 2000, 422–423).

Egypt has the capability of producing and coproducing weapons systems as well

---

Sidebar 1   Egypt on Both Sides of the Cold War

Somalia and Ethiopia were not the only countries to take advantage of the Cold War rivalry between the United States and the Soviet Union. Egypt masterfully used its strategic advantage (the Suez Canal) to bargain for the best economic and military aid from the two superpowers. At first, Egypt allied with the Soviet Union and received thousands of advisors, and millions of dollars of military equipment and economic aid. As Arab nationalism grew in Egypt so too did its demands on the alliance with the Soviet Union. These demands accelerated the decline of an already-strained relationship. Egypt demanded increased military aid both in the form of equipment and technology while also increasing its demands for economic aid, including assistance in the construction of the Aswan High Dam (what was to be a marvel in engineering prowess). With the decline of its relationship with the Soviet Union and its repeated losses at the hands of the Israelis, Egypt looked to peace with Israel as a means to obtain military assistance from the United States. So, upon the signing of the Camp David Accords, Egypt completed a transition from being an ally of the Soviet Union to strategically allying with the United States.

Source
Metz, Helen Chapin. 1991. *Egypt: A Country Study.* Washington, DC: GPO for the Library of Congress.

---

as spare parts. Nevertheless, Egypt still relies heavily on equipment from the former Soviet Union and the United States. The army possesses a wide variety of Eastern and Western equipment, but full interoperability with U.S. and NATO equipment does not yet exist—but it is improving. Older Russian and Eastern bloc equipment is not well maintained, because of a lack of spare parts and because of age. That has quickened the pace with which Egypt has been replacing its equipment with Western matériel. Egypt's military ground transport includes a large number and wide array of trucks from both Eastern and Western sources, including trucks from the United States. The country has a number of armored personnel carriers (APCs), including U.S.-made M113A2s, Russian BTR-50s and OT-62s, as well as Egyptian-made Fahds. It also has a very large tank fleet, including U.S. M60A3s and more than 1,600 Russian T-54s, T-55s, and T-62s. There is an active air force of around 30,000, and a national guard of around 60,000. The Egyptian Air Force is equipped for a wide range of missions and has aerial refueling capability. The country has a large inventory of transport aircraft and modern airfields. Most aircraft are Western in origin, including F-16s from the United States (ibid.).

In the areas of logistics, signals, and engineering, the Egyptian armed forces are capable yet need improvement. Egypt has the capability of deploying three army headquarter units. When deployed, planning and rationing of necessary supplies remain substandard. Egypt's signal corps has substantial experience in interfacing with other forces in multinational operations. They are able to provide command and control for a brigade-size contingent. Within Egypt, there is a fixed signals network that is mobile only within the country. During Egypt's wars with Israel, mines were used extensively throughout the Sinai Peninsula. With this abundance of unexploded ordnance, Egypt's engineer services have become adept at demining. The engineers possess adequate training, equipment, and expertise for such operations. Road and refugee camp construction is another area of expertise for the engineers, but water purification remains weak (ibid.).

As mentioned above, it is estimated that the Egyptian Army consists of 310,000 persons, of whom 240,000 are conscripts. Egypt also maintains a navy of 18,500 that includes 2,000 coast guard personnel and 12,000 conscripts. The main challenges facing the Egyptian military are, first, the transition to an all-mechanized infantry; second, professionalization of the military; third, managing external relations (Arab-Israeli conflict); and fourth, managing internal relations (domestic terrorism and presidential succession).

Currently, the Egyptian military relies heavily on conscription. As such, the education, moral, and overall potential of the armed forces is questionable. Despite the fact that it is one of the largest and best trained militaries in the Arab world, the use of conscripts always raises concerns. Since Egypt has been receiving substantial foreign military assistance from the United States for more than twenty years, the quality of Egyptian military equipment has improved. The equipment that the United States supplies is far superior to that of the Soviet Union, not only in quality but also in technology. Such technology requires substantially more training than in the past, plus better trained individuals to operate and maintain the equipment.

Peace with Israel has permitted Egypt to decrease the size of its military. Before

---

Sidebar 2   The Last Samurai in Egypt

The popular film *The Last Samurai* depicted an American officer training the Japanese military after the U.S. Civil War. Although this film offered cinematic excitement, it did not represent the true extent of U.S. military presence elsewhere in the world. More than fifty American officers served in the Egyptian Khedive's Army after the U.S. Civil War. These officers were deemed superior to French and English officers because the United States had just participated in the most technologically advanced war in history and it did not have the same vested interests in the Suez Canal as did the Europeans. These U.S. officers were placed in the highest positions of the military and began a rigorous training program for the Egyptian military. Although not as glamorous as the movie, American participation in the Egyptian military left a lasting impression in the professionalism and history of the military.

Sources

Butzgy, Michael. *Americans in the Egyptian Army: Ismail's Bold Experiment.* http://home.earthlink.net/~atomic_rom/egypt.htm (accesssed July 17, 2004).

Loring, W. W. 1884. *A Confederate Soldier in Egypt.* New York: Dodd, Mead & Company.

Morgan, James Morris. 1917. *Recollections of a Rebel Reefer.* Boston and New York: Houghton Mifflin Company. Cambridge: The Riverside Press.

---

that peace Egypt maintained a force well over 600,000, while today the number is closer to 300,000. By reducing the size of its force, Egypt can now better focus on training and maintenance. During the wars with Israel, the Egyptian military was very infantry heavy (more than half of its divisions were infantry). Today, as mentioned above, the army has twelve divisions (four armored, seven mechanized, and one infantry). The Egyptian military's goal was to be completely mechanized by 2005.

Within its five military zones, there are a variety of force components. In four of the zones (excluding the Central Zone), the army maintains at least one armored division (two armored infantry brigades and one mechanized infantry brigade) and two mechanized divisions (two mechanized infantry brigades and one armored infantry brigade). In the Central Zone there is a Republican Guard Brigade that is loosely controlled by the leadership of the Central Zone, but more likely it is controlled directly by the president. The units referenced above are supported by four independent armored brigades, two independent infantry brigades, four independent mechanized brigades, seven commando groups, and two heavy mortar brigades. Also, the Army Headquarters unit has a parachute brigade and two surface-to-surface missile brigades. Egypt participates in military exercises with NATO and non-NATO countries, including the United States, the United Kingdom, and other Arab countries that participated in the liberation of Kuwait. These exercises combine all forces in a mock battle similar to that carried out against Iraq (Heyman 2000, 204–205).

Although extremely secretive, the Egyptian military is known to possess weapons of mass destruction (WMD). Egypt's first attempt to acquire WMD came under the leadership of Nasser, who sought to counter the emerging Israeli nuclear weapons program. Although resources were allocated to achieve that goal, the project ended in failure. During the Yemeni civil war Egypt unleashed its arsenal of chemical weapons (mustard type) during military operations. Egypt's use of chemical weapons affected not only the royalist troops but also innocent civilians. It is believed that Egypt continues to produce chemical weapons to offset Israel's strategic advantage of possessing nuclear weapons.

Egypt consistently supports UN resolutions that call for the creation of a Nuclear Weapons Free Zone (NWFZ) in the Middle East. Such resolutions, which usually pass in the General Assembly every year, clearly pressure Israel, not only to admit that it possesses nuclear weapons but also to dismantle its program. The resolution usually receives near universal support, with only the United States and Israel opposed. Egypt does have a nuclear reactor that has been declared to be for only peaceful purposes. The plant does, however, have the capability of creating weapons grade plutonium if modified properly. Egypt has signed the Nuclear Non-Proliferation Treaty and the Biological Weapons Convention, but not the Chemical Weapons Convention (SIPRI 2004). Overall, Egypt possesses a strong unconventional component/deterrent within its armed forces. Such a component, although controversial, may be necessary, in the government's mind, especially in the context of the Middle East (Heyman 2000, 206).

Budget

Although Egypt does not publicize its defense budget, the figures are available. Since Egypt made peace with Israel, Egypt's defense budget has relied heavily on U.S. foreign military assistance (almost one-half of the budget). Since 1988, Egypt's defense budget has gradually decreased, based on the price of the U.S. dollar; however, actual spending in local currency has increased. These variations can be explained by exchange rates. Egypt has averaged between $2 billion and $3 billion per year over the last ten years. As a percentage of gross domestic product, the percentage has also decreased gradually since 1988, ranging from 5 percent in 1988 to about 2.5 percent in 2002. This change in defense spending can be attributed to peace with Israel and a reliable source of funding from the United States.

Egypt's average spending of nearly U.S.$2 billion has gone to increasing its capability to produce weapons systems domestically and toward major capital purchases from the United States, including high-quality fighter aircraft and main battle tanks. Egypt invests in its domestic military production to ensure a reliable source of military equipment and spare parts. As such, the country sets itself apart from its Arab neighbors as both a consumer and producer of military equipment. Although its revenues from domestic production remain small, they do provide additional resources for improving military capabilities. Egypt's position within the Arab world and its perceived threats require Egypt to spend a considerable amount of its financial resources on military matters. That does create additional jobs within Egypt but also takes resources away from economic programs that are extremely important for Egypt's stagnant economy (SIPRI 2004).

Civil-Military Relations/The Role of the Military in Domestic Politics

Since independence Egypt has been ruled by military personnel. Although it calls itself an Arab republic, one can classify Egypt more like other Arab states (for example, Syria, Lebanon, and Saudi Arabia) that have authoritarian types of government. Despite guarantees of democracy, the Egyptian people do not have direct influence on the government (U.S. Department of State 2004). Because of continuing deterioration in the freedoms promised in the constitution, internal pressures for change continue to grow in strength and violence. Most recently, Hosni Mubarak's decision to call for a state of emergency to combat the Muslim Brotherhood and other terrorist groups highlights the influence of the military in domestic politics.

As the guarantor of domestic security and stability, the Egyptian armed forces maintain careful observation of the struggle against domestic terrorist groups. At the first signs of the inability of the police to maintain security and stability, Mubarak can utilize the powers granted under the state of emergency to ensure that the state retains control of the situation. Although the military has remained relatively uninvolved in the political process, certain events could trigger increased unwelcome military participation in politics.

Currently, it is unclear who will replace Mubarak once he decides to step down. When Anwar Sadat was assassinated, Vice President Mubarak rose to the presidency, in accordance with constitutional rules of accession. However, even today Mubarak refuses to choose his heir apparent by selecting a vice president. This, added to his electoral success of four successive elections for six-year terms, adds to his apparent dislike for democracy. When elections do occur, the people of Egypt are more apathetic than the populations of most democracies, when measured by turnout, because they are aware that they have only one choice. That choice is to approve or disapprove the military's candidate for president. It is for this reason that Mubarak regularly receives his mandate with more than 90 percent of the electorate. Clearly, the Egyptian form of republic has more in common with Arab monarchies than with Western republics.

With the continued support of the military Mubarak may go on to yet another term as president, as long as his health lasts. Mubarak has survived several assassination attempts, most notably the attempt on his life in Addis Ababa, Ethiopia, in 1995. As the supreme leader of the military, Mubarak has ruled Egypt with an iron fist for decades. The military's role in domestic politics is secretive, yet strong (Harb 2003, 269–290; Sullivan 2003, 27–31; Sachs 2003, 5; MacFarquhar 2003, 10).

Terrorism

The September 11 terrorist attacks on the United States put Egypt in a difficult position, since several Egyptians were supposedly involved in the planning and implementation of the attacks. President Hosni Mubarak quickly condemned the attacks to ensure that Egypt was not held responsible. The same groups that have caused problems within Egypt were part of the attack. Most notably that includes Islamic Jihad, the organizer of the attacks, Ayman az-Zawahri, and Muhammed Atef, who supposedly piloted one of the planes. Following the terrorist attacks Egyptian authorities conducted a sweep and arrested hundreds of suspected terrorists who had either plotted to overthrow the government or incited demonstrations against the government (*Europa* 2003, 1482; Saleh 2002, 40–44; Frankel 2004, A01; Frankel 2003, A34).

After the terrorist attacks of September 11, 2001, the UN Security Council passed resolution 1373, which requires member states under chapter VII of the charter of the United Nations to take the necessary steps to eradicate terrorism. In operative clause 6, the Security Council created a Counter-Terrorism Committee to monitor the implementation of resolution 1373. Also, within the same clause the Security Council required that member states report to the committee on steps that they have made to implement the resolution. Since that resolution passed, member states have submitted at least three updates that provide a detailed overview of the actions member states have made in the fight against international terrorism (UN Security Council 2001a September 28).

Egypt submitted its first report in December 2001 and subsequently submitted follow-up reports in May 2002 and March 2003. These reports show a concerted effort by Egypt to take legislative, administrative, and executive measures to eradicate terrorism. Terrorism is included in Egyptian criminal law as a serious crime. In 1992, Egypt enacted Law No. 97, which improves Egypt's ability to convict terrorists. Egyptian law does not address terrorism solely within Egypt's boundaries, but throughout the world without discrimination based on nationality.

To clarify its laws, Egypt created a definition of terrorism that leaves no question as to what acts rise to the level of terrorism. The Egyptian legislature has incorporated that definition into all legal texts. Laws address several specific actions that are punishable under Egyptian law. These include, but are not limited to, the supplying of groups with weapons or other matériel that assists them, inviting someone to join a terrorist group, and making monetary contributions to terrorist groups. To facilitate the monitoring of terrorist activities the Egyptian government has enacted laws that make possible better monitoring by the authorities. The bank secrecy law, the banking and credit act, the socialists' public prosecutor law, and the illicit gains law all allow authorities to better monitor illicit financial activities.

Legislation has also been introduced to ensure that money laundering ceases, cutting off an important illicit activity that can be used to fund terrorism. In the areas of weapons and enlistment, Egypt has also implemented several laws to make it illegal to possess weapons without government permits. These laws also address monitoring of domestic and international trafficking, destruction of weapons, control over explosive materials, and severe penalties for recruiting members for terrorist operations. The Egyptian Central Bank has taken measures to implement freezing the funds of terrorist organizations. Cooperation and coordination between other banks has also been streamlined, to allow rapid freezing upon receipt of information on which assets to freeze. The central bank has created standards for controlling assets by registering banks under its supervision to regulate procedures for dealing with the opening of accounts both within and outside Egypt (ibid. 2001b December 21, 2002, 2003).

Another important tool in the fight against terrorism is the exchange of information between countries. Egypt has multiple bilateral and multilateral agreements that facilitate the rapid exchange of information. Mechanisms have been created to facilitate cooperation, including bodies within the International Criminal Police Organization (INTERPOL), the Council of Arab Ministers of the Interior of the League of Arab States, the Organization of African Unity (now known as the African Union), and the Organization of the Islamic Conference. Egypt has laws that forbid sanctuary for terrorists within its borders that include the destruction of terrorist organizations and the provision of resources to ensure that Egypt's vast deserts are not used for terrorist training. This may include not only the police forces but also military forces, if necessary. Egypt has acceded to many international legal instruments, including the Convention for the Prevention and Punishment of Terrorism, the Arab Convention for the Suppression of Terrorism, and nine other conventions that deal with terrorism on an international level. Overall, Egypt has made all the outward proclamations to address the issue of international terrorism. Implementing those proclamations will be the challenge for Egypt. As situations arise that challenge the legal framework that Egypt has devised, the true value of their proclamations will be realized (ibid.).

Relationship with the United States

In general, relations between the United States and Egypt are cordial, strong, and strategic. Although relations remain secure, current U.S. policy in the Middle East has strained the relationship. Despite the strain, however, Egyptian-U.S. relations are important for both sides. Egypt receives substantial military assistance that empowers the Mubarak regime to remain in power, while the United States receives in return a moderate Arab state whose sole purpose is not to remove Israel from the map. Peace in the Middle East is a priority for both sides, especially Egypt, which has fought four wars against

Israel since 1948. Since the U.S.-sponsored peace accords between Egypt and Israel (1979), Egypt's position in the Middle East has varied from one of leadership, to isolation, to open hostility.

Iraq's invasion of Kuwait was Egypt's opportunity to regain its prestigious position in the Arab world. During the lead-up to the war, Egypt was one of the most important coalition partners of the United States. After the United Kingdom, Egypt's troop contribution was the highest after that of the United States. Egypt's strong support for the coalition was strategically important to the United States, since it showed that the coalition was not a neocolonialist construct but a truly global coalition formed to repel an act of aggression in accordance with the charter of the United Nations.

The successful conclusion of the Persian Gulf War not only was a victory over aggression for the United States but also helped a strong ally emerge from more than a decade as a pariah in the Middle East. After the Persian Gulf War the benefits of U.S. military aid (totaling more than $1.3 billion annually) and U.S. development aid (USAID programs totaled over $25 billion between 1975 and 2002) began to show. With Western countries' substantial debt relief, as payment for Egypt's strong leadership of the Arab coalition members, the country moved forward with a strong economic base. Egypt took these benefits and solidified its economy, while expanding its role in the Middle East peace process by hosting several important meetings between Israelis and Palestinians.

Egypt also participates in many joint exercises with the United States and Western militaries, hosts U.S. warships in port, and purchases substantial military hardware from the United States. To increase regional military security, the United States has provided Egypt with the following weapons systems, among others: F-4 jets, F-16 fighter jets, M-60A3 and M1A1 tanks, APCs, Apache helicopters, antiaircraft missile batteries, and aerial surveillance aircraft. Egypt also manufactures military equipment with U.S. assistance. Joint exercises include all branches of the military and deployments within Egypt. Overall, relations between the United States and Egypt are strategic for both sides and will grow stronger in the future (U.S. Department of State, 2004).

Egyptian-U.S. relations follow the course of the Israeli-Palestinian negotiations. If relations between those two entities continue to deteriorate, the United States and Egypt will continue to be plagued by forces that will pull them apart. After years of isolation Egypt again finds itself as a leader of the Arab world. As such, the plight of the Palestinian people has become an issue that Egypt cannot ignore. Despite the extreme importance of U.S. military assistance to Egypt, the country has had to voice its concern over U.S. policy on the Israeli-Palestinian issue. In Egypt's view the United States often supports Israel blindly, even in light of Israeli policies to use military force against its neighbors and the Palestinians, to continue to possess nuclear weapons, to build settlements on Palestinian territory, and to build a barrier between Israeli and Palestinian territory. U.S. support for Israel has drawn strong comments from Egypt but has not drastically changed the relationship.

Peace in the Middle East is only one issue that has strained relations. Egypt's campaign against domestic terrorism remains a borderline case, since many groups are looking for an opening political situation, that is, a more democratic Egypt. Stability within Egypt remains a priority of the United States, but any escalation in terrorist acts could strain the patience of the United States, as human rights in Egypt are continually violated (Sanger and Dao 2003, A1; Wax 2003, A24). U.S. involvement with Egypt has been based on Egypt's importance in providing stability in the Middle East. Peace with Israel was to herald a new age of peace, prosperity, and development in the Middle East. Unfortunately, that has not occurred; therefore, the direction of U.S.-Egyptian relations will adapt to new situations as they arise. But if Egypt's reliability as a stable and modern Arab republic falters, it may be difficult for the United States to continue to provide such large amounts of military assistance.

The Future

The defining moment for the Egyptian military in the next fifteen years will be the transition between the rule of Hosni Mubarak and his successor. Mubarak has not designated a vice president, his constitutional successor; therefore, if Mubarak were to die or become incapacitated, there would be a constitutional crisis wherein the legislature would have to choose a successor. Such a process would surely turn political as the politicians and the military vie for power. Egypt has had successive military men serve as president since Nasser came to power, and the military would surely look to continue that trend. Despite proclamations that Egypt is a republic, democratic institutions have not materialized. Mubarak has "won" four elections with percentages comparable to those of Saddam Hussein in Iraq. That lack of real democracy will make the transition more difficult.

Egypt's relationship with the United States will also dictate the direction of Egypt's military/defense policy over the next fifteen years. The modernization of the Egyptian military relies on nearly $2 billion in military aid from the United States. Therefore it is extremely important that Egypt remain within a reasonable distance of the foreign policy of the United States. However, at the same time, Egypt's leadership role in the Arab world strains its ability to stay in line with U.S. foreign policy. As an Arab state, Egypt must support the Palestinian cause. But as the second Intifada has escalated, support for the Palestinians has propelled Egypt further from U.S. priorities. Egypt has consistently criticized the blind support for Israel's policies in the occupied territories by the United States, viewing such support as a detriment to peace in the Middle East. If the situation in the Middle East does not improve, Egypt and the United States may grow further apart.

Another strain on the relationship between the United States and Egypt is Egypt's record on human rights. As a result of the internal unrest caused by Egypt's battle against terrorists, many countries have criticized Egypt for the treatment of its citizens. The United States has used its leverage over Egypt to press for an improved human rights record. The conflict in Iraq has also strained U.S.-Egyptian relationships. During the period before the war, Egypt attempted to facilitate negotiations that would circumvent the use of force; Egypt did not believe that Iraq posed a threat to the international community, especially after years of debilitating sanctions.

References, Recommended Readings,
and Websites

Books

Ben-Yehuda, Hemda, and Shmuel Sandler.
2002. *The Arab-Israeli Conflict
Transformed: Fifty Years of Interstate
and Ethnic Crises.* Albany: State
University of New York Press.

Berman, Eric G., and Katie E. Sams. 2000.
*Peacekeeping in Africa: Capabilities
and Culpabilities.* Geneva: UN
Institute for Disarmament Research
and Pretoria: Institute for Security
Studies.

Blum, Howard. 2003. *The Eve of
Destruction: The Untold Story of the
Yom Kippur War.* New York: Harper
Collins Publishers.

Cohen, Avner. 1998. *Israel and the Bomb.*
New York: Columbia University Press.

Europa World Yearbook, Vol. I. 2003.
London, England: Europa Publications
Limited.

Goldscheider, Calvin. 2002. *Cultures in
Conflict: the Arab-Israeli Conflict.*
Westport, CT: Greenwood Press.

Hammel, Eric. 1992. *Six Days in June:
How Israel Won the 1967 Arab-Israeli
War.* New York: Scribner's.

Heyman, Charles, ed. 2000. *Jane's World
Armies.* Coulsdon, Surrey, UK, and
Alexandria, VA: Jane's Information
Group.

Karsh, Efraim. 2002. *Arab-Israeli Conflict:
The Palestine War 1948.* Oxford:
Osprey Publishing.

Metz, Helen Chapin. 1991. *Egypt: A
Country Study.* Washington, DC: GPO
for the Library of Congress.

Oren, Michael B. 2003. *Six Days of War:
June 1967 and the Making of the
Modern Middle East.* New York:
Ballantine Books.

Rabinovich, Abraham. 2004. *The Yom
Kippur War: The Epic Encounter that
Transformed the Middle East.* New
York: Schocken Books.

Articles/Newspapers

Eriksson, Mikael, Peter Wallensteen, and
Margareta Sollenberg. 2003. "Armed
Conflict 1989–2002." *Journal of Peace
Research* 40:593–607.

Frankel, Glenn. 2003. "Egyptians Begin
Asking: After Mubarak, What?; Debate
Focuses on Successor, Chances for

Democracy." *Washington Post,*
December 17:A34.

_____. 2004. "Egypt Muzzles Calls for
Democracy; Reformers Say Billions in
U.S. Aid Prop Up Authoritarian Rule."
Washington Post, January 6:A01.

Friedman, Thomas L. 2003. "Expanding
Club NATO." *New York Times,*
October 26, 11.

Harb, Imad. 2003. "The Egyptian Military
in Politics: Disengagement or
Accommodation?" *Middle East Journal*
57:269–290.

MacFarquhar, Neil. 2003. "Egyptians
Wonder if Mubarak's Son Will Stir
Things Up." *New York Times,*
December 21:10.

Ronen, Yehudit. 2003. "Sudan and Egypt:
The Swing of the Pendulum (1989–
2001)." *Middle Eastern Studies* 39:81–98.

Sachs, Susan. 2003. "A Nation at War:
The Regional Fallout; The Question in
Cairo: Will Soap Prices Fall and
Democracy Rise?" *New York Times,*
April 20:B5.

Saleh, Nivian. 2002. "Egypt: Osama's Star
Is Rising." *Middle East Policy* 9:40–44.

Sanger, David E., and James Dao. 2003.
"The President's Trip: Peace Talks;
Bush, in Egypt, Finds Warmth and
Wariness." *New York Times,* June 3:A1.

Sullivan, Dennis J. 2003. "The Struggle
for Egypt's Future." *Current History*
102:27–31.

Tabbara, Acil. 2003. "Israel, Egypt Hit
Low One Quarter Century after Peace
Accords." *Agence France Presse,*
September 16.

UN Security Council. 2001. S/RES/1373
(2001a), September 28,

———. 2001b. S/2001/1237, December 21.

———. 2002. S/2002/601, May 29.

———. 2003. S/2003/277, March 10.

Wax, Emily. 2003. "Mubarak Warns of
Rise in Militancy; Egyptian Defends
U.S. Use of Suez." *Washington Post,*
April 1:A24.

Websites

Central Intelligence Agency, *The World
Factbook*-Egypt: http://www.odci.gov/
cia/publications/factbook/geos/eg.html
(accessed February 17, 2004).

Egyptian Armed Forces:http://www.mmc.
gov.eg.

Ministry of Foreign Affairs: http://www.
mfe.gov.eg.

People's Assembly: http://www.assembly.gov.eg.

President of Egypt: http://www.presidency.gov.eg.

Stockholm International Peace Research Institute (SIPRI), "Facts on International Relations and Security Trends (FIRST) Database, Bonn International Center for Conversion (BICC): Armed Forces, Weapons Holdings and Employment in Arms Production": http://first.sipri.org/ (accessed February 17, 2004).

Shoura Assembly: http://www.shoura.gov.eg.

United Nations. "Contributors of United Nations Peacekeeping Missions" http://www.un.org/Depts/dpko/dpko/contributors/2005/March2005_1.pdf (accessed May 3, 2005).

U.S. Department of State. "Country Reports on Human Rights Practices–2002": http://www.state.gov/g/drl/rls/hrrpt/2002/18274.htm (accessed February 17, 2004).

France

Eben Christensen

Geography and History

France has had one of the most tumultuous histories of any European nation. From Napoleon to de Gaulle to the European Union, France has remained an influential member of the international community. Yet the memories of the glories of the Revolution, and the horrors of both world wars, have had significant impacts on a country that struggles to remain both independent and interdependent.

France is the largest European nation, being of 213,600 square miles (547,030 square kilometers), slightly less than twice the size of the state of Colorado. The terrain is mostly flat or rolling hills in the north and west. These areas hold almost all of the arable land of the country (one-third of the total). The remainder is mountainous, especially the Pyrenees in the south and the Alps in the east. France has 2,130 miles (3,427 kilometers) of coastline on the English Channel to the north, the Bay of Biscay to the west, and the Mediterranean Sea to the south.

As of July 2005 the population of France was 60,656,178, placing it twentieth in the world, ahead of the United Kingdom and behind Thailand. The majority of French citizens are Roman Catholics (83 to 88 percent), while the second largest religious group is Muslim (5 to 10 percent). This immigrant Muslim religious group has been part of the population shifts from the Mediterranean states of Tunisia, Morocco, and Algeria that began in the late 1960s. Although the French state itself is officially secular (since 1905), many social issues such as state subsidies for religious education, and more recently the banning of religious headscarves, have deepened the tensions between groups.

The French economy has traditionally been a mix of private ownership, government ownership, and intervention in the marketplace. This government intervention is particularly noticeable in the large corporations of Air France, France Telecom, Renault, and the defense contractor Thales. Moreover, the French government continues to dominate industries considered important to national security, including the energy production and defense industries. In recent years the French government has scaled back its intervention, with the gradual opening of telecommunications and demonopolizing of the energy sector (allowing 30 percent private ownership), along the guidelines established by the EU. With a GDP of $1.737 trillion (GDP per capita is $28,700) growing at an annual rate of 2.1 percent, the French economy is one of the largest in the world. The services sector comprises the largest share (73 percent) of the national economic strength, followed by the industrial sector (24.3 percent) and a small agricultural sector (2.7 percent) (CIA *World Factbook* 2005).

Modern France was established by the 1958 constitution under the Fifth French Republic. This constitution established a strong presidential system, with a president (as of 2000) that serves seven-year terms. The president appoints a premier and a cabinet who are held accountable to the parliament. The parliament is bicameral, with a National Assembly and a Senate. The deputies for the National Assembly each serve five-year terms for their single-member districts. Senators are elected for nine-year terms from an electoral college made up of the deputies and a number of municipal members. The French government is a highly centralized administrative bureaucracy. In 2003 there were a number of constitutional amendments that yielded some control to regional authorities. Yet the Paris-centered government still maintains most of the control over the delivery of government services. Parliament is responsible for matters of civil law and has budgetary authority; the president appoints the prime minister, the executive ministers, civil servants, and judges. The president is also the commander-in-chief of the military and can dissolve the national assembly.

The country of France was known in Roman times as Gaul; it was conquered by Julius Caesar in the Gallic Wars. After the fall of Rome and throughout the sixth and seventh centuries, Gaul was in perpetual conflict between the Merovingian kings. In 732 the Carolingian Dynasty began with the rise of Charles Martel and his son, Pepin the Short. Pepin dethroned the last Merovingian in 751 and proclaimed himself king with the sanction of the pope. This royal line saw its apex under Pepin's son, Charlemagne. With the death of the last Carolingian heir, the nobles chose Hugh Capet as king in 987. That began the Capetian bloodline, which included the early monarchies of Louis VI and Louis VII. In 1328, Philip VI succeeded to the throne but was contested by Edward III of England, who proclaimed himself king of France in 1337. This dynastic struggle became the Hundred Years War (1337–1453) between the two countries (Haine 2000).

Sidebar 1   Cardinal Richelieu

One of the most famous Frenchmen was Cardinal Richelieu. Born in 1585, Richelieu was appointed Bishop of Luçon in 1606 and Cardinal in 1622. During this time he served as the secretary of state for foreign affairs (1616), and he later became prime minister of France (1624).

The French involvement in the Thirty Years' War in 1636 demonstrated Richelieu's philosophy of the state; he argued that the policies of the state should remain above religion. Although it was a Catholic country, France joined the Protestant forces as a challenge to the Catholic Habsburg Empire given its strategic holdings on the eastern border of France. One of his most famous quotes is "I have never had any [enemies], other than those of the state."

Cardinal Richelieu died in 1642, but only after consolidating power into the hands of the French Monarchy, and providing a model for state action for the next century.

Source
Levi, Anthony. 2000. "Cardinal Richelieu: And the Making of France." NY: Carrol and Graf.

In 1453, Charles VII was crowned king of France at Reims. His descendant Louis XI consolidated French power and defeated the remnants of the feudal lords that remained, controlling the territory that is now all of modern France. The French kings Louis XIII and Louis XIV, under the advice of Cardinal Richelieu and Cardinal Mazarin, saw French victory in the Thirty Years' War against the Hapsburg powers. In 1789 the French Revolution began symbolically with the July 14 storming of the Bastille fortress. The Assembly suspended King Louis XVI and ordered elections for a National Convention to write a new constitution. The first meeting of the Convention was on September 21, 1792, and its first action was to abolish the monarchy and set up the republic. Louis XVI was tried for treason, for which he was executed in January 1793 (ibid.).

Rather than electing a democratic government, the Convention established a civil dictatorship under the Committee of Public Safety, the Committee of General Security, and the Revolutionary Tribunal. This Reign of Terror, led by Georges Danton and Maximilien Robespierre, saw thousands executed. With the eventual execution of Robespierre, and a coup to overthrow the Convention, a four-man Directory was established in 1795. The Directory's control ended after Napoleon Bonaparte seized power and crowned himself emperor in 1804. After Napoleon's defeat at the Battle of Waterloo, the Congress of Vienna restored the borders of 1790 and recognized Louis XVIII as France's legitimate sovereign. The July Revolution in 1830 overthrew his successor, Charles X, and the "citizen king" Louis Phillippe led France. That government fell in the February Revolution of 1848, and in December, Louis Napoleon Bonaparte, nephew of Napoleon I, was elected president of the Second French Republic.

Louis's empire ended with the French defeat in the Franco-Prussian War, which set up the Third French Republic, lasting from 1870 to 1940. After the German

Table 1   France: Key Statistics

Type of government	Republic
Population (millions)	60,656,178 (2005)
Religions	Roman Catholic 83%–88%, Muslim 5%–10%, Unaffiliated 4%, Protestant 2%, Jewish 1%
Main industries	Machinery, chemicals, automobiles, aircraft, electronics, textiles, food processing, and tourism
Main security threats	Terrorist threats; various maritime claims over former colonial holdings including Madagascar, Comoros, Mauritius, Suriname and French Guiana, and Antarctica
Defense spending (% GDP)	2.6 (2003)
Size of military (thousands)	259 (2004)
Number of civil wars since 1945	0
Number of interstate wars since 1945	1

Sources

Central Intelligence Agency Website. 2003. CIA *World Factbook.* http://www.cia.gov/cia/publications/factbook/ (accessed May 15, 2005).

Military Balance, 2003–2004. London: International Institute for Strategic Studies.

occupation of France during World War II, the Fourth French Republic was officially proclaimed in 1946. The Fourth Republic's new constitution reorganized the empire as the French Union, which replaced the colonial system. The French Union began to disintegrate in mid-1950, with the withdrawal of Vietnam, Laos, Cambodia, Morocco, and Tunisia. When the military coup of French military forces in Algeria threatened mainland France in 1958, Charles de Gaulle established the Fifth Republic and became its first president in December 1958 (ibid.; Popkin 1994).

Regional Geopolitics

France has remained one of the most steadfast members of the European Union. This political and economic integration has yielded stable and peaceful relations with the country's neighbors. One exception, however, has been in the troop deployments within Serbia and Kosovo. Those conflicts have remained localized and ethnic in nature, limiting their spillover to France itself. Yet this stability in Europe does not transfer to French interests in its traditional backyard of North Africa. Even so, the colonial history, and shared sociocultural ties that connect France to this region through the Francophonie, reiterate an active French interest (International Organization of the Francophonie Website).

Although the Algerian conflict may have significantly altered French policy in that country, it had little effect on the active interventionist approach noticed in a number of African nations (Nigeria from 1957 to 1964, Senegal in 1962, Gabon in 1964, Niger in 1980, Zaire in 1977, and Togo in 1986, to name a few). This policy has reached a limit, given the inability of France to project its forces in operations within North Africa and farther abroad. Although the need for intervention has increased, resources have become more difficult to muster under total French autonomy. Such limits led Mitterrand in 1985 to declare that France was no longer going to be the gendarme of Africa (Treacher 2003, 127). Although more limited in the number of its interventions, France has continued to be active in policing African interests, most recently in Cote d'Ivoire, Rwanda, and Somalia. The difference with such interventions has been the linkage of French forces with those of other nations, prominently the United States.

One lingering French concern within this region has been the rise of anti-Western terrorist organizations. With the proximity to North Africa, as well as its past policies in the Mideast (notably the Suez conflict, see below), it is possible that France may become a terrorist target in the future. France has relied on finding the underlying reasons for terrorist activities, relying more on tactics including diplomacy, law enforcement, and intelligence cooperation (Gordon 2002).

Conflict Past and Present

The conflicts that have shaped modern France can be traced to the rise of Napoleon, and the series of wars that followed. Napoleon came to power after a soft coup of the executive branch, known as the Directory, in Year III (1795). After declaring that France was done with the "romance of the revolution," Napoleon began a series of events known collectively as the Napoleonic Wars. The quest for territorial expansion began after the defeat of longtime rival Austria in 1800 in Marengo, Italy. That victory strengthened expansionist policies in Italy, Germany, and Switzerland (Schom 1997).

After his own coronation in 1804 in the Cathedral of Notre Dame, famously taking the crown from the hands of the pope, Napoleon became the French emperor. In 1805 a number of states known as the Third Coalition (formed by Great Britain, Austria, Russia, and Sweden) attempted to stop the spread of French power on the Continent. This was met by a show of strength and military genius, with the defeat of a combined Russian and Austrian force at Austerlitz on December 2, 1805. Soon the French occupied Austria, including Vienna. (Prussia met a similar fate after the battle of Jena.) After the defeat of Sweden in 1808 and the tacit truce with Russia, Napoleon controlled Europe, leaving only Britain as a source of resistance.

The Russian rejection of the French-led Continental System led to Napoleon's formation of the Grande Armée, a force of more than 600,000 troops that invaded Russia. The Russian offensive began in June 1812, and while the French forces advanced, the Russians (under Mikhail Kutuzov) retreated into the county's interior. Although Napoleon took Moscow in September, the French forces were beginning to feel the effects of the Russian winter and their overstretched supply lines. That led Napoleon to retreat from Russia on October 19, leading an army now only one-fifth its original size. The emperor was left vulnerable as a result to attacks both from outside and from former supporters (Britt 1985; Schom 1997).

In December, Prussia signed a truce with the Russian czar, later followed by Great Britain, Sweden, and Austria in 1813, beginning the "War of Liberation." At the Battle of Nations in Leipzig (October 16–19), France was forced to retreat. The allies continued on and took Paris on

---

Sidebar 2   Napoleon Goes to Russia

On 23 June 1812, Napoleon sent his Grande Armée into Russia. This force consisted of more than 600,000 men, and Napoleon believed that by taking Moscow he could force Russia to return to the Continental System. Napoleon prepared his army for a push into Russian territory to capture the city.

As the French forces advanced, many of the troops succumbed to typhus and dysentery, with some 80,000 dying from disease. The French forces engaged the Russian Army near Borodino Field, seventy miles from Moscow. After an indecisive battle where 108,000 died, the Russian forces retreated from the battle and abandoned the city. Upon reaching Moscow on 14 September, the French found the city nearly deserted; they were without rations for the troops and, later, without shelter from fire. Soon, in the middle of the harsh winter, Napoleon ordered his troops to begin the 500-mile return to France. Napoleon returned from Russia with only 10,000 troops left, and no victory.

Sources
Britt, Albert Sidney, III. 1985. *The Wars of Napoleon.* Wayne, NJ: Avery.
Schom, Alan. 1997. *Napoleon Bonaparte.* New York: HarperCollins.

March 31, 1814, forcing Napoleon to abdicate and leading to his exile in Elba. While the victors were convening the Congress of Vienna, however, Napoleon landed on the shores of France on March 1, 1815, and established an army of supporters that retook Paris by March 20. Napoleon planned to attack the now unmobilized forces, particularly the British and Prussians. After a number of successful battles against those forces in the north of France, on June 18, Napoleon began a massive attack against the British forces under Wellington at Waterloo. After losing some 32,000 soldiers, Napoleon surrendered himself to a British warship to become a prisoner on the island of Saint Helena, ending the series of conflicts (Britt 1985).

Some fifty years later, France saw the rising Prussian might as a threat to its security. The Prussian victory in the Austro-Prussian War and the unification of the northern German States threatened to embroil France in a war with Germany. Otto von Bismarck's desire to unify north and south Germany led the countries into conflict, and many of the results of the conflict underscored their relations over the next century. The pretext for what is called the Franco-Prussian War involved the French insistence that the Spanish throne not be offered to the Hohenzollern-Sigmaringen house. Bismarck's use of propaganda in the famous Ems dispatch, which described the meetings over this issue, incensed the French, and they declared war on July 19, 1870.

The French declaration drove the states of south Germany to join the North German Confederation for security purposes, thus achieving Bismarck's goal. The well-organized Prussian military defeated the French in a number of battles and began marching on Paris. When Napoleon III attempted to support the forces around Metz, he and 100,000 of his men were captured. When news reached Paris that Napoleon III had been captured, a provisional government of national defense was established. The Germans surrounded Paris itself on September 19, and the forces there withheld the assault until January 28, 1871, when the city fell. The Treaty of Frankfurt (May 21) established a chief executive and a French national assembly (the Third French Republic) that was supported by Germany, but it also required France to pay a $1 billion indemnity and to cede Alsace and Lorraine to the newly formed German Empire (Carr 1991).

Although many point to the assassination of Archduke Ferdinand of Austria-Hungary in the lead-up to World War I, there had been many factors at work since the end of the Franco-Prussian War. The intense conflicts between the European powers over colonial, territorial, and economic issues were at stake. Such territorial claims were evident in the rise of French nationalism over German claims to the Alsace and Lorraine regions. After Serbia's rejection of the punitive measures demanded after the archduke's assassination, war was declared between Austria-Hungary (allied with Germany) and Serbia (allied with Russia). Believing that France was to preemptively attack its country, Germany declared war on August 3, sending troops through Belgium and Luxembourg into France. Soon the war grew to include Great Britain, France, Russia, Serbia, Belgium, the Ottoman Empire, Germany, and Austria-Hungary.

The German strategy, planned by Alfred von Schlieffen, called for an attack on the flank of the French army. These attacks led to the German occupation of Belgium and advances on Paris. One of the most significant battles of the war was undertaken in September 1914. The first battle of the Marne and the battle of Ypres established a grueling war of attrition along a Western Front that extended from Ostend to Luneville and lasted through 1915. In February 1916 the Germans attempted to break the deadlock on the Western Front in the battle of Verdun. With huge losses the French repelled the German offensive. The first U.S. troops landed in France in June 1917 under the command of General Pershing. The German counteroffensive, known as the second battle of the Marne (July/August 1918), stopped just short of Paris. The commander of the unified Allied forces, Marshal Foch, ordered a counterattack that pushed the Germans back to their initial line. This attack continued with a British advance toward Germany and a U.S. push through the Argonne region. An armistice was signed with Germany on November 11 stipulating the removal of all troops west of the Rhine. Moreover the Treaty of Versailles forced Germany to cede Alsace and Lorraine to France and acknowledge guilt for the war (Prior and Wilson 1998; William 1998).

The peace settlement of World War I, the Great Depression, and the rise of German, Italian, and Japanese militarist regimes prompted the second major conflict on European soil. The specter of World War I, and the great loss of French lives, led to the belief that conflict on that scale should be avoided at all costs. The French and British policies of appeasing German military aspirations led to the sacrificing of Czechoslovakia in the Munich Pact in September 1938. With the occupation of all of Czechoslovakia in March 1939 by German forces and the fall of Albania to Italian forces in April, the British and French abandoned that policy and began creating an antiaggression coalition including Turkey, Greece, Poland, and Romania. After the alliance between German and Italian forces, and the Soviet-German nonaggression pact, Germany invaded Poland on September 1, 1939. France declared war on Germany on September 3 and throughout the winter remilitarized behind the famed Maginot Line. That set the stage for what became World War II.

On May 13 the Germans outflanked the Maginot Line in France. By June 22, France had signed an armistice with Germany, setting up the Vichy government, led by Marshal Pétain. Yet the Free French forces under General de Gaulle led resistance movements throughout France, and many regular forces fought alongside the Allies. By early 1944, Allied air strikes had destroyed a number of German cities and severely crippled the German industrial base. These attacks cleared the way for the Normandy campaign by the Allies in northern France, starting on June 6, 1944, and in southern France on August 15. The bloody battles of Normandy led to the Allied push to the Rhine, expelling most of the German forces from France by October. After the German collapse on April 25 at Torgau in Saxony and the suicide of Hitler, there was an unconditional surrender by Germany signed at Reims on May 7 and ratified on May 8 (Winks and Adams 2003).

The aftermath of World War II was not localized to Europe but had an influence on French military policy around the world. This was most evident in the French occupation of Vietnam and the lengthy conflict that embroiled those two countries. While the Japanese occupied Vietnam through World War II, the collapse of the Japanese-supported Bao Dai government in 1945 led to the rise in power of the Viet Minh. The goal of the Viet Minh was to establish an autonomous republic of Vietnam. Following World War II the French attempted to reassert power throughout North Vietnam but were prevented from doing so by the Viet Minh.

An agreement with the leader of the Viet Minh, Ho Chi Minh, in March 1946 recognized Vietnam as a free state and permitted French troops in North

Vietnam. Fighting broke out in November 1946 between Vietnamese and French troops in Haiphong, following the failure of the parties to agree on the status of a separate republic of Cochin China. In December the Viet Minh attacked French forces at Hanoi, thus beginning a long and bloody guerrilla war known as the French Indochina War. By February 1950, France granted Vietnam independence within the larger French Union, under a renewed Bao Dai government. Many Western powers recognized this new government, while the Soviet Union and other communist states recognized Ho Chi Minh. The war eventually led to the French control of the major cities and the Viet Minh controlling the rural areas. This stalemate led to the United States covering as much as 80 percent of the war costs of the French government. In May 1954, Viet Minh forces defeated French forces at Dienbienphu, and the French soon signed an armistice at the Geneva Conference of 1954 (Dalloz 1990).

The nationalization of the Suez Canal by Egyptian president Abdel Nasser was one reason that led to the French involvement in the Suez War, which began on July 26, 1956. France believed that Nasser would close the canal to petroleum tankers bound to Europe from the Persian Gulf. Following a military offensive by Israeli forces on October 29, France and Britain occupied the Canal Zone. After Nasser refused the demands of France for the withdrawal of both Israeli and Egyptian troops, France and Great Britain invaded Egypt on October 31 in "Operation Musketeer." In response, the Soviet Union pledged its support to Egypt. Fearful of a rapid escalation of the crisis by the United States and the USSR, the United Nations put pressure on France to withdraw to the Armistice Line of 1949. The French and British forces complied in December 1956, and the conflict officially ended in March 1957 after the removal of Israeli troops and the deployment of the UN Emergency Force (UNEF) (Schonfield 1969).

French involvement in the Algerian conflict was the most contentious French military involvement in modern times, and eventually the conflict brought down the French government. French involvement in Algeria began in the 1820s and continued until the 1960s with the independence of Algeria. In 1834, France undertook the occupation of the country, which formally became French territory in 1848. By 1880 there were well more than 300,000 Frenchmen in Algeria fighting a strong resistance movement based in the south of the country. The country was given administrative autonomy in 1900 and placed under local command with French control. The French inhabitants and their descendants remained in the modern urban areas, while many of the Muslim inhabitants were forced to live in rural areas or city slums. Although there was an official policy for the assimilation of Muslims into French culture, the local groups (Party of the Algerian People and the Movement for the Triumph of Democratic Liberties) rebuffed this and called for independence.

During World War II, Algeria was the headquarters to both the Allies and de Gaulle, but soon afterward, in 1945, Algerian nationalists killed some ninety Europeans. Those attacks prompted a French crackdown that resulted in the deaths of from 1,500 to 6,000 Muslims, setting the stage for the protracted civil conflict. From 1954 to 1957 the Algerian resistance movement became more violent, and splinter groups (such as the National Liberation Front) began attacking police stations and government offices. That led the French military to raise troop numbers to over 500,000 and to the building of electrified fences along Algerian borders.

The liberal policies of Premier Pierre Mendès-France toward Algeria led to the massive demonstrations of 1958 by colonialists in Algeria and in France. The demonstrations turned into a French military coup in Algeria that began spreading into mainland France. The resulting political chaos led to the resignation of the premier and to the rise of de Gaulle, ending the Fourth French Republic. De Gaulle quelled the protests by colonialists and French Army forces in 1960–1961, and historians note that this may have prevented a French civil war. By 1962, Algeria was given full independence, but the conflict itself did not end. Rogue French military forces in Algeria formed the Secret Army Organization (OAS), which began its own guerrilla war against Algerian forces. The OAS group was soon captured by French military regulars, ending the war only after tens of thousands of lives on both sides had been lost.

More recently, France has been a party to military operations in support of UN peacekeeping missions. For example, French troops participated in the UN-mandated mission in Somalia (UNOSOM). That mission began after Security Council Resolution 794 established Operation Restore Hope to distribute humanitarian relief in that country. Although the project was not supported by the French defense minister, Joxe, the government sent 2,400 troops and four naval vessels to the country. The force was stationed in the southern region, around Baïdoa, and was responsible for the 95,000 square kilometers of land under Opération Oryx. There was some

consternation in Paris that the U.S.-led operations would result in institutionalizing U.S. activity in Africa (Treacher 2003). Such concerns were quelled after the U.S. casualties in Mogadishu led to the quick withdrawal of those forces from the country.

The Gulf War that began with the invasion of Kuwait by Iraq marked a significant policy shift for France. Having no real historical or legal obligations to the Kuwaitis, the early pace of the French force deployment was extremely slow. It wasn't until the Iraqi raid on the French embassy in Kuwait City on September 15 that there was a decision to deploy some 4,500 troops and sixteen warplanes to Saudi Arabia. That force was increased in 1991 to almost 12,000, and, significantly, placed directly under the control of the United States. Among Western European nations only France and the United Kingdom sent ground troops to Iraq, representing the largest military deployment of French troops since Algeria. More important, the Gulf War tested the French ability to project force within a multinational coalition under UN auspices (ibid.). This test was particularly difficult for France as it relied on outdated tactical aircraft and poor troop mobilization. Of 280,000 personnel as part of the FAR designation (earmarked international forces), only 12,000 could be mustered—and those from forty-seven different regiments, a significantly poor showing.

France was also a part of the NATO lead force in the former Yugoslavia. The disintegration of Yugoslavia led to widespread ethnic cleansing and gave France the impetus to join in a conflict with few tangible national interests. Rather, as President Chirac noted, France was fighting for a particular idea of French democratic ideals (ibid., 72). From 1992 through 1995,

French forces under the authority of the United Nations, the WEU, and OSCE were part of the 14,000 troops that made up UNPROFOR. The deterioration of the conflict in 1992 led to the increase of that force to 15,000 troops, of which France contributed 4,500 (which troops were placed under NATO command). During the course of the conflict, and after the humiliation of French soldiers being held hostage, France helped to establish a rapid reaction force of 12,000 troops. These troops employed heavy weaponry to "protect" the UN peacekeepers. With this show of both force and the willingness to employ it, alongside the diplomatic initiatives of the NATO allies, the Dayton Accords were signed in Paris on December 14, 1995. The French continue support with troops deployed as part of SFOR (the Stabilization Force) and a UN police detachment that includes more than 120 French gendarmes.

Alliance Structure

French defense policy was outlined in 1959 with the establishment of the republic. It lays down three comprehensive goals: (1) to defend French national interests as established in the 1958 constitution, which includes the territory and its people, but also allowing for international conflict prevention and peacekeeping; (2) to further European stability, much of which has been established under the WEU, NATO, and OSCE; and (3) to further social cohesion as a means of guaranteeing security and stability (Ministry of Foreign Affairs website). To ensure these goals, France has maintained a high level of international cooperation with its allies in various organizations.

France has been a member of the United Nations from its inception and holds a permanent seat on the Security Council. France has been one of the most vocal supporters of the United Nations and its associated institutions. That was particularly visible from the debate leading up to the U.S.-led invasion of Iraq. In 2003, France contributed $87.3 million, or 6.5 percent, to the operational budget of the United Nations and almost 8 percent of the costs for peacekeeping operations (French Permanent Mission to the UN website).

By 2004, France had backed nine UN peacekeeping missions, sending a total of 958 people to those missions. France's commitment to rapidly deployed peacekeeping forces led it to a standby arrangement system under the United Nations. While the forces remain under the French command structure, these troops are "set aside" and can be deployed in a little over a week for UN needs. As part of the 1999 arrangement, there are 5,000 troops that are part of this rapid deployment force. The force consists of the following: 944 command and support forces, 50 gendarmes, 1,988 army troops, 1,510 sailors (including eleven vessels), and 508 pilots (including seventeen aircraft) (ibid.).

France is a member of the North Atlantic Treaty Organization (NATO), having joined in 1949 as part of the original group of European delegates. A topic of much discussion is de Gaulle's withdrawal from the NATO military structure that took place in 1963 and was completed in 1966. De Gaulle's resentment of the military alliance, and particularly the nuclear guarantee of the United States, was seen as early as 1959.

This withdrawal was based on the belief that the U.S. military would not risk a Soviet attack on its own soil to defend Europe. As a result—or so de Gaulle believed—the military guarantee of

NATO served no real purpose. This allowed France to establish a unique security identity within the broader Atlantic framework (Bozo 1995, 223). There are a number of factors that indicate that this withdrawal from the command structure was relatively risk free. First, there was a significant U.S. presence in Western Europe. Second, there were consistent moves by the West Germans to include France in NATO proceedings. Some have argued that Franco-NATO relations have improved since the separation, with French troops remaining an uncommitted reserve for NATO (Treacher 2003, 38).

France became a member of the Organization for Security and Cooperation in Europe (OSCE) in 1973. During the Cold War, OSCE was established to promote East-West cooperation. Now OSCE plays a more preventative role in crisis management and post-conflict rebuilding (Organization for Security and Cooperation in Europe website). The nations of OSCE came together at the Paris summit to sign the Charter of Paris, which ensured the territorial integrity of Europe and limits the number of conventional troops on the Continent.

France was one of the original ten states that founded the Council of Europe in 1949. Headquartered in Strasbourg, the council was established to promote democracy and human rights within Europe; it now has forty-five member states. The Council of Europe has established a number of institutions that help further its mission, including the European Court of Human Rights, councils for social cohesion, and public health initiatives. France contributes $27,663,878 (12 percent) of the total budget (Council of Europe website).

France has long been a supporter of European integration, and it has been a party to the organizations that have evolved into the European Union. It was in a speech in 1950 that the French foreign minister proposed that the coal and steel industries of France and West Germany be coordinated under a single supranational authority—seen as the "birth" of the EU. This was expanded into the EEC (the Common Market) and Euratom, both established by the Treaty of Rome in 1958. The Treaty of European Union (or the Maastricht Treaty) was ratified in 1993; it established a European central bank and the euro currency, and it expanded the formal authority of the EU in foreign and security policy. Under the Maastricht Treaty the Western European Union (organized in 1948 in part as a defensive organization) was to be the military arm of the EU.

In 1995 the Eurocorps force became operational and drew from the WEU member states, NATO, and EU members. In 1999 the EU completely absorbed the functions of the WEU. The Eurocorps forms part of the Forces Answerable to Western European Union (FAWEU), legally deployable by either the EU or NATO. In 2003, the EU sent peacekeeping forces to replace NATO troops in Macedonia in what was seen as the first troop deployment of the organization (European Union website).

Size and Structure of the Military

One of the most significant areas of French security is the composition of the French nuclear arsenal. As part of a NATO-style flexible response, French security policy states that the nuclear deterrent be the response of last resort. It is composed of two strategic forces, the nuclear ballistic-missile submarine fleet (SSBN), and the air component, which consists of the Air Force Mirage 2000Ns and carrier-borne Navy Super Etendards, equipped with intermediate-range air-to-ground missiles. France currently has approximately 338 warheads, an overall reduction, given the restructuring of land-based systems in favor of sea-launched systems. There are a total of 288 warheads for the sixty-four submarine-launched ballistic missiles (SLBM) in four SSBNs. In 2000, the second of four newly established *Triomphant*-class SSBNs entered service. These are equipped with sixteen M45 SLBMs that are capable of carrying six warheads each. The new M51 will enter service in 2010, phasing out both previous missile systems. The air-launched cruise missile ASMP, with a total of fifty warheads, complements these systems. They will be phased out in 2007 with the introduction of the 500-km ASMP-A (Ameliore) system. France also maintains ten "substrategic" nuclear weapons that are also aircraft delivered (Nuclear Threat Initiative website).

The army has 137,000 active soldiers, excluding the 30,000 civilians. Included in that figure are the Foreign Legion (7,700 troops), the Overseas Marines (14,700 troops), and approximately 2,700 Special Forces troops (*Military Balance, 2003-2004*). The French Army structure includes a land combat forces command (CFAT) and the army logistics command (CFLT), both formed in 1998 as part of the restructuring plan. Under the CFAT command are four Forces Headquarters (EMF), responsible for operational planning. The EMFs are responsible for nine all-arms brigades. The CFLT is responsible for two logistics brigades, as well as specialized support regiments. Lastly, the European corps and the Franco-German brigade (BFA) are part of a joint brigade. The army is made up of a total of eighty-five regiments.

Units of the French Army employ both the AMX-30B2 (244 in active service) and the Leclerc main battle tank (370 in active service), which have been utilized in the Bosnian conflict. Armored infantry units use the highly mobile ERC-09F4 Sagaie, which has a 90mm gun, and the AMX-10C, which has a 105mm gun. Army air brigades utilize the Cougar transport helicopters, and the assault capabilities of that force are complemented by various configurations of the Gazelle helicopter (French Army website; *Military Balance, 2003-2004*).

The navy has a total of 44,250 sailors, which includes 1,700 marines, 6,800 as part of naval aviation, and 10,296 civilians. The French Navy falls under the command of two chains of command: the organic command and the operational

Table 2   French Nuclear Armament Levels, 1964–2004

Year	1964	1965	1970	1975	1980	1985	1990	1995	2000	2004
Warheads	4	32	36	188	250	360	505	500	470	338
	(0.01%)	(0.08%)	(0.09%)	(0.40%)	(0.46%)	(0.57%)	(0.90%)	(1.84%)	(2.15%)	(1.68%)
World Total	36,287	38,118	38,153	46,830	54,706	63,417	55,863	27,131	21,871	20,150

Sources

Military Balance, 2003–2004. London: International Institute for Strategic Studies.

Norris, Robert, and Hans Kristensen. 2002. "NRDC: Nuclear Notebook: Global Nuclear Stockpiles, 1945–2002." *Bulletin of the Atomic Scientists* 58, no. 6 (November/December): 103–104. http://www.thebulletin.org/.

command. The organic command is responsible for preparing the naval forces for readiness. This command is headed by the MoD and is led by the chief of naval staff (CEMM). Under this command are the four organic forces of the navy. The first of these forces is the Naval Action Force (FAN), which consists of the surface fleet of the navy, stationed at Toulon. Under FAN there are seventy-three combat and support ships with 12,200 personnel. Major vessels include the *Charles de Gaulle* aircraft carrier (40,600 tons' displacement, holding forty aircraft), the *Jeanne d'Arc* helicopter carrier, and twelve destroyers (including the *Cassard*, *Suffren*, *Georges Leygues*, and *Tourville* classes). Also under FAN authority is the Anti-Submarine Action Group (GASM), the Minewarfare Force that contains approximately eighty-nine vessels.

The second naval force is the FSM submarine force stationed at Brest, which employs the *Rubis* tactical submarine. This force has ten nuclear-powered attack and ballistic submarines and 3,800 sailors. The third force is the Naval Aviation force, and the naval aviation stations (NAS) in service of the French Navy. This consists of 137 combat aircraft, as well as 6,800 personnel, and is based in Toulon. The Naval Air Force utilizes 10 Rafale, 24 Super Entendard, 14 Atlantique, and 13 Nord 262 combat aircraft. There are 15 Lynx helicopters in active service, with 17 in store, and 21 Alouette III helicopters augmenting this force.

The fourth force consists of the naval fusiliers and commandos (FORFUSCO). This force contains the fusiliers, who protect sensitive facilities, and the naval commandos, the special operations force based in Lorient under a joint command with the gendarmerie maritime. There are fourteen specialized units under this force command, with 1,700 sailors (*Military Balance*, 2003-2004).

The operational command, as with all of the armed forces, is placed under the permanent command of the French chief of defense staff (CEMA). The CEMA is the military advisor to the government, responsible for commanding the active deployed forces. This deployment is often allocated to appointed operations controllers, who control naval operations in their respective operations theater. These commands consist of the following: CECLANT (Atlantic Zone commander), CECMED (Mediterranean Zone commander), ALINDIEN (Indian Ocean maritime zone commander), and ALPACI (Pacific maritime zone commander). The commando forces of FORFUSCO fall under the operational authority of the COS (special operations command) (French Navy website).

The total manpower of the air force is 64,000 airmen, excluding 6,000 civilians. The French Air Force has three hierarchical levels and three complementary structures for training and combat deployment. The top command level is the chief of the air staff (CEMAA); the second are the major commands; lastly follow the air bases. The three complementary structures are as follows: the operational structure, which controls the Strategic Air Force Command (CFAS), and the Air Defense and Air Operations Command (CDAOA). The second structure is the organic specialized structure that controls the Air Combat Command (CFAC), the Air Projection Command (CFAP), the Air Surveillance, Information, Communication Command (CASSIC), the French Air Force Training Command (CEAA), and the Air Force Commando Command (CFCA). The last structure is the organic territorial structure that is made up of three air regions. The main combat equipment for the Air Force includes 380 fighter aircraft including the Mirage 2000, Mirage F1a, and Jaguar. There are approximately 100 tactical and logistic transport aircraft, including the C160 Transall transport and 14 tanker planes. The air force also contains four AWAC detection and communication aircraft, as well as the Cougar combat SAR helicopter (French Air Force website).

There are approximately 101,399 gendarmes, including 1,966 civilians. While under the MoD, the gendarmerie is under the direct control of the General Directorate of the Gendarmerie Nationale (DGGN). The national gendarmerie is a police force with military credentials responsible for the protection of French citizens and infrastructure, both at home and abroad. As part of this mission the gendarmerie is part of the larger criminal investigative and administrative police force. In a military capacity the gendarmerie is part of the nuclear defense force, as well as being used for intelligence gathering, domestic security, and combat operations. The gendarmerie is also stationed abroad as part of NATO and WEU forces, and it can be conceived of as a military reserve force. Gendarmerie units contain eighty armored vehicles and fifty aircraft.

The service is organized into the following subdivisions: the departmental gendarmerie, which has 3,607 brigades and units throughout France, and 700 specialized units (transportation, surveillance, and intervention platoons, mountain units, and air sections) in particular regions. The mobile gendarmerie has 128 squadrons, part of the reserve forces for the other military branches. There are also various specialized units that have individual organizational arrangements, such as security for government officials. Lastly are the overseas detachments of gendarmerie units, which are the French forces stationed primarily in Germany and Africa. Their 20,000 personnel and equipment are permanently stationed in these overseas departments (National Gendarmerie website).

Budget

In 2002, the French government spent $33.59 billion on military expenditures. Total French employment in arms-producing industries was 250,000 in 2001, down 10,000 from the previous year (SIPRI 2003). The most recent data available indicate that France spent $3,550 million on military research and development (a 22 percent decrease from 1995). Military research and development made up 25 percent of the total share of government research and development. France is one of the largest international producers of military armaments, next to the United States and the United Kingdom. There are seven primary arms producers that operate within France. The largest of these is Thales, which totaled $160 million in arms sales in 2000, ranking it seventh among world arms producers. Other important manufacturers include DCN, CEA, SNECMA Groupe, and Dassault Aviation Groupe.

The French state is a 15 percent shareholder in the European Aeronautic Defense and Space Company (EADS), which is a joint venture with Germany and Spain. France ranks fifty-eighth as a recipient of major conventional weapons for the years 1998–2002, importing $297 million in arms for the period. Conversely, France ranks third as a supplier of major conventional weapons, totaling $8.31 billion from 1989 to 2002 (ibid.).

Civil-Military Relations/The Role of the Military in Domestic Politics

France has seen a strained relationship between civilian and military authorities since the end of World War II. These relations could be a product of the military conscription policy, but the transition to a professionalized French military may indicate a strong respect for the rule of law. Some scholars believe that a significant gap will develop between the two (Vennesson 2003). In general, there is a rise in domestic support for the military, particularly among older nonprofessionals within France (ibid., 35). While de Gaulle was the general of the French forces in World War II, it was his ability to firmly put down the unrest during the Algerian conflict that led to his rise as president. While a military figure, however, his authority always came from his civil position. Civilian control over the military has never been questioned in modern France. In general, the public is confident in the loyalty of the military to the state, but much of France believes that the military is separate from general society (Vennesson 2003). Article 15 of the Constitution of 1958 stipulates that the president is the commander-in-chief of the military. Furthermore, Article 21 states that the prime minister is responsible for national defense, while only parliament has the ability to declare war.

Terrorism

The attacks on the United States of September 11 fundamentally altered the way in which the major powers understood their security, and France is no different. The change from terrorism on a local level, over local interests, to the major issue confronting international security has been dramatic. Where France differs from many other Western nations is in its vocal support for addressing terrorism through international organizations. France has stated unequivocally that the forum for fighting international terrorism is the United Nations (outlined in resolutions 1267, 1373, and 1390). Furthermore the G7/G8 is the organization that should address antiterror funding; the EU, through Europol and Eurojust, is the organization to address criminal activities. The official French position is that the underlying causes of terrorism are military actions, such as the U.S. involvement in the occupation of Iraq (French Ministry of Foreign Affairs website).

The French executive does not have one umbrella organization that is responsible for terrorism prevention and emergency response. The French have relied more heavily on the centralized planning and coordination of all state-level actors. There are two new groups that were formed after September 11 to address serious threats to French security on a similar scale. The G.I.G.N. (the national gendarmerie intervention group) and R.A.I.D. (research, assistance, intervention, and deterrence) were established as rapid-response teams designed to counter large-scale terrorist attacks; they were part of the larger Vigipirate plan to increase threat response. French law allows terrorism to be prosecuted as a separable offense, with greater punishments. Acts of eco-terrorism, conspiracy to commit terrorism, and the financing of terrorism are considered criminal offenses. Such offenses are tried under a separate national jurisdiction that has a separate procedural system (French Ministry of Foreign Affairs website).

Relationship with the United States

Franco-American relations have a long tradition spanning 200 years, and a symbol of what brings the two nations together can be seen in New York harbor. Modern relations have seen the two nations brought close during and after the landings of the Allied forces in Normandy to liberate France; troubled under the nationalist policies of President de Gaulle; and distant with the threat of a Security Council veto over the war in Iraq. Although the two nations remain cool to each other as of late, this does not mean that the two can ignore each other.

Despite the visible conflicts over Iraq in the United Nations and the statements made by President Chirac against President Bush's unilateralism, the United States still sees Europe as its traditional global ally, both in security and in economics. Conversely, France sees the United States as the guarantor of both European and Middle Eastern security. There have been many public instances in which the two countries have "snubbed" each other. These disagreements have been countered, however, by the recent deployment of U.S. and French forces to Haiti. That troop action led the French foreign minister Dominique de Villepin to calmly note the "perfect Franco-American co-ordination" in Haiti—unexpected words, given the present climate between the countries. At the same time, President Bush left French authorities in the dark for some time regarding his intention to join the French in the sixtieth anniversary of D-day (*Economist* website 2004). Moreover the recent trade sanctions placed on the United States by the EU, and the public sentiment in the United States toward "French fries," leave lingering suspicions that the political fallout of Iraq has not passed.

The Future

The French defense minister submitted the Military Program 2003–2008 in 2002, outlining the transition to the French 2015 armed forces model. This program makes a number of stipulations regarding increased military expenditures, modernization, and the newly professionalized forces under a new security environment. The stated goals of the new program note the increased need for force flexibility and precision, with the increased threats of biological/chemical/radioactive weapons from terrorists.

As part of this transition the MoD plans on increasing non–Gendarmerie Nationale spending to more than $18.644 billion by 2008. This monetary increase will be coupled by a personnel increase of 446,653 by 2008 (including gendarmerie) (MoD, Military Program 2003–2008 website). One of the most uncertain areas within French security policy is the creation of an independent European military force outside NATO. While the member states have reaffirmed the strengthening of the "European pillar" within NATO, the continued deployment of forces outside Europe may indicate the feasibility of such a force. It is clear that after the intervention of forces in Somalia, the former Yugoslavia, Rwanda, Cote D'Ivoire, and Haiti, France will continue to remain active in the international community. This may indicate a dramatic shift away from the Gaullist-style nationalist policies to an active interventionist state.

References, Recommended Readings, and Websites

Books

Bozo, Frederic. 1995. "France and Security in the New Europe: Between the Gaullist Legacy and the Search for a New Model." In *Remaking the Hexagon: New France in the New Europe*, Gregory Flynn, ed. Boulder: Westview Press, pp. 213–232.

Britt, Albert Sidney, III. 1985. *The Wars of Napoleon*. Wayne, NJ: Avery.

Carr, William. 1991. *The Origins of the Wars of German Unification*. London: Longman.

Dalloz, Jacques. 1990. *The War in Indo-China 1945–54*. Savage, MD: Gill and Macmillan.

Gulick, Edward Vose. 1967. *Europe's Classical Balance of Power*. Ithaca, NY: Cornell University Press.

Haine, W. Scott. 2000. *The History of France*. London: Greenwood Press.

Howorth, Jolyon. 1997. "France." In *The European Union and National Defense Policy*, Jolyon Howorth and Anand Menon, eds. London: Routledge.

Levi, Anthony. 2000. "Cardinal Richelieu: And the Making of France." New York: Carrol and Graf.

Military Balance, 2003–2004. London: International Institute for Strategic Studies.

Popkin, Jeremy D. 1994. *A History of Modern France*. Englewood Cliffs, NJ: Prentice Hall.

Prior, Robin, and Trevor Wilson. 1998. "Eastern Front and Western Front, 1916–1917." In *World War I: A History*, Hew Strachan, ed. Oxford: Oxford University Press.

Schom, Alan. 1997. *Napoleon Bonaparte*. New York: HarperCollins.

Schonfield, Hugh. 1969. *The Suez Canal in Peace and War, 1869–1969*. University of Miami Press.

SIPRI Yearbook 2003. New York: Humanities Press.

Tiersky, Ronald. 1995. *The Mitterrand Legacy and the Future of French Security Policy*. Washington, DC: National Defense University Press.

Treacher, Adrian. 2003. *French Interventionism: Europe's Last Global Player?* Aldershot, UK: Ashgate.

William, Samuel R. 1998. "The Origins of the War." In *World War I: A History*, Hew Strachan, ed. Oxford: Oxford University Press.

Winks, Robin W., and R. J. Q. Adams. 2003. *Europe, 1890–1945: Crisis and Conflict*. New York: Oxford University Press.

Articles/Newspapers

Gordon, Philip H. 2002. "France, the United States and the 'War on Terrorism.'" Brookings Institution. http://www.brookings.edu/fp/cusf/analysis/terrorism.htm.

"Happiness Is Doing Things Together." 2004. (March 4). http://www.economist.com.

Norris, Robert S., and Hans M. Kristensen. 2002. "Nuclear Notebook." *Bulletin of Atomic Scientists* 58, no. 6:103–104.

Vennesson, Pascal. 2003. "Civil-Military Relations in France: Is There a Gap?" *Journal of Strategic Studies* 26, no. 2: 29–42.

Websites

Carnegie Endowment for International Peace. "Proliferation News and Resources": http://www.ceip.org/files/nonprolif/default.asp.

Central Intelligence Agency. *The World Factbook:* http://www.cia.gov.

Council of Europe: http://www.coe.int.

European Union: http://europa.eu.int/.

French Air Force: http://www.defense.gouv.fr/air/index.html.

French Army: http://www.defense.gouv.fr/terre/index.html.

French Ministry of Defense: Military Program 2003–2008: http://www.defense.gouv.fr/english/files/d140/index.htm.

French Ministry of Foreign Affairs: http://www.diplomatie.gouv.fr.

French Navy: http://www.defense.gouv.fr/marine/anglais/present/present.htm.

French Permanent Mission to the United Nations: http://www.un.int/france/.

International Organization of the Francophonie: http://www.francophonie.org.

National Gendarmerie: http://www.defense.gouv.fr/gendarmerie/index.html.

North Atlantic Treaty Organization: http://www.nato.int.

Nuclear Threat Initiative: http://www.nti.org.

Organization for Security and Cooperation in Europe: http://www.osce.org/.

United Nations: http://www.un.org.

Germany

Özgür Özdamar

Geography and History

The Federal Republic of Germany (FRG) is located at the heart of Europe. It has nine neighbors: Denmark in the north, The Netherlands, Belgium, Luxembourg and France in the west, Switzerland and Austria in the south, and the Czech Republic and Poland in the east. Being in the center of Europe, Germany is a link between East and West as well as between Scandinavia and the Mediterranean region. Germany covers 357,021 square kilometers, an area that is slightly smaller than Montana. The geography is diverse. The country has lowlands in the north, uplands in the center, and Bavarian Alps in the south. Germany has a population of 82.3 million, which makes it one of the most densely populated countries of Europe (Kappler and Reichart 1996; CIA *World Factbook*).

The roots of the German nation are usually dated back to the eighth century and initially consisted of people in the eastern part of the Franconian realm. The emperor Charlemagne united people speaking Germanic and Romance dialects. The word *Deutsch* (German) was probably first used in the eighth century to define the language spoken in the eastern part of the Franconian realm. The region's name, *Deutschland* (Germany), stems from that root. The transition to the German Reich is usually dated back to 911, when Conrad I was elected ruler; he is considered to have been the first German king. His official title was first "Frankish King" and later "Roman King." The country was called Roman Empire after the eleventh century and Holy Roman Empire after the thirteenth century (Kappler 1996).

The sixteenth and seventeenth centuries were times of disorder for Germany. The reformation led by Martin Luther, the religious conflicts between Protestants and Catholics, the Peasant's Revolution of 1525, and the Augsburg Peace in 1555—which was a settlement stating that each prince could choose between Lutheranism and Roman Catholicism for his territory—were the milestones of the century. The conflict between Protestants and Catholics continued into the next century; this resulted in the Thirty Years' War, which turned into a systemic war in Europe and ended with the 1648 Peace of Westphalia. The Westphalia agreement is considered the founding document of the modern nation-state system that we live in today.

However, Germany failed to consolidate as a nation-state in the following centuries. The old Holy Roman Empire survived until it was destroyed by the Napoleonic Wars of 1792–1815; instead, German sovereign states established the German Confederation, which lasted until 1866. This was a loose confederation composed of thirty-nine states (Columbia Encyclopedia). Germany as a nation-state was founded in 1871 by Premier Otto von Bismarck. The first seventy-five years of Germany as a nation-state are a history of interstate conflicts; beginning with the Franco-Prussian War of 1871, aggressive German foreign policy has been one of the main reasons behind two world wars. These wars ruined the country and led to its being divided into two states from 1945 to 1990.

With the decline of communism in the early 1990s, East and West Germany unified, and the victorious four allies of World War II lifted the supervision on Germany. No other European country was more deeply affected by the end of the Cold War than Germany. The changes in the alliances, the dissolution of the Warsaw Pact, the withdrawal of the Soviet forces from Eastern Europe, unification of the Federal Republic of Germany (FRG) and German Democratic Republic (GDR)—all shifted the balance of power in Europe in favor of Germany.

More than four decades after the war, Germany regained its full sovereignty in the early 1990s (Bluth 2000).

Presently, Germany is the largest economy and the most populous nation in the European Union. Thus in future Continental issues, such as the economy, politics, and defense, Germany is a key actor. Two world wars, the occupation of Germany by the Allies, and the East-West confrontation in the Cold War have been the important factors that have shaped today's German security and foreign policy.

After the normalization of the status of Germany during early 1990s, the great economic power and influence of Germany in the EU and Europe at first led to suspicion about an increase of German power. However, German foreign and security policy proved to be peaceful. The developments in German foreign policy showed that the country is sincerely in favor of reducing the size of its own military—the Bundeswehr—and basing its security policy on multilateral arrange-

Table 1 Germany: Key Statistics

Type of government	Federal republic
Population (millions)	82,398,326 (July 2003)
Religion	Protestant 34%, Roman Catholic 34%, Muslim 3.7%, unaffiliated or other 28.3%
Main industries	Iron, steel, coal, cement, chemicals, machinery, vehicles, machine tools, electronics, food and beverages, shipbuilding, textiles
Main security threats	Political and economic instability in Southern and Eastern Europe, especially civil wars in Europe
Defense spending (% GDP)	1.38% (2002)
Size of military	active, 284,500; reserves, 358,650 (2002)
Number of civil wars since 1945	none
Number of interstate wars since 1945	none

Sources

Central Intelligence Agency Website. 2004. CIA *World Factbook*. http://www.cia.gov/cia/publications/factbook/ (accessed May 15, 2005).

International Institute for Strategic Studies (IISS). 2003. *The Military Balance 2003–2004*. London: IISS and Oxford University Press.

ments, most of all by emphasizing the European Union.

Today, Germany has the largest economy and is the most populous nation of the European Union. The country's strategic position between East and West also contributes to its further importance for the EU. Germany is not only an important force in Europe but also a major world economy. The total production of the country was $1.976 trillion in 2002, which makes it the third biggest economy of the world, after the United States and Japan (World Bank Group). However, this very powerful and advanced economy slowed during the 1990s. One of the main reasons for this relatively weak performance has been the costs associated with the modernization and integration of the East German economy. Transfers from West to East equal roughly $70 billion each year. In addition, Germany's aging population and high unemployment raised questions about the social security system. Combined with those difficulties are the challenges of European integration. Presently Germany is in breach of the EU's 3 percent debt limit, because of rising government expenditures and a fall in revenues (CIA *World Factbook*).

In terms of its government and politics, Germany is a consolidated democracy. It is a federal republic composed of sixteen states as administrative units. The main political parties are Alliance '90/Greens; Christian Democratic Union (CDU); Christian Social Union (CSU); and Social Democratic Party (SPD). Since 1998, SPD and Greens—the Red-Green coalition—has ruled Germany.

Regional Geopolitics

The end of the Cold War was celebrated by the European nations, in the hope that the East-West conflict would now come to an end. In fact, the last decade proved that to be so: a conflict between Western Europe and the former communist countries is only a remote possibility. Many socialist countries of Eastern Europe have become, and will remain, members of Western political and economic organizations, such as NATO or the EU. However, both Europe and Germany face new challenges in the new century. The threat is no longer the military threat from the Soviets, however. The biggest security challenges for Germany and for most of Europe are the economic instability in the former Warsaw Pact countries and ethnic rivalries that may lead to civil and interstate wars in Europe (Sarotte 2001; Bluth 2000).

Mass migrations from the east because of political upheavals—that is, ethnic conflicts or economic deprivations—are two of the biggest problems for German security. Schlör (1993) suggests that because of its geographical position, Germany is open to mass migration and waves of refugees. By September 1992, Germany had taken in more than 220,000 refugees from the civil war in Bosnia-Herzegovina alone. In addition, Germany's liberal laws on political asylum and generous social service provisions make the country attractive for political asylum seekers. To give an example from the first years of the post–Cold War era, 256,000 people in 1991 and 438,191 people in 1992 sought political asylum in Germany (ibid.). By 1995 the foreign population of Germany amounted to 8.8 percent, leading to the revival of a xenophobia that threatened the political stability of the country (Bluth 2000).

Second, economic instabilities in Eastern Europe can be a source of security problems for Germany. Eastern Europe and Russia are important export markets for Germany, as well as sources of strategic raw materials (Schlör 1993). Third, ethnic issues in the region may take Germany into an interstate conflict. Germany might, for example, be drawn into a conflict to protect a German minority in Eastern or Southern Europe. The Kosovo problem was a prime example, in which Germany would have to be involved militarily. Similarly, if conflicts in Eastern and Southern Europe spill into areas close to Germany, the country could be adversely affected. A worst-case example might be radioactive fallout from an accident or from a terrorist attack on a power plant. Other potential threats include terrorist groups operating in Germany, especially fundamentalist Islamic groups, organized crime moving from East to West, Soviet-design nuclear power stations, and nuclear weapons in former Soviet territory (Bluth 2000). To sum up, then, Germany is in the center of Europe and affected by new security threats from all sides. For that reason Germany has emphasized the importance of collective security in Europe and European defense institutions.

Conflict Past and Present

The history of modern Germany is shaped by the historical rivalries and alliances of Europe in the late nineteenth and twentieth centuries. Conflict with France, Britain, and the United States in the West; Czechoslovakia, Poland, and Russia in the East; and alliances with Austria-Hungary and the Ottoman Empire in World War I and Italy and Japan in World War II are the milestones of German history in the first half of the twentieth century.

In terms of protracted conflicts, certainly the most important is the French-German conflict. The fighting between France and Germany, which lasted at least three centuries, is among the longest and most intense wars in the history of international relations (Brecher and Wilkenfeld 1997).

The great conflicts of this rivalry are the Napoleonic Wars of 1792–1815; the Franco-Prussian War of 1870–1871; World War I (1914–1918); and World War II (1939–1945). During the Napoleonic Wars the French had some initial victories, but they lost the final battle at Waterloo in 1815. In 1870–1871, the Franco-Prussian war resulted in France's defeat and also the unification of Germany. In World War I and World War II, Germany defeated France but was eventually defeated by the Allies. In both conflicts, the two countries suffered enormous losses of men and resources.

In addition to these destructive wars, there were five international crises between France and Germany in the interwar period of 1918–1939: Rhenish rebellions in 1920 (Germany's noncompliance with post–World War I agreements), German reparations in 1921, Ruhr I in 1923, Ruhr II (disagreements about German reparations) in 1924, and the remilitarization of the Rhineland in 1936 (ibid.).

Another important international rivalry that involved Germany was the Czechoslovakia crisis in 1938–1939. According to the International Crisis Behavior (ICB) dataset, that conflict originated in 1919 when the German-speaking areas of the Sudetenland were allocated to the new Czechoslovak state. Hitler claimed those lands from the Czechoslovak state, which led to the escalation of the crisis. As a result, Britain, France, Germany, and Italy were called for the Munich Conference in September 1938, in which Britain and France appeased Germany and gave up Czechoslovakian independence. Germany occupied the claimed lands and a bigger war was avoided—although only for one year.

Both World War I and World War II were initiated by German aggression. In both wars, Germany initially invaded most of Europe but was defeated at the end. In World War II, Germany was occupied by the Allies and given a special status for more than four decades. It was only after 1990 that the legacy of the war was lifted.

After the defeat of Germany in 1945, neither West nor East Germany was involved in a major armed conflict. In the postwar period, West German foreign policy depended mainly on disarmament, influence in international relations as a "civil power," and peaceful unification of East and West Germany. By the end of the Cold War in the early 1990s, Germany had no potential military confrontations with any of its neighbors, for the first time in its history. A relatively secure environment in Europe after the Cold War has led to the restructuring and downsizing of the German armed forces over the last decade (Bluth 2000).

Alliance Structure

The important past and present alliance structure of modern Germany can be analyzed under five headings. Germany participated in the Triple Alliance of 1882, the Central Alliance of World War I, the Axis Powers of World War II, and NATO and the Western European Union since 1955, and at present is the prime advocate for a future European defense system. Thus, the current alliance structure of Germany should be analyzed within a framework consisting of its relations with NATO, the Common Foreign and Security Policy (CFSP) of the EU, and the United States.

The formation of the Triple Alliance began with the foundation of Germany as a nation-state in 1871. In the Franco-Prussian war of 1871–1872, France lost the provinces of Alsace-Lorraine to Germany. That caused an enduring problem and hostility between the two countries that was yet to be resolved in the next century. Against this threat from France, Germany allied with Austria-Hungary and Russia in the Three Emperors' League. However, because of the rivalry between Austria-Hungary and Russia in the Balkans, that alliance was never developed. After the Congress of Berlin in 1878, relations with Russia got worse, and German premier Bismarck made a secret defensive alliance with Austria-Hungary. In 1882, Italy had signed another secret treaty with Germany and Austria-Hungary as a result of its rivalry with France over Tunisia. The Triple Alliance was established and renewed periodically until 1913. Italy was never closely tied to the alliance, however, because of the conflict of interests with Austria-Hungary in the Balkan region (Columbia Encyclopedia).

"Central Powers" is a term used to define the alliance between Germany, Austria-Hungary, the Ottoman Empire, and Bulgaria during World War I. Germany and Austria-Hungary had been allies since 1879, but Italy secretly decided not to be a member of the Triple Alliance in 1902. With the outbreak of World War I in 1914, the Ottoman Empire declared war on Russia in October and thus joined the Germany and Austria-Hungary alliance. Bulgaria was the last nation to enter the war, in October 1915, invading Serbia with Germany and Austria-Hungary. All the Central Powers signed the armistice in the fall of 1918, as a result of the Allies' successful advance on many fronts (Wikipedia).

Between the two world wars, Germany was in a constant crisis with France about various issues. The enduring problems of the Franco-German conflict were not solved by the Versailles Agreement of 1919, and Italy had faced opposition in the League of Nations about its Ethiopia policies. Thus Germany and Italy became allies once again; the term first used by Benito Mussolini was the *Rome-Berlin Axis* when he referred to the treaty of friendship signed between the two countries in 1936. Japan joined the Axis in 1940 with the Tripartite Treaty. Then Hungary, Romania, Slovakia in 1940, and Bulgaria in 1941 joined the Axis as lesser powers. The alliance between the Axis powers came to an end with the end of World War II (Wikipedia).

In 1945, Germany unconditionally surrendered, and it was occupied by four Allied powers. The United States, the United Kingdom, the USSR, and France divided the country into occupation zones and assumed the responsibility for its administration. In 1948, Allied administration ended, and in 1949 the Federal Republic of Germany in the west and German Democratic Republic in the east were established. After the foundation of the two states, the problem of Berlin became more important. However, negotiations with the Soviet Union about a reunification did not solve the problems; beginning in 1954, NATO members regularized their relations with the Federal Republic.

In October 1954 the Paris agreement was signed, in which the three Western powers agreed to terminate the occupation regime, recognize the Federal Republic of Germany as a sovereign state, and invite the Federal Republic of Germany to join NATO and accede to the Western European Union. On May 5, 1955, the FRG became a member of NATO. In 1990, West Germany and the Soviet Union agreed on East Germany's membership in NATO during the unification process (NATO Update 2004).

The 1990s witnessed the end of the Cold War and the formation of new alliances in the world. Although Germany is a firm ally of NATO and the United Sates, German foreign policy–makers emphasize the necessity of a European security and defense policy independent from but coexisting with NATO. To make a finer analysis of the current alliance structure and the transformation of German security policy, we need to focus on the changing German foreign policy, the deepening of the European integration with new institutional designs such as Common Foreign and Security Policy, and the relations with NATO and the United States.

Since the establishment of the Federal Republic, German foreign and security policy has been based on the concept of *Westintegration*. Either under Konrad Adenauer's *Politik der Stärke* (that is, "politics by strength," which entailed a powerful Germany against the Soviets and a closer alliance with the West) or Willy Brandt's *Ostpolitik* (meaning "east politics," suggesting a more neutral stand in the West-East confrontation and détente), the main idea was to be connected to the Western political institutions. That was not only because of the international agreements following World War II; the German government also committed itself to *Westintegration* to complete the rehabilitation of Germany in the international system, to overcome the historical Franco-German rivalry for hegemony in Europe, and to regain the freedom of action in international relations. However, all these aims were difficult to achieve because of the special position of Germany. Thus Germany, to be able to pursue an independent foreign policy, has become an advocate of multilateralism in Europe and using intergovernmental organizations, such as the EU or NATO, to solve international disputes and foster cooperation. In fact, it was argued in the literature that foreign policy and diplomacy emphasizing European policy were the means whereby the new German state constructed its own identity (Duffield 1998; Bluth 2000).

The unexpected end of the Cold War and the opportunity for unification denoted the beginning of substantial changes required in German security and foreign policy. These developments benefited Germany most in political and economic ways. Briefly, Germany is the third largest economy of the world; demographically it is the most populous of the EU, in the center of the continent, in a strategically advantageous position. In addition, the withdrawal of Soviet forces, with Germany gaining and the Soviets losing territory, changed the military balance of power in favor of Germany. Beyond those developments, pressure by the United States and the other Allies on Germany to take a more active role in security issues created such an environment that German policymakers could no longer continue their diplomatically active, militarily pacifist agenda.

The support for further integration of the EU and efforts to create a solid European security system have been key characteristics of German defense policy in the last decade. German policymakers trust the institutional designs of Europe to prevent domestic economic and political instabilities, as well as creating a common defense policy. The first example of an important step for further integration was the Single European Act of 1987, which began the substantial integration of European economic institutions.

In terms of political integration, the milestone has been the Treaty on European Union—or Maastricht Treaty—in 1992. With that treaty, the EU has left the entirely intergovernmental and ineffective European Political Cooperation (EPC) policies and established the Common Foreign and Security Policy. With Maastricht, the members of the EU committed themselves to common and joint action on all issues except defense, and agreed on asking for the help of the Western European Union on defense matters (Forster and Wallace 2000).

The careful language of the treaty, distinguishing common defense issues from others, is important. Germany is the greatest supporter of further integration, especially on foreign policy and security matters. Other than the specific reasons that force German policymakers to suggest multilateralism, pan-Europeanists also believe that without a common foreign and security policy, further development of the economic and monetary union would be limited. That is why Germany insisted on a deeper integration, with the French and Germans at the center. The creation of a significant security policy for the EU is imperative for that aim (Nuttall 2000; Bluth 2000).

However, that view was not shared by all major powers of Europe, such as the United Kingdom, and is approached suspiciously by the United States. CFSP is already the most difficult policy to accomplish because of its connections to high politics issues such as sovereignty, national identity, and statehood. Also, in a union like the EU, in which there are vast differences between the members, there are always various agendas and clashing national interests. Beyond all those political and institutional matters, the way in which members perceive how the institutions should look differs greatly, too. The United Kingdom's continuous Euroskepticism, its different "philosophy" as to the future of the EU—especially on CFSP areas—is an important challenge for Germany and the further development of the CFSP. According to the British perspective, the core of European security and defense is NATO and the alliance with the United States, and there is no need for European defense institutions.

Although Germany would agree with Britain that European defense cannot be established without NATO and U.S. involvement, it still emphasizes the importance of a separate institutional design that will develop a pan-European peace order. According to German policymakers, the EU is the heart of that stability; to extend this beyond the borders of Europe and defend Europe, CFSP and a Common Defense Policy are imperative.

In addition to these pressures, the CFSP and CDP were a result of moves by the United States to push Europe to share the defense burden (Bluth 2000). According to Bluth (ibid.), there are three reasons why Germany suggested the creation of a European pillar of NATO: (1) to convince the United States that the Europeans were serious about making their own defense contributions; (2) to permit the consideration of European interests on a collective basis, in case they are different from those of the United States; and (3) to enable France to be drawn into a framework of European security that was outside NATO but not in contradiction to alliance commitments and objectives.

Although the United States has been a great supporter of European defense in principle, it was nevertheless suspicious of a European Union that might detract from U.S. leadership in NATO (Hyde-Price 2000). Developments in 2002 and 2003, before the Iraq War, might be given as an examples supporting such suspicions.

The next step in creating a European defense mechanism was to establish Franco-German brigades called Eurocorps, created in 1992. How Eurocorps is connected to NATO, the WEU, or the United Nations is left ambiguous, because France and Germany could not agree on the use of force outside of the NATO agreement. While Germany defended the necessity of UN legitimacy, France argued that a UN mandate means the use of Eurocorps by non-Europeans. The compromise suggested that the corps would be used in missions supported by the United Nations wherever member European nations approved. The mission of the Eurocorps was defined as such: (1) The Eurocorps is to be prepared to carry out humanitarian aid missions and population assistance missions following a natural or technical disaster. (2) It can also be made available for peace-restoring or peacekeeping missions, for example within the scope of the United Nations Organization (UNO) or the Organization for Security and Co-operation in Europe (OSCE). (3) The Eurocorps can be employed as well as a mechanized army corps in high-intensity combat operations, in order to ensure the common defense of the Allies in application of Article 5 of the Washington Treaty (NATO), or of the Brussels Treaty (WEU) (Eurocorps website).

British and U.S. reactions to the establishment of a German-French military unit were not quite positive. The U.S. administration at the time expressed explicit concerns that prevented other NATO-WEU members from participating in Eurocorps. Today there are only Belgium, Luxembourg, and Spain participating, in addition to the original two. However, according to some explanations, the Eurocorps project is still a success for Germany: It provides an international framework in which the constitutional and political limitations of German participation in "out-of-area" missions can be gradually overcome by becoming locked in a network of commitments. Also, it draws France closer to NATO (Bluth 2000). Although there are inherent contradictions and weak arrangements, the establishment of Eurocorps is an important step for the institutional design that Germany aspires to establish.

The following very significant step in establishing a common security and defense policy was the Amsterdam Treaty in 1997. Germany has made great efforts to ensure the future consolidation of the defense policy. The Amsterdam Treaty states that the EU can examine all aspects of foreign and security policy. Also, closer links with the WEU are articulated, such as the possibility of an EU-WEU merger, and the EU can avail itself of the WEU on defense matters (Forster and Wallace 2000). This could be a real revolution for the EU and its CFSP and CDP, if the German way of ambitious implementation were taken. Defense could be the fourth pillar of the union. However, because of British opposition to an enhanced and clearer definition of the relations between the EU and the WEU—the United Kingdom obviously wants those two institutions to be separate—the vague nature of the defense policy remains a problem today. Although the treaty clearly refers to the possibility

of an EU-WEU merger, the careful language of the treaty document reveals the disagreeing views of the members on the issue. The biggest obstacle to further consolidation of a CDP is the lack of support for the German approach. Although Germany is willing to take the leadership role in creation of the CDP, only Benelux countries supported the merger of EU and WEU. Even France was in favor of a more intergovernmentalist approach.

However, the Labor Party government in Britain has slightly eased the conflict between Germany and the United Kingdom in terms of defense policy. In 1998, Tony Blair indicated that he will no longer oppose European military cooperation, provided that it does not hurt relations with the United States. Finally, the Nice Treaty, which entered into force on February 1, 2003, contains amendments that reflect the operative development of the European Security and Defense Policy (ESDP) as an independent EU project, and as such it achieves another step for the European defense project (Federal Foreign Office).

The situation between Germany/France and the United States/United Kingdom worsened at the peak of the Iraq crisis in early 2003. Germany and France sought for international legitimacy by UN resolutions, while the United States and the United Kingdom insisted on a military intervention even without a UN resolution. In April of the same year, France and Germany, with Belgium and Luxembourg, proposed that the EU have its own military planning headquarters, situated in the village of Tervuren, just outside Brussels. In addition, the EU constitution, which was planned to be finished by the end of 2003, would include a mutual defense clause. Britain, although not against the European defense idea in principle, expressed its concerns about how this would affect transatlantic relations, especially after such a crisis in early 2003. The draft wording of the EU constitution clause states: "If a member state is the victim of armed aggression on its territory, the other member states shall give it aid and assistance by all the means in their power, military or other, in accordance with Article 51 of the United Nations Charter" (Roxburgh 2003).

But the British insist that the clause should clearly include the fact that commitment in this area shall be consistent with commitments under NATO, which, for those states that are members, remains the foundation of their collective defense (ibid.). The December 2003 EU summit ended in failure, without producing a constitutional document.

The conclusion we can draw from this review is, currently, that as yet there is no institution or treaty providing European defense. Thus the future of the European alliance is ambiguous. There are treaties and attempts to create tangible assets, such as Eurocorps, yet the German push for a solid approach to European defense is far from being accomplished.

Thus, in crisis times, the EU reaction is not, and will not likely be, consistent. Many critics refer to the different responses of the EU members to the Yugoslav crisis in the 1990s and to the Iraq War in 2003 as evidence of the EU's inability to develop foreign and defense policies in times of crisis. The EU responses to such crises are ad hoc.

The German approach to security and defense problems, and the recent cooperation with France, seem to be hopeful for the future of the EU. Such a huge economic and social integration cannot be thought of without a mechanism for defense. The best way to achieve a common

defense policy is to create institutions which recognize that the cooperation of the United States and integration of NATO are vitally important. Although the Franco-German pact seems to acknowledge that fact, in practice they have not yet induced enough U.S. support. The future of European defense depends on assuring the United States that CDP is not against NATO and U.S. interests in Europe.

Size and Structure of the Military

The peacetime strength of the Bundeswehr is some 284,500 personnel, including 94,500 conscripts. The reserve figures are more impressive, with some 358,650 men raising Germany's wartime strength to around 640,000 (*Military Balance 2003–2004*). The army counts 191,350, the navy 25,650, and the air force 67,500 men. The German armed forces are divided into three categories: (1) Basic Military Organization (BMO), which includes the military installations necessary for peacetime command, administration, support, and training; (2) Main Defense Forces (MDF), the backbone of national and alliance defense; and (3) Reaction Forces (RF), with a strength of 50,000 military personnel, which are Germany's readily available contribution to NATO, the WEU, and international military peace standards (Goebel 1999).

In terms of main weapon systems, Germany has modern capabilities by world standards. Germany is not a nuclear power, but the conventional weapon systems of Germany are among the best in the world, even when compared with those of the United States. Major procurement programs of the last couple of years have included Panzerhaubitze 2000 howitzers, Tiger attack helicopters, Eurofighter planes, and U212 submarines, which are all modern conventional platforms. A new command and control system is being introduced to the Bundeswehr, along with the latest information technology–related policies, such as digitalization of the battlefield (ibid.). The Bundeswehr has always been a conscript army, and both the government and public support conscription. According to a survey, two-thirds of Germans wish to keep conscription, on the grounds that it satisfies political and social needs. One of the most important reasons is the fear of the extreme militarism of the past: Germans believe that professional armies are less likely to be controlled by civilian authorities (Fleckenstein 2000).

Since the fall of the Berlin Wall, the German army has faced a series of challenges: the unification of East and West Germany; the imperative to absorb the East German People's Army (NPA); and calls for German out-of-area deployment in crisis areas. In many ways, the Bundeswehr has managed to overcome those difficulties. Yet perhaps the biggest challenge has been how to reform and restructure itself to deal with these tasks (Sarotte 2001).

In the first years of this great transformation, Germany also had to (1) reduce the size of its military from some 600,000 personnel (Bundeswehr and NPA) to 370,000 by 1994; (2) reduce military matériel and equipment on a large scale under the CFE (1990 Treaty on Conventional Arms in Europe); (3) contribute to the German National Program of Unity by establishing new army units in the new German states; and (4) integrate former NVA soldiers into the Bundeswehr (Goebel 1999).

Germany has successfully pursued those policies. However, perhaps the more difficult policy to pursue was participating in the international military actions that the international community pressured Germany into. Having assumed full sovereignty, being a member of the United Nations, and also being one of the richest countries in the world, Germany was expected by its allies in Europe and NATO to participate more actively in international security missions. The problem was that, following two world wars, the Bundeswehr had been designed not to use force abroad. Parliamentary control of the military was firmly established, and noninterventionism was the basic policy of Germany.

Being under such pressures—and especially with regional security concerns such as the Yugoslav War in the 1990s—German policymakers came to the conclusion that they needed to take a more active stand in terms of contributing to NATO, WEU, and UN missions. The German public was prepared for this new role, and in July 1994 the German Constitutional Court ruled that there was no constitutional bar to the use of German armed forces abroad (Sarotte 2001). Step by step, Germany has become more involved in these operations. Bundeswehr personnel participated in various UN missions. In 1992–1993, the Bundeswehr assisted the UN hospitals in Cambodia; in 1992–1994, a force of 1,800 joined the UN in Somalia. German air forces took part in the disarmament of Iraq in 1993–1995 and as a part of NATO mission in *Operation Deny Flight* over Bosnia. In Kosovo, despite the public disapproval of sending ground forces to such a sensitive area, Germany contributed 8,000 soldiers to the *Operation Allied Force* (ibid.). In Kosovo in March 1999, the German military participated in a combat mission for the first time since World War II (CNN).

Currently, German forces contribute significantly to international missions. With some 7,000 personnel participating in multinational missions around the world, Germany is the second largest contributor after the United States. The current deployment of German forces in the world is as follows, as of February 2004: ISAF (International Security Assistance Force), Afghanistan, Uzbekistan: 2,000; KFOR (Kosovo Force): 3,200; SFOR (Stabilization Force), Bosnia and Herzegovina: 1,350; NATO HQ Skopje, Macedonia: 12; UNOMIG (UN Mission in Georgia): 11; Enduring Freedom (Anti-Terror Mission, Horn of Africa): 450; UNMEE (UN Mission in Ethiopia and Eritrea): 2. Together with soldiers on standby in Germany for possible MEDEVAC missions and the naval units in parts of the Mediterranean Sea (Active Endeavour), the total number of Bundeswehr soldiers deployed on missions abroad is about 7,250 (German Ministry of Defense).

As a result of these developments over the last thirteen years, the definition of the major mission and tasks of the Bundeswehr has changed. According to German policymakers, the military in the future must have the following capabilities: (1) to defend Germany and its allies as part of the NATO alliance in NATO operations; (2) to provide military support within NATO, for collective defense or within the crisis management framework through NATO or WEU; (3) to participate in international crisis management and conflict prevention; (4) to help in disaster relief, search and rescue operations, and humanitarian activities (Fleckenstein 2000); (5) to serve world peace and international security in accordance with the UN charter; and (6) to promote military stability and European integration (Goebel 1999).

Budget

The difficulties that the German economy has been experiencing in the last couple of years are reflected in defense spending patterns. Germany announced in 2002 that the defense budget will remain fixed at Ä24.4 billion until 2006. In 2003, research and development received Ä965 million, up from Ä851 million in 2002. Procurement funds rose from Ä3.5 billion to Ä4 billion in the same period. The *Military Balance 2003–2004* claims that although there are extra funds for research and development and procurement in 2003, several programs have been cut as the 2008 procurement bow wave approaches. In addition to these many procurement savings, the defense ministry is reviewing all its operational costs to decrease nonprocurement spending. That may result in some cuts in training and domestic deployments (*Military Balance 2003–2004*). Some detailed information on German defense spending is provided in Table 2.

The transformation that the German Army has gone through is reflected in defense spending issues as well. Since the end of the Cold War, the defense spending of Germany has constantly decreased, in both nominal and relative terms (see Table 2). Although that was the case for major European powers such as the United Kingdom and France as well, there has been growing criticism against Germany for not spending "enough" on defense. For example, Germany spent U.S.$32.4 billion in 1993, U.S.$28.1 billion in 1998, and U.S.$27.7 billion in the year 2002. In percentage of GDP, German defense spending in 1993 was 1.9 percent and only 1.6 percent in 1998 and 2002 (*SIPRI Yearbook 2003*). In both measures there is a certain decline in defense spending.

Table 2   German Military Expenditure by Personnel and Equipment, 1993–2002

	1993	1994	1995	1996	1997	1998	1999	2000	2001	2002
Personnel	19,247	18,370	18,319	18,090	17,607	17,230	17,188	17,078	16,619	16,679
Personnel Change	−8.9	−4.6	−0.3	−1.3	−2.7	−2.1	−0.3	−0.6	−2.7	0.4
Equipment	3,597	3,293	3,383	3,232	3,023	3,575	3,794	3,804	3,865	3,380
Equipment Change	−25.0	−8.4	2.7	−4.5	−6.5	18.3	6.1	0.2	1.6	−12.6

The figures in Table 2 are U.S. dollars (millions) at 2000 prices and exchange rates. The change figures represent the changes from the previous year.

Source
Skönks, Elisabeth, and Petter Stålenheim. 2003. "Appendix 10C: Sources and Methods for Military Expenditure Data." In *SIPRI Yearbook 2003: Armaments, Disarmament and International Security*. London: Oxford University Press.

We observe a decrease in British and French spending in both constant U.S. dollar terms and percentage of GDP. France's military expenditure steadily decreased from U.S.$37.2 billion in 1993 to U.S.$33.5 in 2002; in terms of percentage of GDP, the figures changed from 3.3 percent in 1993 to 2.5 in 2001. For the United Kingdom in the same period, the change was from U.S.$41.6 to U.S.$36 billion and from 3.5 percent to 2.5 percent of GDP. This trend has actually been the case for many developed countries following the Cold War. In the United States, for example, a similar trend has been observed: in terms of dollars spent, the 1993 figure was $354 billion; toward the end of the decade spending decreased to as low as $289 billion by 1998. However, after 9–11 and with wars in Afghanistan and Iraq, defense spending increased significantly to $335 billion in 2002. Defense spending was expected to be $419.3 billion in 2006. In terms of percentage of GDP, the U.S. example shows similarities; spending steadily decreased from 4.5 percent in 1993 to 3.1 percent in 2001 (ibid.).

Although the data from the United Kingdom, France, and the United States show a stable decrease in defense spending, Germany is being criticized for spending the least among these developed countries. However, Gerhard Schröder's security advisors do not agree with such criticisms about German defense spending. They argue that these figures are misleading because so-called defense spending is calculated differently in these countries. For example, the French budget includes "gendarmerie," but the German defense budget does not include that expense. Also, the German government claims that spending which has security implications but is not included in the defense budget—that is, German aid to East Germany and the former Soviet Union for the withdrawal of their forces from the east—should be taken by the Allies as significant contributions to European security (Sarotte 2001)

Presenting all of these examples, Germany denies that its military spending is lower than that of other major powers of Europe. On the contrary, the German government claims that the issues on which Germany prefers to spend are more important in terms of collective European security.

In terms of international arms transfers, Germany is one of the main suppliers. In the 1998–2003 period, Germany accounted for 5 percent of international arms deliveries. After increasing its deliveries slightly in 2002, Germany became the fifth largest arms supplier in the world. Germany's main recipients are Turkey and Israel (*SIPRI Yearbook 2003*).

Civil-Military Relations/The Role of the Military in Domestic Politics

Until the foundation of the Federal Republic in 1949, the German Army had enjoyed autonomy in German society. Parliamentary, or democratic, control of the army was not always achieved. However, the crimes in which the German armed forces participated during World War II led civil authorities to establish full democratic control over the military.

The image of the Bundeswehr in German society today is quite positive. The armed forces are one of the most respected institutions of Germany (Fleckenstein 2000). Parliamentary control over the Bundeswehr and its loyalty to democracy were established in the Basic Law of 1949. The military accepts its position in the democratic system as well, and is responsible to the federal defense minister.

It was not easy for the German society to define its relationship with the Bundeswehr, because of the armed forces' promotion of war and involvement in the Holocaust during World War II (see Sidebar 1). The need for a break with the past was manifest; thus, the society engaged in pacifism. Under these circumstances it was not easy for the Federal Republic to find personnel for the new army. The famous "without me" movement is a clear example of German men's reluctance to join the army. The federal gov-

ernment overcame these problems by introducing new concepts about army services and corporate arrangements. The concept of *Innere Führung* is one of those concepts, meaning that soldiers have fundamental rights protected by the constitution and international human rights standards. *Innere Führung* entails the right of the soldier to oppose orders that violate the Basic Law and international human rights codex. Conscientious objection is also an option for German men (Kümmel 2001). All of these arrange-

---

Sidebar 1　The Holocaust Memorial

A memorial for the victims of the holocaust that was committed by the Nazi dictatorship during World War II is located within walking distance from the Brandenburg Gate in the city center of Berlin. After a decade of discussion, the design created by American architect Peter Eisenman was approved by the German parliament and construction began in 2001. The memorial sits on a 19,000-square-meter open area on which 2,700 concrete steel blocks were erected. The gray steel blocks measure five meters in height and weigh several tons. Eisenman said the site is intended to be a confrontation with the past and that the design should give the impression of an "undulating field." The architect stated the uneven ground and the varying heights of the blocks are designed to create the sense of insecurity, but not overwhelming loss. The memorial was opened May 10, 2005.

Source

Deutsche Welle. "Berlin Holocaust Memorial Takes Shape," 17 August 2003. http://www.dw-world.de/dw/article/0,,949359,00.html (accessed May 18, 2005).

ments and the Soviet threat led German society to believe that the Bundeswehr and conscription are necessary institutions of democracy.

Present civil-military relations in Germany are far from being conflictual. In Germany, the democratic control of the armed forces is complete, and there is no threat of state coup from the Bundeswehr. The mild problems are usually about the defense budget, conscription, or using the Bundeswehr in international missions.

In terms of conscription policy (see Sidebar 2), the majority of Germans still believe it to be necessary, but young people usually subscribe to the "Yes to Bundeswehr but without me" philosophy. Conscientious objectors still remain strong in the society. As to the unification of the Bundeswehr and GDR's National People's Army (NPA), although downsizing and layoffs caused problems—that is, the reaction against the West in the East—it is possible to say that Germany has achieved the great task successfully.

Finally, the use of the German military in foreign crises was an important question at the beginning of 1990s. German constitutional courts in 1994 confirmed the government's interpretation that the Basic Law does not ban such external use of force. Today there is little opposition in Germany about the use of reaction forces with UN mandate—that is, in Afghanistan or Kosovo. In terms of women and homosexuals in the Bundeswehr, there is not a substantial conflict between the society and the politicians. In terms of recruitment to the army, neither women's associations nor homosexual interest groups exert pressure on politicians to alter the existing practices. The German public is uninterested in women's involvement on ac-

count of the sexual harassment of women in other countries' armies, while homosexual men seem to be avoiding the armed forces (Fleckenstein 2000).

Sidebar 2   The German Army

The German army has been a conscript army since the country was unified by Bismarck in 1870. Generally, the public opinion in Germany has been in favor of this policy for various reasons, particularly because the army's involvement in the World War II atrocities made Germans believe that a professional army can be dangerous for the democracy and for the protection of human rights. In the last couple of years, however, a heated debate about abolishing conscription has begun in the government.

The ruling Social Democrat Party recognizes that switching to a professional army, like those found in other NATO countries, might be a better option than the current policy. The Green Party, the smaller partner of the coalition, has long pushed for the elimination of the existing nine-month conscription. German Defense Minister Peter Struck repeatedly has rejected the calls, however, arguing that Germany cannot have a professional army before 2010, mainly because of the German forces committed to international missions and the recent reductions in the number of soldiers serving. The government was expected to reach a final decision on the issue in 2005.

Source
Deutsche Welle. 2004. "Will Germany Abolish the Draft?" May 6. http://www.dw-world.de/dw/article/0,1564,1191774,00.html (accessed May 18, 2005).

Terrorism

Germany suffered from terrorist activities in the 1968–1977 period. The student movements of 1968 led to the emergence of some left-wing terrorist organizations. The Baader-Meinhoff Gang, which also called itself the Red Army Faction (RAF), the Movement 2 June, and Revolutionary Cells (RZ), had some hundred members. Leaders of the RAF—Andreas Baader, Ulrike Meinhoff, and Gudrun Ensslin—who launched the most terrifying era in postwar German history, were captured in 1972. Their followers continued terrorist activities, such as the kidnapping and killing of people, to force the government to release the leaders of the RAF. However, the German government did not appease the terrorists. It was alleged by the German authorities that all three leaders of the RAF and Jan-Carl Raspe—another RAF member—committed suicide in prison on October 17, 1977. Although it was hoped this would end the terror of radical left-wing groups in Germany, the kidnappings and killings continued (Germanculture website). Only in March 1998 was the RAF officially disbanded. Yet German authorities continue to search for several RAF members (Patterns of Global Terrorism 1999).

Authorities in Germany have no evidence of organized, politically motivated right-wing terrorism in the country. With the increase of the foreign population in Germany during the 1990s, however, there were a number of so-called neo-Nazi attacks on minorities. Both at the federal and state level, successful efforts are taken to deal with xenophobic violence (ibid.).

Immediately after the September 11 attacks, the German government announced "unreserved solidarity" with the United States. The German government is in full cooperation with the U.S. government in the war against terrorism. During 2002, Germany played an important role in Operation Enduring Freedom (OEF) and the UN's International Security Assistance Force (ISAF) in Afghanistan. In addition to security-related contributions, Germany also is taking a role in the reconstruction of Afghanistan and humanitarian aid to that country (ibid., 2002).

Since September 11, the government has been taking a harder line against the terrorist organizations operating in Germany. Many al-Qaeda–related terrorists have been captured in the last three years. These efforts are aided by the new legal arrangements introduced by the German state (ibid.).

Overall, Germany does not have a substantial terrorism problem, or terrorist organizations fighting specifically against the German government or people. Terrorist groups—that is, radical Islamist organizations, or the PKK (Kurdish Worker's Party)—operate in Germany, but their main targets are different. Nevertheless, Germany has begun to take more effective measures against these organizations in the last few years.

Relationship with the United States

German-U.S. relations after World War II have been cooperative. Having fought against each other in two world wars, the countries founded their relations on bilateral collaboration over many issues.

After the unconditional surrender in 1945, Germany was occupied by the victorious Allies; disarming, demilitarizing, de-Nazifying, and democratizing Germany were the main objectives of the Allies. However, there were disagreements among the Allies over how to administer Germany—especially on economic and political issues. These disagreements were the principal causes of the Cold War. With the increase of tension between East and West, the United States began a more supportive policy toward the Federal Republic. The Marshall Plan, initiated in 1947, helped the European nations to revive their economies, especially Germany, which was devastated by the war. In 1948, against the Soviet Union's Berlin Blockade, the United States provided 2.2 million people of Berlin with necessary supplies (see Sidebar 3). In 1954 the Federal Republic was invited to join NATO by members in the Paris Conference, and since 1955, Germany has been a NATO member . President J. F. Kennedy's visit to Berlin in 1963 and U.S. support for Germany's membership in the United Nations in 1973 and G-7 meetings since 1975 are other highlights of German-U.S. cooperation during the Cold War (German Embassy to Washington, D.C.).

The beginning of the 1990s witnessed even closer relations between Germany and the United States. With the fall of the Berlin Wall and changing Soviet policy, the unification of East and West Germany had become possible. On this vital matter the United States was the biggest supporter of Germany. Ronald Reagan and George H. W. Bush were the prime advocates of the unification, and the close cooperation continued during the Clinton administration as well. Especially on the question of the expansion of NATO, Germany and the United States consulted with each other and provided a fairly coherent policy on the matter. President Clinton and Chancellor Helmut Kohl agreed on both NATO expansion and EU-U.S. relations (Cox 1995).

The most important disagreement affecting German-U.S. relations today is related to the European Security and De-

---

Sidebar 3   The Berlin Airlift

The Berlin Airlift was one of the first and most important crises of the Cold War. Following World War II, Berlin was divided into four sectors that were controlled by the victorious powers. The city was surrounded by the Soviet occupation zone and, thus, the American, British, and French zones of Berlin did not have borders with their occupation zones in western Germany. As the disagreements among the Allies over the future of Germany and Berlin worsened, the USSR suspended all ground travel in and out of Berlin on 24 June 1948. On 26 June, the United States, followed by the British and French, launched a massive airlift to Berlin mainly providing coal, food, and other supplies. The USSR's blockade was lifted on 12 May, 1949, although the airlift continued until September 30. In thirteen months, the Western powers supplied Berlin with more than 2 million tons of goods. During the operation, an aircraft landed in Berlin every ninety seconds.

Source
USAF. http://www.wpafb.af.mil/ museum/history/postwwii/ba.htm (accessed May 18, 2005).

---

fense Policy (ESDP). Germany is the biggest supporter of a pan-European defense system as an independent entity. Although German governments have been the leader of such an initiative, they have always stated that ESDP is not a substitute for NATO. However, it is not quite clear what direction a Franco/German–led European defense initiative will take, in terms of relations with NATO and the United States. The U.S. position is changing, too; although the United States has always announced its wish for European allies to take more responsibility on defense issues, there are certain suspicions from the U.S. side about the autonomy of such defense institution from NATO. These issues will perhaps become clearer as the EU proceeds to create a solid common security and defense policy.

It should be noted that there were significant disagreements over the Iraq War in 2003 between the United States and Germany. Germany, along with France, opposed unilateral action against Iraq. This was an example of emerging divergent views between Germany and the United States about the future of the world order. Although Germany has contributed significantly to the "War on Terrorism," the Bush doctrine of preemptive action does not seem to have support from the SDP-Green government.

German-U.S. trade relations are developing every year and are usually free of problems. To give an example, from 1997 to 2000, German exports to the United States increased from 76.6 to 119.8 billion deutsch marks (DM), and German imports increased from DM58.6 to DM90.9 billion (German Embassy to Washington, D.C.). Recent figures show similar trends: in the first quarter of 2003, U.S. imports from Germany were up by 17 percent compared with the same period of 2002, and U.S. exports were up by 10 percent. The same good economic relations are also observed in terms of investments: U.S. firms employ about 800,000 people in Germany, and German firms likewise employ about 800,000 people in the United States (U.S. Embassy to Germany).

The Future

Germany is perhaps the most important actor in terms of the defense and security issues of Europe. Research suggests that the normalization of German security and foreign policies through multilateral institutions is the best strategy by which Germany can increase its influence in the international system. Thus, Germany implements such policies and gradually becomes the leader of the EU's security and defense issues. In the next decade, a more active German security and defense policy emphasizing the collective European security and defense institutions can be expected. Concerning these institutional arrangements, German policymakers should recognize that European security and defense are unfeasible without U.S. and NATO involvement. One way of facilitating the further development of CFSP and CDP is to clarify further the relations between institutions such as EU, WEU, and NATO, and to be sure to establish cooperative relations with the United States.

In terms of the defense budget, there is no expectation of change until 2006. After 2006, assuming that there will not be a different security threat than there is today, it would make sense to anticipate that the budget will be affected by the general condition of the German economy. If slow growth, public finance deficits, and unemployment continue, we can expect even lower defense spending. In a scenario in which the German economy revives, increased procurements, research and development spending for the Bundeswehr, and more funds for European defense can be expected to arise.

The security situation in Europe will probably be fairly peaceful in terms of interstate wars in the next decade, given that the current institutional arrangements and Russia's nonaggressive foreign policy will prevail. The greatest security threats in Europe may come from intrastate conflicts—that is, ethnic conflicts in the Balkans or Eastern Europe, and the possible spillover effects of such conflicts.

References, Recommended Readings, and Websites

Books
Bluth, Christoph. 2000. *Germany and the Future of European Security*. New York: St. Martin's Press.
Brecher, Michael, and Jonathan Wilkenfeld. 1997. *A Study of Crisis*. Ann Arbor: University of Michigan Press.
Cox, Michael. 1995. *US Foreign Policy after the Cold War: Superpower without a Mission?* London: Pinter, Royal Institute of International Affairs.
Duffield, John S. 1998. *World Power Forsaken*. Stanford: Stanford University Press.
Hyde-Price, Adrian. 2000. *Germany and the European Order*. Manchester and New York: Manchester University Press.
Kappler, Arno, and Stefan Reichart, eds. 1996. *Facts about Germany*. Frankfurt am Main: Societäs-Verlag.
Military Balance 2003–2004. International Institute for Strategic Studies Publication. London: Oxford University Press.
Nuttall, Simon J. 2000. *European Foreign Policy*. New York: Oxford University Press.
Sarotte, Mary Elise. 2001. *German Military Reform*. Adelphi Papers 340. Oxford; New York: International Institute for Strategic Studies.
Schlör, Wolfgang F. 1993. *German Security Policy*. Adelphi Papers 277. London: International Institute for Strategic Studies.
SIPRI Yearbook 2003. Stockholm International Peace Research Institute. New York: Oxford University Press.

Articles and Book Chapters
Fleckenstein, Bernhard. 2000. "Germany: Forerunner of a Postnational Military?" In *The Postmodern Military*, Charles Moskos, John Allen Williams, and David R. Segal, eds. Oxford and New York: Oxford University Press, pp. 80–100.
Forster, Anthony, and William Wallace. 2000. "Common Foreign and Security Policy." In *Policy-making in the European Union*, Helen Wallace and William Wallace, eds. 4th edition. Oxford: Oxford University Press.
Goebel, Peter. 1999. "German Security Policy." Strategic Forum of National Defense University—Institute for National Strategic Studies, no. 164. http://www.ndu.edu/inss/strforum/SF164/forum164.html (accessed December 10, 2003).
Kümmel, Gerhard. 2001. "Civil-Military Relations in Germany: Past, Present and Future." SOWI-ARBEITSPAPIER, No. 131. http://www.sowi-bundeswehr.de/ap_131.pdf (accessed February 28, 2004).
Stålenheim, Petter. 2003. "Appendix 10.B. NATO Military Expenditure, by Category." In *SIPRI Yearbook 2003*. Stockholm International Peace Research Institute. New York: Oxford University Press.

Websites
CIA *World Factbook:* http://www.cia.gov/cia/publications/factbook/geos/gm.html (accessed February 29, 2004).
CNN Homepage: http://www.cnn.com/WORLD/europe/9903/24/nato.attack.bullet (accessed December 10, 2003).
Columbia Encyclopedia. 6th ed.: http://www.bartleby.com/.
Deutsche Welle Website. 2003. *"Berlin Holocaust Memorial Takes Shape."* August 17. http://www.dw-world.de/english/0,3367,1441_A_949359_1_A,00.html (accessed May 21, 2004).
Deutsche Welle Website. 2004. *"Will Germany Abolish the Draft?"* May 6. http://www.dw-world.de/english/0,3367,1432_A_1191774_1_A,00.html (accessed May 25, 2004).
Eurocorps Website: http://www.eurocorps.org/site/index.php?language=en&content=basic_doc (accessed December 10, 2003).
Federal Foreign Office: http://www.auswaertiges-amt.de/www/en/eu_politik/gasp/esvp_html (accessed February 29, 2004).
German Embassy to Washington, D.C.: www.germany-info.com
http://www.germany-info.org/relaunch/politics/german_us/bilateral.html (accessed February 29, 2004).

http://www.germany-info.org/relaunch/
   politics/german_us/g_a4.html
http://www.state.gov/s/ct/rls/pgtrpt/2002/.
Germanculture.com: http://www.
   germanculture.com.ua/library/weekly/
   aa060499.htm (accessed February 28,
   2004).
German Ministry of Defense: http://
   eng.bmvg.de/bundeswehr/
   buendnisverteidigung/einsatzzahlen.
   php (accessed February 29, 2004).
NATO Update, 2004: http://www.nato.
   int/docu/update/50–59/1954e.htm
   (accessed February 27, 2004).
Patterns of Global Terrorism 1999 and
   2002: http://www.fas.org/irp/threat/
   terror_99/europe.html#Germany
Roxburgh, Angus. "EU Defence Plans
   Baffle NATO." BBC News (December 3,
2003): http://news.bbc.co.uk/1/hi/
   world/europe/3287009.stm (accessed
   December 12, 2003).
United States Air Force in Europe Berlin
   Blockade Website: http://www.usafe.
   af.mil/berlin/berlin.htm (accessed May
   20, 2004).
U.S. Embassy to Germany: http://www.
   usembassy.de/usa/garelations.htm
   (accessed February 28, 2004).
Wikipedia The Free Encyclopedia, 2004.
   http://en.wikipedia.org/wiki/Central_
   Powers; http://en.wikipedia.org/wiki/
   Axis_powers (accessed February 28,
   2004).
World Bank Group Website: http://www.
   worldbank.org/data/databytopic/GDP.
   pdf (accessed December 10, 2003).

India

Timothy D. Hoyt

Timothy D. Hoyt is an associate professor of strategy and policy at the U.S. Naval War College. The opinions presented in this chapter are his own, and do not necessarily reflect the policy of the U.S. Navy, Department of Defense, or any other agency of the U.S. government.

Geography and History

India is the second-most populous state in the world, and the largest democracy. Along with China, it represents one of the two modern states that embody distinct historical civilizations. India has been home to several political systems—each based in the North Indian plain—that eventually encompassed the majority of the South Asian subcontinent. The most important of these are the predominantly Buddhist Mauryan Empire (321–181 B.C.E.), the reign of the Hindu Guptas (319–950 C.E.), and the Muslim Mughal Empire (1526–mid-eighteenth century). The influence of India's rich and generally inclusive religious tradition remains an important factor in the modern secular Indian state—although it also provides abundant opportunity for communal, ethnic, and religious violence.

The Mauryan Empire, roughly coinciding with the unification of China and the rise of Greek civilization in the west, constitutes the first important regional political system in Indian history. During this period the Hindu scriptures (the *Upanishads*) were completed, and Buddhism flourished both in the South Asian subcontinent and in neighboring regions. The most important text on historical Indian statecraft, Kautilya's *Arthashastra,* was written in this period. *Arthashastra* is a manual for princes, similar to Machiavelli's *The Prince* but written at roughly the same time as Thucydides' *History of the Peloponnesian War* and Sun Tzu's *Art of War.* (And, like the *Art of War,* it is almost certainly the product of multiple authors written over decades.) It encompasses not only domestic politics—including a heavy emphasis on the importance of spies and assassins—but also a rich description of Mauryan foreign policy. Kings were advised to adhere to a policy based on the mandala—a concentric vision of international politics wherein a state's immediate neighbors were considered likely enemies, and the exterior neighbors of those states, not immediately bordering the ruler's territory, were seen as potential friends. This vision of geopolitics still influences Indian policy elites today.

The collapse of the Mauryan Empire led to the splintering of the region into a system of competing states. It contributed to the flowering of southern India under the Chola Dynasty, which had extensive maritime contacts with

Southeast Asia, reaching as far as China and Japan. The reign of the Guptas, based in the North Indian plain, faltered at roughly the same time that Islam made a substantial foothold in the region through the capture of Kabul (870 C.E.). Islam gradually increased its control of northern India, and the thirteenth-century Delhi sultanate briefly controlled northern India from the Arabian Sea to the Bay of Bengal. Islam finally consolidated its rule over the North Indian plain under the Mughal Empire in the early seventeenth century, but it still faced fierce resistance in the southern regions. The Mughals also immediately encountered foreign competition—this time a seaborne invasion of Western Europeans led by the Portugese but quickly followed by the French and the British.

The colonial wars of the eighteenth century broke the Mughal Empire once and for all. Mughal forces, based on feudal horse archers and cavalry, were well suited for warfare in the Central Asian steppes, but they proved ineffective against new European military tactics. The European powers and the British East India Company gradually gained control of eastern and southern India, relying on small armies of European troops and native sepoys to defeat much larger Indian armies, such as at the famous Battle of Plassey in 1757. By 1805, the British had virtually eliminated French influence in the subcontinent and defeated the southern Indian princedoms. Over the succeeding decades the British expanded to the north and west, defeating the Sikhs and eventually launching invasions into Afghanistan. The Indian Mutiny of 1857, when sepoys of both Hindu and Muslim faith revolted against their European officers, led to the imposition of direct British rule. India became "the jewel in the crown" of the British Empire—symbolically important, and a source of considerable revenue, but also a strategic responsibility that became too great for British resources by World War II.

India became a republic on August 15, 1947, after an independence struggle that lasted decades and encompassed mass political mobilization under the Indian National Congress (INC) and nonviolent protest led by the renowned Mohandas (Mahatma) Gandhi. Independence came abruptly, and at enormous social cost. The INC, led by Jawaharlal Nehru, first prime minister of India and the dominant political figure in the early years of the republic, was specifically secular—but that was not sufficiently reassuring to at least some of India's many ethnic and religious minorities. The Muslim League, led by Mohammed Ali Jinnah, the founder of modern Pakistan, successfully argued that a separate Muslim state was necessary to protect the large Muslim minority in the subcontinent. Britain agreed to a partition of the subcontinent on the basis of religious demography, which led to chaos, violent ethnic clashes, massive migration of populations, and eventually regional war over Kashmir in 1947–1948. Partition of the subcontinent, and particularly the still unresolved partition of Kashmir, continues to contribute to regional instability today.

For most of its modern history, India has been governed by the Indian National Congress and the descendants of Nehru. Nehru himself was prime minister until his death in 1964. His daughter Indira Gandhi was prime minister from 1966 to 1977, and again from 1980 until her assassination in 1984. Her son Rajiv Gandhi was prime minister from 1984 to 1989 and was running for that office again when he was assassinated in 1991.

The INC is now led by Rajiv's wife, Sonia, who rejected the opportunity to become prime minister after the 2004 elections.

Rajiv's assassination led to a series of coalition governments in the 1990s. The INC's loss of influence was paralleled by the rise of the Bharatiya Janata Party (BJP), a Hindu nationalist party with ties to several violent religious extremist groups (Rashtriya Swayamsewak Sangh [RSS] and its extended family of like-minded organizations, called the Sangh Parivar). In 1996, the BJP briefly held power as part of a coalition government. Elections in 1998 put the BJP firmly in power at the head of a coalition, which led directly to India's nuclear weapons tests in May of that year.

The BJP has weathered two major regional crises with Pakistan, a series of violent riots that murdered thousands of Muslims in Gujarat in 2002, and a military procurement scandal. The INC, led by Sonia Gandhi, was recently elected at the head of a new coalition government, with economist Manmohan Singh as prime minister. India will probably be governed by coalitions for the near future, as neither the BJP nor the INC has proven capable of securing a ruling majority in the past two elections; the INC remains very competitive at the state level of government. Sonia Gandhi's children have also entered politics, suggesting that the Nehru dynasty will continue to play an important role in the INC.

Table 1   India: Key Statistics

Type of government	Federal republic
Population (millions)	1,050 (2003)
Religion	Hindu (81.3%); Muslim (12.0%)
Climate	Tropical monsoon (south) to glacial (in Himalayas)
Area	3,287,590 sq. km (one-third the size of the United States)
Land borders	14,103 km
Terrain	Plateau/plains in south, plains and flatland in east, desert in west, Himalayan mountains in north
Elevation	0–8,598 meters
Main industries	Textiles, chemicals, food processing, steel, transportation equipment, cement, mining, petroleum, machinery, software
Main security threats	Pakistan, China, terrorism/separatism/radicalism
Defense spending (% GDP)	2.3% (FY 2002)
Size of military (thousands)	Active: 1,298; Reserve: 535; Paramilitary: 1,090
Number of civil wars	3 since 1945 (Licklider 1997)
Number of interstate wars	5 (since 1945): Pakistan (1947, 1965, 1971, 1999) and China (1962)

Sources

Central Intelligence Agency Website. 2005. CIA *World Factbook*. http://www.cia.gov/cia/publications/factbook/ (accessed May 15, 2005).

Doyle, Michael W., and Nicholas Sambanis. 2000. "International Peacebuilding: A Theoretical and Quantitative Analysis." http://www.worldbank.org/research/conflict/papers/peacebuilding/index.htm.

International Institute for Strategic Studies (IISS). 2003. *The Military Balance 2003–2004*. London: IISS and Oxford University Press: pp. 129–130.

Licklider, Roy. "Civil War Termination Data" version 2.1. http://www.rci.rutgers.edu/~licklider.

Regional Geopolitics

India dominates the area known in the United States as South Asia, or the Indian subcontinent. Its population far outnumbers the combined populations of the other states in the region (Pakistan, Bangladesh, Nepal, Bhutan, Sri Lanka, and the Maldives—although some analysts include Burma/Myanmar and Afghanistan as part of South Asia as well). It is the dominant economic power in the region, with a gross domestic product (GDP) of $501.8 billion in 2002 (U.S. Department of State 2004). India's GDP doubled in the decade of the 1990s (IISS 2003b, 207), averaging a robust 5.9 percent annual growth rate since instituting economic reforms in the early 1990s (Perkovich 2003, 131). India is also the dominant force in the South Asian Association for Regional Cooperation (SAARC), formed in 1985 and focused primarily on economic issues.

India's security challenges, however, remain complex, and are linked with internal, regional and extraregional actors. In the words of a recent Indian official report:

The country faces a series of low intensity conflicts characterized by tribal, ethnic and left wing movements and ideologies as well as the proxy war conducted by Pakistan and various radical jehadi outfits through the instrumentality of terrorism. India is also affected by the trafficking in drugs and proliferation of small arms and the fact that it is surrounded by two neighbours with nuclear weapons and missiles and history of past aggressions and war. There is also the ever present possibility of hostile radical fundamentalist elements gaining access to the weapons of mass destruction in Pakistan. (Ministry of Defence 2002–2003, 2)

Within the region, most potential threats to India or to regional stability result from ethnic and religious disputes. Sri Lanka has been racked by civil strife for decades, largely at the hands of the Liberation Tigers of Tamil Eelam (LTTE), a Tamil separatist group with strong ties to the international Tamil diaspora. LTTE originally drew on support from the large Tamil minority in southern India, as well as some covert assistance from Indian intelligence organizations. The failure of an Indian peacekeeping intervention (1987–1990) and LTTE's assassination of Rajiv Gandhi eliminated any Indian support for the Tamil movement, but it remains a concern and a constant source of instability in the region. Peace talks with the Sri Lankan government have taken place regularly—in 1981, 1983, 1989, and 1994—and six rounds of recent talks have been brokered by the

Norwegian government without significant breakthroughs or agreements.

Other neighbors also face internal security threats and may contribute to threats to India, but most of those are neither as violent nor as cataclysmic as the decades-long Sri Lankan civil war. Bhutan has good relations with India, but its territory is used by terrorists. These groups—the United Liberation Front for Assam (ULFA) and the National Democratic Front for Bodoland (NDFB)—wage a running conflict with Indian authorities in the Assam region. In late 2003, Bhutan carried out a series of operations to close down ULFA and NDFB training areas and base camps.

Myanmar maintains close relations with China, and it permits the Chinese to operate intelligence-gathering sites bordering the Bay of Bengal. Several insurgent groups carrying on ethnic or ideological conflicts in India's northeast also maintain bases and camps in Burma.

Nepal is the scene of a growing Maoist insurrection—a matter of some concern for India. It is also reportedly the site for continuing infiltration of Islamic extremist terrorists into India, and Kathmandu remains one of the most notoriously insecure international airports in the world. The Maoist United People's Liberation Front and People's Liberation Army maintain a substantial militant presence throughout Nepal. An eight-year war, broken by periodic cease-fires and substantive negotiations in 2001, is now more ferocious than ever. India and the United States have both supplied assistance to the government of Nepal, which remains fractious and disorganized after the tragic assassination of the king and much of the royal family in mid-2001. Violence increased after the breakdown of talks in 2003, and this remains a volatile, if remote, region.

Relations with Bangladesh are generally positive, although there are occasional elements of friction. The two countries share a border of roughly 4,000 kilometers, and illegal emigration across this boundary remains a constant problem. Bangladesh is also viewed as a possible breeding ground for international terrorism; Harakut ul-Jihad-I-Islami/Bangladesh (HUJI-B) aims to establish an Islamic regime in that country, and infighting between the two major political parties raises the possibility that it or other domestic terrorist organizations could play a destabilizing role in the future (Hoyt 2004; U.S. State Department 2003, 133–134). Indian intelligence sources link HUJI-B directly with al-Qaeda, and it also has funding links to Pakistani extremist groups (South Asia Terrorism Portal). The rise of Islamic extremist groups in Bangladesh is viewed with great concern in India, as is the increasing Islamicization of domestic politics.

Pakistan remains India's most pressing security threat. Pakistan was founded on the basis of the "two-nations" theory—the belief that the substantial Muslim population in the subcontinent required a separate nation to avoid discrimination. This theory has been substantially undermined by the independence of Bangladesh—suggesting that multiple Muslim states can safely exist in the region—and by India's relative success at maintaining a secular government and providing special status for the Muslim majority in Jammu and Kashmir. The recent riots in Gujarat suggest that support for Muslim community rights is not universal in the Indian republic, and the fact that Gujarat has a BJP governor and that the rioting Hindu organizations are associated with BJP allies raises concern about communal conflict in the future.

Pakistan can also point to legitimate concerns about India's intentions. Not all Indian governments have pursued status quo policies, and India has taken advantage of past opportunities to liberate Bangladesh, to seize Siachen Glacier, and to intervene—covertly or overtly—in the internal affairs of its neighbors. Some of the Bharatiya Janata Party (BJP) leadership—the leader of India's governing coalitions from 1998 to 2004—and their RSS allies are outspoken regarding their intention to liberate Pakistani-held Kashmir and their intention to roll back special consideration for Indian Muslims. Pakistan's concerns, particularly about Hindu nationalist rhetoric and Indian regional hegemony, have some validity—but they hardly justify fifteen years of support for terrorism in India, or a 1999 covert invasion of Indian-held Jammu and Kashmir.

The status of Kashmir remains both a symbol and a practical manifestation of unresolved Indo-Pakistani disputes. Since the early 1980s, the importance of Kashmir has increased among Pakistani elites—particularly the military leadership.

This increased importance coincided with significant new opportunities for Pakistan to exploit the Kashmir problem—the collapse of Indian governance in Jammu and Kashmir, the rise of an indigenous resistance, the availability of tens of thousands of *jihadist* volunteers willing to strike a blow for Islam as a result of the Soviet withdrawal from Afghanistan, and Pakistan's emerging nuclear capability. These factors increased the risk of conventional war and nuclear escalation in the region and limited India's options for conventional military responses to Pakistani support for Kashmiri separatism (Ganguly 1997; Gunaratna 2002; Swami 2003).

Indo-Pakistani relations have fluctuated violently as a result—near war in 1990, actual war in 1999, and near war in 2001–2002, as well as the historic Lahore Agreement of early 1999, the Agra talks of 2000, and recent efforts to come to some bilateral agreement in late 2003 and early 2004 (Hoyt 2003). The new nuclear environment in the subcontinent has increased the international community's awareness of this volatile region—although that concern has not to date manifested itself as a unified drive for a short-term resolution. Finally, the new global "War on Terrorism" raises the possibility that the forces currently fighting in Kashmir or displaced from Afghanistan may turn against the Pakistani government—a frightening prospect that was nearly realized in two December 2003 assassination attempts against Pakistani president Musharraf.

Relations with China are complicated by unresolved territorial disputes along the 3,500-kilometer border, arising from differing interpretations of the proper boundary and exacerbated by India's defeat in the 1962 Himalayan War (see below). China occupies 38,000 square kilometers of territory that India claims, primarily near Aksai Chin, and at least theoretically claims 90,000 square kilometers of territory that India currently controls. In addition, Pakistan ceded more than 5,000 square kilometers of territory in the northern Kashmir region to China in 1962–1963. Since control of Kashmir remains an unresolved issue between India and Pakistan, India still lays claim to this territory as well. India also sees China as a competitor for the leadership of Asia and views its rapid economic growth, increased international stature, and improved military capabilities with concern. As recently as 1998, Minister of

Defense George Fernandes referred to China as India's primary adversary; security against the Chinese threat was used as a major justification for India's 1998 nuclear tests.

Conflict Past and Present

India has fought five major wars against external powers—against Pakistan in 1947–1948, 1965, 1971, and 1999, and against China in 1962. Most of these wars are the result of either inadequately demarcated boundaries in the region—an ongoing problem—or are rooted somehow in ethnic or religious disputes. Although India portrays itself as a status quo power and perceives itself as nonaggressive, its actions have tended to fluctuate depending on political leadership and opportunity. For example, India invaded Goa in 1961, liberating the former Portuguese colony, but also at least theoretically risking war with NATO and provoking hostility in the United States (Kux 1993). Similarly, India's aggressive posturing in the Himalayas from 1959 to 1962 eventually provoked a devastating Chinese response in 1962 (Hoffman 1990). The justifiable liberation of Bangladesh in 1971 was also an indisputable violation of Pakistani territorial sovereignty, and a deliberately planned offensive campaign utilizing both conventional and proxy forces (Sisson and Rose, 1990).

The 1947–1948 war with Pakistan was a defensive war, fought to determine the territorial status of the princely state of Jammu and Kashmir—a Muslim majority province ruled by a Hindu maharajah. After the Partition, the maharajah refused to join either state—an option made somewhat easier by Jammu's and Kashmir's location between India and Pakistan. Pakistan claimed Kashmir be-

cause of the state's large Muslim majority. The dominant political force in Jammu and Kashmir, however, was the Jammu and Kashmir National Conference, led by Sheikh Mohammed Abdullah—a Muslim ally of the INC. This suggests divided political allegiance in the local population at the time. Jammu and Kashmir also had a substantial Hindu *pandit* community, as well as a large Buddhist community near Ladakh on the Chinese border.

In October 1947, a local Muslim uprising threatened the maharajah's rule; logistic support and tribal paramilitary "volunteers" were promptly provided by Pakistani authorities. Late in the month, as troops approached his capital in Srinagar, the maharajah signed a formal Instrument of Accession and, with the support of Sheikh Abdullah Jammu and Kashmir, formally joined the Indian republic. Indian military intervention prevented the fall of Srinagar and stabilized the military situation. Both sides appealed to the United Nations, and the UN Security Council eventually passed a resolution calling for a cease-fire, the withdrawal of all Pakistani forces from Jammu and Kashmir, followed by a withdrawal of Indian forces.

Both sides were asked to reaffirm their commitment to a plebiscite, and a subsequent Security Council resolution in January 1949 called for a plebiscite to resolve the dispute. That plebiscite never occurred, in part because neither side ever removed its forces from the disputed region. Pakistan continues to control a portion of the territory (known as "Azad Kashmir," or Pakistan-Occupied Kashmir), but the majority of the princedom constitutes the Indian state of Jammu and Kashmir. The territorial boundary between these areas is not recognized as an international border; it is now referred to as the Line of Control (LOC).

The 1962 Himalayan War with China represents India's worst military defeat in the history of the modern state. Skirmishing along the unsettled border began in 1959, and Prime Minister Nehru encouraged the Indian Army to assert Indian territorial claims aggressively, occupying vulnerable forward positions deeper and deeper into regions that China claimed for itself. In late 1962, China responded with overwhelming force, breaking the Indian lines and killing or capturing roughly 25 percent of the Indian troops engaged on the border. India refused to authorize the use of its air force, considered one of the best equipped in Asia. It appealed for help to the United States and the United Kingdom, requesting combat squadrons to provide both air defense and offensive strike capabilities (Kux 1993).

After routing India's ground forces in the northeast, the Chinese forces pulled back, indicating their willingness to allow India to control territory that China claimed in the east. China, however, maintained physical control of valuable strategic territory that India claimed on the western part of the border (Aksai Chin) (Hoffman 1990). India has incorporated those eastern territories into the state of Arunachal Pradesh—a state that China refuses to recognize, much as India refuses to formally accept the status quo in the west.

The defeat in 1962 sparked a major Indian military modernization drive, nearly doubling the size of the army and significantly enlarging India's military industrial base. Faced with a major shift in the regional military balance, Pakistan sought to take advantage of a window of opportunity to resolve the Kashmir conflict before India gained overwhelming military superiority. In early 1965, Pakistani forces probed a poorly defended region of the existing international border in the Rann of Kutch. Nehru had died only months before, and the new Indian leadership responded with restraint. Sensing weakness and opportunity, Pakistani military and political leaders decided to invade Kashmir, authorizing the infiltration of thousands of paramilitary forces into the province, while preparing conventional forces for a follow-up operation if necessary.

India's response surprised Pakistan in three different phases. First, the local population in Kashmir failed to support Operation Gibraltar (the paramilitary infiltration). Second, Indian conventional forces moved beyond the cease-fire line of 1948–1949 into Pakistan-held territory to cut off infiltration routes. Third, after Pakistan launched a conventional invasion across the cease-fire line, India retaliated by striking across the international border, rather than limiting its operations to Kashmir alone. The war ended in a stalemate and a return to prewar boundaries.

In 1971, India took advantage of domestic chaos in Pakistan to firmly establish its regional hegemony. The results of Pakistani elections in December 1970 raised the possibility that political elites in Western Pakistan would have to share power with the Awami League in East Pakistan (now Bangladesh). Rather than acquiesce to a power-sharing agreement or simply nullifying the election and going back to military rule, Pakistani authorities instead launched a reign of terror in East Pakistan. Millions of refugees flooded across into India, and a government-in-exile and armed militant organization—the Mukti Bahini—received support from Indian authorities. India signed

Table 2 The Growth of the Indian Military, 1947–2004

	1947	1962	1965	1971	1982	1991	1997	2004
Army manpower (thousands)	280	550	825	~800	944	1,100	980	1,100
Regiments/ Battalions (a)	~45	n/a	n/a	n/a	n/a	~577	~504	~617
Division HQ (b)	3	9 + 2 bgds.	~16	24 + 9 bgds.	30 + 27 bgds.	33 + 17 bgds.	37 + 15 bgds.	35 + 16 bgds.
Navy manpower (thousands)	11	n/a	16	40	47	52	55	55
Carriers	0	1	1	2	2	2	2	1
Major combatants (c)	n/a	16	13	23	27	25	24	27
Submarines (d)	None	None	0	4	8	19 (incl. one nuclear)	19	19
Air Force manpower (thousands)	n/a	n/a	28	80	113	110	110	170
Combat squadrons (e)	7	~19	~25	33	37	50	38	39
Combat aircraft	~100	n/a	n/a	625	614	833	778	744
Paramil. forces manpower (thousands)(f)	n/a	n/a	n/a	n/a	n/a	922	1,840	~2,000 (1,089 "active")

(a) India's tank and artillery regiments, following the British system, are roughly the size of a battalion in other armies.

(b) These are the numbers of formal divisions and independent brigades that can be formed from the available regiments.

(c) Major surface combatants—roughly 1,000 tons or greater displacement, including light cruisers, destroyers, frigates, and large corvettes.

(d) India leased a *Charlie-I* class Soviet nuclear submarine in the late 1980s.

(e) The total number of fighter/interceptor, fighter/ground attack (fighter-bomber), bomber, and maritime strike squadrons.

(f) Total manpower in various federal, state, and local paramilitary and police organizations, based on available data.

Sources

International Institute for Strategic Studies (IISS). 2003. *The Military Balance 2003–2004.* London: IISS and Oxford University Press.

Kavic, Lorne J. 1967. *India's Quest for Regional Security: Defence Policies 1947–1965.* Berkeley and Los Angeles: University of California Press.

Smith, Chris. 1994. *India's Ad Hoc Arsenal: Direction or Drift in Defence Policy.* Oxford: SIPRI and Oxford University Press.

a Treaty of Peace, Friendship and Cooperation with the USSR in August 1971, ensuring India supplies of military equipment and spares as well as diplomatic support at the United Nations, if necessary. By November 1971, Indian conventional forces were engaging Pakistani forces inside the borders of East Pakistan (Sisson and Rose 1990; Jackson 1975).

On December 3, 1971, Pakistan launched a series of unsuccessful air strikes on Indian bases in the west. Indian forces, which had already been preparing for a December 6 invasion, overran East Pakistan in a masterful two-week campaign, capturing 93,000 prisoners and establishing the modern state of Bangladesh. Warfare in the western sectors was less successful, quickly stalemating near the existing border and LoC. India captured territory in the west that created a slightly more defensible boundary in Kashmir, in addition to 4,500 square kilometers of southern desert (Gill). After the war, India and Pakistan signed the Simla Accord in 1972, in which the Kashmir issue was not formally resolved but both states agreed to negotiate disputes on a bilateral basis, rather than taking them to the international community.

The period from 1972 to 1999 saw no formal wars but a variety of regional crises. India tested a nuclear device in 1974, which accelerated Pakistan's efforts to acquire a nuclear deterrent of its own (neither state is a signatory to the Nuclear Nonproliferation Treaty [NPT]). The Soviet Union's invasion of Afghanistan in 1979 was not formally condemned or supported by India, but it did provide the rationale for a renewed U.S.-Pakistan military and economic relationship. In early 1984, the inadequate demarcation of territorial boundaries led to yet another conflict, this time over the Siachen Glacier at the northern edge of the LoC. Both states continue to fight over this barren, inhospitable region today.

During the 1980s, Pakistan's emerging nuclear capabilities contributed to a series of crises. Many of these were related to military exercises and either poor intelligence or poor communications between the two states. In 1984 an Indian exercise led to the apparent disappearance of several squadrons of the Indian Air Force's (IAF) most capable strike fighters, raising concerns of a possible preemptive strike on Pakistan's nuclear facilities at Kahuta.

In 1986 India carried out a four-stage military exercise named Brasstacks, intended to test new military doctrine and organization in a possible nuclear environment. The final stages of the exercises involved corps-level maneuvers using the Indian Army's heavy mechanized units in positions very close to the international border. Pakistan responded with a countermobilization, repositioning its own mechanized reserves for a strike into Punjab, plagued at the time by separatist violence (Hagerty 1998; Bajpai et al. 1995). The Indian government reportedly authorized, and then canceled, a military operation called Trident, which was apparently intended to recapture significant portions of Pakistani-controlled Kashmir. At roughly the same time, India also carried out a large military exercise in the Himalayas, intended to demonstrate military capabilities and political resolve to China. Finally, another crisis in 1990, linked to military exercises and internal unrest in both Indian-held Jammu and Kashmir and the Sindh province of Pakistan, reportedly led to the assembly of a nuclear device by Pakistan; there followed hasty U.S. diplomatic intervention to prevent escalation from crisis to outright warfare (Hagerty 1998; Krepon and Faruqee 1994).

On May 13 and 15, 1998, India carried out five additional nuclear tests. These demonstrated substantial miniaturization for sophisticated warhead triggers, a verifiable and deliverable fission weapon capability of roughly 10–15 kiloton yield, and a still disputed additional capability for development of boosted fission or thermonuclear designs with higher yields (Tellis 2001, 519–522). Pakistan responded with nuclear tests of its own on May 28 and May 30. Although the number and yield remain disputed, Pakistan clearly demonstrated at least two successful multikiloton detonations.

Many Indian and U.S. analysts hoped that overt nuclearization of the subcontinent would lead to stability and peace. In fact, the region appears more volatile and dangerous after nuclear tests than it was before. In early 1999, at the same time that the prime ministers of India and Pakistan were negotiating the historic Lahore Agreement, Pakistan infiltrated between 1,500 and 2,000 paramilitary troops of the Northern Light Infantry into Indian-held areas of Jammu and Kashmir, threatening the Srinigar-Leh highway—which parallels the LoC and is a major supply line for the forces at Siachen. Pakistan claimed that these forces were mujaheddin—Kashmiri insurgents—and fighting raged in the areas around Dras and Kargil from May until late July, resulting in more than a thousand fatalities. India deliberately limited the fighting to Kashmir, unlike 1965 or 1971, choosing not to cross either the LoC or the international border, although naval forces were mobilized and air strikes were used on Pakistani positions on the Indian side of the LoC. Pakistan eventually withdrew its forces after losing several strategically important positions to Indian assault (Hoyt 2003; Bammi 2002).

Another crisis flared in December 2001, after terrorists belonging to groups based in Pakistan attacked the Indian Parliament in New Delhi. India responded with its most massive mobilization since the 1971 war, moving hundreds of thousands of troops and all of its major armored units to forward positions by the international border and the LoC. These troops stayed in place through the fall of 2002. This exercise in coercive diplomacy was intended to obtain significant concessions from Pakistan, as well as to convince Pakistani leaders that their nuclear forces would not necessarily deter India from waging conventional war. Pakistan's president Musharraf made a landmark speech in January 2002, banning several militant organizations and promising to end infiltration of Kashmiri militants across the LoC. Terrorist attacks in Jammu and Kashmir in May 2002, however, touched off the crisis again. India reportedly prepared for and almost launched conventional attacks in May and June of that year, before the crisis was defused. President Musharraf again pledged to halt infiltration and promised that Pakistan would not allow any terrorists within its borders. None of these pledges have been realized as of this writing, although infiltration rates across the LoC have dropped.

Alliance Structure

India has never been a formal member of an alliance. It signed a Treaty of Peace, Friendship and Cooperation with the Soviet Union in August 1971. That was a defensive agreement which did not involve basing rights. The USSR provided significant amounts of modern military equipment at favorable prices and terms of trade. The two countries cooperated in international forums and the United Nations, and India refused to condemn the Soviet invasion of Afghanistan.

India has been involved in three "neutrality or nonaggression" arrangements, with the USSR (1971–1991), Bangladesh (1972–1997), and Pakistan (1991) (Correlates of War). A recent Ministry of Defence annual report specifically states that a fundamental determinant of Indian security planning is that "India is not a member of any military alliance or strategic grouping, nor is this consistent with our policies necessitating a certain independent deterrent capability" (MoD 2002–2003, 10).

Size and Structure of the Military

India's military is one of the largest in the world, with 1,298,000 on active duty and 535,000 reservists (IISS 2003a). In addition, more than a million are involved in paramilitary forces with internal security duties. According to the Ministry of Defence annual report, the four key elements for Indian security planning are preparing for potential conflicts on two fronts (Pakistan and China), the fact that India is not a member of any military alliance (stated as "consistent with our policies necessitating a certain independent deterrent capability"), the likelihood that India's armed forces will be called upon for significant internal security duties, and India's interests in the Indian Ocean region and beyond (MoD 2002–2003, 10).

The most important service in the Indian military is the army, which not only defends national borders but also serves frequently in international peacekeeping and internal security roles. The army numbers 1,100,000, with roughly 300,000 more first-line reservists (less than five years from the end of their service tenure). The army is stationed in five regional commands and organized in twelve corps. The size and capabilities of each corps are flexible—they are assembled from a total of approximately thirty-five division-size formations and an additional fifteen independent brigades.

The army must respond to several distinctly different threats. The Indian Army operates in some of the most forbidding environments in the world—combat at the Siachen Glacier, for instance, takes place at above 20,000 feet, and Indian forces frequently engaged at over 14,000 feet in the Kargil War of 1999. At the same time, Indian forces may be called on to operate in the deserts of southeastern Pakistan, the jungles and swamps of Sri Lanka and the northeast, or a range of other environments on international peacekeeping missions. As a result, the Indian forces are configured for three primary missions—mountain units, drawing on the nine mountain divisions currently available, which operate primarily in the Himalayas and Kashmir but can be called on for duties at lower altitudes; "holding formations" composed primarily of infantry but with larger complements of heavy artillery and armor than the mountain forces, which are used for border defense and counterinsurgency but lack sophisticated offensive capabilities; and the three strike corps, each configured around an armored division, which are organized for deep advances into Pakistani territory.

The Indian Army is formidable in quantitative terms, but it lacks both the logistic capabilities and the high-technology warfare systems of some Western forces. Half of India's tank force is old, and the more modern T-72 tanks proved unexpectedly vulnerable in recent conflicts in the Persian Gulf. The Indians lack modern self-propelled howitzers, relying heavily on towed guns, and they have few multiple rocket launch artillery systems in service. Indian forces rely heavily on foot infantry and have limited numbers of armored personnel carriers or armored infantry fighting vehicles—a potential liability when fighting in a nuclear environment. Helicopters remain in short supply. These apparent weaknesses, however, are mitigated by the relatively poor equipment available to both

Pakistan and China. India's ground force has some technological advantages over its primary adversaries, and terrain constrains maneuver opportunities on both fronts. The Indian Army, therefore, appears quite adequate to defend Indian territory and interests against China and Pakistan, but its ability to decisively defeat either of those states, particularly in a short war, remains in question.

India is attempting to upgrade its army equipment, utilizing both indigenous and foreign procurement. Some indigenous production efforts, such as the Arjun tank, appear deeply flawed—overweight, reliant on imported technology, mechanically unreliable, and suffering long delays in research and development. The recent Dhruv helicopter project, however, suggests that some Indian indigenous production efforts may be cost effective and useful contributions to India's military capability. India has also sought sophisticated foreign technology through purchase and licensed production. The Bofors FH-77B 155mm howitzer was critical in defeating Pakistan's limited invasion at Kargil in 1999. India is purchasing T-90 tanks, which will eventually be produced in India under license, as well as artillery fire control radars and unmanned aerial vehicles (UAVs) from foreign sources. These will provide substantial force multipliers against its neighbors.

The Indian Army remains considerably short of officers; like most modern armies, it faces the requirement for more highly trained and educated officers for today's complicated electronic battlefield. The fact that the Indian Army maintains 1.1 million men on a budget of less than $8 billion indicates the budget limitations facing the army—particularly when Indians with technical skills are in enormous demand in the information technology

sectors in both India and the United States. India's complex security requirements and limited defense budgets suggest that it will have difficulty rapidly transforming to a more technically sophisticated force with decisive operational capabilities (Mahnken and Hoyt 2000).

The Indian Air Force (IAF) is the next most important service in India, with 145,000 personnel on active duty and an additional 140,000 reservists. The IAF has, in fact, consistently pushed the boundaries of Indian procurement policy, successfully expanding its mission, budget, and force posture during even the most penurious Indian administrations (Smith 1994). The IAF, like the army, is arrayed in five regional commands, controlling more than 700 combat aircraft in addition to transport and helicopter assets.

The IAF relies heavily on Soviet-designed equipment, although many designs have been produced under license by Hindustan Aeronautics Limited (HAL). Twenty-four of thirty attack squadrons, for example, use MiG or Sukhoi designs, as do all nine dedicated interceptor squadrons (IISS 2003a, 130). The combination of older airframes (particularly in the MiG-21 force), heavy demand and wear and tear on the force, inadequate procurement of replacement aircraft (and at times spare parts), and the failure to procure an adequate modern jet trainer has led to a high accident rate that has frequently drawn public attention and condemnation. India recently signed an agreement to purchase HAWK conversion trainers from the United Kingdom, but the requirement for those aircraft has existed for almost two decades.

The IAF is now acquiring some of the force multipliers found in Western air forces. Tanker aircraft for in-flight refueling have recently entered the force, and a contract for Israeli PHALCON airborne early warning and control systems is reportedly pending. Indigenous efforts to create an AEW-type aircraft collapsed after a catastrophic accident in early 1999. Long-range strike aircraft are in relatively short supply—the Su–30, which will be assembled and produced at HAL, has recently entered the force, far outclassing anything in the Pakistani inventory. The older Jaguar attack aircraft has undergone upgrades as well. Mirage 2000 and MiGs fill out the IAF inventory. Long-range strike aircraft also fill a role in India's nuclear deterrent posture, as will be discussed below.

The IAF reportedly hopes to expand from its current authorization of 39 combat squadrons to 60 squadrons in the near future. That objective seems unrealistic, given recent budgets and existing airframes. Current agreements call for procurement of more than 150 Su 30s, and significant upgrades to 125 MiG-21bis. The remaining MiG force, particularly the older MiG-21 and MiG-23 variants, should almost certainly be retired. This leaves an enormous shortfall in aircraft to maintain the existing force structure, much less to expand it by 33 to 50 percent. The hope is that the indigenous Light Combat Aircraft, known as the *Tejas*, will fill the void. The *Tejas* has been marked, like many Indian local production efforts, by long delays and indifferent management. It currently relies on U.S.-supplied engines, because of extensive delays in the Indian Kaveri turbine. Current plans apparently call for procurement of 200 to 250 *Tejas*—a number clearly inadequate to expand the IAF (unless the number of aircraft per squadron is drastically curtailed), and one that might actually diminish the size of the force if procurement takes place in small

annual increments. Again, the IAF also suffers from significant budget constraints; it maintains a force of combat aircraft larger than that of the Royal Air Force on a budget of less than $3.5 billion a year.

Sidebar 2   Indian Military Forces

In periods of relative resource abundance, the Indian armed services frequently have pursued massive expansion programs that could not be sustained or adequately supported. The army's modernization efforts in the late 1980s were frustrated by economic decline, as were efforts to substantially increase the reach and capability of the Indian navy. The Indian air force, capitalizing on the obvious impact of U.S. airpower on foreign adversaries, reportedly hopes to expand from its current authorization of thirty-nine combat squadrons to sixty squadrons in the near future. This objective seems unrealistic, given recent budgets and existing airframes.

The Indian Navy (IN) is the smallest and lowest-funded service in India's military, with 53,000 active duty personnel and an additional 55,000 reservists. The navy has responsibility for force projection, defending India's interests in the Indian Ocean, North Arabian Sea, and Bay of Bengal, and defending India's coastal waters in cooperation with the Indian Coast Guard. The navy operates in three major commands, with regional headquarters at Mumbai, Vishnakhapatnam, and Kochi. The navy suffered particularly badly from a funding crunch in the 1990s—old ships could not be replaced, and either had their service lives extended or were retired without replacement. The destroyer and frigate force, which reached twenty-six in the late 1980s, has declined to nineteen, including several obsolete vessels. Recent orders from both domestic and foreign shipyards will, over time, allow the IN to upgrade its capabilities significantly, but they may not be enough to provide for a quantitative increase in the number of total combatants.

The IN maintains a formidable regional submarine force and a large fleet of surface combatants, and is struggling to maintain or expand its aircraft carrier component. The submarine force includes fourteen modern submarines (ten Russian *Kilo*-class and four German Type 209) and two obsolete Russian *Foxtrots* (with three more in reserve). Two of the Type 209s were built at Mazagon Dockyards Limited in the late 1980s. Despite significant problems with quality control and production delays, this line will be reopened and used to produce French *Scorpene*-class submarines under license, according to recent reports.

The Indian surface fleet was particularly hard hit by the budget crunch in the 1990s. After a significant period of expansion from 1975 to 1988, deliveries of new ships virtually ceased, and those that were delivered suffered long delays. This situation eased in the late 1990s, as domestic orders were finally filled. Three new *Delhi*-class destroyers and one *Brahmaputra*-class frigate recently joined the fleet, providing significant new surface-to-surface capabilities with their SS-N-25 antiship missiles. The *Delhis* complement five older Russian *Kashin*-class destroyers; the *Brahmaputras* (two more are on order) provide a much-needed upgrade to an aging frigate

force based on locally produced versions of the *Leander*-class (twenty to thirty years old), an upgraded variant called the *Godavari* (fifteen to twenty years old), and a pair of obsolete Russian *Petya*-class vessels that should have been retired a decade ago.

The surface fleet is filled out by a range of corvettes and attack craft. Most of the former are fairly recent in construction, including local versions of the Russian *Tarantul* and a larger, more sophisticated local design called the *Khukri*. The attack craft are, by and large, obsolete—but useful for shore patrol and coast defense. The surface fleet will be bolstered by the acquisition of three *Talwar*-class (modified versions of the *Krivak III*) frigates from Russia and additional frigates from domestic shipyards.

India has long sought to expand its aircraft carrier component, with a target force of at least three vessels (one for each regional command, but also ensuring that at least one ship would be available for duty at any given time). The retirement of the *Vikrant* leaves the IN with only the aging *Viraat* (formerly HMS *Hermes*). India is pursuing replacements from two sources—an indigenous design (the Air Defense Ship, or ADS) that will be the largest military vessel ever constructed in India, due for delivery in the 2010–2015 period, and purchase of the former Soviet *Gorschkov*. That latter ship will be completely rebuilt to Indian specifications, and the contract includes provisions for the purchase of MiG-29K fighters for its air component. Another option will be a naval version of the *Tejas*, although converting a land-based fighter for the stresses of carrier landings is not an easy task. The *Gorschkov* will not be delivered until 2007 at the earliest.

In the aftermath of the 1998 nuclear tests, India moved slowly toward the creation of a nuclear force with appropriate weapons and command and control. Potential nuclear delivery vehicles include a range of strike aircraft, particularly the Su–30, Jaguar, Mirage 2000, and MiG-27. The missile force includes the short-ranged, liquid-fueled Prithvi (successfully tested at ranges of 150–250 kilometers, with a solid-fueled 350-kilometer version in development); the Agni–1 short-range ballistic missile (700–800 kilometers, tested in early 2002 and designed specifically for covering Pakistani target sets); and the Agni–2 solid-fueled, medium-ranged ballistic missile (range approximately 2,500 kilometers). Other systems in development include the *Dhanush* (naval *Prithvi* variant), *Sagarika* (sea-launched missile), *BrahMos* (cruise missile with 280-kilometer range, codeveloped with Russia), and the Agni–3 (potential range of 3,500 kilometers). India leased a *Charlie-I* class Soviet nuclear submarine from 1988 to 1991 with mixed results, and reportedly seeks to lease additional Russian nuclear submarines in the near future. India continues to work on the Advanced Technology Vehicle (ATV), a nuclear submarine in development for roughly thirty years, which could serve as the basis for a sea-launched nuclear deterrent force.

Nuclear doctrine was initially codified in the Draft Nuclear Doctrine, released in August 1999 and formally accepted in January 2003. Command of the nuclear force remains in civilian hands, based on the principle of "no first use" (with exceptions in the event of attacks on Indian forces or soil by other weapons of mass destruction) and minimum deterrence. Although India deliberately attempted to control the growth of its nuclear arsenal,

there is some evidence that the region is drifting into a low-level arms race similar to that between the United States and the Soviet Union in the late 1940s and early 1950s (Hoyt 2003; Tellis 2001).

Budget
The anticipated Indian defense budget for 2003–2004 amounts to Rs. 65,300 crores—equal to 650,300,000 rupees, or roughly U.S.$14.429 billion. Some 52.38 percent of the budget ($7.557 billion) is earmarked for the army, 23.61 percent ($3.407 billion) for the air force, and 18.53 percent ($2.647 billion) for the navy, in addition to 5.59 percent ($806 million) for defense-related research and development (MoD 2003, 17). That was the first budget in which the IAF received $3 billion in funding, and the first in which the IN received more than $2 billion.

India's current defense spending is roughly 2.3 percent of GDP, down from a high of slightly more than 4 percent in the late 1980s. The Indian defense budget stagnated throughout the 1990s, because of the pressing need for economic reform and government reluctance to increase defense expenditures. Large increases in 1998 (after the nuclear tests) and 1999 (after Kargil) helped to recapitalize the services, but recent increases have been modest in real terms. These increases were obvious responses to emerging security needs—nuclear deployments and the renewed Pakistani threat. In general, however, Indian military spending is dominated by internal political dynamics rather than any arms race cycle.

In 1995, the Indian government announced a plan to increase research and development spending to 10 percent of the budget by 2005, with the intention of providing 70 percent of India's defense equipment from indigenous sources (as opposed to roughly 30 percent in 1995). These unrealistic goals remain unfulfilled. Given the demand for reequipment in all three services, the competing demands of the strategic forces, the historical mismanagement of India's defense industrial sector, and the rapid advances in international defense technology, India is unlikely to increase its military-industrial independence significantly in the near future.

The Role of the Military in Domestic Politics

India's civil military relations, in the modern era, have been comfortably dominated by democratically elected civilian governments. The new INC leadership significantly reduced the status of the military after independence. Indian political leaders created institutions that kept military leadership largely isolated from major policy decisions, particularly in the case of the army. This reduction in status was the result of the Indian Army's close connection with the British Raj, and its role as one of the last defenders of the British imperial system.

After the Himalayan debacle in 1962, Indian leadership moved toward a less distrustful relationship with the military out of necessity. Closer cooperation between the civilian and political leadership—including shifting priorities in the military-industrial sector—provided the basis for India's victories over Pakistan in 1965 and 1971. The nuclear weapons program, begun before independence by Dr. Homi Bhabha, remained firmly in the hands of civilian authorities, and military planning for a possible nuclear force began on an unofficial basis only in the 1980s (Perkovich 1999; Chengappa 2000). Civil-military cooperation improved dur-

ing this period, partly the result of Prime Minister Rajiv Gandhi's inexperience at foreign policy, but also reflecting the military's increasing role in internal security duties.

Sidebar 3   India's Nuclear Program

India's nuclear program was designed to produce both civilian power and military capabilities, and was managed from 1944 to 1998 by a small core of political leaders and scientists. Although military leaders called for the possible acquisition of nuclear weapons after China's nuclear test in 1964, they were deliberately isolated from nuclear developments and planning. The nuclear weapons program, begun before India's independence, remained firmly in the hands of civilian authorities, and military planning for a possible nuclear force only began (on an unofficial basis) in the 1980s.

It is an indication of the relative status of the military in Indian civil-military relations that when the new Bharatiya Janata Party (BJP) coalition government called a meeting of the Defense Minister's Committee (the minister of defense and the heads of the three services) in 1998, it was the first time that body had met in more than twenty years. The bizarre dismissal of Indian navy chief Admiral Vishnu Bhagwat in 1999 suggests that problems may still exist in civil-military relations. Despite the Bhagwat affair, however, it appears clear that military influence in national security policy has reached a higher point than at any time since the first Rajiv Gandhi administration in the mid-1980s. That includes the continuing evolution of a National

Security Council, the movement toward selection of a chief of defense staff, and the establishment of a nuclear command and control network.

Terrorism

India suffers from a range of terrorist, separatist, and other insurgent threats. Some of these are indigenous, while others are clearly linked to external support. The primary threats exist in the northeast and northwest. In the northeast—particularly in the regions of Mizoram, Assam, Nagaland, Tripura, and Meghalaya—separatist groups based on ethnic or religious separatist movements have been a problem for decades. Maoist groups also menace those regions and neighboring Bihar and Arunachal Pradesh (South Asia Terrorism Portal). International borders in this area are porous, and insurgents opposing India or other regional states (Nepal, Bangladesh) flow across borders seeking sanctuary and support, adding a transnational dimension to a series of primarily local disputes.

In the northwest, particularly Kashmir but also in Punjab, India faces a more serious threat. The Muslims of Kashmir and the Sikhs of Punjab have both taken up arms—and accepted Pakistani support—in separatist struggles since the 1980s. Suppressing Sikh nationalists took a decade (1984–1994), significantly increased the risks of regional war in 1987 and 1990, and cost thousands of lives. The better-known Kashmir conflict began in 1989, primarily as a reaction against Indian misgovernance (Ganguly 1997). Pakistan seized the opportunity to tie up Indian resources, and current estimates suggest that roughly 50 percent of Kashmiri fighters are not locals, being trained in Pakistan or Afghanistan and infiltrated across the LoC. Many of these insurgent groups have links to al-Qaeda and other transnational terrorist organizations (Gunaratna 2002).

Separatist terrorism exists primarily on the periphery of the Indian state and directly affects only a small percentage of the population. These movements do represent an important symbolic threat to the notion of India as a secular multiethnic state. In particular, the simultaneous rise of transnational militant Islamic movements (India has the second or third largest Muslim population in the world) and of militant Hindu nationalism creates the possibility for significant internal tension in more important regions of India in the future. Militant Islamic attacks in Mumbai, Calcutta, and elsewhere, and the murderous riots in Gujarat in 2002, may be an indication of future ethnic and civil strife.

Relationship with the United States

India's relations with the United States have always been mixed. India's commitment to nonalignment prohibited participation in any of the early Cold War alliances. Its reluctance to work with the United States contributed to a U.S. decision to ally with Pakistan, which included substantial arms transfers and military training in the 1950s and early 1960s. India chose to support the Non-Aligned Movement, attempting to create a third force in international politics from Asian and African states once held under European colonial domination. The Non-Aligned Movement, however, lacked both power and cohesion; many members drifted toward the Soviet Union during the late 1950s, and the Himalayan War of 1962 engaged the two most powerful members in a major border conflict.

The 1962 war, and the effort to resolve the Kashmir problem in 1962–1963, represented the first real possibility for closer U.S.-Indian alignment. Nehru requested U.S. forces and military assistance, and the Kennedy administration was committed to a closer relationship with India. The inability to resolve Kashmir, and U.S. unwillingness to provide India with high-technology fighter aircraft, soured the relationship. Relations were seriously harmed by the U.S. decision to embargo arms to both India and Pakistan in 1965, and the conscious micromanagement of grain assistance by the Johnson administration because of concerns about Indian administrative capabilities (Kux 1993; McMahon 1994).

India thus drifted toward the Soviet Union, partly in an effort to obtain modern weapons systems. The 1971 war thoroughly alienated the Nixon administration, which at the time was using Pakistan to facilitate a new U.S. relationship with China that proved instrumental in ending the Vietnam War and establish-

ing détente with the Soviet Union. The 1974 nuclear test further alienated the United States, which was attempting to create a global nuclear nonproliferation regime—at least partly because the plutonium used in the device was created using a U.S.-supplied nuclear facility in violation of U.S. law. The United States imposed economic sanctions on India, denying it access to certain high technologies and critical nuclear components necessary for India's ambitious civilian nuclear energy plans. India's failure to condemn the Soviet invasion of Afghanistan dropped Indo-U.S. relations to new depths, and provided a rationale for a renewed U.S.-Pakistani defense relationship that reshaped the military balance in the subcontinent. As part of that renewed alliance, the United States armed Islamic extremist groups to fight the war in Afghanistan and ignored Pakistani nuclear weapons developments, except when forced to monitor them by congressional pressure.

U.S.-Indian relations began to shift in a more positive direction during the mid-1980s, as the United States eased some technology controls on India and the government of Rajiv Gandhi made a serious effort to recast Indian policy. The collapse of the Soviet Union, and India's internal economic reforms of the 1990s, removed significant obstacles to the relationship. The primary problem in the 1990s remained the issue of nuclear weapons. India pressed for global disarmament, refused to sign the Nuclear Nonproliferation Treaty, and strongly objected to the Comprehensive Test Ban Treaty. Concern over the latter was so great that India attempted to test nuclear weapons in 1995—the tests were canceled under U.S. pressure—and 1996, when the short-lived BJP coalition did not have time to order nuclear tests before falling (Perkovich 1999).

Although the Clinton administration came into office with the intention of fundamentally changing U.S.-Indian relations, those events and the 1998 nuclear tests prevented serious progress until 2000, when Clinton visited New Delhi and signed a Joint Vision statement with Prime Minister Vajpayee. Since that time U.S.-Indian relations have grown much warmer, but they still face significant obstacles. Indian leaders see significant technology transfer, particularly in the nuclear and military sectors, as the first step toward genuine friendship, while U.S. leaders see that kind of cooperation as one of the later steps in a gradually evolving relationship (MacDonald 2002). U.S. and Indian visions of what an alliance actually constitutes remain quite different. Nevertheless, the United States and India are closer today than at virtually any time in the history of modern India.

The Future

Indian national security policy is in the midst of unprecedented change, driven by rapidly evolving domestic, regional, and global conditions since 1990 and, in particular, since 1998. Domestic political change in India, embodied by the implosion of the Congress Party and the rise of the BJP, created a more robust foreign policy aimed at isolating Pakistan and reasserting India's regional leadership and global influence. The formal introduction of nuclear weapons into the region exacerbated, rather than stabilized, relations between India and Pakistan, and provided an incentive for the Kargil war of 1999. The collapse of the Soviet Union, an increasingly friendly relationship with the United States, and India's intensifying defense relationship with Israel transformed India's arms procurement options, as well as its opportunities for partnership and cooperation in other spheres.

India's defense policy remains strained by contradictory requirements. India cannot focus on capital-intensive transformation policies because of the need for manpower-intensive counterinsurgency forces. The heavy armored forces necessary to deter or coerce Pakistan cannot be easily used for counterinsurgency. Nuclear weapons have not permitted India to reduce spending on conventional forces—an experience common among nuclear powers—and even the gradual development of a significant nuclear deterrent will drain resources from the Indian budget. In an effort to reconcile conflicting priorities, India continues to develop a new military doctrine—called Cold Start—for the twenty-first century, incorporating elements of the abortive Limited War Doctrine of 2000 as well as concepts of military transformation emerging from the United States and elsewhere. As India accepts new international responsibilities, including the patrolling of the Straits of Malacca, and possible involvement in nation-building efforts in Iraq, the tension between resources and commitments will remain, barring a significant increase in the defense budget.

References, Recommended Readings, and Websites

Books
Bajpai, Kanti P., P. R. Chari, Pervaiz Iqbal Cheema, Stephen P. Cohen, and Sumit Ganguly. 1995. *Brasstacks and Beyond: Perception and Management of Crisis in South Asia.* Program in Arms Control, Disarmament, and International Security. Urbana-Champagn: University of Illinois.

Bajpai, Kanti P., and Amitabh Mattoo, eds. 1996. *Securing India: Strategic Thought and Practice.* Essays by George K. Tanham with commentaries. New Delhi: Manohar Publishers and Distributors.

Bammi, Y. M. (Lt. Gen., ret.). 2002. *Kargil 1999: The Impregnable Conquered.* New Delhi: Gorkha Publishers.

Bertsch, Gary K., Seema Gahlaut, and Anupam Srivastava, eds. 1999. *Engaging India: U.S. Strategic Relations with the World's Largest Democracy.* New York: Routledge.

Chengappa, Raj. 2000. *Weapons of Peace: The Secret Story of India's Quest to Be a Nuclear Power.* New Delhi: HarperCollins Publishers India Pvt Limited.

Cohen, Stephen P. 1971. *The Indian Army: Its Contribution to the Development of a Nation.* Berkeley: University of California Press.

———. 2001. *India: Emerging Power.* Washington, DC: Brooking Institution Press.

From Surprise to Reckoning: The Kargil Review Committee Report. 1999. New Delhi: SAGE.

Ganguly, Sumit. 1997. *The Crisis in Kashmir: Portents of War, Hopes of Peace.* New York: Woodrow Wilson Center Press and Cambridge University Press.

———. 2001. *Conflict Unending: India-Pakistan Tensions since 1947.* Cambridge, UK: Woodrow Wilson Center Press and Columbia University Press.

Gill, John H. *An Atlas of the 1971 India-Pakistan War: The Creation of Bangladesh.* http://www.ndu.edu/nesa/docs/Gill%20Atlas%20Final%20Version.pdf.

Gunaratna, Rohan. 2002. *Inside Al Qaeda.* New York: Berkley Books.

Hagerty, Devin T. 1998. *The Consequences of Nuclear Proliferation: Lessons from South Asia.* BCSIA Studies in International Security. Belfer Center for Science and International Affairs. Cambridge: MIT Press.

Harrison, Selig S., Paul H. Kreisberg, and Dennis Kux, eds. 1999. *India & Pakistan: The First Fifty Years.* Cambridge, UK: Woodrow Wilson Center and Cambridge University Press.

Hoffman, Steven A. 1990. *India and the China Crisis.* Berkeley: University of California Press.

International Institute for Strategic Studies (IISS). 2003a. *The Military Balance, 2002–2003.* Oxford: Oxford University Press.

———. 2003b. *Strategic Survey 2002/2003.* Oxford: Oxford University Press.

Jackson, Robert. 1975. *South Asia in Crisis: India-Pakistan-Bangladesh.* The International Institute for Strategic Studies. London: Chatto and Windus.

Kanwal, Gurmeet. 2001. *Nuclear Defence: Shaping the Arsenal.* New Delhi: Institute for Defence Studies and Analysis.

Kautilya. 1992. *The Arthashastra.* Edited, translated, and introduced by L. Rangarajan. New Delhi: PenguinBooks India.

Kavic, Lorne J. 1967. *India's Quest for Regional Security: Defence Policies 1947–1965.* Berkeley and Los Angeles: University of California Press.

Koithara, Verghese. 1999. *Society, State & Security: The Indian Experience.* New Delhi: SAGE.

Krepon, Michael, and Mishi Faruqee. 1994. *Conflict Prevention and Confidence-Building Measures in South Asia: The 1990 Crisis.* Occasional Paper No. 17. Washington, DC: Henry L. Stimson Center.

Kux, Dennis. 1993. *Estranged Democracies: India and the United States.* Washington, DC: National Defense University Press.

MacDonald, Juli A. 2002. *Indo-U.S. Military Relationship: Expectations and Perceptions.* Washington, DC: Office of the Secretary of Defense, Net Assessment.

McMahon, Robert J. 1994. *Cold War on the Periphery: The United States, India, and Pakistan.* New York: Columbia University Press.

Menon, Raja (Rear Admiral, ret.). 2000. *A Nuclear Strategy for India.* New Delhi: SAGE.

Ministry of Defence (MoD). *Annual Report 2002–2003.* http://mod.nic.in/reports/welcome.html.

Perkovich, George. 1999. *India's Nuclear Bomb: The Impact on Global Proliferation.* Berkeley: University of California Press.

Roy-Choudhury, Rahul. 1995. *Sea Power & Indian Security.* London: Brassey's.

Singh, Jaswant. 1999. *Defending India.* New York: St. Martin's Press.

Sisson, Richard, and Leo B. Rose. 1990. *War and Secession: Pakistan, India, and the Creation of Bangladesh.* Berkeley: University of California Press.

Smith, Chris. 1994. *India's Ad Hoc Arsenal: Direction or Drift in Defence Policy.* Oxford: SIPRI and Oxford University Press.

Tellis, Ashley J. 1997. *Stability in South Asia.* Santa Monica, CA: RAND.

———. 2001. *India's Emerging Nuclear Posture: Between Recessed Deterrent and Ready Arsenal.* Santa Monica, CA: RAND.

U.S. Department of State. 2003. *Patterns of Global Terrorism 2002.* Washington, DC.

Wirsing, Robert G. 1998. *India, Pakistan, and the Kashmir Dispute: On Regional Conflict and Its Resolution.* New York: St. Martin's Press.

Wolpert, Stanley. 2000. *A New History of India.* 6th ed. New York: Oxford University Press.

Articles and Book Chapters

Bajpai, Kanti. 1998. "India: Modified Structuralism." In *Asian Security Practice: Material and Ideational Influences*, Muthiah Alagappa, ed. Stanford: Stanford University Press, pp. 157–197.

Doyle, Michael W., and Nicholas Sambanis. 2000. "International Peacebuilding: A Theoretical and Quantitative Analysis." http://www.worldbank.org/research/conflict/papers/peacebuilding/index.htm.

Hoyt, Timothy D. 2001. "Pakistani Nuclear Doctrine and the Dangers of Strategic Myopia." *Asian Survey* 41, no. 6 (November–December 2001): 956–977.

———. 2003. "Politics, Proximity, and Paranoia: The Evolution of Kashmir as a Nuclear Flashpoint." In *The Kashmir Question: Retrospect and Prospect*, Sumit Ganguly, ed. London: Frank Cass.

———. 2004. "The War on Terrorism in South Asia." In *South Asia in World Politics*, Devin T. Hagerty, ed. Lanham, MD: Rowman and Littlefield.

Licklider, Roy. "Civil War Termination Data" version 2.1. http://www.rci.rutgers.edu/~licklider.

Mahnken, Thomas G., and Timothy D. Hoyt. 2000. "Indian Views of the Emerging RMA." *National Security Studies Quarterly* 6, no. 3 (summer 2000): 55–80.

Perkovich, George. 2003. "Is India a Major Power?" *Washington Quarterly* 27, no. 1 (winter 2003–2004): 129–144.

Singh, Ravinder Pal. 1998. "India." In *Arms Procurement Decision Making: Volume 1: China, India, Israel, Japan, South Korea, and Thailand*, Ravinder Pal Singh, ed. Oxford: SIPRI and Oxford University Press.

Swami, Praveen. 2003. "Terrorism in Jammu and Kashmir in Theory and Practice." In *The Kashmir Question: Retrospect and Prospect*, Sumit Ganguly, ed. London: Frank Cass.

Websites

Armed Forces of India (official website): http://armedforces.nic.in/.

Bharat Rakshak: http://www.bharat-rakshak.com.

Central Intelligence Agency: *The World Factbook (2003):* http://www.cia.gov/cia/publications/factbook/index.html.

Institute for Defence Studies and Analysis: http://www.idsa-india.org/.

Institute of Peace and Conflict Studies: http://www.ipcs.org.

Ministry of Defence, Government of India: http://mod.nic.in/reports/welcome.html.

Ministry of External Affairs, Government of India: http://meaindia.nic.in/.

South Asia Analysis Group: http://www.saag.org/.

South Asia Terrorism Portal: http://www.satp.org/.

U.S. Department of State. Country Information, 2004: http://www.state.gov/p/sa/ci/in/.

Indonesia

Ken Glaudell

Geography and History

The Indonesian archipelago is composed of thousands of islands, of which 6,000 are inhabited and another 11,000 are uninhabited (see Sidebar 1). Although its landmass is concentrated on four major islands (Java, Sumatra, Borneo, and New Guinea) most of Indonesia's population resides in Java. Its second most populous island, Sumatra, is separated from Java by the Sunda Straits, site of the infamous volcano known as Krakatoa (see Sidebar 2). It shares two of its four largest islands with other governments. Borneo, of which the Indonesian portion is known as Kalimantan, is shared with Malaysia and Brunei. New Guinea, the western (Indonesian) end of which is called Irian Jaya, is shared with Papua New Guinea. Additionally, Indonesia shares the much smaller island of Timor with the newly independent state of East Timor. Consequently, unlike most island countries, Indonesia shares land boundaries with three other political systems: Malaysia (1,100 miles of border), Papua New Guinea (500 miles), and East Timor (an improbably lengthy 140 miles of land boundary on an island only 250 miles long and 50 miles wide; that is partially the result of East Timorese enclave territories situated within the Indonesian [western] portion of the island of Timor).

Sidebar 1   Geography

The unique geography of Indonesia presents serious administrative challenges. With more than 17,000 islands, it is the world's largest archipelago; yet only 6,000 of those islands are inhabited. While many of the remaining 11,000 islands support seasonal populations (typically fishing crews or guano harvesters), the vast majority see little to no "official" human activity. This makes them ideal locations for various criminal enterprises. Consequently, the waters of Indonesia hold the world's highest concentration of ship disappearances—some the result of accidents or forces of nature, but many due to piracy.

Indonesia's territory stretches 3,000 miles from east to west, and 1,000 miles from north to south. Although it covers nearly 3 million square miles of ocean area, the actual land area is less than 700,000 square miles. Approximately 10 percent of its land is cultivable, with an additional 7 percent devoted to permanent crops such as rubber, coffee, and tea. The remainder varies from densely crowded urban complexes such as Jakarta (the capital and largest city) to largely uninhabited steep mountains in eastern Irian Jaya.

Most Indonesians, however, reside in the densely settled farmlands of Java, engaged in traditional labor-intensive wet rice farming. The richness of Java's soil is a result of the region's incessant volcanic activity (see Sidebar 2). Yet many of its small islands are sterile, uninhabitable rock, as noted in Sidebar 1. As with its politics, demography, and economics, Indonesia defies simple generalizations.

Seaborne trade routes linked the archipelago with the wider world from the first century onward. As a consequence,

---

Sidebar 2   Natural Disasters

The Indonesian archipelago contains numerous volcanoes and holds the dubious record for the most cataclysmic volcanic eruption in modern history. Surprisingly, this was not the 1883 eruption of Krakatoa, which killed about 36,000 people through the tsunamis (massive waves) it generated. Krakatoa scored a "6" (colossal) on the 8-point Volcanic Explosivity Index (VEI)—roughly the equivalent of 150 megatons of TNT—in the largest of its explosions, which purportedly could be heard as far away as Australia. The most cataclysmic so far actually is the 1815 eruption of Mount Tambora, which scored a "7" (supercolossal) on the VEI. It killed an estimated 92,000 people outright through blast, heat, and tsunamis, and perhaps an equal number in the famines and chaos that followed. Because the Krakatoa eruption took place during a period of heightened European awareness of, and penetration into, the region, it was much more publicized—including a book (and, ultimately, a twentieth-century film) misleadingly entitled *Krakatoa, East of Java*. Krakatoa is, of course, *west* of Java.

---

the cultures of neighboring South and Southeast Asia began to exercise considerable influence on what would become Indonesia. From the seventh to the fourteenth century, a form of Buddhism flourished on the island of Sumatra, while in eastern Java, Hinduism eventually emerged as the dominant belief system. By 1364 the Hindu kingdom of Java had conquered much of what is now the modern Indonesian heartland. The Javanese language, especially in its high or courtly form, reflected its Indic origins, with heavy dependence on Sanskrit loan words. Culture, from its popular to its most complex elite forms, was heavily imbued with Indic elements.

As also happened in their culturally ancestral homelands of India, the Javanese rulers eventually came into contact with Islam, which arrived during the twelfth century. The nature of the arrival of Islam in the archipelago was a more gradual and peaceful process than in the Indian subcontinent. Islam as a cultural and political force predominated in Java and Sumatra by the end of the sixteenth century. During that same period, Christian proselytizing took place in the eastern archipelago, with the arrival of Portuguese and Dutch political, economic, and cultural forces.

Even though today a sizable majority of Indonesia's population professes Islam in one form or another, the earlier Buddhist and Hindu traditions still persist in pockets of the archipelago, and certain (typically marginal) ethnic groups retain their Catholic or Protestant traditions. Additionally, the folk culture of many nominally Islamic ethnic groups in Indonesia contains significant pre-Islamic (Buddhist, Hindu, or animist) elements. On the small island of Bali, located near the eastern end of Java, a fully articulated and publicly celebrated Hinduism persists. Many of the peoples of the remotest Outer Islands, especially Kalimantan and Irian Jaya, have retained their animist cultures in isolation from the earlier high-culture Buddhist/Hindu political systems or the later (and continuing) proselytizing by Islamic and Christian missionaries.

The bewildering cultural diversity of Indonesia can have serious security consequences, and is, to some extent, the source of its unusually high number of intrastate wars. Where all sources of political and economic position correspond to differences in belief, physical appearance, and social power, the potential for

destructive civil war is extremely high. Ambon, Sulawesi, and East Timor are classic examples of that phenomenon. All have been the site of repeated horrific clashes in the recent past. However, the reinforcing cleavages of language, race, and religion in Indonesia today are partially ameliorated in many regions by the complex intermingling of belief systems in popular culture, as well as by the internal divisions of the otherwise predominant confessional orientation of the country—Islam.

Indonesian Muslims have historically been identified either as *abangan* (a Javanese term for those whose Islam is most heavily influenced by pre-Islamic

Table 1   Indonesia: Key Statistics

Type of government	Transitional presidential republic
Population (millions)	234.9 (2003)
Religion	Muslim 88%, Protestant 5%, Roman Catholic 3%, Hindu 2%, Buddhist 1%, other 1%
Main industries	Petroleum and natural gas; textiles, apparel, and footwear; mining; cement; chemical fertilizers; plywood; rubber; food; tourism
Main security threats	Acehnese separatist insurgency; Irian Jaya separatist insurgency; radical pan-Islamist movement spearheaded by terrorist group Jemaah Islamiyah (JI) seeking an Islamized Indonesia or the creation of a Southeast Asian Islamic state including Indonesia, Malaysia, Singapore, Brunei, the Muslim-populated areas of southernmost Thailand, the northern coastlands of Australia, etc.; localized ethnic and ethno-religious clashes between majority and minority groups (and indigenous and settler groups, which often is fostered by official government policies of resettling Javanese citizens in less densely populated "Outer Islands," especially severe in Kalimantan and the Moluccas); leading region of the globe for seaborne acts of piracy
Defense spending (% GDP)	1.1% (2001)
Size of military (thousands)	297 (1999)
Number of civil wars since 1945	5
Number of interstate wars since 1945	1

Source
Central Intelligence Agency Website. 2003. CIA *World Factbook*. http://www.cia.gov/cia/publications/factbook/ (accessed May 15, 2005).

and especially Hindu folk-cultures) or as *santri* ("pure" or "white" Muslims—those most committed to Islamic orthodoxy and orthopraxy). In its least Islamic form the *abangan* tradition shades into what is termed *kebatinan*—an amalgam of Hindu, Buddhist, and Sufi (mystical Muslim) traditions, given official recognition in the 1945 constitution of Indonesia, which describes legitimate Indonesian religious traditions and creates a Department of Religious Affairs to oversee those traditions. Interestingly, the *kebatinan* tradition (also known as *kejawen* or *agama Jawa*—literally "Javanism") is not subject to the oversight of that department but is instead under the aegis of the Department of Education and Culture.

Although Muslims on the geographic margins of Indonesia—those most likely to be living as minorities within non-Muslim communities, as on the (historically) largely Christian Moluccan Islands—are more likely to profess views closer to the *santri* end of the religious spectrum, the historical and contemporary dominance of *abangan* Javanese culture within Indonesia's population and especially among its political elites has meant that the Indonesia state has generally not been amenable to calls for the imposition of a less tolerant version of Islamic law as the basis for governance.

The notable exception to the persistence of more inclusive and tolerant visions of Islam is the northwestern extremity of Sumatra, in the area known as Aceh. Northern Sumatra has long been a hotbed of political tension between both orthodox (*santri*) and *abangan* Islam. Almost immediately after the country achieved independence, the secularly inclined and nationalist/leftist Indonesian government faced an Islamist insurgency in Aceh (known as the Darul Islam movement) that has flared up occasionally ever since. Aceh currently presents one of the more significant and persistent security threats faced by Jakarta (see Table 2).

Indonesia's demographic parameters are complex, but are roughly as follows: Even though 88 percent of the population professes Islam, only one-fifth of that group embraces the notion that Indonesia should become an Islamic state. Estimates of those in favor of a violent path to achieve that Islamized Indonesian polity vary, but they are generally between 10 and 20 percent of the Islamist fraction. In other words, between 2 and 4 percent of all Indonesians are clearly sympathetic to Jemaah Islamiyah (or similar groups, such as Laskar Jihad).

Ethnically, the single largest segment of the Indonesian population is Javanese, at 45 percent. The next largest group, Sundanese, is less than one-third the size of the Javanese plurality. No other group exceeds 10 percent of the overall population. Linguistic identity tends to be coterminous with ethnicity, with the official language, Bahasa Indonesia, serving as a lingua franca. Bahasa Indonesia was created as a simplified version of the Malay language and is employed as part of Sukarno's efforts to create an Indonesian national identity. In their homes, however, most Indonesians continue to use their local dialect (with Javanese as the most widely spoken of those languages).

During the seventeenth century, the Indonesian archipelago gradually came under the control of The Netherlands, except for East Timor, which remained under the authority of Portugal until 1975. Under Dutch rule for three centuries, Indonesia was known as the Netherlands East Indies, or NEI. Originally colonized

Table 2   Major Insurgencies, Separatist Movements, and Militias in Indonesia

Jemaah Islamiyah (Islamic Group)	Designated an FTO (foreign terrorist organization) by the U.S. State Department. Operations throughout Indonesia, and transnationally. Most dramatic acts attributed to JI are the Bali bombing that killed 202 (2002); Christmas church attacks that killed 19 (2000) (as well as bombings in Manila that same month that killed 20); and the attack on the Jakarta Marriot Hotel that killed 12 (2003). Since the arrest of its lead operative, Riduan Hambali, in Thailand in 2003, JI's capacity to act beyond Indonesia has been limited. Linked to al-Qaeda, recruits come from most ASEAN states (and beyond). More than 100 were arrested in 2003 alone in Indonesia. Of unknown size today.
Laskar Jihad (Army of Jihad)	Originally based in Java, this militant Islamist group moved operations to Maluku and other Outer Islands as Christian-Muslim tensions worsened. With 3,000 to 10,000 men (largely Javans) under arms, LJ is formidable. Government crackdowns since the 2002 Bali bombing eroded its power. Laskar Jihad's leader was arrested in May 2002. al-Qaeda links are widely assumed to exist. Camps on Sulawesi presumed to be at least partially active today.
	Other Islamist Insurgencies: Hizbullah Front, Islamic Defenders Front (FPI), Laskar Mujahidan, Campus Assoc. of Muslim Students (HAMMAS), Mujahidin KOMPAK (on Sulawesi and Java). Similar ideologies and goals to both LJ and JI. 20% of Indonesians embrace Islamist ideology, but only 2% to 4% accept their violent tactics.
Pro-Jakarta Militias in Timor (various groups)	Irredentist rather than separatist; pro-Jakarta rather than anti- government. "Red and White Iron Militia" is best known of many groups. Covert TNI support predates Timorese statehood.
Gerakin Aceh Merdeka (GAM) (Free Aceh Movement)	Active since the 1970s in northern Sumatra (Aceh or Acheh), this group is both separatist and Islamist in orientation. Estimates of total casualties in clashes with TNI forces vary, but most are in the 12,000-plus range. Violence surged in the 1980s. In 1991 civil strife intensified, and TNI dispatched reinforcements to Aceh. Negotiations for a peace settlement, autonomy, and local control of resource revenues (gas) were followed by an international observer mission. By 2002, all of this had collapsed and, in 2003, martial law was imposed. Massive military operations left thousands dead. In May 2004 Jakarta rescinded martial law and declared victory. After this, GAM's strength is uncertain. It draws some revenues from outside sources (Libya in the 1970s) and criminal activities (cannabis, heroin trafficking).
Front Kedaulatan Maluku (Maluku Sovereignty Front)	Founded in Ambon (2000). Small, nominally Christian group seeking Outer Island independence.
Organisasi Papua Merdeka (Free Papua Movement)	Began operations against Indonesian "Act of Free Choice" that gave the Suharto regime control of western New Guinea in 1969. Peaked in 1970s; low-level operations since. While not designated an FTO by the United States, the State Department accuses the OPM of hostage taking and violence. Negotiations between OPM and the Indonesian government collapsed in 2001 when OPM leader was killed. Conducted a symbolic flag raising in Irian Jaya (Papua) on December 1, 2003. Limited but unknown strength.

Sources

Central Intelligence Agency Website. 2003. CIA *World Factbook.* http://www.cia.gov/cia/publications/factbook/ (accessed May 15, 2005).
GlobalSecurity.org.
U.S. Department of State, *Patterns of Global Terrorism, 2003.*

for its role in the lucrative spice trade, Indonesia evolved economically under consciously constructed Dutch colonial policy to become a major supplier of coffee, sugar, tea, and other cash crops. Its role as a major producer of petroleum products emerged rather late in the colonial era. More significant, however, in the history of Indonesia's development than Dutch economic policy was the geopolitical impact of the creation of the NEI. Prior to the establishment of Dutch rule, no political system had ever held sway over the entire archipelago from Aceh to Irian Jaya and from southernmost Timor to the northern tip of Borneo. At most the historical kingdoms of Java had managed to control their home island, the bulk of Sumatra, and a handful of the other Outer Islands. It was only Dutch colonial rule that gave final shape to what would one day become Indonesia. Without the political imposition of the NEI as a geographic entity by The Netherlands, there would have been no Indonesia, as it currently exists on the world stage. The extent of the boundaries of the former NEI precisely defines the borders of Indonesia today.

In the late nineteenth century an independence movement evolved in Indonesia, led by young professionals and students. Although their initial efforts were stymied, World War II and the Japanese occupation of virtually all of the NEI provided them with an opportunity to push for independence. A small group of Indonesians headed up by nationalist leaders such as Sukarno (or Soekarno) and Mohammad Hatta declared the establishment of the Republic of Indonesia in August of 1945, three days after the Japanese armed forces, who had occupied the region during World War II, surrendered to Allied forces.

The Dutch struggled to regain control of Indonesia but were met with strong resistance from the Indonesians, armed with abandoned Japanese weaponry. In 1949, after four years of struggle, hostilities ended between The Netherlands and Indonesian nationalists, with sovereignty transferred to a newly constituted Indonesian government. In 1950, Indonesia was recognized by the United Nations. Born in violence, Indonesia was to have a combative relationship with its neighbors over the next half-century.

Regional Geopolitics

From its inception the state of Indonesia was convulsed with internal rebellions and consumed by the expansionist aims of its leadership. Finding himself surrounded by current and former elements of the British Empire (Australia, eastern New Guinea, and the various components of British Malaya, including Singapore, Sarawak, and Sabah) and the Portuguese colonial outpost of East Timor, President Sukarno developed what can best be described as a self-perpetuating siege mentality. Convinced that soon-to-be-independent British Malaysia would serve as a mechanism to contain and ultimately undo his revolution, Sukarno sought (unsuccessfully) to destabilize and seize those territories. His actions, naturally, produced a Malaysia dependent on British and Commonwealth military support, thereby perpetuating the Anglo-U.S. encirclement he feared.

Internally, he first confronted an Islamist uprising in the Acehnese areas of northern Sumatra, as well as separatist sentiments in the Christian-majority Moluccan islands. He employed the largely Javanese armed forces against the

Darul Islam movement in Sumatra, while exporting (*abangan* Muslim) Javanese populations to the Outer Islands, including the Moluccas, in an effort to "Javanize" (and, to a lesser extent, Islamize) them. Fearing he was becoming too dependent on the army for his security from the Islamist threat, Sukarno fostered an on-again, off-again relationship with the Indonesian Communist Party (PKI).

Dreading an alliance of army officers and Islamists, he pursued an expansionist foreign policy that he hoped would mollify, or at least consume the attention of, the army. In pursuing that expansionist policy and a tacit alliance with the PKI, he compounded the concerns of the regional western powers—first the British and Australians, later the United States. When Sukarno had been driven from power and the PKI crushed in the aftermath of an abortive coup, Western concerns about Indonesian expansionism abated notably. It was after his fall from power that Irian Jaya (western New Guinea) was recognized by the United Nations as part of Indonesia, and in 1976 most of the world acquiesced in Indonesia's occupation of East Timor.

Today Indonesia's focus is largely inward, as a result of a series of separatist movements, ethno-religious clashes, and the continuing dispute over the land borders of the newly created East Timor. The challenge of transnational Islamism, exemplified by Jemaah Islamiyah (but including a variety of other groups, described in Table 2), complicates the relationship of Indonesia with Malaysia, Singapore, Australia, New Guinea, Brunei, the Philippines, and Thailand. Each of these states has been a source of recruits for or a target of the violence of radical Islamists such as JI. The attention of these neighboring states is, however, no longer the expansionism of an Indonesian strongman. Instead, it is the eroding Indonesian state that unnerves bordering countries. An imploding Indonesia could have severe regional security consequences.

The apparent instability of the regime is perhaps exaggerated because of the fact that it had only two leaders from its origins in 1945 until the downfall of Suharto in 1998. Since Suharto's demise Jakarta has had three chief executives in rapid succession (Habibie, Wahid, and now Sukarnoputri), each representing the irreconcilable elements of the Indonesian polity (militarists, Islamists, and leftist-populists). Predictions about the future geopolitics of the region are impossible, given the uncertain future of Indonesia. That uncertain future can be understood only in the context of Indonesia's history of internal and external conflict.

Conflict Past and Present

Conflict History

As noted above, Indonesia was beset by internal conflicts from its inception. In its first decade there was a major uprising in the Moluccas (largely among Christian separatists) in 1950. Shortly thereafter the Darul Islam movement in western Java, northern Sumatra, and southern Sulawesi challenged state authority. While the army captured its main centers of operation in 1960, it continued to threaten the organs of state power at a lower level until its leader was captured in 1962 (Huxley 2002, 31).

A rival provisional state was established by an array of armed factions, including forces in locations as far apart as Ambon and Sumatra, while President Sukarno was on a trip to Thailand in 1958. This semigovernment lasted in some areas until 1961. While it received covert aid from some U.S. elements (flying U.S.-built aircraft out of the Philippines and Taiwan using Chinese, Filipino, and U.S. pilots), its lack of success led to a shift in U.S. official attitudes, with Jakarta ultimately receiving U.S. backing. Following these internal pseudocivil wars, Sukarno consolidated his power and turned his attention (and that of his armed forces) outward, first toward New Guinea and later to the island of Borneo.

At the time of independence, the Dutch-ruled half of New Guinea (the other half was under Anglo-Australian control) remained under the aegis of The Netherlands. The Dutch authorities permitted the region some measure of self-government and independence, in part to forestall local support for liberation via Indonesian occupation. In reality, very few of the indigenes would then (or later) welcome occupation by Jakarta. To gain control of the region, Indonesia's nationalistic and expansionist-minded rulers negotiated with The Netherlands but failed to achieve their aim, the unconditional absorption of what they then called Irian Barat, but would later term Irian Jaya, into the Indonesian polity. Conflict with the Dutch authorities ensued in 1961. In August of 1962 an agreement was reached between Indonesia and The Netherlands for the Jakarta government to assume administrative responsibility for Irian Jaya by May 1963.

Six years later, in 1969, under UN supervision, the Indonesian government conducted what they termed an Act of Free Choice in Irian Jaya. A hand-picked coterie of 1,025 Irianese representatives of local councils agreed to remain a part of Indonesia. After that, the UN General Assembly confirmed the transfer of sovereignty of Irian Jaya to Indonesia. That was followed by sporadic guerrilla activity opposing the Indonesian government's control of the region. Resistance was light at first, but with increasing outmigration of Javanese Indonesians from their home island to the so-called Outer Islands, tensions and conflict with the Irian Jayanese indigenes have steadily increased. This process has been exacerbated by the increased politicization of religious identity in Indonesian politics, given the historical absence of Islam from Irian Jaya prior to the internal colonization of the region by Jakarta since the Act of Free Choice a quarter of a century ago. Since the downfall of President Sukarno and the brief rule of his successor, President Habibie, there have been more explicit (and militant) expressions within Irian Jaya of its indigenes' desire for their homeland's independence. The OPM (Organisasi Papua Merdeka, or Free Papua Movement; see Table 2) has been waging a low-intensity struggle for more than three decades.

Between the onset of Indonesia pressure to control Irian Jaya and the conferral by the United Nations of sovereignty over that area on Jakarta, President Sukarno tried unsuccessfully to expand Indonesia in the opposite geographic direction. That led to the country's one postindependence interstate war (although, notably, the Correlates of War project does not consider it to be a true government-to-government military confrontation, the historical evidence seems to sustain that characterization of the conflict).

The *Konfrontasi* (literally, as one might guess, "confrontation"), as Sukarno styled his efforts at expansion, began with the movement of British Malaya toward independence in the late 1950s. The history of the conflict is complex. Malaya (the peninsular component of modern Malaysia) achieved full independence in 1957. It was at that time composed of only a few of the several British colonies in the region, which also included Singapore and three territories on the northern side of the island of Borneo: Sarawak, Sabah, and Brunei. It should also be noted that the government of the Philippines laid claim to the northernmost extremities of Borneo. A communist insurrection in the area in the late 1950s, led mostly by ethnic Chinese subjects of Britain's Malay territories, had been tacitly supported by Jakarta, although it was ultimately suppressed by British imperial forces, including Australian and New Zealand troops as well as local Malay units. Eager to validate his nationalist and anti-Western credentials, and perhaps also with an eye toward the rich oil fields of Brunei, Sukarno sought to build up a popular movement within both British-controlled Borneo and mainland Malaya for the Indonesia annexation of all of the island (and perhaps, ultimately, of the Malayan peninsula itself, including Singapore).

To that end Sukarno backed the creation of a so-called North Kalimantan National Army (the TKNU). This group launched a rebellion in Brunei in December 1962. The three goals of the TKNU were to seize the sultan of Brunei (he escaped), take the oil fields, and collect as many European hostages as possible. Within a week of the onset of the rebellion British imperial forces, including Gurkhas flown in from Singapore, had reestablished control of the area, and by April 1963 the TKNU leadership had been captured. With no local irregular forces left to contest control of Borneo, Indonesian (and Filipino) authorities acquiesced in the formation of a Malaysian federation, contingent upon the holding of a referendum.

Covertly, however, Sukarno pushed for the arming of approximately 24,000 ethnic Chinese Malaysian citizens (who, while primarily pro-Beijing communists, shared Jakarta's antipathy for the new Malay state and its erstwhile British rulers), and the Indonesian Army infiltrated small units into Malaysian Borneo. Sukarno openly declared a *Konfrontasi* against the creation of a unified Malaysia state that would include any portion of Borneo. Eventually this activity escalated to include the virtually open employment of Indonesia army units within Sarawak and Sabah, as well as less frequent but well-documented small-scale operations on the Malay Peninsula, most notably in Johore province.

In January of 1965, two years after his *Konfrontasi* was launched, Sukarno formally withdrew Indonesia from the United Nations in protest after Malaysia was elected to a seat on the Security Council. By now Sukarno had declared himself the champion of the emerging states ("newly emerging forces," as he called them), which were struggling against the neocolonialists of the formerly British-led, and now U.S.-directed, West. (They were the *Oldefos*, the forces of the old order, which had created Malaysia as a means to encircle him and his greater Indonesian vision.) His ultimate failure to destabilize Malaysian control of Sabah and Sarawak can be attributed to several factors, including the increasingly aggressive and proactive patrols of British, Australian, and New Zealand forces into Indonesian Kalimantan to ambush Indonesian forces prior to their infiltration into Malaysian territory. Additionally, domestic political developments in Java put a stop to Sukarno's efforts to "crush Malaysia" (from a speech in July 1963). For a variety of interrelated geopolitical reasons, Sukarno was toppled from power in a complex coup during 1965 and 1966.

For years Sukarno had played off his two domestic rivals, the Indonesian Communist Party (PKI) and the army, against each other. Along with those two inherently opposed groups, both of which he needed to remain in power, Sukarno had to cope with various Islamist factions, almost all of whom were usually on the opposite side from the president, as well as additional internal and external political forces. Most significantly, the latter group included the People's Republic of China, which backed the PKI, and the United States, which naturally opposed that group. Poised between all of these contradictory forces, Sukarno had remained in power as president for life. He was the creator and enforcer of his own ideology (*Pancasila*—Sanskrit for "the five principles": monotheism; just and civilized humanitarianism; nationalism; popular sovereignty; and social justice). It did seem that in many ways he was politically indestructible, given the apparent unity he imposed upon an utterly diverse Indonesia, and the remarkable way in which he convinced his followers to adhere to his self-contradictory "philosophy"—while daring his opponents to point out his feet of clay, and crushing them whenever they displayed the temerity to do so.

Eventually his juggling act caught up with him, when he put the army in jeopardy of defeat and humiliation in Kalimantan. It was clear that the leadership of the armed forces was becoming increasingly uncomfortable with Sukarno's confrontational style. Lower-ranking officers, conversely, were being exposed to PKI-led proselytizing. When communist-sympathizing junior officers seized some of their superiors and killed them, a complex whirlwind of political events took place that to this day remain obscure. The details upon which everyone is in agreement are the starting and ending points of the coup—from the kidnapping of the generals in September 1965 to the installation of Suharto (also Soeharto) as acting president in March 1966. Everything in between those two events remains controversial. The points of disagreement and probable parameters of the actual events are best summarized by an Australian government archive's retelling:

> It is generally accepted that pro-communist military officers . . . kidnapped six Army generals and murdered them. . . . They claimed that the murdered generals had been in the pay of the [CIA] and had been planning an uprising against President Sukarno. . . .
>
> For months rumours had been circulating that the Army would mount a pre-emptive strike to wound the PKI fatally, while other rumours suggested that the PKI would strike first. . . .
>
> Sukarno, although implicated in the abortive coup, was never formally charged. . . . By nature Sukarno was a survivor and his opponents were reluctant to move against him at this stage. . . .
>
> The PKI and its supporters were not so fortunate. . . . [S]ummary execution, torture and detention were the order of the day. . . . Estimates of people killed . . . vary between 78,000 and 2 million, but the slaughter has never been properly documented, and so widespread were the killings that it probably never will be. (Metcalf 2001, 14–16)

From a regional security perspective, the upshot was that now-president Suharto terminated the *Konfrontasi* of his predecessor—but he did not put an end to other long-cherished Indonesian nationalist goals. After all, it was he that finalized the Irian Jaya takeover in 1969, a year after he had been designated president, and a full three years after the now-deposed Sukarno had conferred upon him the title of acting president.

Following the consolidation of Indonesian hegemony in Irian Jaya, the Jakarta authorities turned their full attention to the remaining European colony in the archipelago, East Timor. East Timor was a Portuguese colony from 1524 to 1975. Late in that year, an East Timorese independence movement with Marxist inclinations declared the island-state's independence. Nine days later the Indonesia army seized the small territory.

In 1976, Indonesia declared East Timor its twenty-seventh province; following the declaration and military occupation by the Indonesian Army, there were widespread political protests and small-scale but relatively deadly guerrilla activity in the region by those opposing Indonesian rule. Unlike the seizure of Irian Jaya, which was sanctioned by the United Nations, international recognition of East Timor was more problematic for Jakarta. Although the major powers acquiesced in the fait accompli, political pressure on (and in some cases, by) Western capitals to undo the conquest was persistent.

When Indonesia's economic and political stability became increasingly tenuous following the Asian financial crises of the late 1990s, and East Timorese separatists found additional international recognition in the form of a Nobel Peace Prize for their leaders, Jakarta grudgingly conceded to international pressure. After UN involvement in January 1999, Indonesia agreed to allow the people of East Timor to choose between autonomy and independence through a direct ballot. The deployment of state-enabled if not centrally controlled antisecessionist militias to the eastern end of Timor—meant to intimidate the occupants of the island into voting to remain part of Indonesia—backfired.

In August 1999 the East Timorese population voted overwhelmingly for independence, in the midst of a paroxysm of violence that killed hundreds of thousands and left East Timor in ruins. Today East Timor has most of the trappings of statehood, but it is only through continued UN-authorized military force that it retains its independence. Absent a significant (largely Australian) armed deterrent it is highly likely that vengeance-minded pro-Jakarta militias (such as the Red and White Iron Militia, described in Table 2) would wreak havoc from their bases on the western side of Timor.

After its officially sanctioned, UN-recognized independence in 1949, Indonesia adopted a new constitution providing for a parliamentary system of government. After 1950, Indonesia saw rebellions on Sumatra, Sulawesi, West Java, and other islands. Failure by the constituent assembly to develop a new constitution further weakened the parliamentary system, with an already divided parliament fragmented among various political parties. As a result, President Sukarno met relatively little effective opposition in 1959 when he revived the old revolutionary nationalist 1945 constitution providing for broad presidential powers.

From 1959 to 1965, Indonesia was under the increasingly authoritarian control of President Sukarno. During that period, Indonesia's relations with certain Asian communist countries (particularly the

PRC, as noted above) were close. Domestically, the Indonesian government (by which one meant President Sukarno in this era) was close with the Indonesian Communist Party, or PKI—and yet, as noted above, not too close. The need to keep the army in his corner meant that Sukarno could not get too close to the PKI. Sukarno designed a system characterized as corporatist or neocorporatist—essentially every social group and economic interest was institutionalized by the state.

Corporatism was a widely employed model at the time, parallel to systems in Mexico under the Institutional Revolutionary Party (PRI), or even in more truly competitive liberal democracies in northern Europe, such as Sweden. But by 1965, many of these mass civic and economic organizations were controlled by the PKI. It was at this point that the army, ultimately under the control of Major General Suharto, moved in to preclude a PKI victory. In that context, the single greatest loss of life in an inter- or intrastate war in Indonesia history took place.

As noted earlier, the exact casualty figures vary widely, from a high of 2 million down to a low of 78,000. The reasons for the ferocity of this virtual civil war are found in many places, including the underlying ethno-religious tensions of Indonesia (the PKI's support base was perceived to be primarily in the ethnic Chinese community); the geopolitics of the region (Sukarno's persistent habit of confronting neighboring states and taking on enemies more powerful than the army wished to deal with—leading to a widespread desire among the military elites to do away with the rival support base that Sukarno often threatened to use against the armed forces—namely, the PKI—so that Sukarno himself could be constrained in his geopolitical ambi-

tions); and in Cold War politics in general (the obvious interests of those who wished to contain communism in reducing the largest active communist party outside of the Sino-Soviet bloc).

Suharto was elected to a five-year term as president in 1968. He was reelected for the next six terms in 1973, 1978, 1983, 1988, 1993, and 1998. Throughout this era the army no longer acted as an open threat to the executive power of the state, nor was that power directed at it. Instead, an era of cooperation, characterized as *dwifungsi*, developed. *Dwifungsi*, or "dual function," meant that the armed forces served both a security role and a social-political function. The officer corps held key positions in Golkar, the holdover Sukarno-era political pseudoparty that was composed of the functional groups of society (that is, the neocorporatist representative body of unions, professional organizations, peasants, bureaucrats, the armed forces, and so forth). Their place in the system was completely institutionalized in the New Order, as Suharto characterized his regime.

Fueled by the windfall from rising oil prices that started with the 1973 October War and subsequent OPEC cartel actions, the Suharto regime embarked on a path of economic development that appeared, on the surface, to be the envy of other developing states. For the next twenty-five years rising foreign earnings coupled with an influx of investment led to the rapid expansion of the Indonesian economy. With economic rehabilitation as its priority, Indonesia's New Order secured a rescheduling of foreign debts and attracted aid through an intergovernmental group of donor countries.

The old nationalist- and socialist-inspired complex regulations governing economic activities were simplified, and a new foreign investment law provided a framework for new private capital investment. In addition to economic development under new economic policies, Indonesia enjoyed a harshly enforced political stability during the Suharto administration that was supported by military power. The military served an openly economic role as well. With state-owned enterprises serving key roles in the development process, higher-ranking officers of the military found themselves holding lucrative positions within the bureaucracy. A posting in Pertamina, the government mineral-extraction concern, was by far the most remunerative (though by no means the only) bureaucratic assignment an aspiring officer could secure.

Current and Potential Military Conflict

The old forces of the left had not entirely disappeared, nor had the advocates for a more Islamist Indonesia—nor, for that matter, had the separatist groups, some of which fed positively (as in Sumatra, where separatist aspirations were fueled by a desire not to be part of a secular or *abangan*/Javanese Indonesia) or negatively (as in Irian Jaya, where separatist aspirations were fueled by a desire not to be part of an Islamized Indonesia) off of the Islamist movements' new prominence.

The military government of Suharto, in other words, was confronted by the same potential for instability as had been the preceding government of Sukarno. To make matters more difficult, in 1993, Megawati Sukarnoputri, the daughter of the former president Sukarno, became a candidate for the Indonesian Democratic Party (PDI), a leading opposition group, and later she was elected chairperson of the PDI. In 1996, in response to her popular support, the Suharto administration acted to remove her from the party chairperson position. This action resulted in nationwide rioting and protesting that was suppressed by the government's security forces.

In mid-1997, economic crises swept across the world, reaching from Brazil to Russia. Southeast Asia in general and Indonesia in particular were severely affected by the crisis. Characterized by capital flight and currency instability, coupled with the inevitable inflation of consumer prices on imports, this crisis struck all classes in Indonesia quite severely. Economic hardship and popular resentment over the government's corruption (previously concealed by the constant influx of foreign investment and petrodollars) brought Indonesia to the brink of chaos. When the armed forces declined to employ massive indiscriminate violence in his defense, President Suharto was forced to resign in May 1998. He handed over power to Vice President B. J. Habibie.

After assuming power, President Habibie hastily enacted some modest (and largely symbolic) political and economic reforms. Several prominent political and labor prisoners were released, and selected limits on the press, political parties, and labor unions were lifted. His fundamental challenge, however, was to achieve economic stabilization. Continued capital flight rendered that impossible. Widespread pogroms against the ethnic Chinese community, a long-established tradition during periods of economic turmoil in Indonesia, did nothing to make Habibie's position any more secure. Finally he responded to the public's demands that he hold new elections, and a special session of the People's Consultative Assembly was convened in November 1998, setting the date for parliamentary elections as June 1999.

In June 1999, Indonesia held elections for the national, provincial, and local parliaments, with forty-eight parties participating in the process. It took nearly two months after the elections for the final results to be confirmed. The primary opposition party, Megawati Sukarnoputri's Indonesian Democratic Party-Struggle, won 37.4 percent of the vote. The previous ruling party, Golkar, won 20.9 percent of the vote. The next largest share of the vote was won by a series of smaller Islamist parties, including both moderate and radical Islamist groups.

In October 1999 the People's Consultative Assembly, assigned the task of indirectly electing the new president and vice president, selected moderate Islamist Abdurrahman Wahid as the new chief executive. To the dismay of her followers, Megawati Sukarnoputri was assigned the presumably lesser role of vice president. Even though expectations of Wahid were high, his power base was much too weak for him to achieve anything of consequence.

In terms of separatist movements' aspirations, this seemed an ideal moment to reassert their power. Wahid conceded, for example, the right of separatists on Irian Jaya to fly their own flag. Such symbolic gestures of rapprochement merely fueled further separatist tendencies (as well as anxieties among the outmigrated Javanese, Madurese, and other populations that previous administrations had settled in the Outer Islands). Shortly after Wahid's accession to power, however, a corruption scandal engulfed his administration, and he was forced to resign.

In 2001, President Wahid's impeachment led to the elevation of Megawati

Sukarnoputri to the presidency. Four years later, in the first direct election of an Indonesian president by popular vote, Sukarnoputri was defeated by retired general Susilo Bambang Yudhoyono, who received 60.6% of the vote to Sukarnoputri's 39.4% in the second stage of a runoff election. The limited tenure of the new administration, combined with the overwhelming scope of the catastrophic tsunami that struck Sumatra late in 2004, limited the ability of observers to gauge the effectiveness of President Yudhoyono to cope with radical Islamist movements, separatist challenges, and other security issues besetting Indonesia.

Under the Suharto regime, there were by law only three political parties. The ruling promilitary and Suharto-supporting "functional group"—not a party—was known as Golkar. The United Development Party, or PPP—composed of various (and mostly moderate, not radical) Islamist groups—was one of two main opposition parties. The other was the Indonesian Democratic Party-Struggle, or PDI-P. It was composed of Christian, socialist, and nationalist elements. Absent from this three-party system were any separatist groups (of which there would have been many in an open, liberal system), radical Islamist groups (reflected primarily in the violent activities of the JI, noted on the first page), and the PKI (the old communist party organization, ruthlessly suppressed in the mid-1960s).

Under the new system, theoretically there is no limit on competitive political parties. From May 1998 onward, some eighty parties emerged. Most new parties, however, were small and local and failed to satisfy party registration criteria. These criteria included a requirement to have party branch offices in at least fourteen of Indonesia's twenty-six provinces and special regions, or to demonstrate support by collecting a million signatures. Such rules preempted the possibility of small separatist parties representing, say, the Acehnese or Irian Jayanese, the Christians of Ambon, or the radically Islamist-inclined of the JI or the Laskar Jihad (all of which have movements noted in Table 2).

These latter two groups are particularly problematic for the Indonesian state, since their membership and ultimate goals transcend the boundaries of Malaysia, Singapore, New Guinea, Brunei, Thailand, and even Australia. As a consequence, any political advancement by the moderate-to-radical Islamist elements in the 2004 elections was expected to have significant consequences for regional relationships, including the unique alliance system known as ASEAN (the Association of Southeast Asian Nations, founded in 1967 at the same time as the transition within Indonesia from the radical expansionist nationalism of Sukarno to the largely status quo–maintaining military government of Suharto). Although conceived of as a largely economic structure, ASEAN has sometimes served a security role.

The continuing problems of East Timor, which create tensions with Indonesia's southern and eastern neighbors (Australia and New Guinea), are a serious obstacle to increased regional cooperation. Of even greater concern is the dispute over the Spratly Islands, claimed by most ASEAN members as well as by China. That territorial dispute, based not so much on the value of the islands themselves but on the potential for petroleum resources below them, renders ASEAN deepening or broadening extremely problematic. As noted below, however, the emergence of transnational terrorist threats may begin to counteract the divisive impact of the Spratlys dispute.

Alliance Structure

Although the status quo–maintaining ASEAN is perhaps Indonesia's best-known semiformal alliance, Jakarta was once known for its role in shaping organizations that symbolically (but rarely practically) challenged the existing distribution of economic, military, and "soft" power in the world. Foremost among these organizations was the Non-Aligned Movement (NAM), of which President Sukarno was a founding member and leading figure from its inception in 1961. NAM grew out of a meeting of heads of emerging states at Bandung, Indonesia, six years earlier. But in practical terms, NAM did not lead to the creation of any meaningful military alliances or even informal security arrangements.

Indonesia's withdrawal from the United Nations in protest over Malaysia's accession to the Security Council (noted above) was also symptomatic of Sukarno's penchant for dramatic but futile global political gestures. In addition to NAM, Indonesia was also prominent in the shaping of the G-77 in 1967 (the counterpoint to the G-7, the annual summit of the leaders of the seven largest market economies in the world). Although Indonesia's continuing prominent role in this organization is notable, its security implications are marginal.

ASEAN, on the other hand, is a much smaller, more focused, and potentially effective organization. Indonesia has, from time to time, suggested that it might serve a more security-focused role in addition to its largely economic function. Recently the government in Jakarta has suggested that ASEAN might have a multilateral military role in defusing the growing Islamist-fueled tension in southern Thailand. ASEAN's members (Brunei, Cambodia, Indonesia, Laos, Malaysia, Myanmar, the Philippines, Singapore, Thailand, and Vietnam) have already agreed to the establishment of a cooperative law enforcement center based in Indonesia to deal with transnational terrorist threats. An overt military role, however, seems unlikely in the short run, but if the security situation in southern Thailand continues to deteriorate, that might change.

Size and Structure of the Military

The precise manpower size of the Indonesian military establishment is not easy to establish, given the historical *"dwifungsi"* role that the military has played in Indonesian society and politics. *Dwifungsi* means that a significant portion of the military—particularly the officer corps—is not committed to military operations, but should, instead, be counted as part of the state bureaucracy.

The weaponry at the disposal of the military reflects the convoluted history of Indonesia. The navy was originally charged with the responsibility for breaking the Dutch blockades that sought to deprive Indonesia's independence movement of the outside support it needed to function in the war for independence (1945–1949). Former Dutch naval vessels were subsequently delivered to the newly formed Indonesian Navy (known as ALRI until 1970, when it became the TNI-AL). This allowed the navy to help Jakarta quell the far-flung separatist and Islamist movements that beset the country in the 1950s. Beginning in 1959, the ALRI obtained Soviet and Warsaw Pact–supplied

vessels and weaponry, and the PKI was perceived by the army to have made deep inroads into the naval officer corps. Consequently, when Sukarno was toppled and the PKI suppressed in 1965–1966, the ALRI was severely downgraded.

With the severing of ties with the USSR in 1970, the ALRI experienced accelerated degradation. The United States and Australia supplied one destroyer escort and one fast attack craft, respectively, following the split with Moscow. The continued decline of the navy's capabilities began to reverse with the acquisition of four U.S. naval frigates in 1974, and an era of modernization and diversification of arms sources from 1978 to 1992 led to plans to acquire West German submarines, Dutch and British frigates, and South Korean fast attack craft. Much of this planned expansion was scrubbed because of the economic crises of 1997. A major influx of former East German equipment in 1992 modestly expanded the naval forces' capabilities.

Although many of Indonesia's larger naval vessels are quite old ("tribal class" Royal Navy destroyers from World War II, for example), its smaller vessels include a more diverse and less antiquated array of boat types, including some locally produced patrol boats. The primary duties of the TNI-AL, to control Indonesian waters, are overwhelming, given the country's enormous coastline, as well as the prevalence of separatists, transnational Islamists, drug smugglers, gun runners, and seaborne pirates (the region leads the world in the disappearance of commercial vessels through piracy).

Given the resources at its disposal, plus its manpower limitations (44,000 naval personnel, including 13,000 marine forces), the performance of naval assets is remarkable. Even though Indonesia asserts sovereignty over all waters between its many islands, it does not obstruct the passage of international vessels through those areas—and it is frankly doubtful that it ever could, given the massive territory it would have to cover with its meager naval resources. Its total complement includes roughly sixty larger vessels (destroyers, destroyer escorts, frigates, and so forth) and a host of smaller coastal craft. Additionally, it operates fixed-wing patrol aircraft.

As with the naval forces, Indonesia's air forces are equipped in a haphazard fashion. Initially armed with largely U.S.-produced World War II–surplus aircraft, in 1958 the Air Force (AURI is its original acronym; it is now known as the TNI-AU) embarked on an ambitious Soviet-supplied upgrade program. Acquiring more than 100 MiG-17 fighters and Ilyushin–28 medium bombers, the AURI, like the navy, acquired a reputation for Marxist influence that cost it dearly in the mid-1960s. The decline was even more precipitous than that of the navy, given the immediate and constant need for spare parts to maintain aircraft airworthiness.

Modernization began with the acquisition of F-5 fighters and A-4 ground attack aircraft from the United States in the late 1970s. Other aircraft acquired since then include C-130 transports, OV-10F Broncos (1960s observation/ground attack aircraft), and, eventually, a handful of F-16s. The F-16s represent the only nonobsolescent combat assets in the current Indonesian inventory. Twelve F-16s were received in 1990, but subsequent deliveries were interrupted by U.S. congressional action to block sales, because of the human rights situation in East Timor. With the end of the Timorese occupation, and the prominence of Indonesia in the "War on Terrorism," that situation may soon change.

The army, once known as ADRI, has begun to refer to itself by its original acronym—TNI (National Army of Indonesia). Before 1999 it was structured in such a way that it shared commanders with the national police forces (paramilitary forces in Indonesia number about 195,000). Additionally, its *dwifungsi* role meant that at any time a third or more of its total manpower would be devoted to nonmilitary civic action projects. Once armed with Soviet bloc weapons, the army has followed the same pattern as the other branches.

Its modest armored force (of relatively little use in a traditional military application in the geographic setting of Southeast Asia) is composed of French-built AMX-13 light tanks (obsolescent) and reconditioned, used armored personnel carriers (AMX-VCI, also French-built), dating to the 1970s. The indigenous small arms industry supplies most of the army's weaponry, which includes mostly Belgian-designed automatic and semiautomatic firearms built under license locally. A few M-16s purchased from the United States in the 1980s are still in service. Critically, the army is in perpetually short supply of ammunition, limiting its ability to train effectively with firearms. Current personnel estimates place TNI strength at 297,000.

Budget

Budgetary estimates for total defense outlays generally do not take into account the civilian functions of the military. Total expenditures are low for a state in which the military has served a political role, in part because its primary costs have been manpower. The acquisition of high-tech weaponry for parades or battlefield applications has not been a high priority of the Suharto regime or its successors. During periods of dramatic rearmament under Sukarno, Soviet weapons of the time were relatively inexpensive.

When Suharto took over and shifted the geopolitical orientation of Indonesia toward the West, there was no dramatic rearming. Indonesia, after all, primarily faced local geopolitical threats of its own creation. By terminating the *Konfrontasi* policy toward Malaysia, Indonesia's longest land border ceased to be a security concern. Relying on small arms produced locally, and with only a modest high-end weapons acquisition program (F-16s from the United States, and naval weapons systems for installation on its obsolescing fleet), Suharto was able to keep military costs at a relatively modest percentage of the overall state budget. The most recently available data (2001) indicates that 1.1 percent of GDP goes to the military, with a total outlay of $1.75 billion annually. Those amounts are, of course, subject to wide variation because of the volatile exchange rate of the Indonesian currency, the rupiah.

Best estimates indicate that military expenditures as a percent of GDP have gone as high as 2 percent (1988) to as low as 0.9 percent (1999). These wide fluctuations in defense outlays are more a function of the rapid expansion of the Indonesian economy and the fluctuation in the exchange rate of the rupiah, rather than a sudden drop in political commitment to maintaining the military establishment. In constant 2003 dollar terms, the highest recent defense budget was $2.096 billion (1996), while the lowest was $1.263 billion (1999—the year of the Asian financial meltdown). The overall trend has been steadily upward, however, rising from below $1.4 billion in 1988 to more than $1.7 billion in 2001, with 1999 as the only year in which defense outlays sank below the 1988 mark.

Civil-Military Relations/The Role of the Military in Domestic Politics

The extensive role of the military in Indonesian civilian life and politics has been described elsewhere in this chapter. The state was born in violence, and Sukarno's role in leading violent resistance to the Dutch led directly to his position as president (and, eventually, to his self-anointing as "president for life"). Under his rule (1945–1965) he paradoxically depended on the military to remain in power while constantly threatening to undercut it (typically by creating a rival popular militia based on the PKI and supplied with Chinese weapons). This complex relationship came to an end with an apparent abortive communist coup from within midlevel officer ranks of the armed forces, followed by an overt coup from the higher ranks of the army. When Suharto took power, however, he did not divert additional resources to the military. Instead, he accelerated the *dwifungsi* role of the army, placing greater numbers of officers in bureaucratic positions throughout the Indonesian state apparatus.

The special role that the military played in the semiofficial pseudoparty known as Golkar will persist long beyond the possible decline of that institution. Future presidents will need to rely on the military to contain the expanding challenges of separatist groups in the east, west, and Outer Islands. They will also need the unwavering support of both the regular armed forces and the paramilitary and intelligence agencies as they confront the emerging transnational Islamist terrorist threat to state power.

In post-Sukarno, post-Suharto Indonesia, the role of the military is less clear. What is clear is that former president Wahid's decision to tolerate the open existence of certain separatist groups did not sit well with traditional nationalistic elements in the officer corps, and the pro-military elements of Golkar were among the most active parliamentary supporters of his impeachment and ouster.

Short of coups and countercoups, the Indonesian armed forces play a key stabilizing role. So many separatist and transnational groups seek to undo part or seize all of the governmental apparatus that no Indonesian leader can do without the support of those forces. That is true in many areas, including in the gathering of intelligence, one of the military functions most central to the emerging Indonesian struggle with terrorist groups on its borders and in its heartland.

Terrorism

As noted elsewhere, Indonesia is beset by a variety of groups that engage in violence, including acts of terrorism. Although in many cases those actions are not directed at the Indonesian state, each such attack further undermines the tenuous rule of law in a country that cannot afford any additional chaos. The nature of Indonesia's terrorist problem varies regionally. In Irian Jaya, for example, separatists target symbols of the state, as well as the assets of companies doing business in the region (mining and timber interests in particular). The Free Papua Movement (Organisasi Papua Merdeka) has engaged in guerrilla activities, with only

infrequent hostage takings. Mass casualty terrorism is not in their repertoire of violent actions.

In the Moluccas a wave of terrorism and counterterrorism between indigenous Christian populations and largely transplanted Indonesian Muslim populations in the late 1990s took hundreds of lives and led to the presence of non-Indonesian (largely Arab) Jihadi elements. Initially ignored by the state, the Laskar Jihad group soon came to challenge the authority of Jakarta. Numbering between 3,000 and 10,000 fighters, Laskar Jihad has operated training camps in the jungles of Sulawesi. The mutual ethnic cleansing campaigns engaged in by Laskar Jihad and its opposite numbers in the Christian communities of the Moluccas (the Maluku Sovereignty Front) have reduced the death toll in recent years (by eliminating mutually vulnerable minority communities), but overall deaths have been in the thousands.

A similar although less violent (or at least less well documented) process is taking place in Kalimantan (Indonesian Borneo), where Madurese settlers and indigenes from the Dayak community have engaged in massacres and countermassacres. This violence generally does not assume the form of classical terrorism. Instead, it fits the paradigm of "clan insurgent forces," as described in *Globalisation and Insurgency* (Mackinlay 2002, 54–66). The violence on Kalimantan has not attracted the same level of unwanted participation by foreign Jihadis.

Finally, the most serious terrorist challenge confronting the Indonesian state is from Islamists who seek not to dismember the polity, but to seize control of it and transform it. The lead group in this process is Jemaah Islamiyah, responsible for a number of attacks over the past several years. The name dates back to the 1970s, although it is not clear that the organization is that old. JI owes its existence to the Darul Islam movement. Abu Bakar Bashir, the head of JI, began his Islamist career as a member of Darul Islam. He was imprisoned, fled to Malaysia in 1985, and began to recruit Islamists to fight in Afghanistan while raising Saudi funds for his group. He returned to Indonesia when Suharto fell from power in 1998 and opened a Javanese religious school. The group was blamed for attacks in the Philippines in 2000, and it was linked to the Ramzi Ahmed Yousef plot to simultaneously hijack eleven U.S. airliners over the Pacific in 1995. Also in 2000, JI supported a wave of bombings against churches in Indonesia. Its most significant action was the mass casualty attack on the island of Bali in 2002.

That attack, which took 202 civilian lives, finally prodded the Indonesian state into action. Before then authorities in Jakarta were reluctant to take on any additional challenges, fearing that they would provoke an even more violent backlash from the radical Islamist community. The United States itself had not designated JI as a foreign terrorist organization (FTO) until it was linked to the Bali bombing. Since 2002 there has been one attack serious enough to gain international attention—the bombing at the Marriott Hotel in Jakarta that took twelve lives. Smaller scale violence, however, has continued in a wide variety of places (JI is not an exclusively Indonesian organization, but seeks to create a single Islamic state across Southeast Asia). Hambali (the nom de guerre of Riduan Isamuddin), thought to be the number two figure in the group, was apprehended in Thailand in 2003, and his

presence there, along with the surge in Islamist violence in the southern extremities of the country, may indicate a shift in JI tactics. Hambali is currently in U.S. custody at an undisclosed location, but Indonesian authorities have begun to prepare for his eventual transferal to their custody. Abu Bakar Bashir, meanwhile, has been tried, convicted, and sentenced for his role as leader of the group held responsible for the Bali attack. Although his trial was an indication of shifting attitudes among top Indonesian politicians about the seriousness of the JI threat, the sentence he received (four years) indicates how intimidated the political system is. In early 2004 his sentence was further reduced to a mere one year of incarceration. Still, the jailing of Bashir, the seizure of Hambali, and the arrest of more than 200 JI members in the last two years may reduce the group's effectiveness for some time to come.

Relationship with the United States

The U.S.-Indonesian relationship has always been strained and difficult, and it is perhaps more complicated now than at any time since the Sukarno regime. Both governments face a common threat in the form of radical Islamism, but one has a sizable population devoted to the imposition of an Islamic state, and a smaller minority dedicated to achieving that goal by indiscriminately violent means. Beyond the "War on Terrorism," which the Bali attack did much to move the two governments closer together on, other issues creating tension between Jakarta and Washington include human rights, national self-determination, and trade. Sales of F-16s to Indonesia were interrupted because of U.S. displeasure with the events in East Timor, and military-to-military contacts were forbidden for many years.

The "War on Terrorism" may have shifted that policy somewhat, and Indonesian officials are seeking a rehabilitated military relationship with the U.S. Department of Defense. The Indonesian justice system and security apparatus are interested in gaining custody of Hambali. It is assumed that after extracting whatever information can be acquired, the United States may accede to those wishes as a goodwill gesture. Indonesia's primary trading relationship is with Japan, both in imports and exports, but given its leading export (petroleum), Washington is quite concerned about the long-term economic and political stability of Indonesia.

The most notable cooperative effort between the states is the annual Cooperation Afloat Readiness and Training (CARAT) exercise, conducted with elements of the Indonesian naval forces, other regional powers, and the U.S. Pacific Command. Although normally focused on seaborne rescue and antipiracy efforts, the CARAT 2002 exercise included an antiterrorist element. Contact between naval forces is less politically complex, as it does not involve U.S. "boots on the ground," nor does it entail contact with the Indonesian Army (TNI), long criticized for its spotty rights record, particularly in the context of East Timor and other separatist conflicts.

The Future

Indonesian security issues defy prediction. The loss of East Timor was a traumatic event for Jakarta. Whether it represents an aberration or a harbinger of the future erosion of Indonesia is not clear. Plainly, the country faces an unpleasant immediate future, beset by separatists, radical Islamists, and an unstable economic environment. How it can survive those challenges in its present form is an open question.

What is certain is that the Indonesian armed forces, including both the regular army as well as paramilitary units and irregular militias, will continue to play a key role in formal and informal policymaking at all levels of the Indonesian polity. The consequences that this military preeminence in national politics hold for regional security relations are ominous. As the apparent decline of the state continues apace, the potential for the externalization of Indonesia's many internal conflicts will increase, as will the need for regional security cooperation and the temptation to divert restive domestic political forces through a return to the regional adventurism of the early years of independence.

References, Recommended Readings, and Websites

Books
Anderson, Benedict. 1991. *Imagined Communities*. Rev. ed. London: Verso.
Emmerson, Donald. 1976. *Indonesia's Elite: Political Culture and Cultural Politics*. Ithaca, NY: Cornell University Press.
———. 1998. *Indonesia beyond Suharto: Polity, Economy, Society, Transition*. London: M. E. Sharpe.
Geertz, Clifford. 1963. *Agricultural Involution*. Berkeley: University of California Press.
Harvey, Barbara. 1977. *Permesta: Half a Rebellion*. Ithaca, NY: Cornell University Press.
Hibbard, Scott, and David Little. 1997. *Islamic Activism and U.S. Foreign Policy*. Washington, DC: U.S. Institute of Peace.
Husain, Mir Zohair. 2003. *Global Islamic Politics*. 2d ed. New York: Longman.
Huxley, Tim. 2002. *Disintegrating Indonesia?* Oxford: Oxford University Press.

Kepel, Gilles. 2002. *Jihad: The Trail of Political Islam*. Cambridge: Belknap Press.

Mackinlay, John. 2002. *Globalisation and Insurgency*. Oxford: Oxford University Press.

Metcalf, Karl. 2001. *Near Neighbours: Records on Australia's Relations with Indonesia*. Canberra: National Australian Archives.

Military Balance, 2003–2004. London: International Institute for Strategic Studies.

SIPRI Yearbook 2003. New York: Humanities Press.

Smith, E. D. 1985. *Malaya and Borneo*. London: Ian Allan.

Weekes, Richard. 1984. *Muslim Peoples: A World Ethnographic Survey*. Vol. 1. 2d ed. Westport, CT: Greenwood Press.

————. 1984. *Muslim Peoples: A World Ethnographic Survey*. Vol. 2. 2d ed. Westport, CT: Greenwood Press.

Wiarda, Howard. 2004. *Political Development in Emerging Nations*. Belmont, CA: Wadsworth.

Articles/Newspapers

Anonymous. 2002. "In the Region." *Defence Brief* 89 (May):1.

Anonymous. 2004. "Who Will Watch the Watchdogs?" *Economist* 370, no. 8363 (February 21):39.

Montaperto, Ronald, James Przystup, Gerald Faber, and Adam Schwarz. 2000. "Indonesian Democratic Transition." *Strategic Forum* (April):171.

Shari, Michael. 2004. "Indonesia: Suharto's Party Is Surging." *Business Week* 3871 (February 23):58.

Websites

Armed Forces of Indonesia Official Website Tentara Nasional Indonesia Angkatan Darat: http://www.tni-ad.abri.mil.id/.

Central Intelligence Agency. *The World Factbook:* http://www.cia.gov.

Council on Foreign Relations. *Terrorism: Q & A: Jemaah Islamiyah:* http://www.cfrterrorism.org/groups/jemaah2.html.

Custom Wire. *Anti-terror Official: U.S. Personnel in Indonesia to Negotiate Possible Access to Hambali:* http://search.epnet.com/direct.asp?an=CX2004039W2218&db=mth.

Custom Wire. *Indonesia Proposes ASEAN Peacekeeping Force, Extradition Treaty to Bolster Regional Security:* http://search.epnet.com/direct.asp?an=CX2004053W8536&db=mth.

Custom Wire. *Southeast Asian Peacekeeping Force Is Unnecessary: Thai FM:* http://search.epnet.com/direct.asp?an=CX2004053H2105&db=mth.

GlobalSecurity.org: *Indonesia* http://www.globalsecurity.org/military/world/indonesia/index.html.

Monterey Institute of International Studies. *2002 Conventional Terrorism Chronology: Incidents Involving Sub-National Actors Resulting in Death or Injury:* http://cns.miis.edu/pubs/reports/pdfs/conv2k2.pdf.

Virtual Information Center-Primer: Separatism in Southern Thailand: http://www.vic-info.org/SEAsia/thailandpage.htm.

Virtual Information Center—Special Press Summary: Unrest in Southern Thailand: http://www.vic-info.org/SEAsia/thailandpage.htm.

Iran

Michael Barutciski

Geography and History

Located in the Middle East between Iraq and Pakistan, Iran borders the Caspian Sea, the Gulf of Oman, and the Persian Gulf, and occupies a strategic maritime pathway for crude oil transport (the Strait of Hormuz). It shares land borders with Afghanistan, Armenia, Azerbaijan, Turkey, and Turkmenistan. The country is slightly larger than Alaska. The terrain is composed of a rugged mountainous rim, a high central basin with deserts and mountains, as well as small discontinuous plains along its coasts. Just over 10 percent of the land is considered arable. The highest point is Kuh-e Damavand, at 5,671 meters.

The country was once known as Persia, a great empire of ancient times. It was also one of the first countries occupied by the Muslim armies that came from Arabia in the seventh century. Conquests by Seljuk Turks, Mongols, and Tamerlane followed this period. The country has long maintained a strong and unique identity within the Islamic world, particularly as a result of its own language and its Shi'a interpretation of Islam.

Iran is the most populous country in the Middle East. The present population of approximately 68.3 million inhabitants is composed of an ethnically diverse mix: Persian 51 percent, Azeri 24 percent, Gilaki and Mazandarani 8 percent, Kurd 7 percent, Arab 3 percent, Lur 2 percent, Baloch 2 percent, Turkmen 2 percent, other 1 percent. Shi'a Muslims represent 89 percent of the population, Sunni Muslims represent 10 percent, and the remaining 1 percent are Zoroastrian, Jewish, Christian, and Baha'i (CIA 2003).

Modern Iranian history begins with the adoption in 1906 of a constitution limiting the royal absolutism of the Persian dynasties that ruled during five centuries. Oil was discovered two years later. A military commander named Reza Khan seized power in 1921 and the parliament voted to make him shah in 1925. He ruled for almost sixteen years. During his reign, the state officially adopted the name of "Iran" in 1935 (it was before that known as Persia). The shah's pro-Axis allegiance during World War II led to a British and Soviet occupation in 1941. He was eventually deposed by the Allies and replaced by his son, Mohammed Reza Pahlavi, who became shah in 1941.

In 1951 the nationalist militant Mohammed Mossadegh was named prime minister. Parliament voted the same year to nationalize the British-owned oil industry. Mossadegh was overthrown in 1953 by the shah, who benefited from Western backing. During the 1960s the shah embarked on a series of economic, social, and administrative reforms known as the White Revolution. The country was modernized and Westernized, and the

307

Table 1   Key Statistics

Type of government	Theocratic republic
Population (millions)	68.3 (July 2003 est.)
Religion	Shi'a Islam 89%, Sunni Islam 10%
Main industries	Oil, textiles, construction materials
Main security threats	U.S. military presence in region
Defense spending (% GDP)	4.6 (2002)
Size of military (thousands)	540 (active, 2003)
Number of civil wars since 1945	1
Number of interstate wars since 1945	1

Sources

Central Intelligence Agency Website. 2003. CIA *World Factbook.* http://www.cia.gov/cia/
   publications/factbook/ (accessed May 15, 2005).
International Institute for Strategic Studies (IISS). 2003. *The Military Balance 2003–2004.*
   London: IISS and Oxford University Press.

economy grew at an unprecedented rate because of its petroleum reserves.

Yet the shah's policies and reliance on the SAVAK (Internal Security and Intelligence Service) to control opposition movements led to riots, strikes, and mass demonstrations in the late 1970s. Shortly after martial law was imposed, the shah and his family were forced into exile in January 1979. The religious leader Ayatollah Ruhollah Khomeini returned after more than fourteen years in exile (in Turkey, Iraq, and France) and directed a revolution that led to the creation of a new theocratic republic based on Islamic principles. On April 1, 1979, the Islamic Republic of Iran was proclaimed following a referendum.

Revolutionary Iran has broken sharply with the foreign policy followed by the shah. That is particularly important in terms of the country's relations with the West. According to the U.S. Department of State, Iran's foreign policy emphasizes the following points: vehement anti-U.S. and anti-Israeli sentiments, elimination of outside influences in its region, support for Muslim political movements abroad, as well as a significant increase in diplomatic contacts with developing countries.

Iran's shift to extremist positions on the world scene is illustrated by Ayatollah Khomeini's 1989 decision to declare Salman Rushdie's *Satanic Verses* to be blasphemous to Islam and to issue a *fatwa* (religious edict) ordering Muslims to kill the British author. Ayatollah Khomeini died on June 3, 1989. The following day, the assembly of experts (an elected body of senior clerics) appointed Ali Khamenei as the new national religious leader.

The 1979 constitution describes the sociopolitical and economic order of the Islamic republic and establishes Shi'a Islam of the Twelver (*Jaafari*) sect as Iran's official religion. The country is governed by both religious and secular leaders with overlapping duties. The constitution provides for the country to be led by a religious leader (or a council of religious leaders). The leader (or council) appoints the six religious members of the council of guardians, appoints the highest judicial authorities, and assumes the role of commander-in-chief of the armed forces. The council of guardians must approve the competence of candidates for the presidency or the National Assembly and must review all bills and legislation to verify their conformity to Islamic principles. The president of the republic is elected (by an absolute majority of votes) by universal suffrage to a four-year term and is responsible for the supervision of the executive branch. The president appoints and supervises the council of ministers and coordinates government policies presented to the National Assembly. The latter consists of 290 members elected to four-year terms by direct ballots containing candidates approved by the council of guardians (see Table 2).

Various power struggles resulted in the clergy dominating political life by the early 1980s, as the center and the left of the political spectrum were eliminated. The Islamic Republican Party was the dominant political party until its dissolution in 1987. Iran now has many parties and associations involved in political activities (U.S. Department of State 2003).

There are twenty-eight provinces in Iran, each headed by a governor-general. The regular military is charged with defending the country's borders, and the Is-lamic Revolutionary Guard forces are responsible primarily for internal security.

Iran's economy is a mixture of central planning, state ownership of oil and other large enterprises, village agriculture, as well as small-scale private trading and service ventures (U.S. Department of State). The main industries are the following: petroleum, petrochemicals, textiles, cement and other construction materials, food processing, meta fabricating, and armaments (CIA 2003). According to the U.S. Department of State, mismanagement and bureaucratic inefficiency have hampered the implementation of coherent economic policies.

Economic development was relatively rapid in prerevolutionary Iran. By the 1970s, the traditional agricultural society had been significantly industrialized and modernized. The rate of growth had slowed prior to the civil unrest in 1978 and has been further stunted since the implementation of the revolutionary government's policies. Banks and important industries such as petroleum, transportation, utilities, and mining were nationalized after the revolution. Economic activity was further handicapped by the

Table 2   Institutions of Governance

Supreme Leader	approves president, supervises government policies, commands armed forces, appoints judiciary
President	nominally heads government
Council of Guardians	reviews legislation in terms of Islamic and constitutional conformity
National Assembly	oversees executive
Assembly of Experts	selects supreme leader
Expediency Council	mediates legislative disputes between consultative assembly and council of guardians

Sources
U.S. Department of State, *Background Note: Iran 2003.* http://www.state.gov/r/pa/ei/bgn/5314.htm.
Independent Task Force Sponsored by the Council on Foreign Relations. 2004. *Iran: Time for a New Approach.* New York.

war with Iraq (1980–1988) and the decline of oil prices beginning in late 1985 (U.S. Department of State).

Iran's GDP grew somewhat after the war with Iraq ended. In 1989, Ayatollah Khomeini approved President Rafsanjani's economic plan that relied on allowing the country to seek foreign loans. Although President Khatami continued to pursue the market reforms initiated by President Rafsanjani (1989–1997), he did not succeed in diversifying the oil-dependent economy (U.S. Department of State). Along with Jordan and Syria, Iran was nonetheless the only state in the Middle East to experience positive economic growth in 2002 (IISS 2003, 273).

The country has recently improved its diplomatic and commercial relations with Western Europe. It has maintained regular diplomatic and commercial ties with Russia and other former Soviet republics. Energy resources from the Caspian Sea represent an area of common concern.

According to some observers, Iran has entered in recent years another era of political and social transformation (BBC 2004). A sea change was heralded by the victory of the liberals over the ruling conservatives in parliamentary elections held in April 2000. President Mohammad Khatami's support for greater civil and political freedom made him popular with young electors (50 percent of the population is under twenty-five years of age). His policies opposed the views of Ayatollah Khamenei and other hard-liners intent on maintaining Islamic traditions.

The early days of the revolution were characterized by severe human rights violations and political turmoil, according to the U.S. Department of State, and the human rights situation continues to represent a serious problem. Political rivalry between President Khatami's supporters (including a large parliamentary majority) and the conservatives favoring Ayatollah Khamenei (including the judiciary and many security officials) contributed to the growing internal tensions. Rising unemployment has also contributed to social discontent among young people eager for more social freedom. According to Amnesty International's 2003 annual report, attacks on freedom of expression and association have resulted in scores of students, academics, and journalists being arbitrarily arrested. Politically motivated criminal charges founded on libel- or security-related laws were commonplace. Torture and ill treatment of prisoners (including prisoners of conscience) occurred throughout 2002, particularly in cases in which detainees were denied access to lawyers and relatives (Amnesty International 2003). A parliament-approved bill outlawing torture was rejected by the council of guardians in June 2002. Delegates from human rights organizations such as Amnesty International and Human Rights Watch are generally denied entry into the country. Iran's first female judge (nominated in 1975 and forced to resign after the 1979 revolution) and present-day civil rights campaigner Shirin Ebadi became the country's first Nobel Peace Prize winner in October 2003.

President Khatami's success in establishing a relatively free press was recently targeted by the conservative judiciary. Proreform publications have been closed. Proreform authors and editors have also been jailed. Television remains very popular in Iran, and restrictions on satellite television are less severe than before (BBC 2004). Many radio broadcasters target Iran, including the U.S.-backed Radio Farda, which plays to a younger audience.

An estimated 7 million Iranians have access to the Internet, which represents an effective way of circumventing the barriers of censorship (ibid.). The Internet constitutes the main forum for dissident voices, despite the prohibition on providers offering access to pornographic or anti-Islamic sites. Internet access is easy to arrange and relatively affordable.

Iran has come under increased pressure from the United States after President Bush declared it part of the "axis of evil" in 2002. The pressure intensified even more after the U.S.-led war against Iraq and Washington's accusations that Iran is developing weapons of mass destruction and subverting U.S. efforts in Iraq. It is worth noting that many countries warn against travel to Iran.

Regional Geopolitics

Iran has assumed the role of a promoter of revolutionary Islam and guardian of oppressed Islamic populations everywhere. As a result, Iran supports extremist Islamic movements in the Middle East and elsewhere in an effort to enhance the regime's credentials in the Islamic world.

The recent U.S.-led war in Iraq has affected defense and security policies throughout the Middle East. Even though most Iranians retain bitter sentiments over their eight-year war with Iraq during the 1980s, they are equally concerned about the effects of Operation Iraqi Freedom on their own internal situation and worried about further U.S. military objectives in the region. Iran's nuclear program is undoubtedly the greatest concern to regional and international actors. Regional powers continue to be worried about the country's continuing support of the Lebanese-based Hizballah and its alleged backing of rebel groups resisting coalition forces in Iraq.

A key factor in revolutionary Iran's defense planning is the sense of isolation that followed after the 1979 revolution. Shortly after the revolution, the country faced Iraqi forces largely without international aid during the eight-year war with its western neighbor. Many Iranians remain angry at the lack of international response to Iraq's use of chemical weapons during that war.

Iran's neighborly relations in the Middle East have been complicated by the country's attempts to export its revolutionary Islamic ideology. For example, Iran supported a plot to overthrow the Bahrain government in 1981. Two years later, Tehran expressed support for Shi'ites who bombed a series of Western embassies in Kuwait. Iranian pilgrims rioted during the pilgrimage to Mecca in 1987. Countries with strong Islamic movements such as Egypt and Algeria are suspicious of Iranian intentions.

The country's defense planning places heavy emphasis on self-reliance in order to respond to potential military confrontations, regardless of foreign aid or sanctions. Likewise, Iran tries to project the image of a society that can take heavy punishment and even glorify martyrdom.

Iran's situation in the region is characterized largely by tensions between two competing orientations: Islamic universalism and Persian nationalism (Eisenstadt 2001). In some ways, Iran finds itself caught in a dilemma: it is a relatively limited regional power with (overly) large ambitions resulting from strong ideological convictions.

Territorial disputes between Iran and its neighbors persist over maritime and land boundaries, as well as navigation channels. There are also existing disputes over Iran's occupation of Tunb Islands and Abu Musa Island. Iran insists on the Caspian Sea being divided into five equal sectors, while other littoral states generally agree to equidistant seabed boundaries (CIA 2003).

Iranian patriotic sentiment encourages the population to see the country as the dominant power in the Persian Gulf region, largely because it has the largest territory and longest coastline in the region. This self-perception positions Iran in direct competition with Saudi Arabia (and Iraq before the defeat of Saddam Hussein's regime).

As a consequence of the tensions associated with these aspirations, the country has been trying to modernize and enhance its military. Yet financial restraints have prevented the country from developing a large and effective military. Iran appears to have been focusing on missile technology and nonconventional weapons in order to compensate.

Since the 1979 revolution, defense planning has focused on perceived threats, particularly from Iraq, Israel, the Soviet Union, Turkey, Azerbaijan, Afghanistan, and the United States. As Iran is a sworn enemy of Israel, its nonconventional weapons and missile systems represent a particular concern to the Jewish state. Iranian officials undoubtedly fear the possibility of a preemptive strike similar to Israel's 1981 air strike against the Osiraq nuclear reactor in Iraq. Israel's recent military cooperation with Turkey is of particular concern to Iran.

Iran remained neutral following Iraq's invasion of Kuwait in 1990, denouncing both Baghdad's aggression and any long-term U.S. military presence in the region. Iran and Iraq resumed diplomatic relations on September 11, 1990. Although the Iranian government is undoubtedly satisfied that Saddam Hussein's regime has been overthrown, the uncertainties relating to Iraq's future present serious strategic challenges, as well as opportunities, for Iran.

The Soviet Union is no longer a threat to the country's independence, but the new independent states in the Caucasus and Central Asia represent a new menace. Iran supported Armenia in its struggle with Azerbaijan. The latter now enjoys special relations with the United States and serves as a potential magnet for the Azeri minority, who compose almost one quarter of the total population of Iran.

Iran also feared that a Taliban-controlled Afghanistan could provoke an uprising among the estimated 2 million Afghan refugees who have found refuge in the country (U.S. Committee for Refugees 2003). This has long been one of the largest refugee populations in the world. Tehran was also concerned that the Taliban could aggravate tensions in eastern Iran, where Sunnis are concentrated and form about 30 percent of the population. As an example of those fears, Iran deployed thousands of troops to its border with Afghanistan in September 1998 after the Taliban admitted responsibility for the deaths of several Iranian diplomats and a journalist (in Mazar-e Sharif).

Relations between Iran and the United States thawed somewhat during the 2001 U.S.-led military intervention against the Taliban and al-Qaeda in Afghanistan. Iran supported the operation by using its influence to mobilize the Shi'a Hazara community (including financing and arming militias), and to a lesser extent the Tadjiks and Uzbeks (Gorce 2002, 20). There were surely national interests at stake, in that Iran perceived the Taliban as an extension of Pakistani influence on the Afghani territory that neighbors some of its most sensitive border areas (Independent Task Force 2004, 24).

Following contacts between U.S. and Iranian officials in Geneva during the weeks preceding the 2003 U.S.-led military intervention against Saddam Hussein's regime, an agreement was negotiated between Iraqi Shi'ite organizations supported by Iran and those protected by Washington. The agreement provided for the establishment of a corridor between Iran and the Shi'a populated areas occupied by U.S. forces in Iraq. Iran's response was effectively subdued during the initial phases of the U.S.-led operation in Iraq. Iran even expelled the Wahhabist group involved in violent political activities in northern Iraq (and suspected by Washington of links with al-Qaeda) that tried to cross the frontier into Iraq after Kurdish forces seized control of the area (Gorce 2003, 8).

However, U.S. secretary of defense Donald Rumsfeld warned Syria and Iran not to assist the Iraqi resistance groups after the fall of Baghdad. Many Iranian officials have undoubtedly concluded that the future of their country will be played out in terms of events in Iraq. U.S. designs for the region, the politico-religious struggles between various Iraqi groups, and the armed Iraqi resistance to the occupation are all seen as key factors affecting Iran's immediate future (ibid.). Tehran responded by creating Al-Olam, an Arab-language continuous news television station focused on events in Iraq.

As the above makes apparent, even though the regime in Iraq has been removed from power, Iran's fears regarding U.S. forces have grown. Although the U.S. presence in the Gulf previously constrained Iran's regional ambitions, its occupation of Iraq now poses a direct threat. The United States has encouraged oil and gas pipelines that circumvent Iran, thereby contributing to Iranian fears that the United States is trying to encircle the country (Eisenstadt 2001).

Iran's nuclear program remains a primary cause for concern in the region. Conceived and initiated under the reign of the shah, Iran's nuclear program was suspended following the 1979 revolution. It appears to have been relaunched following the emergence or possible development of nuclear forces in Pakistan, Israel, and the Gulf states in which U.S. aerial and naval forces have been deployed (Gorce 2003, 9). It is suspected that Iran's missiles can reach population centers in Israel, Turkey, Saudi Arabia, and other Gulf states (Eisenstadt 2001). This could influence regional powers in case of a military showdown.

Conflict Past and Present
Conflict History
Soviet troops stationed in northwest Iran following World War II backed revolts establishing pro-Soviet regimes in Azerbaijani and Kurdish territories. Pressure exerted by the United States and the United Nations forced a Soviet withdrawal. The Azerbaijani revolt consequently disintegrated, and U.S.-backed Iranian forces defeated the Kurdish revolt as the Cold War set in.

Iraqi armed forces invaded Iran on September 22, 1980, following border skirmishes and disputes relating to the sovereignty of the waterway between the two countries, the Shatt al-Arab. That was the beginning of an interstate war that lasted eight years and contributed to the plummeting of the country's oil wealth. A cease-fire was implemented on August 20, 1988. Neither country had made any real gains in the war, according to the U.S. Department of State.

*Current and Potential
Military Confrontations*

The Iranian regime is opposed internally by several armed political groups. An estimated 1,200 to 1,800 opposition fighters from the Kurdish Democratic Party of Iran are suspected of being present in Iran (IISS 2003, 110). Around 200 members of the Kurdistan Organization of the Communist Party of Iran are also believed to be active in the Kurdish territories (ibid., 346). The largest nonstate armed groups opposing the Iranian regime are the Mujahedin-e Khalq Organization, which includes 3,000 members, and its dissident group, the National Liberation Army, which includes several more thousand members (ibid.). There were, for example, a series of terrorist attacks by Mujahedin-e Khalq (originating in Afghanistan) in recent years.

Because of its relatively weak land units, Iran does not represent a significant ground threat to its neighbors. It has the capability to launch limited air strikes against its neighbors, as it did on several occasions against Iraq during the 1990s. In terms of conventional threats, Iran's only real offensive option lies with its naval units in the Persian Gulf and their ability to jeopardize oil exports. Its submarines, coastal missile batteries, and sea mines have the capacity to disrupt oil shipments from the region and threaten the security of some Gulf states. Iran's nonconventional weapons may even be able to block the Strait of Hormuz for a short period. However, Iranian offensive actions of that nature are un-

likely because the country has much to lose from such provocations. It depends as much as its neighbors on the export of oil. Even though the possibility of aggressive posturing and political threats should not be discarded in a confrontational context, these would probably be carried out only in the most extreme scenarios, in which the regime's survival is at stake.

Iran's development of nonconventional weapons and delivery systems, however, has the potential to threaten the entire region. In the event of a confrontation with U.S. forces, Iran's air defenses would pose little difficulty for U.S. airpower. Its naval forces would be easily defeated by the U.S. Navy (Eisenstadt 2001), and the country has fewer armored units than those possessed by Iraqi forces at the time of Operation Iraqi Freedom (IISS 2003, 109, 111). Its most effective weapon would likely be its ability to damage U.S. interests in the region by the use of terrorist and subversive tactics. With the cooperation of the Lebanese Hezbollah, Iran can potentially set off terrorist attacks on several continents. Iran's biological warfare program also represents a serious threat to U.S. forces, which lack the means to effectively counter such mass destruction capabilities (Eisenstadt 2001).

Alliance Structure

Prior to the revolution, Iran relied on access to U.S. and UK military hardware in its defense planning. In recent years, Iran's only significant ally in the Middle East has been Syria. Sudan has also been an ally in the country's efforts to support Islamic movements around the world. Iran has more recently taken significant steps to improve its relations with its Gulf neighbors, particularly Saudi Arabia (U.S. Department of State 2003). This relative lack of allies indicates that the country has limited capabilities to support a war effort and replace combat losses in the event of military confrontation.

Size and Structure of the Military
Size and Structure
According to the constitution, the supreme religious leader (currently Ayatollah Khamenei) is the commander-in-chief of the armed forces, which are estimated to include more than half a million active members. According to the International Institute for Strategic Studies, the armed forces are composed of the regular military (approximately 420,000 active members), the Islamic Revolutionary Guard forces (as many as 120,000 active members), and law enforcement forces (40,000 active members). The regular military and the Islamic Revolutionary Guards fall under the authority of the Ministry of Defense and Armed Forces Logistics. Law enforcement forces fall under the authority of the Ministry of Interior, although it has been alleged that their loyalty lies in fact with the supreme leader (Eisenstadt 2001).

Iran's armed forces have been divided between regular military units and Islamic Revolutionary Guards since the 1979 revolution. According to the constitution, the regular military is responsible for maintaining the security of the country's borders. The Islamic Guards were formed to maintain internal security and protect the ideological integrity of the regime. They have bases near all major cities. The Islamic Revolutionary Guards have a conventional military role as well.

For example, they fought alongside the regular military during the Iran-Iraq war and have continued to hold joint exercises since the end of the war in 1988.

Relations between the regular military and the Islamic Revolutionary Guards remain nonetheless difficult. The Islamic Revolutionary Guards distrust the regular military units because of their association with the shah's regime. In the same way that many of the political structures are checked by religious institutions, the regular military's powers are circumscribed by the Revolutionary Guards. To some extent, the result is parallel military structures that create problems of unity of command and effectiveness. Attempts to bring together the upper echelons of the regular military and the Islamic Revolutionary Guards in order to improve unity of command have been short lived.

The experience of recent years suggests that in case of internal unrest, the law enforcement forces would form the first line of defense. They would be backed up by Basij militia units of the Islamic Revolutionary Guards, followed by other special units of the Guards. The ground forces of the Islamic Revolutionary Guards would then be deployed, with the regular military deployed as a last resort. Interestingly, recent reports concerning election results suggest that the divisions found between conservatives and reformists in the society at large are also present within the ranks of the Islamic Revolutionary Guards.

Although both the regular military and the Islamic Revolutionary Guards have land, air, and naval units, the former is larger and better equipped. Because the regular military would carry out most operations in the event of a war with its neighbors, its status was upgraded in the late 1990s by the creation of its own new supreme commander (ibid.). Following the Iran-Iraq war, the Islamic Revolutionary Guards have been somewhat modernized and have adopted the uniforms and rank structures found in the regular military. Nevertheless, the Islamic Revolutionary Guards units are generally smaller and more lightly equipped than the regular military.

Deployment is influenced to some extent by the concentration of the country's most valuable economic assets (oil, gas) in the Gulf region. Most ground forces are deployed in the border regions with Iraq. The air force is deployed largely in border regions with Iraq and the Gulf, while the navy is deployed essentially in Gulf waters (ibid.).

In terms of equipment for conventional warfare, the armed forces have, for example, an estimated 1,565 main battle tanks (including 480 T-72 and 150 M-60A1), 750 armored infantry fighting vehicles (350 BMP-1 and 400 BMP-2), 3 *Kilo*-class submarines (Russian type–877), 3 frigates (British Vosper Mk 5), 15 naval patrol craft, 7 mine warfare naval craft, and 74 fighter aircraft (including 25 MiG-29A) (IISS 2003, 109–110). The Islamic Revolutionary Guards are in charge of Iran's nonconventional and missile capabilities. The armed forces' overall capabilities appear to be strongest in two extreme forms: nonconventional warfare and terrorism (Eisenstadt 2001).

In terms of cooperation with foreign military personnel, an estimated 150 Islamic Revolutionary Guards are deployed in Lebanon, and an undisclosed number of military advisors may be in Sudan (IISS 2003, 110). As many as 400 foreign military technicians and training staff (from China, Russia, and North Korea) may be present in Iran (ibid.). The Iranian military contributes two observers to UNMEE (Ethiopia, Eritrea).

Budget

Defense spending has increased in recent years, from 3.3 percent of GDP in 2000 to 4.6 percent of GDP in 2002 (ibid., 273, 336). The defense budget has continued to increase more recently from $3.4 billion in 2002 to $4.2 billion in 2003 (ibid., 276).

In October 2001, Iran signed a military-technical agreement with Russia involving up to $4 billion in military sales over the next decade (ibid., 273). In 2002, Iran signed another important defense cooperation agreement with India that provides it with military equipment, training, and maintenance. In return, Iran has granted India the right to use Iranian military facilities in the event of a war with Pakistan (ibid.).

Russia and China represent Iran's most important suppliers in terms of arms deliveries and transfer agreements (ibid., 342–343). For example, Iran received from Russia the delivery of 100 T-72 main battle tanks in 1998, 200 BMP-2 infantry fighting vehicles in 1998, 4 Mi–17 helicopters in 2000, and 30 Mi–8 helicopters in 2001. Iraq returned 29 MiG-29 aircraft in 1999 (ibid., 281).

Despite being a contracting party to the Nuclear Non-Proliferation Treaty, Iran is suspected of trying to acquire nuclear weapons. Although Iran's nuclear procurement activities have been extensive, it may take years for the country to be able to produce fissionable material if it cannot obtain diverted fissionable material abroad. The country has allegedly tried to obtain enriched uranium from a facility in Khazakhstan, fuel fabrication and reprocessing capabilities from Argentina, research reactors from Argentina, India, China, and Russia, nuclear power plants from Russia and China, gas centrifuge enrichment technology from Switzerland and Germany, a gas centrifuge enrichment plant and a laser enrichment plant from Russia, as well as an uranium conversion plant from Russia or China (Eisenstadt 2001).

Russia has recently helped Iran build an $800 million nuclear facility at Bushehr. This suspected covert attempt to establish a nuclear weapons program has been condemned by international actors (such as the European Union and the International Atomic Energy Agency). Indeed, Iran's procurement practices suggest that it is trying to gain the capability to produce plutonium or highly enriched uranium. For example, Iran's uranium mining and establishment of new facilities (particularly recently assembled centrifuge machines and the new heavy water plant at Arak) could give the country the capability to locally develop the fissionable material necessary for nuclear weapons (IISS 2003, 103).

Iran's initial failure to disclose information about these facilities has led to condemnations from the intergovernmental nuclear watchdog (IAEA). In September 2003, the IAEA warned Iran to demonstrate it is not pursuing a nuclear weapons program. Two months later the IAEA concluded that there was no evidence of a nuclear weapons program in Iran, even though the country has admitted producing high-grade plutonium for civilian purposes. After initial obstacles, the IAEA was able to reach agreement with Iran that would allow no-notice snap inspections. That process has recently been complicated, however, by

> ### Sidebar 1   International Atomic Energy Agency Resolution
>
> Following a report by the director general of the International Atomic Energy Agency, in June 2004 its Board of Governors adopted a resolution which deplores that Iran's "cooperation [with the Agency] has not been as full, timely and proactive as it should have been." Iran responded to this resolution by announcing that it has resumed building nuclear centrifuges. Although the Iranian government insists it has not resumed enriching uranium, Washington sources claim that the centrifuges are intended to enrich uranium to weapons-grade for use in nuclear weapons.
>
> **Source**
> Independent Task Force. 2004. *Iran: Time for a New Approach.* New York: Council on Foreign Relations.

Iran's alleged failure to comply with its obligations (see Sidebar 1).

Even though Iran is a contracting party to the Chemical Weapons Convention, it is suspected of having significant stockpiles of weaponized chemical agents (including nerve, blister, choking, and blood agents). These agents are allegedly deployed in bombs, artillery shells, and probably missile warheads (Eisenstadt 2001). Iran has probably also deployed biological weapons, although it may not have developed the technology to disseminate biological weapons agents efficiently (ibid.).

In terms of missile delivery systems, Iran announced in July 2003 completion of the final tests on its Shihab–3 medium-range ballistic missile (range 1,300 kilometers). The missile entered into military service at the end of the month. Its payload of 700 kilograms has led to assessments that it is capable of carrying a small nuclear warhead and possibly chemical and biological warheads (IISS 2003, 103). The country's strategic missile force also includes 300 Shahab–1 (range 320 kilometers), 100 Shihab–2 (range 500 kilometers), and 200 Chinese CSS-8 missiles with a range of 150 kilometers (Eisenstadt 2001). Iran has been working on developing Shihab–4 (2,000 kilometers) and Shihab–5 (5,000–10,000 kilometers) missiles since 1994 (IISS 2003, 281).

There have been several other noteworthy developments concerning the domestic aerospace industry. A first prototype of the Shafagh aircraft is expected in 2008 (ibid., 273). The first local overhaul of a MiG-29 was recently completed, and it was estimated to have cost half the amount of an overhaul in Russia (ibid.).

Civil-Military Relations

Iran has a problematic history of civil-military relations. The 1953 coup and the 1979 revolution continue to affect the country's security situation. Senior officers of the Islamic Revolutionary Guards threatened a coup during the unrest of 1999. Order was quickly restored largely because of the country's ruling clerics. It remains unclear whether the coup could have succeeded, given the political divisions within the armed forces (Eisenstadt 2001).

It is alleged that leaders of the security forces have in effect already intervened in political affairs by participating in the murders of reformists (ibid.). Amnesty International's most recent annual report refers to ill-treatment of prisoners of conscience by Revolutionary Guards in military detention centers (Amnesty International 2003).

Terrorism

According to the U.S. Department of State, Iran is a major state sponsor of terrorism. The country backs a number of groups violently opposed to the Arab-Israeli peace process: Hizballah, Hamas, the Palestinian Islamic Jihad, and the Popular Front for the Liberation of Palestine-General Command.

Terrorism has been an important part of Iran's foreign policy since the 1979 revolution. Its use of terrorism was most concentrated in the 1980s, when the regime participated in kidnappings, assassinations, and bombings in the Middle East, Western Europe, and Asia (Eisenstadt 2001).

Iran allegedly runs terrorist operations out of embassies, consulates, and Islamic cultural centers. Iranian charitable associations have also been suspected of funneling money to extremist groups (ibid.). State officials are known to hunt down dissidents abroad and to use terrorist groups as a tool against enemies (for example, the Kurdish Workers' Party in Turkey).

Aside from attracting attention to the revolutionary Islamic regime, these operations have arguably achieved some success. For example, Hizballah hostage-takings made possible secret deals with the United States (in order to recover impounded financial assets abroad and trade for arms). Hizballah was largely responsible for the Israeli Defense Force's withdrawal from south Lebanon. It also contributed to the breakdown of Israeli-Palestinian negotiations for peace and to the outbreak of the second *intifada* in 2000.

Yet terrorism is also largely responsible for the country's isolation. The high-profile terrorist actions in the heart of Europe, particularly during the 1980s, harmed Iran's relations with European powers. The tensions with Western powers played a role in their pro-Iraqi stance during the Iran-Iraq war. Likewise, Arab Gulf states have built closer ties to the United States for their security guarantees.

Despite these negative consequences on the country's long-term security, terrorism remains one of Iran's main tools to threaten the United States in case of confrontation. For example, it provides the country with a genuine threat to U.S. military facilities in Gulf states. In cooperation with Hizballah, Iran could conceivably initiate a terrorist campaign with the potential of affecting several continents. It is worth noting that Hizballah is arguably the most capable terrorist group in the world (IISS 2003, 358), and that it is armed, trained, and financed by Iran.

There are linkages between Iran's terrorism problem and transnational trafficking. In April 2001, Iran and Saudi Arabia signed a major security deal to combat terrorism, drug trafficking, and organized crime. Iran nevertheless remains a key transshipment point for Southwest Asian heroin to Europe (CIA 2003). In fact, Iran's internal sociopolitical problems may be reflected in the dramatic situation relating to drug dependency: some statistics suggest that the country has one of the highest heroin addiction rates in the world (Gouverneur 2002, 7).

Relationship with the United States

For many Iranians, the starting point for understanding current U.S.-Iranian relations is the alleged U.S. involvement in the 1953 coup against Prime Minister Mossadegh that helped bring the shah back to power. In that sense, the Islamic revolution at the beginning of 1979 is seen as a blow to U.S. interests in Iran. Relations quickly deteriorated.

On November 4, 1979, Islamic militants took fifty-two Americans hostage inside the U.S. embassy in Tehran. The militants demanded the extradition of the shah (who was in the United States for medical treatment) to face trial in Iran. The exiled shah died of cancer in Egypt in July 1980. The U.S. hostages in Tehran were released on January 20, 1981, following 444 days in captivity.

The United States ruptured diplomatic relations with Iran on April 7, 1980, and the Swiss government assumed representation of U.S. interests in Tehran on April 24, 1980. Iranian interests in the United States are represented by the Pakistan government (U.S. Department of State 2003). The Algiers declaration of January 20, 1981, provided for the creation of an Iran-U.S. Claims Tribunal located in The Hague, that has handled claims of U.S. citizens against Iran and of Iranian citizens against the United States.

The United States led an embargo against Iran during the Iran-Iraq war that made it difficult for the country to sustain its war effort. Several high-profile incidents mark U.S.-Iranian relations in the middle of the 1980s, a decade that ended with the United States releasing $567 million of frozen Iranian assets. In a secret arrangement later known as the Iran-Contra affair, the United States attempted to obtain the release of hostages in Lebanon by concluding an arms deal. The USS *Vincennes* also mistakenly shot down an Iran Air Airbus with 290 passengers in July 1988.

The United States imposed oil and trade sanctions against Iran in 1995 for its alleged sponsorship of terrorism, its attempts to acquire nuclear weapons, and its hostility to the Middle East peace process. Commercial relations between Iran and the United States continue to be restricted by U.S. sanctions. As the U.S. government prohibits most trade with Iran, actual commercial activity is restricted to Iranian purchases of food and medical products and U.S. purchases of carpets and food (ibid.).

In January 2002, President Bush described Iran as part of an "axis of evil" in a speech that warned of the proliferation of long-range missiles being developed in that country (as well as in Iraq and North Korea). Unsurprisingly, the speech caused outrage in all political circles of Iran. All political tendencies in Iran also agree that the occupation of Iraq by U.S. forces has achieved the encirclement of their country, which followed from U.S. military deployments in the Gulf region, in the Caucasus, in Central Asia, and in Afghanistan.

However, Iran would be unable to defend itself by conventional means in the event of a military confrontation. Likewise, any open provocations by Iran would invite more sanctions similar to those that weakened neighboring Iraq throughout the 1990s. Although the United States has played a key role in thwarting Iran's nuclear procurement activities, any military confrontation would probably involve the use of some form of nonconventional weapons, as well as terrorism.

According to the U.S. Department of State, areas of objectionable Iranian behavior are defined as follows: Iranian efforts to acquire nuclear weapons and other weapons of mass destruction; Iran's support for and involvement in international terrorism; Iran's support for vio-

lent opposition to the Middle East peace process; and the country's dismal human rights record. Sanctions against Iran have recently been renewed by the United States because of its alleged support for armed groups resisting coalition forces in Iraq (see Sidebar 2).

Sidebar 2   Iran and al-Qaeda

Iran denies U.S. claims that it has harbored or supported al-Qaeda operatives after the fall of the Taliban in Afghanistan, and refutes the suggestion that it has allowed insurgents to cross into Iraq. Although the Iranian government acknowledges that it cannot fully control its long borders with Afghanistan, it claims that it has arrested and deported hundreds of al-Qaeda suspects. The new Iraqi government has announced that about 14 percent of the foreign fighters in detention are of Iranian origin.

Source
Press Association. 2004. "Iran denies fuelling insurgency" (August 1).

The Future

Iran's economy has been performing relatively well over recent years, and it is likely to continue to do so because of strong oil prices and higher oil production. External confidence in its economic prospects is reflected by two successful Eurobond issues in 2002 (IISS 2003, 273). The recent introduction of a single exchange rate should help to reduce the high inflation rates (for example, 16 percent in 2002). The result is that an increase in the country's defense budget can be expected (ibid.), along with further modernization programs concerning its armed forces.

It is unlikely that the United States will launch a military invasion of Iran like the one against Iraq. Iran would represent an operation of a different scale, given its population size and resources. An occupation of Iran would entail the deployment of considerable resources (Gorce 2003, 9). Although Iranian forces could be overwhelmed, significant and prolonged resistance groupings would probably form in the central parts of the country (outside Kurdish zones in the northwest and Baloutchi zones in the southeast).

For some analysts, the risks and uncertainties associated with overt, large-scale military operations against Iran suggest that there may be better possibilities in terms of covert operations. According to that viewpoint, these operations would capitalize on the serious internal dissent and could be more productive in terms of regime change. The large abstention rate in the 2003 elections suggests significant discontent among young voters who have become frustrated with the lack of tangible results from the reformist camp. The recent student revolts are an example of that dynamic. As mentioned in the introduction, the Iranian regime in 2003 was undergoing internal problems which indicated that an eventual shift toward democratic norms associated with good governance is inevitable.

Some analysts nevertheless suggested that the regime was "solidly entrenched and the country not on the brink of revolutionary upheaval" (Independent Task Force 2004, 11). Within this context, the patriotism and strong nationalism that characterize Iranian society should not be underestimated. For those who wish regime change in Iran, it could be counterproductive to show overt support for internal dissent movements. After all, the threat of foreign domination has the ability to unite Iranians of different political persuasions. If a gradual process of change indeed characterizes Iranian politics, selective or limited engagement with the current government may be a more effective approach that will produce results in the long term (ibid., vii). Commercial relations with U.S. businesses also represent a potentially useful diplomatic tool in terms of balancing incentives and punitive measures.

The greatest threat emanating from Iran would be the development of nuclear weapons. Various possibilities need to be pointed out in terms of the country's nuclear program. Iran could pursue its research relating to the necessary technology until it has a sufficiently reliable weapon and until external threats oblige it to develop a nuclear arsenal. The country (like Israel) could secretly produce nuclear weapons and eventually proceed by testing the detonation of a nuclear bomb, as India and Pakistan did in the late 1990s (Gorce 2002, 21). All of these eventualities would be unacceptable from Washington's viewpoint. The United States cannot allow Iran to become a dominant regional force, nor can it provide automatic nuclear protection guarantees to the various Arab monarchies in the Gulf region. Some form of U.S. preemption and preventive doctrine could find its application in relation to this situation. Iran cannot ignore that possibility in its strategic planning (ibid.).

It follows that if Iran insists on continuing its nonconventional weapons program, the most likely military scenario could involve strikes against industrial and nuclear centers capable of producing nuclear capabilities. The Iranian reaction would probably involve destabilization operations in Iraq, Afghanistan, and possibly Pakistan.

As noted above, Iran cannot afford the losses that would follow from a military confrontation with the United States. Yet militant ideology should not be underestimated. Given the Iranian population's generalized hostility toward the United States, it is not clear that negotiations will be privileged over confrontation (ibid. 2003, 8). The Iranian response to perceived threats from the United States will depend to some extent on the internal struggles that have plagued political life in the last few years. If the regime maintains a sufficient degree of internal cohesion, it may be tempted to challenge U.S. interests in the region with terrorism. That approach would be most effective if it is combined with diplomatic and friendly gestures toward its Arab Gulf neighbors.

In any event, Iran will continue to represent one of the most complicated challenges for U.S. foreign policy. Indeed, the country is associated with serious problems relating to nuclear proliferation, state-sponsored terrorism, and the general relationship between religion and politics that have complicated reform in the Middle East. With the unprecedented U.S. presence and engagement in the region, the potential for Iran to create significant difficulties is as great as the possibility for Iran to play an important role in regional stability.

References, Recommended Readings, and Websites

References and Recommended Readings
Amirahmadi, Hooshang, and Manoucher Parvin, eds. 1988. *Post-Revolutionary Iran.* Boulder, CO: Westview Press.
Amnesty International. 2003. *Annual Report.* London: Amnesty International Publications.
BBC News. 2004. *Country Profile: Iran.* http://news.bbc.co.uk/1/hi/world/middle_east/country_profiles/790877.stm.
Buchta, Wilfried. 2000. *Who Rules Iran?* Washington, DC: Washington Institute for Near East Policy.
Central Intelligence Agency (CIA). 2003. *The World Factbook.* http://www.cia.gov/cia/publications/factbook/.
Chubin, Shahram. 1994. *Iran's National Security Policy: Capabilities, Intentions, and Impact.* Washington, DC: Carnegie Endowment for International Peace.
Cordesman, Anthony H. 1998. *Military Balance in the Middle East: Iran.* Washington, DC: Center for Strategic and International Studies.
Cronin, Stephanie. 2003. *The Making of Modern Iran: State and Society under Riza Shah (1921–1941).* London: RoutledgeCurzon.
Eisenstadt, Michael. 1996. *Iranian Military: Capabilities and Intentions.* Washington, DC: Washington Institute for Near East Policy.
———. 2001. "The Armed Forces of the Islamic Republic of Iran: An Assessment." *Middle East Review of International Affairs* 5.
Gorce, Paul-Marie de la. 2002. "Le Sud-Ouest asiatique, au centre de l'offensive américaine." *Le Monde diplomatique* (December):20–21.
———. 2003. "La République islamique d'Iran sous pression." *Le Monde diplomatique* (July):8–9.
Gouverneur, Cédric. 2002. "En Iran, les ravages de la drogue." *Le Monde diplomatique* (March):7.
Human Rights Watch. 2004. *"Like the Dead in Their Coffins"—Torture, Detention, and the Crushing of Dissent in Iran.* New York: HRW Publications.
Independent Task Force. 2004. "Iran: Time for a New Approach." New York: Council on Foreign Relations (July).
International Atomic Energy Agency. 2004. *Implementation of the NPT Safeguards Agreement in the Islamic Republic of Iran—Resolution adopted by the Board of Governors on June 18, 2004.* http://www.iaea.org/Publications/Documents/Board/2004/gov2004-49.pdf.
International Institute for Strategic Studies (IISS). 2003. *The Military Balance 2003—2004.* Oxford: Oxford University Press.

Katouzia, Homa. 2003. *Iranian History and Politics: The Dialectic of State and Society*. London: RoutledgeCurzon.

Katzman, Kenneth. 1993. *The Warriors of Islam: Iran's Revolutionary Guard*. Boulder, CO: Westview Press.

Menashri, David. 1997. *Revolution at a Crossroads: Iran's Domestic Politics and Regional Ambitions*. Washington, DC: Washington Institute for Near East Policy.

Press Association. 2004. "Iran denies fuelling insurgency" (August 1).

Taremi, Kamran. 2003. "Iranian Perspectives on Security in the Persian Gulf." *Iranian Studies* 36:381–391.

U.S. Committee for Refugees. 2003. *World Refugee Survey*. http://www.refugees.org/article.aspx?id=1156.

U.S. Department of State. 2003. *Background Note: Iran*. http://www.state.gov/r/pa/ei/bgn/5314.htm.

Websites

American Institute of Iranian Studies: http://www.simorgh-aiis.org/.

Amnesty International: http://www.amnesty.org.

BBC Middle East: http://news.bbc.co.uk/1/hi/world/middle_east/default.stm.

British Institute of Persian Studies: http://www.britac.ac.uk/institutes/bips/.

Center for Iranian Studies (Columbia University): http://www.columbia.edu/cu/mealac/affiliates/iranianstudies/.

Central Intelligence Agency: http://www.cia.gov.

CIA in Iran: http://www.nytimes.com/library/world/mideast/041600iran-cia-index.html.

CNN Middle East: http://edition.cnn.com/WORLD/meast/archive/.

Human Rights Watch: http://www.hrw.org.

Institut Français de Recherche en Iran: http://www.ifriran.org/.

International Atomic Energy Agency: http://www.iaea.org/.

Iran News Daily: http://www.irannewsdaily.com/asp/iran_news.asp.

Iran Press Service: http://www.iran-press-service.com/.

Irib News: http://www.iribnews.ir/front_en.ASP?sec=front_en.

Ministry of Defence and Armed Forces Logistics (Islamic Republic of Iran): http://www.mod.ir/.

Ministry of Foreign Affairs (Islamic Republic of Iran): http://www.mfa.gov.ir/.

Pars Times: http://www.parstimes.com/.

Tehran Globe: http://www.tehranglobe.com/.

TIME Magazine 1951 Man of the Year: Mohammed Mossadegh: http://www.time.com/time/personoftheyear/archive/stories/1951.html.

U.S. Department of State: http://www.state.gov.

Ireland

Kyle Joyce

Geography and History

The Republic of Ireland is an island located to the west of continental Europe in the North Atlantic Ocean. Ireland shares a land border of 360 kilometers with the United Kingdom, which separates the Republic of Ireland from British-controlled Northern Ireland. The total area of Ireland is 70,280 squared kilometers, with a coastline of 1,448 kilometers (Central Intelligence Agency 2003). In the east, the Irish Sea separates Ireland and the United Kingdom, and the Celtic Sea separates Ireland from continental Europe in the south. The nation's interior is characterized by large areas of peat bogs and grazing pastures, in addition to numerous lakes and rivers. Mountain ranges are found primarily around the coastal regions. Ireland's geographic location makes it a strategic point on major air and sea routes between North America and northern Europe. Enjoying a temperate maritime climate, Ireland has mild winters, cool summers, and a fair amount of rainfall (ibid.).

The total population of Ireland is approximately 3.92 million, with an estimated growth rate of 1.03 percent (ibid.). Ireland's current population is the highest the country has seen since 1871 (Embassy of Ireland 2004). Throughout its history Ireland has experienced large emigration, especially during the nineteenth century in general, and the Great Famine (1842–1845)

in particular. It is estimated that between 1801 and 1921 at least 8 million Irish citizens immigrated to other countries throughout the world, including Great Britain, the United States, Canada, Australia, and New Zealand. It is believed that nearly 70 million people worldwide are of Irish descent (ibid.).

Ireland's largest cities include Dublin (495,000), Cork (123,000), Galway (66,000), Limerick (54,000), and Waterford (44,500). Approximately two-thirds of the population lives in cities and towns of more than 1,000 inhabitants, with over 40 percent of the total population residing within ninety-seven kilometers of Dublin (Central Intelligence Agency 2003).

Ireland's official language is Irish (Gaelic). However, only 35 percent of adults are proficient in the language, and Irish is spoken mostly in the west, in regions known as the Gaeltacht (Embassy of Ireland 2004). English is the language generally used throughout the country. Ireland has two main ethnic groups, Irish (Celtic) and English, and two dominant religions, Roman Catholic (91.6 percent) and Church of Ireland (2.5 percent) (Central Intelligence Agency 2003).

An armed rebellion occurred in Dublin in April 1916, known as the Easter Uprising. The rebellion was partially a result of the suspension of home rule for Ireland until the end of World War I, compounded with the view promoted by the Irish Republican Brotherhood that "England's difficulty is Ireland's opportunity" (Coogan 2003, 41). Leaders of the rebellion viewed the war as an opportunity to strike while Britain's attention was turned toward Europe. The rebellion began with a proclamation declaring an independent Irish Republic, but the movement was crushed in less than a week, ending with the execution of the rebellion's leaders.

Although the armed uprising was not successful in expelling the British from Ireland, the rebellion's momentum, fortified by the Easter Uprising, led to electoral success for the rebellion-rooted political party Sinn Féin ("Ourselves Alone") in the general election of 1918. Following those general elections, members of Sinn Féin refused to take their seats in the British parliament and instead set up Ireland's first parliament, the Dáil Éireann, in 1919.

A guerrilla war began in 1919 between Irish volunteers—namely, the Irish Republican Army (IRA), fighting for national independence against the military and police forces of the British government. The war ended with the signing of the Anglo-Irish Treaty on December 6, 1921, which provided independence for the twenty-six counties of the south who formed the Irish Free State and the partition of six predominantly Protestant counties in Northern Ireland that remained part of the United Kingdom.

Following the establishment of the Irish Free State, a civil war was fought between supporters of the Anglo-Irish Treaty and those who refused to accept portions of the treaty, including an oath of allegiance to the British Crown as well as the partition of Ireland. The antitreaty forces would not accept anything less than a united Ireland containing all thirty-two counties, while the protreaty forces believed they had obtained the best possible terms. The civil war ended with the defeat of the antitreaty forces.

The External Relations Act, signed in 1936, abolished the remaining constitutional, legislative, and executive functions of the British monarch from the internal affairs of the Irish Free State. However, the act confirmed the monarch's role in the external affairs of the Irish Free State because the state remained a member of the British Commonwealth. The Constitution of Ireland, which was passed in 1937, defined the national territory of Ireland as "the whole island of Ireland," with authority limited to the twenty-six counties (Connolly 1998, 112). The Republic of Ireland Act (1948) severed the remaining constitutional links with the United Kingdom and declared Ireland an independent republic.

Ireland is a parliamentary republic with a president who serves as head of state and is elected for seven-year terms with a maximum two-term limit. The prime minister is the head of government and is nominated by the lower house of parliament (Dáil) as the leader of the political party, or coalition of parties, winning the most seats in the national election and approved by the president. The main political parties in Ireland include Fianna Fáil, Fine Gael, the Labour Party, Progressive Democrats, and Sinn Féin. Over the past twenty years every coalition government has included one of the two largest parties, Fianna Fáil and Fine Gael, in combination with the Labour Party or the Progressive Democrats (Embassy of Ireland 2004).

Ireland has a bicameral parliament (Oireachtas) that consists of a senate (Seanad Éireann) and a house of representatives (Dáil Éireann). The Senate contains sixty seats: forty-three are elected from candidates put forward by five vocational panels; eleven are nominated by the prime minister; and five are nominated by the universities. Members of the senate serve five-year terms. The house of representatives, which is based on proportional representation, has 166 members who serve five-year terms (Central Intelligence Agency 2003). Elections are held at least every five years, with all citizens having the right to vote after reaching eighteen years of age.

Local governments are elected by county councils, except in Dublin, Cork, Limerick, and Waterford, where local governments are elected by county borough corporations. However, most authority for governance remains with the central government (U.S. Department of State 2003).

The highest court in Ireland is the Supreme Court, which consists of a chief justice and five additional justices. The Supreme Court has the ability to rule upon the constitutionality of legislation, if asked by the president. In general, judges are nominated by the government and approved by the president. A judge can be removed from office only by resolution of both houses of parliament (ibid.).

Ireland has a workforce of approximately 1.8 million, with 8 percent of those working in agriculture, 29 percent in industry, and 63 percent in services (Central Intelligence Agency 2003). Ireland's main industries include food products, brewing, textiles, clothing, chemicals, pharmaceuticals, machinery, transportation equipment, glass and crystal, and software. Ireland's main agricultural products include meat, dairy products, potatoes, barley, sugarbeets, hay, silage, and wheat. In the service sector, Ireland is a world leader in internationally traded services and international financial services.

Ireland has an open, primarily export-based economy. The modern Irish economy is characterized by high growth

Table 1   Ireland: Key Statistics

Type of government	Parliamentary republic
Population (millions)	3.92 (2003)
Religions	Roman Catholic (91.6% 1998); Church of England (2.5% 1998)
Main industries	Food products, brewing, textiles, clothing, chemicals, pharmaceuticals, machinery, transportation equipment, glass and crystal, and software
Main security threats	None
Defense spending (% GDP)	0.09 (2001)
Size of military (thousands)	10.5 (2002)
Number of civil wars since 1945	0 (2001)
Number of interstate wars since 1945	0 (2001)

Sources

Central Intelligence Agency Website. 2003. CIA *World Factbook.* http://www.cia.gov/cia/publications/factbook/geos/ei.html (accessed May 15, 2005).

Department of Defence. 2002. *Annual Report.* http://www.military.ie/images/ann_report_2002/defence%20forces%20annual%20report%20202.pdf (accessed February 14, 2004).

Ghosn, Faten, and Glenn Palmer. 2003. *Codebook for the Militarized Interstate Dispute Data, Version 3.0.* http://cow2.la.psu.edu (accessed February 4, 2004).

rates and excellent public finances. In 2002, Ireland's unemployment rate was 4.3 percent, with an inflation rate of 4.6 percent. Membership in the European Union (EU), and particularly access to the European single market, are an important component of Ireland's economic success. Ireland was one of the founding members of the Euro and adopted the new European currency in January 2002.

The small relative size of the Irish economy has made it heavily dependent on international trade. In 2002, Ireland's imports totaled $48.6 billion (ibid.). Ireland's primary import partners are the United Kingdom (41.1 percent), the United States (15.3 percent), and Germany (6.8 percent). Ireland's principal imports include data processing equipment, chemicals, petroleum and petroleum products, textiles, and clothing. In 2002, Ireland's exports totaled $86.6 billion (ibid.). Ireland's main export partners are the United Kingdom (23.3 percent), the United States (16.7 percent), and Belgium (14.6 percent). Ireland's main export commodities include machinery and equipment, computers, chemicals, pharmaceuticals, live animals, and animal products.

Ireland is one of Europe's fastest growing economies, averaging 8 percent growth in gross domestic product (GDP) from 1996 to 2001. Ireland's growth slowed in 2003 to 2.7 percent as a result of the global economic slowdown. However, Ireland's GDP per capita ($29,300) remains one of the highest in Europe (ibid.).

Ireland's low corporate tax rate has made it a profitable location for foreign investors. Ireland attracts foreign companies involved in electronics, health care/pharmaceuticals, software, data processing, telemarketing, and financial services. Nine of the world's top ten phar-

maceutical companies and ten of the world's top fifteen medical products companies have significant operations in Ireland (Embassy of Ireland 2004).

Regional Geopolitics

The EU is the central framework within which Ireland pursues its foreign policy objectives. Given the participation of the EU in world affairs, Ireland's view is that active participation in the EU improves Ireland's ability to promote a stable, peaceful, and prosperous European community with respect for the rule of law and human rights (ibid.). Ireland's foreign policy is characterized by support for European integration.

Ireland has been closely involved in the integration of Europe, and it joined the European Community (later the European Union) in 1973. Ireland's cooperation with European countries with regard to foreign policy began in the 1970s, when the European Economic Community established informal political cooperation. The Single European Act (1987) formalized foreign policy relations between member states.

Ireland's foreign and security policies are directly connected through a policy of military neutrality. After achieving independence in 1921, Ireland sought to establish itself on the international stage without appearing as a threat to her closest neighbor and recent occupier, Great Britain. An independent Ireland could establish an independent foreign and security policy only so long as that policy did not threaten Great Britain's strategic interests. In order to assure Great Britain that Ireland would not be a threat to her security, Ireland adopted a policy of military neutrality. That policy prohibits Ireland from forming any alliance with an enemy of Great Britain, as such an alliance would also threaten Ireland's independence.

Relations between Ireland and Northern Ireland are a primary concern of Irish foreign policy. The province of Northern Ireland was created by the Government of Ireland Act (1920). Under that act, the six predominantly Protestant counties of Northern Ireland remained part of the United Kingdom, while the twenty-six mostly Catholic counties of the south obtained independence following the Anglo-Irish Treaty of 1921. Nationalists in Northern Ireland seek a united Ireland, while Unionists want to remain part of the United Kingdom. Northern Ireland has a long history of violent atrocities committed by nationalist or republican paramilitary groups, most notably the IRA, and unionist or loyalist paramilitary groups, including the Ulster Volunteer Force (UVF) and the Ulster Defense Association (UDA). For more than three decades, these groups have engaged in a pattern of violence that has resulted in nearly 3,500 deaths since the "troubles" began in 1969.

A cease-fire was negotiated with the Protestant paramilitary organizations in 1994 and with the IRA in 1997. Following these cease-fires and subsequent intense negotiations, the Good Friday Agreement was signed in 1998. That agreement was approved in a referendum by 71 percent of the voters in Northern Ireland and 95 percent of the voters in Ireland (U.S. Department of State 2003). The Good Friday Agreement established a power-sharing legislative assembly with the authority to administer Northern Ireland. The assembly is led by a first minister and deputy first minister, one from each of the two religious communities. The Good Friday Agreement also provided changes in the British and Irish constitutions. Under the provisions of the Good Friday Agreement, Ireland removed its territorial claim over Northern Ireland, and the United Kingdom agreed that Northern Ireland could become part of a united Ireland if a majority of the island voted to approve such a measure in a future referendum.

Despite the hope that the Good Friday Agreement would resolve the troubles in Northern Ireland, its success has been hampered by suspensions of the assembly because of mistrust on both sides. However, progress has been made, and Ireland is committed to the implementation of the Good Friday Agreement and a lasting peace in Northern Ireland.

The United Kingdom has worked closely with Ireland to find a solution to the troubles in Northern Ireland, and it also supports a successful resolution to the conflict. The likelihood of any militarized conflict in Northern Ireland spreading to Ireland is very low.

Conflict Past and Present

Conflict History

Neutrality has been a component of Irish foreign policy since the country gained independence in 1921 (see Sidebar 1). Following independence, Ireland sought to establish an international presence but was constrained both geographically and by a lack of sufficient resources needed to become established as a military power. As a result of its inability to present itself as a military power, Ireland has relied on military neutrality to defend itself against foreign threats and to preserve Irish sovereignty.

Ireland's informal position on neutrality was transformed into formal legal status in World War II. Military neutrality

Sidebar 1   Irish Neutrality

Following its independence from Great Britain in 1921, Ireland sought to exert its presence in international affairs but encountered several problems. Perhaps most significantly, it was essential that Ireland develop a foreign policy which would not threaten the country's former colonizer. Moreover, Ireland was constrained geographically and lacked sufficient resources to establish itself as a military power. Consequently, Ireland adopted a policy of military neutrality.

This neutrality policy achieved two purposes. First, it allowed Ireland to implement an independent foreign policy, thereby preventing it from forming an alliance with any adversary of Great Britain. Second, it allowed Ireland to preserve its sovereignty and to protect itself against foreign threats. Ireland's neutrality, informal and untested at first, was codified during World War II. During that war, however, Ireland implemented a more liberal interpretation of neutrality and covertly supported the allied powers. While today Ireland still observes a policy of military neutrality, this political stance has not prevented the nation from participating in many regional and international organizations that make no demands on Ireland for assurances that it would participate in a military conflict with another state under certain circumstances.

Source
Connolly, S. J. 1998. *The Oxford Companion to Irish History.* Oxford: Oxford University Press.

was observed during World War II but was not as stringent as the neutrality policies of other neutral countries such as Switzerland. Ireland covertly supported the Allied powers by sharing intelligence information with Great Britain, by granting overflight permission to British and U.S. planes, and by permitting Allied servicemen who landed in Ireland to return to Great Britain (while, in contrast, interning Axis personnel) (Connolly 1998, 505).

After the signing of the Anglo-Irish Treaty in 1921 (the treaty that provided for independence for the twenty-six counties of southern Ireland), those opposed to the partition, including some members of Sinn Féin and the IRA, engaged in a civil war with the new Provisional Government, which had supported and passed the treaty. Vastly outnumbered by the new Irish Army (established in 1922 with the aid of the British government), the antitreaty forces declared a unilateral cease-fire. No negotiations ever occurred, and the cease-fire marked the defeat of the antitreaty forces and an end to the civil war.

Current and Potential Military Confrontation

Ireland is not involved in a current military conflict and has a very small probability of being involved in a future confrontation, because of Ireland's policy of military neutrality. In addition, Ireland benefits from the protection of the collective security structure of the EU.

Alliance Structure

Following its independence, Ireland sought to establish an independent foreign policy in order to achieve international recognition. As a result, Ireland decided to join the League of Nations in 1923. Following World War II, Ireland shifted focus from establishing a presence in international affairs to engaging in international relations on a bilateral and multilateral level. After asserting its position in international affairs, Ireland next sought to affirm its position and later its independence. Irish neutrality continued during the Cold War and was confirmed by Ireland's refusal to join the North Atlantic Treaty Organization (NATO). Despite tension within the Irish government over whether or not to join the United Nations, Ireland submitted an application for membership; it was vetoed by the Soviet Union in 1946 and then again on four additional occasions. However, in the early 1950s, the international community increasingly viewed Irish neutrality as being complementary with diplomacy, a changing perspective evidenced by the fact that Ireland continued to apply for membership in the United Nations. Ireland's application was finally accepted in 1955 as a result of a broader East-West agreement (Tonra 2001).

Ireland's military neutrality prevents the formation of any military alliance with another nation and also influences Ireland's commitment to collective security through international and regional institutions. Ireland's foreign policy is based on the conviction that the country's interests are best achieved through respect for the rules of law in international relations. The constitution of Ireland asserts Ireland's devotion to peace and cooperation among countries founded on international justice and morality. International security and peace are thought to be best achieved through participation in international organizations such as the United Nations and regional organizations such as the Organization for Security and Cooperation in Europe (OSCE), the EU, and NATO's Partnership for Peace.

At the regional level, Ireland is unwavering in its support for the EU, and it takes an active participatory role in the security institutions of the EU. The common foreign and security policy (CFSP), established by the Treaty of Maastricht in 1992, served to centralize foreign policy in the EU. Under the CFSP, member states agree to work together on international issues with mutual political solidarity on all matters of foreign policy, including those in the area of security. The objectives of the CFSP include promoting international cooperation, preserving international peace and security, encouraging the consolidation of democracy, and advancing the rule of law and respect for human rights and fundamental freedoms (Embassy of Ireland 2004). Within the CFSP framework, Ireland participates fully in the formulation and implementation of the EU's foreign policies.

In support of the CFSP, the EU is developing a range of instruments to expand its conflict prevention and crisis management capabilities in an effort to increase its capacity to provide peacekeeping and humanitarian assistance. These tools are being developed under the European Security and Defense Policy (ESDP). Ireland is an active member in developing the ESDP and was working on training military personnel to meet Ireland's commitment to the EU's Rapid Reaction Force by the end of 2003. Ireland expected to have the capability of providing up to 850 personnel (Department of Defence 2002). However, the deployment of any military personnel for peacekeeping operations stills requires a UN mandate.

Ireland's military neutrality prevents the country from joining NATO. However, Ireland became a member of NATO's Partnership for Peace in 1999. That membership allows Ireland to develop closer cooperation with NATO member states without officially joining NATO. The Partnership for Peace, an alliance that is only political in nature, does not require an obligation on the part of its members to comply with Article 5 of NATO, potentially requiring member states to respond with armed force to an attack against another member.

Ireland is also an active participant in the Conference on Security and Cooperation in Europe (CSCE), later called the OSCE. Ireland is committed to the future development of the OSCE as a pan-European security forum and to achieving continentwide security arrangements.

Size and Structure of Military

The Irish Army was established in 1922, following independence from the United Kingdom. Initially, the main military function of the army was intended for internal security, and the army had no voice in defense policy. At the end of the 1920s and beginning of the 1930s, the number of people serving in the military dropped considerably, and the army suffered from an almost total lack of equipment. In response, the Irish government set up a volunteer army in 1934.

The role of the Irish military is to defend the state against armed aggression, assist civil authorities, participate in peacekeeping operations authorized by the United Nations, and provide a fishery protection service under the state's obligation to the EU (ibid.).

Size and Structure

Ireland's Defense Forces are composed of an army, a naval service, and an air corps. Recruitment into the Irish Defense Forces is voluntary. The defense forces consist of a Permanent Defense Force (PDF) and a Reserve Defense Force (RDF). The PDF is authorized to retain a strength of 10,500 personnel, with the additional option of having 250 recruits at any one time. The authorized strength of the PDF was reduced from 17,890 in 1990 to 10,500 in 2002. In 2002 the PDF had an average strength of 10,559 (ibid.). The PDF is a standing force and has the primary responsibility for military operations in Ireland and peacekeeping operations abroad.

The RDF is organized into a first line reserve and a second line reserve. The first line reserve contains former members of the PDF, and the second line reserve contains an army reserve and a naval service reserve. The RDF had approximately 13,500 part-time personnel at the end of 2002. The RDF has a contingent military capability and assists the PDF if necessary. In addition there are approximately 6,000 Civil Defense Volunteers (ibid.).

Ireland's Department of Defense contains both military and civilian components. The department is led by a minister of defense, followed by a secretary general who is the "principal officer" of the department. The civilian component assists in the development and implementation of policy for the department and provides policy advice on defense issues (ibid.). More specifically, the civilian element provides support for promoting Ireland's presence in matters of security and peace, handles procurement, and manages the budget of the department. In 2002, there were approximately 1,500 civilian employees (ibid.).

The military component of the Department of Defense is led by a chief of staff who is responsible for the overall management of the defense forces, including effectiveness, efficiency, military organization, and matters of economy (Embassy of Ireland 2004). The chief of staff is the primary military advisor to the minister for defense. Military command is allocated to the general officers commanding (GOC), who are responsible for the three territorial brigades (Eastern, Southern, and Western), the GOC of the Defense Forces' Training Center and the air corps, and finally to the flag officer commanding, who commands the naval service.

Ireland's army is structured into three brigades: Southern, Eastern, and Western, with each assigned to a specific territorial area with responsibility over that area. Each brigade has infantry, combat support, and combat service elements, including three infantry battalions, an artillery regiment, a cavalry squadron, an engineering and communications company, and a logistics battalion. In 2002 each brigade had 2,330 personnel, giving the army a total strength of 6,990 personnel (Department of Defence 2002). The RDF contains combat, combat support, and three air defense batteries. The RDF works closely with the PDF, with each RDF unit connected to a designated PDF unit.

The air corps contains two operational wings and two support wings. The operational wings contain a light strike squadron, helicopter squadrons, a maritime squadron, a transport squadron, and a fixed wing reconnaissance squadron. The support wings perform specialist maintenance to the aircraft. In 2002, the air corps had a strength of 930 personnel (ibid.).

The naval service contains a logistical command and an operations command. The naval service was reorganized in 2000, at which time its strength was increased. In 2002, the naval service had eight ships and a strength of 1,144 personnel (ibid.). The naval service reserve is divided into an Eastern and a Southern Group, with each group containing two companies.

The Defense Acts of 1954 allow Ireland to participate in peacekeeping missions only if the missions are authorized or mandated by the United Nations (see Sidebar 2). Ireland has been an active participant in peacekeeping operations through international and regional organizations. Ireland's first observer mission was to Lebanon in 1958, and the first peacekeeping mission was to the Congo in 1960. Ireland's first peace enforcement operation took place in Somalia in 1993. Irish military personnel have served on more than 50,000 individual peacekeeping missions in the context of fifty-six peace support operations around the world (ibid.; Permanent Mission of Ireland to the United Nations 2004). Ireland meets the EU peace support operations requirements by providing up to 850 defense force personnel to the EU's Rapid Reaction Force, and it provides military personnel for UN peacekeeping under the UN Standby Arrangements Systems and the Helsinki Headline Goal.

Ireland has participated in numerous UN peacekeeping operations, particularly in the Middle East but also in Somalia, Cambodia, El Salvador, Kuwait, Iraq, Iran, India, Pakistan, Namibia, Angola, Haiti, Macedonia, the Western Sahara, the former Yugoslavia, and the Ivory Coast. Ireland's largest and longest deployment was in Lebanon, where approximately 26,000 troops served between 1978 and 2001. Ireland also participates in peacekeeping missions under the EU and OSCE in Central and Eastern Europe, including missions to the former Yugoslavia, Georgia, Croatia, and Albania, as well as to South Africa and East Timor.

Sidebar 2   Irish Participation in
UN Peacekeeping Missions

The Defense Acts passed in 1954 allow Irish military personnel to serve as peacekeepers on UN-authorized missions. Following admission to the United Nations in 1955, Ireland has been a heavy participant in UN peacekeeping operations. Irish military personnel have served on more than 50,000 individual peacekeeping missions in the context of fifty-six peace support operations throughout the world. Ireland's longest deployment was to Lebanon from 1978 to 2001, and involved 26,000 troops. In addition to Irish military personnel, Ireland's police force began participating in UN missions in 1989, and has contributed more than 400 personnel. Overall, Ireland remains the sixth largest contributor of troops to UN operations.

Source
Irish Defence Forces. 2004. http://www.military.ie (accessed August 1, 2004).

Ireland continues to participate in peacekeeping operations, and Irish military personnel have served recently in seventeen separate international or regional peacekeeping missions, including those to East Timor (UNTAET and INTERFET), Bosnia-Herzegovina (SFOR), Ethiopia and Eritrea (UNMEE), Kosovo (KFOR), Afghanistan (ISAF), Congo (MONUC), Cyprus (UNFICYP), and Liberia (UNMIL). A list of Ireland's current contribution to UN peacekeeping operations is listed in Table 2.

Ireland's police force, the Gárda Siochána, began participating in UN missions in 1989, and it has contributed approximately 400 personnel. There are currently twenty Gárda serving with the United Nations in Cyprus. Additionally, members of Ireland's police force are serving under the EU in Bosnia and Herzegovina and have provided election monitors in South Africa and Palestine (Embassy of Ireland 2004).

Budget
Between 1992 and 2002, Ireland's military expenditures increased from $530 million to $749 million. However, Ireland's military expenditures as a percentage of GDP declined from 1.2 percent in 1992 to 0.7 percent in 2001 (Stockholm Peace Research Institute 2003). The budget allocation for pay compensation for members of the PDF made up 55 percent of the budget in 2002, while compensation for members of the RDF and civilian employees made up only 5 percent of the 2002 budget (Department of Defence 2003).

Expenditures for the air corps, naval service, and defensive equipment make up only 11 percent of the budget. Investment in infrastructure occupies approximately 2 percent of the budget, while less than 1 percent is allocated to research and development.

The air corps operational wing is equipped with thirty-two aircraft. Delivery of eight additional fixed-wing training aircraft was expected in 2004. The naval service possesses a flotilla of eight ships and has commissioned an additional two service ships. The army recently received forty armored personnel carriers, and an additional twenty-five were expected by 2004 (Department of Defence 2002). Ireland's primary import partners for defense hardware are the United Kingdom, the United States, and Switzerland.

Table 2   Ireland: Participation in Current UN Peacekeeping Operations

Name of Operation	Country	Start Date	Number of Personnel
UNMIL	Liberia	11/2003	471
MONUC	Congo	6/2001	12
MINURSO	Western Sahara	9/1991	120
UNFICYP	Cyprus	3/1964	9,647
UNMIK	Kosovo	5/1999	14
UNTSO	Middle East	12/1958	427
UNIFIL	Lebanon	5/1978	31,413

Sources
Irish Defence Forces. http://www.military.ie (accessed August 1, 2004).
UN Department of Peacekeeping Operations. http://www.un.org/Depts/dpko/dpko/index.asp
(accessed August 1, 2004).

Civil-Military Relations/The Role of the Military in Domestic Politics

Ireland's foreign policy is carried out by the Department of Foreign Affairs. Internal security is primarily the responsibility of the national police force, the Gárda Síochána, but the defense forces play a support role. Ireland maintains a volunteer Civil Defense Force with approximately 6,000 personnel. The Civil Defense Force is responsible for emergency relief and support and works closely with local authorities to ensure the operation of vital services and the maintenance of public life (ibid.).

Since Ireland obtained independence in 1921, the military has had an anomalous role in domestic politics (Connolly 1998, 29). Despite tensions within the military during the early years following independence, especially during the Irish civil war, there was only one instance of a split in the Irish military, when a small army mutiny was initiated by IRA veterans in 1924 within the Free State Army. The mutiny was resolved peacefully. Ireland's military acts as a unified body, and there is no threat of a split in the military that might result in a threat to the Irish government.

Terrorism

Several terrorist groups are thought to operate in Ireland without the consent of the Irish government. In a recent statement before the UN General Assembly, the Irish foreign minister remarked that "while Ireland is not a member of a military alliance, the country is not neutral in the struggle against international terrorism" (RTE News 2001). These terrorist groups consist of nationalist and loyalist paramilitary groups opposed to the peace process in Northern Ireland; they include the IRA, the Real Irish Republican Army (RIRA), the Continuity Irish Republican Army (CIRA), and the Loyalist Volunteer Force (LVF). Ireland is committed to establishing a permanent peace in Northern Ireland and desires the end of all paramilitary activity. The Irish government is opposed to terrorism and has arrested and tried members of paramilitary organizations.

The IRA, the most prominent of these terrorist groups, has conducted guerrilla warfare in Ireland, Northern Ireland, and the United Kingdom. Since its inception following the Easter Uprising in 1916, the IRA has undergone several transformations. The goal of the IRA is to remove the British from Ireland and to form a united Ireland. The organization rose to prominence following clashes between Protestants and Catholics in Northern Ireland in 1969. In 1969, the IRA split into two groups: the Provisional Irish Republican Army (PIRA) and the Official IRA, which ceased operations in 1972. Following that split, the PIRA was referred to as the IRA. The height of the troubles occurred in 1972 following "Bloody Sunday," a day on which thirteen unarmed Catholic civil rights marchers were killed by the British Army during a civil rights march in Derry, Northern Ireland. That event led to an escalation of IRA violence which ended with a cease-fire in 1997.

Following the cease-fire, the IRA engaged in several acts of disarmament in support of the Good Friday Agreement. Those measures allowed the political wing of the IRA, Sinn Féin, to take part in the power-sharing assembly in Northern Ireland. However, the IRA retains the ability to conduct paramilitary operations and raises millions of dollars each year through criminal activities (U.S. Department of State 2002). The IRA has several hundred active members with thousands of sympathizers and is thought to operate in Ireland, as well as Northern Ireland, the United Kingdom, and Europe. The IRA has received assistance from various groups and organizations in those countries, as well as backers in the United States. The IRA still considers itself to be an armed force opposed to the illegal occupation of its country (Council on Foreign Relations 2004). The IRA was removed from the U.S. State Department list of terrorist organizations in 2000. In 2002, in support of the ongoing peace process, the IRA apologized to the families of civilian victims.

The RIRA was formed in 1997 as a reaction to the engagement of the PIRA in the Northern Ireland peace process. The RIRA is dedicated to the expulsion of British forces from Northern Ireland and to the formation of a united Ireland. The RIRA has carried out more than eighty terrorist acts since 1999 in Northern Ireland and the United Kingdom (U.S. Department of State 2002). The most prominent attack by the RIRA was the Omagh bombing in Northern Ireland in August 1998, in which twenty-nine people were killed. The strength of the RIRA is estimated to be between 100 and 200 members who have limited support from republicans opposed to the peace process in Northern Ireland (ibid.). The RIRA is believed to operate in Ireland as well as in Northern Ireland and the United Kingdom. The RIRA is suspected of receiving funds from sympathizers in the United States through its political wing, the 32-County Sovereignty Movement, as well as weapons from the Balkans (ibid.). The RIRA is listed on the U.S. State Department's list of terrorist organizations. The founder and leader of the RIRA and approximately forty of its members have been arrested and imprisoned by Irish authorities.

The CIRA formed in 1994 as the armed wing of Republican Sinn Féin, which split from Sinn Féin in 1986. Similar to the RIRA, the CIRA is committed to forcing the British out of Northern Ireland and to establishing a united Ireland. The CIRA has focused its attacks primarily on Northern Ireland, but it is believed to cooperate with the RIRA. Membership of the CIRA is estimated at fewer than fifty (ibid.). The CIRA is listed on the U.S. State Department's list of terrorist organizations.

The Loyalist Volunteer Force (LVF), a Protestant paramilitary group, is committed to preventing a settlement with Irish nationalists in Northern Ireland. The LVF has conducted several attacks against Irish targets along the border separating Ireland from Northern Ireland (ibid.).

Ireland is an active participant in the fight to prevent international terrorism, lending its support to international and regional organizations working to combat terrorism, particularly the United Nations, the EU, OSCE, and the Council of Europe. In 2003, the direct threat to Ireland as a target of an international terrorist attack was assessed as low (Department of Defence 2003). However, as a response to the September 11, 2001, attacks in the United States, an Office of Emergency Planning has been established to meet "the new threat from international terrorism" (ibid. 2002, 18).

Relationship with the United States

Ireland has close political and economic relations with the United States. The strong relationship between the two countries is partially a result of common ancestral ties. Beginning in the 1840s, a large number of Irish citizens immigrated to the United States. Currently there are more than 40 million Americans of Irish origin living in the United States (Embassy of Ireland 2004).

The United States is an active participant in the conflict in Northern Ireland. During the 1990s, the Clinton administration supported the efforts of the British and Irish governments in finding a political settlement. The United States views the Good Friday Agreement, brokered by former U.S. senator George Mitchell, as the best framework for a lasting peace in Northern Ireland.

The United States participates in resolution of the conflict in Northern Ireland through its diplomatic missions and the president's special envoy for Northern Ireland. The United States also provides funding—approximately $25 million annually—through the International Fund for Ireland, for projects to generate economic opportunity and cross-community engagement for Ireland and Northern Ireland (U.S. Department of State 2003).

Economic and trade relations between the United States and Ireland are an important component of the relationship between the two countries. In 2002, Irish exports to the United States were valued at $16.5 billion, while U.S. exports to Ireland were valued at $8.5 billion (ibid.). Irish exports to the United States make up approximately 15 to 20 percent of all Irish exports, making the United States Ireland's second largest export destination, following the United Kingdom. The U.S. investment in Ireland was valued at $35.7 billion in 2002, with more than 507 U.S. companies located in Ireland employing approximately 90,000 people (ibid.).

The Future

The future of Irish foreign and security policy is relatively bright. There are no external or internal threats to Irish security. It is highly unlikely that Ireland will be involved in a militarized internal or external conflict, or that Ireland will be in the unfortunate position of being the target of an international terrorist act. Successive Irish governments have preserved Ireland's military neutrality and have strengthened its international presence by participating in international and regional organizations. Those two actions have significantly reduced the threat to Ireland's security.

While a solution to the troubles in Northern Ireland is a primary foreign policy goal of the Irish government, the likelihood that the conflict will cross the border is very small. Ireland, in conjunction with the international community, will continue to play an active role in securing a peaceful settlement to the conflict in Northern Ireland. While the Good Friday Agreement has served as a foundation for a peace resolution, further implementation of the agreement, including additional disarmament by paramilitary groups and a reform of the police system in Northern Ireland, is likely to be threatened by political and paramilitary groups seeking to undermine and destroy the agreement. Ireland will not accept a return to violent conflict in Northern Ireland and will continue to work toward full implementation of the Good Friday Agreement.

Conflict prevention and management are likely to remain a major goal of the EU and Irish security policy. In the future, Ireland is likely to contribute to numerous peacekeeping operations. A future challenge for the armed forces is to continue Ireland's modernization plan to allow for wider participation in peacekeeping operations under the auspices of the United Nations and the EU.

Ireland supports the roles of international and regional organizations in fostering international peace and security. Ireland will also continue to pursue goals under the auspices of the United Nations, including efforts toward peace between Israel and Palestine, the disarmament of weapons of mass destruction, the eradication of the causes of international terrorism, the establishment of an International Criminal Court, and the promotion of human rights. In addition, Ireland will continue to play an active role in the development of the EU's foreign security policy through the CFSP and ESDP.

Although it is improbable that Ireland will abandon its neutral position, it appears likely that its policy of neutrality will become increasingly flexible, thereby allowing Ireland to play an even larger role in the international community. Given that Ireland maintains its position of military neutrality, this position will always need to be evaluated to ensure that it is commensurate with current events in the world.

References, Recommended Readings, and Websites

Books
Bielenberg, Andy, ed. 2000. *The Irish Diaspora.* Essex: Pearson Education Limited.
Connolly, S. J. 1998. *The Oxford Companion to Irish History.* Oxford: Oxford University Press.
Coogan, Tim Pat. 2003. *Ireland in the 20th Century.* New York: Palgrave Macmilian.
Dwyer, T. Ryle. 1977. *Irish Neutrality and the USA 1939–47.* Dublin: Gill and Macmillian Limited.
Fisk, Robert. 1983. *In Time of War: Ireland, Ulster and the Price of Neutrality 1939–1945.* Philadelphia: University of Pennsylvania Press.
Girvin, Brian, and Geoffrey Roberts, eds. 2000. *Ireland and the Second World War.* Dublin: Four Courts Press.
Kennedy, Michael, and Joseph Morrison Skelly, eds. 2000. *Irish Foreign Policy, 1919–66.* Dublin: Four Courts Press.
Moody, T. W., and F. X. Martin. 2001. *The Course of Irish History.* 4th ed. Lanham, Maryland: Roberts Rienhart Publishers.
Sloan, G. R. 1997. *The Geopolitics of Anglo-Irish Relations in the 20th Century.* London: Leicester University Press.

Tonge, Jonathan. 2002. *Northern Ireland: Conflict and Change,* 2d ed. Essex: Pearson Education Limited.

Tonra, Ben. 2001. *The Europeanisation of National Foreign Policy: Dutch, Danish and Irish Foreign Policy in the European Union.* England: Ashgate Publishing Limited.

Articles/Newspapers

RTE News. 2001. "Ireland Not Neutral in the Struggle against Terrorism." October 2. http://www.rte.ie/news/2001/1002/unreax.html (accessed February 18, 2004).

U.S. Department of State. 2003. "Redesignation of the Real IRA as a Foreign Terrorist Organization." May 13. http://www.state.gov/r/pa/prs/ps/2003/20529pf.htm (accessed February 18, 2004).

Web References

Central Intelligence Agency. 2003. *World Factbook:* http://www.cia.gov/cia/publications/factbook/geos/ei.html (accessed January 14, 2004).

Central Statistics Office: www.cso.ie.

Council of Foreign Relations. 2004. *Terrorism: Questions & Answers:* http://cfrterrorism.org/groups/ (accessed February 18, 2004).

Department of Defence: www.defence.ie.

Department of Defence. 2002. *Annual Report:* http://www.military.ie/images/ann_report_2002/defence%20forces%20annual%20report%202002.pdf (accessed February 14, 2004).

Department of Defence. 2003. *Strategy Statement 2003–2005:* http://www.military.ie/images/Strategy%20Statement%202003–2005.pdf (accessed February 15, 2004).

Department of Foreign Affairs: http://foreignaffairs.gov.ie/.

Embassy of Ireland, Washington, D.C.: http://www.irelandemb.org/govt.html (accessed February 16, 2004).

Ghosn, Faten, and Glenn Palmer. 2003. *Codebook for the Militarized Interstate Dispute Data, Version 3.0:* http://cow2.la.psu.edu (accessed February 4, 2004).

Government of Ireland: www.gov.ie.

Irish Defence Forces: http://www.military.ie (accessed August 1, 2004).

Permanent Mission of Ireland to the United Nations: http://www.un.int/ireland/peacekeeping.htm (accessed February 16, 2004).

Stockholm Peace Research Institute. 2003. The SIPRI Military Expenditure Database: http://first.sipri.org/non_first/result_milex.php?send (accessed February 15, 2004).

UN Department of Peacekeeping Operations: http://www.un.org/Depts/dpko/dpko/index.asp (accessed August 1, 2004).

U.S. Department of State. 2002. *Patterns of Global Terrorism Report:* http://www.state.gov/s/ct/rls/pgtrpt/2002/pdf/ (accessed February 17, 2004).

_____. 2003. *Background Note: Ireland:* http://www.state.gov/r/pa/ei/bgn/3180.htm (accessed February 17, 2004).

Israel

Christopher Sprecher

Geography and History

In the aftermath of World War II and the horrors of the Holocaust, the state of Israel was established in the Middle East. Bordered by Egypt and Lebanon and the Mediterranean Sea, Israel is the only functioning democracy in this troubled region of the world. A climatically temperate country, Israel is not, however, blessed with a vast amount of natural resources. It is dependent upon external sources for oil, grain, raw materials, and military equipment. Despite its limited natural resources, however, Israel has sought to intensively develop its agricultural and industrial sectors over the past twenty years. Israel imports significant quantities of grain but is largely self-sufficient in other agricultural products. Cut diamonds, high-technology equipment, and agricultural products (fruits and vegetables) are the leading exports of the Israeli state, especially within the Mediterranean region (CIA *World Factbook*).

Israel has developed a technologically advanced market economy with substantial government participation. Approximately 50 percent of the government's external debt is owed to the United States, which is its main supporter and supplier of military equipment and foreign aid.

The end of the Cold War caused a large influx of Jewish immigrants from the former Soviet Union during the period 1989–1999. That rapid population growth, when combined with the opening of new markets at the end of the Cold War, energized Israel's economy, which grew rapidly in the early 1990s. By 1995–1996 growth began to decrease, the result of the government's imposition of tighter fiscal and monetary policies. As the twenty-first century began economic growth was 7.2 percent in 2000, but it has declined since then because of the serious dispute between Israelis and Palestinians. This continued conflict has caused difficulties in the high-technology, construction, and tourist sectors, and increased inflation led to overall declines in GDP in 2001 and 2002 (ibid.).

How has a state that is so small, surrounded by enemies and quite devoid of natural resources, survived for over fifty years? This history of Israel is one of sheer determination to survive in the face of insurmountable odds, and the desire of the Jewish people to have a homeland of their own. If we are to understand the Israeli national character today, we need to look back at its inception in the wake of the upheavals caused by World War I.

It should be noted, however, that the concept of a Jewish homeland in Palestine began in the late nineteenth century, when the region was still controlled by the Ottoman Empire and was known as Palestine. At the turn of the century, Ottoman

Palestine had a Jewish population of about 25,000, composing about 5 percent of the total population in the predominantly Arab region.

The early 1880s saw Eastern European Jews, primarily from Russia and Poland, begin immigration to the region to escape persecution in their homelands. This movement became known as Zionism, an attempt to unite the Jews who were dispersed around the world and settle them in Palestine. In his book *The Jewish State* (1896), Theodor Herzl, a Hungarian-born Jewish journalist, discussed the roots of anti-Semitism in Europe and as a solution called for the creation of a Jewish state in Palestine.

In 1897, Herzl convened the first Zionist Congress, representing Jewish communities and organizations throughout the world, in Basel, Switzerland. The congress formulated the Basel Program, which defined Zionism's goal: "To create for the Jewish people a home in Palestine secured by public law." The congress also established the movement's administrative body, the World Zionist Organization (WZO). The Zionist Congress's continued mission for the next fifty years was the creation of a Jewish homeland in the biblical territory of Israel (Freedman 2000).

By 1914 the Jewish population of Palestine had grown to about 85,000, or about 12 percent of the total population, and it became increasingly active in calling for an independent Jewish state. In 1917, during World War I, the British government sought to gain support against its Ottoman adversary by issuing a declaration, known as the Balfour Declaration, which expressed Britain's support for the establishment of a national home for the Jewish people in Palestine. The British rationale behind this document was largely self-serving, given the events of the world war that were taking place (ibid.).

By issuing the declaration Britain apparently hoped to generate support from both U.S. and Russian Jews for the Allied war effort and to preempt efforts by its rival, Germany, to win Jewish support by issuing a similar declaration. Britain's main long-term goal was to retain Palestine as a strategic territory after the war. Despite those underlying motives, of which it was acutely aware, the Zionist movement saw the declaration as an important achievement promoting Jewish settlement and development in Palestine.

Unfortunately for the Jews living in the region, the British had already made two previous agreements with others in the region. In the Sykes-Picot Agreement of 1916, Britain had agreed to split the Ottoman lands into British, French, and Russian areas of control upon defeating the Ottomans. The British had also made vague promises in 1915 and 1916 to support Arab independence in the lands of the former Ottoman Empire in return for Arab support of British forces against the Ottomans. Aided by the Arabs, the British captured Palestine from the Ottomans in 1917 and 1918 (Brecher and Wilkenfeld 1997).

In July 1922 the newly formed League of Nations issued a mandate granting control over Palestine to Britain. One of the main charges of the League to the British was to assist in the formation of a Jewish national state. British support of the Zionist movement led to large waves of Jewish immigrants to the Middle East. Immigration increased as the worldwide Depression deepened, and with it the rise of fascist and communist regimes in Europe and Russia.

By the onset of World War II in 1939, Palestine was in effect two separate functioning states: a Jewish one and an Arab one. During the mandate the British realized that their earlier promises to the Jews and Arabs had led to conflicting expectations by the two communities in Palestine. Both groups laid claim to the territory in Palestine, and both felt that the British had guaranteed them independence. In an effort to ameliorate tensions in the region, the British government issued periodic policy statements that reaffirmed support for a Jewish national home but also limited Jewish immigration and land purchases. However, the Arabs, viewing any British support of Jewish statehood as a threat to Arab independence, continued demonstrations, protests, and attacks on the Jewish community. Arab resistance culminated in a full-scale revolt between 1936 and 1939 (Freedman 2000).

In response to the Arab revolt, the British government in 1939 imposed drastic restrictions on Jewish immigration and provided for the establishment within ten years of a single independent state with Jewish and Arab government participation in proportion to the population. Zionists, who saw this policy as a reversal of the Balfour Declaration and a denial of mandate obligations, emphatically rejected the document. However, the onset of World War II delayed any settlement of the issue.

In 1945, exhausted and depleted by six years of war, Great Britain sought to reassess its position and policy in Palestine. After efforts to negotiate with the Arabs and the Zionists, the British government referred the Palestine issue to the United Nations in February 1947. After extensive evaluation of the situation, the UN Special Committee on Palestine (UNSCOP) proposed that the territory of the British mandate west of the Jordan River be partitioned into Jewish and Arab states with Jerusalem under international control. On November 29, 1947, the United Nations adopted a partition plan. Both the United States and the Soviet Union voted in favor, while Britain abstained. Zionists reluctantly accepted the plan as the best resolution they could expect, given the political circumstances, but the Arab world denounced and rejected it. The Arabs felt that the United Nations had no right to make such a decision and that Arabs should not be made to pay for Europe's crimes against the Jews. Fighting in

Table 1   Israel: Key Statistics

Type of government	Parliamentary democracy
Population (millions)	6.1 (June 2002)
Religion	Jewish (80%), Muslim (14.6%), Christian (2.5%), other (3.2%)
Main industries	Agriculture, high technology equipment, cut diamonds
Main security threats	Palestinian terrorists, Egypt (until 1979), Syria, Jordan
Defense spending (% GDP)	8.75% (2002 estimate)
Size of military (thousands)	2,500,000 (2003 estimate)
Number of civil wars since 1945	0
Number of interstate wars since 1945	4

Source
Central Intelligence Agency Website. 2003. CIA *World Factbook*. http://www.cia.gov/cia/
   publications/factbook/geos/is.html (accessed May 15, 2005).

Palestine escalated rapidly in the months after the plan was adopted (Safran 1969).

In 1948 the British withdrew from their mandate of Palestine, and the fledgling United Nations partitioned the area into Arab and Jewish states, an arrangement rejected by the Arabs. Subsequently the Israelis defeated the Arabs in a series of wars without ending the deep tensions between the two sides. As time has progressed, the Arab-Israeli conflict has somewhat subsided, but the conflict between the Israeli state and the Palestinians has increased. In the sections below I discuss in more detail the wars that Israel has been involved in, and the switch that the Israeli state has made from focusing on interstate conflict to one that resides primarily within its borders.

Regional Geopolitics

Israel as a state has been surrounded since inception by states that have pledged nothing less than the obliteration of the Israeli people from the world stage. In that context Israel has faced, and still faces, grave danger every day that it continues to exist. The relationship that Israel has had with its Arab neighbors since 1948 can be classified as conflictual—a prime example of the concept of an enduring rivalry.

As various scholars have discerned (Diehl and Goertz 2000; Thompson 2001), a surprisingly small number of states are responsible for the majority of conflict that occurs within the international system. As Diehl and Goertz (2000, 7) noted, since 1816 more than 45 percent of all militarized disputes have been the result of enduring rivalries, and 53 percent of all wars have taken place within the context of enduring rivalries. Enduring rivalries possess numerous features that make them unique; in regard to the Arab-Israeli conflict, I focus on two elements: the notion of recurring conflict and the stability that shapes these long-term relations.

According to Diehl and Goertz (2000, 36), an enduring rivalry is an antagonistic relationship between two states that engenders a military component and witnesses three militarized disputes between the two states in fifteen years. The rivalry terminates if it goes for ten years without a dispute. That is largely an empirical definition, based upon patterns of behavior, rather than a theoretically driven definition, as Diehl and Goertz acknowledge. However, it does serve to demonstrate that certain pairs of states are overwhelmingly more hostile than others.

A main characteristic of enduring rivals is that their relationship represents an inherent stability. Their behavior is predictable, even if it is hostile. This stability leads to a balance between the two rivals. Within the context of enduring rivals, Sorokin (1994, 299) notes that "regional rivalries are characterized by high levels of animosity between neighboring states and the potential for intervention by outside states that are militarily stronger than any of the regional powers." And Huth and Russett (1993) note that general deterrence between enduring rivals is a common security issue for such states because they are continually preparing for hostilities.

This is especially so in the two most prominent enduring rivalries of the post–Cold War era, that between Israel and its Arab neighbors and between India and Pakistan. Both of those rivalries have deep-rooted animosities based upon territorial and ideological issues that are not readily solved. In the case of Israel, the issue at stake is survival, and the continued integrity of her state.

Conflict History

On May 14, 1948, when the British mandate over Palestine expired, Jewish authorities declared the establishment of the State of Israel. The declaration recalled the religious and spiritual connections of the Jewish people to the land of Israel, without mention of specific boundaries; guaranteed "freedom of religion and conscience, of language, education, and culture"; provided a framework for a democratic Jewish state founded on liberty, justice, and peace; and called for peaceful relations with Arab neighbors. The state declared itself open for Jewish immigration. A provisional government was established; David Ben-Gurion became the first prime minister and Chaim Weizmann its first president. The United States and the Soviet Union, along with many other states, quickly recognized the new government (Safran 1969).

Declaring a new state and ensuring its survival are two different things, however. The Arab states of Egypt, Transjordan (now Jordan), Syria, Lebanon, and Iraq announced that their armies would enter the area to restore order, and they immediately declared war on the nascent Israeli state. The newly established Israel Defense Forces (IDF) shocked the world when they successfully repelled Arab forces. Fighting continued into early 1949, when Israel and each of the bordering states signed truce agreements that established the borders of the new state.

The agreements left Israel in control of territory beyond what the partition plan allocated to it. Portions of territory that the UN plan had allocated to Palestinian Arabs came under Egyptian and Jordanian control (Egypt took over the Gaza Strip, and Jordan gained control of the West Bank). Jerusalem was divided between Israel and Jordan. Several hundred thousand Arabs fled Israel for more secure areas in the Gaza Strip, the West Bank, and in neighboring Arab states. Of the original Arab population in Palestine, only about 160,000 remained in the territory that was now Israel. Permanent peace negotiations were supposed to follow the armistice agreements but did not. The Arabs refused to recognize or negotiate with Israel (Brecher and Wilkenfeld 1997).

Besides vocal support, there was little Great Power involvement in the Arab-Israeli conflict in the early years. The one exception was Great Britain. Continued British involvement in Palestine occurred through much of the 1950s. Great Britain and Jordan signed an alliance agreement in 1936, when the Jordanian state was granted autonomy. Although tensions between the states flared during World War II, they cooled with the formation of the Israeli state in 1948 and the subsequent war. In 1949, Great Britain issued a public pledge, saying that it would protect Jordan from Israeli aggression. In return, the British were able to maintain their rights to airfields and military bases within Jordan.

Although numerous border skirmishes occurred after 1948, only two major crises erupted before the end of the British-Jordanian alliance in 1957. In 1953, as a response to Jordanian infiltration into Israel, Israeli troops fired upon the Jordanian village of Qibya. After Jordan appealed to the United Nations and the British, Israel promised to cease its border incursions against Jordan. In 1956, Israeli forces retaliated for Jordanian raids against the city of Qalqilya. Jordan responded by asking for Iraqi assistance militarily, and inviting Iraqi troops into Jordan. Israel threatened retaliation if that occurred. The crisis ended with a British show of planes, and an Israeli promise not to invade Jordan unless she were physically attacked (ibid.).

The years between 1949 and 1956, notwithstanding the crises and incursions from Jordan, were ones in which Israel sought to build up its new state and solidify its existence in the Middle East region. However, tensions soon erupted again in 1956, this time over issues pertaining to the Suez Canal.

The year 1956 saw an additional involvement by the British, as well as the two superpowers, in the Middle East. The lack of comprehensive peace settlements between Israel and the bordering states after the 1949 armistice agreements caused continual tensions in the region. The Arab states continued to regard the establishment of Israel as an injustice and sustained a political and economic boycott on the new state. Egypt refused Israel access to the Suez Canal, and had earlier, in 1951, blocked the Strait of Tiran. These actions were to wholly land lock Israel (ibid.; Tal, 2000).

At the same time, Palestinians from the West Bank and the Gaza Strip began raiding Israeli communities near the borders. Israel held Jordan and Egypt responsible for those attacks and launched retaliatory raids. Further conflicts arose over control of demilitarized zones along the border and over Israeli use of water from the Jordan River—which borders Israel, Jordan, and the West Bank—for domestic development. Syria soon became involved as well.

In February 1955 Israel launched a raid against an Egyptian army base in the Gaza Strip. In response, Egyptian president Gamal Abdel Nasser began supporting Palestinian guerrilla operations against Israel, and he intensified Egypt's military buildup. In September, Egypt concluded an arms deal with the communist government of Czechoslovakia (acting for the USSR).

Israel found these developments, along with Nasser's emergence as the leader of a new Arab nationalist movement, threatening and began to prepare for war. In July 1956, Egypt nationalized the Suez Canal, transferring ownership of the company that controlled its daily operations from British and French shareholders to the Egyptian government. Through secret negotiations with Britain and France, which sought to regain control of the canal and topple the Nasser regime, Israel planned a military offensive against Egypt.

In October 1956, Israel invaded the Gaza Strip and the Sinai Peninsula, quickly capturing those areas and advancing toward the Suez Canal. As planned in the meetings with Israel, the British and the French issued an ultimatum demanding withdrawal of both Israeli and Egyptian forces from the canal. When Nasser refused, British and French forces bombed Egyptian bases. The United States and the USSR demanded an immediate cease-fire, and a UN resolution soon forced the British, French, and Israelis to withdraw from Egyptian territory. The UN Emergency Force (UNEF) stationed troops on the frontier between Israel and Egypt, which helped ensure quiet along the border for the next decade. The Egyptian government reopened the canal, and Israel gained access to the Strait of Tiran. However, no comprehensive Arab-Israeli peace talks followed the crisis, and continued border incursions persisted (Brecher and Wilkenfeld 1997; Safran 1969).

In a period of relative peace in the decade after the 1956 war, Israel's economy developed rapidly. Industrial and agricultural development allowed the government to end its austerity measures, unemployment almost disappeared, and living standards gradually improved. Exports doubled, and the gross domestic product increased dramatically. Israel now manufactured previously imported items such as paper, tires, radios, and refrigerators. The most rapid growth occurred in the manufacture of metals, machinery, chemicals, and electronics. Farms began to grow a larger variety of crops for the food-processing industry, and fresh produce for export. To handle the increased volume of trade, a deep-water port was built on the Mediterranean coast at Ashdod.

Foreign relations expanded steadily. Israel developed ties with the United States, the British Commonwealth countries, most Western European nations, and nearly all the countries of Latin America and Africa. Hundreds of Israeli experts and specialists shared their knowledge and experience with people in other developing countries in Africa, Asia, and Latin America. Israel strengthened its military and political cooperation with France; the United States agreed to supply Israel with arms in 1962; and West Germany continued to provide economic and military aid. In 1965, Israel exchanged ambassadors with West Germany, a move that had been delayed because of bitter memories of the Holocaust.

The Six Day War broke out on June 5, 1967, following three weeks of tension that began on May 15, 1967, when it became known that Egypt had concentrated large-scale forces in the Sinai Peninsula. Egypt's force buildup in the Sinai was accompanied by other serious steps: the UN Emergency Force stationed on the border between Egypt and Israel and at Sharm el-Sheikh in 1957, and which had provided an actual separation between the countries, was evacuated on May 19 upon the demands of the Egyptian president at the time, Gamal Abdel-Nasser; the Egyptian Navy blocked the Straits of Tiran, located at the end of the Gulf of Eilat, on the night of May 22–23, 1967, preventing the passage of any Israeli vessels; and on May 30, 1967, Jordan joined the Egyptian-Syrian military alliance of 1966 and placed its army on both sides of the Jordan River under Egyptian command. Iraq followed suit. It agreed to send reinforcements and issued a warning order to two brigades; contingents arrived from other Arab countries including Algeria and Kuwait. Israel was confronted by an Arab force of some 465,000 troops, more than 2,880 tanks, and 810 aircraft.

In this way, a direct threat along the whole length of Israel's territory was created. The Egyptian Army was deployed in the Sinai, the straits were closed, signaling the failure of Israeli deterrence, and Jordan joined the military alliance, closing the circle of the states threatening Israel's borders. As the situation deteriorated, Israel increased its reserve forces call-up, which had already been under way, and established a National Unity government that included representatives of the opposition parties at that time. Moshe Dayan was appointed minister of defense. Although the government of Israel viewed the closing of the straits as a belligerent act and a warning bell, the government tried to solve the crisis through political channels. The government of Israel approached the Great Powers, which had guaranteed the freedom of Israeli navigation. Britain and France reneged on their commitment, and the president of the United States proposed a plan for breaking the blockade by an international armada. Israel agreed to wait and give the plan a chance, and Prime Minister Eshkol announced his government's intentions in a radio broadcast on May 28. Israel's decision to wait was taken despite the fact that the country was well aware that the main threat had now become the Egyptian deployment in the Sinai and not the closing of the straits. When it became clear later that the political demarches had failed, the government, on June 4, gave approval to the Israel Defense Forces to undertake a military offensive to eliminate the threat to Israel's existence (Oren 2003; Safran 1969).

This dramatic development was the height of continued deterioration in the relations between Israel and her neighbors. The state of war that had existed since 1948 had already intensified between 1964 and 1967 with the increase in the number of dangerous incidents on the Syrian border following Israel's activation of the National Water Carrier from the Sea of Galilee to the Negev in 1964. That tension came against the backdrop of Syrian attacks on Israeli farmers cultivating land in the demilitarized zone and on Israeli fishing boats and other craft in the Sea of Galilee. The Arabs opposed the National Water Carrier project and tried to destroy it by diverting the subsidiaries of the Jordan River located in their territories. In addition, at the start of 1965, Palestinian terrorist organizations, under the patronage of both Syria and Egypt, began to operate against Israeli settlements. Their attacks led to Israeli military reprisals against their bases located in neighboring countries.

The Arabs were strengthened in their stand by the consistent support of the USSR, through both the supply of weapons and military advisers and through political support in the frame-

work of the Cold War between the East and West. It was the Soviets who spread the false report in 1967 that Israel had concentrated large forces on the border with Syria in preparation for attack, after the Syrians had already "heated up" the border area. That fraudulent report was the declared reason for the concentration of Egyptian forces in the Sinai, in support of the military alliance between Egypt and Syria. The concentration of forces gradually led the Arabs to believe that an opportunity had been created to realize their nineteen-year aspiration to destroy Israel. In the light of this development, Israel had no choice but to preempt (Oren 2003).

Nasser died in 1970; soon after, newly elected Egyptian president Anwar al-Sadat sought to regain the Sinai Peninsula from Israel through diplomatic means. Negotiations to resolve the dispute failed, and on October 6, 1973, Egyptian and Syrian military forces launched a surprise attack on Israeli positions along the Suez Canal and in the Golan Heights. Despite initial Egyptian and Syrian advances, Israel pushed Syria back beyond the 1967 cease-fire line and crossed the Suez Canal to take a portion of its west bank in Egypt. During the fighting, the USSR supplied arms to Egypt and Syria, and the United States provided arms to Israel. The Yom Kippur War (called the Ramadan War by the Arabs) ended with a cease-fire in late October. Israel suffered heavy losses in the fighting, despite its ultimate military successes. Parliamentary elections were postponed until December. The Labor Party remained in power, and Golda Meir retained her position as prime minister.

As conflict escalated between Israel and Egypt, the United States became gravely concerned about the ramifications of the fighting. Traveling back and forth between the countries in a process known as shuttle diplomacy, U.S. secretary of state Henry Kissinger helped negotiate a military disengagement between Israeli and Egyptian forces in January 1974, and another between Israel and Syria in May. Kissinger arranged a second agreement between Egypt and Israel in 1975. A tense but relatively peaceful stalemate resulted. Israel agreed to withdraw from the canal zone, and Israel and Syria returned to the 1967 cease-fire boundaries.

The costly war caused increased unrest in Israel and the growing criticism of the country's leaders. The government appointed a commission of Supreme Court justices, the state comptroller, and two former military chiefs to investigate Israel's lack of preparedness for the Arab strike. The commission's report was highly critical of the military. Meir resigned following the report in the spring of 1974 and was replaced by Yitzhak Rabin. Economic problems and turmoil within the Labor Party undermined Rabin's tenure.

The year 1977 saw Sadat announce his willingness to meet with Israel publicly and openly to discuss peace. In November he arrived in Israel to address the Knesset, calling on Begin to negotiate peace. After nearly a year of stalled negotiations, U.S. president Jimmy Carter brought the parties together at Camp David, Maryland, in September 1978 to break the stalemate. Carter, Begin, and Sadat concluded the Camp David Accords, which were agreements that provided the outline and basis for a peace treaty between Egypt and Israel and for a comprehensive Middle East peace focusing on the Palestinian issues and the future of the West Bank and Gaza Strip (Freedman 2000).

In March 1979, Egypt and Israel signed a peace treaty calling for Israel's gradual withdrawal from the Sinai Peninsula and the establishment of diplomatic relations between the two countries. Egypt and Israel opened their borders, established direct communication links, opened embassies, and exchanged ambassadors in 1980. Israel completed its Sinai withdrawal in 1982. The treaty eliminated the threat of Israel's primary Arab adversary with the largest military capacity. It also led to increased U.S. economic and military assistance to both Israel and Egypt. However, it failed to bring about a comprehensive Middle Eastern peace. On the contrary, the Arab League condemned Egypt and suspended its membership.

Despite peace with Egypt, hostilities continued between Israel and other Arab nations. In June 1981, Begin sent Israel's air force to destroy an Iraqi nuclear reactor near Baghdad, claiming that it was being used for development of nuclear weapons. Later that year Israel effectively annexed the Golan Heights by extending Israeli civil law to the region; Syria refused to recognize Israel's authority. Begin continued to push for Israeli settlement in all of the Occupied Territories, heightening tensions in those regions (Kuperman 2002).

The Lebanon border, which had been relatively quiet through the preceding Arab-Israeli wars, became the focus of Israeli security concerns in the early 1980s. Tensions between Lebanese Muslims and Christians had been heightened when the PLO, which had been expelled from Jordan in 1970, arrived in Lebanon. The situation was further complicated by the presence since 1976 of Syrian forces, which had originally intervened in behalf of Christians but soon allied with the PLO and other Muslims. PLO raids from

Lebanon into Israel and the presence of Syrian missiles in Lebanon since early 1981 prompted Israel to launch a major military action, called Operation Peace for Galilee, into southern Lebanon in June 1982. The objectives of the raid were to ensure security for northern Israel and to destroy PLO infrastructure in Lebanon. Israel allied with Lebanese Christians, who also sought to expel the PLO. Under orders from Defense Minister Ariel Sharon, the Israeli military pushed north to Beirut, defeating PLO and Syrian forces. U.S. envoy Philip Habib negotiated a cease-fire, and the PLO withdrew its forces from Lebanon in August 1982 (Barnett 1996; Brecher and Wilkenfeld 1997) (see Sidebar 1).

As evidenced by Table 2, the Israeli military has been quite successful in its battles with its Arab adversaries. Israel, despite its smaller population, has more effectively and efficiently trained its military, and it has used that training (along with superior military technology) to prevail in the interstate wars it has fought.

Current and Potential Military Confrontation

The roots of the current military confrontations that Israel faces now can be traced to events beginning in 1987. It is at this time that Israeli conflict behavior turned largely from external enemies to adversaries within her borders. The rela-

---

Sidebar 1 The Palestine Liberation Organization (PLO)

The PLO is a political body working to create a state for Palestinian Arabs in some or all of historic Palestine, particularly within the Israeli-occupied West Bank and Gaza Strip. The PLO was established in 1964 as a channel for Palestinian demands for a state. The PLO grew in regional and international prominence after Arab armies proved unable to defeat Israel in the Six-Days' War of 1967, and Israel occupied the Gaza Strip and West Bank.

After years of deep animosity between Israel and the PLO, the two sides signed a series of agreements between 1993 and 1998 that transferred almost all Palestinian towns and cities and most of the Arab population in the West Bank and the Gaza Strip to Palestinian administration. The agreements created an interim body, the Palestinian National Authority (PNA), to administer these Palestinian areas until their final status was determined. In 1994, the PNA took over many of the PLO's administrative and negotiating roles with respect to these territories, while the PLO continued to act as an umbrella group representing Palestinian interests both inside the West Bank and the Gaza Strip and elsewhere in the world. Despite having entered into diplomatic negotiations, the PLO and Israel remain at odds and are often engaged in periods of profound violence.

Sources
Arian, Asher. 1989. *Politics in Israel.* 2d rev. ed. Chatham, NJ: Chatham House Publishing.
Heller, Mark. 2000. *Continuity and Change in Israeli Security Policy.* London: International Institute for Strategic Studies.
Tal, Israel. 2000. *National Security: The Israeli Experience.* Westport, CT: Praeger.

Table 2   Comparison of Israeli and Arab Battle Deaths in Major Arab-Israeli Wars

Years	Conflict	Israeli Deaths	Arab Deaths
1947–1949	Israeli War of Independence	2,131	15,000
1967	Six Days' War	983	4,296
1969–1970	War of Attrition	641	5,000
1973	Yom Kippur War	2,838	8,528
1982	Lebanon War	215	2,600

Source
Clodfelter, Micheal. 2002. *Warfare and Armed Conflicts*. 2d ed. London: McFarland.

tive quiet in the West Bank and Gaza Strip ended in December 1987, when a series of widespread demonstrations, strikes, riots, and violence known collectively as the *Intifada* broke out. Encompassing the Gaza Strip and the West Bank, the *Intifada* began as a spontaneous expression of frustration and resentment at twenty years of Israeli rule and Jewish settlement in the Occupied Territories. As the movement expanded and became more violent, Israel responded with increasingly harsh reprisals, which drew international criticism.

The United States excluded the PLO from negotiations as long as the PLO refused to accept Israel's right to exist, and Palestinians would not participate in negotiations that excluded the PLO. The PLO's claim to be the representative of the Palestinian people was further strengthened when Jordan ceded to the PLO its territorial claim to the West Bank in July 1988.

The 1988 Israeli elections were again inconclusive, and a new national unity government was installed, but this time Shamir was to remain as prime minister throughout the tenure of the government. Peres became finance minister, while Rabin remained as defense minister. At this time PLO chairman Yasir Arafat acknowledged Israel's right to exist by ac-

cepting UN Security Council Resolution 242 (originally adopted by the United Nations in 1967), and Arafat renounced terrorism. As a result the United States and the PLO began a formal dialogue. In the spring of 1989 the Israeli government proposed a comprehensive peace initiative, but efforts to work out the details soon failed. Negotiations suffered a further setback when the United States suspended its dialogue with the PLO following Arafat's refusal to condemn a terrorist raid on a beach near Tel Aviv by a group affiliated with the PLO.

The Iraqi invasion of Kuwait in August 1990 and the subsequent Gulf War between the United States and Iraq in 1991 further postponed efforts to seek an Arab-Israeli peace. During the war the United States and other members of an international coalition against Iraq excluded Israel from participation, so as not to alienate the coalition's Arab members. Soon after hostilities broke out, in January 1991, Iraq fired Scud missiles at Israel and Saudi Arabia in an effort to split the coalition by diverting Arab attention from its anti-Iraqi stance to its opposition to Israel. The plan failed because Israel, at the request of the United States, did not retaliate.

In the aftermath of the Gulf War of 1991, Israel saw itself faced with increased violence from Palestinean terrorists in the

Occupied Territories. This threat of terrorist violence has replaced Israel's fears about external enemies. The conclusion of the Lebanese war in 1983 and the signing of a peace treaty with Jordan in 1994 made great strides toward preserving Israel's sovereignty, but it is in internal terrorism that the threat to Israel's stability now lies.

Size and Structure of the Military

Founded in 1948, the Israel Defense Forces (IDF) acts as a unified command over all of Israel's air, land, and sea forces. In 2001, Israel maintained a standing army of 161,500, with an additional 430,000 in reserve forces.

Israel as a state does not have any military alliances with other countries. It does tend to align its foreign behavior with other states, however, particularly the United States. Ward (1982, 5–10) makes a good first cut in distinguishing between alliances, alignment, and coalitions. Alignment differs from alliance in that it is not signified by formal treaties, and it is not focused on only a military dimension. Coalitions tend to be short-term alliances, established in the face of a specific threat. Once the threat passes, the coalition ceases to exist.

More recent work by Walt provides an expanded definition of alliances. According to his study, "an alliance is a formal or informal arrangement for security cooperation between two or more sovereign states" (Walt 1987, 12). Unfortunately, that classification blurs the distinction between alliances and alignments, but it does describe the relationship between Israel and the United States. Although there exist no formal security ties between the two states, they are quite similar in their foreign policies in the region.

Israel has maintained a nonallied policy because of its view on wanting to maintain its own course of self-determination without external interference. It has, however, developed a nuclear program to ensure its survival. Even though its nuclear program is ambiguous, it has helped deter a fair amount of Arab aggression through the years. Throughout its history Israel has maintained a policy of noncommital regarding its nuclear program. It has never officially declared its nuclear status, or signed any international treaty pertaining to the spread or development of nuclear weaponry. This ambiguity has served Israel well, since its Arab rivals are uncertain about the status of the Israeli nuclear program, and the potential threat it poses (Maoz 2003). Israel's nuclear weapons program has its roots in the period from 1955 to 1957, when a heated debate took place within the small scientific and policy community in Israel regarding the feasibility and desirability of the nuclear weapons option. When Shimon Peres put together the Dimona deal in 1957 and obtained massive French assistance, Ben Gurion gave the go-ahead to the project.

The United States "discovered" the Dimona project in late 1960, almost three years after it had been launched. President Kennedy was the only U.S. president who made serious efforts to curb the Israeli nuclear project. U.S. scientists were invited to visit Israel and investigate the site.

The visiting U.S. scientists never found direct evidence that Israel engaged in weapons-related activities. The CIA, at least since the early mid-1960s, understood and presumed that Israel was determined to develop nuclear weapons (Cohen 1998). By late 1966 the CIA circulated reports that Israel had completed the development phase of its nuclear program and was only weeks away from having a fully assembled bomb. Such information was never shared with the inspection teams that visited Dimona, nor was it accepted by the State Department. By late 1966, Israel had completed the development phase of its nuclear project. Yet Prime Minister Eshkol forcefully disallowed a nuclear test, knowing that such an act would violate the unique set of tacit understandings he had with the United States.

The June 1967 War had an important nuclear dimension. New and little-known Israeli and U.S. sources suggest that Israel had improvised two nuclear devices and placed them under alert. Cohen (ibid.) suggests that sometime prior to the Six-Days' War, Israel had achieved a rudimentary nuclear weapons capability, and during the tense days of the crisis in late May it placed that capability under "operational alert." By the eve of the war Israel had two deliverable explosive devices.

The advent of the Non-Proliferation Treaty (NPT) in 1968 set the stage for the most direct confrontation between the United States and Israel on the nuclear issue, during the Johnson era. Based on newly declassified documents and oral history, Cohen (ibid.) delineates the details of the last U.S.-Israeli confrontation on that issue. The two prime players in the confrontation were Ambassador Yitzhak Rabin and Assistant Secretary of Defense Paul Warnke. The end result of the confrontation was that Israel declined to join the NPT.

A new set of U.S.-Israeli understandings on the nuclear issue came into being in 1970, through meetings between President Richard Nixon and Prime Minister Golda Meir. The United States no longer pressed Israel to sign the NPT; it also ended the visits at Dimona. In return, Israel is committed to maintaining a low profile nuclear posture: no testing, no declaration, no acknowledgment. With these "Don't Ask, Don't Tell" understandings, nuclear opacity was born. Those understandings persist today.

Budget
The annual budget of Israel's military is quite substantial. In 2002, Israel spent $8.97 billion on defense. Much of that goes toward conventional forces, for its nuclear budget is secret.

The country's conventional budget, however, has declined somewhat in the last twenty years. Israel's constant-dollar defense expenditures fell steeply over the ten-year period between 1984 and 1994—by more than 70 percent. As a proportion of the GNP, the decline has been even steeper, with the relative decrease approaching 300 percent.

Given the current trends of inadequate expenditures combined with far-reaching territorial concessions, many Israeli policymakers envision a scenario in which the United States may be called upon to commit troops to active combat in order to prevent Israel from suffering military defeat (Ariel Center for Policy Research). The operational difficulties and expense involved in such an enterprise would be immense, especially as—unlike the case of Kuwait—no Arab country would be likely to offer its territory as a staging point for U.S. forces rushing to the aid of the Israeli state. If, on the other hand, the United States decided to forswear her obligation to Israel, the political repercussions are likely to be severe, both domestically and internationally, with the United States appearing as an unreliable ally.

Increased outlays on her own security would significantly reduce the possibility of Israel placing her greatest ally and major source of international support in such an unenviable predicament. Thus it would appear that not only would the Israeli national interest be well served by a considerable boost in defense expenditure, but so would that of the the United States as well.

In 2000 the defense budget was cut by approximately U.S.$140 million, and it now accounts for less than 18 percent of the overall budget, the lowest percentage since the establishment of the state of Israel. The budget has become less flexible over the years because of large fixed components—that is, rehabilitation and compensation payments, sharp increases in operational costs, and growing R&D expenses—making less funding available for procurements. At the same time, the U.S. Defense Aid package to Israel is growing as part of a bilateral agreement to compensate Israel for the reduction in U.S. civilian aid. As a result of these developments, the Ministry of Defense has little choice but to increase its procurements in the United States.

The Israel Ministry of Defense has in recent years been shifting some of its procurements from its local currency (shekel) budget to its U.S. Foreign Military Assistance budget. This development has been the result of recurring reductions in Israel's defense budgets and increases in U.S. defense aid. The diversion of procurements from the local market to the United States has resulted in strong protests from local manufacturers, some of which have in the course of the years become dependent on MOD orders. The major goals of the civilian defense system are to develop and prepare infrastructure and resources for implementing IDF objectives; to design and implement procurement, manufacture, development, construction, and service arrangements in order to give the IDF the means it needs to do its job; to rehabilitate disabled veterans and members of bereaved families; to develop and administer the defense export system; to administer, plan, and control the defense budget; and to handle all civilian aspects of the defense system (ibid.).

Civil-Military Relations/The Role of the Military in Domestic Politics

In Israel, as in most democratic societies, there is civilian control of the military. Although serving in the military is not a prerequisite for political office in Israel, many of its prime ministers have military experience, because of the compulsory nature of military service in Israeli society. The government has ultimate control over the military (Telhami 1995). Most Israelis are inducted into the army at age eighteen. Jewish and Druze men serve for three years, and unmarried Jewish women serve for twenty-one months. Men continue in reserve duty until age fifty-five for up to forty-five days a year (or longer in the event of emergency). Women are rarely called for reserve duty, but technically, unmarried women may be called until age fifty. Arabs are exempt but may serve voluntarily.

By an agreement dating from the late 1940s, Israel's minister of defense could grant religious Jews exemptions from military service. However, in December 1998 the Supreme Court ruled that this agreement was illegal and instructed the Knesset to pass legislation to regularize the situation within one year. A government-appointed chief of staff heads the IDF and is responsible to the cabinet minister of defense. Although the IDF as an institution has no formal or informal role in the political process, retired senior officers have become significant political figures. Although the military may often-times disagree with the civilian leadership, the general staff of the IDF reports to the government of Israel at any given time (Israeli Defense Force website).

Terrorism

Israel has been plagued with terrorist attacks since its inception. In 1972 the violence of a Palestinean terrorist organization against Israeli athletes at the Munich Olympics underscored that fact to the entire world. However, it was not until the late 1980s, as Israel made peace with its external enemies, that terrorism became an almost daily experience for the citizenry of Israel.

In the late 1980s, Palestinians began the *Intifada*, a widespread campaign against the continuing Israeli occupation of the Gaza Strip and the West Bank. The campaign combined elements of mass demonstrations, civil disobedience, riots, and terrorism. The *Intifada* put the Israeli army on the defensive and forced it to devote significant resources to patrolling the West Bank and Gaza Strip as a police force. Many soldiers, including civilian reservists, were injured or killed, and the army in turn often used brutal tactics against Palestinians.

As a result of the *Intifada*, pressure grew within Israel to broaden the peace process. The opportunity to do so was provided in 1991 by the Gulf War against Iraq. In that war a multinational coalition of Western and Arab armies expelled Iraq from Kuwait, which Iraq had invaded in 1990. One of the coalition's chief partners was the United States, a strong advocate for Israel. Following the Western-Arab victory, the United States, along with the Soviet Union, pressed Arabs and Israelis to pursue peace at the Madrid Conference of 1991. For the first time, all sides sat together to conduct bilateral and region-wide peace talks. Although little progress was made, the conference paved the way for future agreements.

In 1993, while the official negotiating teams of the Palestinians and Israelis were engaged in deadlocked negotiations in the United States, the two sides achieved a major breakthrough with the Oslo Accords, which were secretly negotiated in Oslo, Norway. The Oslo Accords and the resulting Declaration of Principles set the stage for a gradual transfer of power to the Palestinians. Further agreements in 1994 and 1995 gave the Palestinians autonomy over most aspects of life in the Gaza Strip and in urban areas of the West Bank through a new administrative body, the Palestinean National Authority.

In the first elections for the PNA, in 1996, PLO chairman Yasir Arafat was chosen as its president. Finally, the agreements stated that soon after those elections Israel would conduct further withdrawals from rural areas of the West Bank, after which talks addressing the final status of the Palestinian areas would begin.

Meanwhile, with the initial progress on the Palestinian issue, many Arab states felt freer to engage Israel openly and formally, though still with caution. On the heels of the 1993 agreements, Israel and Jordan took steps to negotiate a cooperative relationship. Despite opposition from other Arabs on the basis that Jordan's King Hussein was abandoning Palestinian interests in pursuit of a treaty with Israel, Hussein was undeterred. Jordan and Israel signed a peace agreement in 1994. By the mid-1990s, Israel had also achieved diplomatic relations with Arab countries in North Africa and the Persian Gulf.

Despite these accomplishments toward peace, some terrorism and bloodshed continued. Palestinians conducted terrorist attacks on Israeli citizens, and on a number of occasions Israeli extremists responded in kind. Israeli prime minister Yitzhak Rabin was assassinated in 1995 by an Israeli student opposed to the peace process. Under Israeli prime minister Benjamin Netanyahu, the peace process stalled in 1997. Even though Netanyahu completed some elements of the peace agreements, such as removing Israeli troops from the West Bank town of Hebron, some of his policies—including the building of Israeli settlements in Arab East Jerusalem—angered Palestinians and earned rebukes from many nations.

In October 1998, Netanyahu and Arafat signed an accord by which Israel would withdraw from additional West Bank territory in return for Palestinian security measures against terrorist attacks on Israel. The Palestinians also agreed to remove articles that called for Israel's destruction in their national charter. In November, Israel completed the first of three scheduled withdrawals but froze the implementation of the accord the following month. Israel claimed that the Palestinians had not carried out their part of the accord and had placed new conditions on further withdrawals. These developments again stalled the peace process and delayed negotiations on the final status of the West Bank and Gaza Strip. In 1999 elections, Netanyahu was defeated by Labor Party leader Ehud Barak, who vowed to move the peace process forward.

Negotiations between Barak and Arafat were encouraging at first, but they foundered over expansion of Israeli settlements in the West Bank and Gaza Strip and the issue of how Israelis and Palestinians could share the city of Jerusalem. Despite the active participation of U.S. president Bill Clinton, the two sides were unable to come to an agreement after marathon negotiating sessions held at Camp David, Maryland, in the summer of 2000. That failure generated bitter frustration among both Israelis and Palestinians. The volatile situation erupted in September with the outbreak of a second *Intifada* (known as the Al Aqsa *Intifada,* after the holy Al Aqsa Mosque in Jerusalem), the resumption of widespread resistance to Israel in the West Bank and Gaza Strip, and a string of devastating terrorist attacks in Israel proper. At the same time, the Israeli Army increased its restrictions on the Palestinian population and stepped up its military tactics. During the second *Intifada* loss of life was heavy on both sides, and peace negotiations broke down. In the absence of meaningful diplomacy, the situation was marked by increased use of force by the Israeli side and frequent suicide and ambush attacks by the Palestinian side.

In a February 2001 election Likud Party leader Ariel Sharon defeated Barak and became prime minister of Israel. In late 2001, Sharon asserted that Arafat was either unwilling or unable to represent the Palestinian people adequately and was therefore irrelevant to the peace process. Arafat, however, remained entrenched as the Palestinian leader. With mounting pressure from both Palestinian and Israeli extremist groups, the subsequent period was marked by pessimism and bitterness on both sides.

Relations with the United States

As evidenced throughout this essay, the United States has been one of the major supporters of Israel since 1948. Since 1972, as Organski (1990) has noted, the United States has been the primary supplier of military and foreign aid to Israel. In return, the United States has come to expect some levels of cooperation from Israel on security concerns in the Middle East region, and it has found Israel to be a strong supporter of U.S. interests.

The United States has sought to broker peace in the Arab-Israeli conflict on numerous occasions, and it has had some limited success. President Carter's Camp David Accords, and the Oslo Accords of fifteen years later, helped pave the way for some sense of stability between Israel and her adversaries. Have there been differences of opinion? Certainly. However, they have been largely contained, primarily because of the desire by both parties to see Israel, as a flourishing democracy, continue to exist and prosper.

The George W. Bush administration has supported greater Palestinian autonomy by advocating a "road map for peace" (see Sidebar 2). That road map has become a controversial topic within Israel and abroad, because of the continued terrorist attacks on Israel that emanate from the occupied territories. It remains to be seen if Israel and the Palestinians can coexist peacefully.

The Future

Israel faces a future clouded with uncertainty. It faces frequent terrorist attacks

> ### Sidebar 2   The Road Map to Peace
>
> From July 2002 forward, the United States and Israel have been involved in a plan called "The Road Map to Peace," which seeks to ameliorate the Israeli-Palestinian conflict. The plan is centered around three main phases. In the first phase, the Palestinians were to agree to cease attacks on Israel, and work toward building viable political institutions. In the second phase, begun in the latter half of 2003, transition to statehood was to take place, with the establishment of a government under the auspices of the Palestinian National Authority and a formal constitution. In 2004–2005, the permanent status of a Palestinian state and an end to hostilities with Israel were intended.
>
> As of this writing, the Road Map is at a dead end. Continued terrorist attacks and wrangling between Arafat and his opposition curtailed the Road Map's potential for ending the Israeli-Palestinian conflict. The death of Arafat on November 11, 2004, led to a lessening of tensions between Israel and the Palestinians, and the hope that the Road Map may finally be implemented.
>
> *Sources*
> Jewish Virtual Library. http://www.
>   jewishvirtuallibrary.org/.

from Hamas and other radical terrorist organizations. One of the main goals of the current Sharon government is to isolate Israel from potential Palestinian terrorists through the use of a security wall.

Construction of the wall is the latest Israeli step to fight suicide bombers and militants battling Israeli control over the Occupied Palestinian Territories. Likud and Labour, Israel's two main political parties, both backed the move, and a June 2002 poll in *Ma'ariv* newspaper showed that 69 percent of Israelis backed the plan.

However, most Palestinians are in an uproar over its construction and estimate that 10 percent of West Bank land will be confiscated by the time it is completed. Spokesmen say that 2 percent of their land has already been appropriated to build the 120-kilometer first phase, in the northern part of the West Bank.

Variously known to Israelis as the Separation Wall, the Security Wall, or the Terror Wall, the fence began to go up late in 2002. When completed it will be an eight-meter-high barrier of metal, concrete, or barbed wire, backed by electronic sensors, razor wire, trenches, and parallel security roads for the military.

The security wall is Israel's latest answer to the violence that erupted anew in September 2003. To date approximately 1,800 Palestinians and 700 Israelis have died in the clashes, and the wall is seen by Israelis as further protection, along with closures and checkpoints, against Palestinian violence (Jewish Virtual Library website).

The proposed road map to peace has its advantages, but it calls upon Israel to grant more autonomy to the Palestinians, something the Sharon government is loath to do. As time progresses, the Israeli state endures, but at what cost?

References, Recommended Readings, and Websites

Books
Arian, Asher. 1989. *Politics in Israel.* 2d rev. ed. Chatham, NJ: Chatham House Publishing.
Barnett, Michael, ed. 1996. *Israel in Comparative Perspective.* Albany: State University of New York Press.
Brecher, Michael, and Jonathan Wilkenfeld. 1997. *A Study of Crisis.*
Ann Arbor: University of Michigan Press.
Clodfelter, Micheal. 2002. *Warfare and Armed Conflicts.* 2d ed. London: McFarland.
Cohen, Avner. 1998. *Israel and the Bomb.* New York: Columbia University Press.
Diehl, Paul, and Gary Goertz. 2000. *War and Peace in International Rivalry.* Ann Arbor: University of Michigan Press.
Freedman, Robert O., ed. 2000. *Israel's First Fifty Years.* Gainesville: University of Florida Press.
Heller, Mark. 2000. *Continuity and Change in Israeli Security Policy.* London: International Institute for Strategic Studies.
Institute for International Strategic Studies. 1961–1984. *The Military Balance.* London: Institute for International Strategic Studies.
Mintz, Alex, and Bruce Russett. 1992. "The Dual Economy and Arab-Israeli Use of Force: A Transnational System?" In *Defense, Welfare, and Growth*, Steve Chan and Alex Mintz, eds. London: Routledge, pp. 179–196.
Oren, Michael. 2003. *Six Days of War.* Oxford: Oxford University Press.
Organski, A. F. K. 1990. *The $36 Billion Bargain: Strategy and Politics in U.S. Assistance to Israel.* New York: Columbia University Press.
Russett, Bruce, and Gad Barzilai. 1992. "The Political Economy of Military Actions: The United States and Israel." In *The Political Economy of Military Spending in the United States*, Alex Mintz, ed. London: Routledge.
Safran, Nadav. 1969. *From War to War.* New York: Pegasus.
Shakak, Israel. 1997. *Open Secrets: Israeli Nuclear and Foreign Policies.* Chicago: Pluto Press.
Shimshoni, Jonathan. 1988. *Israel and Conventional Deterrence: Border Warfare from 1953–1970.* Ithaca, NY: Cornell University Press.
Stockholm International Peace Research Institute (SIPRI). Various years. *World Armaments and Disarmament.* London: Taylor and Francis.
Tal, Israel. 2000. *National Security: The Israeli Experience.* Westport, CT: Praeger.
Telhami, Shibley. 1995. Israeli Foreign Policy: A Realist Ideal Type or a Breed

of Its Own?" in Michael Barnett, ed., *The Politics of Uniqueness: The Status of Israeli Case.* Albany: State University of New York Press.

Walt, Stephen. 1987. *The Origins of Alliances.* Ithaca, NY: Cornell University Press.

Ward, Michael Don. 1982. *Research Gaps in Alliance Dynamics.* Denver: University of Denver Press.

Journal Articles

Blechman, Barry. 1972. "The Impact of Israel's Reprisals on Behavior of the Bordering Arab Nations Directed at Israel." *Journal of Conflict Resolution* 16:155–181.

Huth, Paul, and Bruce Russett. 1993. "General Deterrence between Enduring Rivals: Testing Three Competitive Models." *American Political Science Review* 87, no. 1:61–73.

Kuperman, Ranan. 2001. "The Impact of Internal Politics on Israel's Reprisal Policy during the 1950s." *Journal of Strategic Studies* 24:1–28.

———. 2002. "The Extent of Dissent: The Effect of Group Composition and Size on Israeli Decisions to Confront Low Intensity Conflict." *European Journal of Political Research* 41, no. 4:493–511.

Maoz, Zeev. 2003. "The Mixed Blessing of Israel's Nuclear Policy." *International Security* 28, no. 2: 44–77.

Sorokin, Gerald. 1994. "Alliance Formation and General Deterrence: A Game-Theoretic Model and the Case of Israel." *Journal of Conflict Resolution* 38, no. 2:298–325.

Sprecher, Christopher, and Karl DeRouen, Jr. 2002. "Israeli Military Actions and Internalization-Externalization Processes." *Journal of Conflict Resolution* 46:244–259.

Thompson, William. 2001. "Identifying Rivals and Rivalries in World Politics." *International Studies Quarterly* 45:557–586.

Wilkenfeld, Jonathan, Virginia Lee Lussier, and Dale Tahteninen. 1972. "Conflict Interactions in the Middle East, 1949–1967." *Journal of Conflict Resolution* 16:135–154.

Websites

Ariel Center for Policy Research: http://www.acpr.org.il/.

Central Intelligence Agency. *The World Factbook:* http://www.cia.gov.

Federation of American Scientists: http://www.fas.org.

Israeli Defense Force: http://www.idf.il/newsite/english/main.stm.

Israeli Knesset: http://www.knesset.gov.il/main/eng/home.asp.

Jewish Virtual Library: http://www.jewishvirtuallibrary.org/.

Stockholm International Peace Research Institute: http://www.sipri.se/.

Italy

Neal G. Jesse

Geography and History

Italy is one of the largest of European democracies, yet most in the United States know very little about it (Hughes 1979, 3). However, most can identify Italy on a map because of its unique "boot" appearance. Specifically, Italy occupies a peninsula in southern Europe extending into the central Mediterranean Sea. The country also includes the islands of Sardinia and Sicily. The area of Italy is roughly 294,020 square kilometers, or slightly larger than the state of Arizona (CIA World Fact Book 2003). Italy borders a number of countries: Austria, France, Switzerland, and Slovenia. One country, San Marino, and the Holy See (or Vatican City) are independent political entities inside Italian borders.

The Italy that most recognize today came into existence only in the nineteenth century. Italy organized under a constitutional monarchy in 1861 but did not consolidate the nation-state until 1870. Before that the territory that is now Italy was divided into numerous kingdoms, principalities, the Papal States, and other political jurisdictions. Italian democracy succumbed in the early 1920s to the world's first fascist regime, under the rule of Benito Mussolini. Italy's subsequent defeat in World War II led to the "reconstruction" of Italy in the postwar period. The Italian economy rebounded dramatically, so much so that its impressive growth into one of the top-ten largest economies in the world has become known as "the Italian Miracle" (Wiskemann 1971, ch. 3; Sassoon 1997, pt. 1).

To an outsider, Italian politics appear tranquil; to an Italian it is anything but tranquil. Foreigners know of Italian culture, scenic beauty, cuisine, and soccer. What they do not know is the political turmoil that Italy has experienced since 1945. The reconstruction of democracy led to the ascendancy of the Christian Democratic Party (DC) and their four-decade rule until 1994. A strong, institutionalized bureaucracy, a predictable party system, a strong system of checks and balances, corruption from inside and outside the government, secret societies, and domestic terrorism—all of these have played a part in Italian politics.

In 1994 the underlying system of corruption that extended all the way to the DC prime minister was swept aside by judicial inquiries, a process that became known as Clean Hands. Italian politics is now reorganizing again. Strong personalities, such as the current prime minister, Silvio Berlusconi, mix with a strong right and a strong left. Regionalism splits Italy into three parts: a north, a center, and a south. The country is seemingly chaotic, yet the economy moves forward as does the nation (Bufacchi and Burgess 1998).

This has led to what LaPalombara (1987, ix) calls "Democracy Italian Style."

Table 1   Italy: Key Statistics

Type of government	Republic
Population (millions)	57,998 (2003)
Religion	Roman Catholic (majority), Muslim, Jewish, Protestant
Main industries	Tourism, machinery, iron and steel, chemicals, food processing, textiles, motor vehicles, clothing, footwear, ceramics
Main security threat(s)	Bilateral property disputes with Croatia
Defense spending (% GDP)	1.64 (2002)
Size of military (thousands)	14,450 (2003)
Number of civil wars since 1945	0
Number of interstate wars since 1945	1

Source
Nils Petter Gleditsch, Peter Wallensteen, Mikael Eriksson, Margareta Sollenberg, and Håvard Strand. *Armed Conflict 1946–2002*, International Peace Research Institute, Oslo (PRIO); Department of Peace and Conflict Research, Uppsala University.

Italy appears like a country "engaged in an unremitting political war of all against all and on the verge of total disintegration." Yet the great tension leads to an almost perfect balance of forces. When one understands that amid all the chaos there is stability, one understands Italy. Italian defense and security policy is an understated part of that stability.

In describing Italian foreign policy since 1945, Sassoon (1997, 279) writes: "Foreign policy has always taken a back seat [to domestic policy] and foreign economic policy has been virtually nonexistent. The main reason why this book has not got a separate chapter on foreign policy is that there is not much to say." Regarding Italian defense and security policy, one could come to the same conclusion. Italian defense and security policy has rested, and continues to rest, on membership in two organizations: the North Atlantic Treaty Organization (NATO) and the European Union (EU), and specifically the Common Foreign and Security Policy (CFSP). Italian defense and security has typically been passive, and it is not a trend that Italy appears willing to change any time in the near future.

Regional Geopolitics

The regional geopolitics of Europe has changed dramatically since 1989. From 1945 to 1989 the division of Europe by the superpowers (that is, the United States and the Soviet Union) resulted in a Cold War tension between eastern and western Europe. The security alliances maintained by the two superpowers resulted in an "iron curtain" being drawn between the two camps and their satellite countries. The Bloodless Revolutions of 1989–1991 that swept through the former Soviet Union and eastern Europe swept communism aside, and with it the division and tension in Europe.

Italy finds itself in the post–Cold War Europe at the border between the industrialized, democratic Western states and the developing Eastern states. The disintegration of the former Yugoslavia and the resulting civil and ethnic wars destabilized the Balkans and led to a refugee crisis. Although the potential for spillover from the former Yugoslavia into the rest of Europe is now quite low, during the 1990s it was of major concern to the western European powers. Continuing territorial disputes and tension between Macedonia, Serbia, and Greece are still of concern but are currently being addressed through diplomacy.

Because of the decadelong crisis, Albanians, and other ethnic minorities, fled from the war-torn region into Italy. Migration, immigration, and immigration control play a major part in the new politics of south-central Europe. Italy is a destination country for immigrants, but many do not stay there. Rather, they seek to immigrate into other European Union countries. As such, other EU member-states are putting pressure on Italy to tighten its immigration policies and enforcement mechanisms.

European Union expansion into eastern Europe also plays a major role in the contemporary politics of Europe. The fifteen-member-strong EU is seeking to expand with the ascension of up to twelve new member-states, almost all of which are in eastern Europe. The ratification of the Treaty of Nice paves the way for the merging of the two former camps into one united European free-trade zone and political union. With ascension into the EU comes an obligation for the East European states to improve their economic and democratic performance. These pressures and tensions between the Eastern and Western states shape most of the politics of the region in the first decade of the twenty-first century and quite possibly for some time to come.

Conflict Past and Present

Conflict History

Italian history is long, but the history of the Italian nation-states is not. One of the major misperceptions among world citizens is that while Italian culture, tradition, and history can be traced back to prehistorical time, the nation-state that we call Italy has existed for a much shorter period. Therefore, I take as my departing point the consolidation of the Italian state that flowed from the Risorgimento—the "resurrection" or "rediscovery" of a national Italian identity—in the nineteenth century (Di Scala 1995). Despite the pronouncement in 1861 by the new Italian Parliament of Victor Emmanual II as Savoy king of Italy, the modern Italian state did not truly exist until the cessation of the insurrections and civil war that prevailed during the "difficult decade" from 1861 to 1870 (Hughes 1979).

Following the unification of Italy and the French withdrawal from Rome in late 1870, successive Italian governments followed a cautious foreign policy. An avoidance of entangling alliances and a tacit policy of neutrality became the basis for dealing with an uncertain Europe. However, the French occupation of Tunis in 1881 led to calls by the Italian public for the government to engage in imperialist behavior more in line with that of other European powers and empires. King Umberto successfully persuaded the parliamentary government to align Italy's fortunes with those of the two conservative empires in east-central Europe: Germany and Austria-Hungary. In May of 1882 the three signed the Triple Alliance Treaty. Italian imperial ambitions led the government to send the army into eastern Africa. That led to some success and also some defeat, mainly at the hands of the Ethiopians, especially the loss of nearly 17,000 troops to an Ethiopia army in 1896 (ibid., 248).

Italy's next major conflict was the Libyan War, which began in 1911. Turkey formally controlled the North African country of Libya, but it maintained a fairly small armed force protecting it. Italian imperial ambitions, awakened by Italy's growing industrial power, turned toward Libya as an easy conquest. The conquest of Libya, however, was more difficult and expensive than expected. Turkey ceded control over Libya in October 1912, but a local guerrilla movement continued to harass the Italian occupiers for years afterward (ibid., 259–260).

Italian involvement in the Triple Alliance almost led to its siding with those powers during World War I. However, circumstances proved to be the undoing of Italian participation in the alliance. Leaders of the Italian armed forces wanted to commit to the Triple Alliance and in particular to the defense of Germany and the restraint of Austrian ambitions. Italy was a party to the renewal of the Triple Alliance in 1912. The Italian left was sympathetic to republican France. The Italian public disliked the Austrian occupation of Trento and Trieste and probably would not have accepted a war in which Italy was on the same side as Austria. Fortunately for Italy, the Austrian attack on Serbia allowed Italy to declare neutrality in the ensuing conflict. Once World War I began, the public divided into two camps: the neutralists who wished to keep Italy out of the war and the interventionists who wanted Italy to enter on the side of the Triple Entente (Britain, France, and Russia). Prime Minister Salandra was an interventionist who signed the secret Treaty of London on April 26, 1915, in which he pledged Italian participation in the war.

But 1915 was a turbulent year in Italian domestic politics. Numerous political groups fought for control of the government. The socialists maintained that Italy should stay out of the war. An emerging radical and republican movement sought entry as a crusade for Italian nationalism in the spirit of the Risorgimento. The most important event occurred in November 1914, when a young socialist journalist named Benito Mussolini split from the Socialist Party and founded his own newspaper in order to campaign for war (Sidebar 1 explains Mussolini's transformation). In May 1915 the interventionist forces drove the government from power and entered the war against the Austrians (and later the Germans). The initial gratification of the interventionists wore off soon, when Italy failed to score any significant military victories. It turned to panic when the Austrians almost broke through the Italian line in early 1916. The Italian government became more and more repressive at home, often using national security as a justification to clamp down on socialists, the Parliament, or any other group that dared to challenge it. Italian participation in the war did not solve Italy's problems; rather it polarized political division, exacerbated class division, centralized the state, and increased hostility to that state (ibid., 267–268).

Socialist agitation by the end of the war continued into 1919 and 1920. Workers' unions found themselves at odds with industrialists and landowners. The unstable government could not meet the demands of both groups. Mussolini and his fascist movement began to take hold of both political and economic power in northern Italy. In October 1922, with his

Sidebar 1   Mussolini Was a Socialist before He Was a Fascist

Benito Mussolini was born on July 29, 1883, in the agricultural Romagna region. His father was a blacksmith and revolutionary socialist. In 1902, Mussolini emigrated to Switzerland and there he met several leaders of Italian socialism and became acquainted with the works of Karl Marx. He adopted the Socialist rejection of reformism, advocacy of revolutionary action, and emphasis on the political party. In 1912, Mussolini was offered the editorship of *Avanti!* the socialist newspaper. Mussolini split from the socialists when the latter opposed Italian participation in World War I. Mussolini became editor of *Il Popolo d'Italia,* a newspaper that encouraged Italian war participation and was sponsored by industrialists. Thus, Mussolini turned from support by the workers to support by industry and his move toward Fascism began.

Source

De Grand, Alexander. 2000. *Italian Fascism: Its Origins and Development.* 3d ed. Lincoln: University of Nebraska Press.

exile and imprisoning and executing others. The Italian economy suffered a steep devaluation crisis by the late 1920s. Urban unemployment rose dramatically and fueled opposition against Mussolini's government. Mussolini turned toward economic isolationism, national self-sufficiency, and aggressive expansionism to counter the crisis. The Concordat of 1929 between Mussolini's government and the Catholic Church removed the latter from the ranks of possible opposition.

By the early 1930s a number of events would lead to Italian aggression against Ethiopia. The 1933 ascension of Adolph Hitler to power in Germany and the rejection of Mussolini's proposed four-power agreement (the United Kingdom, France, Germany, and Italy) turned Italian ambitions away from eastern Europe and toward North Africa. Italy invaded Ethiopia in 1935, deposed Emperor Haile Selassie, and declared itself an empire. The League of Nations imposed weak and meaningless sanctions, which seemed only to embolden Mussolini. The war with Ethiopia was savage, long (pacification continued until 1938), and costly, but nonetheless it ended in an Italian victory.

Personal diplomacy between Mussolini and Hitler in the late 1930s made it certain that Italy would be drawn into any war in which Germany was a participant. On May 22, 1939, Italy signed the Pact of Steel with Germany. It pledged the two to a military alliance. Italy assumed that war would probably begin within three years and was surprised when Germany launched its offensive in September 1939. Italy was not ready for war and did not even participate until June 1940, when it launched an abortive invasion of southern France. Italian military action in Greece and North Africa failed so miserably that the operations

hold on the north consolidated and his two main opponents, the socialists and Catholics, hopelessly divided against each other, Mussolini led a fascist march on Rome that was more ceremony than actual conquest. The king refused to order the army to intervene and consequently invited Mussolini to form a government.

Mussolini and the fascists ruled Italy, initially with the help of other groups and then by themselves. From 1925 to 1927 the fascist regime increased its repression of political opponents, driving most into had to be rescued by German units. Italian participation in the German invasion of the Soviet Union went equally badly, and by the winter of 1942 most Italian troops involved had been either captured or killed. By 1943 there was an Allied invasion of Sicily and a U.S. aerial bombardment of the mainland. Given those events, public opinion, the workers' unions, and even the conservative forces in society (such as the Catholic Church and industrialists) now turned against Mussolini. Mussolini was deposed, and peace was made with the Allies on September 8, 1943. Germany invaded Italy, and on October 13, 1943, Italy declared war on Germany. The Germans rescued Mussolini, and he promptly set up the Italian Social Republic (RSI), or Republic of Salo, in northern Italy. In April 1945 the partisans liberated Milan, captured Mussolini, murdered him, and displayed his body in public.

The end of the war brought occupation by the Allies (primarily the United States and Britain) and disarmament. The largest political faction in Italy was the Communist Party (PCI), which had played a major role in the partisan resistance. Britain and the United States intervened in Italian domestic politics to ensure that the communists would be excluded from government. The 1948 election led to a slim Christian Democrat (DC) majority and the beginning of their dominance in Italian politics until 1994 (Sidebar 2). In 1949, Italy had joined the North Atlantic Treaty Organization (NATO), and its defense and security policy has remained under the NATO umbrella ever since. Italy joined the fledgling European Coal and Steel Community (ECSC) in 1953 and became party to the treaties that later would produce the European Union. In 1993, Italy ratified the

Maastricht Treaty, or Treaty of European Union (TEU), which included the Common Foreign and Security Policy (CFSP). Therefore Italian security was guaranteed not by the Italians themselves, but by the U.S.-led NATO, and later, the complementary EU CFSP.

Sidebar 2   The Reign and Fall of the Christian Democrats

The Christian Democrats (DC) controlled government in Italy from 1948 to 1994. Following the 1946 referendum, the DC was the largest party, controlling 35 percent of the representation. In 1947 the party expelled the Communists and the pro-Communist Socialists from the legislature, thus making the DC synonymous with democracy, pro-Americanism, and anti-Communism. The DC maintained its position as the largest party in every election up to 1994. While never having a majority of seats in the legislature, the DC formed successive coalition governments with numerous smaller parties. In 1992, numerous cases of scandal and corruption (known as *Mani Pulite* or "Clean Hands") within the DC and some of its coalition partners empowered Italian magistrates to destroy much of the DC's power base.

Sources
Bufacchi, Vittorio, and Simon Burgess. 1998. *Italy since 1989: Events and Interpretations.* New York: St. Martin's Press.
Partridge, Hilary. 1998. *Italian Politics Today.* Manchester: Manchester University Press.

The history of Italian aggression from 1945 to 2002 is the null set. Italy did not engage in any interstate war during that time. The terrorist attack on the United States on September 11, 2001, led to the first Italian participation in an interstate conflict of its post–World War II life. Prime Minister Silvio Berlusconi sided with U.S. president George W. Bush, on both the U.S.-led intervention in Afghanistan and his interpretation that Iraq posed a threat to the Middle East or the Western states. Under Berlusconi's leadership Italy committed itself to help the 2003 U.S.-led coalition against Saddam Hussein and Iraq. Thus did Italy enter into its first post-Mussolini interstate conflict.

Current and Potential Military Confrontation

As mentioned before, Italian defense and security policy rests under the umbrella of NATO and the CFSP of the European Union. As such, many of its post-1990 security concerns were related to the Cold War and deterring any communist invasion of western Europe. With the "bloodless revolutions" of 1989–1991, communism is no longer a threat to Italian sovereignty. To put it bluntly, Italy has no immediate security risks, either internally or externally. International terrorism is a nuisance but not a direct threat to the Italian government or Italian democracy.

Italy's only pressing military engagement is with the U.S.-led coalition forces in Afghanistan and Iraq. But that is more foreign policy than security or defense policy. It involves the projection of Italian military might as part of a larger foreign policy in congruence with the U.S. "War on Terrorism." As such, there is little potential for any extended military confrontation between Italy and any other nation. Italy's most important dispute is with the new Republic of Croatia. Croatia

and Italy are negotiating property and ethnic minority rights issues stemming from border changes dating back to the end of World War II. Specifically, Italy has sought restitution for Italian landowners expelled after World War II near Trieste and Gorizia from areas that were incorporated into Croatia. There is also a small Italian minority in the Croatian county of Istria. The recent democratization of Croatia has led to the two nations being free to address these issues, which they could not do when Croatia was a republic in the communist former Yugoslavia. There is little potential for this dispute to escalate to any meaningful confrontation.

Alliance Structure

Italy is a member of only one military alliance: the North Atlantic Treaty Organization (NATO). Italy is a founding member of that defense alliance between western Europe and North America, established in 1949. Article 5 of the NATO Treaty defines each member's commitment to respond to an armed attack on any party to the treaty. With the end of the Cold War, NATO has expanded to include members from eastern Europe. The 1999 NATO Strategic Concept states that the alliance will seek to prevent conflict or contribute to its effective management beyond just the common defense policy articulated in Article 5.

Italy is also a party to some nonmilitary cooperation structures that tie it to other nations. Italy is party to the 1954 Western European Union (WEU) agreement. The WEU comprises most of the European states (both Western and Eastern) and seeks to facilitate cooperation on foreign and security policies. Most operational activities of the WEU transferred to the EU in 2000. In February

2003 the assembly of the WEU reconstituted as the Interparliamentary European Security and Defence Assembly. Seated in Paris, it scrutinizes intergovernmental cooperation in the Western European Armaments Group (WEAG) and the Western European Armaments Organisation (WEAO).

Italy is also a member of the NATO-Russia Council. Established in May 2002, this council seeks to promote itself as a mechanism for greater cooperation between Russia and NATO on security issues (Stockholm International Peace Research Institute).

In addition, Italy is a member of the European Union and is party to the Treaty of European Union (TEU). The Common Foreign and Security Policy (CFSP) included in the TEU mandates that Italy consult with the other EU members in security and foreign policy. The CFSP calls for an eventual common defense, but as of yet the EU has not moved very far in this direction. The establishment of a European Regional Defense Force independent of NATO is barely in the planning stages. As a member of the EU, Italy coordinates its defense and security policy with the other West European powers through the EU.

Italian defense and security policy tries to unite the two umbrella organizations into one coherent policy. Italy is a strong supporter of closer collaboration between NATO and the EU. Italy supports NATO's Mediterranean Dialogue, which seeks to get North African and Middle Eastern countries to work more closely together to keep conflict from erupting in the Mediterranean Sea. Italy sees the EU's Euro-Mediterranean Partnership program to be complementary to the NATO efforts in the region.

Size and Structure of the Military

In 2000, the Italian armed forces contained more than 374,000 personnel. That figure has been declining since the end of the Cold War in 1991, when the Italian armed forces numbered over 440,000. The defense force is an all-volunteer force. The armed forces are divided into four components: army, navy, air force, and Carabinieri (a collective name for a historical army formation that now covers most of the Italian territory and has some policing functions—much like a national guard). The army comprises three army corps, having disbanded the divisional commands in 1975. The army has about 165,600 personnel. The three corps comprise thirteen brigades (down from twenty-five in 1989), of which five are mechanized infantry, three are alpine infantry, two are armor, one is armored cavalry, one is paratrooper, and the last is airmobile (Italian Army Website). The air force employs 63,600 personnel and the navy 40,000 (Italian Defense Ministry Website).

Weapon holdings include more than 5,200 heavy weapons, of which over 1,100 are battle tanks, over 1,400 are heavy artillery, and nearly 500 are aircraft. The Italian armed forces are modern and well equipped. Italy does not have any nuclear weapon capacity or any nuclear weapons program (SIPRI). As a member of NATO, Italy hosts important U.S. military forces at Vicenza (army); Aviano (air force); Sigonella, Gaeta, and Naples (navy)—home port for the U.S. Navy Sixth Fleet. The United States has about 16,000 military personnel stationed in Italy. Italy hosts the NATO War College in Rome.

Italy engages in UN and other peacekeeping operations. Since just 1997 Italy has engaged in more than 107 missions (ibid.). Most of these are as UN peace-keepers or as UN observers. As of January 31, 2004, Italy had 161 personnel abroad as part of UN peacekeeping operations (see Table 2). Of those 161, some 47 were civilian police, 20 were military observers, and 94 were military troops (UN Peacekeeping Operations). Italy also contributes to NATO regional peacekeeping activities and observers. The Italian army currently embarks on observation missions in seven countries or regions of the world: India/Pakistan, the Middle East, West Sahara, Iraq, Ethiopia, the former Yugoslavia, and Kosovo (Italian Army Website). The army also has experts deployed in three countries: Malta, Morocco, and Albania (ibid.). Detailed information on Italian commitments to UN peacekeeping and casualties is in Table 2.

Budget
In 2002, Italy had the eighth-largest military expenditure in the world. Italy spent more than 24 trillion Lira (approx. $21 billion), surpassed only by the United States, Japan, Britain, France, China, Germany, and Saudi Arabia (SIPRI). As a share of gross domestic product (GDP), this amounted to 2 percent. Italian military expenditure has held steady since the 1980s at about the same level as a share of GDP. The share of research and development in the military expenditure budget in 1998 was about 1 percent (ibid.). Further, military research and development has been an ever-decreasing share of government expenditures since 1985 (ibid.). Military research and development was only 3 percent of all government research and development (ibid.). It is clear then that Italy spends a great deal on its military but has not recently spent a great deal on developing new weapons.

Some of the world's largest arms-producing companies are Italian. Einmeccanica was the thirteenth-largest producer of arms in the world as of 2000. The company makes artillery, aircraft, electronics, military vehicles, missiles, and small arms and ammunition. Einmeccanica was publicly owned until June 2000, when the state share was reduced from more than 50 percent to 5 percent. Other major Italian arms-producing companies include Alenia Marconi Systems (subsidiary of CEA—France), Fiat (forty-fourth largest), Marconi Mobile (subsidiary of DRS Technologies—USA), IVECO (subsidiary of Fiat), IRIf (eightieth

Table 2   Italian Commitments to UN Peacekeeping and Italian Casualities, January 2004

Mission	Location	Units	Number	Fatalities
MINURSO	Morocco	Military Observers	5	0
UNIFIL	Lebanon	Troops	50	5
UNIMEE	Eritrea	Troops	44	0
UNMIK	Kosovo	Military Observers	1	0
		Civilian Police	47	1
UNMOGIP	India & Pakistan	Military Observers	7	0
UNTSO	Middle East	Military Observers	7	1
			161	7

largest), and FIAT Aviazione (subsidiary of Motorola—USA) (ibid.).

Italy is a significant arms exporter. Over the course of the years 1998 to 2002, Italy was the world's seventh-largest supplier of major conventional weapons (ibid.). During those years Italy delivered more than $1.7 billion in weapons to other countries. Major Italian exports include the delivery of frigates to Turkey and Brazil; helicopters to Sweden, Canada, Nigeria, Albania, Ghana, the United States, and India; radar systems to Argentina, Oman, Pakistan, Singapore, Croatia, Hungary, India, Turkey, and Brazil; smaller naval vessels to Thailand, Malaysia, and Australia; torpedoes to India; armored personnel carriers (APCs) to Macedonia and Bulgaria; surface-to-air missiles to Spain; and antiship missiles to Peru and Bangladesh (ibid.).

Italy is also an arms importer. Typically it imports fighter aircraft from the United Kingdom, main battle tanks from the United States, missiles from the United States, mortars from France, aircraft radar from France, and reconnaissance APCs from France. From 1998 to 2002, Italy imported the twenty-sixth largest amount of conventional weapons (in U.S.$) in the world (ibid.). It also imports small arms from Canada, Finland, Norway, Sweden, and the United States (ibid.).

Civil-Military Relations/The Role of the Military in Domestic Politics

Since the end of World War II the military has had no official role in domestic politics. The reconstruction of Italian democracy in the late 1940s left no role for the military. Typically, an analysis of political power and Italian democracy focuses on other questions. What is the role of the political parties? Are the political parties too strong (that is, the *Partitocrazia*)? Why is Italian government so big? Is it too bureaucratic? Does anyone actually govern Italy? It even has been asked, "Who Governs Italy?" (LaPalombara 1987). What is not asked is if the military governs Italy. The military is subservant to the domestic government.

Where the military has typically been implicated is in secret plots to overthrow the government. Of particular note was the infamous P2 plot, uncovered in 1981 and slowly unraveled for the next ten years. It came to light surrounding a list of 962 persons belonging to a Masonic lodge called Propaganda 2 (or P2). The membership of P2 contained the "names of all the head of the secret services, 195 officers of the various armed corps of the Republic, among whom were twelve generals of the Carabinieri, five of the Guardia di Finanza, twenty-two of the army, four of the air force, and eight admirals" as well as hundreds of public officials, news media members, and politicians (Ginsborg 2003: 144–145). A commission reported in 1984 that the P2 had devoted itself to "the pollution of the public life of a nation . . . [and] aimed to alter . . . the correct functioning of the institutions of the country" (ibid., 147). The implication of the involvement of the armed forces in the P2 plot showed that elements within it still favored a return to a less democratic system. There has also been some connection between elements in the armed forces and the radical right (Ferraresi 1996).

Despite the secret societies and backward-looking elements, the armed forces are not influential in the domestic political process. The military responds to domestic control and follows the orders of the government. As such, it is one of the most subservant in the Mediterranean.

Terrorism

Terrorism in Italy peaked during the decade of the 1970s. Mounting civil unrest led to terrorist campaigns on both the right and the left. Terrorist threats to the government and the very fabric of Italian society so pervaded those times that the 1970s have become known as the "years of the bullet" (*anni di piombo*) (Domenico 2002, 123; Partridge 1998, 130). Of particular note is that the terrorism derived primarily from domestic sources. The "Red" terrorism of the 1970s and 1980s was communist inspired and sought to topple the Italian democracy. The "Black" terrorism of the right was a reaction to the strength of the communists and the introduction of the Italian Socialist Party (PSI) into government since 1963. Thus one must view terrorism in Italy as part of the larger domestic political scene rather than as part of the international environment. That view is enhanced by the nature of organized crime in Italy, the Mafia. The terrorist acts of the Mafia are aimed mainly at government officials and seek to intimidate the government to prevent or reduce anti-Mafia activities. Terrorist acts by the Mafia have more to do with organized criminal activity than any outright political agenda or international source; interested readers may consult the recommended readings for further information.

The largest sustained terrorist campaign in post–World War II Italian history was committed by the Red Brigades (*Brigate Rosse*, BR). The BR emerged during the early 1970s from the widespread and legal struggle of other revolutionary groups. A general workers' struggle to gain more rights clashed with right-wing trade unions and managers. The BR initially targeted these right-wing elements and subjected them to beatings or car burnings. Around 1977 the BR changed its tactics. Kidnapping and murder became more commonplace as the BR hoped to provoke a right-wing backlash and, they hoped, expose the true nature of the state as a coercive force in society.

Successive Italian governments engaged in a policy of firmness and non-negotiation with the Red Brigades. No single incident epitomizes the government's position more than the kidnapping and eventual murder of Aldo Moro, a notable Christian Democrat (DC) politician, by the BR. In early 1978, Moro facilitated discussions between the DC and the Italian Communist Party (PCI). Although the public was divided on whether to negotiate with the terrorists, the government refused to do so. The BR held Moro for two months before murdering him and leaving his body halfway between the buildings housing the DC and PCI headquarters (Partridge 1998, 132). By the 1980s the firm no-negotiation policy, active antiterrorism campaigns, and laws that persuaded BR members to collaborate with the government in exchange for shorter prison sentences eventually weakened and silenced the Red Brigades. However, in March 2001 a new generation of BR engaged in two shootings. Police raids uncovered munitions and weapons, and the Italian government suspects that the BR might be reforming (UPI, December 22, 2003).

Neofascist groups and other right-wing groups also participated in terrorist activities during the 1970s and early 1980s. The right typically used bomb explosions to maim and kill, while pointing the finger at leftist or anarchist groups as the culprits. The agenda of the right-wing terrorists was to force the government to deal severely with left-wing terrorists and, in particular, to defeat any communist movements. The right wing's gambit of forcing the government's hand became known as the "strategy of tension" (Partridge 1998, 131–138). The Italian secret services were implicated as being behind the right-wing terrorism. Giovanni De Lorenzo, a former head of military intelligence and eventually a member of the Italian Parliament and neofascist Italian Social Movement Party (MSI), planned a coup d'état in the summer of 1964 in order to prevent a center-left government from coming to power. In 1970 a judicial investigation found that De Lorenzo "had acted against the law and the constitution," but he was never prosecuted because of his parliamentary immunity (ibid., 135). In December 1970, Prince Junio Valerio Borghese, who had been a former naval commander in the fascist Republic of Salo, led a small group of men and occupied the Ministry of the Interior in an attempt to overthrow the government. Borghese had connections to the military and secret services, and a larger plot was eventually uncovered (although everyone brought to trial was acquitted).

Right-wing terrorism flared up again in 1993 as the corrupt political system engineered by the DC began to unravel. A number of bombings occurred, an indication that the right wing might be returning to the "strategy of tension" in order to preserve its privileged position in society. The sacking of the chiefs of the two secret service organizations by Prime Minister Carlo Azeglio Ciampi quickly confirmed rumors that the right wing terrorists were again being led by ele-

ments inside the state. Right-wing terrorism has since subsided dramatically.

Following the terrorist hijackings and attacks of September 11, 2001, Italy has become engaged in the antiterrorist campaigns aimed at Islamic fundamentalists. Italy has moved to unite with other countries to defeat international terrorism. For example, Italy signed an agreement with Algeria in July 2003 in which both countries agree to cooperate to fight international terrorism (BBC, July 18, 2003). Prime Minister Silvio Berlusconi, a firm ally of the United States, urged Italy to stand united with Russia and Russian president Vladimir Putin in fighting international terrorism (Agence France Presse, February 3, 2003). On November 23, 2003, Interior Minister Guiseppe Pisanu said after a truck bomb killed twenty-eight Italian soldiers in the southern Iraqi town of Nasiriyah on November 12 that Italy was one of the "major targets of Islamic terrorism" (AFX News Limited, November 23, 2003). It is clear from recent events that while domestic sources of terrorism in Italy have subsided, the increasing challenges of international terrorism have forced Italy to become more active in combating international terrorism.

Relationship with the United States

Since 1945 the relationship between the United States and Italy has been vital to both countries (Hughes 1979, 3). It can be said that "Italy's emergence as a major Western industrial power owed much to the USA" (Partridge 1998, 177). After World War II, Italy received economic assistance in the form of Marshall Aid, much like other West European countries. However, Marshall Aid was never a significant proportion of the gross domestic product of Italy. The economic relationship between the two countries was part of a larger political relationship. The United States wanted to strengthen the Italian economy in order to keep communism at bay. Italy wanted to help the U.S.-led anticommunist effort in order to benefit economically. It was a win-win situation for both countries. This early agreement that cooperation would be beneficial to both has led to a continued pattern of peaceful and cooperative relations.

Following World War II, and during the U.S. occupation of Italy, the acting U.S. secretary of state wrote: "Our objective is to strengthen Italy economically and politically so that truly democratic elements of the country can withstand the forces that threaten to sweep them into a new totalitarianism" (ibid.). The Italian geostrategic position was important to the United States at the start of the Cold War. Italy had the potential for dominating the Mediterranean while also being close to Tito's Yugoslavia. Moreover, from a U.S. perspective, the Soviet Union had written off Italy, allowing the United States to make Italy a client state.

From the Italian perspective, U.S. intervention into its politics was a blessing. Italian foreign policy following World War II had three aims: to recover politically from the damage of Mussolini's foreign policy, to gain acceptance into the emerging European/Western community, and to secure economic aid for reconstruction (Spotts and Wieser 1986, 268). When Italy accepted the April 1948 invitation to join the Organization for European Economic Cooperation (OEEC), it succeeded in starting down the path of accomplishing all three goals.

The Italian public and government were more hesitant about accepting an invitation into the North Atlantic Treaty Organization. The public mood was of "neutralism, pacifism and apathy" (ibid., 269). Prime Minister Alcide De Gasperi, as well as his foreign minister, Carlo Sforza, feared that the United States (and the British) would relegate Italy to an inferior position in the newly proposed military alliance. Italy did indeed agree in January 1949 to join NATO. Italy's acceptance of membership in the OEEC and NATO transformed the first of the three Axis powers from an enemy to an ally of the United States.

Spotts and Wieser suggest that the period from 1945 to 1949 set the entire subsequent course of Italian foreign policy, and in particular the Italian relationship with the United States. They point out that Italy's reliance on the Western economic and military alliances allowed the country to withdraw from world affairs. Italian foreign policy has been "passive and pacific" because it can be (ibid., 263). Foreign policy thus takes a secondary position to domestic policy, because most of the authority for Italian foreign policy is diffused across the rest of western Europe and the North Atlantic. Italy stays behind a cover of multilateral institutions and thus protects itself from direct confrontation in international conflicts. Italian foreign policy relies on "NATO and the United States to provide a strategy, to develop plans, and to establish goals" (ibid., 276). The United States benefits from the use of bases in Italy to protect the southern flank of Europe. Italy benefits by making few decisions.

The major disruptor of smooth relations between the United States and Italy has been the existence of the Italian Communist Party (PCI). The Italian postwar political party system can be characterized as "polarized" between the Christian Democrats on the center-right and a strong left, of which the PCI was a strong component (Farneti 1985). The United States has always feared the PCI because it is large and potentially strong enough to share power or lead a government in Italy. At the start of the Cold War, a communist-led Italy would not only create a domestic problem for any U.S. president but also possibly divide NATO. U.S. fears of a communist Italy have led the American government to intervene, both covertly and overtly, into Italian domestic politics. That has included U.S. encouragement and funding for rival political parties, trade unions, groups, and individuals. The United States has interfered in Italian elections, supporting non-PCI parties with millions in U.S. dollars and other aid. U.S. government officials and ambassadors have also made public statements at key times in order to oppose the entry of the PCI into any Italian government (Spotts and Wieser 1986, 280–282). U.S. hostility to the Italian communists diminished some in the 1960s, when President Kennedy encouraged the Italian Christian Democrats to allow the Italian Socialists (PSI) into a coalition government. With the end of the Cold War, U.S. anticommunist activities have stopped, and the United States no longer considers any left-leaning Italian government to be a threat. Moreover, throughout the years a partisan consensus regarding foreign policy gradually replaced disagreement (ibid., 272).

With the end of communism, Italy has become important to U.S. foreign policy in southern Europe and the Middle East. Italy provided key logistics and basing operations for NATO involvement in both the Yugoslavian and Kosovo conflicts of the 1990s. Along with Turkish bases, Italian bases are a major source of NATO projection into the Middle East, especially Iraq. Although the Italian public has not been supportive of the U.S.-led invasion of Iraq in 2003, the Italian government under Silvio Berlusconi and his Forza Italia Party have been very supportive (Sidebar 3 provides details about Silvio Berlusconi).

Sidebar 3   Forza Italia, Soccer, Berlusconi, and Elections

Silvio Berlusconi, an entrepreneur, media magnate, and billionaire, entered politics in the 1994 election. He named his new party *Forza Italia*, literally "Go Italy," a cheer used to spur on the national soccer team. At the time, Berlusconi owned the three largest private media networks, roughly 150 more businesses under his umbrella company Fininvest, and the highly successful soccer team AC Milan. Behind a slick campaign Forza Italia gained the most votes in the elections and Berlusconi became Prime Minster of Italy. His government was fractious and did not last long, with new elections being called in 1996. Beroluscicni returned to power in 2001. He has been a strong supporter of the American "War on Terror" and the American-led invasion of Iraq in 2003.

Source
Bufacchi, Vittorio, and Simon Burgess. 1998. *Italy since 1989: Events and Interpretations.* New York: St. Martin's Press.

The Future

The future of Italian defense and security policy is not clear. Domestically, Italian politics are more unstable than ever before. Constantly changing coalitions, governments, and prime ministers are a mainstay of the post-1994 landscape. The reshaping of the party system into two large blocs, one on the left and the other on the right, has led to an alternation of governance between the two blocs, bringing some consistency to the otherwise fragmented party system. Realignment of government between elections is common (as occurred in 1995, when Dini's government gave way to Berlusconi's). Also, D'Alema's communist-led leftist government of the late 1990s illustrates that the wide swath of Italian ideological positions can all eventually find their way into government. Italian domestic politics is also divided geographically, between the richer north and the poorer south (Agnew 2002).

Foreign and defense policy remains of a secondary nature. Moreover, the continued presence of NATO ensures that Italy can continue to take foreign policy for granted, allowing it to be dictated by the security concerns of the larger alliance. Further, the emergence of a Common Foreign and Security Policy (CFSP) in the Treaty of European Union has given Italy another umbrella under which to hide. European calls for a European Defense Force move Italy further in the same direction. Or perhaps it is the recent upswing in immigration, particularly from Islamic nations, that will provide an impetus for future foreign policy. Anti-immigration policies may indeed be the front line of security policy in the twenty-first century.

Mapping the course of Italian politics is both easy and troublesome. The domestic political system is in flux, and political parties are short-lived. The government changes hands often, and the nation-state is rended by geographical and ideological divisions (ibid.). In defense and security policy there will most certainly be continuity with the past fifty years: a focus on European security under the two umbrellas of NATO and the EU. If change is to come to Italian defense and security policy, it will most likely not be initiated by Italy. Rather, it would be the product of a fundamental change in thinking and policy by either NATO or the EU. Thus, if you want to know where Italy is headed—look first at where the two umbrella organizations are headed.

References, Recommended Readings, and Websites

Books

Agnew, John A. 2002. *Place and Politics in Modern Italy.* Chicago: University of Chicago Press.

Baker, John A. 1989. *Italian Communism: The Road to Legitimacy and Autonomy.* Washington, DC: National Defense University Press.

Bufacchi, Vittorio, and Simon Burgess. 1998. *Italy since 1989: Events and Interpretations.* New York: St. Martin's Press.

Cammett, John. 1967. *Antonio Gramsci and the Origins of Italian Communism.* Palo Alto: Stanford University Press.

De Grand, Alexander. 2000. *Italian Fascism: Its Origins and Development.* 3d ed. Lincoln: University of Nebraska Press.

Di Scala, Spencer M. 1995. *Italy: From Revolution to Republic.* Boulder, CO: Westview.

Domenico, Roy Palmer. 2002. *Remaking Italy in the Twentieth Century.* Lanham, MD: Rowman and Littlefield.

Farneti, Paolo. 1985. *The Italian Party System (1945–1980).* New York: St. Martin's Press.

Ferraresi, Franco. 1996. *Threats to Democracy: The Radical Right in Italy after the War.* Princeton: Princeton University Press.

Forgasc, David. 1990. *Italian Culture in the Industrial Era.* Manchester: Manchester University Press.

Ginsborg, Paul. 2003. *Italy and Its Discontents: Family, Civil Society, State 1980–2001.* New York: Palgrave Macmillan.

Gleditsch, Nils Petter, Peter Wallensteen, Mikael Eriksson, Margareta Sollenberg, and Håvard Strand. *Armed Conflict 1946–2002.* Oslo: International Peace Research Institute, Oslo (PRIO), Department of Peace and Conflict Research, Uppsala University.

Holmes, George. 1997. *The Oxford History of Italy.* New York: Oxford University Press.

Hughes, H. Stuart. 1979. *The United States and Italy.* 3d ed. Cambridge, MA: Harvard University Press.

LaPalombara, Joseph. 1987. *Democracy Italian Style.* New Haven: Yale University Press.

Levy, Carl. 1996. *Italian Regionalism: History, Identity and Politics.* Oxford: Berg.

Morgan, Philip. 2004. *Italian Fascism, 1915–1945.* 2d ed. New York: Palgrave Macmillan.

Newell, James, ed. 2004. *The Italian General Election of 2001: Berlusconi's Victory.* Manchester and New York: Manchester University Press.

Partridge, Hilary. 1998. *Italian Politics Today.* Manchester: Manchester University Press.

Ranney, Austin, and Giovanni Sartori, eds. 1978. *Eurocommunism: The Italian Case.* Washington, DC: American Enterprise Institute for Public Policy Research.

Sassoon, Donald. 1997. *Contemporary Italy: Economy, Society and Politics since 1945.* 2d ed. New York: Longman.

Schnapp, Jeffrey T. 2000. *A Primer of Italian Fascism.* Lincoln: University of Nebraska Press.

Schumann, Reinhold. 1986. *Italy in the Last Fifteen Hundred Years: A Concise History.* Lanham, MD: University Press of America.

Seton-Weston, Christopher. 1967. *Italy from Liberalism to Fascism.* London: Methuen.

Smith, Dennis Mack. 1997. *Modern Italy: A Political History.* Ann Arbor: University of Michigan Press.

Spotts, Frederic, and Theodor Wieser. 1986. *Italy: A Difficult Democracy: A Survey of Italian Politics.* New York: Cambridge University Press.

Stille, Alexander. 1995. *Excellent Cadavers: The Mafia and the Death of the First Italian Republic.* New York: Vintage Press.

Wiskemann, Elizabeth. 1971. *Italy since 1945.* London: Macmillan/St. Martin's Press.

Zamagni, Vera. 1997. *The Economic History of Italy, 1860–1990.* Oxford: Clarendon Press.

Articles/Newspapers

AFX News Limited. 2003. "Italy Is a Major Target for Terrorism." November 23.

Agence France Presse. 2003. "Italy's Berlusconi Urges 'Complete Unity' against Terrorism." February 3.

British Broadcasting Company Monitoring International Reports. 2003. "Algeria, Italy Sign Agreement to Combat Organized Crime, Terrorism." July 18.

Facts on File World News Digest. 2003. "Germany, Italy: Terrorism Arrests." November 28.

Gibler, Douglas M., and Meredith Sarkees. 2004. "Measuring Alliances: The Correlates of War Formal Interstate Alliance Data Set, 1816–2000." *Journal of Peace Research* 41, no. 2 (March 2004): 211–222. COW Database.

United Press International (UPI). 2003. "Analysis: Italy's Homegrown Terrorism Back." Byline: Roland Flamini. December 22.

Websites

Area Studies Italy: http://www.psr.keele.ac.uk/area/italy.htm.

CIA World Fact Book 2003: http://www.cia.gov/cia/publications/factbook/.

Facts on International Relations and Security Trends (FIRST): http://first.sipri.org/.

General Information: http://www.italyemb.org/generalinfo.htm (English).

International Peace Research Institute, Oslo (PRIO): http://www.prio.no/.

Italian Air Force: http://www.aeronautica.difesa.it/home.htm (Italian)/.

Italian Army: http://www.esercito.difesa.it/root/sezioni/Sez_English.asp (English).

Italian Constitution: http://www.giurcost.org/fonti/cost_ingl.html (English).

Italian Defense Ministry: http://www.
difesa.it/ (Italian).

Italian Government (portal site): http://
www.italia.gov.it (Italian).

Italian Interior Ministry: http://www.
interno.it/ (Italian).

Italian Navy: http://www.marina.difesa.it/
(Italian).

Italian Prime Minister: http://www.
palazzochigi.it/ (Italian).

Stockholm International Peace Research
Institute (SIPRI): http://www.sipri.
se/.

UN Peacekeeping Operations: http://
www.un.org/Depts/dpko/dpko/home.
shtml.

Japan

Woondo Choi

Geography and History

Japan is composed of thousands of islands, among which Hokkaido, Honshu, Kyushu, and Shikoku are the four largest. The country is separated from the Asian continent by the East Sea (the Sea of Japan). Comparable to California and larger than Germany in total land area, the islands of Japan extend from the latitude of Oslo to that of Naples, lying in one of the most earthquake-prone regions in the world.

Located at the farthest eastern point in Asia, Japan was the final destiny for the imperial encroachment of the Atlantic powers. After 1633 traveling abroad was forbidden in Japan, and foreign trade was limited to a few ports. By the end of the eighteenth century, however, pressure from the West for trade was mounting, but it occurred only in 1853, when Commodore Perry succeeded in forcing the Tokugawa government to open Japan for international trade. Japan's volume of trade was still very limited at the time, and full-scale interaction with the rest of the world was not realized until the inauguration of a new government.

The Meiji Restoration, which put an end to the rule of Tokugawa Bakufu (1603–1867), brought back the sovereignty of the emperor in Japan. With the enactment of a European-style constitution in 1889, the Diet, Japanese Parliament, was established. While the ruling clique, composed of a small group of nobles and former samurai, exercised actual power, the emperor held the top position in army, navy, executive, and legislative affairs. After the Restoration, Japan became fully devoted to catching up with the Western powers, eventually succeeding in joining the group of modernized nations.

However, with the atomic bombs dropped on Hiroshima and Nagasaki, Japan accepted its unconditional surrender to end World War II. Headed by General MacArthur, the general headquarters (GHQ) led the Allied occupation of Japan, ruling Japan for seven years (1945–1952) with an initial policy orientation that can be summarized as "democratization" and "demilitarization." The GHQ drafted the new constitution of Japan, which came into effect in 1947. Although escaping accusations of being a war criminal, the emperor was deprived of any political and military power, recognized only as a symbol of the state. Sovereignty came to rest with the people through the Diet, for which the cabinet, composed of the prime minister and ministers, was responsible. Japan's armed forces were completely abolished, and arms industries were dismantled along with Japanese business conglomerates, the so-called *zaibatsu*.

With the outbreak of the Korean War, the occupation took policies upstream. Given new U.S. interests of having Japan serve as a bulwark of the market economy against Soviet communism, Japan was allowed and requested to possess its own armed forces and arms industries. In addition, labor union activities in Japan came to be regulated, and educational administration was recentralized again. For this "reverse course" to be realized, the occupation was terminated through the San Francisco Peace Treaty, after which Japan and the United States signed an alliance treaty.

The trend toward bipolarity in international politics provided a window of opportunity for Japan, whose primary goal lay in recovering its economy and building its status in the international community. Achieving this through the Yoshida Strategy, named after Prime Minister Yoshida Shigeru, Japan could focus its energy on economic recovery while entrusting the defense of Japan to the U.S. forces stationed on Japanese soil. The Japanese economy in the early 1960s subsequently recovered its prewar indus-

trial capability, which had been comparable to that of England at the beginning of World War II. Japan maintained an average economic growth rate of 10 percent during the 1960s and 5 percent during the 1970s, placing its economy among the first class of the world by the end of the 1970s. At present, it is the third-largest economy (with 7.5 percent of world GDP), after the United States (23 percent) and China (12 percent) (CIA World Factbook 2003), and the second most technologically powerful economy in the world after the United States.

In the post–Cold War era, Japan experienced two trends in the area of economy and security: long-term depression and conservatism. Entering the 1990s, the unprecedented Japanese economic growth showed a marked decline. This began with the burst of the bubble in the real estate sector and the accumulation of bad loans by banks, which spread to bring the eventual collapse of Japan's whole financial system. Coupled with the decline and

Table 1   Japan: Key Statistics

Type of government	Constitutional monarchy with a parliamentary government
Population (millions)	127 (2003)
Religion	Both Shinto and Buddhist 84%, other 16% (including Christian 0.7%)
Main industries	Motor vehicles, electronic equipment, machine tools, steel and nonferrous metals, ships, chemicals, textiles, processed foods
Main security threats	Missile test of North Korea; potential threat from China
Defense spending (% GDP)	1.0% (2002)
Size of military (thousands)	240 (2002)
Number of civil wars since 1945	0
Number of interstate wars since 1945	0

Sources
Central Intelligence Agency Website. 2002. "CIA World Factbook." http://www.cia.gov/cia/
    publications/factbook/ (accessed May 15, 2005).
Hand Book for Defense 2003. Tokyo: Chouwoon Shinbunsha.

stagnation of domestic consumer demand, Japan fell down into the long tunnel of complex depression. In the area of security, on the other hand, the conservative trend has been rising. Japan's alliance relationship with the United States and the Japanese role in security cooperation has also been intensified and expanded. Following the test launch of the Daepo-Dong missile by North Korea and the 9–11 terrorist attacks in the United States, Japan is determined to effect a fundamental reestablishment of its fifty-year-old security arrangements.

Regional Geopolitics

The Cold War took the form of a confrontation between the two forces of sea power and land power. In the process of Japan's disarmament following its unconditional surrender in World War II, the Soviet Union and the United States landed on the north and south of the Korean peninsula, respectively. After the Korean War, that division led to the establishment of the communist regime in the north and the pro-U.S. regime in the south.

Defeated after several decades of conflict with the Chinese Communist Party (CCP), Chiang Kai-shek, the leader of the Nationalist Party (KMT), retreated to Taiwan and relocated the Republic of China on that island. On the mainland across the Taiwan Strait, the Chinese communists declared the establishment of the People's Republic of China on October 1, 1949. China decided to enter the Korean War to support the North Koreans a few months after the war's outbreak, and the United States and Japan signed the Mutual Security Treaty in San Francisco on September 8, 1951. The U.S.-led group of countries, composed of Japan, South Korea, and Taiwan, were aligned to contend with the communist regimes of the Soviet Union, China, and North Korea.

This geopolitical landscape was altered in 1972, when the United States and China terminated two decades of hostility and promised to work toward establishing a full diplomatic relationship. Following the reconciliation, normalization of relations was reached between Japan and China on October 10, 1972, and between the United States and China on January 1, 1979. For its part, the United States had to shift its diplomatic recognition from Taiwan to China and acknowledge China's "One China" policy. The three major powers of the region, the United States, China, and Japan, subsequently started the honeymoon period in their trilateral relationship, which lasted until the end of the Cold War.

The advent of the post–Cold War era brought about more uncertainty in regional politics than had the collapse of the Soviet Union. Disappearance of the external enemy caused a weakening of internal cohesion. The honeymoon among the three major powers was over, and China's rapid growth began to be perceived as a possible threat to the future of U.S. hegemony.

In the new era, international relations in this region are likely to be characterized more by conflict than by cooperation. Historical legacies of suspicion and antagonism have the potential to make the high level of regional economic interdependence fall into a momentum of conflict rather than cooperation. Backwardness in the development of institutions and organizations that can funnel economic interdependence into security cooperation is a key feature of the region, and the lack of experiences of cooperation and collaboration has been indicated as the most crucial factor of the problem (Buzan and Segal 1994; Friedberg 1993/1994).

Since the latter part of the 1990s, however, East Asia has begun to present a picture quite different from the above scenario. Confidence, multilateralism, talks and meetings, cooperation and conferences are ideas often found in discussions on the security environment of the region, along with concepts such as alliance, deterrence, balance of power, and sanction. Although the realist argument still dominates the rhetoric of regional security, the liberalist approach to regional stability is increasingly being reflected in government policies and scholastic arguments.

The realist picture is made up of several aspects of regional politics. First, Joseph Nye (1995), who shaped U.S. engagement policy in East Asia as deputy minister of the Department of Defense under the Clinton administration, argued that maintaining U.S. forces at a level of 100,000 was necessary to secure U.S. national interests in the region, advocating the idea that "security is like oxygen." The policy was directed toward the potential threat of China and North Korea and called for the security cooperation of Japan. By now, the United States is also in the process of developing a missile defense system on a global scale to defend its mainland and its allied countries from possible attack from the "rogue states."

Second, China did not hesitate to emphasize its military might toward Taiwan whenever its presidential candidates showed support for the independence of the island. The United States, having maintained strategic ambiguity on the matter, sent its air force carrier *Independence* and war ships to the area to respond to the Chinese missile threat in 1996. China's startling rate of economic development and its double-digit increases in military spending over a period of more than a decade pose a potential threat to this region.

Third, North Korea, struggling to maintain its regime since the collapse of the Soviet Union, has been advancing its nuclear weapons program to reach crisis situations with its neighboring countries and the United States. In addition to the nuclear program, North Korea has demonstrated its rapid advancement in missile technology by test-launching its missiles over Japan.

Fourth, in response to the request by the United States, and to defend against the direct threat of North Korea and the potential threat of China, Japan has been expanding its sphere of activities. In the name of cooperation with the United States, Japan has passed a law permitting military operations in its "surrounding area," which can be interpreted as encompassing the Taiwan Strait. In the name of international cooperation and humanitarian relief, Japan began to send its troops to the disputed area as a participant in peacekeeping operations and to the Indian Ocean for the antiterrorism war in Afghanistan and the postwar reconstruction of Iraq.

According to the liberalist picture, multilateral organizations, which work toward regional cooperation in the areas of security and economics, began to play a role in regional politics during the last decade. At the government level (Track I), programs such as the ASEAN Regional Forum (ARF), Northeast Asian Security Dialogue (NEASeD), and the Singapore "Shangri-La Dialogue" are working for consultation on security matters and confidence building among member countries. Such activities at Track I are supported by the research and exchange of institutions at the civilian level (Track II), such as the Council for Security Cooperation in the Asia-Pacific (CSCAP) and the Northeast Asia Cooperation Dialogue (NEACD) (Cossa 2002, 1996). However, even ARF, which is the meeting between foreign ministers and the most conspicuous among Track I activities, is not producing any binding agreement and is limited to the level of consultation.

In the economic arena, interdependence among the major powers is progressing rapidly. China is the second-largest export partner for Japan (¥3.764 billion, 7.6 percent of total exports) and imports (¥7.027 billion, 16.6 percent), next to the United States (¥14.711 billion in exports and ¥7.627 billion in imports) in 2001 (Japan Statistical Yearbook 2003). Japan has become the largest partner for China's imports and the second largest for exports following the United States, and these three countries represent the largest trading partners in the world. In the area of foreign direct investment, Japan is the second-largest contributor next to Hong Kong, with the United States ranked the fourth largest. In addition, Japan, China, and South Korea are keen on concluding a Free Trade Agreement with ASEAN countries. The geopolitical landscape of East Asia can thus be summarized as a coexistence of strategic competition and economic cooperation (Choi 2003).

Conflict Past and Present

Between 1868 and 1945, Japan waged four major wars: the Sino-Japanese War (1894–1895), the Russo-Japanese War (1904–1905), the second Sino-Japanese War (1937–1945), and the Pacific War (1941–1945) (Katzenstein 1996, 53). During that period Japan rose as a member of the imperialist powers, but it suffered as a country devastated by war. These wars occurred over the process of modernization, leaving a deep legacy on Japanese national strategy in the following period. The war experiences of this period are briefly introduced below. After the Meiji Restoration, Japan rapidly installed modern state organs and began to extend its influence in competing with the Western imperialist powers. The first clash of the Sino-Japanese War involved dispute over the control of Korea. When the Tonghak farmers' rebellion erupted in Korea, the Korean government had requested Chinese assistance for suppression. Although encouraging Chinese intervention in Korea on the one hand, Japan was also looking for the excuse to dispatch its own troops. The Japanese army eventually defeated the Chinese in the Korean peninsula and marched into Chinese territory, with the Japanese navy also crushing the Chinese fleet off the mouth of the Yalu River.

The Sino-Japanese War was terminated with the signing of the Treaty of Shimonoseki. By recognizing Korea as a sovereign state, China had to give tacit approval for Japanese domination in the peninsula. China also ceded to Japan Taiwan, the Liaodong peninsula, and the Pescadores Islands, located in the Taiwan Strait, in addition to a huge amount of war reparations. This contract, which favored Japan's position in China, invited the intervention of the Western imperialist countries, the so-called Triple Intervention. Russia, France, and Germany pressured Japan to return the Liaodong peninsula, which was substituted for by an increase in war reparations. After the war there occurred a surge in modernization in China; also, competition between the Western imperialist countries and Japan, the latecomer, intensified.

The Russo-Japanese War was waged by Japan for the control of Korea and Manchuria. After the Triple Intervention, in 1896, Russia signed an alliance relationship with China to stand against Japan. China granted Russia the right to construct the Trans-Siberian Railroad, extending across Manchuria to Vladivostok, while also being pressured by Russia to lease the strategic post of Port Arthur, located at the tip of the Liaodong peninsula. Russia was establishing its occupation in Manchuria and expanding its sphere of influence southward to Korea, where Japan had won the initiative through its war victory over China. At the time the Russian occupation in the region was not yet established because of the country's limited armed forces and transportation facilities. Japan was sustaining its superiority over Russia with ground troops in Manchuria, and it decided to exploit the chance before losing its advantage. The war started with Japan's surprise attacks on Port Arthur and Incheon, which were directed toward Manchuria and Korea, respectively. The battles on land inflicted heavy casualties on both sides, with the demolition of the Russian Baltic Fleet at the Tsushima Strait marking the turning point of the war.

U.S. president Theodore Roosevelt mediated the subsequent peace conference, held at Portsmouth, New Hampshire. In the Treaty of Portsmouth, Japan secured control of Port Arthur and the Liaodong peninsula, in addition to the concession of the South Manchurian railroad and half of Sakhalin Island. Japan's exclusive privilege in Korea was also recognized, and it annexed Korea as a Japanese colony in 1910. As for Russia, it promised to evacuate from southern Manchuria; following defeat, it succumbed to the domestic turmoil of revolution. For Japan, the Russo-Japanese War represented the first war in which a non-Western country defeated a Western country, which encouraged Japanese nationalism. These postwar conditions were shaped under the England-Japan alliance and the Taft-Katsura agreement between the United States and Japan. The war victory was lamented by some critics as a catalyst for the imperial expansion of Japan, which was headed toward eventual collapse.

In the covenant of the League of Nations at the Paris Peace Conference following World War I, Japan proposed a revision of a racial equality clause, but that was rejected by the United States, England, and Australia. After that, the relationship between Japan and the West began to deteriorate rapidly. At the same time, Japan was forcing China to participate in unequal treaties and was consolidating its control over Manchuria with the establishment of the puppet state "Manchukuo." Anti-Japanese sentiment was rising among the Chinese, and a minor incident involving the Marco Polo Bridge developed into a full-scale war in 1937, the second Sino-Japanese War. The Japanese Guandong Army occupied almost the entire coast of China and committed several atrocities, such as the Nanjing Massacre, in which an estimated 300,000 Chinese were killed. With the worsening Chinese sentiment toward Japan, neither the Kuomintang nor the communists wanted to be involved in a full-blown war against Japan.

Meanwhile Japan joined the group of Axis powers that included Germany and Italy and marched to occupy Vietnam, a French colony at the time. This worsened Japan's relationship with the United States and the British, who suspended the supply of oil to Japan. The impending shortages of fuel and natural resources, combined with the intensified diplomatic conflicts, pushed Japan to challenge the hegemonic powers of the United States and England, Japan's former partners.

The Japanese surprise attack on Pearl Harbor in December 1941, without warning or declaration of war, was successful. Within the first six months of the subsequent Pacific War, Japan would bring under its control a huge territory that extended to the border of India in the west and the islands of New Guinea in the south. However, it soon became clear that the declaration of war was a wrong decision. The United States prevented Japan's invasion of the Midway Islands, destroying four Japanese air force carriers, ships that Japanese industry could not replace. This debacle became the turning point in the Asian theater of World War II, putting the Japanese on the defensive.

The United States and the Allied forces began to take back the captured islands against the eager defense of Japanese troops, from Guadalcanal in mid-1942 to the Philippines in late 1944. When the islands of Iwo Jima and Okinawa fell under the occupation of Allied forces, the homeland of Japan was brought within range of naval and air attack. When Tokyo was bombarded and the two atomic attacks devastated Hiroshima and Nagasaki, the Japanese emperor declared Japan's unconditional surrender. The Soviet Union declared war on Japan in early 1945, but it began its military attack in Manchuria only three days after the U.S. atomic bomb was dropped on Hiroshima, on the same day that the atomic bomb was dropped on Nagasaki.

Current and Potential Military Confrontation

The Japanese constitution, drafted by the GHQ, is called the Peace Constitution because it renounces war as an instrument for settling disputes. Even the Self Defense Forces (SDF) were established as part of a reverse course only after the reinterpretation of the constitution as permitting Japanese military activity if its role is confined only to the passive defense of Japan. Although Japan willingly maintained its exclusively defense-oriented policy while institutionalizing the Yoshida strategy, international pressure from neighboring countries also contributed to the minimal defense posture of Japan (Milford 2002). The United States, as well as China and Korea (which had suffered from past conflict), was wary of the remilitarization of Japan. During the Cold War, however, there occurred no military confrontation involving Japan under the ebb and flow of tension between the blocs of East and West.

With the end of the Cold War, the military threat seemed to have disappeared from East Asian regional politics. Into this seemingly peaceful situation there arose three territorial disputes, which had taken root since the end of the Pacific War. These disputes so far remain at the diplomatic level and are quite unlikely to develop into military conflict.

First, Japan resumed its request for the return of the four islands off the north of Hokkaido that had fallen under the sovereignty of the Soviet Union. Immediately after Japan's unconditional surrender, Soviet troops moved southward, occupying the southernmost point of the Kurile Islands. Finding U.S. forces absent, by September 3 Soviet troops had occupied Etorofu, Kunashiri, Shikotan, and the Habomai Islands, which are recognized as inherent territories of Japan. With regard to the Soviet seizure of the four Japanese islands, the Soviet Union has argued that it was recognized in the Yalta Agreement between the United States, England, and the Soviet Union. The Soviet Union did not sign the San Francisco Peace Treaty, for the reason that international society did not recognize the four islands as part of Soviet territory. No peace treaty has been concluded so far between Japan and the Soviet Union and the Russian Federation. Negotiations concerning the islands, which had been suspended since 1956, were resumed in 1991 when President Mikhail Gorbachev visited Japan. Several summit meetings have been held without any resolution, but both sides are committed to reach consensus based on law and justice.

Second, Japan also claims rights for the rocky island of Dokdo (Takeshima), which has been a matter of territorial dispute between South Korea and Japan since the 1950s. Although Japan asserts that the island was incorporated within the control of the Shiname Prefecture government in 1905, South Korea argues that it was initially under the control of Korea's Shilla Dynasty in 512 C.E. and that Korea could not effectively protest against the Japanese control because of the Protectorate Treaty of 1905 (also known as the Ulsa Treaty). The San Francisco Peace Treaty of 1952, concluded between Japan and the Allied powers without the presence of Korea, did not settle the ownership of Dokdo. This dispute over Dokdo is the major reason why diplomatic relations between Japan and Korea were not normalized, even after the end of the Pacific War. The issue remained unresolved in the ROK/Japan Basic Relations Treaty

of 1965, and it resurfaced in the process of negotiation for EEZ and the fishery in 1996. Currently, while a small group of Korean coast guards are stationed on the island, the Japanese continue at times to claim sovereignty.

Japan's third territorial confrontation has involved the Senkaku/Diaoyu Islands, located between Taiwan and Okinawa. Japan insists that the Senkaku Islands have been under Japanese sovereignty since its occupation of Okinawa in 1879 and were formally incorporated as Japanese territory after the Sino-Japanese War of 1895. The United States occupied the islands at the end of the Pacific War, returning them along with Okinawa in 1972. On the other hand, China has historically regarded the islands as part of the Chinese province of Taiwan, and it argues for their return as part of the San Francisco Peace Treaty. The most recent related dispute was in the summer of 1996, when the nationalist organization of the Japan Youth Federation built a lighthouse on the islands, landing again on September 9 to repair the structure. The Chinese government responded by launching a formal protest against the Japanese government's tacit consent, and the People's Liberation Army (PLA) sent several naval ships to the area of the Senkaku Islands. On September 13 and 14 the PLA conducted a large-scale exercise of combined forces in landing operations, and on September 18 the Chinese navy conducted a comprehensive supply exercise in the East China Sea. China adopted tough measures, such as the mobilization of warplanes and naval vessels to the disputed area, and after a series of visits between top officials, Chinese vice foreign minister Tang Jisxuan and Japanese prime minister Hashimoto reached an agreement. With no solution for the dispute over sovereignty of the islands, the potential crisis between China and Japan still persists.

If any, the North Korean nuclear threat is the most clear and present danger to Japan. That threat, which has existed in the region since 1994, when the North Korean nuclear program was first brought to question, was directly sensed by the Japanese only when the Daepo-Dong missile was test-launched successfully over Japanese territory in 1998. Suspicion about the North Korean nuclear program still remains, and it provides the best excuse for the purchase of new armaments and the installation of new legal institutions in Japan. The emergency situation on the Korean peninsula served as a test bed for the planning backup rear area support to the activities of U.S. forces, as suggested in the new Guideline for U.S.-Japan Defense Cooperation. The Daepo-Dong missile test provided Japan with the rationale for the hurried launch of a reconnaissance satellite, a decision that resulted from Japan's active participation in the research of the Theatrical Missile Defense system and from open discussion on the emergency legislation.

At the present time, China is posing only a potential threat (Sato 1998). Even though a spectrum of various views is presented on the threat of China, the Japanese government has taken a critical position, with its policy toward China recognizing "China as a threat" (Zhang and Montaperto 1999). *The Basic Strategy of Japanese Foreign Policy of the 21st Century*, a document issued in November 2002 by a task force team composed of scholars, retired bureaucrats, and businessmen, clearly expresses Japanese apprehension about China's military buildup and expanding military expenditure (Task Force on Foreign Relations for Prime Minister 2002).

In contrast to scholars, the pessimists among politicians exhibit their security-first propensity as follows. Deepening Japan's interdependence with China will not guarantee a friendly relationship between the two countries. The current market condition in China appears to be overstated, and the future is not that rosy. In terms of bilateral trade, the volume of trade is not a concern, and Japan's vast trade deficit with China may worsen. In addition, China's economic growth and the deepening of Japan's and China's interdependence could bring serious repercussions in the form of shortages of resources and fuel, environmental devastation, and to some extent, economic competition and challenges in military hegemony. Moreover, Japan still cannot ensure its influence over China's policy decisions resulting from their greater interdependence (Green and Self 1996).

Alliance Structure

Immediately following the onset of the Korean War, John Foster Dulles, special emissary of the U.S. secretary of state, formulated a regional defense alliance of a NATO type in order to encourage Japanese rearmament, while placing it under the control of the proposed international organization. The crescent that contains communism at the Eastern Front was conceived to connect together the United States, Japan, Australia, New Zealand, the Philippines, and Indonesia. Dulles's proposal was rejected, however, by Japan's incumbent prime minister, Yoshida, who wished to maintain Japan's cultural and political distinctiveness. Although it was necessary for the United States to conclude an individual alliance treaty with each of the countries, the security treaty, concluded in 1951 on the same day as the

San Francisco Peace Treaty, was highly unequal (Pyle 1996). In simple terms, it endowed all the privileges of overseas bases to U.S. forces but did not specify the obligation to defend Japan (Hara 1991). The treaty was revised to set a more equal footing in 1960.

Upon consultation with its U.S. counterpart, the Japan Defense Agency (JDA) issues a National Defense Program Outline (NDPO) that is approved by the cabinet. The NDPO specifies the midterm strategic goal of the appropriate defense posture for the international and domestic situation and sets the direction of armament. Based upon the NDPO, the United States and Japan produce a U.S.-Japan Defense Cooperation Guideline, which formulates the division of labor and cooperation between SDF and U.S. forces at the tactical level. To put the guideline into practice, new laws and regulations are introduced, if necessary.

The NDPO was drawn up for the first time in 1976. Previously, the armament of SDF had been focused on its role only in localized conflicts. After revision, however, the operational goal was aimed at building the capability to defend independently against a limited aggression or to resist the enemy until the arrival of U.S. assistance, and the goal of the defense buildup was aimed at the qualitative improvement of existing armament. Based on this strategy, the following basic postures of mutual cooperation were prescribed in the U.S.-Japan Defense Cooperation Guideline of 1978: (1) posture for deterring aggression; (2) actions in response to an armed attack against Japan; (3) Japan-U.S. cooperation in the case of situations in the Far East outside Japan affecting Japan's security. Contrary to the detailed stipulations on (1) and (2), a short commitment to "con-

duct studies in advance" on the scope and modalities of facilitative assistance to be extended to U.S. forces by Japan was attached to (3). Under this arrangement between the two countries, Japan continued its minimum defense strategy. Just as Japan's actual contribution in the alliance partnership was increasingly falling short of U.S. expectations of the Japanese burden-sharing level, the Cold War was over and peace was restored.

The collapse of the Soviet Union, the former common enemy of the United States and Japan, put the "alliance adrift" (Funabashi 1999). The so-called Nye Initiative (proposed in 1994 by an assistant deputy minister of the Defense Department at the time, currently a Harvard professor) to recover and upgrade the U.S. alliance relationship with Japan provided a momentum for communication between the two countries. Those efforts bore fruit in the form of a reassurance policy on the bilateral relationship and U.S. engagement policy in East Asia.

Under the uncertainties of the post–Cold War international order, Japan issued a new NDPO in November 1995, suggesting the direction of Japanese defense policy. Two points deserve attention here. First, SDF was mentioned for the first time as being tasked to contribute to building a more stable security environment for Japan, in addition to being responsible for Japan's defense and for handling severe disasters. Second, the new NDPO emphasized the importance of allied operations with the United States. Regarding defense capability, it suggested restructuring SDF to make it compact and efficient.

At the U.S.-Japan summit meeting in 1996, the Joint Declaration promised further cooperation in the alliance framework and the forward deployment of

100,000 U.S. troops in East Asia. This political commitment was supported by a working-level agreement of the new Guideline for the U.S.-Japan Defense Cooperation. It developed practical activities for cooperation in resolving issues of the Far East that had remained at the consultation level in the old guideline. The activities mentioned in the new guideline came into effect with the enactment of the Law on the Area Surrounding Japan (Mochizuki 1997).

Development of the alliance relationship between the United States and Japan is restrained by the question of collective self-defense. According to the UN charter and the U.S.-Japan Security Treaty, collective self-defense is recognized, but depending on the interpretation of the constitution, it can be illegal. Japan's official position is that Japan has the right to collective self-defense, although Japan does not exercise it in practice. It means that Japan can join in bilateral alliance and international collective security as a partner as long as SDF is not involved in the use of force. That is why activities such as ship inspection operation, and search and rescue, which are highly likely to invite armed conflict, are excluded from the series of laws newly enacted in the post–Cold War era, such as the PKO Law (1994), Law on the Area Surrounding Japan (1998), Anti-Terror Special Measures Law (2001), and the Special Measures Law for Iraq (2003). A separate law (the Ship Inspection Operations Law) was passed to stipulate deliberate avoidance of such conflict situations.

Size and Structure of the Military

SDF, Japan's armed forces, belongs to the Japan Defense Agency (JDA), which was established in 1954 as an external bureau of the prime minister's office (it became an external bureau of the cabinet office after the reorganization of the central government in 2001). Initiated as a part of a self-help principle of the U.S.-Japan Security Treaty in a country in which armed forces had been abolished and prohibited, it is different in status and structure from the armed forces of other foreign countries. The director general of JDA is a state minister and a member of the cabinet, but his power does not parallel that of other cabinet members, reflecting the agency's organizational status, which is not equivalent to that of the ministry.

The JDA consists of internal bureaus, three military services of SDF, the Joint Staff Council (JSC), the Defense Facilities Administration Agency, and other defense-related organizations. Among them, the internal bureaus, which deal with defense policy, personnel and education, and equipment, are the most powerful organs and the conduit of influence from other ministries such as the Ministry of Foreign Affairs (MOFA), Ministry of Finance (MOF), and the Ministry of International Trade and Industry (MITI), under the name of civilian control (Katzenstein and Okawara 1993).

The three services of SDF are known as Ground SDF, Air SDF, and Maritime SDF. The total manpower of SDF is 237,000, which is smaller than the forces of other major powers of East Asia. In 2000, China (2,810,000), Russia (1,520,000), and the United States (1,366,000) composed the top three; South Korea placed fifth (683,000) (www.nationmaster.com). (According to the *Military Balance 2000/2001* [IISS], North Korea's military personnel is estimated at 1,170,000.) In 2002 Japan's total SDF personnel included 148,197 members of Ground SDF, 44,404 of Maritime SDF, 45,582 of Air SDF, and 1,656 of JSC. Since the announcement of the new NDPO in 1995, the number of personnel was to be reduced by 10,000, and that reduction is still in process (*Hand Book for Defense 2003*).

Ground SDF is made up of five regional armies: the Northern Army (Sapporo), Northeastern Army (Sendai), Eastern Army (Tokyo), Middle Army (Itami), and Western Army (Kumamoto). Each army is composed of divisions and brigades and is in charge of its own region. MSDF is composed of two groups: regional district units and a Self-Defense Fleet. The former are divided according to five regional districts: the Ominato Regional District Unit (RDU), Yokosuka RDU, Kure RDU, Maizuru RDU, and Sasebo RDU. These district units are responsible primarily for their assigned district and support the Self-Defense Fleet.

The Self-Defense Fleet is divided into three groups: four fleet escort forces (Yokosuka, Sasebo, Maizuru, Kure), the Fleet Air Force (including fixed-wing patrol aircraft units and others), two submarine forces (Yokosuka, Kure), and two minesweeper flotillas (Yokosuka, Kure). These are responsible for the defense of the sea around Japan (ibid.). Among these, each fleet escort force is well known by another name, "88 Fleet." Eight escort ships (one helicopter-on-board escort ship, two missile escort ships, five destroyers) and eight antisubmarine helicopters compose a fleet escort force. The helicopter-on-board escort ship carries three helicopters, and each destroyer carries one helicopter. One destroyer of each 88 Fleet is equipped with the Aegis system.

The SDF, however, has never been involved in real warfare. It began to dispatch its troops outside of Japan's territorial seas only after the end of the Cold War. With the revision of the Law Concerning the Dispatch of International Disaster Relief Teams, the SDF began to engage in international relief operations. Japan made significant contributions to the international community through the air transportation of relief materials to aid earthquake recovery in India, through the dispatch of SDF units to aid in hurricane recovery in Honduras, and through the marine transportation of relief materials to aid the 1999 earthquake recovery in Turkey (*Defense of Japan 2001*, 215–217).

Since 1992, when Japan began its involvement in UN Peacekeeping Operations (PKO) in Cambodia, Japan has participated in four PKOs (Cambodia, Mozambique, the Golan Heights, and East Timor) and carried out two humanitarian aid assignments, for Afghan and Rwanda refugees (*East Asian Strategic Review 2003*, 309–310) (see Sidebar 1). With the enactment of the Anti-Terrorism Special Measures Law after the 9–11 terrorist attacks, Japan has provided active support to U.S. forces in Afghanistan. Between November 2001 and December 2002, Japan dispatched seventeen MSDF vessels, refueled U.S. supply ships and destroyers 131 times and British supply ships 9 times, and sent C-130H cargo airplane of ASDF for 112 flights (ibid., 301).

The SDF, whose deployment was in the past confined to Japanese territory, has been expanding its radius of activities overseas in the cause of international cooperation.

Budget

Japanese defense policy is moving toward activism and expansion. Japan is involved in disputes with neighboring countries with claims of territorial sover-

Sidebar 1   Public Opinion on PKO

According to the polls conducted by the Cabinet Secretary Public Information Office, there has been a tremendous transformation in public opinion on the SDF's participation in PKO. People who indicated that they "approve" and "tend to approve" of the SDF's participation increased from 44.9 percent in February 1991 to 79.5 percent in January 2000. During the inspection tour of East Timor, then Director General of JDA General Nakatani remarked that "the time for apprenticeship is over."

Source
East Asian Strategic Review 2003.
   Tokyo: Defense Institute for National Defense.

While the reduction by 10,000 SDF personnel has been under way since the issue of the new NDPO, the share of expenses for personnel and provisions consistently increased from 40 percent (1991) to 45 percent (2003). On the other hand, the share of equipment and material purchases decreased from 27.73 percent (1991) to 18.31 percent (2003), contrary to expectations when considering the list of new armaments. The share of R&D fluctuated between 2.35 percent (1991) and 2.98 percent (2003), but in any case, the size of R&D was not large enough to compensate for the loss in equipment and material purchases. Japan has been expanding its host nation support since the early 1990s, occupying 4.05 percent in 1991, 5.6 percent in 1999, and 4.99 percent in 2003. The sum of other items fluctuated between 25 percent and 30 percent during the period.

How can we explain the activism in Japanese defense policy during the last decade? First, the current level of defense expenditure is higher than at any previous time. Furthermore, the size of Japan's expenditure has been standing second among the major powers of the world. In 2002, the United States spent $341 billion, Japan $47 billion, England $37 billion, France $34 billion, and China $30 billion on defense (see Table 2). The current size of Japan's defense expenditure is large enough for the limited expansion of burden sharing under the U.S.-Japan alliance relationship.

The second aspect of note of Japanese defense expenditure is its inefficiency in the past. Besides the 1 percent ceiling and the Three Non-Nuclear Principles, Japan also proclaimed the Three Principles of Arms Export in 1976, which prohibited the export of weapons to countries in the communist bloc, countries under sanction

eignty over the islands located on three sides of its territorial waters. It has been introducing new laws expanding the scale and scope of its activities and already possesses or will possess new arms and equipment to implement the new activities, such as the following: F-2 support fighters, Early-Warning Aircraft (AWACS), in-flight refueling aircraft, Aegis escort ships, and 13,000-ton escort ships and cruisers.

In contrast to these new trends, few changes have occurred in Japanese defense expenditure. Compared with the previous period, there have been only trivial changes in the amount of expenditure. In terms of share of GNP, Japan has not violated its self-imposed rule of a 1 percent ceiling, which was announced in 1976 by the cabinet. The share of government expenditure, which reflects the priorities of policy, has not deviated from the average of 6.24 percent for a decade (Hand Book for Defense 2003).

Table 2   Military Expenditures of Major Powers (U.S. $ [millions] at constant 2000 prices)

Year	United States	Japan	United Kingdom	France	China
1988	426,798		46,581	38,337	
1989	422,133	40,140	46,746	38,807	11,300
1990	403,701	41,311	45,604	38,635	12,100
1991	354,284	42,259	47,111	38,887	12,700
1992	374,386	43,278	42,586	37,663	15,300
1993	354,778	43,753	41,626	37,246	14,200
1994	334,539	43,958	40,268	37,438	13,500
1995	315,107	44,398	37,119	35,584	13,900
1996	298,058	45,293	37,719	34,729	15,300
1997	296,530	45,510	35,401	34,856	15,500
1998	289,658	45,394	35,605	33,922	17,800
1999	290,480	45,479	35,171	34,209	20,000
2000	301,697	45,793	35,677	33,814	22,000
2001	304,130	46,259	36,414	33,708	25,900
2002	341,489	46,773	36,738	34,394	30,300
2003	417,363	46,895	37,137	35,030	32,800

Source
Stockholm International Peace Research Institute (SIPRI). 2004. *SIPRI Yearbook 2004: Armaments, Disarmament and International Security.* London: Oxford University Press.

of the United Nations, and countries involved in international conflicts. Japan maintained defense industries in order to sustain the foundation of technology and as a part of manufacturing capability. In arms imports, Japan was ranked second in the world, next to Saudi Arabia during the 1980s. With limited domestic and overseas demand and with the huge amount of imports, Japanese defense production could not escape from the vicious circle of inefficiency, despite the tremendous success in the development of dual-use technology. From the experience of the coproduction project of the F-2 support fighter, Japan changed its strategy from catching up with the total level of technological capability of arms exporters to developing unrivaled technologies that are essential for arms development (Green 1998; Samuels 1994). The NDPO of 1995 pointed out the need for developing the procurement and supply system to promote efficiency in acquisition. Arms imports have also been consistently decreasing since the 1990s.

The third explanation can be found in the effort to build compact and efficient SDF. The restructuring of Ground SDF is focused on reducing personnel while developing armaments of a higher caliber. The number of tanks was reduced from 1,200 to 1,040, mobile guns from 680 to 570, and armored vehicles from 720 to 680 during the last decade. In the case of Maritime SDF, the change can be summarized as a reduction of vessels combined with the construction of vessels of large tonnage. The number of vessels decreased from 163 to 138 and the total tonnage increased from 328,000 tons to 382,000 tons. Air SDF adopted high technology and high efficiency in its equipment. There were increases of 33 F-15s and 32 F-2s, while there were 12 and 42 retirements in F-4s and F-1s, respectively. The former aircraft display the cutting edge of technology, while the latter are of the old model. This restructuring within SDF might have made the purchase of new equipment possible (*Hand Book for Defense 2003, 1994*).

Civil-Military Relations/The Role of the Military in Domestic Politics

Japan experienced two great losses during World War II: first, the loss caused by the two atomic bombs dropped by the United States, and second, the sacrifices necessitated by their own government. The lesson learned by the Japanese highlighted the dangers of a strong state. Not only the public but also the elites of Japan had suspicions about the instability of Japanese democracy and military rule, and that has evolved to form the background of their culture of pacifism and antimilitarism (Berger 1999). The public mood toward the military is supported and strengthened by the principle of civilian control in the Peace Constitution. Article 66 states: "The Prime Minister and other Ministers of State must be civilians." The commander-in-chief of the SDF is the prime minister, and the director general of JDA is a state minister and must be a civilian. Article 77 prohibits court-martial.

With the policy priorities on economic rehabilitation and economic growth, the Japanese government's macroeconomic policies and budget allocation are solely directed toward economic purposes. The budget increase demanded by SDF was perceived as the most nonproductive of expenditures. In the process of budget allocation, the authority of JDA is considerably limited compared with the dominant control of MOF and the political influence of MITI and the Economic Planning Agency (Campbell 1977).

For LDP politicians, membership in the National Defense Division (which grants status as a National Defense tribesman [*kokuho-zoku*]) of the Policy Affairs Research Council (PARC) was not helpful for the election. Considering the fact that public opinion stood against defense policy in general, it was rather a negative move for the politician's career. Therefore, the old members of the Diet, or Diet members who had a career in the Defense Agency, had to compose the National Defense Division for a long period of time. Even though the role of tribesmen expanded during the 1980s, the National Defense tribesmen did not receive any support from society, bureaucrats, or members of the same party (Calder 1988).

The Japanese election law of the medium-size electorate makes LDP candidates compete against each other in the same election, and politicians have come to form alliances with supporters' associations, such as small and medium-size enterprises, construction companies, and local industries. Japan's politicians cannot find clear linkages between their political interests and defense issues. Also, the norm of pacifism by ordinary citizens, and their demands for economic development and equal income distribution, have challenged politicians against an enthusiastic pursuit of defense issues (Ozawa 1994).

During the last decade, there occurred significant changes in Japan's civil-military relationship. Ever since the Nye Initiative of 1994, JDA and SDF conducted close consultations with their counterparts, the U.S. Department of Defense and armed forces. They discussed all issues, such as the restructuring of the alliance relationship and the measures of security cooperation in the surrounding area. In drawing up the new guideline, revising the Acquisition and Cross-Servicing Agreement (ACSA), and assisting the activities of the Japan-U.S. Special Action Committee (SACO), the expertise of SDF in defense matters played a significant role.

Political parties and politicians also began to play important roles in the area of foreign and defense policies. While the power of bureaucrats declined, LDP members were able to put their policy ideas into practice, based on the vast network of bureaucrats and their ability to invent new policies, acquired from the LDP's long experience in power. The leadership of politicians is also supported by the conservative trend followed by the Japanese public. The generation change of LDP members made the hawkish conservative politicians in their forties dominate the National Defense Division of PARC. Furthermore, the new election system that combines the small-constituency system and the proportional representation system was enacted for the first time in the Lower House election of 1996. Since then, politicians have been expected to play a leadership role in defense matters as a part of policy competition.

So far, meaningful changes have occurred at almost all levels of the political process concerned with the civil-military relationship. What is missing is only the evidence of corresponding changes in social norms.

Terrorism

Until the mid-1990s, Japan was virtually a crime-free society. Katzenstein (1996) presented pacifism as a cultural norm of postwar Japanese society, citing that the Japanese police and military have been unusually reluctant to use violence (pp. 1–2). Given this social environment, Japan has been free from threats of terrorist attack. However, the Aum Shinrikyo doomsday cult launched two consecutive gas attacks in 1994 and 1995, the first in Matsumoto and the second in Tokyo. In the former, the targeted judges survived, but seven residents were killed and fifty-four were hospitalized. The latter sarin gas attack on the Tokyo subway system was catastrophic, killing twelve people and injuring more than five thousand.

Japan's engagement with terrorism has also occurred overseas. As a reaction to the September 11 attacks, the Japanese Diet passed the Anti-Terrorism Special Measures Law on October 29, 2004, under the initiative of Prime Minister Koizumi. Based upon that law, Japan's SDF provided logistical support for the war in Afghanistan, including intelligence collection, supply shipments, and humanitarian relief. This was Japan's first case of military participation in international conflict since the end of World War II. Besides participating in these military support activities, the Japanese government has also provided refugee assistance and economic assistance to countries surrounding Afghanistan, and has engaged in the freezing of transactions of terrorist-related assets.

This rapid and dramatic response to September 11 can be understood from several background explanations. First, with the deaths of twenty-four Japanese in the World Trade Center attack in New York representing double the toll of the 1995 subway attack in Tokyo, Japan could not ignore the importance of international terrorism. Second, Japan did not want to repeat its regretably inactive role in the 1991 Gulf War, in which, despite the country's financial contribution of U.S.$13 billion, Japanese foreign policy was branded as "checkbook diplomacy" for the lack of personnel contributed. Third, September 11 provided Japan with an opportunity to make a major step toward realizing its expanded role in security burden sharing with the United States, which had been in progress in an incremental manner.

Relationship with the United States

With the conclusion of the Security Treaty, Japan was integrated into the Western bloc against communism. In the sphere of security, Japan allowed the stationing of U.S. forces in return for minimum spending on its own defense. In the economic sphere, Japan supported the economic leadership of the United States by joining the Bretton Woods System and GATT, in pursuit of its strategy of export-driven economic growth. Article 2 of the revised security treaty of 1960 (the Treaty of Mutual Cooperation and Security between Japan and the United States of America) states that both parties "will seek to eliminate conflict in their international economic policies and will encourage economic collaboration between them." In practice, however, Japan unilaterally benefited from the favorable conditions in its trade with the United States.

Until the 1960s, when the Cold War was at its peak and when Japan was still under recovery, this Japanese strategy was accepted by the United States. Entering the 1970s, the U.S. withdrew its defense commitment to its allies by announcing the Guam Doctrine; it renounced the dollar standard of the Bretton Woods monetary system and raised questions on the unfairness of Japanese trade practices. Facing the rising demands of the United States for sharing the burden of defense, the Ohira government coined the concept of Comprehensive Security. The emphasis was then placed on the nondefense aspect of Japanese security, which meant that securing the supply of natural resources (supply security) and securing markets to sell Japanese goods were as important as defending against armed aggression. Japan avoided spending on defense matters and continued to exploit the international order of trade for its own profit.

While Japan adhered to the strategy of minimum defense under the security threat that was to be termed the Second Cold War of the 1980s, the hegemonic power of the United States fell on the track of relative decline. Japan was accused of being a free rider because it was enjoying the security alliance without meeting its burden sharing; it was also called a "developmental state" (Johnson 1995) and the harbor of "mercantile realism" (Higenbotham and Samuels 1998) because its trade policy did not consider the relative position of its trade partners.

As long as it remained within the U.S. strategic framework, Japan could resist the accusations and demands of the United States. That was possible because of the Cold War—that is, the existence of an imminent major enemy. When the Cold War was over, a Japanese scholar evaluated Japan's international role in a selected area (Inoguchi 1993). In trade, Japan behaved more as a free rider, a spoiler, or a challenger than as a supporter of international structure, even though it altered that practice in the latter half of the 1980s by doubling its imports and reducing its exports. In the area of technology transfer also, Japan was labeled as a free rider for its protectionism but was moving toward a supportive role. In the international monetary system, Japan was a supporter through its policy on debt relief and developmental assistance.

When the Cold War ended, neither the United States nor Japan could withstand the situation any longer, and the alliance went adrift. The U.S.-Japan relationship became unstable because the early Clinton administration, absorbed in economic matters, dissembled the ties with its trade partners into conflict. The United States had been recording the largest trade deficit with Japan at the turn of the 1990s, and, blaming Japan for undertaking unfair trade practices, it pressed for changes. At that time Japan began to experience the most serious economic depression since the end of the Pacific War, and the thirty-eight-year longevity of the Liberal Democratic Party was terminated in 1993. Japanese politics was in a fluid state of unstable coalition, with bureaucrats under attack for their mismanagement of the country's economy.

U.S. engagement policy under the second Clinton administration successfully restored the bilateral relationship, and the continued stationing of U.S. forces (39,691 in 2001) on Japanese soil was responded to by Japan's expanded burden sharing in the form of rear-area support under the emergency of the surrounding area. However, the Clinton administration failed to bring confidence to the U.S.-Japan partnership by mismanaging the trilateral relationship with China.

In the latter part of the 1990s, the uncertainty during the post–Cold War era evolved into a unipolar international order. In a short report known as the Armitage-Nye Report, the bipartisan research committee called for a closer and firmer relationship between the United States and Japan and suggested that Japan could become the England of the Pacific (Armitage and Nye 2003). For the construction of an international order that will last for another century, dominant military power, backed by a strong economy and the active support of allied partners, is inevitable (Zoellick 2000). With the inauguration of the Bush administration, the two governments of the East and West started mending the bilateral relationship. After the 9–11 attacks, Japan passed two bills to mobilize the SDF to the Gulf region in a quick response to the U.S. request; in that process the Japanese government tried to bring out the restraint of the Peace Constitution. Japan's denial of collective self-defense, which prohibits any activities that may involve armed conflict, became a main obstacle in international cooperation (see Sidebar 2).

Until the enactment of the Law on the Area Surrounding Japan, Japan pursued

---

Sidebar 2   Collective Self-Defense

"Japan's prohibition against collective self-defense is a constraint on alliance cooperation. . . . We see the special relationship between the United States and Great Britain as a model for the alliance." Collective self-defense is the focal point of the Japanese domestic discussion on the Constitutional revision. Japan's Cabinet Legislation Bureau in Article 9 states that while Japan possesses the right of collective self-defense, it cannot exercise it.

Source
Armitage, Richard L., and Joseph S. Nye, Jr. 2000. "The United States and Japan: Advancing toward a Mature Partnership." *INSS Special Report.* Asahi Shimbun, November 10, 2003.

its burden sharing under the constraint of the laws. Since the North Korean test launch of its Daepo-Dong missile, Japan has been willing to remove the legal constraints to its international cooperation. If the previous period can be called "passive burden sharing," the current orientation can be called "active burden sharing." So far, the United States has been pushing Japan for a more active position in defense, but from now on, the United States might rather have to play the role of a "cap on the bottle."

The Future

Entering the new millennium, two major questions hover over Japan. The first asks when Japan will escape the long tunnel of economic depression. The Japanese have referred to the 1990s as a "lost decade" for the Japanese economy. Delay in dealing with the remaining bad loans from the collapsed bubble economy of the late 1980s, failure to keep up with the information revolution, loss of corporate and consumer confidence, and inept government policy are often emphasized as the reasons for an average annual growth rate of a mere 0.7 percent from 1991 to 2003. The cost of the recession has been high, both domestically and internationally. It has been suggested that if the needed structural reform of the Japanese economy is possible, it can serve as the basis for sustained economic development in Japan and the rest of the world.

The Japanese government has released statistics showing that Japanese GDP in the fourth quarter of 2003 grew by 1.7 percent in real terms, tantamount to an annual growth rate of 7 percent. That marked the best growth of the Japanese economy in thirteen years and was interpreted as a promising sign of the recovery

of Japan's economic vitality. It is not yet clear, however, whether Japan has escaped its thirteen-year-long depression. Previously there were several upsurges in economic indicators in Japan during the last decade, but with no incidences of sustained recovery.

The second question asks whether the Japanese constitution will be revised, and if so, when. Japan plans to revise its constitution in the near future. In January 2000, constitutional reform councils were set up in both houses of the national Diet to debate the outlook of the constitution and its possible reform. Currently, the LDP, the leading coalition party, and the Democratic Party, the major opposition party, are working on this matter and are committed to issuing the drafts for revision soon. According to Asahi Shimbun's opinion poll following the Lower House election of November 9, 2003, more than two-thirds of the 480 newly elected Diet members support revision of the constitution. To submit a proposal of constitutional revision, agreement from more than two-thirds of the total number of seats is required.

The election has also showed two important trends. First is the failure of progressive parties such as the Communist Party and the Social Democratic Party. Furthermore, young politicians in their forties, who are taking up key positions in the LDP and leading the Nation Defense Division of PARC, are oriented toward a right-wing conservative stance. These LDP members are trying to upgrade the JDA to the level of ministry. The two leading conservative parties of the LDP and the Democratic Party took up 79 percent of all seats. This illustrates the second trend, toward a two-party system. If it is established as a new political system, party members will compete with policy proposals, and that is likely to bring improvements in defense matters.

When this domestic political environment is coupled with the U.S. demand for Japan's revision of its constitution, legalizing the right of collective self-defense, the revision of the Japanese constitution will soon be realized. In that case, it is clear that Japan will rapidly shift toward becoming a "normal country" (Ozawa 1994).

If there is a single most important factor that can decide the shaping of Japanese defense policy in light of the above-mentioned trend, it is the role of China. As can be seen from Table 2, China's military expenditure is rapidly catching up with that of the major powers, recording double-digit growth rates for more than ten consecutive years. In addition China has been the largest arms importing country in recent years. Its huge GNP is already the second largest in the world. The future of the international as well as the regional order depends on whether or not China accepts the existing order of U.S. hegemony. The United States is preparing for the future with the deployment of its Missile Defense System and the restructuring of overseas U.S. forces. Currently, Japan is adjusting its defense establishment with expanded international cooperation, under the leadership of the United States. As long as China does not take a challenging route, Japan is unlikely to move beyond the position of a "normal country."

References, Recommended Readings, and Websites

Books
Calder, Kent E. 1988. *Crisis and Compensation: Public Policy and Political Stability in Japan*. Princeton: Princeton University Press.

Campbell, John C. 1977. *Contemporary Japanese Budget Politics*. Berkeley: University of California Press.

Defense of Japan 2001. Tokyo: Urban Connections.

East Asian Strategic Review 2003. Tokyo: Defense Institute for National Defense.

Funabashi, Yoichi. 1999. *Alliance Adrift*. New York: Harold Pratt House.

Green, Michael J. 1998. *Arming Japan: Defense Production, Alliance Politics, and the Postwar Search for Autonomy*. New York: Columbia University Press.

Hand Book for Defense 1994. Tokyo: Chouwoon Shinbunsha.

Hand Book for Defense 2003. Tokyo: Chouwoon Shinbunsha.

Hara, Yoshihisa. 1991. *Nichbei kankei no kozu (Framework of the U.S.-Japan Relations)*. Tokyo: Nippon Hososhupansha.

Inoguchi, Takashi. 1993. *Japan's Foreign Policy in an Era of Global Change*. New York: St. Martin's Press.

Johnson, Chalmers A. 1995. *Japan, Who Governs?: The Rise of the Developmental State*. New York: Norton.

Katzenstein, Peter J. 1996. *Cultural Norms and National Security: Police and Military in Postwar Japan*. Ithaca, NY: Cornell University Press.

Katzenstein, Peter J., and Nobuo Okawara. 1993. *Japan's National Security: Structures, Norms, and Policy Responses in a Changing World*. Ithaca, NY: East Asia Program, Cornell University.

Mochizuki, Mike M. 1997. *Toward a True Alliance: Restructuring U.S.-Japan Security Relations*. Washington, DC: Brookings Institution Press.

Ozawa, Ichiro. 1994. *Blue Print for a New Japan: The Rethinking of a Nation*. New York: Kodansha International.

Pyle, Kenneth B. 1996. *The Japanese Question: Power and Purpose in a New Era*. Washington, DC: AEI Press.

Samuels, Richard J. 1994. *Rich Nation, Strong Army: National Security and the Technological Transformation of Japan*. Ithaca, NY: Cornell University Press.

Zhang, Ming, and Ronald N. Montaperto. 1999. *A Triad of Another Kind: The United States, China, and Japan*. New York: St. Martin's Press.

Articles/Newspapers

Armitage, Richard L., and Joseph S. Nye, Jr. 2000. "The United States and Japan: Advancing toward a Mature Partnership." *INSS Special Report.* Asahi Shimbun, November 10, 2003.

Berger, Thomas U. 1999. "Alliance Politics and Japan's Postwar Culture of Antimilitarism." In *The U.S.-Japan Alliance: Past, Present, and Future,* Michael J. Green, Patrick M. Cronin, and Patrick M. Cronin, eds. New York: Council on Foreign Relations Press.

Buzan, Barry, and Gerald Segal. 1994. "Rethinking East Asian Security." *Survival* 36:23–41.

Choi, Woondo. 2003. "Persistence and Change in Japan-China Relationship." *Journal of International and Area Studies* 10:75–92.

Cossa, Ralph A. 1996. "Multilateralism and National Strategy in Northeast Asia." *NBR Analysis* 7:25–38.

———. 2002. "Asian Multilateralism Takes on New Energy." *Korea Times,* July 29.

Evera, Stephen Van. 1990/1991. "Primed for Peace: Europe after the Cold War." *International Security* 15:7–57.

Friedberg, Aaron. 1993/1994. "Ripe for Rivalry: Prospects for Peace in a Multipolar Asia." *International Security* 18:5–33.

Green, Michael J., and Benjamin L. Self. 1996. "Japan's Changing China Policy: From Commercial Liberalism to Reluctant Realism." *Survival* 38:35–58.

Higenbotham, Eric, and Richard J. Samuels. 1998. "Mercantile Realism and Japanese Foreign Policy." *International Security* 22:171–203.

Mearsheimer, John J. 1990. "Back to the Future: Instability in Europe after the Cold War." *International Security* 15:5–56.

Milford, Paul. 2002. "The Logic of Reassurance and Japan's Grand Strategy." *Security Studies* 11:1–43.

Nye, Joseph S., Jr. 1995. "The Case for Deep Engagement." *Foreign Affairs* 74:90–102.

Sato, Hideo. 1998. "Japan's China Perceptions and Its Policies in the Alliance with the United States." Asia/Pacific Research Center. http://www.ciaonet.org/wps/sah02/sah02.pdf (accessed February 29, 2004).

Task Force on Foreign Relations for Prime Minister. 2002. *The Basic Strategy of Japanese Foreign Policy of the 21st Century.*

Zoellick, Robert B. 2000. "A Republican Foreign Policy." Foreign Affairs 70: 63–78.

Websites

Central Intelligence Agency. *The World Factbook:* http://www.cia.gov.

Institute for International Policy Studies: http://www.iips.org/.

Japan Defense Agency: http://www.jda.go.jp/.

Japan Statistical Yearbook: http://www.stat.go.jp/english/data/nenkan/.

Ministry of Foreign Affairs: http://www.mofa.go.jp/.

National Graduate Institute for Policy Studies: http://www.grips.ac.jp/.

National Institute for Defense Studies, Japan: http://www.nids.go.jp/english/main.html. www.nationmaster.com.

Prime Minister of Japan and His Cabinet: http://www.kantei.go.jp/foreign/index-e.html.

SIPRI Yearbook. Stockholm International Peace Research Institute: http://www.sipri.se/.

Lebanon

Faten Ghosn

Geography and History

After fifteen years of sectarian contention between 1975 and 1990, Lebanon, a small country on the eastern shores of the Mediterranean, has made progress toward rebuilding its political and economic institutions. Situated in the Levant, Lebanon's shoreline extends 225 kilometers (150 miles) from north to south and 85 kilometers (53 miles) from east to west (at its greatest width), with a total area of 10,452 square kilometers (4,500 square miles). It shares a 322-kilometer (200-mile) border with Syria to the north and east, and to the south it shares a disputed border of about 100 kilometers (161 miles) with Israel, demarcated by the Blue Line, as defined by the United Nations in 2000.

Lebanon's beauty is illustrated by its geography. It is divided into four distinct regions: (1) a narrow coastal strip that runs from north to south along the Mediterranean coast, where the major port cities of Tripoli, Beirut (the capital), Sidon, and Tyre are located; (2) a western mountain range known as Mount-Lebanon; (3) an eastern mountain range known as Anti-Lebanon, which runs along the eastern border with Syria; and (4) the fertile Bekaa valley, situated between the Mount Lebanon and the Anti-Lebanon mountains (Congressional Quarterly 2000, 310) (see Sidebar 1).

Since its creation, Lebanon has experienced large waves of migration, making it a safe haven for religious, ethnic, and political minorities. Characteristic of Lebanese society is the wide spectrum of religious sects it houses, including Christian Maronite, Roman Catholic, Greek Orthodox,

Roman Orthodox, Protestant, Armenian Catholic, Armenian Orthodox, Sunni Muslim, Shi'a Muslim, Alwaite, and Druze. The Lebanese population is estimated at 3,532,000, with about 70 percent of the population being Muslim and 30 percent Christian (*Military Balance* 2003, 277). There are also about 390,000 Palestinian refugees registered with the UN Relief and Works Agency (UNRWA), almost all of whom fled to Lebanon after the 1948 and 1967 Arab-Israeli wars and the civil strife in Jordan in 1970.

From 1516 to 1918, Lebanon was under the administrative rule of the Ottoman Empire; Lebanon did not exist in its current territorial form until 1920. After World War I, the League of Nations placed Lebanon under French mandate. On May 25, 1926, a constitution was adopted establishing a democratic republic with a parliamentary system of government. Although the French commander general, Catroux, proclaimed Lebanon an independent sovereign state in 1941, Lebanon remained under French influence until 1943. In September 1943, Parliament members came into conflict with the French authorities over the transfer of administrative services, and in November the Lebanese government approved the amendment of the constitution removing all stipulations considered to be inconsistent with the independence of Lebanon (Fisher 2001, 801). As a result, the French delegate general arrested the president and some members of Parliament and suspended the constitution. This caused uproar in Lebanon, and after pressures from the international community, the Parliament members were released and Lebanon declared its independence on November 22, 1943. In 1945, Lebanon became a founding member of the League of Arab States, as well as the United Nations.

The structure of the Lebanese government is based on the constitutional principle of division of power among the executive, legislative, and judicial branches. The members of the National Assembly (about 128 members) are elected directly by universal adult suffrage every four years, based on a system of proportional representation for the various confessional groups. In turn, the National Assembly (that is, the Parliament) elects a president every six years, and after consultation with the Parliament the president appoints a prime minister who heads the Lebanese government.

The development of Lebanon's political structure was strongly affected by two important events that helped the diverse religious sects reach common terms of agreement concerning the role and representation each one would have in government. The first of these was the National Pact of 1943, which was not a formal agreement but rather a verbal one between Bshara al-Khoury (a Maronite leader) and Riyad al-Solih (a Sunni leader). This agreement asserted that Lebanon was a sovereign, independent, and neutral country, and it also allocated power on an essentially confessional system based on the 1932 census, which had identified the ratio of Christians to Muslims as being six to five. Positions in the government were also allocated along confessional/religious lines, with the top three positions in the ruling "Troika" (as they are called) distributed as follows:

- The president is a Maronite Christian
- The prime minister is a Sunni Muslim

• The president of the National Assembly is a Shi'a Muslim

However, not until the second agreement, the Ta'if Accord of 1989, was the ratio between the Christians and Muslims changed to 50–50. Under the Ta'if, the president maintains some of his influential power, holding the authority to transmit the laws passed by the National Assembly, issue supplementary regulations, ensure the execution of laws, and negotiate treaties. However, the Ta'if strengthened the position of the prime minister, who now heads the meetings of the Council of Ministers (if the president is not present) and supervises the work of ministries, whereas the president can attend the meetings but cannot vote on issues. As for the National Assembly, it is responsible for levying taxes and passing the budget. It also exercises political control over the cabinet through its right to question ministers on policy decisions.

Lebanon has a competitive free market economy and a strong laissez-faire commercial tradition. The Lebanese economy is mainly service oriented, with services and banking sectors representing 70 percent of the country's GNP (Ministry of Finance Website). Services include banking and finance, hotels and restaurants, media and advertising, as well as consulting and engineering. Some of the main industries in Lebanon are agriculture, manufacturing, construction, trade, and tourism.

Lebanon's economic infrastructure was damaged by the civil war (1975–1990) and the Israeli occupation of the south (1978–2000). However, the economy has made remarkable improvement since the launch of "Horizon 2000" in 1993, the government's $20 billion reconstruction program (CIA World Factbook). Moreover, the government has taken measures to maintain the stability of the Lebanese pound and to improve fiscal performance through a reduction in the debt service burden and privatization of state assets. The GDP registered high growth rates between 1993 and 1995, averaging an estimated real growth rate of 7.2 percent. However, real GDP grew at a slower rate from 1996 to 2000, with real growth estimated to have been 1.5 percent in 2002, while GDP was estimated at $17.61 billion (*Military Balance* 2003, 275) (see Sidebar 2).

Table 1   Lebanon Key Statistics

Type of government	Parliamentary republic
Population (millions)	3.5 (2003)
Religion	Muslims 70%; Christian 30%
Main industries	Banking, tourism
Main security threats	Regional instability from the war in Iraq; Arab-Israeli conflict
Defense spending (% GDP)	8.8% (2003)
Size of military (thousands)	72 (2003)
Number of civil wars since 1945	2
Number of interstate wars since 1945	1

Source
International Institute for Strategic Studies (IISS). 2003. *Military Balance 2003–2004.* London: IISS and Oxford University Press.

Sidebar 2   Illicit Drugs

During Lebanon's civil war, which lasted from 1975 to 1990, the Bekaa valley became a key center of opium production as a result of the breakdown of the government and the rising global trend. By the end of the war, about one-third of the valley's land (75,000 acres) was dedicated to drugs, and the profits of cannabis and opium growing were estimated at $80 million per year.

With pressure from the United States government as well as with millions of dollars in international assistance, however, the Lebanese government began to sponsor programs that encouraged farmers who grew opium to switch to staple crops and to raising cattle. Unfortunately, farmers still do not have enough access to credit to restore their business and, given the severe economic problems, farmers throughout the region are longing to revive their outlaw tradition of growing cannabis and opium poppies.

Sources
Abdelnour, Ziad. 2001. "The Revival of Lebanon's Drug Trade." *Middle East Intelligence Bulletin* 3, no. 6. http://www.meib.org/articles/0106_l3.htm.
MaCfarquhar, Neil. 2001. "Cattlemen in Lebanon Miss Lucre of Hashish." *New York Times*, April 5.

Regional Geopolitics

The consequences of the September 11, 2001, terrorist attacks in the United States have affected the Middle East and North Africa more than any other regions (ibid. 2002, 95), and Lebanon's strategic location in the Middle East has made it extremely vulnerable to events in the area. Syria, Iran, Israel, and the Palestinians have all influenced Lebanon's political system, and each continues its involvement in Lebanon's internal affairs, with their conflicts jeopardizing the future of the region and Lebanon itself (Ellis 2002a, 25). In addition, the recent tension in U.S. relations with Syria as well as Iran following the war in Iraq has made the region very susceptible to another war.

The United States today is more entangled in Middle Eastern affairs than at any other time in history (Morris 2004). This is clearly seen in President Bush's declaration of his intentions of reforming the Arab and Islamic world. Almost a year after the U.S. invasion of Iraq, that country remains deeply unsettled, and anti-American sentiment against the U.S. occupation in Iraq is on the rise. U.S.-led military forces face guerrilla-style attacks daily. The unstable situation in Iraq, especially a protracted military conflict, could create more insurgencies and a spillover to other parts of the region.

The United States has accused Syria of helping Iraq by harboring Iraqi leaders and scientists, as well as by allowing fighters to cross over the border to fight in Iraq. It also believes that Syria is developing chemical weapons, an allegation that Syria has denied, arguing that they support making the Middle East, including Israel, free of weapons of mass destruction. However, on November 11, 2003, the U.S. Senate voted for the Syrian Accountability and Lebanese Sovereignty Act, which mandates economic sanctions against Syria if it does not end its support for terrorism, halt its development of weapons of mass destruction, refrain from illegal importation of Iraqi oil, and end its occupation of Lebanon (U.S. Department of State Website).

Another tense relationship in the region is that between the United States and Iran. Since the Iranian revolution in 1979, the relationship between these two countries has been tumultuous. The U.S. government has condemned Iran's effort to acquire nuclear weapons, its support for Hizballah, Hamas, the Palestinian Islamic Jihad, and the Popular Front for the Liberation of Palestine (all of which violently oppose the Arab-Israeli peace process), as well as its bleak human rights record (U.S. Department of State Website). Having been defined as part of a tripartite "axis of evil," as well as witnessing the U.S. attack on Iraq, Iranian policymakers are concerned that the United States also intends to pursue a "regime change" in Iran. Moreover, there is fear that if the military conflict in Iraq continues and interfactional fighting begins to emerge, the fighting may spill over into Iran, heightening the tensions along the border (Royal Institute of International Affairs 2003, 11).

To make tensions in the region even worse, the Palestinian-Israeli conflict continues to spiral out of control. The failure of the July 2000 Camp David meeting, followed by then opposition leader Ariel Sharon's controversial visit in late September to the area known as Haram al-Sharif to Muslims and as Temple Mount to Jews, sparked off the second *Intifada*, on September 29, 2000 (*Military Balance* 2002, 95). Since then, thousands of innocent civilians have been killed, and the violence is only increasing. Friedman summed up the situation by stating that it is an "utterly self-destructive vicious [circle] (in the article the author uses cycle and not circle) that threatens Israel's long term viability, poisons America's image in the Middle East, undermines any hope for a Palestinian state, and weakens pro-American Arab moderates" (Friedman 2004).

U.S. preoccupation with the situation in Iraq and its "War on Terrorism," the tense relationship between the United States and Syria, as well as tension between the United States and Iran and the continuing escalation of the Palestinian-Israeli conflict could all have a devastating effect on the region in general and Lebanon in particular. Of greatest concern for Lebanon's proximity to tensions in the region is that the call for the termination of Syrian and Iranian support of Hizballah, and the impending refusal of such demands, would lead to military confrontations between the United States, Syria, Iran, and Hizballah.

Conflict Past and Present

Conflict History

Since its independence in 1943, Lebanon has found itself involved in the Arab-Israeli War of 1948 and two civil wars (1958 and 1975–1990) (see Table 2), as well several skirmishes with its neighbors, Israel and Syria.

Even though the Lebanese government had officially opposed the partition plan of the United Nations for Palestine, it did not have the capability to participate actively in the conflict. Nonetheless, being a member of the Arab League required that at minimum it provide some military support, and so Lebanon did send a force, estimated at 2,000 men, to its border. Prior to the outbreak of hostilities, some Maronite Christian leaders "adopted a policy favorable to Zionism in the belief that this would counter pan-Islamic and pan-Arabist movements that saw Lebanon as part of the Syrian Arab hinterland" (Ellis 2002a, 26). That view, nonetheless, was not a popular one, and on May 14 Lebanese troops were mobilized along the Lebanese southern border. On May 15, 1948, war broke out between Egypt, Iraq, Jordan, Lebanon, and Syria against the

Table 2   **Civil Wars in Lebanon**

	Dates	Winner	Casualties	Intervention	Side of Intervention
First Civil War	May 9, 1958 to September 15, 1958	Government	>1400	United States	On Side of Government
Second Civil War	April 13, 1975 to October 13, 1990	Opposition	167,000	Syria	On Side of Opposition
				Israel	On Side of Government

Source

Sarkees, Meredith Reid. 2000. "The Correlates of War Data on War: An Update to 1997." *Conflict Management and Peace Science* 18, no. 1:123–144.

newly created state of Israel. After initial Arab expansion, Israel counterattacked, thereby enlarging its territory. Separate armistice agreements were reached with each of the Arab countries that participated. The war resulted in the killing of 6,000 Israelis and 15,000 Arabs and the wounding of 15,000 Israelis and 25,000 Arabs, in addition to exiling approximately 750,000 Palestinians (Cook 2001, 294).

After the 1956 Suez Canal crisis and the creation of the United Arab Republic (UAR), which united Egypt and Syria, Arab nationalism was at its peak. Many Lebanese Muslims wanted to join the UAR, especially as sentiments rose among many who felt that they were second-rate citizens in their own country, since they lacked a political role proportionate to their numbers. As a result these citizens began demanding that a new census be taken, which they believed would indicate a Muslim majority. However, Lebanese Christians, especially the Maronites, were not fond of the idea, since a new census could lead to the annulment of the National Pact, which acknowledged a Christian majority. Lebanese President Camille Chamoun attempted to amend the constitution in

order to serve a second term. His main aim was to increase his power and reduce the influence of the traditional leaders. In fact, he was accused of manipulating the 1957 parliamentary results.

On July 14, 1958, the Nasserites in Iraq staged a coup and succeeded in overthrowing the monarchy. President Chamoun feared that the same fate might be facing Lebanon. As a result, he turned to the United States for protection by invoking the Eisenhower Doctrine. On July 15, 1958, the U.S. Marines landed in Beirut. The marines helped in stabilizing the situation and in mediating a cease-fire. General Fouad Shehab was elected as the next president to succeed Chamoun, and the Lebanese political system survived its first major internal shock.

The union between Egypt and Syria was doomed from the start. However, the final blow came in July 1961, when Nasser called for the elimination of local autonomy and the unification of Egyptian and Syrian currencies, which would have dissolved Syrian economic independence. On September 28, 1961, a group of army officers staged a successful coup and announced the separation of Syria from Egypt. The relationship between the pro-Nasserites and the new government remained strained, with various coup attempts ending with the establishment of a Baathist regime in 1963.

The conflict between the Baathist regime in Syria and the pro-Nasserites led to increased tensions between the Syrian regime and the Lebanese government. On February 5, 1963, Syrian troops violated Lebanese borders by entering and searching a Lebanese village for pro-Nasserites. The Lebanese government protested the incident, arguing that there were no Syrian rebel camps in Lebanon. However, between August and October there were several Syrian army incursions across the Lebanese borders, and on October 20, 1963, Syrian army patrols ambushed and killed three Lebanese soldiers. The Lebanese government and the Syrian government ended their border dispute on November 8 of that same year, when Syria promised to conduct a joint investigation with the Lebanese government and to punish all those involved in the October incident.

The Arab-Israeli war left Lebanon host to about 142,000 Palestinian refugees. However, today that number is estimated to be about 390,000, making the future of the Palestinian refugees in Lebanon the most critical concern for the Lebanese government in any settlement between the Palestinians and the Israelis, as well as between the Lebanese and the Israelis.

Lebanon's concerns with the Palestinian refugees are different from those of Syria and Jordan. First, its economic capacity to take in Palestinian refugees, given its small population, is very limited. Second, the overwhelming majority of Palestinians are Muslims, who cannot be easily absorbed into the country without upsetting the delicate sectarian balance, which is a highly sensitive issue for the Lebanese (Ellis 2002a, 27).

As time passed, the Palestinians began to realize that their dream of returning home was never going to turn into reality. The issue of Palestinian refugees became a convenient way by which Arab leaders could divert attention from their domestic problems, focusing popular discontent instead toward the Israeli state. Palestinians inside the refugee camps, growing disgruntled and desperate, began to form groups with the belief that in order to free their homeland they needed to rely on themselves.

One of the battlefields for the Palestinian struggle was southern Lebanon. The relationship and the status of the Palestinians in Lebanon, as well as the relationship between Lebanon and Syria, began to change as the Palestinian-Israeli violence on the border created resentment among some Lebanese who wanted their government to deal forcibly with the Palestinians. The Israeli bombing raids were becoming more and more frequent, and the Israeli attack on Beirut International Airport on December 28, 1968, as a protest to the hijackings that were being carried out by a Palestinian group based in Lebanon served as a major turning point. Conflict broke out between the Palestinian groups in Lebanon and the Lebanese army. However, President Nasser of Egypt intervened, and the Cairo Agreement was reached in 1969. While that agreement recognized Lebanese military control over Lebanese territory, it also allowed for the Palestinian Liberation Organization (PLO) to maintain a military presence in the country. Therefore, rather than resolving the crisis, the agreement strengthened the PLO's role in Lebanon, especially after 1970 when the PLO authority was driven out of Jordan and Arafat reestablished himself and his fighters in Lebanon. In fact, Lebanon emerged as the principal arena of the Palestinian-Israeli conflict, placing immense strain on the Lebanese political system, which eventually erupted in civil war in 1975 (Congressional Quarterly 2000, 46).

The second Lebanese civil war, which broke out in April 1975, was not so much a conflict between Christians and Muslims as it was a conflict between the militia of the dominate Maronite leaders who were in control of the government and the various militias, who wanted to overthrow the traditional political system. That civil war can be divided into several distinct stages because of the different parties involved.

In the first stage two major forces confronted each other: the Lebanese National Movement (LNM), which mainly included leftist parties as well as Arab nationalist parties, and the Lebanese Front (LF), which was primarily composed of Maronite militias. One of the main disagreements between the two fronts was the existence of the Palestinians in Lebanon. The LNM supported the Palestinian presence, arguing that it was part of the Arab cause; however, the LF believed that the Palestinians should be removed from Lebanese soil. The LNM also wanted to advance a political reform program that would abolish political sectarianism, an issue that was highly contested by the LF, believing that such a shift would be disadvantageous to them.

On April 13, 1975, masked gunmen killed three Christian militiamen belonging to the Phalange Party, a Maronite militia, outside a church in Beirut. The Phalange Party assumed that the culprits had been Palestinians, and so that same day they ambushed and killed twenty-seven Palestinians who were returning to their camp by bus. News of the bus ambush spread quickly, and almost instantly fighting broke out throughout the country.

As various groups took sides, the conflict began to spread, forcing residents to leave their homes and seek refuge in towns in which their sect was a majority. Additionally, the Lebanese army, which had originally stayed out of the conflict, began to fall apart as soldiers took sides with the militias of their sect.

In March 1976, Syrian forces were dispatched to Lebanon at the request of the Maronites (LF) in order to protect the presidential palace and to restore the political balance that had begun to tip in favor of the LNM-PLO front. The Syrians were afraid that if the LNM-PLO joint forces were victorious over the LF, an Israeli invasion would be imminent. As a result, fighting between the Syrian army and the LNM-PLO forces began to intensify until October, when a cease-fire was reached in Riyadh, Saudi Arabia. Later that month an Arab League summit was held in Cairo to ratify the Riyadh agreement, which called for the establishment of an Arab Deterrent Force (ADF) that would provide security and stability throughout Lebanon. The ADF was to be composed of units of several Arab states, but it was understood that the Syrian forces would be the main component.

Although the Syrians had intervened on behalf of the Maronites against the PLO, they did not by any means put an end to PLO activity in Lebanon. As a result, the Maronite-Syrian alliance broke down, and since the Maronite leaders had entered into covert arms deals with the Israelis, the LF challenged the Syrians with the assurance that Israeli support would be provided if needed (ibid., 319).

Under the Riyadh agreement the PLO relocated to the south, where they continued to carry out their attacks against Israel. As a result, tensions began to rise between the PLO and the Shi'ites in the south, especially after the Israeli invasion in 1978 that led to the creation of an Israeli self-declared "security zone" within the Lebanese border.

Internal conditions were worsening as the LF attempted to gain political power through the presidential seat in the face of Syrian opposition. The assassination attempt on the Israeli ambassador in London, however, led to a full-scale Israeli invasion on June 6, 1982. The United States sent a special envoy headed by Philip Habib to stabilize the situation. As a result, the PLO was expelled from Lebanon, and the Parliament elected Bashir Gemayel as president. However, he was assassinated before taking office; his brother Amin was elected to take his place. The Israelis blamed the Palestinians for the assassination.

Lebanese resistance against the Israeli occupation intensified. In August 1982 the United States, France, the United Kingdom, and Italy sent a peacekeeping force to support the Lebanese government and help in evacuating the PLO. However, the fighting between different militias continued, and on October 23, 1983, a suicide bombing of the U.S. and French barracks in Beirut left 241 U.S. Marines and 58 French paratroopers dead (ibid., 321). Shortly thereafter, the Lebanese government collapsed, and in February 1984 the United States began to withdraw its forces from Lebanon, followed quickly by the withdrawal of French, British, and Italian forces.

In 1985, Israeli forces withdrew to the "security zone" that they had established in 1978. However, factional conflicts continued to intensify. In 1985 and 1986,

Amal, a Shi'ite militia, sought to crush the Palestinian stronghold in Lebanon. In 1987, the Druze joined with the Palestinian Front for the Liberation of Palestine (PFLP) and their allies against Amal. Violent clashes continued in 1988, especially between Amal and Hizballah. Also, in September 1988, President Gemayel appointed Lebanese general Michel Aoun, a Maronite Christian, as the new prime minister for a transitional government before stepping down from his office. That caused a major uproar among the Muslim community, since the appointment violated the National Pact agreement, which called for the prime minister to be a Sunni Muslim. Hence, Lebanon witnessed the emergence of two governments with no president: one in east Beirut headed by a Christian prime minister and another in west Beirut headed by a Muslim prime minister.

In 1989, General Aoun attacked the LF and later turned his attention against the Syrians and their Lebanese militia allies in his "War of Liberation." In October 1990, he was forced to take refuge in the French embassy in Beirut, and later into exile in Paris.

In October 1989, all the Lebanese parliamentary members were invited to a meeting held in Ta'if, Saudi Arabia, at which they agreed to the National Reconciliation Accord, which gave Muslims, especially Sunnis, a greater role in the political process while institutionalizing the sectarian divisions in the government. It transferred executive power from the president to a cabinet of ministers, with portfolios divided equally between Christians and Muslims. The number of seats in the National Assembly was expanded from 99 to 108, and the assembly was also divided equally between Christians and

Muslims; in 1992 the number of seats was raised to 128.

Upon their return to Lebanon the agreement was ratified, and on November 4 Rene Moawad was elected president. However, he was assassinated on November 22 during the Independence Parade, and Elias Hrawi was elected to take his place. President Hrawi remained in office until 1998, when President Emile Lahoud was elected.

Current and Potential Military Confrontation

Since the establishment of the state of Israel in 1948, the relationship between Israel and Lebanon has been tumultuous. Having joined the Arab League in 1945, Lebanon was bound as a charter member to participate in the Arab-Israeli war of 1948. In 1949, Lebanon signed an armistice agreement with Israel. Between 1965 and 1967, Israeli forces repeatedly violated Lebanese territory in order to strike at Palestinian fedayeen (resistance fighters) that were carrying out attacks against Israel across the Lebanese border. In 1968, Lebanese and Israeli forces clashed several times as the activities of the Palestinian guerrilla group intensified on the border. And on December 28, 1968, Israeli forces attacked Beirut International Airport, leading to the destruction of thirteen civilian aircraft. Skirmishes between the Lebanese army and Israeli forces, as well as Israeli attacks on Palestinian bases in Lebanon, culminated in the first Israeli invasion of Lebanon, in 1978.

On March 14, 1978, Israeli forces invaded Lebanon (Operation Litani) with the aim of establishing a ten-kilometer-wide security zone. However, upon entering Lebanese territory, the Israeli forces did not stop until they had occupied about half of southern Lebanon, destroying eighty-two villages, displacing 160,000 Lebanese, and killing 1,000 people in the process (Hiro 1993, 52). On March 19, Security Council Resolution 425 was passed, calling for the withdrawal of Israeli forces from Lebanon and establishing a UN Interim Force in Lebanon (UNIFIL) to confirm the withdrawal as well as to assist in the restoration of the Lebanese authority into southern Lebanon. Three months after their invasion, Israeli forces withdrew from southern Lebanon, but they relinquished control not to the UNIFIL forces but instead to a Christian militia headed by Major Saad Haddad, a former Lebanese army officer who had established his Southern Lebanese Army by recruiting former Lebanese army soldiers.

Between 1980 and 1982, Syrian armed forces clashed with Israeli forces on Lebanese soil, and despite the Israeli-PLO cease-fire agreement of 1981, the assassination attempt on the Israeli ambassador in London led to the second Israeli invasion of Lebanon, on June 6, 1982 (Operation Peace for Galilee). The goal was to capture about forty kilometers of Lebanese territory and eradicate the area of the Palestinian fedayeen in order to establish a new Lebanese government under the presidency of Bashir Gemayel, with the view of developing and signing a peace treaty, thereby making northern Israel safe from attack (ibid., 82). However, once the Israeli forces entered Lebanon, they continued their incursion all the way to Beirut and Mount Lebanon. Israeli forces encountered opposition from the Lebanese and Palestinian militias as well as the Syrian forces. By July 3, Israeli forces had tightened their siege around west Beirut by cutting off the water and electricity and by limiting the entry of food, fuel, and medical items. However, after the assassination of Bashir Gemayel, the Israelis surrounded the Palestinian camps, claiming that the Palestinians were responsible. The Phalangist militia and the Israel Defense Forces reached an understanding that the Israeli forces would allow the Phalangists to enter the camp and capture PLO men in order to hand them over to Israeli forces.

On September 16, 1982, the Phalangists entered under the command of Elie Hobeika and massacred the inhabitants of the camps (ibid., 92–93). The precise number of the victims is unknown, but the International Committee of the Red Cross estimated the total at around 2,750, a figure that is disputed by Israeli as well as Lebanese authorities. Nevertheless, an Israeli investigative commission (Kahane Commission) concluded that Ariel Sharon, who was then the Israeli defense minister, was "personally responsible" for the massacre. In August 1983, Israel began its withdrawal, and by September they had withdrawn from all but the southern security zone, where they remained until May 2000.

After the end of the civil war, the dispute between Lebanon and Israel over the occupation of southern Lebanon continued. Hundreds of militarized incidents took place between 1993 and 2001 between the two countries, with Syria participating infrequently on the side of Lebanon. The majority of these incidents occurred as a result of Israeli attacks on Hizballah in southern Lebanon in response to Hizballah attacks on Israeli troops, mainly within the security zone. Israel also violated Lebanese borders in order to monitor Hizballah's activities. The Lebanese government constantly protested the border incursions and often fired antiaircraft missiles at the Israeli jets.

In early April 1996, Israel conducted its operation dubbed "Grapes of Wrath" in response to Hizballah's rocket attacks on villages in northern Israel. The operation caused hundreds of thousands of civilians in southern Lebanon to flee their homes. On April 18, an Israeli attack on a UN compound at Qana caused the death of 102 civilians sheltered there (Fisher 2001, 822). As a result of that incident, an Israel-Lebanon Monitoring Group (ILMG) was set up in order to assess complaints submitted by both parties. The ILMG was cochaired by France and the United States and included Syrian representatives. However, the ILMG was dissolved after the Israeli withdrawal from southern Lebanon on May 24, 2000.

Despite the Israeli withdrawal, however, a major disagreement related to the so-called Shebaa Farms remained unsettled. The Lebanese government has raised the issue with the United Nations, arguing that this area, captured in 1967 by Israel, in fact belongs to Lebanon. Israelis argue that the Shebaa Farms region is Syrian territory and that any resolution over the territory is part of an Israeli-Syrian agreement.

Alliance Structure

The Lebanese alliance structure is characterized by three main alliances. Two of the alliances stem from its membership in the Arab League, while the third is the 1991 Treaty of Brotherhood, Cooperation and Coordination between Lebanon and Syria.

The Arab League was established in 1945 with the aim of fostering cultural, economic, and communication links between the Arab states. It also meant to mediate disputes between Arab states, to represent them in international negotiations, and last but not least, to coordinate economic and diplomatic offensives against Israel (Cook 2001, 2–3), an aim that has become less of a focus as Egypt and Jordan have signed peace treaties with Israel. On April 13, 1950, a treaty was drafted in Cairo dealing with the joint defense and economic cooperation between the states of the Arab League. The treaty was first ratified by Lebanon, Syria, Egypt, Saudi Arabia, and the Yemen Arab Republic on June 17, 1950. Jordan and Iraq joined in 1952, followed by Tunisia in 1956, Morocco and Kuwait in 1961, Algeria, Sudan, and Libya in 1964, the Yemen People's Republic, Qatar, Bahrain, and the United Arab Emirates in 1971, Somalia in 1974, and Yemen in 1990, after its unification. According to Article 2 of the treaty, any armed aggression against one member is an attack against them all (Arab League Website). This treaty binds all member states to undertake any measure necessary, including the use of armed force, to aid any fellow state under attack. Lebanon also has an entente with all the members of the Arab League.

In 1991, after the end of the civil war, Lebanon and Syria signed a pact aimed at facilitating cooperation and coordination between the two countries on a range of political, cultural, and economic issues, as well as on matters of security and defense (Hiro 1993, 241–245). According to this treaty, an agreement between the two governments would determine the strength and duration of the presence of the Syrian forces after the period that was specified in the Ta'if had expired. Moreover, a Higher Council was established that included the presidents of the two countries as well as the prime ministers, deputy prime ministers, and the heads of the Parliament, designed to facilitate coordination and to oversee implementation. Several committees, such as Foreign Affairs, Defense and Security Affairs, and Economics and Social Affairs, were also established, each charged with the duty of making recommendations to the Higher Council.

Size and Structure of the Military

The Lebanese Armed Forces (LAF) has about 72,100 active military personnel. About 97 percent (70,000) of the forces are in the army (ground forces), divided among the 11 mechanized infantry brigades, 5 regional commands, 5 special forces regiments, 2 artillery regiments, 1 Republican Guard brigade, 1 commando regiment, 1 airborne regiment, and 1 navy commando regiment. The navy has about 1,100 personnel, while the air force has about 1,000 (*Military Balance* 2003, 114). The LAF's weaponry system is somewhat outdated, however equipment readiness and sustainability is slowly improving. The army has more than 300 military battle tanks, 125 armored fighting vehicles, 1,300 armored personnel carriers, 100 towed artillery pieces, 25 rocket launchers, 250 mortars, several antitank weapons including 30 ENTAC, 16 Milan, RPG-7s, M-65 89-mm rocket launchers, and 50 recoilless rifles, as well as 20 surface-to-air missiles (SAMs). As for the navy, it has 5 UK-made Attacker inshore patrol craft, 2 UK-made Tracker inshore patrol craft, 25 armed boats, as well as 2 Sour tank landing ships (LSTs) capable of carrying 96 troops each. The air force has no real combat capability. It is limited to 6 Hunter F9 aircraft and 5 Fougas, about 40 helicopters, and 3 Bulldog training aircraft (ibid., 114–115).

At the end of the fifteen-year civil war, the Lebanese army found itself fragmented and in need of unification. The role of the LAF has been largely confined to internal security. However, the LAF has also engaged in important developmental as well as construction activities (Lebanese Army Website). They have implemented a range of social programs mainly intended for use by the military, such as housing projects and post exchange stores. Moreover, they have provided assistance to those who had been displaced as a result of the civil war, helping to return these individuals to their villages as well as rehabilitating the infrastructures of war-torn villages. In addition, they have helped in restoring historical and cultural sites. Since the Israeli withdrawal from southern Lebanon, the LAF forces have been slowly deployed to the south and have been working with the UNIFIL to clear land mines.

Budget
Lebanon's defense budget fell in 2003 to U.S.$498 million from $U.S.539 million in 2002. Today the defense budget accounts for only 8.8 percent of government spending, in comparison to 1992, when it accounted for 24 percent (*Military Balance* 2003, 275). Some 84 percent of the defense budget goes to military salaries and wages, with the remaining share going to equipment, repairs, operational tasks, and various subsidies. As a result very few funds are available to buy new weapons, and there are no resources for research and development. The aid received from Syria, the United States, France, the United Kingdom, and other countries has played a major role in assisting Lebanon to bridge the gap between equipment needs and the means to obtain those needs. In particular, the United States has provided the LAF with 750 armored personnel carriers, 3,000 tactical wheeled vehicles, and 27 CSB bridge boats at a very low price (Lebanese Army Website). In addition, the LAF has received 7 patrol boats and other accessories from the United Kingdom and spare parts from France.

Civil-Military Relations/The Role of the Military in Domestic Politics
The sectarian character of Lebanese society is also reflected in the structure of the military, wherein the general of the armed forces must be a Maronite and the army's chief of staff is a Druze. As a result of the sectarian divisions within society, the Lebanese army has almost never been a coherent body capable of carrying out a coup and setting up a military regime. For the most part, Lebanese soldiers have found themselves loyal to their own sect rather than to their country. One exception, however, was the 1958 civil strife.

In 1958, when a full revolt broke out between the pro-Chamounist allies and the Muslim factions, President Chamoun ordered the military, which was under the command of General Fouad Shehab, to put down the revolt. However, General Shehab refused to involve the military, arguing that the role of the military was to defend the country against external threats and not to get involved in domestic affairs. By keeping the army neutral he was able to save it from fracturing along sectarian lines if ordered to fight, as was the case in the civil war between 1975 and 1990.

During the second civil war, the Lebanese army broke down as a result of insubordination, desertion, and divided loyalty. Most of the soldiers joined the militias of their own sect and in many cases clashed with the army. Not until the end of the civil war and the sanctioning of the Ta'if agreement was the

Lebanese army restored under the command of General Emile Lahoud. After the disarming of the militia groups, an estimated 20,000 militiamen were incorporated into the Lebanese army, and in 1991 the army was deployed to different areas throughout the country. Today the LAF plays a significant role in helping those that had been displaced during the civil war to return to their homes.

Terrorism

After the September 11 attacks, the United States included Hizballah, an Iranian backed Shi'ite group in Lebanon, on a list of twenty-two foreign terrorist organizations whose financial assets would be frozen. However, the Lebanese government stated that it would refuse any request to freeze the assets of Hizballah, arguing that there is a difference between terrorist organizations and freedom fighters or resistance organizations. To the Lebanese authority, Hizballah falls in the latter category, since it played a major role in forcing Israel to withdraw its troops from southern Lebanon (see Sidebar 3).

Hizballah has enjoyed a wide support among the Shi'ite Muslims and holds about 8 seats out of 128 in the Lebanese Parliament. The organization has several branches, including a political, social, and militant branch. It has its own TV station (al-Manar), as well as its own radio station (al-Nour). Hizballah runs several hospitals and medical centers, schools, supermarkets, gas stations, department stores, and other commercial networks. For a long time, Iran has financed Hizballah's social programs.

Frustration and anger within the Shi'ite community has been fueled by several factors, which include the Arab defeats by

---

Sidebar 3   Hizballah

While the United States government has included Hizballah on its list of foreign terrorists, the Lebanese authority has maintained that Hizballah is a resistance organization and not a terrorist group. The position of the Lebanese government stems from its belief that Hizballah played a major role in forcing Israel to end its twenty-two-year occupation of southern Lebanon. Moreover, Hizballah has several branches, including a political, social, and militant branch, holds about eight seats in parliament, and had a clear victory in the 2004 municipal elections over its main rival, Amal.

Sources
Raad, Nada. 2004. "Analysts Dissect Election Results: Hariri Seen as Loser in This Round, But Premier Not Counted Out for 2005." *Daily Star*, June 1.
U.S. Department of State. http://www.state.gov.

Israel in 1948, 1967, and 1973, in addition to the failure of the Lebanese government to achieve balanced socioeconomic development among the different communities, leading to the rise of Shi'ite movements in Lebanon. Moreover, the activities of the Palestinian armed groups in southern Lebanon, the Israeli retaliation aimed mainly at the Shi'ites who constitute about 80 percent of the population in the south, and the inability of the Lebanese government to protect its citizens made the situation worse.

Hizballah was one of the most notable Shi'ite movements to emerge from this widespread discontent, and while its main aim was resistance to the Israeli occupation of Lebanon, it had also called for the establishment of an Islamic republic in Lebanon. However, it has dropped the call for an Islamic republic in Lebanon and has decided to participate in the existing political system. Hizballah is believed to have accomplished what no other Arab country has been able to do—namely, to defeat Israeli forces and oust them from an Arab country without making any concessions.

Hizballah's victory, however, has brought with it serious issues and decisions that must be made regarding the future. That is to say, it was the successful struggle against the Israeli occupation that strengthened the group's standing within the Shi'ite community and made it popular in Lebanon's public opinion and political system. Now questions are beginning to surface around the role that Hizballah will play in Lebanon and whether giving up its militancy will damper its position and popularity.

After the Ta'if agreement was signed in 1989, all the militia groups were required to disarm and surrender their weapons to the government. Hizballah was also required to give up some of its weapons, but it was allowed to continue carrying arms in southern Lebanon in its struggle against the Israeli occupation. Hizballah participated in the first parliamentary elections after the civil war and was able to win eight seats. It also participated in the 1996 and 2000 elections. It has continued to provide social welfare, to help in the reconstruction of houses damaged by Israeli forces, as well as to pave roads and supply water to Shi'ite villages in the south. With the Israeli withdrawal, however, the Lebanese government is slowly beginning to assert its sovereignty in the south. This transition could mark the beginning of the decline of Hizballah as a militant party, forcing it to become one of the many political parties in Lebanon.

One issue that will dominate Hizballah's affairs will be its rivalry with Amal, another prominent Shi'ite party (Zisser 2000, 37). The tension between these two groups can be clearly seen in the escalating confrontations that have taken place between the two since the Israeli withdrawal. The first incident between the two took place several weeks after the withdrawal, when fighters from the two factions clashed for control of the area from which Israel had pulled out. Several other minor clashes have occurred between Hizballah and Amal, and the struggle for influence promises to remain intense.

Amal, however, has been viewed as a more moderate political party, with a largely secular leadership that is well established in Lebanese society. The head of the Amal party, Nabih Berri, is currently the president of the National Assembly. Moreover, in the parliamentary elections of the 1990s and in the 1998 municipal elections, Amal candidates gained control over many Shi'ite strongholds (ibid.). However, in the 2004 municipal election, Hizballah was clearly the winner, sweeping to victory both in the south and in the Bekaa (Raad 2004).

Hizballah, of course, remains a prominent Shi'ite movement that has considerable support within the Shi'ite community, not to mention the backing of Syria and Iran. The strength of this group was clearly demonstrated once again in its ability to force Israel to acknowledge its demands by releasing more than 400 Arab prisoners in January 2004. The prisoner deal came after Germany was able to mediate an agreement between Israel and Hizballah in which Israel agreed to free 429 prisoners and return the corpses of 60 Lebanese killed as far back as 1984 in return for the bodies of 3 soldiers killed on the Lebanese border in 2000 and the release of a kidnapped Israeli businessman (Rees 2004). This deal has bolstered Hizballah's image, but with the current U.S. military troops in Iraq and U.S. demands for the dismantling of Hizballah, only time will tell what move the party will make next.

Relationship with the United States

Since World War II, the United States has attempted to balance its support for Israel with the need to maintain influence in the Arab countries in order to have access and control over Middle Eastern oil (Ellis 2002b, 91). Therefore, the United States has always had an interest in promoting a stable, independent, and democratic Lebanon, for a strong Lebanon will not only open new opportunities for U.S. investment and export sales but also make an important contribution to a comprehensive peace plan in the Middle East (U.S. Department of State Website).

The first U.S. intervention in Lebanese affairs was in 1958, when that country came to the aid of Lebanon by invoking the Eisenhower Doctrine, which promised military or economic aid to any county in the Middle East needing help in resisting communist belligerence. On July 15, 1958, 10,000 U.S. Marines and airborne ground troops landed on the shores of Beirut, putting an end to the civil strife that had broken out between Muslims and the pro-Chamounist allies.

The United States also came to the aid of Lebanon in 1982, when it brokered the evacuation of Israeli and Syrian troops as well as PLO fighters from Beirut. A multinational force consisting of U.S., French, British, and Italian soldiers was also deployed to help oversee the evacuation. On May 17, 1983, Lebanon, Israel, and the United States signed an agreement in which Israel agreed to a withdraw from Lebanon, conditional upon Syrian withdrawal. However fighting continued, and the U.S. presence in Lebanon created resentment, because the Muslim factions believed that the United States was there only to aid the Christian Maronite militias and to protect the interests of Israel. That resentment, combined with the virtual collapse of the Lebanese army in February 1984 after the defection of many Muslim and Druze units, and following the suicide attacks on the U.S. Marine barracks that led to the withdrawal of those marines, set the stage for the termination of the agreement on March 5, 1984.

In 1987 the United States imposed a travel ban to Lebanon that was not lifted until 1997, as a result of the kidnapping and murder of Americans in Lebanon. In an effort to resolve the situation in Lebanon, the United States turned to Syria to exercise military control and deliver the foreign hostages held by Hizballah. In return, the United States endorsed Syrian primacy in Lebanon and supported Lebanese presidential candidates that had Syria's blessing (Ellis 2002b, 98). Thus, when the Ta'if agreement was signed in 1989, it became the centerpiece of U.S. policy in Lebanon because it was seen as the best way to create a settlement among Lebanon's divergent political and religious factions.

Between 1993 and 2000, Lebanon found itself in a cycle of violence as Hizballah continued to resist the Israeli occupation in southern Lebanon. The tension in southern Lebanon put a strain on the U.S.-Lebanese relationship. Following the September 11 terrorist attacks, the relationship between the two countries has been increasingly strained by the Syrian presence in Lebanon and the Lebanese government's support of Hizballah. In fact, President Bush has endorsed the Syrian Accountability and Lebanese Sovereignty Act, which mandates economic sanctions against Syria if it does not comply with U.S. demands, including those for Syria to cease all support of Hizballah and its occupation of Lebanon. However, the Syrian government as well as the Lebanese government have both rejected these demands, arguing that the relationship between Syria and Lebanon is the concern of both governments and not that of the United States.

The United States has repeatedly asked the Lebanese government to hand over more than forty suspected terrorists, many of them believed to be Hizballah activists. However, the Lebanese government has refused, arguing that it does not consider those active in resisting the Israeli occupation of Lebanon to be terrorists. Nonetheless, Lebanon has cooperated with the United States in cracking down on other Islamic opposition groups, such as Usbat al-Ansar, which is based in the Palestinian refugee camp of Ein al-Hilweh and is believed to have ties with Osama bin Laden; it has also been accused of planning several attacks on westerners.

The United States continues to promote its relationship with Lebanon. The Economic Support Fund (ESF) had requested $32 million for FY 2004, and the Bush administration has earmarked $35 million to Lebanon in its 2005 budget for foreign aid. The aid is to be used to promote economic growth, as well as to foster democratic institutions. Also, $700,000 was requested by International Military Education and Training (IMET) in order to reinforce civilian control of the Lebanese military as well as to reduce sectarianism in one of the country's major institutions—that is, the Lebanese Armed Forces (U.S. Department of State Website).

Future

Lebanon's strategic location in the Middle East and its delicate internal balance have made it extremely susceptible to events in the area; reverberations from conflicts with, as well as within, neighboring countries will continue to influence the external and internal stability of the country. Since its independence in 1943, Lebanon has been involved in one interstate war, two civil wars, and several disputes with its neighbors, Israel and Syria. Even though the chances of Lebanon's going to another interstate war are relatively low, there are several ongoing issues that will continue to predominate with Lebanese decision makers.

The U.S. presence in Iraq as well as the mounting pressure that the United States is exerting upon Syria and Iran will continue to occupy the security calculations of Lebanon. Perhaps even more important to Lebanese politics will be the decisions adopted by Hizballah on the extent to which they should convert themselves into a nonmilitary political organization.

Moreover, despite the Israeli withdrawal from southern Lebanon on May 24, 2000, a major disagreement related to the Shebaa Farms remains unsettled. The Lebanese government's stance has been that this area is part of the Lebanese territory, whereas the Israeli authorities argue that they had captured the area from Syria, and therefore any resolution over this territory is part of an Israeli-Syrian agreement. Dispute over the area has left the Lebanese-Israeli borders vulnerable, with tensions mounting on both sides. In fact, since the end of the Iraq war, Israel has been increasing its calls that Hizballah be disarmed and dismantled and for the deployment of the LAF to the south. Another contentious issue between Israel and Lebanon is the Palestinian refugees in Lebanon. The Israeli government has argued that the Palestinian refugees should be settled in the countries that they are currently residing in; however, the Lebanese stance has been that the Palestinians should be allowed to return to their homeland, or to the Palestinian state that will be created, since Lebanon is sensitive to sectarian imbalances.

At the end of the second civil war, the Lebanese military was fragmented and lacked the necessary equipment to fulfill its role. Lebanon's defense budget has fallen in the last couple of years. In fact, in 2003 the defense budget accounted for only 8.8 percent of government spending, in comparison to 1992, when it accounted for 24 percent (*Military Balance* 2003, 275), and it is unlikely that the Lebanese defense budget will change dramatically. Moreover, most of the defense budget is allocated to military salaries and wages, thus leaving no room for either buying new equipment or research and development.

However, the Lebanese government has taken several measures to revitalize the economy by developing the private sector and integrating Lebanon into the global economy. In fact, Lebanon applied for membership in the World Trade Organization (WTO) and was given observer status in 1999. Also, in 2002, Lebanon initiated an association agreement with the European Union that aims mainly at liberalizing trade between Lebanon and the EU. Moreover, significant private investment is being made to modernize and expand the tourism sector, which accounted for 20 percent of the GDP prior to the outbreak of the second civil war (Ministry of Finance Website). Nonetheless, Lebanon's fate is tied to the peace and stability within the country, as well as within the region.

References, Recommended Readings, and Websites

Books

Congressional Quarterly. 2000. *The Middle East.* 9th ed. Washington, DC: Congressional Quarterly Press.

Cook, Chris. 2001. *The Facts on File World Political Almanac: From 1945 to the Present.* 4th ed. New York: Checkmark Books.

El-Khazen, Farid. 2000. *The Breakdown of the State in Lebanon 1967–1976.* Cambridge, MA: Harvard University Press.

Ellis, Kail. 2002a. "The Regional Struggle for Lebanon." In *Lebanon's Second Republic: Prospects for the Twenty-first Century,* Kail Ellis, ed. Gainesville: University Press of Florida.

———. 2002b. "U.S. Policy toward Lebanon." In *Lebanon's Second Republic: Prospects for the Twenty-first Century,* Kail Ellis, ed. Gainesville: University Press of Florida.

Firro, Kais. 2003. *Inventing Lebanon: Nationalism and the State under the Mandate.* New York: I. B. Tauris.

Fisher, W. B. 2001. "Lebanon." In *The Middle East and North Africa. 2001* London: Europa Publications Limited, pp. 801–857.

Fisk, Robert. 2002. *Pity the Nation: The Abduction of Lebanon.* New York: Thunder's Mouth Press/Nation Books.

Friedman, Thomas. 1995. *From Beirut to Jerusalem.* New York: Anchor Books.

Hallenbeck, Ralph. 1991. *Military Force as a Instrument of U.S. Foreign Policy: Intervention in Lebanon August 1982–February 1984.* New York: Praeger.

Hiro, Dilip. 1993. *Lebanon: Fire and Embers.* New York: St. Martin's Press.

Khalaf, Samir. 2002. *Civil and Uncivil Violence in Lebanon: A History of the Internationalization of Communal Conflict.* New York: Columbia University Press.

Military Balance, 2002–2003. 2002. London: International Institute for Strategic Studies.

Military Balance, 2003–2004. 2003. London: International Institute for Strategic Studies.

O'Ballance, Edgar. 1998. *Civil War in Lebanon, 1975–1992.* New York: St. Martin's Press.

Picard, Elizabeth. 2002. *Lebanon, A Shattered Country: Myths and Realities of the Wars in Lebanon.* New York: Holmes and Meier.

Salibi, Kamal. 1988. *A House of Many Mansions: The History of Lebanon Reconsidered.* Berkeley: University of California Press.

Articles/Newspapers

Abdelnour, Ziad. 2001. "The Revival of Lebanon's Drug Trade." *Middle East Intelligence Bulletin* 3, no. 6. http://www.meib.org/articles/0106_l3.htm.

Friedman, Thomas. 2004. "War of Ideas." Part 4. *New York Times,* January 18.

Ghosn, Faten, and Glenn Palmer. 2003. "Codebook for the Militarized Interstate Dispute Data, Version 3.0." http://cow2.la.psu.edu.

Gibler, Douglas M., and Meredith Sarkees. 2004. "Measuring Alliances: The Correlates of War Formal Interstate Alliance Data Set, 1816–2000." *Journal of Peace Research* 41, no. 2:211–222.

Gill, N. S. 2003. "Lebanon—The Phoenicians." http://ancienthistory.about.com/library/bl/bl_lebanonphoenicians.htm.

Hamzeh, Nizar. 1997. "Islamism in Lebanon: A Guide." *Middle East Review of International Affairs* 4, no. 3:43–52.

Held, Colbert. 2004. "Lebanon (country)." Microsoft Encarta Online Encyclopedia. http://encarta.msn.com.

MaCfarquhar, Neil. 2001. "Cattlemen in Lebanon Miss Lucre of Hashish." *New York Times,* April 5.

Middle East Briefing. 2003. "Hizbollah: Rebel without a Cause?" *International Crisis Group,* July 20.

Morris, Mary. 2004. "At a Crossroads: American Policy and the Middle East." Paper presented at conference hosted by the California State University, January 22, San Bernardino, CA.

New York Times. 1963. "Lebanon Charges Syrians Killed 3 In Border Ambush." October 20.

Raad, Nada. 2004. "Analysts Dissect Election Results: Hariri Seen as Loser in This Round, But Premier Not Counted Out for 2005." *Daily Star,* June 1.

Rees, Matt. 2004. "A Devil's Bargain? Germany Brokers a Prisoner Swap between Israel and Hizballah. Arafat's Frozen Out—But the Killing Goes On." *Time Europe Magazine,* February 1.

Royal Institute of International Affairs. 2003. "Iraq: The Regional Conflict." Briefing paper, February. London: UK.

Sarkees, Meredith Reid. 2000. "The Correlates of War Data on War: An Update to 1997." *Conflict Management and Peace Science* 18, no. 1:123–144.

Zisser, Eyal. 2000. "Hizballah: New Course or Continued Warfare." *Middle East Review of International Affairs* 4, no. 3:32–42.

Websites

Al-Mashriq: http://faculty.winthrop.edu/haynese/mlas/al1.html.

Arab League: http://faculty.winthrop.edu/haynese/mlas/al1.html.

Central Administration for Statistics (CAS): http://www.cas.gov.lb.

Central Intelligence Agency. The World Fact Book: http://www.cia.gov.

CLS Lebanon-related internet resources: http://users.ox.ac.uk/~shehadi/links_m.htm.

Governments on the Web—Lebanon: http://www.gksoft.com/govt/en/lb.html.

Hizballah: http://www.hizballah.org.

Lebanese Army: http://www.lebarmy.gov.lb.

Lebanese Links: http://www.middleeastnews.com/LebaneseLinks.html.

Lebanese Parliament: http://www.lp.gov.lb/english.html.

Lebanon Research Guide: http://www.sipa.columbia.edu/regional/mei/lebanon.doc.

Lebanon—UNIFIL: http://www.un.org/Depts/dpko/missions/unifil/index.html.

Lebanon—UNRWA: http://www.un.org/unrwa/refugess/lebanon.html.

Lebanon-Global Policy Forum-UN Security Council: http://www.globalpolicy.org/security/issues/lbisindx.htm.

Lebanon-Wikipedia: http://en.wikipedia.org/wiki/Lebanon.

Library of Congress: http://lcweb2.loc.gov/frd/cs/lbtoc.html.

Ministry of Finance: http://www.finance.gov.lb.

Prime Minister of Lebanon: http://www.rafik-hariri.org.

U.S. Department of State: http://www.state.gov.

Libya

Darius Watson

Geography and History

Libyan geography is one of the starkest in Africa. Covered more than 90 percent by desert, the country's coastal region is the only area that offers respite, as it enjoys typical Mediterranean weather patterns: relatively dry, hot summer weather mixed with cooler wet winters. Because of its climate, Libya suffers substantially from desertification and a lack of potable water. The former has led to Libya's having only 1 percent of its land considered arable, with only 0.17 percent of the total area (1,759,540 square miles) dedicated to permanent agriculture (CIA World Factbook). The latter has led Libya to develop what is currently the largest water project in the world aimed at tapping aquifers deep under the Sahara desert in southern Libya and linking those freshwater sources to the coastal cities. This may in fact be a considerable source of future regional instability, as Libya's current and future water use projects had already led to declines in the underground water levels within Libya, as well as for their neighbors (www.fao.org).

The population of Libya is ethnically almost exclusively Arab and Berber. There is also, however, a sizable foreign population consisting of French, Italian, Greek, and Egyptian ethnicities, alongside black Africans from other central and southern African nations. The Arab population represents both the dominant and predominant group, residing primarily in the coastal cities of the regions of Tripolitania and Cyrenaica. In particular, the cities of Tripoli (the capital of Libya), Beghazi, and Tobruk have a rich history as primary ports for the flow of trade between Europe and the African interior. The less numerous and more tribal Berbers reside primarily in the southern, more desolate areas of the Libyan interior, specifically the Fezzan region and the northern areas of the Sahara desert as it demarcates the southern boundaries of Libya with Niger, Chad, and Sudan. Although most of Libya's population is in fact of a mixed Arab-Berber ancestry, some of the more nomadic tribes in the south do still have pure Berber lineages and speak their own dialects. Much of Libya's history has been cast as the struggle of the northern, more developed areas—especially when under foreign control, and at times operating outside the normal government and legal systems—to reign in the activities of these groups.

Libyan society has been fundamentally transformed by their current ruler, Mu'ammar al-Qadhafi, and his drive to create Libya as a *Jamahiriyya*—a state ruled directly by its citizens. Qadhafi came to power as result of a military coup on September 1, 1969, against the government of King Idris al-Sanusi. Sanusi had come to power in 1951 as the chosen leader of the newly independent Libyan state, which was composed of the highly disparate regions of Tripolitania, Cyrenaica, and Fezzan.

Before the establishment of Libya as an independent monarchy, its modern history was a litany of various periods of domination by European powers, the most important of which for this study was Italy. The main legacy of the Italian domination was the destruction of the few fledgling economic and bureaucratic institutions during occupation that may have aided in Libya's development as a state following World War II. At the point of their independence, Libya was among the poorest states in the world, with what little infrastructure development they had achieved being decimated by the war (Vandewalle 1998, 46). In the eight years of rule between independence and the discovery of oil, Sanusi fought against an ill-conceived federal governmental structure that tilted national distributive capability into the hands of provincial and local governments, as well as against an associated fear of separatist and anti-

governmental movements within Tripolitania and Fezzan (Sanusi was a native of Cyrenaica). One major development was an expansive system of favor and paternalism as Sanusi appointed only proven allies and supporters to key positions in the Libyan Parliament and national government. This situation was exacerbated by his outlawing of political parties in 1952.

The discovery of oil in 1959 was transformational on several levels within Libya. The most important was the rapid switch from a federal government to a unified one that was led by King Sanusi, whose reasons for this radical change were multiple and reinforcing. "The adoption of the unitary system, at least according to the amended constitution, thus gave the king—and his *diwan*—inordinate power. The evisceration of the provincial bureaucracies and the new administrative organization enabled Idris to staff the new governmental organizations that started to proliferate in 1963. . . . The newly created national bureaucracies, which replaced the provincial machinery,

Table 1   Libya: Key Statistics

Type of government	Military dictatorship (see below)
Population (millions)	5.5 (2002)
Main religion(s)	Sunni Muslim (97%)
Main industries	Petroleum (main export), food processing, textiles, handicrafts, cement
Main security threats	Egypt, United States
Size of military (thousands)	45,000 (active)
Military spending	$1.3 billion (2002 est.)
Military spending as % of GDP	3.9% (2002 est.)
Number of civil wars since 1945	0
Number of interstate wars since 1945	1 (Ugandan-Tanzanian conflict, 1978)

Sources

Central Intelligence Agency Website. 2005. "CIA World Fact Book." http://www.cia.gov/cia/publications/factbook/ (accessed May 15, 2005).

Correlates of War 2. http://cow2.la.psu.edu/ (accessed May 24, 2005).

Stockholm International Peace Research Institute (SIPRI). 2002. *SIPRI Yearbook 2002: Armaments, Disarmament and International Security.* London: Oxford University Press.

provided ample opportunities for the government to provide large-scale patronage" (ibid., 52–53).

What made this a smooth transition was that, despite the conflict between the Sanusi government and the provincial and tribal political units during the 1950s, these same groups also quickly grasped the importance of the oil discoveries, the resulting massive capital inflows, and ultimately, their need to be more involved in the newly evolving national institutions of Libya. The result was that Sanusi was unopposed in his use of a dual approach to creating "the Kingdom of Libya" from "the United Kingdom of Libya." On the one hand, he practiced a conservative approach to state building that was aimed at keeping as much control as possible of the critical elements of the government. At the same time he reinforced his position by an intricate system of patronage that was now centered upon the distribution of lucrative oil and land contracts to specific elites within Libya. In combination with the failings of state development that existed from the first decade of Idris's rule, this created a tense situation of rapidly growing inequality that, contrary to all efforts, led to social and political unrest by the mid-1960s.

It was during this period that Qadhafi would come to power. Although at first his machinations were centered on protests against foreign military bases in Libya and increasing societal inequalities represented in part by a lack of state-sponsored health care or labor standards, it was the 1967 Arab-Israeli war that accelerated his rise to power. This was due primarily to an impression on the part of more radical Muslim elements within Libyan society that the Sanusi government had failed to fully back the Arabs,

and Egypt in particular, during the war. It was also due to the charismatic influence that Abdul-Nasser, president of Egypt, and his Arab-centric Nasserism had had on the more religious elements of Libyan society, particularly the young men of the small Royal Army. It was believed by Qadhafi in particular that the rampant corruption in the government resulting from cronyism associated with oil economics had stunted the real goals of Libya, as well as the establishment of a *Jamahiriyya* and the proper observance of a greater Libyan understanding of Arabism. This essentially revolved around the understanding that belonging to the Arab nation entailed a specific obligation to help bring about its greater unity (LeMarchand 1988, 20). Although the specific impact of Qadhafi's policies on the security and military status of Libya will be discussed at length later in this study, it is important to note the effect he has had on Libyan society in general.

Modern economic activity within Libya is tied almost exclusively to the manufacture and export of its sizable crude oil reserves. Furthermore, some analysts argue that Libya represents a state typology that is important to study, as they have played a central role in many modern conflicts: newly independent or developing countries inundated with massive cash inflows resulting from oil sales. Libya is similar to many countries in the Middle East that have seemingly attempted to use these revenues to hasten or alter what is commonly accepted as the proper path of development for newly emerging states. In particular, "distributive states" are able to circumvent many of the assumedly "natural" methods of progress because the importance of development of social and political institutions aimed at creating social

Table 2   Libya: Economic Indicators

Gross domestic product	U.S.$41 billion PPP (2002 est.)
GDP real growth rate	1.2% (2002 est.)
GDP per capita	$7,600 PPP (2002 est.)
Unemployment rate	30% (2001)
Notable industries	Petroleum (main export), food processing, textiles, handicrafts, cement
Primary trading partners	Italy (39.6%), Germany (15.5%), Spain (14%) (2002)
Electricity production by source	Fossil fuel (100%) (2002)
Oil production	1.319 million bbl (2002)
Total export earnings	U.S.$11.8 billion (2002 est.)
Total import value	U.S.$6.3 billion (2002 est.)

Sources

Central Intelligence Agency Website. 2005. "CIA World Factbook." http://www.cia.gov/cia/publications/factbook/ (accessed May 15, 2005).

Stockholm International Peace Research Institute (SIPRI). 2002. *SIPRI Yearbook 2002: Armaments, Disarmament and International Security.* London: Oxford University Press.

welfare is mitigated by the rise of paternalism and cronyism (Vandewalle 1998, 12–13).

In this case, the rise of Qadhafi in relation to the jumps in oil revenues associated with the "oil shocks" of the 1970s allowed him to institute radical socialist economic and political reforms that arguably would have been ruinous for other countries. Through various edicts and laws, the practice of private enterprise has been essentially eliminated, as has private property (Harris 1986, 56–61). Almost all important aspects of the economy have been nationalized including the banking and insurance systems as well as the oil industry that had, prior to the 1969 revolutionary coup, been dominated by foreign companies. It is this last point that so soundly set the stage for Libya's current relations with the West. This is because despite his drive for autarky both economically and militarily, "insufficient indigenous technical personnel, incorrect planning ill-advised spending, and, most of all, the lack of a comprehensive and realistic develop-

ment strategy have all contributed to Libya's present state of economic deterioration and, in some sectors, near chaos" (Harris 1986, 110; El-Kikhia 1997, 61–82). Although that was written some fifteen years ago, it still rings true today as Libya finally crawls from under sanctions imposed upon the country by the international community.

A second key consideration for the analysis of Libya's economy was the long-term prosecution of a strict international embargo against the country. The development of the sanctions regime has been an evolutionary process spearheaded by the sometimes questionable use of unilateral sanctions on the part of the United States. Beginning in 1978, the target of U.S. sanctions was initially Libyan oil exports and military imports. The impetus for these sanctions was clear evidence of Libyan support for Islamic terrorists in the Middle East, as well as a more general Libyan obstruction of the search for peace in the region. However, early in the process, U.S. security interests—specifically the CIA—believed that Libya still represented a possible ally because of the anticommunist aspects of Qadhafi's ideologies. At that point the primary U.S. concern was the possible resale of military equipment purchased by Libya to more militant Arab countries, specifically Syria and Nasser's Egypt. The situation was exacerbated by the 1972 sale of 100 Mirage fighters to Libya by the French that were then used by the Egyptians against Israel in the 1973 Arab-Israeli war. The interesting development is that in his anger over being "left out of the loop" regarding war planning between Syria and Egypt, Qadhafi played a significant role in getting the United States out of Egypt during and immediately following the war, to the degree that Nixon would send a personal note of thanks. This further led certain U.S. officials to believe Libya might still hold promise (Cooley 1982, 159–161).

This lingering but fading impression, combined with the continued interest of U.S. oil companies in investment in Libya, would be the main basis of the initially hesitant nature of the sanctions. As the links between terrorism and Qadhafi were strengthened in the early 1980s, so were the sanctions. The key events to discuss with regard to the effects the sanctions had on the Libyan economy are Reagan's invoking of the International Emergency Economic Powers Act in 1986, the bombing of Pan Am Flight 103 over Lockerbie, Scotland, in 1988 and the subsequent imposition of an international air and arms embargo based upon UN Resolution 748 in 1992, and finally, the Iran-Libya Foreign Oil Sanctions Act (ILSA) of 1995. The importance of these events as a whole is that they represent critical moments in which the sanctions were increasingly tightened and the impact on the Libyan economy was both direct and, at times, acute.

What cannot be ignored, however, is that the sanctions regime seems to have worked. According to Libyan sources the sanctions have cost them $33 billion in trade revenues, while the World Bank puts the figure at $18 billion—still a considerable sum for an economy of its size. In either case, what is interesting is that the reliance on oil revenues that allowed Qadhafi to build up a system of terror also allowed the international community to respond in a strong and unified manner (Takeyh 2001, 64–65).

After a steadily declining sponsorship of international terrorist groups, the move by Qadhafi to negotiate for the extradition of the Lockerbie bombing suspects was to many an indication that Libya was finally beginning to take responsibility for its actions during the 1970s and 1980s regarding the promotion of global terrorism. Furthermore, this change in Libyan foreign policy was a direct result of the sanctions regime headed up by the United States.

When in 1999 the suspects were finally handed over to UN authorities, the embargo was partially suspended. Although the suspension theoretically allowed for the reopening of diplomatic and economic ties with the international system, the few successes they have had have predictably centered upon investment and development in the petroleum sector. Libya enjoyed 4.4 percent GDP growth in the year following the suspension of the UN sanctions, and that number continued to grow dramatically, reaching 9.8 percent growth in 2003 with U.S. Department of Defense estimates for 2005 at 6.8 percent (Energy

Just as Libya was once the symbol of the rising problem of state-sponsored terrorism, they now appear as proof of the effectiveness of comprehensive international sanctions in altering the behavior of pariah states. In particular, Libya's recent activities in relation to the settlement of the 1988 Lockerbie bombing case have gone far in allowing them to reenter the international community as a full member. Specifically, Libya in August of 2003 officially accepted responsibility for the bombing leading to the full removal of United Nations sanctions in September 2003. This was followed by the unprecedented establishment by Libya of a compensation fund for victims of the bombing, which earmarked $4 million apiece for each victim. Libya also established a similar fund in February of 2004 for victims of the 1989 bombing of UTA flight 772 over Niger, an incident that had also been directly traced back to Libya. This change in Libya's stance toward international terrorism was mirrored by an internal effort to divest themselves of all contacts with terrorist groups. Beginning in 1997 with the expulsion of the Palestinian terrorist group Abu Nidal, Libya has appeared determined to leave this part of the past behind them with the United States State Department reporting that there has been no credible evidence that Libya has supported international terrorist activity since 1994.

Source
Boucek, Christopher. March 2004. "Libya's Return to the Fold." *Strategic Insights*, Vol. 3, No. 3.

Information Agency, 2005). Despite these increases, however, unemployment has remained high, and rigid government structures along with extremely high public sector spending continue to serve as impediments to attracting foreign investment.

In September 2003 the UN Security Council voted to remove the sanctions fully. That move was not without continued controversy, as the United States maintained its own sanctions against Libya; it also continued to keep Libya on its Terrorist Watch List as a state implicated in sponsoring terrorism. It remains to be seen what effect this new series of developments will have on a Libyan economy that suffers from 30 percent unemployment and a severe lack of development and trade-initiated projects. But what seems to be widely accepted is the premise that Libya is now set to begin to attempt to reintegrate itself as a functioning member of the international community, perhaps leaving behind its legacy as the prototype pariah state.

Regional Geopolitics

Libya's recent history in relation to its neighbors in North Africa and the international community in general is typified by alternating acts of aggression and reconciliation aimed at friend and foe alike. Qadhafi's foreign policy is firmly grounded in his interpretations of Islam and the closely associated concept of Arabism, or Arab unity. The latter is crucial in understanding that Libyan foreign policy as religion and ideology has most often served as the lightning rod for Libya's establishment of both allies and enemies. However, the importance of ideology seems to be a function of the proximity of the threat to Libya. In other words, the closer the threat to Libya's territory, the more likely Libya is to respond with real, geostrategic considerations. The farther away the threat, the more likely Libya is to respond on a more ideological and rhetorical level. "It is precisely this dichotomy that exists in Libya's foreign policy behavior. When core Libyan interests are at stake, Libya's foreign policy is dictated primarily by practical and political considerations, which might even be contrary to its ideological stands, without, for that matter, rendering the policy irrational or capricious" (Deeb 1991, 14). In establishing this first level of understanding regarding Libyan foreign policy, the conclusion to be drawn is that, contrary to the opinions of some outward observers, Qadhafi has not necessarily acted like a "madman" bent on chaos and disruption. Rather, he tends to recognize the utility of ideology in dealing with the larger international community as a whole, whereas the limits of Libya's practical foreign policy restrict Qadhafi's interventions and alliance formation predominantly to North Africa.

Qadhafi's exact implementation of his doctrine is based upon not only his interpretation of Arabism but also the role he envisions that all Arab rulers (especially himself) should play in promoting Arab unity, which in turn is based upon Nasser's vision of concentric circles of power. Nasser believed that there were circles of power that emanated from Egypt and encompassed in successive order Arab, Islamic, and finally, African unity. Qaddafi's approach altered only slightly the idea of African unity to a broader sense of the unity of nonaligned states. Although the practical aspects of this policy have been confined to calls for unity with neighboring North African

states (Vandewalle 1998, 56–60), it has at times allowed Qaddafi to take leadership roles within various international IGOs predisposed to the position of the developing or nonaligned world. Most recently, in July 2002, Qadhafi all but disrupted the inaugural meeting of the new African Union with calls for the creation of "a single African country" (Mungo and MacAskill 2002). This served as a clear indication that the sanctions have not dulled his greater ideologically based foreign policy goals.

Overall, Libya's relationship with the rest of its neighbors in North Africa can be summed up in terms of the expansions and contractions of Qadhafi's attempts to export his concept of *Jamahiriyya* in the face of international resistance and lukewarm acceptance in the region at best. A better understanding of Libya's relationship with the rest of the region will develop when its conflict history is examined. Currently, Libya seems to be in as stable a position as ever regarding its relationships with neighboring states, especially Egypt and Sudan, which have historically represented the greatest security concerns for Qadhafi's Libya. That, combined with an apparent renunciation of support for international terrorism in the last decade, has led to improved relationships with Tunisia and Sudan, as well as the EU and some eastern European countries.

Conflict Past and Present

Libya's history since independence, and especially during the Qadhafi era, has been characterized by successive periods of intense security concern, most often instigated or initiated by Libya. The country's aggressiveness, especially with regard to its neighbors, was a key factor in the rest of the world's viewing Libya essentially as a pariah state. Even though Libya has also obviously been implicated in support of international terrorism, much of its subversive activity has in fact been focused on destabilizing unfriendly local regimes. It is this fact that has set the foundation for Libya's "conflict history." To understand this history and how it has led to Libya's current positioning world politics, we must briefly examine some key rivalries.

Conflict History

With regard to regional security, Egypt has always been the most important consideration for Libyan foreign policy. Egypt is the only contiguous state that has both the power and prestige to threaten Libya, whether unilaterally or through alliance formation. But Egypt has at times been Libya's most capable ally. Considering the direct influence of Nasser on Qadhafi and the "Revolution of 1969," that may not be a surprise. In fact, what is surprising is the relatively antagonistic nature of their relationship for most of the Qadhafi regime. Egypt perhaps is the clearest example of Qadhafi's willingness to target Arab states as readily as non-Arab ones in his ultimate goal of spreading Arabism and Islamic socialism (Sicker 1987, 51–52).

At the time of Qadhafi's assumption of power in 1969, Egypt was in fact keener on some sort of Arab union with Libya than Libya was. Although Qadhafi admired and respected Nasser, so did many of the opponents that he would remove from power over the first five years of his rule. This meant that his initial policy goal regarding Egypt was to try to establish some sort of parity with Egypt, both within the region politically and also in the broader pan-Arab community. Ultimately, he would prove more dedicated (at times fanatically so) to promoting Nasser's dream than either Nasser or his successor, Sadat. The result was that, by 1974, Egypt would represent Libya's most dangerous enemy. Egypt and Libya had a minor border skirmish in July 1977 that lasted four days (21–25) and was precipitated by increasing social unrest in Egypt fueled by Qadhafi from Libya. This was followed by approximately a decade of mutual militarization of the border, accompanied by traded recriminations and covert actions against each other. This new relationship would play itself out predominantly through intervention by both Egypt and Libya within Chad and Sudan.

The key events in the development of the modern relationship between Libya and Egypt were the 1973 Arab-Israeli war and its aftermath, culminating with the 1977 Libyan-Egyptian border clash and the 1992 sanctions against Libya. The former event was crucial insofar as it precipitated the break between Libya and Egypt, while the latter event seems in hindsight to have been a primary factor in the repair and development of a new relationship between the two countries. That is because while the sanctions were upheld by most Arab countries including Egypt, Qadhafi took care not to overly antagonize the Mubarak regime in Egypt. It seemed that again his practical geopolitical outlook overrode his ideological stance, in that Libya had reacted much more aggressively toward Egypt following the Arab-Israeli war, a point at which Egypt was much less pro-Western than they were to become by the early 1990s. Ultimately, Qadhafi saw Egypt as a bridge between a hostile West and his desire to reintroduce Libya as a legitimate actor in international relations.

This new relationship appears to be more dynamic than the one that was being promoted between the two countries immediately following the 1969 coup. After a "plenary meeting" between Qadhafi and Egypt in the spring of 2001, the Joint Higher Egyptian-Libyan Committee was created as a vessel through which closer ties between the two nations could be examined. The result of the work of this committee was the signing of nearly a dozen "agreements, executive programs and protocols on cooperation in the commercial, economic and investment fields" (Arabicnews.com, "Egypt, Libya . . . Bilateral Relations" 2002). Although the impact of this new cooperative relationship on the development of Libya is still unclear, what is clear is that Libya has already begun to experience economic growth that is approaching their presanction status.

The second nation that is highly placed in discussion of Libya and its conflict history is Chad. The two countries' postcolonial histories have been closely entwined yet have matured in radically different ways. The result has been a long history of pronounced Libyan interventions in Chad that have directly contributed to the continuation in that country of one of Africa's longest and most brutal civil wars.

When Libya gained independence in 1951, power was vested in what seemed to be a stable and accepted authority in King Idris. Although Libya had its problems, in relation to most of the newly independent African states of the period, it was politically stable, economically self-sufficient, and ultimately a viable member of the international community. The same could not be said of a newly independent Chad in 1960. As Libya represents the prototypical "oil state," so Chad represents the typical newly independent Third World state, struggling with postcolonial and postimperial legacies during the 1960s.

In this case the former colonial power, the French, sought to retain most of their substantial influence in the region, and thus power in the new Chadian government was vested in the pro-French Sara tribes of the south, whose allegiance was owed to French protection of those tribes during the slaving period of colonialism. The Christian Sara tribes were opposed by the Muslim Tebu tribes of the central and northern areas, who resisted the southerners' imposition of essentially alien laws and civil codes. "So long as the French were in control, Chad had a certain enforced cohesion. . . . While not originally responsible for such divisions, France exploited rather than ameliorated them" (Wright 1989, 126). Thus Chad was set up to be as inherently instable as Libya would seem stable. Although French intervention in Chad would fluctuate over the first two and a half decades of its independence, it was almost always pro-Sara and anti-rebel. It was this relationship that would lead to a direct and negative interaction between the French and Libya.

The major efforts of Qadhafi in Chad were concentrated in a period from 1977 to 1987, beginning with the seizure of the Anzou strip in northern Chad and ending with a defeat at the hands of the U.S.- and French-backed Habre regime. Libya's adventures in Chad were their most direct attempt to establish themselves as a power in North Africa. It included the now familiar call for Libyan unity with a neighboring state (which was defeated by the combined diplomatic efforts of the OAU) and the extensive use of Soviet hardware purchased with oil revenues. All of these efforts, however, would fail as renewed French and U.S. assistance helped weaken the pro-Libyan rebels that composed the Transitional Government of National Unity (GUNT). By 1987 stability appeared to have returned to Chad, and "the whole Libyan position in Chad, built up at such expense and with so great effort over 20 years, appeared to be in ruins" (ibid., 133). Over the next five years Libya's position on the Anzou softened considerably as backlash from the Lockerbie incident continued to mount. With the assistance of the UN Anzou Strip Observer Group (UNASOG), the withdrawal of the Libyans from the territory was negotiated and concluded by 1994. Since then, relations between Chad and Libya appear to have stabilized, with both nations joining the same regional and international organizations in recent years.

Libya has been actively engaged with almost all of its neighbors in one aspect or another since the revolution. Although Egypt and Chad represent the most direct activity on the part of Libyan foreign policy, they have also intervened in the activity of other nearby states. During the turbulent period of relations with Egypt, Libya also targeted Sudan as an ally of Egypt's. In particular, Qadhafi made several attempts at destabilizing the country, both politically and economically. Although he was initially unsuccessful, the rise of Sadiq al Mahdi as the prime minister of Sudan signaled a warming in Libya-Sudan relations. Since the end of the Chadian conflict, however, relations between the two states have been generally neutral.

Libyan relations with its smallest neighbor, Tunisia, have been as erratic as with other states. Initially Qadhafi seemed finally to have found a serious partner in his drive for unity with another state. However, Qadhafi was much more dedicated to the project than his neighbors, with the relationship deteriorating steadily until 1984. Following continued failed attempts by Libya to ferment a coup or revolution within Tunisia, they seemed poised to invade the much weaker country by mid-1985. It was at this point that Algeria gave indications that they would support Tunisia militarily in such a conflict. "It has long been evident that Qadhafi is wary of any serious confrontation with Algeria," and that fact seemed verified by Libya's backing down in their stance toward Tunisia immediately following the Algerian statements (Sicker 1987, 73). Since then, Libya and Tunisia have reestablished cordial relations, signing several economic agreements since the lifting of the UN sanctions.

It is fair to conclude by stating that Libyan regional policy has been characterized by wildly vacillating relations with all of its neighbors. At one time or another the country has been both allied with or at war against every neighboring state. Although Libya's methods and justifications may at times have appeared to be rational and cohesive, it was too often mixed with irrational acts that seemed to have nothing more than disruption and anarchy as their goal. It is truly encouraging that Libya has sought to mend old fences and establish amiable relations with all of its neighbors to one degree or another. Just as the country's regional policies prior to 1990 seemed to be the manifestation of Qaddafi's egomaniacal view of the world, perhaps its current "good neighbor" approach is also illustrative of a true desire to become an accepted member of the international community.

Alliance Structure

For all of Libya's attempts at unity with other nations, its ability to form useful and durable security alliances has been dismal. The reality is that all of the acknowledged alliances Libya has entered into since Qadhafi came to power have been simply a symbol of his ideological policy goals, bereft of any real strategic worth, or fragile and short-lived agreements made in response to a particular event, such as regional conflicts and coups. An example of the former would be the numerous ill-fated attempts to actually achieve state unity with almost every one of its neighbors. Although some produced named agreements such as the 1969 Tripoli Agreement with Egypt and Sudan, the 1973 Hassi Messaoud Accords with Algeria, and the 1984 Oujda Treaty with Morocco, none produced any tangible security relationships, either at the time or now (Vandewalle 1998, 72n). In fact, in most cases Libya has often been at odds with those other states soon after the signing of these treaties, some cases involving armed conflict either directly or through proxies.

Without question, Libya's most important ally up until the late 1980s was the Soviet Union. Following the change of regimes between Nasser and Sadat, Egypt after 1971 began to warm toward the West, leaving Libya as the primary target of influence for Soviet goals in North Africa. Between 1975 and 1979, Libya imported almost $7 billion (1981 $U.S.) in arms, with the Soviet Union providing $5 billion of that total; the next closest African state was Algeria, which imported just under $2 billion in arms during the same period (Nation and Kauppi 1984, 134–135). The result was that although the Soviets tended to maintain diplomatic relationships only with African states avoiding more stipulated security agreements, it is obvious that Libya represented a more involved target for the Soviets.

In fact, Libya by the mid-1980s was becoming a major resupplier of arms to other African states and nonstate actors, with Soviet arms provided them for exactly that purpose. One other crucial aspect of this relationship was the fact that Libya was one of the few Soviet clients that paid regularly with hard currency gained from oil sales. To be sure, the Soviets were never actively supporting or allied with Libya in the same manner that they were with Cuba. However, this meant that Qadhafi was very much left to his own devices, while being provided with just about any tool needed short of weapons of mass destruction. It was during this period that Libyan foreign policy was most aggressive, both regionally and internationally, and it was consequently the fall of the Soviet Union that signaled the decline of Qadhafi's ability to act. Subsequently, the U.S. and UN embargoes on Libya eroded the country's ability to support the only means left them to promote his goals, terrorism.

As of 2003, Libya enjoyed no security agreements of note. Although the lifting of sanctions against the country by the United Nations and the EU during the same year precipitated a number of new economic and trade agreements, it has not yet led to any substantive security treaties. It seems that Libya is simply continuing its attempts to improve relations with all of its neighbors, most of which have not forgotten the recent past. More recently, Libya has been involved in OAU- and UN-sponsored peacekeeping missions in Chad and Congo. It is fair to say that, combined with the country's continually stated goals of African Union, rather than establishing traditional security arrangements, Libya is pursuing a predominantly regional approach to strengthening its position—one that so far has been hesitantly accepted by both the region and the international community at large.

Size and Structure of the Military

The Libyan military is a paradox in regard to other modern military establishments. On the one hand, the country's extensive oil revenues since the early 1970s have allowed it to purchase and maintain one of the most advanced militaries in North Africa, second only to Egypt. Beginning with the purchase of French Mirage jet fighters in the early 1970s, Libya has been able to maintain highly developed air forces in regard to force structure, capability, and strength. Specifically, they have developed dynamic capability with a total of 130 MiG-23, 81 *Mirage*, 45 MiG-21, 70 MiG-35, and numerous lighter combat aircraft being split between recon, ground attack, and fighter squadrons. This airpower is aided substantially in defense by an extensive air defense network consisting of a wide variety of Soviet AA missile systems linked to a relatively modern radar network. They also have developed support capacity in one squadron of heavy and two squadrons of light transport helicopters, including CH-47C and Mi–18/17 variaties. Transport aircraft are also available to them and include C-130 and An–26 heavy transports (IISS 2002 Yearbook). A last dimension to their air force is a sizable cache of a wide variety of missiles, including air-to-surface and antiship missiles, which has led to a higher level of integration of the air force with the other military bureaucracies, as they tend not to have their own support capacities.

The army itself stood at 45,000 active regulars as of 2002. In addition, there are approximately 25,000 reservists and conscripts that could be called up to defend Libya's eleven border defense and four security zones. Its equipment is extensive, varied, and modern, representing a highly modern army, especially in the context of most African states. The core of Libya's ground forces are some 500 Soviet T-55, T-62, and T-72 main battle tanks, purchased during the late 1970s and early 1980s. They were able to complement that heavy firepower with purchases of Soviet BTR-50 and BMP1 armored infantry vehicles, as well as some Brazilian *Caravel* armored personnel carriers (between 1,700 and 2,000), carriaged and self-propelled heavy artillery pieces (close to 2,000), and technologically advanced battlefield equipment including night vision apparatus (IISS 2002 Yearbook).

Libya has put considerable effort into developing its antitank capabilities, as the country's vast, open desert terrain makes it potentially vulnerable to fast armored attack. They currently have some 3,000 pieces, ranging from modern *Milan* and AT-5 *Spandrel* antitank guided weapons to older RPG-7s. Basic force structure includes 10 tank, 22 artillery, 18 infantry, 10 mechanized, and 6 parachute/commando battalions, supplemented by a variety of support brigades. Overall, Libyan ground forces represent a formidable force on paper, one whose variation and technological level could pose significant problems for any future operation against them.

The weakest of the three armed forces, the navy is limited to coastal defense and missile boats, with the goal ostensibly being to harass an approaching enemy in conjunction with Libyan air attacks. Its mainstay is 8 missile frigates: 5 French *Combattante* II and 3 Soviet *Osa II*. The missile capability of these ships is limited in comparison to both the army and air force, as they rely on just a few *Otomat* and *Styx* ship-to-ship systems. They also have a single *Koni*-class Soviet frigate, as well as one older Soviet *Foxtrot* attack submarine (IISS 2002 Yearbook). Although they have a handful of LST and LCT landing craft as well, overall their naval forces can be considered relatively underdeveloped.

The paradox of the Libyan military lies in the fact that for the most part it has never fully possessed the number of technically proficient personnel to independently man their military forces. The history of the Libyan armed forces has always included a sizable foreign presence aimed at filling those vacancies. Prior to 1977 the majority of these positions were filled by Egyptians who even went to European training exercises under Libyan visas. After the Libyan disengagement with Egypt, those roles were filled by Soviet and eastern European personnel who became a mainstay in the Libyan armed forces. From training positions to fully operative Soviet reconnaissance air wings, these personnel have played a significant role in the training and development of the modern Libyan military. While those relationships began to dwindle significantly during the mid- and late 1980s, Libya still maintains a sizable foreign influence within its military.

Another key component is the relationship between Qadhafi and the established military. Following the struggles that led to Qadhafi's ousting of key Islamic clerics from the Libyan political system after his rise to power, the military became his greatest source of opposition—and thus, to a certain degree, his greatest source of instability. Depending on the source consulted, Qadhafi has survived between four and ten coups since 1970, all of which originated or were promoted by disgruntled military officers and groups. This led to the Sibha Declaration of 1977, in which he called for a program to develop his concept of the "armed people," which would in turn create a 50,000-strong militia that would in theory be fanatically loyal to both Qadhafi and the revolution. The creation of this militia coincided with a decommissioning of thousands of regular military personnel, and Qadhafi hoped that it would lead to a fully militarized society capable of deterring any thoughts of aggression on the part of neighbors. The development of this militia went hand in hand with his concept of *Jamahiriyya*, insofar as the entire society would be mobilized, including teachers and women. For all of the efforts Qadhafi expended on this project, it seems the only tangible development has been a lessening of military resistance to his rule, as the decommissioning has also been described as a "purge" (Bearman 1986, 238–243). The practical uses of the People's Armed Forces have been minimal at best, but politically their development has been noteworthy.

Much of the accessible data on Libya's military budget has been estimated, because of a simple lack of reported data over the last three decades: Libya's published governmental budget numbers have only sporadically included a number for military outlays. The more important consideration is that the numbers that have been supplied have grossly underrepresented the amount of money that Libya spends on its military. It is well known that the first arms agreement signed between the Soviets and Libya, in 1974, totaled $12 billion, the largest state-to-state arms agreement in history at the time. Yet the projected annual spending by Libya of $1 billion in relation to the agreement appears nowhere in Libya's published budget from 1975 to 1979. By the mid-1980s, Libya had stopped providing any information at all. That is most likely associated with a peak in Libyan spending, which the U.S. Arms Control and Disarmament Agency (ACDA) estimates reached $5.1 billion annually by 1984. The important point about Libyan military expenditure up to this period is that Qadhafi specifically focused upon diversifying his sources for arms purchases, so that while the Soviets were their main supplier, they also made notable purchases from Brazil, Pakistan, Italy, France, Syria, and Czechoslovakia.

Another important consideration is that, while Libya's expenditures exceeded by far the average per capita expenditure of other African states (U.S.$1,360 vs. U.S.$34, respectively, in 1984), they were well supported by their oil revenues. The result is that Libya in fact enjoys one of the lowest defense burdens of any state in Africa. Qadhafi has been able to maintain highly mobile and technically modern armed forces without the attendant social and economic trouble that most developing nations attempting similar programs have encountered. The irony is that while producing a quality, modern military and avoiding any serious defense burden, the lack of social development continues to impede the country's ability to independently staff their own technically demanding military positions.

Civil-Military Relations/The Role of the Military in Domestic Politics

The military tends to enjoy a prominent status in newly developing states, as it may often be the most stable bureaucracy in the country. That is particularly true of the oil states, as the military also becomes a source of regional or international prestige and thus a target for the substantial revenue increases those nations enjoy. For the most part, Libya also fits that pattern. The military coup that initiated the Qadhafi period was based solidly on the influence that Nasserism had within the Royal Libyan Army during the 1960s. Before that they were known as the Sanusi Army, a force trained and equipped by the British to fight against the Axis during the North African desert campaigns. During the reign of King Idris, the armed forces were divided into an armed police force and the Royal Army. Although Idris did attempt to enlarge the army, which was approximately half the size of the police forces in 1960, by the time of the coup it was still small and relatively antiquated.

Qadhafi's modernization plans for the military were substantial. But he also kept the division between the internal and external security forces in place. Although Idris's separation was perhaps the combination of expediency and need (Libya faced essentially no major external threats at that time), Qadhafi had a more fundamental reason for enforcing this division. Ultimately, his establishment of the Revolutionary Committees and the militia (Popular Resistance Force) in 1971 had "arisen from his desire to move toward the day when a professional military—and the threat it poses to his authority—is no longer necessary" (Harris 1986, 73). Those who have remained in the armed forces for long periods have tended to be the officers most dedicated to Qadhafi and his ideology. There is also a relatively high rotation rate with regard to postings that further discourages possible rivals from building any sort of lasting base of support that could then be used to threaten Qadhafi's rule. Finally, all of this combines with the fact that a high number of their technically demanding military positions continue to be filled by foreigners to ensure that the military is not currently a major source of concern for Qadhafi and his goal to maintain power.

Terrorism

Libya has played a pivotal role in the development of international terrorism as we know it today. Between being the prototypical state that supports global terrorist activities and Qadhafi's vocal and active denunciation of the West, Libya in many ways created our conception of international terrorism and the people associated with it. That said, Libya is also coming to represent the hopes and ambitions of the international community, as it is the only state on the U.S. terrorist list that has made significant strides toward leaving those activities behind. Whether one attributes the recent changes to UN and U.S. sanctions or a softening of Qadhafi's global vision and his pursuit of it, it is undeniable that Libya is an example of both the worst and the best aspects of the struggle against international terrorism over the last three decades.

Almost immediately after seizing control in 1969, Qadhafi began to establish a network designed to support various international terrorist activities. The primary focus of these activities was the Arab-Israeli peace process, which Libya was adamantly opposed to. But that was only a part of his larger target, which was essentially the international system that he believed was dominated by the imperialist activities of the United States and the USSR. By the early 1970s, Libya was being implicated in funding and support-

ing several of the more aggressive groups in the Middle East and the world, including the Palestine Liberation Front (PLF), the Irish Republican Army (IRA), Abu Nidal, the "Black September Movement," Hamas, and Hezbollah, to name a few (Institute for International Economics, Cases 78–8 and 92–12). There were two key aspects to Libyan support of international terrorism that led the country to become the focal point of efforts to combat terrorism: Qadhafi's assumption of a coordinating role for several of these disparate groups and the escalating level of violence that was being used in the attacks. By the late 1970s it was well known that Libya had become a primary training ground for many of the world's most dangerous terrorist organizations. Libya was also providing essential financial and intelligence support for those groups, which in turn led to a rapid decline in their relationship with the West—and the United States in particular. However, it would be Qadhafi's attempts to confront the United States directly that would truly begin to define the face of international terrorism and the world's response to it.

The Islamic terrorist group Abu Nidal is perhaps the most important link between Libya and international terrorism, as they were found to be the key actor in two of the larger terrorist attacks against the West prior to the attack on the World Trade Towers in 2001: the bombing of the La Belle Discothèque in Berlin on April 14, 1986, and the bombing of Pan Am Flight 103 over Lockerbie, Scotland, on December 21, 1988. Both incidents were linked directly to Libyan intelligence agencies through eyewitness testimony, and enough evidence was gathered to support claims that Qadhafi himself had ordered the attacks (St. John 2002, 165–168).

The result was that the international community began to fall in line with the U.S. hard-liner stance against Libya, culminating in severe economic and diplomatic sanctions against them (see UNSC Resolutions 731, 743, and 883).

As central as these events were to the evolution of international terrorism, the key is that they were actually only part of the global campaign of terror being promoted by Libya. The country's activities involving their neighbors have been well documented, but Qadhafi also managed to influence destabilizing efforts in wide variety of other states throughout Africa and the world (Tanter 1998, 124). Further, the Libyan promotion of terrorism was being done in a systematic manner, with the close cooperation of both Iran and Syria. The result was a terrorist network that had the backing of substantial oil revenues and thus was well funded and capable of higher levels of destruction than had been previously associated with terrorism. In addition to being directly linked to the Lockerbie and La Belle attacks, Libya was also either suspected or known to be behind the PLF's seizing of the *Achille Lauro* on October 7, 1985, the hijacking of Egypt Air Flight 648 in 1985, the bombing of UTA Flight 772 on September 19, 1989, in Niger, and the 1972 Munich Olympic massacre perpetrated by the "Black September Movement." The breadth and depth of Libya's involvement is what sets that country apart from most other terrorist states. In contrast, Iran, which also has been a heavy supporter of international terrorism, tended to focus the majority of its efforts against Israel. Libya's leadership role as a main supporter of international terrorism throughout the 1970s and 1980s was not an accident or a random application of Libyan power; rather, it was the result of a specific Libyan foreign policy in turn based upon Qadhafi's rejection of the two dominant ideologies in the world at the time, capitalism and communism.

An associated aspect of Libya's terrorist activities was its attempted development of both chemical and nuclear weapons capability. Even though Libya achieved significantly more progress with chemical than nuclear weapons, Qadhafi's search for weapons of mass destruction in general elevated the West's concern over Libya as a potential threat. The key considerations were Libya's development of possible chemical production facilities at Rabta and Tarhunah, as well as an initial Soviet agreement with Libya to help the country construct a small 10-megawatt reactor for research. In 1977 the reported size of the planned facility was significantly enlarged to 440 megawatts. The latter reactor easily could have served to produce weapons-grade material in large quantities; thus, upon Qadhafi's third visit to the USSR in October 1985, the West saw Libya's search for weapons of mass destruction as a first-level concern (ibid., 133–135; St. John 1987, 77–79). However, growing Soviet misgivings about both their own and Libya's economic situation eventually spelled doom for the deal. Thus, real concerns voiced more recently by the United States in relation to Libya's procuring those materials have been met with relative skepticism. That has been reinforced by a lack of evidence supporting claims that the Rabta and Tarhunah sites are in fact producing chemical weapon agents. The relative changes in Qadhafi's foreign policy, combined with no new evidence that Libya is currently trying to acquire these weapons, has eased tension over the issue considerably. As of February 2004, Libya had signed all of the major

WMD agreements, including the Chemical Weapons Convention (CWC), the Nuclear Nonproliferation Treaty (NPT), and the Biological Weapons Convention (BWC). Inspections in relation to all three agreements have yielded no significant proof that Libya is currently violating these agreements.

Relationship with the United States

Undoubtedly, the United States has been Libya's greatest adversary since Qadhafi's coming to power. From the closure of U.S. air bases following the revolution, through air strikes and military showdowns, and culminating in the current U.S. insistence that sanctions be maintained against Libya, the relationship between the two states has always been the most critical one for Libya. The United States has consistently shown a desire not only to check Qadhafi's ambitions but also to punish his regime for real or perceived threats to the international system. The result has been a historically antagonistic relationship that at times has hindered both Libya and the United States in fulfilling their goals. While admittedly the impact has been far greater on Libya than the United States, it is important to note that it has affected the relationships of the United States with other states, particularly within Europe.

Initially the U.S. viewed Libya only as a growing concern. Although Libyan activities immediately following the revolution were scrutinized closely by the United States and other Western states, for the most part Qadhafi was viewed as a regional annoyance. That view of Qadhafi as only a minor problem contributed directly to initial attempts by the United States and its intelligence community to establish at least cordial relations with

the new regime. It was not long, however, before it became apparent that Qadhafi would not be a friend of the United States. Three key developments typified this early relationship: the rapid growth of the Libyan-Soviet relationship, culminating in the 1975 Arms Agreement; the inconspicuous Libyan support of a wide variety of revolutionary and "terrorist" movements in the mid- and late 1970s; and the concerted Libyan effort to destabilize the Middle East peace process, as well as the failure of Libya in 1979 to protect the U.S. embassy in Tripoli when it was stormed by students sympathetic with those leading the Iranian revolution. "In sum, Libyan initiatives from the Mediterranean to the Caribbean opposed U.S. global policies on virtually every front" (St. John 2002, 119). All of these considerations served as clear signals to the United States that there would be no rapprochement with Qadhafi, even if the signal was not clearly received or understood. The result was that until the election of Ronald Reagan in 1980, U.S. policy toward Libya was essentially reactive, as officials tended to focus on larger, more systemic concerns, such as the Soviet Union and the Arab-Israeli conflict.

The Reagan era represented the most conflicted period in U.S.-Libyan relations. Between 1980 and 1988 the United States conducted several air strikes against Libya and also constructed the sanctions regime that would come to symbolize Libya's relationship with the rest of the international community. However, Libya was just as active against the United States during that period, as evidenced by the high number of terrorist activities that targeted U.S. interests and citizens and that were supported or initiated directly by Qadhafi. So, while the Ford and Carter administrations tended to deal with Libya on an ad hoc basis, Reagan formulated a clear and aggressive policy aimed minimally at reducing Libya's power as a revisionist state, and at the most at removing Qadhafi from power all together. It is clear that the latter policy goal was never achieved, but what is less clear is whether or not the military aggressiveness toward Libya contributed to the country's reduction of terrorist activity and, ultimately, Qadhafi's renunciation of his more radical foreign policy initiatives.

The direct military confrontations between the United States and Libya outwardly centered upon Libya's claim of sovereignty over the Gulf of Sirte. That claim conflicted with international law, as well as broader Mediterranean trade and security issues; thus it was perceived as a direct challenge to both Europe and the United States. The United States, however, would prove to be much more aggressive in taking up this challenge. The first contact between Libyan and U.S. forces was in 1973, and it initiated a recurring pattern that would culminate with the 1986 U.S. air strikes against Tripoli and Benghazi. Almost all of the military clashes were between aircraft, and a surprising number of them over the thirteen years of the standoff were initiated by the Libyans (ibid., 124–146). Also, the development of the U.S.-Libyan conflict mirrored an escalating propaganda war between the two states. The result was an intrinsic link between the events described and the broader ideologies of both Qadhafi and Reagan. For the United States, the vehemence with which they pursued Qadhafi at critical times produced political backlash that in fact hindered their attempts to mitigate Libyan power. Key illustrations of this were Europe's relative rejection of U.S. attempts

to paint Qadhafi as a madman, evidenced directly by French refusals to assist the 1986 attacks in any way; real long-term resistance to the unilateral use by the United States of sanctions, culminating in severe responses to the 1996 Iran-Libya Sanctions Act (ILSA); and the domestic and international furor associated with the Iran-Contra Affair, which eroded the moral foundation of Reagan's crusade against terrorism.

For Libya the conflict with the United States represented a dynamic influence on the development of both their internal and external politics. Domestically, the small and progressive military rebukes delivered by the U.S. 6th Fleet had the effect of weakening the traditional role of the Libyan military within the society. It was in fact in the immediate aftermath of the 1986 strikes that Qadhafi took steps to strengthen the capability of the "Armed People" to help in civil defense. Ironically, it was the Libyan military that the CIA had identified as the most probable ally in the event that they could foster Qadhafi's removal. It seemed again that competing U.S. strategies for implementing policy reduced the effectiveness of all of the policies, for not only did they lose the only real alternative to Qadhafi's rule of Libya, but it was also in the few years following the attack that international terrorism entered a new more aggressive stage, one that seemed fueled by Qadhafi in response to U.S. activity (ibid., 143).

Although it is true that eventually Libya succeeded in becoming the textbook pariah state, they did so with the considerable assistance of the United States. Despite evidence that Syria and Iran were larger supporters of terrorism, Libya was clearly singled out by the United States and the Reagan administration in particular as the primary target of

U.S. foreign action, both overt and covert. The nature of the rhetoric put Qadhafi at the center of global efforts to combat terrorism, a position that he probably did not deserve yet eagerly accepted. More significantly, the U.S.-Libyan relationship at this time critically helped to shape the common U.S. perception of a single identifiable enemy behind major threats to their interests. This has been a continuing aspect of U.S. antiterrorism policy, one initiated and formed around the personality of Muammar Qadhafi and continued in the demonization of Osama bin Laden and Saddam Hussein.

Currently the United States is resisting what seems to be a real reversal within Libyan foreign policy. Although UN and EU sanctions have been lifted, the United States continues to hold its sanctions in place, ostensibly because they feel that Qadhafi has not fully complied with every aspect of the UN resolutions. That position has been further supported by International Atomic Energy Agency (IAEA) inspectors reporting a more advanced nuclear program within Libya than was previously suspected (CNN 2003). A large portion of the international community, however, seems to

---

Sidebar 2   Libya and Weapons of Mass Destruction

Libya has made significant gains with regard to reentry into the international community in the area of weapons of mass destruction. Although a signatory of the Nuclear Nonproliferation Treaty (NPT, 1975) and the Biological Weapons Convention (BWC, 1982), it was widely acknowledged that Libya had pursued both types of weapons in addition to its previously confirmed chemical weapon capability. In December 2003, however, after months of negotiations with the United States and Great Britain, Libya formally announced that it would dismantle its WMD programs as well as its missile program. This action has moved the United States significantly closer to the removal of unilateral sanctions, an event that would open Libya to possibly extensive western investment resources. Initial evidence of this has been the $2.5 million disbursement through the U.S. Nonproliferation and Disarmament Fund for assistance in Libya's dismantling of its programs.

Specifics in its new approach have been the elimination of Libya's intermediate range missile forces and the signing of the Missile Technology Control Regime (MTCR) guidelines. Libya also has allowed international supervision of the destruction of chemical munitions and the dismantling of related facilities. This latter point has been the most promising sign of a new internationalist foreign policy in Tripoli as it has been coupled with a much broader submission to inspections by the International Atomic Energy Agency (IAEA) as well as by UK and U.S. officials. These inspections have thus far yielded higher than expected returns, chief among them the uncovering of Pakistani scientist A.Q. Khan as a key international broker in nuclear technology.

Sources
Sinai, Joshua. 1997. "Libya's Pursuit of Weapons of Mass Destruction." *The Nonproliferation Review*, Spring–Summer.
Squassoni, Sharon A. and Andrew Feickert. 2004. *Disarming Libya: Weapons of Mass Destruction.* CRS Report for Congress; Foreign Affairs, Defense and Trade Division.

believe that the dogmatic aspects of U.S. antiterrorism policies during the Reagan administration are being revived and unfairly used against Qadhafi. That is predominantly because it appears that Qadhafi has completely abandoned all attempts to acquire WMDs and has done so in both a transparent and verifiable manner.

Many of the most historically determined enemies of the Qadhafi regime have started to thaw relations as a result of this most recent turn in Libyan foreign policy—so much so that the United States is now one of the last states not to have reestablished diplomatic relations with Libya. That too may be changing; many have taken a recent congressional visit to Libya (the first since the revolution) as a signal that the United States is looking for new ways in which to engage Libya. Just as in the 1970s and 1980s, the United States will be a critical determinant of Libya's relationship with the international community. In the post 9–11 era, the United States has proven itself to be committed to aggressive response to international terrorism, especially when supported by states, and thus the United States is understandably wary of rapprochement with Libya. That fact surely must be included in Libya's current policy calculations. However, the United States must also recognize that Qadhafi is still an adept diplomat with considerable influence in the regional politics of Africa and the Middle East, as well as within the legacy of the Non-aligned Movement and other "development-based" international political movements. Whether one attributes the changes in the U.S.-Libyan relationship to U.S. aggressiveness and fortitude in confronting terrorism or to Qadhafi's practical understanding of international

relations and his subsequent changes in Libyan foreign policy, what is apparent is that the two countries are finally poised to leave behind them a history of confrontation—a move that will invariably improve almost every aspect of Libya's relationship with the rest of the world.

The Future

Compared with its recent past, the diplomatic and economic future of Libya looks promising. As it emerges from nearly two decades of international sanctions that crippled its economy, signs that economic regeneration is already under way are evident. But even more important, many in the world community seem to be willing to give Libya a second chance to participate as a full member, despite a widely publicized history of promoting violence and anarchy. Thus Libya's future will be determined by the intersection of key considerations—and more important, how Qadhafi responds to the opportunities they present. The tension of Libya's economic promise balanced against its political legacy represents the first of those intersections. Oil will ensure that Libya will continue to be courted by Western states as an economic power. Further, oil will also fuel whatever level of development Libya is able to find within the next five to ten years. The question yet to be answered is what form that development will take, as it was Libya's militarization that acted as the foundation of past foreign policy. Although it is certain that Libya will again see large revenues from reinitiated oil exports, channeling those funds into productive programs and ventures in Libya rather than toward old terrorist and extremist groups throughout Africa and the Middle East will be the primary task of both Libya and the rest of the world.

A second intersection consists of U.S. foreign policy and Qadhafi's own ideologies. Even though it is true that most of the aggressiveness is now gone from Qadhafi's speeches and actions, the bravado and at times incomprehensible policy goals are still evident. The United States will continue to play a key role in Libyan politics only if it believes that the former is again guiding the latter. As Libya continues to reinvigorate itself economically, it is likely that the European Union will be the primary concern for Libya. That concern, however, will be over trade agreements and oil exports rather than sanctions and air strikes. As long as Libya is committed to this new path, they will find a willing partner in the EU, as it is European countries that are leading the current charge to reestablish links with the Libyan petroleum sector in particular; there is no reason to believe this will change in the near future.

Perhaps the largest concern for Libya's future revolves around Qadhafi and his design of the Libyan state. Libya has developed in accordance with the specific goals of establishing a *Jamahiriya*, or Islamic state, based loosely upon socialist and traditional Islamic ideals, and, at least domestically, Qadhafi has been extremely successful in meeting those goals. The key has been his institutionalization of central aspects of the society, which in turn has helped establish considerable legitimacy and staying power for Qadhafi's government. The concern is whether these institutions and the *Jamahiriya* concept in general will last beyond Qadhafi. Considering Libya's history, it cannot be assumed that pressures of democratization or economic liberalization are present and waiting to be released. Rather it appears that future attempts at regime change will center on traditional versus "Qadhafi-ized" views of Islam. It is this conflict that will most directly determine Libya's future, as it will also help to determine whether Libya returns to more extremist policies that set it at odds with the rest of the international community. This struggle will also encompass a conflict between the military and the political segments of the society, inasmuch as the military is the traditional source of strength and stability within Libya. Even though Qadhafi has gone to great lengths to mitigate the power of the military, he has also been careful not to permit alternative sources of political power. Thus the military establishment may come back into a position of power by default rather than through a real and protracted struggle with other groups vying for power.

As long as Qadhafi is in power, there will be very little variation in Libyan foreign and security policy. Currently Libya is fully dedicated to reestablishing political and diplomatic relations that will allow it to participate in the international community. They are specifically attempting to reduce the impact of their own legacy of violence and terrorism on the way in which they are viewed by the rest of the world community. In that regard, Qadhafi has indeed made a remarkable transformation. What remains to be seen, however, is what his new policy goals are. Although he has not given up his quest for African Union, he also is no longer exporting that vision through support of extremist and revolutionary groups. Just as the balance between the practical and the rhetorical was at the center of Qadhafi's foreign policy over the last two decades, it will continue to be a focus of the postsanction Qadhafi regime. Ultimately, Libya and Qadhafi will need to formulate a specific plan for the country's development in order to avoid even the impression of a return to past practices. The question remains what that program will be, and, finally, whether the program will be of Qadhafi's design. For Libya, the first point depends directly upon the last, as does ultimately Libya's future in the world community.

References

Bearman, Jonathan. 1986. *Qadhafi's Libya*. London: Zed.

Bender, Gerald J., James S. Coleman, and Richard L. Sklar, eds. 1985. *African Crisis Areas and U.S. Foreign Policy*. Berkeley: University of California Press.

CNN. "Bush Official: Libya's Nuclear Program a Surprise." December 19, 2003. http://www.cnn.com/2003/WORLD/africa/12/19/libya.nuclear/ (accessed May 24, 2005).

Cooley, John K. 1982. *Libyan Sandstorm*. New York : Holt, Rinehart, and Winston.

"Egypt, Libya to Promote Bilateral Relations." ArabicNews: May 10, 2002. http://www.arabicnews.com/ansub/Daily/Day/010510/2001051028.html (accessed May 10, 2005).

Energy Information Agency. 2005. "Libya Country Analysis Brief." http://www.eia.doe.gov/emeu/cabs/libya.html. February.

Fergiani, Mohammed Bescir. 1983. *The Libyan Jamahiriya*. London: Darf.

Global Policy Forum—UN Security Council. "Sanctions Bibliography." http://www.globalpolicy.org/security/sanction/bibliog.htm (accessed April 3, 2004).

Institute for International Economics. "Case Studies in Sanctions and Terrorism: Case 78–8, United Sates v. Libya (1978: Gadhafi, Terrorism); Case 92–12 United Nations v. Libya (1992–99: Pan Am 103)." http://www.iie.com/research/topics/sanctions/libya3.htm (accessed April 3, 2004).

International Institute for Security Studies (IISS). 2002. *Strategic Survey*. London: IISS.

LeMarchand, Rene, ed. 1988. *The Green and the Black: Qadhafi's Policies in Africa*. Bloomington: Indiana University Press.

Lesser, Ian O. "Countering the New Terrorism: Implications for Strategy." In *Countering the New Terrorism*, Lesser et al., eds. Santa Monica, CA: RAND, 1999.

"Mubarak Reviews the Agreement between Egypt and Libya for Increasing Trade and Investment." ArabicNews: May 20, 2002. http://arabicnews.com/ansub/Daily/Day/020520/2002052038.html (accessed April 3, 2004).

Nation, Craig R., and Mark V. Kauppi, eds. 1984. *The Soviet Impact in Africa*. Lexington, MA: D. C. Heath.

Nelson, Harold D., ed. 1979. *Libya: A Country Study*. Washington, DC: American University Press.

Nolutshungu, Sam C. 1996. *Limits of Anarchy: Intervention and State Formation in Chad*. Charlottesville: University Press of Virginia.

O'Balance, Edgar. 2000. *Sudan, Civil War and Terrorism, 1956–99*. New York: St. Martin's Press.

Pillar, Paul R. 2001. *Terrorism and U.S. Foreign Policy*. Washington, DC: Brookings Institution.

Prados, John. 2002. *America Confronts Terrorism: A Documentary Record*. Chicago: Ivan R. Dee.

Shinn, David H. 2003. "Situation Report: Sudan and Her Neighbors." Institute for Strategic Studies: March 7. http://www.iss.co.za/AF/current/Sudan03.html (accessed April 3, 2004).

SIPRI Yearbook 2002. 2002. Oxford: Oxford University Press.

Skreslet, Paula Youngman. 2000. *Northern Africa: A Guide to Reference and Information Sources*. Englewood, CO: Libraries Unlimited.

Soggot, Mungo, and Ewen MacAskill. 2002. "Gadafy Hijacks Africa's New Union with His Federal Fantasy." *The Guardian*, July 11. http://www.guardian.co.uk (accessed April 3, 2004).

St. John, Ronald Bruce. 1987. *Qaddafi's World Design: Libyan Foreign Policy, 1969–1987*. London: Saqi.

———. 1998. *Historical Dictionary of Libya*. 3d ed. Lanham, MD: Scarecrow.

Sturman, Kathryn. 2003. "The Rise of Libya as a Regional Player." *African Security Review* 12, no 2. http://www.

iss.co.za/Pubs/ASR/12No2/C2.html (accessed April 3, 2004).

Takeyh, Ray. 2001. "The Rogue Who Came in From the Cold." *Foreign Affairs* 80, no. 3 (May/June).

Tanter, Raymond. 1998. *Rogue Regimes: Terrorism and Proliferation*. New York: St. Martin's Press.

U.S. Congress. "Public Law 104–172: *The Iran and Libya Sanctions Act of 1996*." http://www.parstimes.com/law/iran_libya.html (accessed May 24, 2005).

U.S. Congress. "Public Law 107–24: *ILSA Extension Act of 2001*." http://www.state.gov/e/eb/c9998.htm (accessed April 3, 2004).

U.S. Department of State. "2003 Report of Foreign Terrorist Organizations." http://www.state.gov/s/ct/rls/fs/2003/12389.htm (accessed April 3, 2004).

Vandewalle, Dirk, ed. 1995. *Qadhafi's Libya, 1969–1994*. New York: St. Martin's Press.

Wilkinson, Paul. 2001. *Terrorism versus Democracy*. London: Frank Cass.

Wooldridge, Mike. 2003. "Analysis: Lifting Sanctions on Libya." BBC News: November 24. http://news.bbc.co.uk/1/hi/world/africa/3199551.stm (accessed April 3, 2004).

"World Military Expenditures and Arms Transfers 1997." U.S. Arms Control and Disarmament Agency. http://dosfan.lib.uic.edu/acda/wmeat97/wmeat97.htm (accessed April 3, 2004).

Wright, John. 1982. *Libya: A Modern History*. London: Croom Helm.

———. 1989. *Libya, Chad and the Central Sahara*. Totowa: Barnes and Noble.

Recommended Reading

Deeb, Mary-Jane. 1991. *Libya's Foreign Policy in North Africa*. Boulder, CO: Westview.

El-Kikhia, Mansour O. 1997. *Libya's Qaddafi: The Politics of Contradiction*. Gainesville: University Press of Florida.

Harris, Lillian Craig. 1986. *Libya: Qadhafi's Revolution and the Modern State*. Boulder, CO: Westview.

Sicker, Martin. 1987. *The Making of a Pariah State*. New York: Praeger.

St. John, Ronald Bruce. 2002. *Libya and the United States: Two Centuries of Strife*. Philadelphia: University of Pennsylvania Press.

U.S. Department of State, Bureau of Near Eastern Affairs. 2003. "Background Notes: Libya." November. http://www.state.gov/r/pa/ei/bgn/5425.htm (accessed April 3, 2004).

"Use of Sanctions under Chapter VII of the UN Charter: Libya." 2003. Office of the Spokesman for the Secretary-General, February. http://www.un.org/News/ossg/libya.htm. (provides links to all relevant UN resolutions; accessed April 3, 2004).

Vandewalle, Dirk. 1998. *Libya since Independence: Oil and State-Building*. Ithaca, NY: Cornell University Press.

Internet Sites

CIA World Fact Book: http://www.cia.gov/cia/publications/factbook/geos/ly.html.

Columbia University, Middle East Studies: Libya: http://www.columbia.edu/cu/lweb/indiv/mideast/cuvlm/Libya.html.

Electronic Resources: Libya: http://ssgdoc.bibliothek.uni-halle.de/vlib/ssgfi/subject/almisbah_ssg0302030703_on_en.html.

International Institute of Security Studies (IISS): http://www.iiss.org/.

Library of Congress, Federal Research Division, Country Studies: http://lcweb2.loc.gov/frd/cs/.

Libya: Our Home: http://ourworld.compuserve.com/homepages/dr_ibrahim_ighneiwa/.

Libya Online: http://www.libyaonline.com/.

Nationmaster: http://www.nationmaster.com/country/ly/People.

Permanent Mission of the Great Socialist People's Libya Arab Jamahiriyya: http://www.libya-un.org/index_f.html.

University of Pennsylvania, African Studies: Libya: http://www.sas.upenn.edu/African_Studies/Country_Specific/Libya.html.

Malaysia

Ken Glaudell

Geography and History

Malaysia is a unique geographic construct composed of a mainland peninsula (Malaya) and two provinces on the island of Borneo, a territory that it shares with Indonesia. The Indonesian portion of Borneo is called Kalimantan and the oil-rich microstate of Brunei comprises the other portion. More than half of Malaysia's landmass is located in the less densely populated island territories of Sabah and Sarawak on Borneo, while the bulk of the country's population is on the Malayan mainland. Kuala Lumpur, the nation's capital and largest city, is also on the mainland. Insular Malaysia is also differentiated from peninsular Malaysia in economic terms. Although only 5.5 percent of Malaysian land is cultivable (with another 17.6 percent devoted to permanent crops, primarily rubber trees and oil-bearing palms), the vast majority of farm and plantation land is located on the mainland. Tin mining is also an important peninsular industry, as is light and medium manufacturing (Malaysia is a major exporter of electronics). The island zones depend more on logging and the lucrative petroleum industry (both extraction and refining).

As a result of its location on traditional sea-lanes and trade routes, and due to British colonial transmigration policies, the population of modern Malaysia is diverse in terms of religion, language, and race. The largest portion of Malaysia's population (at roughly 50 percent) is Malay, a group that speaks Bahasa Melayu (the national language) and practices Islam. The so-called *bumiputera* (sons of the soil), the Malay dominate the political system and security apparatus of the state. The economy, however, is often perceived (especially by the Malay) to be largely controlled by the second-largest group in Malaysia, the ethnic Chinese. Members of this group—approximately a quarter of the total Malaysian population—speak a variety of Chinese dialects (Cantonese, Mandarin, Hokkien, Hakka, Hainan, Foochow) and manifest a wide array of religious identities including Buddhism, Daoism, Hinduism, and Christianity (but notably not Islam). The remaining quarter of the population is composed of multigenerational Indian immigrant groups (comprising 8 percent of the population, mostly composed of Tamil and Telugu speakers with some Punjabis as well, and largely Hindus with some Sikhs and a small Muslim minority) and a wide array of indigenous peoples. Some of the indigenes (Javanese, Minangkabau, Sama, Melanau; most of these four groups follow Islam) are only indigenous in the sense that they have been in place longer than the Chinese or Indian communities. Others are indigenous in the classic sense and are found largely in

Table 1   Malaysia: Key Statistics

Type of government	Constitutional monarchy
Population (millions)	23 (2003)
Religion	Muslim (more than 60%), Buddhist, Daoist, Hindu, Christian, Sikh; note: Shamanism is practiced in East Malaysia
Main industries	*Peninsular Malaysia*—rubber and oil palm processing and manufacturing, light manufacturing industry, electronics, tin mining and smelting, logging and processing timber; *Sabah*—logging, petroleum production; *Sarawak*—agriculture processing, petroleum production and refining, logging
Main security threats	Radical pan-Islamist movement spearheaded by terrorist group Jemaah Islamiyah (JI) seeking an Islamized southeast including Malaysia, Indonesia, Singapore, Brunei, the Muslim-populated areas of southernmost Thailand, the northern coastlands of Australia, etc.; endemic localized ethnic and ethno-religious clashes between majority and minority groups (Malay-Chinese clashes in *Peninsular Malaysia*; Malay-Indigene clashes in *Sabah* and *Sarawak*)
Defense spending (% GDP)	2.03% (FY 2000)
Size of military (thousands)	96
Number of civil wars since 1945	3
Number of interstate wars since 1945	1

Source
Central Intelligence Agency Website. 2005. CIA *World Factbook.* http://www.cia.gov/cia/publications/factbook/ (accessed May 15, 2005).

Malaysia's Borneo territories (Dayaks and others, many of whom have converted to Christianity, while others follow shamanistic practices). It is from within the Chinese (and, to a lesser extent, the indigenous) community that past leftist insurgencies have drawn their internal support.

The evolution of a cultural and political Malay identity was a slow and complex process. In the first century C.E., while searching for alternative sources of gold and metals, Indian ships arrived in Southeast Asia, including the Malayan peninsula. Malaysia's rich mineral deposits attracted settlers, and through trade with India and other countries the region prospered. During the next two centuries, small Malayan kingdoms appeared in the region, and Indic culture, religion, and politics were brought to the region through maritime linkages.

From the ninth to thirteenth centuries C.E., the Srivijaya kingdom dominated much of the Malay Peninsula from modern-day Thailand down to Singapore. In the fourteenth century, another Hindu kingdom known as Majapahit controlled much of the peninsula. Hindu (and, to a lesser extent, Buddhist) influences were strong during this period. In the following century a Muslim prince took power, resulting in the conversion of the Malays in the region to Islam. Attracted by re-

Sidebar 1   A Unique Monarchical Structure

Malaysia is unlike any other constitutional monarchy. The "Paramount Ruler" (constitutional monarch) serves a five-year term. He is elected by and from the nine hereditary sultans of those Malay states that retained this structure under British colonial rule. Only Sabah and Sarawak (the two Malay states on Borneo), plus Melaka and Penang on the mainland, have elected or appointed governors. While the Paramount Ruler occupies a largely ceremonial role, he is more actively engaged in the political process than modern European constitutional monarchs.

gional trade, Portuguese forces arrived in 1511 and exerted control over much of the area, initiating the era of European expansion in Southeast Asia. Arriving in 1641, the Dutch drove the Portuguese from peninsular Malaya. In 1786, the British occupied Penang, on the Malayan peninsula. They eventually ejected the Dutch and by 1795 managed to exercise hegemonic control over what would eventually become modern Malaysia and Singapore.

In 1826, Melaka, Penang, and Singapore were combined by the British to form the colony of the Straits Settlements. In the nineteenth and early twentieth centuries, the British established protectorates over the more remote Malay sultanates on the peninsula. British economic and security interests in the area expanded, and four of the Malay sultanates were consolidated in 1895 as the Federal Malay States. During this era, a British public administration system was established in these states, and large-scale rubber plantation opera-

tions were introduced. In addition, tin production was promoted.

The British imperial forces were ejected from the region during World War II. Malaya and Borneo experienced Japanese occupation from 1942 to 1945. The British returned to the region after the war, and they established the Federation of Malaya in 1948 to unify all of the peninsular territories. However, the movement toward independence was strong among the Malays during World War II, in part due to conscious policies pursued by the Japanese occupation forces. After the war, the independence movement gained momentum, and a complex struggle between the various Malayan ethnic communities and their British colonizers ensued. While the Malay people generally sought independence, they and their minority neighbors (especially the Chinese, but also the Indians and indigenes) were concerned about the postindependence power-sharing arrangement.

Civil war ensued in parts of Malaya and British Borneo, with ethnic riots and counterriots, as well as an armed insurrection by a largely ethnic Chinese communist guerrilla force. Seeking an exit from this complex and costly struggle, but fearful of the consequences of a leftist victory in the guerrilla war, British forces eventually sought help from other Commonwealth countries, the United States, and the Malay peoples. By the mid- to late 1950s sufficient order was established to satisfy British concerns about the nature of an independent Malaysia. The official state of emergency that had prevailed since 1948 was finally suspended in 1960. In August 1957, the Federation of Malaya (consisting of peninsular but not insular Malaysia) obtained independence. Led by Tunku Abdul Rahman (who became the first Malayan prime minister), the flag of this new state reflected its complex political and social structure (see Sidebar 2). The federation eventually expanded to include Singapore, Sabah, and Sarawak after a lengthy low-intensity conflict with Indonesia and a diplomatic quarrel with the Philippines over the fate of British Borneo. That struggle, known in Indonesia and Malaysia as the *Konfrontasi* (literally, confrontation), complicated Indo-Malaysian relations for much of their early years.

Sidebar 2 What's in a Flag?

The modern Malaysian flag is representative of the complex nature of Malaysian society. It has horizontal red and white stripes with a blue field in the upper left-hand corner. This reflects the federal structure of the state, based on the U.S. model. The flag has fourteen stripes, representing the original fourteen Malay states. These included the nine traditional Malay sultanates (noted in Sidebar 1) plus two states on Borneo and two mainland nonmonarchical Malay states. The fourteenth state was Singapore. When Singapore seceded, its stripe was left in place. In the blue field there is a crescent moon and star, traditional Islamic symbols. Uniquely, the star has fourteen points (reflecting the original fourteen Malay states). The star is intended to be the sun—a traditional Chinese symbol, as seen on the flag of the Republic of China—and both it and the moon are yellow, rather than the Islamically traditional white.

Following the tense years of the Konfrontasi, Malay-Indonesian relations have steadily improved. The recently departed prime minister of Malaysia, Ma-

hathir, and his counterpart in Indonesia, former president Suharto, were the longest and second longest serving executives in Asia (indeed, in virtually the entire world, with a handful of exceptions such as Castro in Cuba). To the extent that tension sometimes defined the relationship of these two leaders, it ceased to be a function of territorial disputes on Borneo. Instead, concerns about transnational terrorism, illegal immigration, and economic rivalry replaced the traditional military-political confrontation of the past.

With recent elections in both states leading to changes in leadership, it is difficult to predict what the shape of regional relations will be in the immediate future. The clash over Borneo, however, now seems to be a relic from a distant past, unlikely to be resurrected in future regional relations. The same cannot be said for the more recently emerging rivalry over the Spratly Islands, claimed not only by Malaysia but by virtually every other state with any coastline abutting the South China Sea.

Regional Geopolitics

Although Malaysia's relationship with each of its immediate neighbors has involved at least verbal hostilities (and, in the case of the Konfrontasi, an actual interstate war), past acrimonious exchanges are fading into the background. There is now a broad consensus among the regional states (Malaysia, Singapore, Indonesia, Thailand, Brunei, the Philippines, Vietnam, Cambodia, and Laos) that the primary long-range security concern is China. Since many of these states were once "tributary fiefdoms" to the Middle Kingdom (as China was known), there are long-standing fears of an eventual reassertion of Chinese hegemony in the region. Other states are concerned about their large Chinese minority populations (especially Malaysia, which once experienced a leftist insurrection based within that ethnic bloc). To some extent this drives the region's governments to maintain close ties with the United States, while openly attacking U.S. foreign policies in the rest of the world. Malaysia's recently retired prime minister Mahathir bin Mohamad perhaps best exemplified this ambivalent attitude.

The primary geopolitical fact that orients Washington's policy in the region is the global war on terrorism, particularly with respect to Indonesia and Malaysia, but increasingly with regard to Thailand as well. Prior to 9–11, China loomed much larger in the U.S. perspective on the region, and it still plays a role in shaping policy there, but radical Islamism has replaced Beijing's expansionist nationalism as a primary American security concern.

Conflict Past and Present

Conflict History
From its inception the state of Malaysia was convulsed with internal ethnic strife and imperiled by the expansionist aims of its much larger neighbor, Indonesia. As Indonesia's leader from independence until his ignominious ouster in 1965, Sukarno claimed that an independent Malaysia would simply be a proxy British imperialist presence designed to contain the revolutionary nationalism of Indonesia. Surrounded by current and former elements of the British Empire (Australia, eastern New Guinea, and the various components of British Malaya, including Singapore, Sarawak, and Sabah) and the Portuguese colonial outpost of East Timor, President Sukarno developed what can best be de-

scribed as a self-perpetuating siege mentality. Convinced that the soon-to-be-independent British Malaysian possessions would serve as a mechanism to contain and ultimately undo his Indonesian nationalist revolution, Sukarno indirectly and directly sought (unsuccessfully) to destabilize and ultimately seize those territories. His actions, of course, produced a Malaysia dependent on British and Commonwealth military support, thereby perpetuating the Anglo-American encirclement he feared.

The Konfrontasi, as Sukarno referred to his efforts at expansion, began with the movement of British Malaya toward independence in the late 1950s. Although the history of the conflict is complex, a simple outline of its parameters will have to suffice. Malaya (the peninsular component of modern Malaysia) achieved full independence in 1957. It was comprised of only a few of the several British colonies in the region, including Singapore and three territories on the northern side of the island of Borneo—Sarawak, Sabah, and Brunei.

It should also be noted that the government of the Philippines laid claim to the northernmost extremities of Borneo, including Sabah province. A communist insurrection in the area in the late 1950s, led mostly by ethnic Chinese subjects of Britain's Malay territories, had been tacitly supported by the Indonesian government in Jakarta. The insurrection was ultimately suppressed by British imperial forces, including Australian and New Zealand troops as well as Gurkha units. Anxious to validate his nationalist and anti-Western credentials, and perhaps also with an eye toward the oil fields of Brunei, Sukarno sought to build a popular movement within both British-controlled Borneo and mainland Malaya for the Indonesia annexation of all of the island (and perhaps, ultimately, of the Malayan peninsula itself, including Singapore). To this end he backed the creation of a so-called North Kalimantan National Army (the TKNU). This group launched a rebellion in Brunei in December 1962. The three goals of the TKNU were to seize the sultan of Brunei (he escaped), take the oil fields, and collect as many European hostages as possible. Within a week of the onset of the rebellion, British imperial forces—including Gurkhas flown in from Singapore—had reestablished control of the area, and by April 1963 the TKNU leadership had been captured. With no local irregular forces left to contest control of Borneo, Indonesian (and Filipino) authorities acquiesced in the formation of a Malaysian federation, contingent on the holding of a referendum.

Covertly, however, Sukarno pushed for the arming of approximately 24,000 ethnic Chinese Malaysian citizens (who, while primarily pro-Beijing communists, shared Jakarta's antipathy for the new Malay state and its erstwhile British rulers), and the Indonesian army infiltrated small units into Malaysian Borneo. Sukarno openly declared a Konfrontasi against the creation of a unified Malaysia state that would include any portion of Borneo. Eventually this activity escalated to include the virtually open employment of Indonesia army units within Sarawak and Sabah, as well as less frequent but well-documented small-scale operations on the Malay Peninsula, most notably in Johore province.

In January 1965, two years after his Konfrontasi was launched, Sukarno formally withdrew Indonesia from the United Nations in protest after Malaysia was elected to a rotating seat on the Security Council. His ultimate failure to destabilize Malaysian control of Sabah and Sarawak can be attributed to several factors, including the increasingly aggressive and proactive patrols of British, Australian, and New Zealand forces into Kalimantan to ambush Indonesian forces prior to their infiltration into Malaysian territory. Additionally, domestic political developments in Java put a stop to Sukarno's efforts to "crush Malaysia" (from a speech in July 1963). For a variety of interrelated geopolitical reasons, Sukarno was toppled from power in a complex coup during 1965 and 1966 (Smith 1985, 99–101).

Even though the Konfrontasi ended satisfactorily for Malaysia (with the demise of Sukarno and his replacement by the less threatening Suharto), Indonesia now presents a new sort of security challenge for Malaysia. Currently Indonesia's attention is turned largely inward, due to a series of separatist movements, ethnoreligious clashes, and the continuing dispute over the land borders of newly created East Timor. Additionally, the challenge of transnational radical Islamists, exemplified by Jemaah Islamiyah (JI) (but including a wide variety of other groups, as noted in Table 2), complicates the relationship of Indonesia with Malaysia, Singapore, Australia, Papua New Guinea, Brunei, the Philippines, and Thailand. Each of these states has been a source of recruits for and/or a target of the violence of radical Islamists such as JI.

The attention of these neighboring states is, however, no longer focused on the expansionism of a radical nationalist Indonesian strongman. Instead, it is the apparent lack of power of the decaying Indonesian state that unnerves bordering countries. The fear is that an imploding Indonesia could have drastic security consequences for all regional states. The apparent instability of the regime in Jakarta

Table 2   Islamist Groups Operating on the Fringes of Malaysia

Jemaah Islamiyah (The Islamic Group)	Designated an FTO (foreign terrorist organization) by the U.S. State Department. Operations primarily in Indonesia, but also transnational. Worst act attributed to JI was the Bali bombing that killed 202 (2002). Links to Malaysia, where it once was headquartered clandestinely. Since the arrest of its lead operative, Riduan "Hambali" and his Malaysia-born ethnically Chinese Muslim convert wife in Thailand in 2003, JI's capacity has been reduced. Linked to al-Qaeda, recruits come from most ASEAN (Association of Southeast Asian Nations) states (including Malaysia). Apparently facilitated al-Qaeda summit in Malaysia for planning phase of 9–11 attacks. Of unknown size today.
Al-Ma'unah	Tiny, exclusively Malay Islamist "cult"; supports groups listed below.
Abu Sayyaf Group (ASG)	Designated an FTO, the ASG is a Filipino Muslim separatist group with increasingly radical Islamist ideology. It often operates from Malaysian territory as it raids the Filipino islands where it seeks political control. ASG has taken tourists at Malaysian resorts hostage. ASG actions inimical to Malay interests have eroded its support.
Barasi Revolusi Nasional (BRN); BERSATU; Mujahideen Islamic Pattani Group; Pattani United Liberation Organization (PULO); Mujahideen Pattani Movement (BNP); Barsian National Pember-Basan Pattani (BNPP); Gerakan Mujahideen Islam Pattani (GMIP)	These Thai Islamist movements are, in part, based in the northernmost Malay states. They draw on support from Malay Islamist groups, as well as global forces like al-Qaeda. Some blur the lines of clan warfare, criminal gangs, and political insurgent movements.

Sources
Patterns of Global Terrorism. 2003.
GlobalSecurity.org.
U.S. State Department. http://www.state.gov/s/ct/rls/pgtrpt/2003.

is perhaps exaggerated due to the fact that it had, in essence, only two leaders from its de facto independence in 1945 until the downfall of Suharto in 1998. Since Suharto's demise, Jakarta has had three chief executives in rapid succession (Habibie, Wahid, and now Sukarnoputri), each representing the contradictory and irreconcilable elements of the Indonesian polity (army-dominated nationalism, political Islam, and leftist populism). Predic-tions about the future geopolitical contours of the region are impossible, given the uncertain future of Indonesia. But the demographic dominance of Indonesia, as well as its geographic size and chaotic character, make its future stability a prime security concern for Malaysia and all of its neighbors.

Malaysia's other neighbors present very different geopolitical challenges. Singapore, a tiny city-state on the southern margins of peninsular Malaysia, has a developed economy and living standard that is the envy of the region. Singapore joined with the Malayan Federation in 1963, as noted previously, but left abruptly in 1965. The complex nature of that breakup had much to do with the relative positions of Malay and Chinese peoples within the city-state and the wider Malaysian polity. In Singapore, ethnic Chinese were the single largest community, outnumbering Malays by five to one, while in the rest of Malaysia the Malays were the largest ethnic bloc. The secession of Singapore from Malaysia was precipitated by the ethnic deadlock of these two groups. Once the split was finalized, Singapore had a clear Chinese majority, while the dominant role of the bumiputera Malays of the countryside was ensured through the departure of many Chinese from the wider Malayan polity. Lingering boundary disputes complicate their current relationship.

On Borneo the small enclave of Brunei (actually composed of two noncontiguous landmasses) was a British protectorate prior to its independence in 1984. Although some Malay nationalists sought its inclusion in a postcolonial Malaysian state, this did not occur. Brunei was (perhaps due to its small size and enormous petroleum reserves) the first target of Indonesian expansionism on the island of Borneo as part of the Konfrontasi in the early 1960s. Today Brunei has some lingering boundary disputes with the Malaysian state that surrounds it, but the primary source of friction between Malaysia and the sultan of Brunei is their competing claim to islands in the South China Sea (also claimed by Vietnam, China, Taiwan, and the Philippines). The disputed Spratly Islands may sit atop significant petroleum reserves.

Just to the north of Borneo, the Philippines present another geopolitical hot spot for Malaysia. As noted earlier, the government of the Philippines claimed the territory of Sabah, on the northernmost tip of British Borneo. Although both Jakarta and Manila relinquished their claims to this area, the consequences of their earlier assertions still color regional cooperative efforts. The Philippines is also one of several governments laying claim to the Spratly Islands, perhaps the most disputed islands on the globe. The southern extremities of the Philippines, including Mindanao, are home to most of that country's Muslim minority population. Separatist groups including the Moro National Liberation Front (MNLF), Moro Islamic Liberation Front (MILF), and Abu Sayyaf Group (putatively linked to al-Qaeda) have connections to communities on Malaysia's northern coastal areas and operate both from and within those territories on occasion. There have been recent hostage-taking events within Malaysian territory that have crossed into Filipino areas. Although there may be little sympathy in the halls of power in Kuala Lumpur for Abu Sayyaf, MILF, and MNLF, there is broad popular concern among Malaysia's slim Muslim majority about the fate of their coreligionists in Mindanao, as noted in Table 2.

The same can be said of Malaysian-Thai relations. Even though the border is relatively undisputed (except for a small segment on the Kolok River), there is increasing Malaysian government concern over the lawlessness in Thailand's southern Muslim-populated areas (while a small fragment of the overall Thai population, at less than 4 percent, they are geographically concentrated in the south on the Thai-Malay frontier). Groups with a dizzying array of names (Pattani United

Liberation Organization; Mujahideen Islamic Pattani Group; United Front for the Independence of Pattani [Bersatu]; Barasi Revolusi Nasional; Barisan National Pember-Basan Pattani, etc.) operate in the region. Recent efforts by some of these groups have led to the deaths of soldiers and police on the Thai side of the border, including one dramatic raid in which the rebels seized numerous automatic weapons and explosives from a Thai army depot. Although some of these groups are no more than bandit organizations with imaginary political agendas, many are potentially linked to the broader radical Islamic movement that has spread across the region.

The regional Islamic movement is spearheaded by the high-profile JI, whose founders and main operatives originated in Indonesia but whose base of operations in the late 1980s and early 1990s was peninsular Malaysia. As noted in Table 2, JI is the most prominent of the many violent radical Islamic movements in the region. Riduan Isamuddin, better known as Hambali (the apparent instigator of the 2002 Bali bombing in Indonesia), lived and worked openly in Malaysia, only going underground in 2000 when a wave of church bombings swept across Indonesia. He and his ethnic Chinese (but Muslim) Malaysian wife were arrested in Thailand in 2003. In an effort to avoid additional U.S. pressure (while still trying to avoid serious radical Islamic violence in Malaysia), the authorities in Kuala Lumpur have taken an increasingly active role in disrupting JI and like-minded groups within the country. In many cases this apparently has meant that they have simply driven the problem north into Thailand, which has fewer domestic public opinion-related constraints on acting violently and in open concert with U.S. forces against these organizations.

Current and Potential Military Conflict
The old threat of Sino-Malay ethnic tensions seems remote in comparison to the more immediate radical Islamic challenge facing Malaysian authorities. Even more unlikely is the emergence of a credible conventional (or unconventional) threat from neighboring states such as long-time rival Indonesia. In the short run, radical Islamic violence appears to be the most likely peril confronting Kuala Lumpur. Yet while neighboring states have seen a spike in such violence (including the 2002 Bali bombing and 2003 Jakarta Marriott Hotel attack in Indonesia, plus a host of less well-publicized incidents there; thwarted al-Qaeda efforts in Singapore to attack U.S. and other interests; the sudden explosion of Islamic violence in southern Thailand; and the arrest of Hambali north of Bangkok), very little seems to have transpired within Malaysia. This may be due to the rigorous enforcement efforts of an effective police state (Malaysia's Internal Security Act has long been a mainstay of the autocratic prime minister Mahathir bin Mohamad's efforts to silence his opponents). The absence of violence may also be due to the lack of a large-scale public movement sympathetic to radical Islamism (as the most developed Muslim majority state, perhaps Malaysia cannot serve as an effective incubator of radical Islamism). At least equally likely is the possibility that a tacit agreement has existed among radical Islamic elements that Malaysia would be one of the places to be kept off-limits from attacks, so as to use it more freely as a base for rest and refitting, logistical support, and so forth. The 2000 al-Qaeda summit meeting (noted in

Table 2) that took place in Malaysia may be an indication that this latter explanation applies (or at least applied in the pre-9–11 world).

Whatever the explanation, it seems clear that the outgoing administration of Mahathir bin Mohamad, as well as the newly minted regime of Prime Minister Abdullah bin Ahmad Badawi, cannot help but be seen by Washington as fully supporting the campaign against al-Qaeda. To do less in a climate of finger-pointing, preemption, and evidence of a pre-9–11 al-Qaeda presence in Malaysia would be foolhardy. Both the former and current leaders have, therefore, made the best of a bad situation, linking their domestic opponents to radical Islamism in its most virulent form. The second-largest political party in Malaysia, ranking after the long-ruling UMNO (United Malays National Organization) of Mahathir bin Mohamad, is the PAS, or Islamic Party of Malaysia. In the context of the global war on terrorism, to be able to link his closest opponents (rightly or wrongly) with al-Qaeda would be of considerable advantage to the prime minister.

In mid-1997, economic crises swept across the world, reaching from Brazil to Russia. Southeast Asia in general and Indonesia in particular was severely affected by the crisis. Characterized by capital flight and currency instability, coupled with the inevitable inflation of consumer prices on imports, this crisis struck all classes in the region quite severely. Although Malaysia weathered the storm better than most other countries in the region, economic hardship and popular resentment of the government's corruption (previously concealed by the constant influx of foreign investment and petrodollars) increased. Internal political pressures on the UMNO government of

Mahathir increased, to which he responded by attacking his erstwhile allies. Anwar Ibrahim, a onetime student leader of the Islamic movement in Malaysia coopted by UMNO and groomed for succession to the throne, became a particularly prominent target of Mahathir's wrath. His trial, conviction, and imprisonment on widely assumed-to-be trumped-up charges created a regional and even global political firestorm.

In reality the challenge posed by mainstream moderate Islamic politicians like Anwar Ibrahim to the Malaysian state pale in comparison to the threats from transnational radical groups such as JI and other al-Qaeda-affiliated organizations. Since JI's membership and ultimate goals transcend the boundaries of Malaysia, Singapore, Indonesia, Papua New Guinea, Brunei, Thailand, and even Australia, the response to its threat requires a regional effort. With Indonesian elections on the horizon in 2004, the political fate of moderate-to-radical Islamic elements in that voting will have significant consequences for all regional relationships, especially the Malaysian-Indonesian dyad. Other affected linkages will include the unique alliance system known as the Association of Southeast Asian Nations (ASEAN), founded in 1967 at the same time as the transition within Indonesia from the radical expansionist nationalism of Sukarno to the status quo military government of Suharto. Although conceived as a largely economic structure, ASEAN has sometimes served security roles.

Alliance Structure

Even though ASEAN is perhaps Malaysia's most well-known semiformal alliance, Malaysia's Mahathir was once known for his role in touting organizations that symbolically (but rarely practically) challenged the existing distribution of economic, military, and soft power in the world. Foremost among these organizations was the Non-aligned Movement (NAM), which held meetings in Malaysia just prior to the onset of the 2003 war in Iraq. Much noise was made at the meeting, particularly by Mahathir himself, but in practical terms, NAM did not lead to the creation of any meaningful movement toward developing world unity against U.S. policy. The security aspects of NAM remain marginal at best, as does the Organization of the Islamic Conference, of which Malaysia is also a prominent member.

ASEAN, on the other hand, is a much smaller, more focused, and potentially effective organization. Indonesia has, from time to time, suggested that ASEAN might serve a more security-focused role in addition to its largely economic function. Recently the government in Jakarta has suggested that ASEAN might have a multilateral military role in defusing the growing Islamic-fueled tension in southern Thailand. ASEAN's members (Brunei, Cambodia, Indonesia, Laos, Malaysia, Myanmar, the Philippines, Singapore, Thailand, and Vietnam) have already agreed to the establishment of a cooperative law enforcement center based in Indonesia to deal with transnational terrorist threats. An overt military role, however, seems unlikely in the short run, but if the security situation in southern Thailand bordering Malaysia continues to deteriorate, that might change. Although Malaysia may have common security concerns with its neighbors, the problem of illegal immigrants in the country creates obstacles to cooperation. Over 70 percent of the estimated 380,000 illegal immigrants come from Indonesia, and efforts by Malaysia to expel them for either security or economic reasons have led to great discord within ASEAN.

Size and Structure of the Military

The Malaysian armed forces have a total of 96,000 active and 49,800 reserve forces available, with the bulk of them concentrated in the army. The army consists of 80,000 active-duty troops, organized in four combat divisions and equipped with relatively little in the way of heavy weaponry. Although estimates from the late 1990s indicate that the army possessed fewer than thirty armored fighting vehicles, the most recent defense budgets call for a massive increase in armaments (purportedly as much as a tenfold increase in tanks alone).

The Royal Malaysian Navy consists of only four large combat vessels, with ten times as many coastal combat and patrol boats of various sizes. Plans exist for the acquisition of at least one submarine. Its 8,000 personnel are precisely matched in the Royal Malaysian Air Force, which fields a variety of aircraft from 1960s-era MiGs to the latest high-tech fighters and fighter-bombers. As noted previously, Malaysia is in the process of trying to acquire F/A-18 Hornets from the United States. Additionally, it is seeking MiG-29 multirole fighters from Russia and European-built Hawk–2000 ground attack aircraft. Collectively, the total personnel in the armed forces of Malaysia number 145,800, including active (96,000) and reserve (49,800) elements of all four branches.

Budget

The aggressive proposed armaments program for the period ending in 2005 would see a massive increase in Malaysia's defense budget, much above the current level of $1.7 billion or a fraction over 2 percent of its gross domestic product (GDP). Whether Malaysia can sustain such an ambitious program in light of the global financial downturn of 2000–2001 is an open question. Many of the armed forces' proposed outlays were deferred into the indefinite future, reflecting the rather volatile trajectory of the Malaysian defense budget over the last fifteen years. From 1988 to 2003, the lowest commitment to defense expenditures (expressed as a percent of GDP) occurred in 1998 and 2000 (1.6 and 1.7, respectively). The highest outlays were seen in 1991 (3.0), 1992 (3.0), and 1993 (2.9). Since then, the budget has slowly declined, with precipitous drops before and after the Asian financial crisis of the late 1990s. In dollar terms the fluctuations seem less drastic, with defense expenditures of $882 million in 1988 rising to a peak of $1.879 billion in 1995, declining to a recent low of $1.248 billion in 1998, then returning to the $1.5–2.0 billion range in the aftermath of the 9–11 attacks.

Civil-Military Relations/The Role of the Military in Domestic Politics

A paramilitary force of roughly 20,000 men often fills the space between the military and civilian governing apparatus in Malaysia. Unlike most other states in the region (especially Indonesia), the military does not play an obviously dominant role in the political process. Instead, UMNO, a national political party dedicated to ethnic Malay predominance in the political process, serves as the primary enforcer of state will against would-be opponents. The armed forces are overwhelmingly composed of ethnic Malays, in spite of their overall share of Malaysia's population (50 percent).

The most important role the armed forces have played historically in Malaysian domestic politics have come during periods of regional tension, especially with Indonesia. Fears—real and imagined—that portions of the nonethnic Malay community might serve as a fifth column at the behest of regional rivals (Indonesia and China) have led to internal military deployments to intimidate those minority communities and forestall any unrest. Since the demise of President Sukarno of Indonesia (who almost single-handedly created and sustained the Konfrontasi over Borneo), the internal use of the Malaysian military to contain threats from minority ethnic communities has markedly declined.

In the contemporary period it is the threat of transnational nonstate actors—regional Islamic terrorist movements in particular—that consume the domestic security concerns of the military. Although the 2004 elections saw an increase in the power of the ruling UMNO party—largely at the expense of Islamic political movements—this does not imply a rapid erosion of violent pro-Islamic groups in Malaysia and surrounding areas. In fact, the failure of democratically oriented political Islam will probably lead to increases in Islamic political violence, including terrorism, since the ballot path has not proven successful for Islamists. This leads to heightened pressure on the military to serve as a domestic security force (indeed, it was employed in that way during the elections of 2004). An attack similar to the one in Bali is expected to come sooner or later to Malaysia, leading to constant tension among defense and security forces in the country. The parameters of these tensions are spelled out in the following section.

Terrorism

As noted elsewhere, Malaysia has perhaps unintentionally played host to a variety of groups that engage in violence, including acts of terrorism. Although in most cases these actions are not directed at the Malaysian state, the potential for a sudden upsurge in terrorism is palpable. Especially given the continued expansion of Malaysian security sweeps against radical Islamists (and moderate Islamists deemed political threats to the hegemony of the long-ruling UMNO), it is not unlikely that problems on the scale of those confronting Indonesia or the southern extremities of Thailand may emerge at some time in the near future.

The nature of Malaysia's terrorist problem varies on a regional basis. In Sarawak and Sabah, for example, the primary source of political tension (and therefore likely generator of political violence and terrorism) is the ethnic Malay-indigene rivalry. In this context, indigenous resistance may take the form of *lumpen insurgency*, where tribal organization is not present, or *clan insurgency*, where traditional social structures remain intact (Mackinlay 2000, 44, 55–56). On mainland Malaysia, Sino-Malay tensions often run high, but are unlikely to manifest themselves in a violent manner, although spontaneous ethnic rioting may move into the realm of lumpen insurgency. But given the strength of the Malaysian state, it seems unlikely that any form of violence other than a popular insurgency (waged, presumably, by Islamic elements against the government) could be sus-

tained for very long (Mackinlay 2000, 66–67). The historical guarantee of Malay hegemony over the non-Malay minority (which is just barely outnumbered by the bumiputera) makes such a conflict unlikely, although the parallels with Indonesia are intriguing and disturbing.

In the case of both states, an ethnic bloc comprising around half of the overall population dominates the levers of political power while struggling to work out the precise relationship between its Islamic identity and the broader national community (in Malaysia, the 50 percent bumiputera Malay population; in Indonesia, the 45 percent Javanese population). The more compact geography of Malaysia, coupled with its superior economic performance, has thus far spared the country the widespread jihadi struggles that have plagued the geographic, economic, and cultural margins of the Indonesian archipelago.

In conclusion, the most serious terrorist challenge confronting the Malaysian state is from transnational Islamists who seek not to dismember the polity, but to seize control of it and transform it. The lead group in this process is JI, responsible for a number of attacks over the past several years. The name dates back to the 1970s, although it is not clear that the organization is that old. JI owes its existence to the Darul Islam movement, which sought to impose an Islamic theocracy in Java, Sumatra, and other islands of the Indonesian archipelago. Abu Bakar Bashir, the head of JI, began his radical Islamist career as a member of Darul Islam. He was imprisoned for his affiliation with the outlawed group, fled to Malaysia in 1985, and began to recruit radical Islamists to fight in Afghanistan while raising funds from Saudi Arabia for his group. He returned to Indonesia when

Suharto fell from power in 1998 and opened a religious school on Java. The group has been held responsible for attacks in the Philippines in 2000 and was linked to the Ramzi Ahmed Yousef plot to simultaneously hijack eleven U.S. airliners over the Pacific in 1995. Also in 2000 JI supported a wave of bombings against churches in Indonesia. Its most significant action was, of course, the mass casualty attack on the island of Bali in 2002. Thus the counterterrorist challenges of Malaysia and Indonesia are fused together and defy resolution without regional cooperation.

The Bali attack, which took the lives of 202 civilians, finally prodded the Indonesian state into action. Before that event, authorities in Jakarta were reluctant to take on an additional challenge, fearing that they would provoke an even more violent backlash from the radical Islamic community. The United States had actually not designated JI as a foreign terrorist organization until it was linked to the Bali bombing. Since that attack there has been one other attack serious enough to gain international attention—the bombing at the Marriott hotel in Jakarta that took 12 lives. Meanwhile, in Malaysia the authorities have been much slower in turning their attention to such Islamic groups. Hambali (the nom de guerre of Riduan Isamuddin), thought to be the number two figure in the group, has a wife who is an ethnic Chinese Malay convert to Islam. He operated openly in the country before going underground in 2000. He and his wife were apprehended in Thailand in 2003, and his presence there, along with the surge in Islamic violence in the southern extremities of the country, may indicate a shift in JI tactics away from Indonesia and toward southern Thailand. This shift may indicate a significant amount of

JI travel through, over, or around Malaysia, something about which the government in Kuala Lumpur is quite concerned.

Hambali is currently in U.S. custody at an undisclosed location (presumably Diego Garcia, the British Indian Ocean Territories), but Indonesian authorities have begun to prepare for his eventual transferal to their custody. The JI spiritual leader, Abu Bakar Bashir, meanwhile has been tried, convicted, and sentenced for his role as leader of the group held responsible for the Bali attack. Although his trial was an indication of shifting attitudes among top Indonesian politicians about the seriousness of the JI threat, the sentence he received (four years in jail) indicates how intimidated the political system is by JI. Still, the jailing of Bashir, the seizure of Hambali, and the arrest of over 200 JI members in the last two years may reduce the group's effectiveness—in Indonesia at least—for some time to come. A large-scale sweep has netted many Malaysian citizens as well, including current and former officers of the Malaysian armed forces active in Indonesia, Mindanao, Singapore, and Malaysia itself. The linkages between the global jihadi movement and Malaysian citizens are of great concern to U.S. and Malaysian authorities.

Relationship with the United States

The U.S.-Malaysian relationship has always been paradoxically close and distant and is perhaps more complicated now than at any time since the rise to power of Mahathir bin Mohamad in 1981. Simultaneously an advocate for world trade and a staunch protectionist, an anti-Islamist and a pseudo-Islamic nationalist, a semi-elected democrat and an autocrat, Mahathir remains a collection of contradictions. When he stepped down from power after more than twenty-two years in office, Mahathir had some sharp parting words for the United States. Attacking both U.S. policy toward the Islamic world (especially in Israel and Iraq, but also as it related to the toppling of the Taliban regime in Afghanistan) and the radical Islamic response to the United States (i.e., al-Qaeda-style mass casualty terrorism), the Malaysian strongman lived up to his lifelong reputation for alienating all sides and staking out his own unique political position. Mahathir's closing remarks included a significant element of anti-Semitic conspiracy mongering, and when the world press took him to task he acerbically retorted that their response only proved his point that a Judaic cabal was "out to get him." Mahathir's successor has shown less rhetorical flash or confrontational hyperbole, but Prime Minister Badawi had only been in office a few weeks at the time of this writing. The uncertain path facing Malaysia is made less clear by lack of a public track record for the new leader, given his predecessor's penchant for total control of the levers of power.

Both governments face a common threat in the form of radical Islamism, but one has a sizable population devoted to the imposition of an Islamic state and a smaller minority dedicated to achieving that goal by indiscriminately violent means. Notwithstanding the war in Iraq, which did much to move the two governments farther apart (at least rhetorically), Washington and Kuala Lumpur have much in common. The aggressive stance that Malaysia takes toward drug trafficking wins many supporters at the conservative end of the U.S. political spectrum. At the same time, Malaysia horrifies the human rights advocacy community. The

long-term threat posed by China remains a central Malaysian concern, more so since its sizable ethnic Chinese minority has, more than once, provided a bridgehead for Beijing-sponsored leftist insurgencies in Borneo and mainland Malaysia. Proposed sales of F/A-18 Hornets to Malaysia reflect the mutual desire of the two states to continue to pursue a doctrine of containment toward Chinese influence in the South China Sea. The global war on terrorism has accelerated direct contacts between the U.S. Department of Defense and Malaysian authorities, including the training and operation of U.S. Special Operations Command elements in the country and the presence of roughly 1,500 Malaysian officers and other ranks in various U.S. military educational programs.

The most notable cooperative effort between the two states is the annual Cooperation Afloat Readiness and Training (CARAT) exercise, conducted with elements of the Malaysian naval forces, other regional powers, and the U.S. Pacific Command. Although normally focused on seaborne rescue and antipiracy efforts (obvious areas of shared interest), the CARAT 2002 exercise included an antiterrorist element as well.

The Future

As in neighboring Indonesia, the demise of the long-ruling autocratic regime of Malaysia leaves ample room for speculation regarding the security challenges confronting the government. Prime Minister Badawi has not been in office sufficiently long to form conclusions regarding how he will act toward the moderate and extremist forces of political Islam that battle his UMNO party and each other. His own multiethnic origin (he is a

Muslim of partially Chinese descent) indicates at least the symbolic choices that the UMNO will make in the coming years. Attempting to retain both ethnic harmony and a special place for Islam within the polity is a difficult balancing act, which Badawi may or may not be able to execute. Meanwhile, neighboring Indonesia teeters on the brink of either a new era of democratic openness or a cataclysmic internal conflict—or, perhaps Jakarta will find a way to negotiate the difficult waters between radical Islamism and ethnic harmony as well. Meanwhile, the question of China's regional hegemony looms to the north. How—and if—the transforming Malaysian state deals with these multiple security concerns is a difficult question.

References, Recommended Readings, and Websites

Books
Anderson, Benedict. 1991. *Imagined Communities*. Rev. ed. London: Verso.
Djiwandono, J. Soedjati. 1996. *Konfrontasi Revisited: Indonesia's Foreign Policy under Soekarno*. Jakarta: Centre for Strategic and International Studies.
Harvey, Barbara. 1977. *Permesta: Half a Rebellion*. Ithaca, NY: Cornell University Press.
Hibbard, Scott, and David Little. 1997. *Islamic Activism and U.S. Foreign Policy*. Washington, DC: U.S. Institute of Peace.
Husain, Mir Zohair. 2003. *Global Islamic Politics*, 2nd ed. New York: Longman.
Huxley, Tim. 2002. *Disintegrating Indonesia?* Oxford: Oxford University Press.
Kepel, Gilles. 2002. *Jihad: The Trail of Political Islam*. Cambridge, MA: Belknap Press.
Mackie, J. A. C. 1974. *Konfrontasi: The Indonesia-Malaysia Dispute, 1963–1966*. Oxford: Oxford University Press.
Mackinlay, John. 2000. *Globalisation and Insurgency*. Oxford: Oxford University Press.

The Military Balance, 2003–2004. London: International Institute for Strategic Studies.
Smith, E. D. 1985. *Malaya and Borneo*. London: Ian Allan Ltd.
Stockholm International Peace Research Institute (SIPRI). *SIPRI Yearbook 2003*. New York: Humanities Press.
Weekes, Richard. 1984. *Muslim Peoples: A World Ethnographic Survey*, Vol. 1, 2d ed. Westport, CT: Greenwood Press.
———. 1984. *Muslim Peoples: A World Ethnographic Survey*, Vol. 2, 2d ed. Westport, CT: Greenwood Press.
Wiarda, Howard. 2004. *Political Development in Emerging Nations*. Belmont, CA: Wadsworth.

Articles/Newspapers
Anonymous. 2002. "In the Region." *Defence Brief*, 89, May:1.
———. 2004. "Who Will Watch the Watchdogs?" *The Economist* 370, no. 8363:39.

Websites
Center for Defense Information. *Malaysia:* http://www.cdi.org/issues/Asia/malaysia.html.
Central Intelligence Agency (CIA). 2005. *World Factbook:* http://www.cia.gov.
Council on Foreign Relations. *Terrorism: Q&A: Jemaah Islamiyah:* http://www.cfrterrorism.org/groups/jemaah2.html.
Custom Wire. *Anti-Terror Official: U.S. Personnel in Indonesia to Negotiate Possible Access to Hambali.* http://search.epnet.com/direct.asp?an=CX2004039W2218&db=mth.
———. *Indonesia Proposes ASEAN Peacekeeping Force, Extradition Treaty to Bolster Regional Security:* http://search.epnet.com/direct.asp?an=CX2004053W8536&db=mth.
———. *Southeast Asian Peacekeeping Force Is Unnecessary: Thai FM:* http://search.epnet.com/direct.asp?an=CX2004053H2105&db=mth.
GlobalSecurity.org. *Malaysia:* http://www.globalsecurity.org/military/world/malaysia/index.html.
Kementerian Pertahanan Malaysia (Official Website of the Ministry of Defense): http://www.mod.gov.my/ [try to find official govt military Website].

Monterey Institute of International Studies. 2002. *Conventional Terrorism Chronology: Incidents Involving Sub-National Actors Resulting in Death or Injury:* http://cns.miis.edu/pubs/reports/pdfs/conv2k2.pdf.

Virtual Information Center. *Primer: Separatism in Southern Thailand:* http://www.vicinfo.org/SEAsia/thailandpage.htm.

———. *Special Press Summary: Unrest in Southern Thailand:* http://www.vicinfo.org/SEAsia/thailandpage.htm.

Mexico

Marc R. Rosenblum

Geography and History

Mexico is bordered on the north by the United States; on the east by the United States, the Gulf of Mexico, and the Caribbean Sea; on the south by Belize and Guatemala; and on the west by the Pacific Ocean. It is located between 32°32″ and 144°54″ north latitude and 117°01′ and 86°83′ west longitude. The country's total landmass is 1.97 million sq. km, approximately three times the size of the state of Texas. Mexico is located in one of the earth's most dynamic tectonic areas, and its capital (Mexico City) was struck by a magnitude 8.2 earthquake in 1985. The climate ranges from desert in the north, through temperate mountainous regions in the center of the country, to tropical jungles in the south. Approximately 13.3 percent of the land is considered arable.

Mexico is divided into thirty-one states and a federal district, and its geographic diversity has produced highly variegated settlement patterns among its 104.9 million residents. The large northwestern states of Baja California Norte, Sonora, Chihuahua, and Coahuila are dominated by deserts and have population densities of less than 10 people per sq. km. But the states of Mexico and Puebla surrounding the capital city have population densities of more than 200 people per sq. km. Mexico City is one of the world's largest cities with over 17 million inhabitants in the metropolitan area and has a population density of 5,500 people per sq. km. The national average is 52 people per sq. km (2002 estimate). Mexico's population growth rate peaked at 3.2 percent in 1970 and has fallen since that time to 1.43 percent (2003 estimate). The United Nations projects Mexico's population to increase by 50.3 percent between 2000 and 2050.

The Spanish colonial viceroyalty of New Spain was founded in 1519 following the conquest of the Aztec empire by Hernán Cortés and his army of conquistadors. Cortés' army was heavily outnumbered, consisting of fewer than 1,000 men and two dozen horses, against a heavily militarized Aztec empire with a population approaching 30 million people. Nonetheless Cortés exploited technological advantages (muskets and cannons), made strategic alliances with non-Aztec peoples who resented their imperial Aztec masters, and benefited from a smallpox outbreak that decimated the indigenous population. Thus, in less than two years Cortés' army extracted a surrender from the Aztec king Moctezuma and destroyed the imperial capital city of Tenochtitlán, possibly the largest city in the world at the time (150,000–250,000 residents).

The colony of New Spain included all of Central America with the exception of Panama and extended north throughout the modern states of Texas, New Mexico,

Arizona, Colorado, Utah, and California. The sovereign state of Mexico that emerged following the colony's war of independence from Spain (1810–1821) initially sought to hold these territories. But the states of Central America declared independence in 1824, and Texas seceded as an independent republic in 1836. Texas secession remained unresolved until the U.S.-Mexican War (known in Mexico as the War of the North American Invasion) of 1846–1848, during which the United States seized almost half of Mexico's territory. Mexico's final territorial change occurred in 1855 when the United States purchased the Mesilla Valley in southern New Mexico for $10 million through the Gladsen purchase.

In addition to these territorial changes, Mexico's first forty years of independence were characterized by a high degree of instability and internal conflict as regional military strongmen, or *caudillos,* battled for control of the national territory. Indeed, Mexico was ruled by fifty separate presidents between 1823 and 1861, including thirty-five army officers. The modern state was finally consolidated under the leadership of the economically liberal but politically autocratic general Porfirio Díaz, who led a coup in 1876 in the name of competitive democracy and no presidential reelection, but then went on to rule the country for all but four years between 1876 and 1910, a period known as the Porfiriato.

Díaz's liberal economic policies produced high levels of foreign investment, economic modernization, and growth, but failed to satisfy elites' demands for competitive elections. Thus, Francisco Madero's 1910 Plan de San Luís Potosí called for armed resistance to this end, setting in motion the Mexican Revolution (1910–1920). Four distinct revolutionary armies contended for power before moderate Constitutionalists consolidated their hold on the government between 1917 and 1920.

Nonetheless, more radical elements had a lasting influence, shaping the Mexican constitution of 1917. Article 27 of the constitution promised that the land that had been consolidated during the Díaz period would be redistributed to communal peasant groups and also established that any land not serving a useful social function could be appropriated by the state. Article 3 of the constitution radically limited the role of the church by placing restrictions on its right to hold property or organize political parties and by mandating free public secular education for all Mexicans. Article 123 established the most far-reaching labor rights of any country at the time, including an eight-hour workday and six-day workweek, a minimum wage, wage equality regardless of gender or nationality, and the right to organize labor unions and to strike for higher wages. Although later governments were selective in their enforcement of these provisions, Mexico's revolution is recognized as the first social revolution of the twentieth century.

The victorious northern "revolutionary family" consolidated its military position over the next decade, but political stability remained elusive until a 1928–1929 settlement brought rival factions into a single political party that resolved succession disputes and centralized policymaking. Eventually known as the Institutional Revolutionary Party (PRI), the party became the foundation for what Peruvian novelist Mario Vargas Llosa referred to as Mexico's "perfect dictatorship": exploiting revolutionary rhetoric, a rigid monopolistic corporatist structure, and patronage politics that ruled without interruption for seventy-one years.

PRI's hold on power began to unravel after the massive 1985 Mexico City earthquake. A liberal faction split from PRI to form the Party of the Democratic Revolution and probably won a majority of votes in the 1988 presidential election, though electoral officials eventually certified the PRI candidate as the winner. Nonetheless, a series of reforms ensued to expand opportunities for opposition parties and to improve electoral oversight, culminating in PRI's loss of its majority status within congress in 1997 and the presidential election of Vicente Fox of the pro-business National Action Party in 2000.

As with most of Latin America, Mexico's economic development strategy throughout most of the post–World War II period was heavily influenced by *dependencia* thinking, which called for a strategy of import-substituting industrialization (ISI). That is, Mexico employed tariffs and state subsidies to create manufacturing jobs primarily for the domestic market. The strategy was initially highly successful as the creation of a new urban workforce fueled demand for the consumer goods being produced, and the Mexican economy grew at a real annual rate of over 6 percent between 1940 and 1970.

ISI faced a number of structural limitations. First, Mexico's emphasis on domestic sales failed to generate the hard currency needed to pay for imported technology and manufactured inputs. As a result, ISI growth was highly dependent on government deficits and sovereign debt accumulation. Second, ISI growth during the 1950s and early 1960s was, in retrospect, easy because a large previously unmet market for consumer and durable goods existed. As that market became saturated, however, Mexican industry faced a problem of overproduction, and job creation became difficult. The latter problem was exacerbated by high population growth and rural-urban migration in the postwar period. While a national population growth rate of around 3 percent meant that the overall population doubled every twenty-five years, growth of major cities approached 7 percent, and the population of Mexico City increased from 3 million to 4.5 million in just six years after 1952. A fourth obstacle to sustained growth through ISI was the inefficient and corrupt Mexican state, which employed subsidies as a political tool rather than for economic reasons.

An economic crisis was postponed by discovery of vast new petroleum reserves during the 1960s, followed by the 1973 global oil shocks, which combined to produce an increase in Mexican oil production from 0.55 to 3.0 million barrels per day between 1973 and 1982. Nonetheless, rising global interest rates, the 1981 U.S. recession, and a sharp drop in oil prices in 1982 brought inevitable collapse. In August of that year, after three successive peso devaluations, Mexico defaulted on payments of its foreign debt (see Sidebar 1).

The elimination of foreign financing forced Mexico to make radical economic adjustments during the 1980s, including privatizing state-owned industries, cutting state spending, minimizing inflation, and opening trade markets. These changes undermined economic growth during Latin America's so-called lost decade, as Mexico's economy grew at an annual rate of just 0.1 percent over the next eight years while inflation and unemployment remained high.

Nonetheless, Mexico's unified political system facilitated its successful implementation of the Washington consensus

Sidebar 1   The Mexican Debt Crisis

Following the advice of leading economists, Mexico pursued a policy of import-substituting industrialization (ISI) after 1930, with the state actively promoting domestic manufacturing. Postwar demand and urban-rural migration fueled growth, but industry relied on subsidies and tariffs. This shortcoming was relatively unproblematic during the 1950s, thanks to high levels of foreign direct investment, and during the 1960s, thanks to high levels of U.S. aid through the Alliance for Progress. But during the 1970s these sources dried up; and European banks—flush with OPEC petrodollars—targeted the developing world for sovereign loans. Thus, Mexico's debt climbed from U.S.$6 billion in 1970, to U.S.$20 billion in 1976, to U.S.$80 billion—a staggering 42 percent of gross domestic product (GDP)—with the collapse of global oil markets (and Mexico's main source of revenue) in 1982. When Mexico subsequently failed to make a regularly scheduled interest payment, it ushered in a new era of strict conditionality and economic austerity (the "lost decade") throughout Latin America.

Source
World Bank. 2001. World Development Indicators [CD-ROM]. Washington, DC: World Bank.

reforms, and by the 1990s Mexico's relatively high growth rate (average of 5 percent, 1997–2000) was considered a neoliberal success story. Nonetheless, growth remains problematic (–0.3 percent in 2001; 0.9 percent in 2002), and Mexico's 40 percent poverty rate continues to loom as a major social problem in the twenty-first century.

Mexico's 2002 gross domestic product (GDP) was US$637 billion. Of this, 69 percent consists of services (employing 56 percent of the labor force, 27 percent consists of industry (employing 24 per-

Table 1   Mexico: Key Statistics

Type of government	Federal republic (democracy)
Population (millions)	104.9 (2003)
Religion	Roman Catholic 89% (2003)
Main industries	Food and beverages, tobacco, chemicals, iron and steel, petroleum, mining, textiles, clothing, motor vehicles, consumer durables, tourism
Main security threats	Domestic guerrilla movements
Defense spending (% GDP)	.5 (2002)
Size of military (thousands)	193 (2001)
Number of civil wars since 1945	0
Number of interstate wars since 1945	0

Sources
Central Intelligence Agency Website. 2005. CIA *World Factbook*. http://www.cia.gov/cia/publications/factbook/ (accessed May 15, 2005).
Stockholm International Peace Research Institute (SIPRI): SIPRI Internet. www.sipri.org.

cent of the labor force), and 4 percent of the economy consists of agricultural product (employing 20 percent of the labor force). Mexican trade and foreign investment is overwhelmingly oriented toward the United States, which buys 83 percent of Mexico's exports (next largest source: Canada, 5 percent), provides 71 percent of Mexico's imports (Germany, 3.5 percent), and provides 67 percent of Mexico's foreign direct investment (European Union, 19 percent).

Regional Geopolitics

Civil wars in Central America were a source of instability between the mid-1970s and early 1990s. The wars in El Salvador (1980–1992) and Nicaragua (1981–1990) both pitted explicitly Marxist groups (the guerrilla Farabundo Martí Liberation Front [FMLN] in El Salvador and the ruling Sandinista Party in Nicaragua) against anticommunist forces enjoying substantial U.S. support. The effects of these conflicts within Mexico mainly impacted the increased transmigration of war refugees en route to the United States and generated strong U.S.-Mexican tensions over the resolution of the conflicts.

Guatemala's civil war was longer lasting (1961–1996), occurred immediately across the border from Mexico, and was especially bloody, with at least 200,000 (mainly civilians) killed or "disappeared" during the thirty-six-year conflict. In addition, while the war began as an economic conflict between Marxist guerrillas (the Guatemalan National Revolutionary Unity [URNG] movement) and groups loyal to the landed aristocracy, most of the fighting after the 1960s reflected ethnic conflict between European and mixed-race elites and ethnic Mayans, who had

historically moved freely between Guatemala and the Mexican state of Chiapas to work in seasonal agriculture. For all of these reasons, the Guatemalan civil war had an enormous impact on southern Mexico, which hosted 40,000 official Guatemalan refugees and an estimated 50,000 to 100,000 undocumented Guatemalan immigrants by the end of the war. Mexican sources blame Guatemalan guerrillas for contributing to the emergence of the Zapatista National Liberation Army in Chiapas during the 1980s.

All three of these regional civil wars were resolved during the 1990s. In Nicaragua, the Sandinistas stepped down following the election (with substantial U.S. financial support) of the opposition candidate Violeta Chamorro in 1990. In El Salvador, Mexico and the United States both participated in negotiations that eventually produced a peace treaty signed by the government and the FMLN in 1992. Mexico also played a role in support of Guatemala's UN-brokered peace process, which culminated in the signing of a series of treaties between the URNG and the government of Guatemala between 1994 and 1996.

El Salvador is often cited as a successful model of the negotiated settlement of a civil war, as former guerrillas participate widely in civil society and, through their political parties, within the national government. Nonetheless, the transition to neoliberal economics has depressed postwar economic growth in all three countries (ten-year average per capita GDP growth rates are 1.2 percent in Guatemala, 1.6 percent in El Salvador, and 1.8 percent in Nicaragua). In Nicaragua, future economic prospects are further dimmed by rampant corruption within both major political parties and a growing wave of crime and urban violence. In

Guatemala, economic tensions have contributed to lingering civil unrest, including a 2003 national teachers' strike. Nonetheless, there are no active guerrilla movements or armed conflicts within the region and little likelihood of spillover effects within Mexico.

Indeed, whereas regional geopolitics between the 1960s and early 1990s were characterized by armed conflict and refugee flows, the trend in the last decade has been toward increased cooperation and economic integration. Between 1995 and 2000, Mexico signed bilateral free trade agreements with every Central American country except Panama. In 2001, the Fox administration initiated the Plan Puebla Panama, designed to expand infrastructure (especially roads, telecommunications equipment, and electrical connections) and promote trade among the nine southernmost states in Mexico and the seven countries of Central America.

Conflict Past and Present

Although Mexico had an exceptionally violence-prone "long nineteenth century" (beginning with its war of independence in 1810, and lasting through the final battles of the Mexican Revolution in 1930), its position just south of the United States has limited its external conflicts. Thus, Mexico was involved in four international wars prior to 1900, but none (apart from World War II) since the Mexican Revolution. Domestic conflict was also common throughout most of the nineteenth century, but has been limited since 1930 (see Table 2).

In comparison with the rest of Latin America, Mexico's war for independence from Spain (1810–1821) was especially protracted and geographically dispersed.

Battles were characterized by numerous overlapping cleavages including church-state relations; conflicts between *creole* elites (i.e., aristocrats born within Mexico), *peninsulares* (elites born in Spain), and *mestizo* (mixed race) and indigenous peasants and workers; and conflicts between Lockean enlightenment thinkers and those favoring a continued monarchy. Although the war for independence was initiated by a Jesuit-educated creole favoring a republican form of government (Miguel Hidalgo), the final armistice with Spain was signed by a pro-monarchy *peninsulare*, who opposed Spain's Enlightenment-influenced 1812 constitution. Thus, after gaining independence, the victorious Mexican general Agustin De Iturbide established a European-style monarchy, naming himself Emperor Augustín I. Nonetheless, the empire was short-lived as Augustín was removed in a coup just three years later.

In August 1829, a force of 3,000 Spanish soldiers landed at the Mexican port of Tampico and sought to retake Mexico. The Spanish surrendered following a three-month siege of the city, and the main legacy of the so-called Mexican-Spanish War was that it launched the thirty-year political career of victorious Mexican general Antonio López de Santa Anna.

As president, Santa Anna led the Mexican army during the Texas War for Independence six years later. North Americans (predominantly non-Catholic) had settled in Mexico's sparsely populated northern region beginning in 1821 and quickly grew to outnumber the (Catholic) Mexican population. A series of laws sought to reinforce Mexican control, including an emancipation proclamation (1829), a prohibition on new North American migration to Texas (1830), and a new

Table 2   Major Internal and International Conflicts

War	Dates	Major Parties[a]	Mortalities
War for Independence	1810–1821	**Pensiulare loyalists** Spain Pro-independence creoles	23,000
Texas War for Independence	1836	**North American "Texicans"** Mexico	2,000
Mexican-American War (War of the North American Invasion)	1846–1848	**United States** Mexico	17,000
Caste War	1847–1855	State of Merida[b] Regional Maya Indians	250,000
Reform War (La Reforma)	1858–1861	**Liberals** Conservatives	10,000
Franco-Mexican War	1862–1867	**Liberals** Conservatives + France	40,000
Mexican Revolution	1910–1920	**Consitutionalists** Zapatistas Villistas Diaz loyalists United States[c]	1,500,000
Cristero War	1926–1930	**Mexico** Catholic rebels	10,000
Mexico's "Dirty War"	1968–1982	**Mexico** Revolutionary Armed Movement (MAR) Revolutionary Armed Forces of the People (FRAP)	1,000
Chiapas Insurrection	1994 to present	**Mexico** Zapata National Liberation Army (EZLN)	400+
Guerrero Insurrection	1996 to present	**Mexico** Popular Revolution Army (EPR)	<100

[a]Victorious party in **bold.**
[b]There was no clear victor in the Caste War.
[c]The United States intervened in the Mexican Revolution on two occasions and helped prevent the Pancho Villa army from sharing in the revolutionary settlement.

Sources
Armed Conflict Events Data: Mexico 1800–1999: http://www.onwar.com/aced/nation/may/mexico/findex.htm.
Harvey, Neil. 1998. *The Chiapas Rebellion: The Struggle for Land and Democracy.* Durham, NC: Duke University Press.
Meyer, Michael C., William L. Sherman, and Susan M. Deeds. 1999. *The Course of Mexican History.* 6th ed. New York: Oxford University Press.

Constitution (1836) that established a centralized Catholic monarchy. The latter prompted rebellious Texans to declare independence.

Santa Anna's 6,000-man army won a victory at the Battle of the Alamo (March 2–6, 1836) in modern San Antonio, but the death of all 183 Texan defenders (as well as Mexico's execution of 352 Texan prisoners two weeks later following the Battle of Goliad) became rallying cries for the Texans and mobilized support from the United States. A reorganized Texas army then caught Santa Anna's troops off-guard at the Battle of San Jacinto (April 21, 1836), near modern-day Houston, and Santa Anna was forced to recognize the Republic of Texas (see Sidebar 2).

Sidebar 2   The Battle of San Jacinto (April 21, 1836)

The Battle of San Jacinto was one of the greatest military defeats in Mexican history—and a decisive victory for the Texans. Outmanned by a count of 1,500 men to 900, the Texan rebels mounted a surprise assault during the Mexicans' traditional afternoon siesta. Rallied by cries of "Remember the Alamo" and "Remember Goliad," the Texans attacked ruthlessly, and slaughtered retreating Mexicans over the objections of their commanding general Sam Houston. The battle lasted only eighteen minutes and resulted in the death of nine Texans and injuries to thirty others. The Mexicans were devastated, however, with 630 killed, 208 wounded, and 730 taken prisoner. Captured the next day, Mexican general and president Santa Anna accepted the unconditional withdrawal of Mexican forces from the entire Texas territory, including the modern U.S. states of Texas, Arizona, California, Nevada, New Mexico, Utah, and parts of Colorado, Kansas, Oklahoma, and Wyoming.

Source
Sons of DeWitt County Texas. *The Battle of San Jacinto:* http://www.tamu.edu/ccbn/dewitt/batsanjacinto.htm.

The U.S. Congress voted to annex Texas nine years later, setting in motion a chain of events leading to the Mexican-American War (1846–1848). The annexa-

tion prompted a diplomatic break, but negotiations continued over the location of the Texas-Mexico border, in dispute because Santa Anna's troops had retreated across the Rio Grande River (Rio Bravo in Mexico), rather than stopping at the Nueces River, recognized as the boundary at the time. When word leaked in Mexico that U.S. negotiators sought additional land, including modern California, an outcry ensued, and negotiations broke down.

President James Polk ordered U.S. troops into the disputed border area, and sixteen U.S. soldiers were killed or wounded in the skirmish that followed. Having essentially invaded Mexico, President Polk called for a congressional declaration of war on the grounds that Mexico had "shed American blood on American soil."

Partly as a result of political divisions within Mexico, the war was a rout. In the West, American troops claimed all of New Mexico and Colorado without firing a shot and moved into California and the Mexican state of Chihuahua with minimal resistance. A second front was established in north-central Mexico, where U.S. General Zachary Taylor marched on the Mexican city of Monterrey. Taylor's 6,000 men defeated 7,000 Mexican troops in September 1846, but Santa Anna led 20,000 reinforcements to hold the line at Monterrey in February 1847.

With Mexican troops thus spread thin, U.S. General Winfield Scott landed near the Mexican port of Veracruz in March 1847 and attacked the well-fortified port city from its unprotected interior. In a three-day siege, the Americans bombarded the city with 6,700 mortar shells, killing 1,500 Mexicans, mainly civilians. Scott's troops then began their march to Mexico City, skirting Santa Anna's defenses to attack from the rear at the Battle of Cerro Gordo (April 16–18, 1847), taking the town of Puebla without a fight. The fiercest fighting of the war occurred in the final push for Mexico City, including the bloody battle at Molina del Rey (September 7, 1847). The final battle came September 13 at the heavily fortified Chapultepec Castle; Mexican military cadets fought to the death during its defense, and these *niños heroes* (boy heroes) remain national martyrs.

Under the Treaty of Guadalupe Hidalgo that formally ended the war February 2, 1848, Mexico agreed to give up half of its national territory, including the modern U.S. states of Texas, New Mexico, Colorado, Arizona, and California, and the United States made a onetime payment of $18 million. This one-sided war and its aftermath—made more bitter by the discovery of gold in California one year later—remains a defining moment in the Mexican consciousness.

The Caste War (1847–1855) was a broadly successful rebellion by Mayan Indians seeking independence from Mexico. The central state remained weak during this period, as noted previously, and Yucatan elites revolted in 1839, relying heavily on Mayan Indian support. The resulting Merida government (which rejoined Mexico in 1843) pursued a liberal economic agenda, allowing the consolidation of large-scale plantations over Mayan objections.

Mayan leader Manueal Antonio Ay organized opposition to the reforms, but was executed on conspiracy charges in July 1847. Two of his followers staged an offensive beginning with a massacre of non-Mayas in Tepich on July 30 and spreading to the outskirts of Merida by the middle of 1848. The Mayan offensive stalled when insurgents returned to cultivate their fields, and a creole force counterattacked, killing 200,000 Mayas by the end of 1849. A final stage in the war began in 1850 when a group of Mayas underwent a religious awakening and successfully seized the eastern half of the Yucatan Peninsula. The region remained essentially autonomous from Mexico, trading with Belize, until 1901 when the Mexican army finally invaded and established the modern state of Quintana Roo.

The Reform War (*La Reforma*, 1858–1861) was, in a sense, the final battle of Mexico's war for independence: a civil war between liberals who favored a modern, secular, economically rationalized state and conservatives who favored a return to the monarchy and a strong Catholic Church. The prelude to the war was President Santa Anna's 1855 sale of the Mesilla Valley to the United States for $10 million as the latter sought a southern rail route to California. With most Mexicans still viscerally angry about the loss of territory seven years earlier, Santa Anna's opponents took advantage of popular outrage to force the conservative president from office and to pass a series of liberal, anticlerical reforms.

Conservative General Félix Zuloaga issued the Plan de Tacubaya as a call to arms in defense of the Church. When the moderate President Comonfort resigned, the liberal Chief Justice of the Supreme Court Benito Juárez and General Zuloaga each declared themselves president, with the conservatives setting up a government in Mexico City and the liberals in Veracruz. The conservatives won a series of battles in 1858, but the liberals resisted an assault on Veracruz in the spring of 1859, turning the tide of the war. At least 8,000 soldiers were killed prior to the final battle of San Miguel Calpulapan, and civilians were regularly brutalized by both sides in what was the bloodiest of Mexico's nineteenth-century civil wars.

The final international war fought on Mexican territory, the Franco-Mexican War (1862–1867), was prompted by President Juárez' subsequent decision to declare a two-year moratorium on Mexico's mounting foreign debt. Spain, Britain, and France agreed in the October 1861 Convention of London to seize the customs-house at Veracruz in order to collect payments on the debt. But once military representatives from the three states arrived, it became clear that the French intended to reestablish an imperial presence in the Americas, and British and Spanish forces withdrew.

A French army of 6,500 men marched forth from Veracruz, and were repelled in the Battle of Puebla on May 5, 1862 (in commemoration of which Mexicans now celebrate the Cinco de Mayo holiday), with Mexican General Porfirio Díaz playing a key role in the battle. A second Battle of Puebla was fought almost a year later following the arrival of 30,000 French reinforcements, who took the city after a two-month siege. With the fall of Puebla, the French occupied Mexico City without a fight and were enthusiastically welcomed by the city's conservatives and the Catholic Church.

Under the Convention of Miramar signed in October 1863, Austrian Archduke Ferdinand Maximilian agreed to become emperor of Mexico, taking on the responsibility for Mexico's debts and for the payment of 20,000 French troops remaining in Mexico. Maximilian's French army won a series of battles and forced the Juárez government in exile to retreat all the way to the northern town of El Paso (the Mexican portion of which is now known as Ciudad Juárez). But the tide turned with the end of the American Civil War, which allowed U.S. diplomatic and financial resources to lend support to Mexico against the foreign invaders (and in defense of the U.S. Monroe Doctrine). Diplomatic pressure (as well as military conflicts within Europe) forced Napoleon to withdraw his troops beginning in 1866, and Juárez's army won a series of battles during the summer before defeating Maximilian's French army at the Battle of Querétaro in February 1867.

The Mexican Revolution (1910–1920) was actually a series of overlapping civil conflicts involving a dozen separate armies and a half dozen presidential transitions. The fighting also caused between 1.5 and 2 million deaths out of a prewar population of only 15 million. The revolution was set in motion by disaffected economic elites who shared Porfirio Díaz's liberal economic ideology but demanded competitive elections. After pressing unsuccessfully for Díaz to step down prior to the 1910 presidential race, the wealthy rancher Francisco Madero announced his own candidacy for office and was promptly arrested and jailed by Díaz loyalists. Madero's Plan de San Luis Potosí called for armed resistance in support of the principle of no reelection; and when his supporters seized the town of Juárez, Díaz fled the country and Madero claimed the presidency.

Madero immediately faced a series of revolts. In the southern state of Morelos, Emiliano Zapata's Plan de Ayala (November 1911) inspired a broad-based peasant movement demanding land reform. Within months, Zapata's army occupied towns and disrupted railroad and telegraph service throughout south-central Mexico. A second challenge came from former Madero ally Pascual Orozco, who also called for land redistribution as well as labor reforms and an end to government nepotism. After initial successes, the 8,000-soldier Orozco army was defeated by General Victoriano Huerta in the Battle of Rellano (May 1912). A third challenge came from the right five months later when Díaz's nephew, Félix Díaz, led a revolt in Veracruz.

Though Díaz was quickly captured and jailed in Mexico City, he conspired from jail with fellow counterrevolutionaries and on February 9, 1913, was released by complicit federal troops. For the next ten days, known as the *Decena Trágica*, full-scale civil war raged within Mexico City, resulting in thousands of civilian casualties. Fighting came to a stop on February 18 after U.S. Ambassador Henry Lane Wilson negotiated a pact between Díaz and Madero's chief of staff Huerta that removed Madero from office and installed Huerta following a sham congressional ratification. Madero and his vice president were executed without trial.

Opposition quickly coalesced against Huerta. In the north, Madero supporters Venustiano Carranza, Alvaro Obregón, and Pancho Villa led Constitutionalist armies in the states of Coahuila, Sonora, and Chihuahua, respectively. In the south, Zapata's army also remained intact. Though not allied with the pro-Madero forces, Zapata rejected Huerta's government as equally hostile to peasant interests. Intense battles raged on both fronts, and Huerta dissolved the congress and employed conscriptions to expand the federal army tenfold to 250,000.

Although Americans had been instrumental in bringing Huerta to power, U.S. President Woodrow Wilson (elected in 1912) refused to recognize the authoritarian Huerta regime. A turning point occurred in April 1914 when U.S. sailors buying gasoline in Tampico were briefly arrested. Though the Americans were immediately released and an official apology was issued, Wilson used the incident as an excuse to intervene against Huerta, occupying the port of Veracruz and blocking Huerta's arms imports. Although the Constitutionalists objected to the U.S. occupation, which resulted in hundreds of civilian casualties, they took advantage of the diversion of federal troops to Veracruz by moving decisively on the capital, forcing Huerta to flee the country.

The various rebel armies met in the town of Auguascalientes in October 1914 to choose a provisional government, but the meeting broke down over fundamental issues. While delegates loyal to Carranza and Obregón focused on the rallying call of "effective suffrage and no reelection," Villa and Zapata supporters sought land reform and economic redistribution. When the convention chose Eulalio Gutiérrez as compromise president, Carranza rejected the choice and established a rump government in Veracruz.

The Constitutionalists gradually consolidated their military position against Villa and Zapata over the next three years. Obregón won a decisive victory over Villa's forces at the Battle of Celaya (April 1915) by employing World War I–style barbed-wire barricades and machine-gun nests against Villa's charging cavalry, killing 4,000 Villa troops and capturing 6,000 others while losing only 138 of his own men in the process. A second turning point came in March 1916 when Villa invaded the U.S. town of Columbus, New Mexico (killing eighteen Americans), to punish the United States for its diplomatic recognition of the Carranza government. In response, 6,000 U.S. soldiers under General John Pershing pursued Villa throughout northern Mexico. Though Villa was not captured, his flight prevented any future contribution to the revolution. A third turning point came the following May, when Constitutionalists passed the constitution of 1917. The progressive document, discussed previously, broadened Carranza's base of support. Fourth, in April 1919, Constitutionalist Colonel Jesús Guarjado pretended to throw his support to Zapata, and then assassinated the peasant leader.

Thus, by 1920, Carranza had effectively won Mexico's civil war, but his Constitutionalist rallying cry ("effective suffrage and no reelection") ensured that political succession remained contentious. When Carranza sought to install a political loyalist as his successor, Obregón joined forces with two other Constitutionalist generals, Adolfo de la Huerta and Plutarco Calles, and marched on the capital. Carranza fled in May and was assassinated, and Obregón assumed the presidency. Calles became president in 1924 and finally resolved the succession by establishing the official Party of the National Revolution.

A final postrevolutionary conflict erupted in 1926 when Mexico's archbishop called on Catholics to reject the anticlerical constitution of 1917. Calles responded by deporting foreign priests and closing church schools, and the archbishop declared a clerical strike beginning on July 31, 1926. In the Cristero War (1926–1930) that ensued, the federal army and pro-church forces traded atrocities, resulting in 10,000 deaths by 1930, including the assassination of Obregón. Finally, U.S. Ambassador Dwight Morrow negotiated a settlement in which Calles promised to respect the legal integrity of the Church and allow church-based religious instruction, and the Church agreed that priests would register with the state and called on clerics to lay down their arms and resume church services.

Mexico largely escaped the large-scale guerrilla movements and counterinsurgency campaigns that characterized the rest of the region during the 1960s and 1970s—but not completely. Tensions mounted in 1968 as Mexico prepared to host that year's summer Olympics, and the state responded with a heavy hand against student protesters celebrating the July 26 anniversary of the Cuban Revolution. A national student strike committee demanded the resignation of the chief of the riot police, and 500,000 protesters joined an August rally in Mexico City's Zócalo (main square), the largest antigovernment demonstration in Mexico's history. Six weeks later, on October 2, riot police opened fire on a smaller rally at Mexico's Plaza de las Tres Culturas in the district of Tlatelolco. Official reports acknowledged 43 student deaths, but unofficial estimates are that 400 were killed and at least 2,000 jailed, many for years.

The Tlatelolco massacre demobilized student protesters but spawned a number of revolutionary guerrilla groups. Two of these groups, the Movimiento Armado Revolucionario and the Fuerzas Revolucionarias Armadas del Pueblo, carried out a series of bank robberies, kidnappings, and assaults on police stations and tourists between 1970 and 1974. The most notorious guerillas were based in the state of Guerrero, under the leadership of Lucio Cabaña. When the Guerrero insurgents kidnapped the PRI gubernatorial candidate in May 1974, 10,000 army troops were dispatched to the state, eventually tracking down and killing Cabaña a year later. Partial records of this period have only recently been released, and Mexico's Human Rights Commission estimates that at least 532 dissidents were "disappeared" between 1968 and 1982. In July 2004, a Mexican special prosecutor formally accused former president Luís Echeverría and several other former government and military officials of genocide for their role in a June 10, 1971, massacre of twenty-five or more protestors in Mexico City.

Current and Potential Military Confrontation

Given its deep integration with the United States, Mexico faces no external threats, but the current period of economic and political transition has sparked substantial domestic discontent, especially among peasants whose traditional agricultural production has been jeopardized. The most significant internal threat is the Zapatista movement in the southern state of Chiapas, named for the revolutionary peasant leader. Peasant and Marxist activities in Chiapas dates from the post-1968 period, when the Maoist Fuerzas de Liberación Nacional began working with indigenous leaders seeking land distribution. The Zapata National Liberation Army (EZLN) formed in 1983 as a coalition of several peasant organizations and announced its presence to the world on January 1, 1994, when 1,600 insurgents declared war on the Mexican government and took control of seven Chiapas towns. After two weeks of intense fighting, 20,000 Mexican army troops, supported by air strikes, gained control of the area. The military reported 120 rebel deaths, but local church leaders estimated over 400.

The rebel leadership, including its media-savvy spokesperson Subcommander Marcos, retreated into the jungle highlands, and an armed truce has been in effect since February 1995. In 1996 the Zapatistas announced their willingness in principle to lay down their arms and become a legal political party, and negotiations intensified following the election of the opposition president Vicente Fox. But after the EZLN participated in a national conference on indigenous rights (accepting government protection during a caravan to the capital), they rejected the results of the meeting. As of 2004, several hundred Zapatistas soldiers continue to hold about thirty communities spread out over 15 percent of the state of Chiapas.

A number of smaller armed movements and potential movements also merit attention. The most significant of these is the Popular Revolution Army (EPR), based in the state of Guerrero. The EPR announced its presence in 1996 when 100 masked men armed with AK-47s joined 6,000 civilian mourners at a memorial service marking the one-year anniversary of a massacre of 17 unarmed peasants at Aguas Blancas. The EPR issued a manifesto that it sought "to overthrow the antipopular, antidemocratic, demagogic, and illegitimate government which panders to national and foreign capital interests" and carried out at least thirty attacks against Mexican army convoys over the next three years. Although the EPR has been less active since two of its main leaders were captured in October 1998, sporadic attacks continue in and around Guerrero. At least three other guerrilla groups have also claimed credit for attacks within Guerrero: the Democratic Popular Revolutionary Party, the People's Revolutionary Insurgent Army, and the Armed Front for the Liberation of the Marginalized People of Guerrero.

Altogether, there may be as many as eight separate guerrilla organizations spread out across Mexico, though only the Zapatistas are thought to number more than a couple hundred insurgents. In addition, in Quintana Roo, which shares a border with Chiapas, EZLN supporters have not taken up arms, but have drawn on their collective memory of the Caste War to call for Yucatecan independence. In Chiapas, a peasant squatter movement unrelated to the EZLN has seized several large estates. In Morelos, a local peasant group occupied the Tlalnepantla town hall in 2004 to protest fraudulent local elections.

Alliance Structure

Mexico was formally allied with the United States between 1936 and 1945 as an original signatory to the Buenos Aires Declaration of Principles of Inter-American Solidarity and Cooperation. With the formation of the Organization of American States (OAS), the Buenos Aires Treaty was replaced in 1947 by the Rio Treaty (the Inter-American Treaty on Reciprocal Assistance), which bound signatories to mutual defense against attack from outside the hemisphere. After years of disuse, the OAS invoked the treaty on September 21, 2001, to unanimously support a resolution to use "all legally available measures to pursue, capture, extradite and punish" anyone who might have assisted in the September 11 attacks.

Nonetheless, U.S.-Mexican tension in the post-9–11 period has placed Mexico's formal alliance structure in flux. Indeed, Mexico formally pulled out of the Rio Treaty in September 2002 on the grounds that it was obsolete. Then, in October 2003, Mexico hosted a special OAS conference that produced a Declaration on Security in the Americas, supplementing the Rio Treaty by requiring signatory states to work together on traditional security issues, such as arms dealing, terrorism, and drug trafficking, as well as on nontraditional security issues, such as HIV/AIDS, poverty, natural disasters, and environmental degradation. In the words of Mexico's foreign minister Luis Ernesto Derbez, the new declaration "leaves behind the doctrinaire logic of the Cold War" and moves toward a more realistic understanding of post-9–11 regional security threats. Nonetheless, the new declaration imposes no concrete requirements on signatory states.

Size and Structure of the Military

Although the military ballooned to 250,000 soldiers during the Mexican Revolution, Presidents Obregón and Calles downsized forces during the 1920s. Since that time, with the vastly larger United States representing both Mexico's greatest external threat and its reliable protector against other possible enemies, Mexico has been remarkable within Latin America for its relatively modest military budget and personnel structure. Indeed, while Latin America as a whole averaged 3.5 soldiers per 1,000 population in 1991, the corresponding figure for Mexico was just 1.9 per 1,000. Although the overall size of the military has roughly doubled since 1970, military growth has kept pace with population growth, and the ratio of soldiers per 1,000 civilians has remained roughly constant.

As of 2001, Mexico's active armed forces consist of 193,000 personnel, or about 1.87 per 1,000 civilians in the country. The majority of these (130,000) serve in Mexico's army, including 60,000 conscripts. Mexico's navy consists of 37,000 personnel (all volunteers), and its air force consists of 8,000 personnel (all volunteers). The remainder of the armed forces is divided among military police, special forces, paratroopers, presidential guards, and rural defense forces. All Mexicans are required to perform a year of part-time national defense service overseen by the secretary of national defense, but the majority of these service hours consist of nonmilitary activities including educational service, promotion of public health, and cultural activities.

In contrast with other nations in Latin America (and in contrast with the United States), the Mexican armed forces are governed at the cabinet level by two distinct government ministries: the Secretariat of National Defense (including the army and air force) and the Secretariat of the Navy. Heads of each secretariat report directly to the president. In 1988, Mexico created a National Security Council (renamed the National Public Security Council in 1995), including representatives of the Naval and Armed Forces secretariats, as well as representatives of the foreign ministry, interior ministry (concerned with governance in Mexico, not the environment), and attorney general's office, to coordinate all aspects of internal and external security.

Mexico's armed forces have been governed since 1926, with minor modifications, by the Organic Law, which defines a threefold mission "to defend the integrity and independence of the nation, to maintain the constitution, and to preserve internal order." The National Defense Ministry currently describes its fivefold mission to include external defense, internal security (including antinarcotic efforts, public security, and internal order), public works (including reforestation, education, and national sports programs), assistance of civil officials, and disaster relief.

Given Mexico's history of episodic internal conflict and (since the last U.S. incursion into Mexican territory in 1916–1917) limited external conflict, much of the army's focus has been on domestic security concerns. In particular, the army has been involved in narcotic crop eradication since the early 1970s, and since 1995 the army has also played a direct role, in cooperation with the attorney general's office, in antinarcotics interdiction and law enforcement. Counterinsurgency efforts have also been a major focus, including during Mexico's "dirty war" and more recently within the states of Chiapas and Guerrero.

The Mexican army consists of seven brigades, including one armored, two infantry, one motorized infantry, one airborne, one combined military police and engineering brigade, and the presidential guard. In addition, independent regiments and battalions are assigned to thirty-five geographic zones. These independent regiments include an armored cavalry regiment, nineteen motorized cavalry regiments, a mechanized infantry regiment, and seven artillery regiments.

The army employs a number of light armored vehicles, including French-made Panhard ERC-90 Lynx six-wheeled reconnaissance vehicles and Panhard VBL M-11 light armored cars, German-made HWK-11 tracked armored personnel carriers (APCs), and Mexican-made DN-3 and DN-5 Caballo and Mex–1 APCs. Mexico deployed M4 Sherman tanks transferred from the United States after World War II through the 1970s, but these tanks were retired during the late 1990s and no replacement has been developed or purchased. The army also employs a small number of self-propelled 75-mm howitzers, a larger number of towed 105-mm howitzers, and French Milan antitank missiles.

The Mexican navy is defined by the Organic Law as "a national military institution, of permanent character, whose mission is to employ its power for the external defense of the Federation and to contribute to the internal security of the country." In particular, naval activities have focused on the transportation of army forces, policing of territorial waters, protection of maritime traffic, search and rescue operations, disaster prevention and relief, and antinarcotics efforts.

Mexico's navy is divided into six geographic divisions, including three responsible for Mexico's 7,800 km of Pacific coastline (headquartered at the port of Manzanillo) and three responsible for Mexico's 3,300 km of Caribbean/Gulf of Mexico coastline (headquartered at the Gulf of Tuxpan). Including territorial waters, the Mexican navy patrols a total of 3.1 million sq. km and makes use of 28 separate naval bases.

Mexico's major naval equipment includes three frigates, two destroyers, two amphibious assault ships, eleven patrol ships, fourteen auxiliary support ships, and numerous reconnaissance airplanes and helicopters.

The Mexican air force was conceptualized as early as 1911 as the "eyes of the military" by revolutionary president Francisco Madero and was formally established in 1915. Its primary activities in recent years have consisted of the rapid transportation of personnel and equipment in cooperation with the Mexican army, reconnaissance (especially related to Mexico's counternarcotics cam-

paign), medical evacuations, disaster relief, and fighting forest fires. The air force is divided into four regionally defined divisions, with forces distributed among a total of eighteen bases dispersed throughout the country.

In addition to more than two dozen types of aircraft and helicopters employed for reconnaissance and troop transport, the air force employs Northrop F-5e Y F5f Tiger fighter planes, MD530-F combat helicopters, and Sikorsky UH-60 Blackhawk combat helicopters.

Budget

In the years prior to the onset of the 1982 debt crisis, Mexico funded substantial research and development related to military use, including the deployment of an advanced military communications system in 1982. Defense spending almost tripled between 1979 and 1981 (from $567 million to $1.403 billion) (Serrano 1995), as Mexico worked on developing short-range missile technology and a domestic tank design. Mexico also entered discussions to coproduce armored vehicles and/or aircraft in cooperation with German, Israeli, and French defense industries.

The 1982 debt crisis derailed these programs, none of which ever reached the production stage. Spending remained flat during the 1980s, before climbing from $1.624 billion in 1988 to $2.96 billion in 2002 (Stockholm International Peace Research Institute [SIPRI] 2005). Estimates from the Central Intelligence Agency (U.S. CIA) and Center for Defense Information (CDI) are higher, placing the Mexican defense budget at $4 billion in 1999 (CIA 2005) and $5.9 billion in 2004 (CDI 2005). Although these numbers represent an increase in defense spending—especially relative to the federal budget, which has otherwise fallen since 1994— Mexican military spending still remains relatively low compared to other countries in the region (between 0.5 and 1.0 percent of GDP, depending on the source).

According to current estimates, Mexico's defense budget is primarily devoted to personnel and equipment maintenance. Maintenance expenses include those related to a total of 1,100 armored land vehicles and 170 combat aircraft (Strategy Page). Military hardware is disproportionately employed in counternarcotics efforts, which involved 25 percent of the country's military personnel in the late 1990s, but consumed 60 percent of the country's operation and maintenance budget.

Relatively few resources are devoted to arms imports and research and development (R&D). Arms imports totaled US$80 million in 1996 (U.S. ACDA), making Mexico the fifty-fifth-ranked arms importer in the world, falling to US$13 million in 1998 (Nationmaster. com), or sixty-ninth in the world. More recent purchases include eight Star Safire II multisensor infrared surveillance systems for CASA C-21–200 fixed-wing aircraft (US$5.5 million) in August 2002 and four P-3B Lightweight Orion surveillance aircraft in March 2002. A substantial proportion of Mexican arms imports fall within counternarcotics programs, including US$51 million in counternarcotics, military, and policy aid under various U.S. programs in 2002 and U.S.$10 million in counternarcotics arms sales from the United States.

Data available from the Organization for Economic Cooperation and Development (OECD) (of which Mexico is a member state) and other sources do not report Mexican defense R&D spending, but the country does have a small domestic arms industry, employing about 5,000 persons. Arms production in 2003 was limited to small arms and ammunition, as well as military uniforms. Mexican arms exports totaled US$10 million in 1996 (U.S. ACDA), forty-second in the world, and US$13 million in 1998 (Nationmaster. com), fifty-second in the world.

Civil-Military Relations/Role of the Military in Domestic Politics

In contrast with most Latin American states, the Mexican military remained squarely under civilian control throughout most of the twentieth century, and Mexico is the only large Latin American state to not experience a military coup since 1917. In part, civilian dominance is a function of Mexico's shared border with the United States and its overwhelming military superiority.

A second important basis of civilian dominance of the Mexican military is the legacy of the Mexican Revolution. In the aftermath of the economic and human devastation of the civil war that followed, both the military and the general population were strongly averse to further civil conflict or a prominent role for the Mexican military. A more important legacy of the Mexican Revolution was the creation of Mexico's hegemonic political party, originally known as the National Revolutionary Party (PNR), and subsequently renamed (and reorganized) as the Party of the Mexican Revolution (PRM) and then the PRI. From the beginning, the PNR included military leaders among the party elites, and in 1937 President Lázaro Cárdenas made the military one of four formal corporatist branches of the party, along with peasants, labor, and small businesses. Thus, by bringing the military into the hegemonic governing coalition, the postrevolutionary settlement prevented the civil-military conflict that plagued the rest of Latin America during the twentieth century.

The Cárdenas era marked a high point for the military's formal political role. The establishment of the PRI in 1946 eliminated the military branch of the party, and President Miguel Alemán, elected that year, was the first civilian president since Francisco Madero. All presidents since have also been civilians. At the same time that the military's formal role diminished, its budget and prominence expanded in response to student protests and guerrilla insurgencies during the 1960s and 1970s.

Mexican democratization during the 1990s and the elimination of the PRI's hegemonic role raise a new question about the future of civil-military relations: Has the Mexican military been truly subservient to civilian leaders, or have military and civilian leaders never before taken conflicting positions on substantive questions? The question is important as nongovernmental organizations (NGOs) allege serious human rights violations in Chiapas and Guerrero during the last decade. A 1998 lawsuit in Mexican federal court found in favor of survivors of the Tlatelolco massacre and initiated an investigation of the military's role in that event. As a result, a special presidential prosecutor has begun investigating Mexico's "dirty war," and 160,000 secret government documents from the period were released in 2002. But civilian control remains uncertain. In 2002 the national security adviser's military oversight role was abolished, and

Fox appointee Adolfo Aguilar Zinser was forced to resign.

Terrorism

There is no evidence of terrorist groups operating within Mexico, but the country's cooperation with U.S. antiterror efforts is considered important given its strategic location. Mexico has cooperated in the fight against global terrorism through a number of formal agreements and concrete steps. First, Mexico is a signatory to all twelve UN conventions related to terrorism passed between 1963 and 1999, and Mexico also supported UN Security Council Resolution 1373 (September 28, 2001), which requires member states to adjust domestic legislation to combat terrorism and prevent its financing. Mexico likewise voted for a pair of OAS measures designed to promote hemispheric antiterror cooperation: the 2002 Inter-American Convention against Terrorism and the 2003 Declaration of San Salvador on Strengthening Cooperation in the Fight against Terrorism. Finally, Mexico allowed the expanded deployment of U.S. agents at Mexican airports and throughout the state of Chiapas in 2003 and early 2004 to supervise increased security efforts, though this deployment was scaled back following a large public outcry against this "assault on Mexican sovereignty."

Nonetheless, Mexico has not been unqualified in its support for the U.S. "War on Terrorism." Mexico was a prominent no vote in the UN Security Council prior to the 2003 Iraq war despite intense U.S. lobbying. Mexico has also taken the lead within the hemisphere in rejecting the U.S. position that terrorism represents the gravest threat to countries in the

Western Hemisphere, and has sought instead to frame hemispheric security in terms of economic and social issues. As Mexican Ambassador to the OAS Miguel Ruiz-Cabañas explained in 2003, "the military concept of security is being set aside to include, in keeping with a consensus, specific commitments in favor of poverty, the environment, AIDS, and social justice."

Relations with the United States

Even 150 years later, Mexico's memory of the War of the North American Invasion and subsequent U.S. incursions remain central to its relationship with the United States. Relations were especially strained in the years after the revolution, mainly because U.S. businesses feared that the revolutionary government would employ Article 27 of the Mexican constitution to expropriate their property. The United States only recognized the new government in 1923 after the two states signed the Bucareli Agreement, through which Mexico promised not to appropriate any properties that had been improved through investments (e.g., oil rigs).

Nonetheless, relations deteriorated during the 1930s, initially over migration issues as the United States deported 500,000 Mexican migrants during the Great Depression. Tens of thousands were stripped of their U.S. property and many were packed into cattle cars for hours or days during forced trips across the border. A second controversy came in 1938, when a Mexican industrial arbitration board ruled in favor of striking oil workers, mandating large wage increases on the part of British, Dutch, and U.S. oil firms. When the firms refused to comply

with the ruling, President Lázaro Cárdenas responded by nationalizing the firms, worth a total of $500 million. Negotiations to resolve the dispute were complicated by the intensifying war in Europe, and when the U.S. boycotted Mexican oil in response to the expropriation, Mexico expanded its oil sales to the Axis powers.

The crisis was resolved as part of a multidimensional settlement in 1942 that ushered in a new era of bilateral cooperation. First, the U.S. State Department negotiated an agreement between Mexico and the foreign firms on $24 million (plus interest) in compensation for the oil expropriation—highly favorable terms for Mexico. Second, although Mexicans were still concerned about migration issues, Mexico agreed to assist American labor recruiters through the so-called Bracero Program, which eventually coordinated the temporary migration of 4 million Mexicans to the United States between 1942 and 1964 (see Sidebar 3). Third, though neutral throughout World War I, Mexico broke diplomatic relations with the Axis states following the attack on Pearl Harbor and formally declared war on the Axis states following German attacks against Mexican oil tankers in May 1942.

Mexico joined Brazil as one of two Latin American states to substantially contribute to the Allied war effort. Three air force squadrons deployed to the Asian theater and the "Aztec Eagles" Squadron 201 saw extensive combat in the Philippines, where five of the squadron's thirty-one pilots were killed in action. In addition, Mexico permitted the United States to establish three radar stations within Mexico, staffed by Mexican personnel. Mexico was also a primary foreign supplier of raw materials to the U.S. war effort, passing

---

Sidebar 3   The United States–Mexico Bracero Program

With the United States both dependent on Mexican labor for its war effort and eager to improve bilateral relations, Mexicans dominated 1942 guestworker negotiations. According to the treaty signed that year, Mexicans received higher wages than their U.S. counterparts; U.S. employers were required to provide housing, food, and transportation; and the U.S. and Mexican governments collaborated to ensure contract enforcement. Although employers successfully demanded deregulation in 1948, Mexico again extracted a state-to-state contracting agreement during the Korean War. But with the end of that conflict and the inaugurations of new governments in Mexico and the United States in 1954, U.S. President Dwight Eisenhower forced Mexico to accept an agreement which denied Mexico any role in the setting of wages or the enforcement of contracts; and this pro-grower treaty remains the blueprint for contemporary guestworker immigration to the United States.

Source
Rosenblum, Marc R. 2003. "The Intermestic Politics of Immigration Policy: Lessons from the Bracero Program." *Political Power and Social Theory* 17: 141–184.

---

and enforcing strict price controls to prevent war profiteering.

Relations again deteriorated thereafter, beginning with Mexico's refusal to send troops to the Korean War. Presidential elections in both countries in 1952 ushered in a new wave of conflict. In the United States, Dwight Eisenhower explicitly rejected the Good Neighbor policy toward Latin America that had been emphasized by the Truman and Roosevelt administrations. In Mexico, Adolfo Ruiz Cortines appointed a hard-line anti-Yankee cabinet after a narrow (by Mexican standards) electoral victory over a leftist candidate who criticized Ruiz Cortines's collaboration with the United States during his term as governor of Veracruz in 1914. Bilateral disputes flared in 1953–1954 over the Bracero agreement, a boycott of Mexican cattle due to hoof-and-mouth disease, a dispute over ocean and boundary waters, Mexico's lone no vote against a U.S.-backed OAS anticommunism resolution, and Mexico's 1954 peso devaluation. More profound disagreements also arose over Mexico's opposition to the U.S. role in the 1954 coup in Guatemala and Mexico's support for the Castro regime in Cuba after 1959.

A new phase in Mexican foreign policy and bilateral relations was initiated with the 1973 oil price shocks and simultaneous discovery of vast new Mexican petroleum reserves. With the sudden infusion of wealth, Mexico sought to adopt a more aggressive position as a regional leader and head of the global Non-aligned Movement. Mexico initiated new weapons programs and loudly boycotted the 1973 OAS General Assembly meeting to protest the military coup in Chile. When the Ford and Carter administrations sought Mexican support during the U.S. energy crisis, including offering a deal involving new guestworker flows (as Mexico had previously sought), the nationalistic Echeverría and Lopez Portillo administrations rejected their overtures.

The 1980 election of Ronald Reagan followed by the 1982 Mexican debt default marked the demise of Mexico's aggressive foreign policy and another turning point in bilateral relations. Throughout the decade, the two countries clashed over Mexico's economic crisis, Mexico's slow pace of democratization, undocumented migration, narcotics flows, and Mexico's opposition to the U.S.-backed civil wars in Central America. A low point came in 1985–1986 when U.S. Drug Enforcement Agent Enrique Camarena was kidnapped and killed in Mexico; U.S. Customs Director William Von Raab testified before the Senate that Mexican officials and members of President Miguel de la Madrid's family personally profited from the drug trade, and the United States passed the restrictionist 1986 Immigration Reform and Control Act.

Presidents Bush and Salinas, both elected in 1988, sought to repair damaged relations. Fundamental economic disagreements were replaced by Mexico's deep commitment to the U.S.-backed neoliberal economic agenda, including the North American Free Trade Agreement (NAFTA), and in 1997 Mexico surpassed Japan as the United States' second-largest trading partner. Conflict over Central America was eliminated by the settlement of civil wars in Nicaragua, El Salvador, and Guatemala between 1990 and 1996. Mexican Presidents Salinas and Zedillo dramatically expanded Mexican antinarcotics efforts, replacing many corrupt police units with cleaner military units. In addition, after initiating a process of "Mexicanization" of drug enforcement early in the 1990s (i.e., replacing joint programs with unilateral enforcement), U.S.-Mexican cooperation on drug enforcement intensified under the Clinton and Zedillo administrations. Finally, although the U.S. Congress continued to pass harshly restrictionist immigration policies during the 1990s, Presidents Clinton and Zedillo reached a series of agreements in 1995–1997 establishing new bilateral migration institutions that Mexican officials credit with improving respect for migrants' rights and conditions along the border.

Migration cooperation appeared poised to be the centerpiece of improvements in the bilateral relationship in 2001 following the inaugurations of Presidents George W. Bush and Vicente Fox, but the 9–11 terror attacks derailed high-level talks on the subject. Relations have remained strained since that time as the Fox administration suffered severe domestic setbacks as a result of the U.S. retreat from the migration talks and as the Mexican economy suffered ripple effects from the U.S. recession. Additional disputes over U.S. unilateralism in the run-up to the Iraq war, including Mexico's refusal to offer its support within the Security Council and Mexico's withdrawal from the OAS Rio Treaty, seemed to signal a further decline. However, in 2004 the Bush administration appeared to offer an olive branch by revisiting the issue of a major migration agreement in a pair of summit meetings in January and March.

The Future

Questions about Mexico's future relate to the resolution of domestic insurgencies, the direction of civil-military relations, and the nature of regional economic integration and relations with the United States. With regard to the first of these issues, the consolidation of Mexican democracy seems secure in most parts of the country, but political corruption continues in various regions, including Chiapas and Guerrero in particular. The further incorporation of competitive elections and honest institutions in these troubled regions could go a long way to undermine the appeal of insurgent groups over time. On the other hand, Mexico's economic restructuring and integration into the world economy has struck these same regions particularly hard as peasants and others dependent on traditional modes of production have been forced to undertake difficult adjustments. The absence of substantial economic assistance to the regions will foster continued tensions.

Those who are concerned about civil-military relations under the liberal Fox administration highlight a third scenario in Chiapas and elsewhere: the possible increased military deployment within Mexico, perhaps similar to the "dirty war" of the 1960s and 1970s. In light of these concerns, it is noteworthy that human rights organizations have documented substantial tension between pro-Zapatista villagers and Mexican troops and illegal paramilitary forces. By the same token, continued vigilance from Mexican and international NGOs makes it unlikely that civil-military relations will spin out of control in the region. Mexico's role in hemispheric counterterror and counternarcotics efforts will likely involve continued expansion of domestic military actions, and the increased role of regular army and special forces regiments in counternarcotics campaigns has already been associated with more military involvement in drug gangs.

Mexico's deep integration with the United States and other states in the region and around the world is a final factor pointing to moderation and continuity. In addition to its NAFTA membership, Mexico has formal economic relations with Colombia and Venezuela (the Group of Three) and the countries of Central America (Plan Puebla Panama), and, as of 2004, Mexico had signed the largest number of bilateral free trade accords (thirty-two) of any country in the world. The two largest political parties are both deeply committed to continued economic neoliberalism, and an increasing number of Mexicans see further democratic consolidation and international integration as squarely in the country's best interests. Although such integration makes Mexico—like other countries in the region—vulnerable to U.S. and international economic shocks, it is also a source of stability that makes future regional conflict or militarization seem unlikely.

References, Recommended Readings, and Websites

Books

Altman, Ida. 2003. *The Early History of Greater Mexico.* Upper Saddle River, NJ: Prentice-Hall.

Camp, Roderic A. 1992. *Generals in the Palacio: The Military in Modern Mexico.* New York: Oxford University Press.

———. 1999. *Politics in Mexico.* 2d ed. New York: Oxford University Press.

Colson, Harold. 1987. *Civil-Military Relations and National Security in Modern Mexico: A Bibliography.* Auburn, AL: Auburn University Press.

Domínguez, Jorge I., and Rafael Fernández de Castro. 2002. *The United States and Mexico: Between Partnership and Conflict.* New York: Routledge.

Dunn, Timothy. 1996. *The Militarization of the U.S.-Mexico Border, 1978–1992: Low Intensity Conflict Doctrine Comes Home.* Austin: CMAS Books, University of Texas.

English, Adrian J. 1984. *Armed Forces of Latin America: Their Histories, Development, Present Strength, and Military Potential.* London: Jane's.

Fauriol, Georges A. 1989. *Security in the Americas.* Washington, DC: National Defense University Press.

Goodman, Louis W., and Johanna M. Forman. 1990. *The Military and Democracy: The Future of Civil-Military Relations in Latin America.* Lexington, MA: Lexington Books.

Harvey, Neil. 1998. *The Chiapas Rebellion: The Struggle for Land and Democracy.* Durham, NC: Duke University Press.

Joseph, Gilbert. M. 2002. *The Mexico Reader: History, Culture, Politics.* Durham, NC: Duke University Press.

Lieuwen, Edwin. 1968. *Mexican Militarism: The Political Rise and Fall of the Revolutionary Army, 1910–1940.* Albuquerque: University of New Mexico Press.

Meyer, Michael C., William L. Sherman, and Susan M. Deeds. 1999. *The Course of Mexican History.* 6th ed. New York: Oxford University Press.

Ronfeldt, David, ed. 1984. *The Modern Mexican Military, a Reassessment.* San Diego: Center for U.S.-Mexican Studies, University of California.

Rosenblum, Marc R. 2003. "The Intermestic Politics of Immigration Policy: Lessons from the Bracero Program." *Political Power and Social Theory* 17:141–184.

Rugley, Terry. 1996. *Yucatan's Maya Peasantry and the Origins of the Caste War.* Austin: University of Texas Press.

Suchlicki, Jaime. 2001. *Mexico: From Moctezuma to the Fall of the PRI.* 2d ed. Washington, DC: Brassey's.

Van Young, Eric. 2001. *The Other Rebellion: Popular Violence, Ideology, and the Mexican Struggle for Independence, 1810–1821.* Stanford, CA: Stanford University Press.

World Bank. 2001. World Development Indicators [CD-ROM]. Washington, DC: World Bank.

Articles/Newspapers

Ackroyd, William S. 1991. "Military Professionalism, Education, and Political Behavior in Mexico." *Armed Forces & Society* 18:81–96.

De Cordoba, Josie. 2000. "Mexican Army Takes Greater Public Role as Democracy Grows." *Wall Street Journal,* January 31:A1.

Fernandes, Deepa. 1999. "Militarization Continues in Southern Mexico." *NACLA Report on the Americas* 33:2–3.

Hurst, Andrew. 2002. "Mexicans Hope to Close Case on 1968 Massacre." *Houston Chronicle,* February 15, 2002:A35.

Katz, Friedrich. 1978. "Pancho Villa and the Attack on Columbus, New Mexico." *American Historical Review* 83:101–130.

Mandel-Campbell, Andrea, and Thomas Omestad. 2000. "A Time of Change for Mexico's Military." *U.S. News & World Report,* December 11:48.

Schwab, Stephen I. 2002. "The Role of the Mexican Expeditionary Air Force in World War II: Late, Limited, but Symbolically Significant." *Journal of Military History* 66:115–1141.

Serrano, Mónica. 1995. "The Armed Branch of the State: Civil-Military Relations in Mexico." *Journal of Latin American Studies* 27:423–448.

Thompson, Ginger. 2001. "Rights Group Says Mexico Ignores Abuses by Military." *NewYork Times,* December 6:A18.

Weiner, Tim. 2003. "U.S. and Mexico Coordinate Military Efforts for Mutual Protection against Terror." *New York Times,* March 23:B13.

Websites

All Refer.com. *Country Study and Guide: Mexico:* http://reference.allrefer.com/country-guide-study/mexico/.

Armed Conflict Events Data. *Mexico 1800–1999:* http://www.onwar.com/aced/nation/may/mexico/findex.htm.

Center for Defense Information: http://www.cdi.org/.

Mexico Connect: http://www.mexconnect.com/mex_/history.html.

Mexican Department of Defense (including air force): http://www.sedena.gob.mx.

Mexican Department of Interior Web Portal: http://www.gob.mx/.

Mexican Department of the Navy: http://www.semar.gob.mx.

Nationmaster.com: http://www.nationmaster.com/country/mx/Military.

Sons of DeWitt County Texas. *The Battle of San Jacinto:* http://www.tamu.edu/ccbn/dewitt/batsanjacinto.htm.

Stockholm International Peace Research Institute (SIPRI): http://www.sipri.org.

Strategy Page. *Armed Forces of the World Database:* http://www.strategypage.com/fyeo/howtomakewar/databases/armies/default.asp.

U.S. Arms Control and Disarmament Agency (ACDA): http://dosfan.lib.uic.edu/acda/.

U.S. Central Intelligence Agency. 2005. *World Factbook:* http://www.cia.gov/cia/publications/factbook/geos/mx.html.

Washington Office on Latin America: http://www.wola.org/.

World History Archives. *The History of the Estados Unidos Mexicanos (Mexico):* http://www.hartford-hwp.com/archives/46/index.html.